AF214204

OXFORD STUDIES IN EUROPEAN LAW

*Series Editors*

PAUL CRAIG

*Professor of English Law at St John's College, Oxford*

GRÁINNE DE BÚRCA

*Professor of Law at New York University School of Law*

# The Human Rights of Migrants and Refugees in European Law

# OXFORD STUDIES IN EUROPEAN LAW

*Series Editors:*
Paul Craig, Professor of English Law at St John's College, Oxford and
Gráinne de Búrca, Professor of Law at New York
University School of Law

The aim of this series is to publish important and original research on EU law. The focus is on scholarly monographs, with a particular emphasis on those which are interdisciplinary in nature. Edited collections of essays will also be included where they are appropriate. The series is wide in scope and aims to cover studies of particular areas of substantive and of institutional law, historical works, theoretical studies, and analyses of current debates, as well as questions of perennial interest such as the relationship between national and EU law and the novel forms of governance emerging in and beyond Europe. The fact that many of the works are interdisciplinary will make the series of interest to all those concerned with the governance and operation of the EU.

OTHER TITLES IN THIS SERIES

**An Ever More Powerful Court? The Political Constraints of Legal Integration in the European Union**
Dorte Sindbjerg Martinsen

**The Concept of State Aid under EU Law From Internal Market to Competition and Beyond**
Juan Jorge Piernas López

**Justice in the EU The Emergence of Transnational Solidarity**
Floris de Witte

**The Euro Area Crisis in Constitutional Perspective**
Alicia Hinarejos

**The European Fundamental Freedoms A Contextual Approach**
Pedro Caro de Sousa

**National Identity in EU Law**
Elke Cloots

**The Constitutional Foundations of European Contract Law A Comparative Analysis**
Kathleen Gutman

**The Criminalization of European Cartel Enforcement Theoretical, Legal, and Practical Challenges**
Peter Whelan

**Fundamental Rights in Europe Challenges and Transformations in Comparative Perspective**
Federico Fabbrini

**The Principle of Loyalty in EU Law**
Marcus Klamert

**Constitutional Pluralism in the EU**
Klemen Jaklic

**EU Consumer Law and Human Rights**
Iris Benöhr

**The Principle of Mutual Recognition in EU Law**
Christine Janssens

**The Coherence of EU Free Movement Law Constitutional Responsibility and the Court of Justice**
Niamh Nic Shuibhne

**European Law and New Health Technologies**
Edited by Mark Flear, Anne-Maree Farrell, Tamara Hervey, and Thérèse Murphy

**European Agencies Law and Practices of Accountability**
Madalina Busuioc

# The Human Rights of Migrants and Refugees in European Law

CATHRYN COSTELLO

*Andrew W Mellon Associate Professor in International Human Rights and Refugee Law*

OXFORD
UNIVERSITY PRESS

**OXFORD**
UNIVERSITY PRESS

Great Clarendon Street, Oxford, OX2 6DP,
United Kingdom

Oxford University Press is a department of the University of Oxford.
It furthers the University's objective of excellence in research, scholarship,
and education by publishing worldwide. Oxford is a registered trade mark of
Oxford University Press in the UK and in certain other countries

© C. Costello 2016

The moral rights of the author have been asserted

First Edition published in 2016

All rights reserved. No part of this publication may be reproduced, stored in a retrieval system, or transmitted, in any form or by any means, without the prior permission in writing of Oxford University Press, or as expressly permitted by law, by licence or under terms agreed with the appropriate reprographics rights organization. Enquiries concerning reproduction outside the scope of the above should be sent to the Rights Department, Oxford University Press, at the address above

You must not circulate this work in any other form
and you must impose this same condition on any acquirer

Crown copyright material is reproduced under Class Licence
Number C01P0000148 with the permission of OPSI
and the Queen's Printer for Scotland

Published in the United States of America by Oxford University Press
198 Madison Avenue, New York, NY 10016, United States of America

British Library Cataloguing in Publication Data
Data available

Library of Congress Control Number: 2015945916

ISBN 978–0–19–964474–2

Links to third party websites are provided by Oxford in good faith and
for information only. Oxford disclaims any responsibility for the materials
contained in any third party website referenced in this work.

Do mo mháthair
agus
i gcuimhne m'athair agus Mícheál

# *Series Editors' Preface*

Cathryn Costello's book is important and timely, more especially in the light of the current EU migration crisis and the difficulty in securing political agreement between the Member States on the appropriate way forward. The effect of the crisis, and the political response, on the existing body of EU legal rules that regulate asylum and immigration remains to be seen. Whatsoever that turns out to be, there is no doubt that the issues discussed in this book will remain salient and central.

The book considers the legal status, broadly conceived, of a range of migrants, with the principal focus being on admissions, conceived in terms of access to territory and authorization of presence and residence. It examines the leading measures concerning the rights of third-country nationals to enter and stay in the EU, and the way in which the EU conceptualizes illegal immigration. There is, as Costello notes, a duality in the EU's treatment of migration, in that it both supports Member States in their admission control dictates, while also establishing its own rules on admissions. There is much to be learned from the insightful treatment of complex EU legislation concerning border control, returns, family reunification, and the asylum measures on qualification, asylum procedures, and the Dublin schema.

The legislative and judicial analysis is conducted against the backdrop of human rights protection. It is a further strength of this work that the rights-based analysis draws on three bodies of law: the case law of the ECtHR on migrant rights; EU law on migration and asylum, and the judicial interpretation thereof that draws on EU conceptions of fundamental rights and the Charter; and international refugee law.

This complex tapestry is set against and is reflective of broader themes, with implications over and beyond the specific area of migration. There is, as the author notes, a real connection between the issues addressed in this study, cast in terms of the end points of migrants' journeys, and the very telos of the EU, framed as it is in terms of 'ever closer union among the peoples of Europe', with inevitable contestation as to the definition of peoples for this purpose. There is, moreover, the tension between statist assumptions that underlie much of traditional international law thinking in this area, and the emergence of international human rights law. The extent to which EU law may embody transformative potential in this regard, breaking the mould of statist tradition, is one of the principal themes explored in the book.

There is no doubt that Cathryn Costello's book will be of interest to all those concerned with EU law and governance, and that it constitutes a rich resource for those interested to learn more about the EU's approach to these difficult issues.

Paul Craig and Gráinne de Búrca

# *Acknowledgements*

This book reflects many years of academic interest in migration and asylum, and the potential, limits, and temptations of EU and human rights law in these fields. Many of the ideas took shape in my doctoral thesis, written whilst I held the Francis Reynolds Fellowship in EU and Public Law at Worcester College, Oxford. I would like to therefore first thank my doctoral supervisors. Timothy Endicott initially gave me great confidence in the importance of the topic, and later Stephen Weatherill helped me bring the doctoral project to fruition. I received much helpful guidance from David Miller and Derrick Wyatt at the end of the first year of my doctoral work. I also owe a weighty debt of gratitude to my two final examiners, Paul Craig and Dora Kostakopoulou, for their helpful comments made during and after the viva and for their consistent support and encouragement.

When commencing my DPhil studies, the late Peter Birks, the then Director of Graduate Studies, warned that combining my full-time teaching commitments and DPhil studies would be a challenge. My law colleagues at Worcester over the years, Jeremy Horder, Donal Nolan, Maris Kopke-Tinturé, and Michelle Madden Dempsey, were a source of much inspiration and support. Particular thanks must go to my college advisor, Judith Freedman, for frequent words of encouragement. Worcester generously facilitated my sabbatical leave when I took up a Global Emile Noel Fellowship at NYU School of Law. My doctoral project was then in its incipient phase, and I received helpful guidance from Ruth Rubio-Marín and Willem Maas, as well as from my fellow academic visitors at NYU, including Marian Ahumada Ruiz, Alicia Cebada Romero, Jean d'Aspremont, Gareth Davies, and Julie Ringelheim. I also benefitted greatly from attending a class on theory of international law convened by Philip Alston, Benedict Kingsbury, and Matthias Kumm.

The Oxford Law Faculty has provided much support, in the form of research support funding, sabbatical leave, and most of all supportive and inspiring colleagues. No doubt I omit many when I thank explicitly from my DPhil cohort, for their enduring friendship and support, Jeff King, Tarun Khaitan, and Kirsty Maclean. From my Oxford law colleagues, I am grateful to many for their inspiration and encouragement, particularly Dapo Akande, Alan Bogg, Anne Davies, Sionaidh Douiglas-Scott, Pavlos Eleftheriadis, Sandy Fredman, Mark Freedland, Guy Goodwin-Gill, Les Green, Barbara Havelkova, Aileen Kavanagh, Liora Lazarus, Denise Réaume, and Catherine Redgwell. Thanks in particular go to Alan Bogg and Mark Freedland for support when despair would otherwise have set in. At Oxford, I have not only benefitted from my college and faculty affiliations but I have also been privileged to be a part of the migration and refugee studies communities. At COMPAS, I thank in particular Bridget Anderson, Rob McNeil, Martin Ruhs, and Sarah Spencer. Taking up a new post at the Refugee Studies Centre (RSC) in 2013 provided a new and exciting environment and the support of many colleagues. Even before I took up my post at the RSC, I was grateful for the many opportunities for scholarly exchange provided by RSC colleagues over the years, including that of Roland Banks, Alexander Betts, Dawn Chatty, Jean-Francois Durieux, Elena Fiddian-Qasmiyeh, Matthew Gibney, and Violeta Moreno-Lax. At the European Studies Centre at St Antony's College, my colleagues Othon Anastasakis, Kalypso Nicolaïdes, and Timothy-Garton Ash continue to inspire and support me. I am grateful for the welcoming, supportive intellectual environment provided by my new college, St Antony's, and to its inspiring warden, Margaret Macmillan, in particular.

This book has been informed by many different encounters with asylum seekers, migrants, and refugees, and the legal processes that determine their fate. I am grateful to numerous individuals and organizations that have afforded so many valuable learning opportunities to me very early in my academic studies. As an ERASMUS exchange student in Germany in the 1990s, I was fortunate to work as an intern with Gunther Christ RA, a distinguished asylum practitioner. It was in his office that I first came across the notion of tolerated presence ('Duldung') and the other vagaries of asylum seeking in Europe. As an intern at the Los Angeles Federal District Court the following year, I heard the argumentation on the constitutionality of Proposition 187, which sought to prevent 'illegal aliens' from accessing rights to education and healthcare in that state. As a master's student at the College of Europe, Bruges, I followed an inspirational course taught by Joseph H.H. Weiler, and read his 'Thou Shalt Not Oppress a Stranger: On the Judicial Protection of the Human Rights of Non-EC Nationals—A Critique' (1992), a piece that has remained key to my thinking. Much later, during a stint on the Board of the Irish Refugee Council and later when campaigning to preserve automatic *jus soli* citizenship laws in Ireland, I saw the interaction between EU, asylum, and nationality law played out to restrictive effect. In the UK, I found myself cajoled by the inspirational Elspeth Guild to write a critique of the then draft Asylum Procedures Directive for ILPA, opening a line of inquiry that has continued. In turn, the opportunity to present that work to audiences of practitioners (at ECRE and ELENA events) and judges (under the auspices of the International Association of Refugee Law Judges) has greatly enhanced my own understanding. Alice Edwards at UNHCR provided an inspiring research opportunity, examining asylum processes and alternatives to detention up-close. Meeting those most affected by migration controls and in greatest need of refuge in the context of that project continues to inspire.

I was privileged to have the opportunity to present parts of this book, and related papers, at various stages of development. Chapter 6 contains an updated and extended version of a previous article, 'Courting Access to Asylum in Europe: Recent Supranational Jurisprudence Explored' (2012) 12 HRLR 287, while Chapter 7 draws on 'Human Rights and the Elusive Universal Subject: Immigration Detention under International Human Rights and EU Law' (2012) 19(1) Indiana Journal of Global Legal Studies 257, albeit significantly updated. I thank the publishers for permission to reprint this material. I am grateful to repeat invitations to address events convened by the European Council on Refugees and Exiles (ECRE), European Legal Network on Asylum (ELENA), the International Association of Refugee Law Judges, the Odysseus Network, and the Refugee Law Initiative (RLI). Two organizations with which I have long-standing links, the Irish Centre for European Law and the Irish Refugee Council, provided me with early opportunities to consider the impact of EU and human rights law on migration and asylum. I thank in particular my hosts and commentators at the following institutions: the Faculty of Law, University of Zagreb; the Institute for International Law and the Humanities (IILAH), Melbourne Law School; Monash University at Prato; the Danish Human Rights Institute, Copenhagen; Faculty of Law, University College London; Faculty of Law, University of Glasgow; Faculty of Law, University of Fribourg; the Nordic Asylum Law Seminar; the Dutch Council for Refugees; the Academy of European Law (ERA), Trier; and the Faculty of Law, Indiana University Maurer School of Law.

Two scholars who inspired and encouraged me along the way include the late Neil MacCormick and Sarah van Walsum. Their intellectual prowess matched their great generosity, kindness, and humour. I acknowledge an intellectual and personal debt of gratitude to them both. For much-appreciated comments on draft chapters and related papers, and for sharing their insights into political and judicial processes more generally, I thank in particular the following: Samantha Besson, Gráinne de Búrca, Joseph Carens, David Cantor, Nicola Countouris, Catherine Dauvergne, Jean-Francois Durieux, Michelle Foster, Thomas Gammeltoft-Hansen, Madeline Garlick, Iris Goldner Lang, Elspeth Guild, Alison Harvey, Mark Henderson, Maria Hennessy, Raza Husain, Esra Kaytaz, Jeff King, Susan Kneebone, Nico Krisch, Jane McAdam, Audrey Macklin, Virginia Mantouvalou, Violeta Moreno-Lax, Catherine Meredith, Valsamis Mitsilegas Nuala Mole, Bríd Moriarty, Kai Möller, Chris Nash, Niamh NicShuibhne, Gregor Noll, Síofra O'Leary, Maria O'Sullivan, Irini Papanicolopulu, Kris Pollett, Aaron Rathmell, Bernard Ryan, Flip Schuller, Eleanor Sharpston, Jo Shaw, Rachel Sheppard, Ciara Smyth, John Stanley, Dallal Stevens, Mark Symes, Daniel Thym, and Jens Vedsted-Hansen. Visits to the Faculty of Law of the Vrije Universiteit of Amsterdam over the years, including to participate in their Bergen aan Zee seminar, have been particularly inspiring. I thank Juan Amaya Castro, Hemme Battjes, Evelien Brouwer, Gareth Davies, Galina Cornelisse, Karen Geertsema, Marcelle Reneman, and Thomas Spijkerboer, and the greatly missed Sarah van Walsum, for various invitations, challenging comments, and of course, for their rigorous and inspiring scholarship.

As a sometime nomadic academic, I enjoy the privilege of relatively free movement that so often eludes the migrants and refugees this book is concerned with. The book was written in Oxford, Kerry, New York, and Mysore (India). I thank Sudhir Krishnaswamy for organizing my time as a visiting professor at the National Law School of India University, Bangalore. Living in nearby Mysore and practicing yoga at the Ashtanga Yoga Research Institute provided a period of both respite and focus.

All books are team efforts. I must thank many research assistants for their work on the manuscript, in particular Emma Dunlop, Emily Hancox, Minos Mouzourakis, and Aaron Rathmel. At OUP, the patient and professional team of Alex Flach, Natasha Flemming, Elinor Shields, Shalini Puthiyedam, and their colleagues have brought this book to fruition. I am grateful to Kate Buckley for the beautiful cover art, inspired by Norway, discovered in Dingle, and made in New Zealand.

The years spanning the thesis and this book have been the best and worst of times. I have drawn on the support of too many friends, relatives, and colleagues to mention. My mother, Celine, has continuously and unreservedly supported my endeavours. She will be much relieved by the completion of this one. To Huseyin, thank you for your love and patience. Here's to the next project.

Cathryn Costello
Kerry,
31 July 2015

# *Contents*

# *Table of Cases*

CJEU CASE LAW (NUMERICALLY)

## CJEU CASE LAW (ALPHABETICALLY)

## EU CIVIL SERVICE TRIBUNAL



## EUROPEAN COURT OF HUMAN RIGHTS

## INTER-AMERICAN COMMISSION OF HUMAN RIGHTS



## UNCAT



## UN HUMAN RIGHTS COMMITTEE



## NATIONAL CASE LAW

### United Kingdom Case Law

## OTHER NATIONAL CASE LAW

**Australia**



**Austria**



**France**



**Germany**



**Ireland**



**Italy**



**Netherlands**



**US**

# Table of Legislation

## EU DIRECTIVES

EU REGULATIONS

## INTERNATIONAL TREATIES AND INSTRUMENTS

## NATIONAL LEGISLATION

### France



### UK



### UK Secondary Legislation

# *List of Abbreviations*

| | |
|---|---|
| ACHR | American Convention on Human Rights |
| AFSJ | Area of Freedom, Security and Justice |
| AG | Advocate General |
| AJIL | American Journal of International Law |
| ARI | Análisis del Real Instituto Elcano |
| ATD | Alternatives to Detention |
| BVerfG | Bundesverfassungsgericht (Federal Constitutional Court of Germany) |
| CAT | Convention Against Torture and other Cruel, Inhuman or Degrading Treatment |
| CD | Citizenship Directive |
| CEDAW | Convention to Eliminate All Forms of Discrimination Against Women |
| CEPS | Centre for European Policy Studies |
| CERD | Committee on the Elimination of Discrimination |
| CJEL | Columbia Journal of European Law |
| CJEU | Court of Justice of the European Union |
| CLP | Current Legal Problems |
| CMLRev | Common Market Law Review |
| CPT | Committee for the Prevention of Torture |
| CSR | Convention relating to the Status of Refugees |
| EASO | European Asylum Support Office |
| EAW | European Arrest Warrant |
| EC | European Community |
| ECHR | European Convention on Human Rights |
| ECmHR | European Commission on Human Rights |
| ECtHR | European Court of Human Rights |
| ECR | European Court Reports |
| EHRLRev | European Human Rights Law Review |
| EHRR | European Human Rights Reports |
| EJIL | European Journal of International Law |
| EJML | European Journal of Migration and Law |
| ELJ | European Law Journal |
| ELR | European Law Review |
| EMN | European Migration Network |
| EPC | European Policy Centre |
| ESC | European Social Charter |
| ESD | Employer Sanctions Directive |
| ETUC | European Trade Union Confederation |
| EU | European Union |
| EUCFR | European Union Charter of Fundamental Rights |
| Eur Const LR | European Constitutional Law Review |
| FOM | Swiss Federal Office for Migration |

| | |
|---|---|
| FRA | EU Fundamental Rights Agency |
| FRD | Family Reunification Directive |
| *FRD Ruling* | CJEU ruling on the validity of the FRD (2006) |
| GCIM | Global Commission on International Migration |
| GISTI | Groupe d'information et de soutien des immigrés |
| Harv LR | Harvard Law Review |
| HRC | Human Rights Committee |
| HRLR | Human Rights Law Review |
| HRW | Human Rights Watch |
| IACtHR | Inter-American Court of Human Rights |
| ICCPR | International Covenant on Civil and Political Rights |
| ICESCR | International Covenant on Economic, Social and Cultural Rights |
| ICMPD | International Centre for Migration Policy Development |
| ICTD | Intra-Corporate Transferees Directive |
| IGO | intergovernmental organization |
| IHRL | International Human Rights Law |
| IJCLLIR | International Journal of Comparative Labour Law and Industrial Relations |
| IJRL | International Journal of Refugee Law |
| ILC | International Law Commission |
| ILO | International Labour Organization |
| INTEC | Integration and Naturalisation Tests, the new way to European Citizenship |
| IOM | International Organization for Migration |
| JCMS | Journal of Common Market Studies |
| JRS | Jesuit Refugee Service |
| LIBE | Civil Liberties, Justice and Home Affairs Committee of European Parliament |
| LTR | Long-term Resident |
| LTRD | Long-term Residents Directive |
| Mich JIL | Michigan Journal of International Law |
| MLR | Modern Law Review |
| NGO | non-governmental organization |
| Nord JIL | Nordic Journal of International Law |
| Northwestern U LR | Northwestern University Law Review |
| OAU | Organisation of African Unity |
| OHCHR | Office of the UN High Commissioner for Human Rights |
| OJLS | Oxford Journal of Legal Studies |
| PACE | Parliamentary Assembly of the Council of Europe |
| Pal YIL | Palestinian Yearbook of International Law |
| PD | Asylum Procedures Directive |
| PROSINT | Research Project on Promoting Sustainable Policies for Integration |
| QD | Qualification Directive |
| QMV | Qualified Majority-Voting |
| RCD | Reception Conditions Directive |
| RD | Returns Directive |
| RPD | Recast Procedures Directive |
| RQD | Recast Qualification Directive |
| RRCD | Recast Reception Conditions Directive |

| | |
|---|---|
| RS | refugee status |
| RSQ | Refugee Survey Quarterly |
| SBC | Schengen Borders Code |
| SD | Students Directive |
| SIC | Schengen Implementing Convention |
| SIS | Schengen Information System |
| SP | Subsidiary Protection (under QD and RQD) |
| STC | Safe Third Country |
| SWD | Seasonal Workers Directive |
| TCN | Third Country National |
| TEU | Treaty on European Union |
| TFEU | Treaty on the Functioning of the European Union |
| UDHR | Universal Declaration of Human Rights |
| U Ill LR | University of Illinois Law Review |
| UNHCR | United Nations High Commissioner for Refugees |
| UNHCR ExCom | UNHCR Executive Committee |
| UNRWA | United Nations Relief and Works Agency for Palestine Refugees in the Near East |
| UNTS | United Nations Treaty Series |
| VfGH | Verfassungsgerichtshof (Constitutional Court of Austria) |
| VIS | Visa Information System |
| WGAD | Working Group on Arbitrary Detention |
| Wisconsin LR | Wisconsin Law Review |
| Yale LJ | Yale Law Journal |

# 1

# Destination Europe

## I. Introduction: The Scope of This Book

This book examines some of the ways that human rights law responds to challenges to migration control and migration status, in particular where migrants and refugees seek to establish rights to enter, stay, live with their families, and remain at liberty in Europe. Migration controls and migration status determine the legal predicament in which migrants and refugees find themselves. To best understand the limits and potential of European human rights law, I focus on those areas where migrants and refugees (latu sensu) invoke human rights norms as regards their rights to enter, stay, and be at liberty in Europe. As such, this is not a general human rights treatise—I do not examine how and whether migrants and refugees enjoy the full range of human rights to which they are entitled simply in virtue of being human, such as the right to freedom of expression or to freedom of association, to education, or to fair and just working conditions. Rather, this book examines some of the main areas where migration control and status encounter human rights challenges. The focus of the book is, in other words, on access to territory and authorization of presence and residence, as well as on some related questions of security of residence, as revealed when migrants contest their expulsion from Europe or seek to live with their close family members. The 'human rights' of the title are principally legally enforceable rights, particularly as protected under the European Convention on Human Rights (ECHR) and in European Union (EU) law, which has its own Charter of Fundamental Rights (EUCFR). However, it also assumes that human rights protections should not be 'incarcerated' in the juridical frame, to borrow Sen's memorable phrase.[1] Human rights law has its limits, jurisdictional and practical ones. In some parts of this work, I identify how human rights law fails to meet the promise of human rights ethics. It is assumed that the latter is broader than the former.

'Migration control' refers to the enforcement apparatus surrounding migration and asylum, which extends far beyond the territorial borders of the European States. Migration control also pervasively takes place within the State,

[1] A Sen, 'Elements of a Theory of Human Rights' (2004) 32(4) Philosophy and Public Affairs 315, 319–20.

routinely reaching into family life, workplaces, and educational establishments. 'Migration status' refers to the fact that immigration and asylum law create particular statuses (or none), packages of rights, and obligations of enduring significance. Migration status dictates not only the nature, extent, and duration of rights of entry and residence but also often determines rights in other contexts, in the political realm, in family life, in the workplace, and in economic life generally.[2]

The title of this work refers to 'migrants and refugees'. 'Migrants and refugees' are in the main those who do not hold the nationality of an EU Member State, although the legal position of EU Citizens is referred to for contrast. I examine the key measures concerning both the rights of third-country nationals (TCNs) to enter and stay in the EU *and* the EU's construction of migration status, in particular irregular status.[3] The personal scope is accordingly broad, encompassing those who seek admission for various purposes, be it protection, opportunity, to join family, or a combination of these. I refer to these compendiously as 'admission-seekers'. The figure of the admission seeker is deliberately ambiguous. It assumes that those who seek to enter and live in the EU have many purposes and aims. Some are refugees entitled to international protection, others may have strong moral (and legal) claims as family members of those present in the EU. Although a relatively small proportion of those seeking admission to the EU each year are asylum seekers and refugees,[4] they attract great legal and political attention. This book reflects that phenomenon, with Chapters 5 and 6 focusing on asylum seekers and refugees. Yet, there is also the related phenomenon of the 'disappearing'[5] or 'vanishing' refugee,[6] where migration controls obscure refugeehood. A premise of this book is that the EU blocks access to protection for many refugees (as Chapter 6 examines), and also fails to recognize many of them.[7] The figure of the 'rejected

[2] This book focuses on admissions (rights of entry and residence), but for a collection examining the impact of migration status in work, see C Costello and M Freedland (eds), *Migrants at Work: Immigration and Vulnerability in Labour Law* (OUP 2014).

[3] Throughout, when I refer to migrants or admission-seekers, I mean third-country nationals (TCNs), unless otherwise specified.

[4] By way of example, in 2012, Eurostat reported 1.7m third-country nationals entering the EU, and 319,000 asylum applications (which include pending and subsequent applications). See Eurostat, *Migration and Migrant Population Statistics* (2014) <http://epp.eurostat.ec.europa.eu/statistics_explained/index.php/Migration_and_migrant_population_statistics> accessed 10 April 2015; Eurostat, *Asylum Applicants and First Instance Decisions on Asylum Applications* (2013) KS-QA-13-005-EN-N, 5.

[5] A Macklin, '"Disappearing Refugees": Reflections on the Canada–US Safe Third Country Agreement' (2005) 36(2) Columbia Human Rights Law Review 101.

[6] JF Durieux, 'The Vanishing Refugee: How EU Asylum Law Blurs the Specificity of Refugee Protection' in H Lambert, J McAdam, and M Fullerton (eds), *The Global Reach of European Refugee Law* (Cambridge University Press 2013) 225.

[7] While it is difficult to establish definitely that asylum processes are unreliable, we have copious evidence that asylum procedures in many EU Member States are unfair, and often lead to the rejection of strong claims. See *IM v France*, App No 9152/09 (ECHR, 2 May 2012); *AC v Spain*, App No 6528/11 (ECHR, 22 April 2014); UNHCR, *Improving Asylum Procedures: Comparative Analysis and Recommendations for Law and Practice* (UNHCR, 2010) <http://www.unhcr.org/4c7b71039.pdf> accessed 10 April 2015.

asylum seeker with unmet protection needs', or the 'unrecognised refugee' caught up in the EU's migration control apparatus, emerges in various guises in this book. Also, with refugees in mind, I note that many who ought to be recognized as refugees have no legal route to the EU.

No doubt there are some privileged migrants and even some refugees who glide into the EU with ease. They meet all applicable legal prerequisites, overcome bureaucratic hurdles, and settle in the EU. Over time, they gain a permanent right to reside, and if they naturalize, EU Citizenship. For them, the migration controls of 'Destination Europe' entail no obvious human rights violations—they are afforded a right to reside in the country of choice at the outset, and across the EU in time. However, for many others, migration controls are increasingly intense, blunt, and even arbitrary. Their migration status is often precarious. The cases examined throughout this book emerge from diverse contexts, where people enter the EU irregularly to live with their family members, or to seek international protection. They also concern long-term residents, whose migration status may fail to recognize their deep connections with their host countries, or impede their freedom to live with their families. Precarious migration status is all too common, resulting in many migrants being increasingly constructed as deportable, and in turn detainable. In this context, migrants have recourse to human rights law to seek to remedy or at least mitigate their legal predicament.

While international law creates a privileged status for refugees, they too are subject to migration controls, and are often granted only a precarious status, if any. Refugees, asylum seekers, and rejected claimants with unmet protection needs thus also turn to human rights law, when their protection claims are wrongly rejected or when they face detention or other human rights restrictions in the name of migration control. Access to protection is the most acute human rights issue facing those fleeing persecution and serious harm: without access to territory and fair, reliable determination procedures, the privileged status envisaged for refugees is a mirage.

Accordingly, the 'European Law' of the title encompasses the human rights law of the ECHR and that of the EU. Indeed, the focus of the work is on the interactions, tensions, and frictions across those two systems, in particular as manifest in the overlapping jurisdiction of the European Court of Human Rights (ECtHR) and the Court of Justice of the European Union (CJEU).[8] The central contention of this book is that while the ECtHR provides important protections for the human rights of migrants, when issues of admissions are at stake, that court is too deferential to the States' migration control prerogatives. EU law offers transformative potential. It is to understanding the role of the EU in this field that this opening chapter now turns.

[8] The pervasive overlapping of ECHR and EU on these topics is evident in the joint publication of the Council of Europe and the EU's Fundamental Rights Agency *Handbook on European Law Relating to Asylum, Borders and Immigration* (2nd edn, Council of Europe/FRA 2014).

## II. *Telos* and *Chora:* The Contested Project of European Union

The 'Destination Europe' of the chapter title refers not only to the end-point of migrants' journeys, their chosen *chora*, but also the EU's own destination, its telos. The EU is a contested project. It has thrived on its cryptic *telos* of 'ever closer union among the peoples of Europe'. Despite episodic talk of finalité politique, ambiguity and becoming-ness are likely to remain a defining feature of European integration. Indeed, we seem to be at a point in EU development where 'ever closer' may need to be understood as 'ever looser' with differentiation embraced as a feature of unity, not a threat thereto. Nonetheless, in deciding on the location and nature of its external boundaries, the EU is engaging in a crucial process of self-definition.

This book examines a key aspect of that process of self-definition, namely how the EU sets up the legal structures, institutions, and rules governing who may live in the *chora* that is the EU, the container defined by presence and interaction, a condominium for those who live together, characterized by their disparate nationalities, defined by unity in diversity. While the EU project has transformed some migration between Member States into liberalized 'mobility', its engagement with formal law-making on immigration and asylum of those from outside the EU (so-called 'third-country nationals' or 'TCNs'[9]) dates to the Treaty of Amsterdam[10] and is usually regarded as following an exclusionary logic, in contrast to the internal liberalization. This book takes issue with the sharp insider-outsider dichotomy that account suggests, and instead identifies complex stratifications of status and rights in this field.

Making a human rights claim may be a last recourse for many. However, as human rights protections are institutionalized at the supranational level in the EU and under the ECHR, human rights law sets up a process to adjudicate whether migration status and migration control violate human rights. The migrant, by definition a non-citizen, is nowadays a rights-bearer. Staking a human rights claim may be a last recourse, but given the institutional and in particular judicial protection of rights in the EU, that claim is not as futile as was imagined by Arendt.[11] And yet, the human rights of migrants remain precarious and contested when they seek to use human rights protections to secure rights of entry and residence.

[9] 'Third-country national' defines migrant as a person holding the nationality of a State other than an EU Member State. Of course, the problem of statelessness persists in Europe and globally, raising a distinct set of problems not directly addressed in this book. But see further A Edwards and L Van Waas, *Nationality and Statelessness in International Law* (Cambridge University Press 2014).

[10] Treaty of Amsterdam [1997] OJ C 340/1.

[11] 'No paradox of contemporary politics is filled with more poignant irony than the discrepancy between the efforts of well-meaning idealists who stubbornly insist on regarding as "inalienable" those human rights, which are enjoyed only by citizens of the most prosperous and civilized countries, and the situations of the rightless themselves.' H Arendt, 'Decline of the Nation-State: End of the Rights of Man' in *The Origins of Totalitarianism* (Harcourt Brace 1985) 267–302.

The EU both bolsters and limits the Member States in their admission control dictates and itself shapes and determines the matter of admissions. The chapter structure reflects the peculiar shared competence of the EU and its Member States over migration and asylum. The EU does not subsume the Member States' migration control prerogatives entirely: in some respects, it bolsters their control prerogatives and capacity to refuse entry and residence by deeming migration (and migrants) 'illegal'. Thus the substantive analysis begins in Chapter 3, which examines how migration status emerges. It sets out the EU's border control instruments, and the Returns Directive (RD)[12] and Employer Sanctions Directive (ESD).[13] Concerning EU rights to enter and reside, Chapter 4 focuses on the Family Reunification Directive (FRD),[14] while Chapters 5 and 6 examine aspects of the three key asylum Directives and their recasts: the original and recast Qualification Directive (QD);[15] the original and recast Asylum Procedures Directive (PD);[16] the original and recast Reception Conditions Directive (RCD),[17] as well as the Dublin II Regulation[18] and its recast version, the Dublin III Regulation,[19] and related instruments.[20] The examined EU measures, the FRD, the recast QD and PD in

[12] Directive 2008/115/EC of the European Parliament and of the Council of 16 December 2008 on common standards and procedures in Member States for returning illegally staying third-country nationals (RD) [2008] OJ L348/98.

[13] Directive 2009/52/EC of the European Parliament and of the Council of 18 June 2009 providing for minimum standards on sanctions and measures against employers of illegally staying third-country nationals (ESD) [2009] OJ L168/24.

[14] Council Directive 2003/86/EC of 22 September 2003 on the right to family reunification (FRD) [2003] OJ L251/12.

[15] Council Directive 2004/83/EC of 29 April 2004 on minimum standards for the qualification and status of third country nationals or stateless persons as refugees or as persons who otherwise need international protection and the content of the protection granted (QD) [2004] OJ L304/12; Directive 2011/95/EU of the European Parliament and of the Council of 13 December 2011 on standards for the qualification of third-country nationals or stateless persons as beneficiaries of international protection, for a uniform status for refugees or for persons eligible for subsidiary protection, and for the content of the protection granted (recast QD) [2011] OJ L337/9.

[16] Council Directive 2005/85/EC of 1 December 2005 on minimum standards on procedures in Member States for granting and withdrawing refugee status (PD) [2005] OJ L326/13; Directive 2013/32/EU of the European Parliament and of the Council of 26 June 2013 on common procedures for granting and withdrawing international protection (recast PD) [2013] OJ L180/60.

[17] Council Directive 2003/9/EC of 27 January 2003 laying down minimum standards for the reception of asylum seekers (RCD) [2003] OJ L31/18; Directive 2013/33/EU of the European Parliament and of the Council of 26 June 2013 laying down standards for the reception of applicants for international protection (recast RCD) [2013] OJ L180/96.

[18] Council Regulation (EC) No 343/2003 of 18 February 2003 establishing the criteria and mechanisms for determining the Member State responsible for examining an asylum application lodged in one of the Member States by a third-country national (Dublin II Regulation) [2003] OJ L50/1.

[19] Regulation (EU) No 604/2013 of the European Parliament and of the Council of 26 June 2013 establishing the criteria and mechanisms for determining the Member State responsible for examining an application for international protection lodged in one of the Member States by a third-country national or stateless person (recast) (Dublin III Regulation) [2013] OJ L180/31.

[20] The Dublin System comprises the Dublin Regulation and the Eurodac database, set up by Council Regulation (EC) No 2725/2000 of 11 December 2000 concerning the establishment of 'Eurodac' for the comparison of fingerprints for the effective application of the Dublin Convention (EURODAC Regulation) [2000] OJ L316/1. This has now been recast by Regulation (EU) No 603/2013 of the European Parliament and of the Council on the establishment of 'Eurodac' [...] (recast EURODAC Regulation) [2013] OJ L180/1.

particular, deal with those border crossings where human rights norms have already established some constraints on State discretion.[21] Chapter 7 looks at immigration detention. Accordingly, the chosen focus is on the interaction between established human rights norms, in particular the ECHR and international refugee law, principally the 1951 Convention on the Status of Refugees and its 1967 Protocol (the 'Refugee Convention' or 'CSR').[22]

These fields of EU law map onto established European Court of Human Rights (ECtHR) case law. The book thus re-examines some well-trodden issues, where migrants have invoked ECHR protections in seeking rights to enter and to establish rights to stay. My focus is on the migration-related case law, or even more accurately case law where migration status has a bearing on the human right claimed. Cases include those seeking admission at Europe's frontiers, or more commonly rejected asylum seekers and other migrants seeking protection against removal, for instance on grounds that deportation would expose them to violations of Article 3 ECHR, claims to enter or remain based on family ties and other connections framed under Article 8 ECHR, and immigration detention under Article 5 ECHR. The unifying theme, accordingly, is how the EU has incorporated and transformed human rights norms concerning admission-seekers.

There are thus two, if not three, dynamic bodies of law under scrutiny here: The case law of the ECtHR on migrant rights, which contains notable unstable features, which are highlighted and, where appropriate, critiqued throughout. Then, there is EU law on migration and asylum, which has been subject to legislative revision and progressive judicial interpretations. Thirdly, we have international refugee law, in particular the CSR, which lacks a central enforcement authority, but is characterized by dynamic interpretation and cross-fertilization across jurisdictions, viewed by many as an exemplar of transnational judicial dialogue.[23] Unsurprisingly then, given that the focus is on the interactions across these three domains—EU–ECHR–international refugee law—this work must take some liberties with each domain in seeking to capture each regime's internal dynamic. Of course, it cannot attempt an exhaustive, all-embracing description of each domain, so much is bracketed out for the purposes of exposition.

The importance of the EU's engagement in this human rights sensitive field is of general significance to contemporary debates on the role of human rights in Europe. The place of human rights in the EU remains contested, with some

[21] Throughout, 'human rights' is used in a broad sense to include national constitutional rights and international human rights law (IHRL), in particular the ECHR and fundamental rights protected within the EU legal order. Where it is necessary to differentiate, I refer to IHRL as a generic term for international instruments, and 'constitutional rights' for those human rights generally found in national constitutional bills of rights. I conceive of both sets of rights as interlinked. See further G de Búrca and O Gerstenberg, 'The Denationalization of Constitutional Law' (2006) 47 Harvard International Law Journal 243.

[22] Convention relating to the Status of Refugees (adopted 28 July 1951) 189 UNTS 137.

[23] G Goodwin-Gill and H Lambert, *The Limits of Transnational Law: Refugee Law, Policy Harmonization and Judicial Dialogue in the European Union* (Cambridge University Press 2010).

suggesting that the EU should re-orientate itself as a human rights organization.[24] With the entry into force of the Lisbon Treaty on 1 December 2009, the EU's constitutional commitment to fundamental rights was made more explicit: The EU Charter of Fundamental Rights (the 'Charter' or 'EUCFR') became binding, the EU committed to accede to the ECHR, and reaffirmed that fundamental rights were general principles of EU law.[25]

In 2014, the Court of Justice of the European Union (CJEU) ruled that the Draft EU Accession Agreement to the ECHR was incompatible with EU law.[26] All the EU institutions and 28 Member States intervening argued that the agreement was compatible. The mode of accession aimed to take into account the shared human rights obligations of the EU and its Member States under the ECHR, as exemplified in the co-respondent mechanism.[27] To understand that ruling, we must go back to Opinion 2/94,[28] in which the CJEU ruled that the European Community (as it then was) could not accede to the ECHR for lack of specific competence. That Opinion was open to criticism for privileging the Court's hegemony in matters of EU law over establishing external accountability in human rights matters.[29] A Treaty amendment was required to enable accession, so in 2009 the Treaty of Lisbon included a duty to accede to the ECHR in Article 6(2) TEU.[30]

The hard work of accession required adaptations on the ECHR side, too, and the EU had to negotiate an accession treaty with the Council of Europe and its 47 members, a process which took several years. The resulting Accession Agreement sought to create mechanisms to adapt ECHR membership to the particularities of the EU constitutional set-up.[31] Opinion 2/13 is complex and already has attracted much criticism,[32] with one commentator arguing that the EU should accede to the

[24] A Von Bogdandy, 'The European Union as a Human Rights Organization? Human Rights and the Core of the European Union' (2000) 37 CMLRev 1307; S Besson, 'The European Union and Human Rights: Towards a New Kind of Post-National Human Rights Institution' (2006) 6 HRLRev 323.

[25] Art 6 TEU [2012] OJ C326/1.

[26] *Opinion 2/13 on EU Accession to the ECHR* [2015] OJ C 65/C.

[27] T Lock, 'EU Accession to the ECHR: Implications for the Judicial Review of Strasbourg' (2010) European Law Review 777; T Lock, 'End of an Epic? The Draft Accession Agreement on the EU's Accession to the ECHR' (2012) 31(1) Yearbook of European Law 162; C Eckes, 'EU Accession to the ECHR: Between Autonomy and Adaptation' (2013) 76(2) MLR 254; V Kosta, N Skoutaris, and V Tzevelekos (eds), *The EU Accession to the ECHR* (Hart Publishing 2014).

[28] *Opinion 2/94 (Accession to the ECHR)* [1996] ECR I-1759.

[29] P Alston and JHH Weiler, 'An "Ever Closer Union" in Need of a Human Rights Policy: The European Union and Human Rights' (1998) 9 European Journal of International Law 658.

[30] The Lisbon Treaty also included Protocol No 8 relating to Article 6(2) of Treaty on European Union on the Accession of the European Union to the European Convention on the Protection of Human Rights and Fundamental Freedoms [2012] OJ C326/1 and Declaration on Article 6(2) of the Treaty on European Union [2012] OJ C326/390, requiring that accession to the ECHR must comply with the 'specific features' of EU law.

[31] See Lock, 'End of an Epic?' (n 27).

[32] S Douglas-Scott, 'The Relationship between the EU and the ECHR Five Years on from the Treaty of Lisbon' in S de Vries, U Bernitz, and S Weatherill (eds), *The EU Charter of Fundamental Rights as a Binding Instrument: Five Years Old and Growing* (Hart Publishing 2015, *forthcoming*); S Peers, 'The CJEU and the EU's Accession to the ECHR: A Clear and Present Danger to Human Rights Protection' *EU Law Analysis*, 18 December 2014.

ECHR notwithstanding the Opinion.[33] That move would be a legal and political rupture, so it looks more likely that accession is stalled. In the meantime, the two courts will continue to interact. If anything, now that accession has been stalled, greater frictions may emerge.

The scope of EU human rights obligations remains contested, with resistance from governments evident in their keenness to avoid the development of a general EU human rights jurisdiction to scrutinize all national acts.[34] The examination throughout this work emphasizes that 'human rights' cannot be regarded as a matter of settled law, which the EU must simply respect or import from other systems. Rather, human rights claims beg questions about access and allocation of rights, which demand a distinctive EU answer. The EU must not only respect international standards, but also inform their progressive development in a way that fits its own distinctive legal and constitutional context. After Opinion 2/2013, the challenge may well be to ensure that its own way does not become one of isolation, but remains constructively engaged with other human rights instruments. The reasoning of the CJEU has wider implications for its conception of the EU legal order, and so is explored further in Chapter 2.

## III. Human Rights and Migration Control

Chapter 2 sets out the approach to human rights pluralism espoused, one in which mutual engagement and interaction across different human rights regimes is encouraged. But crucially, divergence is also embraced, in particular where there are good reasons for higher standards of protection within the EU system.[35] That chapter identifies several reasons why the EU can and should establish human rights standards within this zone of upward flexibility, escaping some of the limitative features of the ECtHR, which are rooted in that institution's particular institutional context. I identify the constitutional, institutional, and legislative aspects of the EU which warrant distinctive human rights protections for migrants. In key areas, this book examines how the EU's approach to migrants' rights should (and in some instances does already) depart from the ECHR pan-European minimum, namely on family migration, the scope of protection for refugees, the allocation of responsibility for asylum claims, and detention standards.

[33] L Besselink, 'Acceding to the ECHR notwithstanding the Court of Justice Opinion 2/13' *Verfassungsblog*, 23 February 2015.

[34] See on the scope of EU review over national acts, Case C-617/10 *Åkerberg Fransson* [2013] OJ C 114/7. See further, E Hancox, 'The Meaning of "Implementing" EU Law under Article 51(1) of the Charter: *Åkerberg Fransson*' (2013) 50(5) CMLRev 1411.

[35] cf J Callewaert, 'The European Convention on Human Rights and European Union Law: A Long Way to Harmony' (2009) 6 HRLR 768.

In spite of its universal premises and aspirations, international human rights law, of which the ECHR is an exemplar, acknowledges and accommodates States' migration control imperatives. In contrast, when we turn to the EU domain, the State is no longer the same plenipotentiary actor. Its competences in the migration field are transformed by being shared both horizontally with other States and vertically with the EU authorities.

For the purposes of this book, I assume that strong judicial protection of human rights is appropriate. Under many accounts of human rights adjudication, in those instances when there is reasonable disagreement about rights-protection, democratically-accountable institutions ought to be afforded leeway in determining the scope of rights. However, in examining migrants' rights at the European level, this concern plays out differently. To put it strongly, when the human rights of the unenfranchised migrant are at issue, the democratic credentials of elected bodies are lacking. While some aspects of migration control and migration status may be justified, by definition, the bodies setting these standards are not representative of those affected interests. Accordingly, majoritarian concerns about judicial review and human rights dissipate. On this point we may helpfully recall the statement of Advocate-General (AG) Maduro in *Panayotova*:

> Judicial protection of fundamental rights is particularly important with regard to the treatment accorded to [TCNs], since the latter constitute 'discrete and insular minorities'. These are often particularly vulnerable groups that are deprived of other means, in particular political means to influence legislation and the political process, for the protection of their rights. Aliens, by the very nature of the political community, cannot benefit from all the rights granted to the citizens of that political community, but it is precisely for the same reason that they deserve added judicial protection where rights granted to them are affected by decisions of the same political community.[36]

No doubt that normative claim may be contested, but settling that debate is not the purpose of this work. For the purposes of this book, a robust judicial role in protecting migrant and refugee rights is assumed to be right and proper, as I hope will be borne out by the substantive analysis in the ensuing chapters. Moreover, as is explored further in Chapter 2, that judicial role varies according to the constitutional and institutional context of the judicial body concerned, so divergent interpretations of human rights are not only inevitable, but also desirable. In particular, my work is informed by the inclusive, rights-protective dynamic observed in other fields of EU law.

In the next section, I provide a sketch (perhaps a caricature) of the 'statist assumption' under IHRL. My assertion is that this explains at least some of why human rights law fails to protect migrants' and refugees' rights appropriately. Then I turn to the 'transformative potential' of the EU context.

[36] Case C-327/02 *Panayotova* [2004] ECR I-11055, Opinion of AG Maduro, para 47, citing the United States Supreme Court in *United States v Carolene Products* 304 US 144 (1938). See further D Strauss, 'Is *Carolene Products* Obsolete?' (2010) U Ill. LR 4 1251.

## 1. IHRL and the statist assumption

Human rights are understood as universal, in that they inhere in all persons simply by virtue of their being human.[37] That promise sits uneasily with statist border control, which presupposes rights enjoyed within bounded States, with States having a sovereign right to control admissions. The figure of the refugee stands out as the exception that constitutes this rule: while international law does not afford refugees a right to protection in any particular State, or even a right to enter any particular State to seek protection in most circumstances, the norm of *non-refoulement* is understood to apply at the border (and under certain circumstances further afield),[38] in a manner that limits whether States may turn away those seeking protection. The exception to statist border controls for refugees has hugely important symbolic dimensions, and it serves to justify the institutionalization of exclusion that would otherwise be ethically and politically indefensible.

When it comes to entry and residence rights, the notion of the State's 'sovereign' right to exclude sometimes seems to obviate any need for justification of its actions. Here, we encounter a version of old-style sovereignty, which elides sovereignty and unfettered State discretion. I refer throughout to the 'statist entry control assumption' or simply the 'statist assumption' to connote this notion that States have a sovereign right to exclude aliens without justification. Undoubtedly, this notion warrants challenge on ethical grounds,[39] and cries out for historical corrective.[40] The statist assumption seems out of place in an age of human rights, and increasing transnational economic and social interpenetration. Yet, in the migration context, it remains stubbornly ingrained.[41]

This statist assumption is reflected in the Universal Declaration of Human Rights (UDHR),[42] and percolates through other instruments. The UDHR speaks of a 'right to nationality' but not in the country of one's residence or choosing. It affirms the right 'to freedom of movement and residence' but only 'within the borders of each state'[43] and everyone's 'right to leave any country, including his own, and to return to his country',[44] but not to enter another. Other binding

[37] Tasioulas refers to this as the 'orthodox view' of human rights. J Tasioulas, 'Towards a Philosophy of Human Rights' (2012) 65 CLP 1.

[38] *Hirsi Jamaa v Italy* (2012) 55 EHRR 21; C Costello, 'Courting Access to Asylum in Europe: Recent Supranational Jurisprudence Explored' (2012) 12(2) HRLR 287.

[39] Even without endorsing an open borders position, many facets of migration control and migration status are ethically problematic. See further, C Wellman and P Cole, *Debating the Ethics of Immigration* (OUP 2011).

[40] For critiques of the presentation of the statist assumption in light of the historical development of public international law, see J Nafziger, 'The General Admission of Aliens under International Law' (1983) 77 AJIL 804; S Juss, 'Free Movement and the World Order' (2004) 16 IJRL 289.

[41] See further, C Dauvergne, 'Sovereignty, Migration and the Rule of Law in Global Times' (2004) 67 MLR 588; M Schain, 'The State Strikes Back: Immigration Policy in the European Union' (2009) 20(1) EJIL 93.

[42] Universal Declaration of Human Rights (UDHR), UN General Assembly Resolution 217 A (III), 10 December 1948.

[43] Art 13(1) UDHR. [44] Art 13(2) UDHR.

instruments follow this pattern.[45] As Benhabib puts it, 'a series of internal contradictions between universal human rights and territorial sovereignty are built into the logic of the most comprehensive international law documents in our world'.[46] Of course, these contradictions create instabilities and sites of contestation, with diverse outcomes when migrants and refugees seek to draw down universal protections into particular contexts.

Scholars examining these tensions between human rights and migration control and status have tended to fall within three broad categories. Soysal exemplifies the universal. She argued that the development of IHRL marked a transition from nationality to humanity as the primary reference for the enjoyment of rights, diminishing the distinction between citizens and aliens.[47] Her 1994 thesis seems to have a naïve 'end of history' ring to it twenty years on. On the other extreme, we find scholars who emphasize the persistent significance of migration control and alienage within IHRL.[48] IHRL, rather than opening up space to resolve tensions between admissions control and sometimes tending to freeze this conflict, reify it, supporting the statist assumption. In this vein, it has been suggested that the international legal character of IHRL instruments ties them to the State system.[49] Accordingly, norms which manifest State sovereignty 'alter and shape human rights provisions'.[50] International refugee law similarly may be characterized at either pole, either as the sole exception to the statist assumption, rendering it barely palatable, or as a yawning chasm which reflects the illusory nature of States' border control myths.

This work locates itself on the more ambivalent middle terrain, drawing on the work of Benhabib. She identifies the apparently 'irresolvable contradiction' between universal human rights and democratic self-determination within bounded polities.[51] Yet, while she accepts that this contradiction cannot be overcome, she argues that it can be mediated and mitigated through 'democratic iterations', including 'jurisgenerative politics'.[52] These are the deliberative processes in which universalist rights claims are contested and contextualized.[53] Courts are amongst the 'strong public bodies' engaged in these processes.

[45] See International Covenant on Civil and Political Rights (ICCPR), 16 December 1966, UN Treaty Series vol. 999, 171, Arts 12 and 13.

[46] S Benhabib, *The Rights of Others: Aliens, Residents and Citizens* (Cambridge University Press 2004) 11. In her later work, these ideas are further developed. See S Benhabib, *Dignity in Adversity: Human Rights in Troubled Times* (Polity Press 2011), in particular Chapters 8–10.

[47] Y Soysal, *Limits of Citizenship Migrants and Postnational Membership in Europe* (University of Chicago Press 1994).

[48] L Bosniak, 'Universal Citizenship and the Problem of Alienage' (2000) 94 Northwestern U LR 963.

[49] See further, S Meckled-García and B Çali, 'Lost in Translation: The Human Rights Ideal and International Human Rights Law' in S Meckled-García and B Çali (eds), *The Legalization of Human Rights: Multidisciplinary Perspectives on Human Rights and Human Rights Law* (Routledge 2006), 11.

[50] ibid, 18. [51] Benhabib (n 46) 19.

[52] ibid, 176–81, drawing on R Cover, 'Foreword: Nomos and Narrative' (1983) 97 Harv LR 4 and F Michelman, 'Law's Republic' (1988) 97 Yale LJ 1493.

[53] ibid, 179.

## 2. From ECHR to the EU: Interfaces and interactions

Admission-seekers' claims place courts in a position where they must at least recognize the migrant as a rights-bearer, a legal subject. In so doing, courts may legitimately act as agents of inclusion, or potentially exclusion. Accordingly, as is explored throughout the book, the ECtHR- the human rights institution at the heart of this work- has unsettled statist border control assumptions, albeit in tentative fashion. My starting intuition was that relocating matters of asylum and immigration into the EU realm was replete with further transformative potential, in particular in shifting admissions to shared EU-Member State competence with the aim of creating an 'Area of Freedom, Security and Justice' (AFSJ). That intuition has proved correct as regards some migrants. The CJEU has asserted that, where EU law sets out exhaustive and clear admissions criteria, national authorities must accord a right to enter, not merely unsettling, but effectively inverting the statist assumption.[54] However, in other contexts, the EU amplifies Member States' discretionary control over migration, and even amplifies 'illegality' across the EU, as Chapter 3 explores.

Accordingly, in this dynamic domain, the central question addressed is how the EU has incorporated and transformed human rights norms concerning admission-seekers, focusing in particular on those of the ECHR and international refugee law. A process of mutual influence is revealed. While the main concern is to identify when and why it is appropriate for EU standards to exceed the Strasbourg minimum, EU law may in turn influence Strasbourg developments. The EU emerges in this process from its previous role as passive human rights 'standard receiver' to a more active 'standard setter'.[55] In large part then, this book is unabashedly doctrinal. It examines in detail the EU legislative measures, Luxembourg case law, and Strasbourg jurisprudence. Yet, the underlying supposition is constructivist, prompted by Benhabib's view of 'jurisgenerative politics'.

Following other EU constructivist literature, I share the view that:

> Agents [including courts] have the capacity to capitalize on the normative surplus of meaning and the progressive possibilities already present in accepted logics and existing conceptual resources nested within institutions in order to develop new conceptions, to construct and extend norms and to act in complex environments. On this basis, institutional change is not iterative, that is reproducing the same ideas, norms, patterns

[54] On Regulation (EC) No 810/2009 of the European Parliament and of the Council of 13 July 2009 establishing a Community Code for Visas (Visa Code) [2009] OJ L243/1, see Case C-84/12 *Koushkaki* [2014] OJ C 52/7; Case C-575/12 *Air Baltic Corporation* [2014] OJ C 395/8. On Council Directive 2004/144/EC of 14 December 2004 on the conditions of admission of third-country nationals for the purposes of studies, pupil exchange, unremunerated training or voluntary service (Students' Directive) [2004] OJ L375/12, see Case C-491/13 *Ben Alaya* [2014] OJ C 409/18. See further D Kostakopoulou, D Acosta Arcarazo, and T Munk, 'EU Migration Law: The Opportunities and Challenges Ahead' in D Acosta Arcarazo and C Murphy (eds), *EU Security and Justice Law after Lisbon and Stockholm* (Hart Publishing 2014) 129–45.

[55] O De Schutter, 'The Division of Tasks between the Council of Europe and the European Union in the Promotion of Human Rights in Europe: Conflict, Competition and Complementarity' (2007) REFGOV-FR-11 Working Paper, 3.

and practices. It is instead more fluid, contingent, unpredictable, and more importantly, transformative.[56]

The EU's own distinctive human rights standards are now embodied in the Charter and the general principles of EU law.[57] Both sources draw on the ECHR, and indeed there are references to the CSR in the Charter and in EU primary and secondary law. The Charter sets up an interface whereby the rights therein which correspond to ECHR rights should be interpreted in a similar way, unless EU law provides additional protection.[58] The wording of this interface in Article 52(3) EUCFR is worth setting out in full. It states that: 'In so far as this Charter contains rights which correspond to rights guaranteed by the [ECHR] the meaning and scope of those rights shall be the same as those laid down by the said Convention.' The crucial addendum is that: 'This provision shall not prevent Union law providing more extensive protection.' The Charter also protects the right to asylum 'with due respect for the rules of [CSR] and in accordance with the [EU Treaties].[59]

In this context, interpretative harmony between the EU, ECHR, and Refugee Convention might seem like the most legally appropriate option. However, this book argues, to the contrary, that the distinctive features of the EU warrant a different approach to human rights claims by migrants. It does so by seeking to understand the extant limits of the ECtHR case law (which of course may be overcome in time), and the distinctive constitutional context of the EU. Chapter 2 develops that argument. The next part seeks to explore the constitutional and institutional context of the EU, and its transformative potential.

## IV. The EU's Transformative Potential: Beyond Statism to Shared Competence

### 1. The common market and 'free movement'

In order to appreciate the significance of the EU's role in relation to admissions, a brief excursus into the development of its competence on migration and asylum is necessary. The 1957 Treaty of Rome aimed to create that advanced form of economic integration, a common market, in which not only products (goods and services) but also the factors of production (labour and

[56] D Kostakopoulou, 'Ideas, Norms and European Citizenship: Explaining Institutional Change' (2005) 68 Modern Law Review 233, 236–37.

[57] Art 6 TEU.

[58] Charter of Fundamental Rights of the European Union (EUCFR) [2007] OJ C-303/1, Art 52(3).

[59] Art 18 EUCFR.

capital) would be liberalized. The original economic rationales underlying the common market could have, and arguably should have, embraced migration of at least those TCNs settled within the territory of the Member States. If the rationale for internal free movement was efficient allocation of products and the factors of production, excluding some residents from that market defies the efficiency rationale. However, early on it became clear that such an interpretation was not acceptable to most Member States, and the first admission and further movement of TCNs was viewed as originally escaping the Community context.[60]

There are two defining features of internal free movement of persons as it evolved, which means it differs greatly from migration under the statist assumption. Firstly, as Chapter 3 explores in greater detail, EU law creates secure migration status, with rights of entry and residence that take precedence over national law. Although EU Citizens may have to comply with certain conditions of residence, and may be amenable to deportation *in extremis*, the right to entry and residence has a particular weightiness that constrains domestic discretion. Crucially, the rights to entry and residence subsist irrespective of domestic authorization.[61]

Secondly, internal free movement is not only for those who fall into narrowly defined migration categories (seasonal worker, high-skilled migrant, family migrant and so on). Although originally conceived of as being for defined economic purposes (work, service provision, establishment), these were not narrowly drawn categories. Now, they have been largely subsumed into the overarching category of EU Citizenship.[62] The effect is that rather than temporally and functionally defined status, which depends on meeting strict legal requirements, internal free movement can genuinely be characterized as mobility, with 'rights allowing people to send their children abroad to study, shop internationally with consumer protection, buy houses in sunnier climes, retire and collect pensions, get emergency medical treatment, marry and have normal family life and social benefits with a foreign European spouse, and countless other shorter and longer term cross-border mobilities'.[63] It could be argued that this process is the creation of a European *ersatz* nationality, but that is precisely the outcome I seek to avoid. Rather, as Chapter 2 elaborates, these developments are not reflective of insider privilege, but arise from immanent features of the EU legal order, in particular its approach to individual rights.

[60] The exception related to the free movement of services, where the original Treaty provided for the extension of the freedom to TCNs—ex Art 49(2) EC, now Art 56(2) TFEU.

[61] Case 48/75 *Royer* [1976] ECR 497; Case C-413/99 *Baumbast* [2002] ECR I-7091.

[62] Admittedly, economic activity still matters, but much less than for other migrants. N Nic Shuibhne, 'The Resilience of EU Market Citizenship' (2010) 47(6) CMLRev 1597; M Everson, 'The Legacy of the Market Citizen' in J Shaw and G More (eds), *New Legal Dynamics of European Union* (Clarendon Press 1995) 73.

[63] A Favell, 'The UK has been one of the main beneficiaries of free movement of labour in the EU' (*EUROPP*, 1 July 2014) <http://blogs.lse.ac.uk/europpblog/2014/07/01/the-uk-has-been-one-of-the-main-beneficiaries-from-free-movement-of-labour-in-the-eu/> accessed 10 April 15.

## 2. The control ethos of Schengen

Internal free movement evolved largely in the judicial arena, and was largely politically uncontroversial in an EU of 9, 12, and even 15 Member States. A core group of States, keen to facilitate cross border movement, set up the Schengen arrangements in order to abolish internal border controls. Engagement with immigration and asylum policies regarding TCNs was treated as a necessary response to internal free movement. This 'compensatory measures rationale' provided the institutional rationalization for much of the activity in the admissions field under the Schengen arrangements,[64] and continues to be a feature of EU policy discourse on asylum and migration today. In a typical policy statement, the Commission set out the linkages thus:

> The lifting of controls at internal borders in the Schengen area [of then twenty-five countries] has enabled people to travel from the Iberian Peninsula to the Baltic States and from Greece to Finland without having to go through any border checks. This potentially benefits over 400 million EU Citizens, and implies that Member States trust in each other's ability to guard effectively the external borders on behalf of the EU and to issue visas for the whole Schengen area.[65]

In this context, positing the 'need' for EU external control policies as a result of the creation of internal free movement (which is still predominantly for EU Citizens) is like saying a Free Trade Area must have a Common External Tariff (a leap the trade lawyers would presumably question). As long as internal free movement rights are only for EU Citizens, there is no logical requirement for common immigration or asylum policies. As Bigo argues, '[t]he debate on compensatory measures and the security deficit created by the opening of the internal borders [is] one of the strongest myths of EU self-presentation'.[66] Its mythic nature is revealed by scrutinizing the unexplained linkages. In particular, stating that the lack of internal border controls requires an external immigration and asylum policy cannot explain the restrictiveness of admissions policies. If internal free movement extends to all within the territory, it is still agnostic as to the restrictiveness or otherwise of external barriers. It simply requires the application of common rules. For example, for internal free trade in goods in a customs union, there must be a common external tariff and commercial policy, but not of any particular restrictiveness. In contrast, in relation to the admissions of persons, the EU's role at least initially was to develop an entry control system, rather than common rules on admissions, which have

[64] J Monar, 'The Dynamics of Justice and Home Affairs: Laboratories, Driving Factors and Costs' (2001) 39 JCMS 747, 754.

[65] European Commission, *Justice, Freedom and Security in Europe Since 2005: An Evaluation of the Hague Programme and Action Plan*, COM(2009) 263 final, 4.

[66] D Bigo, 'Border Regimes, Police Cooperation and Security in an Enlarged European Union' in J Zielonka (ed), *Europe Unbound: Enlarging and Reshaping the Boundaries of the European Union* (Routledge 2003). See also P Andreas, *Border Games: Policing the US–Mexico Divide* (Cornell University Press 2000) 116.

emerged only for some categories of migrants, and of late. The lie that this system is required by the imperative of internal free movement is also revealed in relation to the UK and Ireland's participation in a range of external border control measures, without any commitment to the abolition of internal border controls.[67]

The institutional features of Schengen arrangements, and, post-Maastricht, the intergovernmental EU, contributed to the adoption of measures treating immigration and asylum as demanding a control response.[68] Wallace characterizes these interactions as 'intensive transgovernmentalism',[69] wherein officials from interior ministries overcame their domestic legal and political constraints,[70] bringing a particular security dominated view of migration and asylum issues.[71] Criticism has been harsh: officials from national interior ministries created an institutional framework marred by lack of 'coherence, consistency, democratic accountability, respect for the rule of law and for human rights, and effectiveness'.[72] In this respect, the EU level served as one amongst many networks and loose consultative bodies, largely dominated by governments keen to restrict admissions or at least 'manage migration', all of which tend to underpin, indeed bolster, the statist assumption. The EU's defining feature was the capacity for policy transfer across Member States and to the then Central and Eastern European States then seeking EU Membership.[73] The output of this era, the original Dublin Convention and various non-binding resolutions, have had an enduring impact on EU migration and asylum policy.[74]

To summarize, the EU evolved with a strong rights-based approach to internal free movement, but immigration and asylum from outside the EU were addressed in different policy contexts, with no EU judicial scrutiny. The Treaty of Amsterdam marks a huge institutional shift, with formal EU lawmaking competence over immigration and asylum, under the new overarching aim of creating an Area of Freedom, Security, and Justice (AFSJ).

[67] This point has been repeatedly raised by the House of Lords EU Committee. See, e.g. *Fighting Illegal Immigration: Should Carriers Carry the Burden?*, 5th Report Session, 2003–2004 and *A Common EU Policy on Illegal Immigration*, 37th Report, Session 2001–2002. For an overview of the UK, Ireland, and Denmark's selective participation in this field, see Annex 1.

[68] D Kostakopoulou, 'The "Protective Union": Change and Continuity in Migration Law and Policy in Post-Amsterdam Europe' (2000) 38 JCMS 497, 498.

[69] H Wallace and W Wallace (eds), *Policymaking in the European Union*, (4th edn, OUP 2000) 28.

[70] V Guiraudon, 'European Integration and Migration Policy: Vertical Policy-making as Venue Shopping' (2000) 38 JCMS 251.

[71] See also J Huysmans, 'The EU and the Securitization of Migration' (2000) 38 JCMS 751.

[72] Kostakopoulou (n 68) 498.

[73] See further, R Byrne, G Noll, and J Vedsted-Hansen, 'Understanding Refugee Law in an Enlarged European Union' (2004) European Journal of International Law 355.

[74] On the 1992 London Resolutions and Asylum Procedures, see C Costello and E Hancox, 'The Recast Asylum Procedures Directive: Caught between the Stereotypes of the Abusive Asylum-seeker and the Vulnerable Refugee' in V Chetail, P De Bruycker and F Maiani (eds), *Reforming the Common European Asylum System: The New European Refugee Law* (Martinus Nijhoff 2015 forthcoming).

## 3. The Treaty of Amsterdam and the 'Area of Freedom, Security and Justice': An offering to citizens?

In the Treaty of Amsterdam, the aim was to 'to maintain and develop the Union as an area of freedom, security and justice, in which the free movement of persons is assured in conjunction with appropriate measures with respect to external border controls, asylum, immigration and the prevention and combating of crime'. So, free movement was for 'persons', and only 'appropriate' (to what end?) policies on asylum and immigration. The TEU now provides in Article 3(2):

> The Union shall offer its citizens an area of freedom, security and justice without internal frontiers, in which the free movement of persons is ensured in conjunction with appropriate measures with respect to external border controls, asylum, immigration and the prevention and combating of crime.

Note the enduring notion that the EU Area of Freedom, Security and Justice (AFSJ) is an offering to citizens, and its position, ahead of the internal market in the EU's aims. Article 67 of the Treaty on the Functioning of the European Union (TFEU) sets out greater detail, namely that 'The Union shall constitute an area of freedom, security and justice with respect for fundamental rights and the different legal systems and traditions of the Member States.' And, again reiterating the linkage between internal free movement and external asylum and immigration policies, it states:

> It shall ensure the absence of internal border controls for persons and shall frame a common policy on asylum, immigration and external border control, based on solidarity between Member States, which is fair towards third-country nationals. For the purpose of this Title, stateless persons shall be treated as third-country nationals.

My opening claim was that the EU provides a transformative political space, in institutionalizing shared competence over admissions. Before turning to understand the contours of this shared competence, the AFSJ concept is explored.

The AFSJ signals no particular objective or 'finalité', rather a 'continuing adherence to a highly abstract triumvirate of values'.[75] Yet, in casting these three values as features of an 'area', there is vision of sorts. It may be read as more of the same (security-dominated and exclusionary), or mined for its transformative potential. In the embers of the EU Constitutional Treaty we find a reference to the EU as 'a Special Area of Hope'.[76] It is difficult to read that designation without cringing at the hubris, if not Euro-narcissism. Given what we know about developments in the fifteen years since Amsterdam entered into force on 1 May 1999, positing a transformative reading may seem too optimistic, but the inert and the transformative (hopeful even) readings are contrasted here.

[75] N Walker, 'In Search of the Area of Freedom, Security and Justice: A Constitutional Odyssey' in N Walker (ed), *Europe's Area of Freedom, Security and Justice* (OUP 2004) 5.

[76] A Ferrara, 'Europe as a "Special Area for Human Hope"' (2007) 14(3) Constellations 315.

### *i. Area of territory*

The term 'area' avoids the loaded term 'territory'. Legally, we only speak of the 'territory of the Member States' implying that the territorial hallmark of statehood remains out of the EU's reach. The German Constitutional Court's Lisbon ruling, in traditional statist vein, asserts that a Europe without borders is merely 'accessory to the state territory of the member states'.[77] The EU is not a State,[78] but a 'new kind of legal order'. This suggests that 'area' is chosen simply not to be 'territory', for its inert nature. This reading fits the account of the EU as simply serving to bolster national sovereignty.

However, the notion of the 'territory of the Union' has figured in the CJEU's case law on Citizenship of the Union, to great effect, bringing EU legal principles into areas which would previously have been deemed 'internal' to the home Member State of EU Citizens, namely deprivation of nationality[79] and residence rights for those who had not exercised their free movement rights.[80] Without getting caught up in the specificities of those rulings, it is notable that the invocation of the 'territory of the Union' was specifically tied to Citizenship of the Union: one might go further to say that Citizenship posits unified territory only in some contexts, and not others. As has been noted, even for EU Citizens, the EU remains a place of delimited national territories, as the case law on expulsion of 'bad' EU Citizens shows. Indeed, it has been powerfully argued that the expansion of Citizenship rights in *Zambrano* has its flipside in the territorial retrenchment in *PI*, a case where the expulsion of an EU Citizen from a host Member State was justified in terms which were in tension with the applicable Directive and existing case law. [81]

So where does the 'area' of the AFSJ fit, if there is both national and EU territory? The argument here, the transformative potential, lies in transcending the either/or binary. The spatial metaphor of *chora* invoked at the outset is used precisely in order to transcend the familiar. The *chora* contains, rather than constrains. Like 'area' it does not have a delineated border, yet is a space with limits, a clear inside and outside. That those limits might need to be designed and institutionalized differently to 'traditional' borders[82] seems not only a hopeful aspiration, but also fitting the EU's central achievement, which is inherently transformative of

[77] *Lisbon Case*, BVerfG 2 BvE/08 30 June 2009, para 345. I rely on the translation of D Halberstam and C Möllers 'The German Constitutional Court says "Ja zu Deutschland!"' (2009) 10 German Law Journal 1241, 1247.

[78] *Opinion 2/13*, para 156.

[79] Case C-135/08 *Rottmann* [2010] ECR I-1449.

[80] Case C-34/09 *Zambrano* [2011] ECR I-1177.

[81] There are new trends in the case law on deportation, as exemplified in Case C-348/09 *PI v Overbürgemeisterin der Stadt Remscheid* [2012] OJ C 200/2. See further D Kochenov and B Pirker, 'Deporting the Citizens within the European Union: A Counter-Intuitive Trend in Case C-348/09, P.I. v. Overbürgemeisterin der Stadt Remscheid' (2013) 19 Columbia Journal of European Law 369; L Azoulai, 'The (Mis)construction of the European Individual: Two Essays on Union Citizenship Law' (2014) EUI Working Papers in Law 2014/14.

[82] Here, I catch myself, as we know that the border controls on the movement of persons which we now view as 'normal' are of recent origin: J Torpey, *The Invention of the Passport: Surveillance, Citizenship and the State* (Cambridge University Press 1999).

the State, with territory, authority, and people contained within borders. Ferrara reminds us that:

> the European Union is the one political space on the entire planet where this separation of governance and state apparatus, of constitution and state, of the monopoly on the legitimate use of force and the monopoly on the attribution of legitimacy to the use of force, is being thoroughly explored and put into practice—a separation that might function as an example for an even more extended cosmopolitan governance of the future.[83]

'Area'/'chora' has a second transformative dimension. Territorial limits normally serve two different purposes. As well as regulating flows (of people or things), they also track the limits of the law, captured in the notion of jurisdiction. As Chapter 5 explores, there are moves in IHRL to expand the notion of jurisdiction beyond the State's territorial boundaries in order to assert accountability. Does the notion of an 'area' not suggest one in which a distinctive account of jurisdiction is required for the EU context? To date, the supranational EU has been parasitic on the orthodox notion of jurisdiction in both public international and international human rights law when asserting that EU law becomes the law of the land within each Member State's bounded territory. Yet, as suggested in Chapter 5, and as I have explored elsewhere with Violeta Moreno-Lax, the time may be ripe for such a development.[84]

### *ii. Freedom*

In official AFSJ documents, freedom still tends to refer to internal free movement, with the measures on migrants and refugees from outside the EU merely accessory to creating 'freedom' for insiders. As explained above, this 'compensatory measures' rationale is a long-standing trope in this field, but is ultimately unconvincing. Moreover, it fails to articulate the aims that immigration and asylum policy should pursue. The *glissage* between 'people' and 'Citizens' is frequent, also in the Treaty formulations of the AFSJ, which posits the AFSJ as an offering for Citizens, while not clarifying which 'people' benefit from migration opportunities into the EU. If the Area is for Citizens, then to what end are TCNs to be admitted? And by whom? Other than a reference to 'fairness' to TCNs, and respect for refugee rights, there are no positive formulations of what aims EU policies should pursue. Moreover, by positing an EU role in 'combatting illegal immigration', the EU is put at the service of all aims and none, as 'illegality' comes out of multifarious national laws, practices, and oversights, as Chapter 3 explores. Not only does internal free

[83] Ferrara (n 76) 329.

[84] For instance, Art 1 ECHR states that Contracting Parties are obliged to protect the human rights of 'everyone within their jurisdiction'. See further C Costello, 'Courting Access to Asylum in Europe: Recent Supranational Jurisprudence Explored' (2012) 12(2) HRLR 287; C Costello and V Moreno-Lax, 'The Extraterritorial Application of the EU Charter of Fundamental Rights: From Territoriality to Facticity, the Effectiveness Model' in S Peers, T Hervey, J Kenner, and A Ward (eds), *The EU Charter of Fundamental Rights: A Commentary* (Hart Publishing 2014) 1657 on an EU conception of the extraterritorial scope of human rights duties.

movement not demand restrictions on the rights of entry and residence of TCNs but, by treating internal free movement as given, that basic discrimination at the heart of the EU escapes proper scrutiny.

As well as defining freedom as internal mobility, a further trope is evident in EU documents, namely treating the freedom in the AFSJ as '[f]reedom to live in a law-abiding environment in the knowledge that public authorities are using everything in their individual and collective power... to combat and contain those who seek to deny or abuse that freedom'.[85] This invites a reading of freedom as being free from criminal and other threats to public order. This posits the 'other' as a threat to the internal order, the oldest trope in the flanking measures rationale. Both these freedom tropes ('freedom' as 'internal market freedom' and 'freedom' as 'freedom from disorder from outsiders') leave the objects of immigration and asylum law, migrants, and refugees themselves, as just that, objects of policies made in the interests of others, namely EU Citizens.

The transformative reading treats freedom as including the freedom of migrants and refugees, if not to migrate as of right, but at least to be free from human rights violations arising out of migration controls and migration status. Chapter 2 explores the notion of 'living in a law-abiding environment' as evoking positive freedom to live within the law. Individuals who are subject to too much law may have an insufficient zone of autonomy to plan their lives. Those who are unable to stake legal claims may experience the 'naked life' subject to brute power. Chapter 2 suggests that some forms of migration status are such that migrants lurch from one pole to another, with forms of legal precariousness meaning that they lack the freedom to live in a law-abiding environment.

### *iii. 'Security'*

Adding 'security' to the AFSJ brings all the pre-Amsterdam ideological and institutional baggage back into play. Positing 'freedom' and 'security' suggests the freedom of insiders from the security threat posed by outsiders. The Preamble to the Treaty on European Union (TEU) refers to free movement of persons 'while ensuring the safety and security of their peoples, by establishing an area of freedom, security and justice'. Similarly, Article 67(3) TFEU refers to the need 'to ensure a high level of security' within the AFSJ. These references may be read as positing the security of EU nationals *from* threats posed by TCNs. Crowley therefore suggests that, while:

> there is perhaps no *inherent* difficulty in an area of 'freedom, security and justice'; once, however, 'security' has been defined by reference to a protean threat attached, even vaguely, to a group of people not susceptible to precise legal definition, the erosion of freedom by considerations of security becomes depressingly likely.[86]

[85] European Commission, *Towards an Area of Freedom, Security and Justice* (The Vienna Action Plan) COM(1998) 459 final. For discussion see J Monar, 'The Area of Freedom, Security and Justice' in A Von Bogdandy and J Bast (eds), *Principles of European Constitutional Law* (2nd edn, Hart Publishing 2009) 558.

[86] J Crowley, 'Differential Free Movement and the Sociology of the Internal Border' in E Guild and C Harlow (eds), *Implementing Amsterdam: Immigration and Asylum Rights in EC Law* (Hart Publishing 2000) 25.

No doubt the ongoing dominance of the security perspective has practical ramifications. It ensures the continued dominance of interior ministry officials over immigration and asylum issues. The interlinkages between immigration, asylum, and policing remain evident in the EU Treaties.[87]

A transformative reading would develop the point made in the previous section; 'security' could also include a human security dimension, in particular security of residence for migrants and refugees.

### *iv. 'The primacy of justice'*

Seeking 'balance' between the triumvirate of values 'freedom', 'security', and 'justice' may seem like the appropriate move. We can certainly critique EU policies for privileging insiders' freedom over an imagined security threat from outsiders, and seek to re-establish the appropriate 'balance'. While this is an important argument, it leaves too little room for 'justice', which in many political theoretical discussions should be accorded primacy.[88] In the inert reading of the AFSJ, 'justice' tends to be associated with formal judicial institutions, in particular criminal law enforcement and adjudication. For Kochenov, this is a distortion, 'justice to an unfamiliar narrow reading of judicial efficiency' fails to capture the concept's deep potential.[89] The AFSJ promises that third-country nationals will be treated 'fairly'. This commitment needs to be realized by testing the impact of migration controls and migration status on migrants and refugees. That would be a minimal understanding of justice, but at least one that avoids treating 'justice' as synonymous with the administration of justice in a juridical sense, and no more.

Where would that consideration of justice as fairness to migrants and refugees take us? Most political theoretical discussions of justice and migration have been State-centric. They are often polarized even in their responses to the basic question as to whether the distribution of access to territory and membership are subject to constraints of justice at all.[90] For some, open borders are a requirement of justice,[91] for others justice has no relevance to the distribution of membership within polities.[92] Once we acknowledge duties in justice across borders, much migration control in developed countries stands reasonably accused of constraining individual freedom and perpetuating an unjust global economic order.

[87] Ex Art 61 EC, now Art 67 TFEU, ex Art 31(e) of the pre-Lisbon TEU, now replaced by Arts 82, 83, and 85 TFEU.

[88] Rawls characterized justice as the 'first virtue' of political institutions. J Rawls, *A Theory of Justice* (Harvard University Press 1971).

[89] D Kochenov, 'The Ought of Justice' in G de Búrca, D Kochenov, and A Williams (eds), *Debating Europe's Justice Deficit* (Hart Publishing 2015).

[90] C Wellman and P Cole (eds), *Debating the Ethics of Immigration: Is There a Right to Exclude?* (OUP 2011).

[91] J Carens, *The Ethics of Immigration* (OUP 2013).

[92] M Walzer, *Spheres of Justice: A Defense of Pluralism and Equality* (Basic Books 1983) Chapter 2. Note, however, even on this account there are important moral constraints on how States choose migrants, and how refugees should be protected.

However, unpicking the relationship between migration control and global injustice is beyond the scope of this work.[93] These questions go much wider and deeper than enforceable legal duties, but suffice here to note that discussing the human rights claims of migrants and refugees in the juridical sense does not claim to exhaust the discussion of justice. Any developed institutional[94] or interactional[95] account of justice would go much further than the scope of actionable human rights duties at present.

This book does not purport to identify a just immigration and asylum policy for the EU. It is much more limited in scope and ambition. By focusing on human rights claims, I focus particularly on those aspects of migration control that reach the standard of a legally cognizable human rights violation, a mere sub-set of injustice. Rather than congratulating ourselves that a human rights compliant migration and asylum policy is a lofty aspiration, it would be better to recall the modesty of that objective, and that many injustices may fail to reach the standard of human rights violation in the legal sense.

The focus here is rather on the extent to which migration controls and migration status in themselves violate human rights. Irrespective of the broader question of the justice in the distribution of migration opportunities, the coercive character of migration controls means that human rights must be protected.[96] As is discussed further in Chapter 3, social membership should be recognized with legal security of residence as a matter of human rights. And the human right to family life of migrants and refugees ought to be respected, as Chapter 4 sets out. Detention must be examined for its human rights impact, not assumed to be required as a matter of migration control, as Chapter 7 discusses.

Regarding refugees, most ethicists take the view that the CSR refugee definition is under-protective, and that those fleeing a wider range of existential threats should be afforded protection.[97] The ECHR has extended the protection against *non-refoulement* in some respects beyond the CSR (although *non-refoulement* is not co-extensive with refugee protection, which is all about status and rights). EU law too has contributed a supplementary status in the form of subsidiary protection under the QD, but it only extends existing protections to a micro-degree. In contrast, in different political contexts, other regional definitions have significantly

[93] See, e.g. T Pogge, 'Migration and Poverty' in V Bader (ed), *Citizenship and Exclusion* (Macmillan 1997) 12–27; A Shachar, *The Birthright Lottery: Citizenship and Global Inequality* (Harvard University Press 2009); M Risse, 'On the Morality of Immigration' (2008) 22 Ethics and International Affairs 25.

[94] As exemplified by T Pogge, *World Poverty and Human Rights: Cosmopolitan Responsibilities and Reforms* (Polity Press 2002).

[95] As exemplified by O O'Neill, *Bounds of Justice* (Cambridge University Press 2000).

[96] See, e.g. D Miller, 'Border Regimes and Human Rights' (2013) 7(1) Law and Ethics of Human Rights 1.

[97] A Shacknove, 'Who Is a Refugee?' (1985) 95 Ethics 274; M Gibney, *The Ethics and Politics of Asylum: Liberal Democracy and the Response to Refugees*, (Cambridge University Press 2004). Even theorists who defend discretionary immigration control on liberal nationalist grounds agree the refugee definition ought to be expanded. See D Miller, *Citizenship and National Identity* (Polity 2000).

extended the Refugee Convention definition, in particular to those fleeing armed conflict and general unrest.[98] The EU contribution, extending protection to those who can demonstrate that they are at 'individual risk' of 'indiscriminate violence' seems parsimonious in contrast.[99] So even taking the State-centric standards of justice, the EU seems to be falling short in defining those who should be allowed to stay due to the existential threats they face.

However we assess the EU's contribution to refugee protection, we must immediately confront the lack of safe means to access the EU. Long recognized as the most pressing issue of refugee protection, the ongoing catalogue of horrors at EU borders (drownings in the Mediterranean of those seeking protection in the EU,[100] asylum seekers in squalid detention conditions[101] and living in make-shift camps,[102] shootings by EU border guards at external borders[103]) is the serrated edge of Europe's ostensibly 'porous' borders. The most pressing human rights issue is how to provide access to those desperately seeking protection within the EU, a matter making a glimmer of an appearance in EU policy discussions in the form of 'protected entry procedures' and 'humanitarian visas'.[104]

In this context, addressing the most egregious injustices perpetuated by the EU would be a good start.[105] Some of these injustices are undoubtedly human rights violations. Others may be difficult to establish legally as human rights violations not because the suffering inflicted is not sufficiently serious, but because the EU facilitates Member States' external cooperative practices, which make seeking asylum more difficult and more perilous.[106]

[98] Organization of African Unity (OAU) Convention Governing Specific Aspects of Refugee Problems in Africa (adopted 10 September 1969) 1001 UNTS 45; Cartagena Declaration on Refugees (22 November 1984).

[99] Art 15(c) QD.

[100] For a recent commentary, see Amnesty International, *Lives Adrift: Refugees and Migrants in Peril in the Central Mediterranean* (2014) EUR 05/006/2014.

[101] *MSS v Belgium and Greece* (2011) 53 EHRR 2.

[102] UNHCR, *Observations on the Current Asylum System in Bulgaria* (UNHCR, April 2014).

[103] F Govan, 'Spain Admits Firing Bullets at Migrants Swimming to Enclave' *The Telegraph* (14 February 2014).

[104] J Hathaway and T Gammeltoft-Hansen, '*Non-refoulement* in a World of Cooperative Deterrence' (2014) U of Michigan Law & Econ Research Paper No 14-016; UNHCR, 'Syrian Refugees in Europe: What Europe Can Do to Ensure Protection and Solidarity' (UNHCR 2014). European Commission, *An Open and Secure Europe: Making it Happen*, COM(2014) 154, develops the idea of Protected Entry Procedures (PEP), defined by Noll as 'an overarching concept for arrangements allowing a non national to approach the potential host state outside its territory with a claim for asylum or other form of international protection and to be granted an entry permit in case of a positive response to that claim, be it preliminary or final', in G Noll, J Fagerlund, and F Liebaut, 'Study on the Feasibility of Processing Asylum Claims Outside the EU' (2002) The Danish Centre for Human Rights, European Commission. See also C Hein and M Damato, *Exploring Avenues for Protected Entry in Europe* (Italian Council for Refugees 2012). Based on the wording of the Visa Code, and the application by analogy of the recent CJEU judgment in Case C-84/12 *Koushkaki* (n 54), it is argued that there may be a duty to issue humanitarian visas under some circumstances. See U Iben Jensen, 'Humanitarian Visas: Option or Obligation?' (2014) Study for the LIBE Committee, PE 509.986.

[105] See further S Douglas-Scott, 'Justice, Injustice and the Rule of Law in the EU' in de Búrca et al. (n 89).

[106] Hathaway and Gammeltoft-Hansen (n 104).

However, as currently framed, by employing the flanking measures rhetoric and positing 'legal' and 'illegal' immigration as primordial categories, EU policy making obscures the ethical questions that ought to be addressed in immigration and asylum policy-making. These include difficult questions regarding the definition of the refugee, the circumstances (if any) in which it is permissible to use guest workers (resurgent in Europe—see the recent Seasonal Workers Directive,[107] as transient a status as could be imagined), and the acceptability of various selection criteria when choosing refugees and migrants more generally.

Some of these questions are addressed in this book. However by focusing on court-to-court interactions, there is an iterative quality to the discussions which fails to open up the full range of ethical issues at stake. Accordingly, to return to the concept of the AFSJ, it is at once an inert acronym and a tantalizing suggestion of a different approach to mobility and migration. The space, the 'area', the 'chora' creates new opportunities to realize core political values. Whether these values may be realized depends at least in part on the institutional context and structures, to which the next section turns.

## V. Institutionalizing Shared Competence

### 1. Beyond statism?

The premise underlying the statist assumption is that excluding aliens needs no justification. It is simply a corollary of statehood. However, when admission decisions come to be taken on the basis of EU law, Member States can no longer rely on *ipso facto* justifications for their acts *qua* States. At the very least, the EU adjudicatory context opens up space for reasoned argument, not pre-emptive assertions. Hence, we might expect that the troublesome 'weightiness' attached to migration control does not distort appraisal. Transferring competences once conceived of as integral to statehood to the EU level is not to confer statehood on the EU, even by stealth. Nor does it entail simply a shift in venue. The EU is a transformative political space, and in taking decisions out of the exclusive domain of the State, the underlying assumption of the confluence of territory, authority, and rights is undone, destabilizing the statist migration control assumption.

The EU project as a whole stands to contradict the illusion underpinning statism, namely that decisions of the bounded polity only concern insiders. Once we shatter this illusion, it is apparent that the admission-seeker is profoundly affected, and sometimes coerced or harmed, by the decision whether to admit her. If it is accepted that exclusion is (even sometimes) coercive, closure becomes harder

[107] Directive 2014/36/EU of the European Parliament and of the Council of 26 February 2014 on the Conditions of Entry and Stay of Third-Country Nationals for the Purpose of Employment as Seasonal Workers (Seasonal Workers Directive) [2014] OJ L94/375.

to justify.[108] On many accounts then, rejection requires justification. The migrant should not be automatically suspect or unwelcome. The EU context opens up this justificatory space, wherein both the Member States and the EU should be required to articulate reasons, acknowledging that statism is ill-fitting once competence is shared. That common interest should be articulated in terms not of creating a State with common (State-like) frontiers, but rather mining the transformative potential of the AFSJ. While this normative prescription is unlikely to gain immediate acceptance, the changed institutional context opens up a crucial contestatory space.

MacCormick was once correct that European integration left 'a compendious "external sovereignty" of all the member states intact and even in a sense strengthened'.[109] Benhabib in a somewhat similar vein suggests that the EU is potentially caught 'in contradictory currents which move it towards norms of cosmopolitan justice in the treatment of those who are within its boundaries, while leading it to act in accordance with outmoded Westphalian conceptions of unbridled sovereignty toward those who are on the outside'.[110] Those accounts, to the extent that they evoke the EU's support for the Member States' admissions capacity, no longer hold: The EU is in a process of defining itself as it not only facilitates, but also divides and constrains external competence over admissions.

Admittedly, we still find contrasting readings of the EU. On a liberal intergovernmental view of the EU, European integration does not supplant the Member States, but rather provides a framework to enable their exercise of national sovereignty, bolstering the capacity of the individual States.[111] In this vein, European integration appears as a national sovereignty gain, lending credence to the statist assumption. While individually the Member States may lack the capacity to control their own borders, the EU enhances their capacity to act. Without becoming a State itself, the EU rescues national sovereignty. Much of the pre-Amsterdam activity on admissions does fit this account of the EU. Yet, this liberal intergovernmental view has patent shortcomings. In particular, the binding EU rules constrain national discretion, determining, at least in part, which admission-seekers may lawfully reside in the EU. Moreover, the account of the EU rescue of statism belies the fact that when the EU is engaged by its Member States in this vein, it tends to '[reinforce] national cleavages'[112] and pits Member States against each other, such as within the Dublin System for allocation of asylum seekers discussed in Chapter 5. Zero-sum engagement ensues, undermining the putative bolstering of State capacity. This account therefore does not fully capture the EU's transformative impact.

[108] See further A Abizadeh, 'Democratic Theory and Border Coercion: No Rights to Unilaterally Control your Own Borders' (2008) 36 Political Theory 37.

[109] N MacCormick, 'Liberalism, Nationalism and the Post-Sovereign State' (1996) 33 Political Studies 553, 561–62.

[110] S Benhabib, *Another Cosmopolitanism*, (OUP 2005) 47.

[111] For a pithy synthesis, see P Craig, 'The Nature of the Community: Integration, Democracy and Legitimacy' in P Craig and G de Búrca (eds), *The Evolution of EU Law* (OUP 1999) 1, 8–16.

[112] To borrow a phrase from Menéndez: A Menéndez 'The European Democratic Challenge: The Forging of a Supranational *Volonté Générale*' (2009) 15 ELJ 277, 300.

At the other extreme, we may imagine the inexorable development of a comprehensive binding EU *acquis* on admissions, suggesting a shift to a statist[113] reading of the EU itself, where the EU would come to supplant the Member States and ultimately assert its own exclusive right to exclude, control its borders, and to decide on admissions. On this view, the EU role in admissions would come to resemble its role in trade in goods, where it has exclusive competence to set the rules and represent the EU externally.[114] European integration on this view may be seen as leading inexorably, if gradually, towards EU statehood. While it may be all too easy to dismiss this vision, it certainly has some resonance with contemporary developments, particularly when we examine some of the institutional claims for the exhaustiveness of EU harmonization measures,[115] or the desirability of the EU becoming the sole entity with responsibility for at least some types of admissions, or even the legal-rhetorical claim of the 'territory' of the Union. Nonetheless, the notion of EU statehood seems politically completely out of tune with moves to limit and even repatriate EU competences. Moreover, even those who advocate further European integration in asylum and immigration often leave nationality law within the purview of the Member States, reflecting the Member States' continuing primacy over the question of who belongs in Europe.

Both the above accounts, the EU rescue of the State and the EU *qua* State, miss the interesting bits. Focusing on the EU or national level exclusively fails to capture the interlocking reflexive character of their relationship, and ignores the importance of transnational interactions across the Member States. This book is accordingly concerned with the more intriguing phenomenon of sharing competence over admissions.[116] It thus aims to assist in 'giving up the fetishism of indivisibility'[117] of sovereignty. Indeed, admissions present a fruitful area of exploration as they are traditionally conceived of as an aspect of the 'hard core' of sovereignty.[118]

[113] I avoid the term 'federal' as it may connote a federal State with unitary sovereignty at the centre, or federal union with shared sovereignty. Cf R Schütze, 'On "Federal" Ground: The European Union as an (Inter)national Phenomenon' (2009) 46 CMLRev 1069. Schütze has powerfully demonstrated that 'federal' may connote shared sovereignty, and so is the apt term for the EU.

[114] Admittedly the external trade competence under what was before Art 133 EC [now Art 207 TFEU] is limited. As the CJEU explained in *Opinion 1/94* (WTO) [1994] ECR I-5267, at the current state of EC law, admission of TCNs fell outside of the common commercial policy in Art 133 EC, and so the cross-border movement of service providers under the GATS agreement fell outside of Art 133 EC. See further Craig and de Búrca (n 112) 182–85.

[115] See discussion in Part V.4 on the QD's scope.

[116] Such shared authority is not unprecedented. Although it is usually assumed that in federal States admissions are for the federation to determine, in Canada a mode of dividing authority has been devised, in particular to accommodate Quebec's distinctive culture. See further, A Shachar, *Multicultural Jurisdictions: Cultural Differences and Women's Rights* (Cambridge University Press 2001) 151–54.

[117] R Howse and K Nicolaïdis, 'Democracy without Sovereignty: The Global Vocation of Political Ethics' in T Broude and Y Shany (eds), *The Shifting Allocation of Authority in International Law: Considering Sovereignty, Supremacy and Subsidiarity* (Hart Publishing 2008) 163, 165.

[118] D Kostakopoulou, 'Floating Sovereignty: A Pathology or Necessary Means of State Evolution?' (2002) 22 OJLS 135, 150.

## 2. Limited competences

Before I turn in Chapter 2 to the framework of human rights protection, some detail on the modes of sharing competence and their implications for human rights are developed in the next and final part of this chapter. The aim is both to develop a more practical, institutionally grounded understanding of two key modes of shared competences, and the human rights challenges they pose. Moreover, a closer examination of the operation of such legislation is warranted. In particular, it is important to clarify that the Member States still remain competent to offer asylum or migration opportunities beyond the EU measures. As discussed further in Chapter 3, they retain an important power to regularize and naturalize. These national competences are important to note, and fit the account of the EU as a distinctive *chora*, which contains the Member States, but which does not constrain their inclusive capacities.

The Treaty of Amsterdam brought immigration and asylum lawmaking under Title IV EC, bringing some, but by no means all, of the legal and institutional constraints of typical supranational processes.[119]

During the first five years post-Amsterdam, unanimity was required in the Council for the adoption of measures, with the European Parliament merely consulted. Most of the original measures discussed in this work were adopted under these old procedures, the exceptions being the Visa Code, the Schengen Borders Code (SBC),[120] the Returns Directive (RD) and the Employer Sanctions Directive (ESD), discussed in Chapter 2, which were adopted under qualified majority voting (QMV) in the Council with co-decision of the Parliament. The Council in 2004 used the Treaty power to alter the lawmaking procedures.[121] With the entry into force of the Lisbon Treaty, the normal lawmaking procedure, involving QMV in the Council and a strong role for the European Parliament as co-decision-maker, became the norm. The Recasts of the Asylum Directives and Dublin Regulation were adopted under these procedures, initially raising hopes for a radical rehaul. That the outcome of the recasting process led merely to incremental change suggests some path dependency based on the original legislative framework, such that the new institutional context did not produce significantly new thinking.[122]

[119] See C Costello, 'Administrative Governance and the Europeanisation of Asylum and Immigration Policy' in H Hofmann and A Türk (eds), *EU Administrative Governance* (Elgar Publishing 2006) 287; D Kostakopoulou 'The "Protective Union": Change and Continuity in Migration Law and Policy in Post-Amsterdam Europe' (2000) 38 JCMS 497, 508.

[120] Regulation (EC) No 562/2006 of the European Parliament and of the Council of 15 March 2006 establishing a Community Code on the rules governing the movement of persons across borders (SBC) [2006] OJ L105/1.

[121] Council Decision 2004/926/EC providing for certain areas covered by Title IV of Part Three of the Treaty establishing the European Community to be governed by the procedure laid down in Article 251 of that Treaty [2004] OJ L396/45. See S Peers, 'Transforming Decision Making on EC Immigration and Asylum Law' (2005) 30 ELRev 285.

[122] D Acosta, 'The Good, the Bad and the Ugly in EU Migration Law: Is the European Parliament Becoming Bad and Ugly? (The Adoption of Directive 2008/115: the Returns Directive)' (2009) 11(1) EJML 19; A Ripoll Servent, 'Point of No Return? The European Parliament after Lisbon and Stockholm' (2010) 19(2) European Security 191; A Ripoll Servent, 'The European Parliament and

The EU measures examined in this book are of different degrees of intensity in terms of how much discretion they leave to nationality authorities. The bulk of the book is concerned with the exercise of shared competence over family (Chapter 4) and refugee admissions (Chapters 5 and 6), where the EU established minimum standards. These measures effectively create an EU right to enter, yet one where the Member States retain a role as bearer of both legislative discretion and administrative capacity, although its extent remains contentious. In contrast, in the areas where EU legislation sets out exhaustively the conditions for admission, an EU right to enter the EU is created, albeit in limited fields.[123] On the issue of pre-deportation immigration detention under the RD, the Court's interpretation has been dictated by the fact that those rules set out the conditions for detention exhaustively. Accordingly, national measures are pre-empted (effectively set aside) and the constraints on national discretion greater than under directives which are more loosely drafted.[124]

Under the statist assumption, admissions fall within the realm of exercise of executive discretion. Yet, now we find that the EU has brought a determined legislative dominance to the immigration and asylum field. Not only do we find a proliferation of binding EU legislation, but the adopted EU Directives also require domestic *legislative* implementation, where previously administrative circulars and shady guidance would have been commonplace, flimsy sources of constraint on executive power. The SBC, a binding EU Regulation, now governs border crossings, replacing measures of ambiguous legal status. The European Parliament successfully secured the inclusion of additional criteria therein, including procedural protections.[125] The Visa Code similarly sets out the criteria for at least some visas issued to enter the EU.

Nonetheless, immigration admissions as defined in Title V of Part 3 TFEU are far from comprehensive in scope, and the competence not fully exercised. The EU has set minimum standards only for some TCNs' entry and residence into the EU, in particular that of Students and Researchers.[126] It has also adopted the so-called Blue Card Directive[127] on highly skilled immigration, although strictly speaking, it does not create a right to enter the EU at all, but merely requires Member States to afford this particular permit to those they choose, and then only if they fulfil its

the Returns Directive: The End of Radical Contestation; The Start of Consensual Constraints' in B Anderson, M Gibney, and E Paoletti (eds), *The Social, Political and Historical Contours of Deportation* (Springer 2013) 43–58; M Mouzourakis, '"We Need to Talk about Dublin": Responsibility under the Dublin System as a Blockage to Asylum Burden-Sharing in the European Union' (2014) RSC Working Paper No 105.

123 On the Visa Code, see *Koushkaki* and *Air Baltic Corporation* (n 54). On the Students' Directive, see *Ben Alaya* (n 54).

124 See Chapter 7 for discussion of the pertinent case law.

125 Art 5a SBC.

126 Council Directive 2005/71/EC of 12 October 2005 on a specific procedure for admitting third-country nationals for the purposes of scientific research [2005] OJ L289/15.

127 Council Directive 2009/50/EC on the conditions of entry and residence of third-country nationals for the purposes of highly qualified employment (Blue Card Directive) [2009] OJ L155/17. See further S Peers, 'Legislative Update: EC Immigration and Asylum Law Attracting and Deterring Labour Migration: The Blue Card and Employer Sanctions Directives' (2009) 11 EJML 387.

strict criteria concerning high-skilled employment. Most recently, Directives on Seasonal Workers and Intra-Company Transferees[128] have been adopted. In other respects though, common rules on immigration admissions have not emerged.[129]

Comprising shared competences, the exercise of what was until recently Title IV EC [now in essence Title V of Part 3 TFEU] is subject to the principle of subsidiarity.[130] The principle provides that the EU should act only when it is demonstrably better at achieving the given objective than the Member States. Given the open-textured nature of the objectives of this Title, it seems unlikely that subsidiarity would act as a significant constraint on action under this Title.[131] Subsidiarity also has a positive dimension, requiring the EU to exercise its competences if the Member States are ineffective. On this basis, Noll argues persuasively that sharing the responsibility for processing asylum claims across the EU is a duty arising out of the positive dimension of subsidiarity, as it is intrinsically a task which confounds individual States.[132] However, it is precisely this sort of task, one which poses a genuine collective action problem, that the EU political institutions are ill-designed to tackle.[133]

## 3. Minimum standards legislation

Some of the legislation in this field merely establishes minimum standards, as is set out in the applicable Treaty bases.[134] The immigration competences

[128] Directive 2014/66/EU of the European Parliament and of the Council of 15 May 2014 on the conditions of entry and residence of third-country nationals in the framework of an intra-corporate transfer [2014] OJ L157/1.

[129] Even an attempt to bring convergence to national primary immigration law through the softer coordinative mechanism of the Open Method for Coordination appears to have floundered. See European Commission, *On an Open Method of Coordination for the Community Immigration Policy*, COM(2001) 387, 11 July 2011; A Caviedes 'The Open Method of Co-Ordination in Immigration Policy: A Tool for Prying Open Fortress Europe?' (2004) 11 JEPP 289.

[130] See Art 4(2) (j) TFEU and Art 5(3) TEU [ex Art 5(2) EC].

[131] Compliance with the legal principle of subsidiarity requires that the EU demonstrate that it is better able to achieve the objectives of the proposed action. The matter should be left to the Member States if they are able to 'sufficiently' achieve them. However, as well as the uncertainties intrinsic in the comparative efficiency test, the identification of the objectives of EU acts is a crucial prior stage. If, as under Title IV EC, the objectives are ambiguous, the likelihood is that the creation of common standards will in itself be regarded as the object, in which case the comparative efficiency test becomes loaded in favour of the EU level.

[132] G Noll, *Negotiating Asylum* (Martinus Nijhoff Publishers 2000) 330–37.

[133] Again, developing an EU or Europe-wide mechanism to distribute responsibility for processing asylum claims fairly has crept up the EU political agenda. For an overview of relevant policy proposals, see E Guild, C Costello, M Garlick, V Moreno-Lax, and M Mouzourakis, 'New Approaches, Alternative Avenues and Means of Access to Asylum Procedures for Persons Seeking International Protection' (2014) Study for the LIBE Committee, PE509.989, 50–59.

[134] The exceptions to the minimum standards competence are Art 63(1)(a) EC [now found in Art 78(2)(e) TFEU] on the allocation of responsibility for processing asylum claims, and the immigration competence in Arts 63(3) and 63(4) EC [now found in Arts 79(2)(a) and (c) TFEU and 79(2)(b) TFEU respectively], which seems to permit both higher and lower domestic standards. See R Schütze, 'Cooperative Federalism Constitutionalised: The Emergence of Complementary Competences in the EC Legal Order' (2006) 31 ELRev 167, footnote 15. cf Peers: 'The most logical interpretation is...that EC immigration legislation can allow more restriction *or* more protection *or* impose full

permit the adoption of measures on legal admissions, including for family reunification and illegal immigration. The Treaty stated in Article 63(4) [now replaced by Article 79 TFEU] that legislation adopted thereon 'shall not prevent any Member State from maintaining or introducing in the areas concerned national provisions which are compatible with this Treaty and with international agreements.'

In the context of minimum standards legislation, the Member States may set higher domestic standards. Creating space for further national inclusive measures is an important aspect of shared competence, so understanding the degree of upward flexibility is important. In the *FRD Ruling*,[135] AG Kokott examined the legal base for this measure, and rejected reading it either as a typical minimum standards competence,[136] or as leaving the Member States completely free to set their own standards, as the German government had argued.[137] Rather, applying the principle of 'practical concordance', she opined that legislation based on Article 63(2) EC *was* binding.[138] The article was to be read not as 'limiting the legal effect of legislation' but rather 'enjoining the Community legislature... to leave Member States an appropriate degree of latitude,' as it had done in the 'range of options' left to Member States in the FRD itself.[139] The CJEU's interpretation of the FRD refutes any contention that the legal base precludes binding, or even directly effective, EU rights.[140]

On illegal immigration, the ESD expressly permits Member States to set higher standards for the benefit of TCNs as regards their back-pay and complaint entitlements 'provided that such provisions are compatible with' the ESD.[141] Yet it also expressly permits 'more stringent rules' on subcontractors.[142] Even more broadly, the Preamble stipulates that 'Member States should remain free to adopt or maintain stricter sanctions and measures and impose stricter obligations on employers.'[143]

Many areas of EU competence are restricted to setting down minimum standards. Normally, legislation in these areas contains a standstill clause, explicitly precluding Member States from lowering their domestic standards in implementing the Directive in question. Such clauses are notably absent from the FRD, QD, PD, and RCD. The capacity to adopt higher standards, or upward-flexibility, usually means measures affording a more stringent form of regulation to protect the interest concerned: workers in the case of the legal base on the health and safety of workers, or the environment in the case of environmental policy, for instance.[144] These Treaty bases make explicit that the more stringent measures are for the protection of working conditions and the environment respectively.

harmonization, depending on the choice of the legislator.' S Peers, 'EU Immigration and Asylum Law: Internal Market Model or Human Rights Model?' in T Tridimas and P Nebbia (eds), *European Union Law for the Twenty-First Century* (Hart Publishing 2004) 345, 358.

[135] Case C-540/03 *Parliament v Council (Family Reunification)* (FRD Ruling) [2006] ECR I-5769.

[136] *FRD Ruling*, Opinion of AG Kokott, para 35.

[137] ibid, paras 36–38.

[138] ibid, para 39.

[139] ibid, para 41.

[140] ibid, para 60.

[141] Art 15 ESD.

[142] Art 8(4) ESD.

[143] Recital 4 ESD.

[144] Arts 137(4) and 176 EC respectively [now Arts 153(4) and 193 TFEU].

On the same logic, 'higher' in asylum policy means affording greater protection to asylum seekers and refugees. The alternative, that higher standards could mean 'higher' protection of domestic control prerogatives verges on the absurd.[145] Such an interpretation is also inappropriate from a human rights perspective. It is both legally necessary and politically desirable that EU measures and national implementation should contribute to, rather than stifle, positive developments in IHRL.[146]

Although the Treaty competence was confined to setting minimum standards, the text of both the QD and PD qualify their minimum standards clauses, in contrast to the RCD and FRD. Article 3 QD provides that: 'Member States may introduce or maintain more favourable standards for determining who qualifies as a refugee or as a person eligible for subsidiary protection, and for determining the content of international protection, *insofar as those standards are compatible with this Directive*' (emphasis added). A similar formulation is found in Article 5 PD. The Recasts keep this wording, although they also purport to move from 'minimum' to 'common' standards. In contrast, the FRD straightforwardly states that it 'shall not affect the prerogative of Member States to adopt or retain more favourable conditions'.[147] The Preambles of the QD, PD, and RCD contain provisions reiterating that:

> [i]t is in the very nature of minimum standards that Member States should have the power to introduce or maintain more favourable provisions for third country nationals or stateless persons who request international protection from a Member State.[148]

The extent to which Member States could set higher standards, notwithstanding qualification in Articles 3 QD and 5 PD, remained, until the changes brought to Title V of Part 3 TFEU by the Treaty of Lisbon, highly contested and consequential. The predominant view is that the EU legislature could not use a minimum standards competence to harmonize exhaustively any particular issue. Following Schütze, even if we accept that there is some doubt on this constitutional point,[149] there is at least a strong presumption against total harmonization, under what he terms the 'soft constitutionalist' position. Regrettably, the CJEU has limited the extent to which States can grant the EU status of subsidiary protection, in a manner that suggests that the QD is being treated as a ceiling rather than a floor of rights.[150]

145 Peers (n 134) 357.

146 Along these lines, McAdam argues that Member States must be able to adopt more protective standards so as not to 'stunt the development of the law.' J McAdam, 'The European Union Qualification Directive: The Creation of a Subsidiary Protection Regime' (2005) 17 IJRL 461, 515.

147 Art 3(5) FRD.

148 Recital 8 QD, and the analogous Recital 7 PD and Recital 15 RCD.

149 See Schütze's discussion of Case C-203/96 *Chemische Afvalstoffen Dusseldorp BV v Minister van Volkshuisvesting, Ruimtelijke Odening en Milieubeheer* [1998] ECR I-4075, and Case C-318/98 *Criminal Proceedings Against Giancarlo Fornasar* et al [2000] ECR I-4785 in R Schütze, 'Cooperative Federalism Constitutionalised: The Emergence of Complementary Competences in the EC Legal Order' (2006) 31 ELRev 167.

150 Case C-542/13 *M'Bodj* [2015] OJ C 65/12.

Minimum standards legislation is a means of sharing competence over admissions in the EU. It offers a useful way for the EU to set a floor of entitlements while ensuring that Member States may offer further migration and asylum opportunities, and contribute to the progressive development of international human rights and refugee law. However, this claim depends on the content of the minimum standards legislation: If it is too low, or offers no constraint against implementation in a manner that undermines existing protections, then it fails to meet this aim. Much is left to the CJEU, which is called on to interpret the minimum standards legislation. In so doing, as I contend throughout, it should be mindful of the ECHR standards, but not precluded from developing higher human rights standards if they are more fitting in the EU legislative and institutional context.

## 4. EU mutual recognition and human rights

### *i. A primer on mutual recognition*

Minimum harmonization sets up a shared vertical competence between the EU and its Member States. Also familiar to EU lawyers are systems of mutual recognition. In the context of the AFSJ, mutual recognition often raises human rights issues, which demand an EU response. Internal market mutual recognition sets up duties to accept goods, services, or professionals on the basis that they comply with the regulatory standards of other Member States. In so doing, mutual recognition of laws underpins the transnational dimension of the EU. Familiar from the internal market context, that recognition has many virtues. It preserves national autonomy to regulate domestic products, professions, and activities, yet also opens up national spaces to transnational actors. If a good, person, or service is to be excluded, it must be justified, so that the impact of the national regulatory choice on outsiders is subject to scrutiny.

Mutual recognition is not then an end in itself, but a tool to achieve a particular aim. For instance, in order to facilitate trade, national authorities are obliged, under certain conditions, to recognize products that comply with the regulatory standards of other Member States (and implicitly thus those standards) as apt for marketing in that other State.[151] As regards nationality law, the current structure of EU Citizenship, being a derivative status from Member State nationality, means that Member States must in effect recognize those who hold the nationality of the Member States as EU Citizens, again within certain limits.[152] Even on this cursory examination, mutual recognition emerges as a diverse tool, which may be stricter or looser depending on its context and purpose. Mutual recognition requires trust, in that there must be some basis for a general acceptance that other Member States' acts are worthy of legal recognition.

151 Case 120/78 *Rewe-Zentral (Cassis de Dijon)* [1979] ECR 649.

152 C Costello, 'Citizenship of the Union: Above Abuse?' in R Feria and S Vogenauer (eds), *Prohibition of Abuse of Law: A New General Principle of EU Law* (Hart Publishing 2011).

Mutual recognition usually works in tandem with some minimum harmonization. One of the main lessons of the institutionalization of mutual recognition in the internal market context is the possibility for judicial moves to prompt legislative action. As is now a familiar tale in the annals of European integration, the CJEU's turn to mutual recognition in *Cassis de Dijon* prompted the EU political institutions to rethink their approach to harmonization, focusing on minimum standards to underpin mutual recognition, rather than exhaustive common standards.[153] However, in the AFSJ, mutual recognition appears to be treated as an end in itself, not an instrument of wider political goals that may also require harmonization of standards.

### *ii. The (ostensible) democratic underpinnings of mutual recognition*

The idealized and simplified version of mutual recognition portrayed above is often posited as addressing one of the shortcomings of statism, namely that internal decisions impact unenfranchised outsiders. Writing of the internal market context, Maduro thus explains that mutual recognition corrects the twofold deficit of States. These deficits are that:

> [O]n the one hand, [states] do not control many decision-making processes which impact on those polities but take place outside their borders; on the other hand, national polities exclude from participation and representation many interests which are affected by their decisions.[154]

While this account has been challenged,[155] it reflects the destabilization of territory and authority across the EU. Laws that impact on outsiders require an additional layer of justification, underpinned by the commitment to mutual openness and justification within the internal market context.

### *iii. Mutual recognition in the AFSJ*

If the account in the preceding section portrays the virtuous vision of mutual recognition, then its institutionalization in the AFSJ has some vicious elements. Lavenex suggests that mutual recognition in the AFSJ is distinguished by the fact that 'those benefiting from mutual recognition are... not societal actors but state representatives'.[156] However, as Nicolaïdis points out, it was ever thus, with national rules and practices being the subject of the duty of recognition

[153] K Nicolaïdis, 'Kir Forever? The Journal of a Political Scientist in the Landscape of Recognition' in L Azoulai and M Maduro (eds), *The Past and Future of EU Law: The Classics of EU Law Revisited on the 50th Anniversary of the Rome Treaty* (Hart Publishing 2007).

[154] M Maduro, 'Europe and the Constitution: What If This Is as Good as It Gets?' in JHH Weiler and M Wind (eds), *European Constitutionalism Beyond the State* (Cambridge University Press 2003) 74, 83.

[155] A Somek, 'Monism: A Tale of the Undead' in M Avbelj and J Komarak, *Constitutional Pluralism in the European Union and Beyond* (Hart Publishing 2012) 343.

[156] S Lavenex, 'Mutual Recognition and the Monopoly of Force: Limits of the Single Market Analogy' (2007) 14 Journal of European Public Policy 762, 764.

even in the internal market context.[157] Yet, mutual recognition of asylum and immigration decisions *is* profoundly different when we examine the particular ways it is institutionalized in the EU.

The difference is manifest in the prevalence of negative mutual recognition, which is explicable by the absence of the democratic corrective we find in the traditional mutual recognition contexts. The standard idealized account explains mutual recognition as establishing at once a limit to the external application of national decisions, and an expansion of democratic justificatory structures. In contrast, under admissions decision-making, the affected interests are not enfranchised in the first State, the 'home' State. The restrictive tendency is amplified in the process of mutual recognition. To subject the home State's decision to mutual recognition is to grant it an even greater overreach. To be more concrete, imagine a decision to expel a TCN from her Member State of residence. That TCN is by definition not enfranchised in her State of residence, so the democratic underpinning of the expulsion decision is not fully democratic in the sense that the most affected interest is not represented.[158] When that expulsion decision is subject to mutual recognition across the EU, it means 27 other Member States join in recognizing that expulsion. The argument that mutual recognition permits the affected outsider to contest decisions or policies that would exclude her no longer applies. Instead, the mutual recognition takes one decision (which may be legitimate or legal, but is not obviously democratic) and requires other authorities to enforce it.

In the admissions field, EU measures more often require mutual recognition of negative decisions (i.e. those to exclude or not admit) than positive ones, serving to amplify exclusionary tendencies. As Chapter 2 illustrates, those regarded as 'illegal' or 'unwanted' in one Member State must be so regarded by all the others. Under the Schengen Information System (SIS), a migrant may find herself unwanted throughout *Schengenland* on the basis of one national administrative decision, based on a minor infraction of national immigration procedures. Under the RD, a migrant subject to a national expulsion order must in principle be treated as unlawfully present by the other Member States, subject to certain exceptions.

Asylum seekers find themselves not only confined to the Member State in which they lodge an application for asylum, but also confined in their choice of EU destination by the Dublin regime for the allocation of responsibility for asylum seekers, as explored in Chapter 6. Even recognized refugees do not then have an EU right to have their status recognized in other Member States, although they do benefit from the Long-Term Residents Directive (LTRD)[159] now.[160] Yet, if they

[157] K Nicolaïdis, 'Trusting the Poles? Constructing Europe through Mutual Recognition' (2007) 14 Journal of European Public Policy 682, 690.

[158] See Council Directive 2001/40/EC of 28 May 2001 on the mutual recognition of decisions on the expulsion of third country nationals [2001] OJ L149/34.

[159] Council Directive 2003/109/EC of 25 November 2003 concerning the status of third-country nationals who are long-term residents (Long-Term Residents Directive) [2003] OJ L16/33.

[160] Directive 2011/51/EU of the European Parliament and of the Council of 11 May 2011 amending Council Directive 2003/109/EC to extend its scope to beneficiaries of international protection [2011] OJ L123/1.

are refused asylum, that refusal ordinarily applies across the EU, due to the Dublin aim of avoiding multiple applications.

There is some positive mutual recognition in the AFSJ, but it tends to be highly qualified and limited to privileged categories. The Schengen short-term visa applies throughout *Schengenland*. Longer-term visas for immigrants do not normally entail duties of mutual recognition. Ordinarily, until naturalized, a lawful immigrant to one Member State has no right to reside elsewhere in the EU, unless he or she meets all the requirements of the LTRD. As discussed in Chapter 3, the LTR status is elusive in practice. Even the most highly privileged categories of migrants only enjoy qualified free movement entitlements.[161]

The most significant example of positive mutual recognition is the strict duty of mutual recognition of nationality designation that underpins EU Citizenship. In *Micheletti*,[162] the CJEU established two key propositions concerning nationality designation. The first recognizes Member State competence over nationality, but subject to unspecified EU legal constraints: '[u]nder international law, it is for each Member State, having due regard to Community law, to lay down the conditions for the acquisition and loss of nationality'. The second proposition establishes a strict mutual recognition regime, such that:

> [I]t is not permissible for the legislation of a Member State to restrict the effects of the grant of nationality of another Member State by imposing an additional condition for recognition of that nationality with a view to the exercise of the fundamental freedoms provided for in the Treaty.[163]

While TCNs are mainly subject to 'negative mutual recognition', EU Citizenship rests on the duties of positive mutual recognition of Member State nationality. Insisting on strict mutual recognition creates greater pressure for some trust-enhancing common principles. Yet, in the absence of formal EU legislative competence, these can only emerge through informal coordination and/or judicial intervention.[164] The aftermath of *Chen*[165] illustrates some informal coordination at work. The Advocate General's (AG) Opinion in *Chen* was issued after the Irish government had called a referendum to change Ireland's constitutional all-island *jus soli* rule. AG Tizzano stated that 'the problem, if problem there be, lies in the criterion used by the Irish legislation granting nationality [*iure soli*]' and that 'to avoid such situations, the criterion could have been moderated by the addition of a condition of settled residence of the parent'.[166] The referendum passed, so we can infer that the institution of EU Citizenship exercised an exclusionary pull on nationality designation. The pitfalls of the informal process are evident. The reforms were rationalized as needed to bring Ireland into line with the European norm, yet that norm is non-existent. There

161 See, e.g., Art 16 Blue Card Directive, which contains more generous rules than the LTRD.

162 Case C-369/90 *Mario Vicente Micheletti* [1992] ECR I-4239.

163 ibid, para 10.

164 See further K Rostek and G Davies, 'The Impact of Union Citizenship on National Citizenship Policies' (2006) 10 European Integration Online Papers No 5.

165 Case C-200/02 *Zhu and Chen* [2004] ECR I-9925.

166 ibid, paras 124–25. Opinion of AG Tizzano.

was little opportunity to debate the virtues of *jus soli* or invoke comparisons from other (admittedly non-EU) countries which have retained that system.[167]

Common principles may also emerge from the judiciary. *Rottmann* provides a crucial first elucidation on the EU limits on nationality designation, and suggests shallow but broad requirements with which Member States must comply in their nationality designation and withdrawal. For now though, their scope and limits remains to be explored, and the strict duty of mutual recognition remains.

### *iv. Mutual recognition and human rights*

So mutual recognition has no particular intrinsic value and is merely an instrument, but of what? As the horizontal dimension of EU Citizenship, its institutional purpose and rationale is clear. Without it, or without common membership criteria (in the form of common nationality rules), EU Citizenship as a status would not work. However, as regards the panoply of diverse decisions taken under the immigration and asylum aspects of the AFSJ, rationales are under-articulated and elusive.

The problems are best illustrated in the Dublin System, which concerns the allocation of asylum seekers to particular Member States for processing their asylum claims. Portrayed as a matter of mere allocation for bureaucratic purposes, it also determines the living conditions, chances of recognition as a refugee, naturalization, and onward migration prospects over years. In this context, even using the term 'mutual recognition' understates the range of official consequences imposed under the Dublin System. In particular, and often behind the human rights case law, is a legal attempt to resist deportation to another Dublin State, often as the asylum seeker contends his or her human rights will be violated on return. As will be discussed at length in Chapter 6, the CJEU in *NS/ME*[168] confirmed that human rights obligations would require a Member State to refuse a Dublin transfer but only as regards certain breaches of Article 4 EUCFR (Article 3 ECHR). Noteworthy is that mutual recognition is posited as the rationale for rejecting the argument that in the case of any likely breach of fundamental rights, transfer should be refused. This argument was apparently rejected on the following grounds:

> At issue here is the raison d'être of the European Union and the creation of an area of freedom, security and justice and, in particular, the Common European Asylum System, based on mutual confidence and a presumption of compliance, by other Member States, with European Union law and, in particular, fundamental rights.[169]

[167] The Constitution of Ireland was amended so that citizenship is granted to children born on the island of Ireland if they have 'at least one parent who is an Irish citizen or entitled to be an Irish citizen.' For a critique, see C Costello, 'Accidents of Place and Parentage: Birthright Citizenship and Border Crossings' in *The Citizenship Referendum: Implications for the Constitution and Human Rights* (Law School Trinity College Dublin 2004) 5.

[168] Joined Cases C-411/10 and C-493/10 *NS v Secretary of State for the Home Department and ME v Refugee Applications Commissioner and Minister for Justice, Equality and Law Reform* [2011] ECR I-13905.

[169] ibid, para 83.

This paragraph fails to distinguish between the aims (creating the AFSJ) and means (mutual recognition and mutual confidence). Suffice to note for now that the Dublin System's aims are clear (avoiding multiple asylum applications across the EU) but some of the means used to secure that aim (deporting people from one State to another to undergo an administrative procedure) seem like an extreme way to achieve it. Invoking 'mutual recognition' as an obligation in this context serves to avoid the examination of the aims and means of the actions concerned, and their proportionality. In contrast, in the internal market context, for good or ill, the Court has at least implicitly placed a high value on the market openness that is secured through mutual recognition, or the other-regarding embracing of mutual recognition of nationality designations. In contrast, in the different areas of the AFSJ, mutual recognition and the mutual trust that underpins it, are treated as ends in themselves, rather than tools to achieve particular ends subject to a proportionality assessment.

Human rights law tends to demand individual case-by-case assessment. Yet, if mutual recognition is conditional on establishing human rights compliance in each individual case, it is scarcely worth the name. The account of the Dublin System in Chapter 6 reveals the apparently endless stream of Strasbourg cases seeking to temper governments' reliance on Dublin to institutionalize blind trust across the EU.[170] Yet, less well-recognized, but also evident, is that case-by-case assessment also seems inadequate. As de Schutter puts it, the case law often posits a human rights exception to mutual recognition, which tends to be 'purely reactive and *ad hoc*, rather than proactive and systematic.'[171] Systems of mutual recognition instead ought to prompt serious *ex ante* monitoring mechanisms to ensure that human rights compliance is real and effective, rather than simply assumed.

Normally, for mutual recognition to function, States need some common minimum framework. In the AFSJ, human rights (usually assumed to be at the ECHR minimum) are sometimes portrayed as providing that framework. However, the intensity of the interaction under mutual recognition systems suggests that it requires greater commonality than the ECHR minimum. Taking an example from the criminal sphere, where the EU has attempted to establish higher standards, de Schutter explains that while the ECHR:

> [C]ertainly constitutes a common minimum threshold of protection,... its requirements are not detailed enough to create the necessary cement between Union Member States justifying mutual recognition; mutual trust between Member States could be threatened, not only when a Member State violates this minimum standard which should be respected by all, but also when there are excessive differences between Member States.[172],

[170] From *TI v UK* to *Tarakhel v Switzerland*. See Chapter 6 for a full exposition.

[171] O de Schutter, *International Human Rights Law* (Cambridge University Press 2010) 27. See further, O de Schutter, 'The Promotion of Fundamental Rights by the Union as a Contribution to the European Legal Space (I): Mutual Recognition and Mutual Trust in the Establishment of the Area of Freedom, Security and Justice' (2006) REFGOV-FR-2 Working Paper.

[172] ibid, 33.

As is explored throughout, establishing appropriately higher human rights standards to underpin mutual recognition of decisions rejecting people from the whole 'territory of the Union' (expulsion, Dublin, rejecting asylum claims) is urgently required. The particular context must be borne in mind: Mutual recognition in the Dublin context is unlike the transnational execution of an arrest warrant, where an individual is sought by the authorities of one Member State to face criminal prosecution or to serve a criminal sentence. In the arrest warrant scenario, if transfer is refused, the individual will not face justice and the system fails in its aim. In contrast, under Dublin, there is no duty to transfer, only a duty to take back: the internal logic of the system has always accepted that States may consider asylum applications themselves. A refusal to transfer, where it coheres with the wishes of the asylum-seeker, may actually better meet the objectives of the system than transfer. The CJEU has admitted as much in its case on unaccompanied minors, *MA*,[173] where it held that refusal to transfer would be the best way to ensure swift processing of asylum claims.

In Opinion 2/2013, the CJEU regarded mutual recognition as a constitutional requirement in EU law, rather than a flexible policy tool suitable to meet some EU objectives, but not others. The Court expressed the principle thus:

> [T]he principle of mutual trust between the Member States is of fundamental importance in EU law, given that it allows an area without internal borders to be created and maintained. That principle requires, particularly with regard to the area of freedom, security and justice, each of those States, save in exceptional circumstances, to consider all the other Member States to be complying with EU law and particularly with the fundamental rights recognised by EU law.[174]

However, the Treaty does not treat mutual trust as constitutive of the AFSJ, but rather states in Article 67(1) TFEU that the EU must 'constitute an area of freedom, security and justice *with respect for fundamental rights*'. In contrast, for the CJEU, the 'principle of mutual trust' necessitated duties 'to presume that fundamental rights have been observed by the other Member States, so that not only may they not demand a higher level of national protection of fundamental rights from another Member State than that provided by EU law, but, save in exceptional cases, they may not check whether that other Member State has actually, in a specific case, observed the fundamental rights guaranteed by the EU'.[175] Accordingly, the Court opined that the Protocol had failed to reflect the feature of the EU legal order which meant that in the relations between each other, Member States should not be treated as subject to the same relations as if they were acting with third States. This seems to elevate the duty of mutual recognition to a necessary feature of the EU legal order. One may question this move, which elevates mutual recognition from an adaptable tool in certain areas of EU policy to a constitutional necessity.

[173] Case C-648/11 *MA v Secretary of State for the Home Department* [2013] OJ C 255/18.

[174] Opinion 2/13 of 18 December 2014, para 191, citing *NS and ME*, paras 78–80, and *Melloni* paras 37 and 63.

[175] ibid, para 192.

## VI. Conclusion

This chapter has set out the content and aim of this book, to examine those areas of EU law that regulate the admission of migrants and refugees, focusing on areas that have also been the subject of litigation before the ECtHR. The limits of the human rights of migrants have been sketched, and in particular it has been suggested that human rights bodies, including the ECtHR, defer to statist border controls in a manner that shapes human rights protections of migrants. This opening suggestion figures in the substantive analysis in the subsequent chapters, and will, I hope be borne out there. This is not to suggest that the human rights of migrants under the ECHR are unimportant. On the contrary, in many respects that Court's rulings on migrants' rights are ground-breaking and legally innovative.

Nonetheless, my central contention is that moving immigration and asylum policy into EU law has further transformative potential. That potential is explored in this chapter at both the constitutional and institutional level. At the constitutional level, the aim of the creation of an Area of Freedom, Security and Justice has been examined. While the inert acronym AFSJ is uninspired and uninspiring, there is transformative potential in attaching these basic political values to the 'area', the *chora* that is the EU. The institutional dimension examines shared competences, minimum standards legislation, and the institutionalization of mutual recognition across the EU. While these are the familiar tools of European integration, their institutionalization in the AFSJ is different: they may be harnessed either to exclusionary or inclusionary effect.

The next chapter returns to the unifying theme of this book, namely how the EU has incorporated and transformed human rights norms concerning admission-seekers. It sets out the approach to human rights pluralism espoused, one in which mutual engagement and interaction across different human rights regimes is encouraged, but crucially, divergence also embraced, in particular where there are good reasons for higher standards of protection within the EU system.

# 2

# The Human Rights of Migrants and Refugees in a Pluralist Setting

## I. Introduction

This book examines areas where migrants have already sought to clarify the protections of the European Convention on Human Rights (ECHR) as regards their rights to enter, reside, have their claims for protection assessed, and be free from detention. European Union (EU) law has come into play after the ECHR, bringing not only its own legislative standards, but also its own human rights norms, and court, the Court of Justice of the European Union (CJEU). It might seem desirable to ensure a harmonious approach between the ECHR and EU systems as regards migrants' rights. Why should a migrant be treated differently as regards her human rights depending on whether an issue happens to be regulated by EU law or not? This chapter aims to bring together the various legal and institutional reasons why EU law should take a different approach to the ECHR, in particular in order to overcome some of the limitative features of the Strasbourg jurisprudence. I do not suggest that the EU ignore, undermine, or sideline the ECHR—quite the contrary. My prescription is for a constructive engagement between the two systems, which I call 'constructive human rights pluralism'.

EU human rights law comprises largely judge-made general principles, and the Charter of Fundamental Rights of the European Union (EUCFR or 'the Charter'). The Charter was initiated in 1999, with the aim of rendering more visible existing protections in EU law, not only drawing on the ECHR but also on other international instruments and the common constitutional traditions of the Member States.[1] The drafting process was an open, deliberative one, leading to an extensive catalogue of rights, much broader than the ECHR.[2] The Charter was proclaimed in 1999, and became legally binding in EU law with the entry into force of the Lisbon Treaty.[3] The Charter contains detailed final provisions regarding its interpretation. These include a licence, if not an invitation for the EU to establish distinctive higher standards of human rights protection than the ECHR, even where the rights

[1] Presidency Conclusions of the Cologne European Council, 3 and 4 June 1999, Annex IV, para 2.

[2] G de Búrca, 'The Drafting of the European Charter of Fundamental Rights' (2001) 26 European Law Review 126.

[3] Art 6 (1) TEU.

correspond to those in the ECHR. Article 52(3), headed 'Scope of guaranteed rights', states:

> In so far as this Charter contains rights which correspond to rights guaranteed by the [ECHR], the meaning and scope of those rights shall be the same as those laid down by the said [ECHR]. *This provision shall not prevent Union law providing more extensive protection.*[4]

Part II sets out the sense in which the relations between the EU and ECHR (and indeed other aspects of international human rights law) are 'pluralistic'. While pluralism in the EU is often characterized as 'constitutional' I avoid this term so as to embrace the external elements of pluralism fully, noting the interfaces between EU–ECHR and EU–international refugee law. I identify various pluralist pitfalls, and so set out to avoid them by setting out some prescriptions for a 'constructive human rights pluralism', a mode of engagement between regimes which is characterized by openness and mutual regard, but is also attuned to when each system may develop distinctive approaches.

A central aim is to identify when it is appropriate for the EU to set higher human rights protections than the ECHR, which it should be noted does not damage the integrity of the ECHR—indeed, it may inform higher ECHR protections in time. Like all International Human Rights Law (IHRL), the ECHR encourages the development of higher domestic standards. Thus, whilst drawing on existing meta-principles that aim to inform interactions across systems in a pluralist setting, the rest of the chapter sets out more specific reasons why the EU standards on migrant rights should be higher than the ECHR. It identifies how the sources of EU human rights transcend the ECHR, a point which needs little elaboration given the broad range of sources that evidently inform the EUCFR—see Part III of this chapter. While Chapter 1 set out some constitutional and institutional reasons why the EU context lends itself to overcoming the statist migration control assumption, this chapter engages more closely with the judicial arena. Part IV compares and contrasts the European Court of Human Rights (ECtHR or 'Strasbourg') and CJEU in terms of their jurisdictions, institutional positions, and decisional autonomy. This institutional account provides an explanatory frame for their different case law on migrant status and remedies, and their contrasting jurisprudential styles. This framing serves to set up the substantive analysis in the remaining chapters.

## II. Human Rights Pluralism

In examining how EU law has incorporated and transformed ECHR norms, this book is situated in the 'ontological reality'[5] of overlapping EU–ECHR human

[4] (Emphasis added). See further S Peers and S Prechal, 'Article 52—Scope of Guaranteed Rights' in S Peers, T Hervey, J Kenner, and A Ward (eds), *The EU Charter of Fundamental Rights: A Commentary* (Hart Publishing 2014).

[5] N Walker in M Avbelj and J Komárak, 'Four Visions of Constitutional Pluralism—Symposium Transcript' (2008) 2(1) European Journal of Legal Studies 325, 347.

rights systems. I use the term 'human rights pluralism' throughout, to capture these overlapping human rights systems and bring (at suitable moments) international refugee law into the mix. Pluralism has its pitfalls, so to avoid them a 'constructive' approach is advocated, the features of which are identified in this section, and fleshed out through the detailed analysis in the substantive chapters.

## 1. A plurality of pluralisms?

To the extent that pluralism is concerned with conflicting validity claims,[6] it is often cast as inevitably concerned with constitutions or legal orders, leading to 'legal pluralism' or 'constitutional pluralism'.[7] However, for some, 'constitutionalism' and 'pluralism' remain distinct concepts, the former connoting unitary authority (within a legal system or constitutional order), while the latter suggests interactions between legal orders and their constituent parts where the relationships 'are governed not by legal rules but primarily by politics, often judicial politics; where we find heterarchy, not hierarchy'.[8] Still others use the term 'pluralism' to capture the contestation between constitutional authorities even *within* constitutional orders.[9] I use the term 'pluralism' in a broad, capacious sense, to capture EU–ECHR relations (even post-accession) and EU–IHRL relations. While these legal relations are different, they are characterized by interfaces set up within each respective system, so in this sense the interactions are pluralist as each regime approaches the other from within its own logic. By interface I mean loosely the rules or practices developed within one system or instrument to set out the mode of incorporation, engagement, or consideration of the other system or instrument. There are of course overarching principles of public international law, but given that the EU has not yet ratified either the ECHR or the 1951 Convention on the Status of Refugees and its 1967 Protocol (CSR or 'the Refugee Convention'),[10] the engagement from within each system is my main focus.

The 'constitutional' label is sometimes applied to the ECHR regime. The ECtHR has itself called the ECHR 'a constitutional document' of European public law.[11] In scholarship on the ECHR, 'constitutional pluralism' is sometimes used to capture the state of evolution of the ECHR *qua* regime, in which the Convention is effectively incorporated into the legal orders of all its States, and enforced by national judges,

[6] See, e.g., M Kumm, 'The Jurisprudence of Constitutional Conflict: Constitutional Supremacy in Europe before and after the Constitutional Treaty' (2005) 11(3) ELJ 262.

[7] N Walker, 'The Idea of Constitutional Pluralism' (2002) 65 MLR 317. See further M Avbelj and J Komárak (eds), *Constitutional Pluralism in the European Union and Beyond* (Hart Publishing 2012) Chapter 1.

[8] N Krisch, 'The Open Architecture of European Human Rights Law' (2008) 71 MLR 183, 185.

[9] D Halbertam, 'Constitutional Heterarchy: The Centrality of Conflict in the European Union and the United States' (2008) Michigan Law School Public Law & Legal Theory Working Paper No 111.

[10] Convention relating to the Status of Refugees (28 July 1951) 189 UNTS 137; Protocol Relating to the Status of Refugees (4 October 1967) 606 UNTS 267.

[11] *Loizidou v Turkey* (1995) 20 EHRR 99.

with all States now permitting individual petition to the ECtHR.[12] On this view, the ECHR is constitutional (in its scope and effects) and pluralist (in the sense that each domestic legal order accommodates it on its own terms). However, for others, the 'constitutional' label is one mode of adjudication employed by the ECtHR, and a normative rallying cry for a bolder ECtHR.[13] These usages are distinct, and while I do not disagree with the characterization of the ECHR as having some constitutional features, the label 'constitutional' is used to different effect in different contexts in the scholarship on the ECHR. I avoid its application to the ECHR, for the reason that even if it is a 'constitutional' regime, its constitutional character is unlike that of the EU, where the breadth and depth of its political and legal commitments are 'constitutional' by any measure.

The pluralist turn in studying the EU has its origins in studying the relationship between the EU and its Member States.[14] The label 'constitutional pluralism' seems particularly apt in the context of the internal relationships between the Member States, and EU constitutional orders. Within the EU, this label is appropriate to theorize the competing supremacy claims of domestic and EU legal orders, as manifested in clashes (latent or blatant) between the CJEU and national constitutional courts on human rights protection. This 'internal pluralism' is preoccupied with jurisdictional conflict, as the EU's overt supremacy claim was a direct confrontation with the claim of unitary authority within domestic constitutional orders. That story is now well-told and well-worn, but suffice to recall that this internal pluralism is not specifically about human rights, but rather human rights provided both the source and solution of tensions between overlapping legal orders.[15] The CJEU's incorporation of human rights as general principles was prompted by national judiciaries, and the latter continue to keep check on the content and intensity of the CJEU's review. I confine the term 'constitutional pluralism' to this context.

In contrast I resist reaching for a 'constitutional' glue across the systems in the context of 'external pluaralism'. It adds little to the endeavour of seeking to understand EU–ECHR interactions, nor does it assist the inquiry into the place of International Refugee Law under each system. Instead, I focus on points of interaction, interfaces which reveal pluralistic engagement, friction, and contestation. In this discussion, coherence across systems may appear to be of value, and indeed it may reflect appropriate equality of treatment and legal certainty. However, there are situations when divergence and disparity are appropriate, not least so that one system can offer a corrective to the other, or inform its progressive development. The vigour of the interaction and mutual engagement is better assured by avoiding

[12] A Stone Sweet, 'A Cosmopolitan Legal Order: Constitutional Pluralism and Rights Adjudication in Europe' (2012) 1(1) Journal of Global Constitutionalism 53.

[13] See, e.g., S Greer and A Williams, 'Human Rights in the Council of Europe and the EU: Towards "Individual", "Constitutional" or "Institutional" Justice?' (2009) 15 European Law Journal 467.

[14] Neil MacCormick's towering contribution to that endeavour must be noted: N MacCormick, *Questioning Sovereignty: Law, State and Nation in the European Commonwealth* (OUP 1999).

[15] P Craig and G de Búrca, *EU Law: Text, Cases and Materials* (5th edn, OUP 2011) 379–410.

overarching constitutionalism across systems. Accordingly, I omit the adjective 'constitutional' given its diverse usages and connotations of uniformity, and refer instead to 'human rights pluralism' to capture the peculiarities of the interactions on which I focus. While my embrace of contestation is wholehearted, I acknowledge some challenges and pitfalls.

## 2. Pluralist challenges and pitfalls

The combined impression of internal pluralism within the EU and domestic legal orders, external pluralism in the international order, and the transnational and supranational interactions between and across these domains raises the spectre of legal fragmentation.[16] However, interpretation is a mode of 'defragmentation', so this work has affinities with the scholarship which looks to courts to avoid fragmentation.[17] Importantly, not all forms of divergence are 'fragmentation', and for the EU to develop higher standards of human rights protection for migrants' rights would not be fragmentation at all, provided it is properly reasoned. The CJEU–ECtHR relationship, a principal focus of this work, is also a fairly cosy case, where the interfaces of interpretative engagement are well established: both Courts purport to apply analogous rights. The EUCFR contains all the ECHR rights, and then some more. As mentioned at the outset, the EUCFR sets up an interface whereby the rights therein which correspond to ECHR rights should be interpreted in a similar way, unless the EU provides additional protection.[18] This work identifies several contexts in which the EU should establish human rights standards within this zone of upward flexibility.

Even within the domain of international human rights law, there are more challenging cases. For instance, the CJEU's use of sources *other than* the ECHR has been 'parsimonious'.[19] So looking at the question of how, say, the legal commitment to insulate refugees from the punitive effects of border controls (a matter dealt with by Article 31 CSR) should be applied in EU law[20] is more challenging than ECHR–EU relations. Questions about interactions between say international refugee law and international humanitarian law, touched on briefly in Chapter 5, are more complex also.[21] The pluralist frame opens up questions of

[16] The spectre of fragmentation is raised often by public international lawyers, as exemplified by the International Law Commission (ILC) report on that topic. M Koskenniemi and E Castrén, *Fragmentation of International Law: Difficulties Arising from the Diversification and Expansion of International Law* (Erik Castrén Institute of International Law and Human Rights, University of Helsinki 2007).

[17] See, e.g., P Webb, *International Judicial Integration and Fragmentation* (OUP 2013); O Fauchald and A Nollkaemper, *The Practice of International and National Courts and the (De-)Fragmentation of International Law* (Hart Publishing 2014).

[18] Art 52(3) EUCFR; see also Peers and Prechal (n 4).

[19] I de Jesús and O de Schutter, 'Binding the EU to International Human Rights Law' (2008) 27 Yearbook of European Law 277, 282.

[20] In Case C-481/13 *Qurbani* [2014] OJ C 315/24, the CJEU's refusal to rule on the interpretation of Art 31 CSR was regrettable.

[21] For an example on the meaning of 'armed conflict' in international humanitarian law and the Qualification Directive (QD), see Case C-285/12 *Diakité* [2014] OJ C 93/6. See generally,

how different branches of international law should interact together, and how to foster appropriate cross-fertilization and engagement. Far more challenging questions concerning interaction between legal regimes abound at present, where the commonality of purpose between the EU and the ECHR is lacking. While the mutual openness that characterizes legal pluralism is apt to the interlocking, mutually regarding positions of both national–EU law and EU–ECHR relations, it may not be appropriate to the relationship between EU and all international law, in particular where international norms need a check on their legitimacy.[22] So in some ways then, this work focuses on an easy case, identifying how EU law can and should establish higher human rights standards than the ECHR, taking into account commitments in International Refugee Law.

Nonetheless, even in the EU–ECHR context, there are pitfalls to the pluralist approach, which a constructive approach would seek to avoid. One shortcoming of the current mode of engagement is that it is often muted and tacit. Mutual influence between the CJEU and ECtHR goes well beyond express citation. As Douglas-Scott has identified:

> [M]uch of [it] is not directly acknowledged—express references being the tip of an iceberg of far greater depth of influence, interest and respect. Each court wants to retain autonomy and control, while avoiding conflict out of ignorance. Each recognizes the significance of human rights in European integration but also recognizes the need to tread carefully in the present complex jurisdictional arena.[23]

This work identifies various examples of oblique rather than open engagement. A downside of this phenomenon is that some shifts are so subtle as to be barely detectable, undermining the process of public reasoning which contributes to judicial review's legitimacy.

A further under-explored downside of pluralism is complacency. The proliferation of rights sources and adjudicative bodies with overlapping jurisdiction may give the appearance of a rights surfeit. Yet, if rights claims are resolved by mannered, polite, mutual reference rather than reasoned scrutiny, the appearance will belie the reality. The desire for mutual accommodation can all too easily include excessive deference, rather than the constructive engagement and rigorous scrutiny demanded by human rights accountability. Pluralist practice could quite easily become conservative, with synthesis robbing human rights litigation of some of its transformative potential. Coherence may come at the expense of vigour, with compatibility etiolating rights. Chapters 4, 5, and 6 identify evidence of this phenomenon.

D Cantor and JF Durieux (eds), *Refuge from Humanity? War Refugees and International Humanitarian Law* (Brill/Nijhoff 2014).

[22] See, for example, S Besson, 'European Legal Pluralism after *Kadi*' (2009) 5 European Constitutional Law Review 237, 260.

[23] S Douglas-Scott, 'A Tale of Two Courts: Luxembourg, Strasbourg and the Growing European Human Rights Acquis' (2006) 43 CMLRev 619, 660.

To avoid these pitfalls, a constructive approach to human rights pluralism is advocated.

## 3. Constructive human rights pluralism

This book is premised on the 'ontological reality' of human rights pluralism in Europe. It sets out to examine its workings, in particular the interpretative stances it should engender.[24] Human rights pluralism requires courts to cultivate a certain openness to outside sources, yet maintain the integrity of their own legal orders. AG Maduro's Opinion in *Elgafaji* sets out an idealized vision of human rights pluralism in action, which is worth setting out in full:

> [T]he ECHR is reproduced in [EU] case-law for two main reasons. First of all, because the commitment which each Member State has expressed to the Convention demonstrates the status of those rights as corresponding to values common to the Member States, which therefore necessarily wish to safeguard them and reproduce them in the context of the European Union. Next, the protection of fundamental rights in the Community legal order exists alongside other European systems of protection of fundamental rights. These include both systems developed within the national legal systems and those stemming from the ECHR. Each of those protection mechanisms certainly pursues objectives which are specific to it and the mechanisms are certainly constructed from legal instruments particular to them, but sometimes they apply none the less to the same facts. In such a context, it is important, in respect of each existing protection system, while maintaining its independence, to seek to understand how the other systems interpret and develop those same fundamental rights in order not only to minimise the risk of conflicts, but also to begin a process of informal construction of a European area of protection of fundamental rights. The European area thus created will, largely, be the product of the various individual contributions from the different protection systems existing at European level.[25]

In his scholarly writings, Maduro has developed this ideal further.[26] It comprises a set of meta-principles to be internalized by courts within pluralistic settings, in order to oil the machine as it were. The requirements for successful pluralistic relations are a degree of systemic compatibility between the orders, regimes, or systems (as is present in the EU Member States' context of internal pluralism, or the EU–ECHR context externally); institutional awareness of the other regime, and a shared hermeneutic framework. Again, this is present between the EU and ECHR, albeit latently, to the extent that the two Courts routinely read and cite the other,

[24] M Maduro, 'Interpreting European Law: Judicial Adjudication in a Context of Constitutional Pluralism' (2007) 1 EJLS 1.

[25] Case C-465/07 *Elgafaji v Saatssecreteris van Justitie* [2009] ECR I-921, Opinion of AG Maduro, para 22.

[26] M Maduro, 'Courts and Pluralism: Essay on a Theory of Judicial Adjudication in the Context of Legal and Constitutional Pluralism' in JL Dunoff and JP Trachtman (eds), *Ruling the World: Constitutionalism, International Law and Global Governance* (Cambridge University Press 2009); M Maduro 'Three Claims for Constitutional Pluralism' in Avbelj and Komárek (n 5); M Maduro 'In Search of a Meaning and Not in Search of the Meaning: Judicial Review and the Constitution in Times of Pluralism' (2013) Wisconsin LR 541.

and have some shared interpretative techniques, notably in the near-ubiquity of the principle of proportionality. We can also find interfaces between the EU and the CSR, in particular given the commitments to respect the CSR in the EUCFR and the EU Treaty.[27] These interfaces make mandatory the constructive approach to pluralism. Maduro's meta-principles operate at a high level of generality, and prescribe an institutional stance and ethos, rather than particular outcomes. The aim of this chapter, in contrast, is to identify more particularly when and why EU human rights standards should be higher—in other words when their application should lead to divergence, rather than convergence. Accordingly, while I endorse these principles of active engagement across regimes, I am concerned with the discrete set of circumstances within that pluralistic setting in which EU law ought to develop distinctive higher standards.

As Maduro indicates, the key is 'to understand how the other systems interpret and develop those same fundamental rights'. As the next sections explore, the different institutional features of the CJEU and ECtHR lead to different jurisprudential outputs, prompting the questions: How should 'is' and 'ought' interact here? In other words, how should the fact of the contrasting institutional positions of the two Courts influence how they ought to interpret and integrate each another's jurisprudence? I argue that the CJEU should, when interpreting EU human rights law, even when drawing on the ECHR, be wary of those aspects of the ECtHR case law that are ill-fitting in the EU's own constitutional and institutional context. In Chapter 1, I outlined the transformative potential in the EU's constitutional engagement with migrant and refugee rights, aiming to create an 'Area of Freedom, Security and Justice'. Moreover, I suggested that institutionalizing shared competence over admissions itself demands a rethink of the statist assumption. In the next section, I suggest that the institutional position of the two Courts means that different interpretations of human rights are not only acceptable, but desirable. While Luxembourg should pay close attention to Strasbourg's minimum standards, it should not be hemmed in by Strasbourg's accommodation strategies and incrementalism. Luxembourg has no institutional reason to limit its review of EU acts to the ECHR standard alone nor should Luxembourg's application of EU fundamental rights settle on the ECHR minimum. As is explored throughout, there are instances where reliance on the Strasbourg approach is simply wrong for Luxembourg.

## III. EU Human Rights: Multiple Sources

This part expands the central unifying theme of this book, namely that the EU is legally obliged to develop human rights standards within its zone of upward flexibility, escaping some of the limitative features of the ECtHR, which are rooted in that institution's particular institutional context. In contrast, I identify the legal (in

[27] Art 18 EUCFR; Art 78(1) TFEU.

the narrow sense of binding rules), constitutional, and institutional aspects of the EU which warrant distinctive human rights protections for migrants.

In key areas, the EU's approach to migrants' rights does and should depart from the ECHR pan-European minimum, namely on family migration, the scope of protection for refugees, the allocation of responsibility for asylum claims, and detention standards. One other straightforward reason why EU law, and the CJEU in particular, should not slavishly follow the ECtHR is that the latter's case law may be internally contradictory, or 'wrong', even within the confines of the ECHR. An outside supranational court cannot directly question the ECtHR, but may offer a corrective alternative from this form of pluralism, and vice versa.[28]

The first important feature of EU human rights law (both under the EUCFR or the general principles) is the multiplicity of sources from which it can and should draw inspiration. The Charter itself is a manifestation of that plurality of sources, with the Cologne European Council mandate requiring the drafters to draw on sources other than the ECHR.[29] The result is a bill of many rights. As its Preamble indicates, the Charter is informed by the indivisible, universal values of human dignity, freedom, equality, and solidarity. The legal commitment to human dignity has legal effects, as can be seen in the important ruling of *ABC* on dignity in the asylum process.[30] Particularly important, although its full potential has yet to be explored, is the right to asylum in Article 18 EUCFR. Article 18 provides that 'the right to asylum shall be guaranteed with due respect for the rules of the [Refugee Convention]'.[31] Article 19 expressly refers to the principle of *non-refoulement*.[32]

Both the Charter and the general principles of EU law draw on the 'common constitutional traditions of the Member States' and appropriate international norms other than the ECHR. The EUCFR, and even more evidently the EU general principles, purport to engage with the 'common constitutional traditions' of the Member States. As Maduro puts it, 'A comparative law approach mindful of constitutional pluralism will not only see in national law a source of inspiration but recognise to it a particular authority.'[33] Making room for national constitutional standards raises the vista of entrapment in the maximum

[28] e.g. AG Sharpston in *Radu* critiques the 'flagrant breach' standards of the ECtHR case law, setting a particularly high standard to establish protection against removal to face breaches of rights other than Art 3 ECHR (as examined in Chapter 5). Case C-396/11 *Radu* [2013] OJ C 86/5, Opinion of AG Sharpston, paras 82–83.

[29] Presidency Conclusions of the Cologne European Council (n 1).

[30] C-148/13, C-149/13, and C-150/13 *A, B & C v Staatssecretaris van Veiligheid en Justitie* [2015] OJ C 65/2.

[31] See further MT Gil-Bazo, 'The Charter of Fundamental Rights of the European Union and the Right to Be Granted Asylum in the Union's Law' (2008) 27 Refugee Survey Quarterly 33; M den Heijer, 'Article 18' in Peers et al. (n 4) 519.

[32] Art 19(2) '[n]o one may be removed, expelled or extradited to a State where there is a serious risk that she or he would be subjected to the death penalty, torture or other inhuman or degrading treatment or punishment.'

[33] Maduro, 'Interpreting European Law' (n 24). The article is a working out of the interpretative implications of his vision of constitutional pluralism in M Maduro, 'Contrapunctual Law: Europe's Constitutional Pluralism in Action' in N Walker (ed), *Sovereignty in Transition* (Hart Publishing

standard.[34] That is not the prescription here, but rather that the comparative distillation process should be open to and mindful of domestic constitutional standards. Chapter 4 illustrates, for instance, that the CJEU ought to have engaged with constitutional jurisprudence in order to develop a distinctive EU human rights standard on migrants' right to family life, beyond the ECHR minimum.

The other legal source that should inform EU human rights standards comes from the EU legislature itself. Of course, EU human rights are normatively superior to EU legislation.[35] Nonetheless, EU legislation is capable of amplifying human rights standards, embodying more elaborate and more progressive human rights norms than the ECHR. In this context, it is appropriate that those legislative norms that articulate human rights standards should inform the CJEU's judicial construction of human rights as general principles of EU law, and indeed in suitable cases, the EUCFR. In turn, we can identify examples where the EU standards feed into the Strasbourg system.

An example from a field outside the scope of this work, but useful for illustrative purposes, is EU equality law.[36] In this field, the EU legislature developed the concepts and frameworks, which the CJEU in turn deemed to reflect fundamental rights commitments.[37] In turn, the concepts have come to inform ECtHR case law in some respects. In this context, the CJEU was correct to look to its own legislature to identify the commitments that *were* human rights, albeit ones that had their genesis in legislative standards. The EUCFR reflects much that has its origins in EU legislation too, such as the right to reconciliation of family and working life, including paid maternity leave.[38] In Chapter 4, I bemoan the failure to use the Family Reunification Directive (FRD) to articulate a distinctive higher EU human rights standard, but identify the potential for such a move in light of subsequent cases.[39]

2003) 501, and M Maduro, 'Europe and the Constitution: What If This Is as Good as It Gets?' in JHH Weiler and M Wind (eds), *European Constitutionalism Beyond the State* (Cambridge University Press 2003) 74.

[34] cf L Besselink, 'Entrapped by the Maximum Standard: On Fundamental Rights, Pluralism and Subsidiarity in the European Union' (1998) 35 CMLRev 629.

[35] Case C-236/09 *Test-Achats* [2011] ECR I-773; Joined Cases C-293/12 and 594/12 *Digital Rights Ireland Ltd* and *Seitlinger and others* [2014].

[36] The impact of Council Directive 2000/43/EC of 29 June 2000 implementing the principle of equal treatment between persons irrespective of racial or ethnic origin (Race Directive) [2000] OJ L180/22; and Council Directive 2000/78/EC of 27 November 2000 establishing a general framework for equal treatment in employment and occupation (Framework Employment Directive) [2000] OJ L303/16 on the interpretation of Art 14 ECHR is evident, inter alia, in *Nachova v Bulgaria* (2006) 42 EHRR 43.

[37] See, e.g., Case C-144/04 *Mangold* [2005] ECR I-9981.

[38] Art 33 EUCFR. See further C Costello, 'Article 33—Family and Professional Life' in Peers et al. (n 4).

[39] See in particular Case C-578/08 *Rhimou Chakroun v Minister van Buitenlandse Zaken* [2010] ECR I-01839.

## IV. Institutional Pluralism: Contrasting Courts

A constructive approach to pluralism also takes into account that different human rights adjudicators are differently situated from an institutional point of view. In particular, the CJEU and ECtHR are differently situated institutionally. This awareness can inform an understanding of their outputs, which in turn can determine how each should regard the standards articulated by the other. In particular, this section develops the argument that the ECtHR has particular accommodation strategies that constrain its developments of human rights jurisprudence, which should not be imported into the EU context.

### 1. ECtHR jurisdiction

The ECtHR's main jurisdiction is hearing cases from individual applicants who have exhausted domestic remedies.[40] ECHR Protocol No 11 entered into force in 1998, abolishing the European Commission of Human Rights and centralizing authority in the ECtHR. Acceptance of individual applications and compulsory jurisdiction became mandatory for all Contracting States. The requirement of exhaustion of domestic remedies reflects the subsidiary nature of the ECtHR's jurisdiction: its entire structure is premised on Contracting States' duties to develop effective domestic remedies. Strasbourg may also hear interstate disputes under Article 33 ECHR, and the fact that any State may litigate any human rights violation reflects an important collective recognition that all have an interest in human rights protection.

While Strasbourg ostensibly provides judgment only in individual cases, many of its rulings condemn domestic legislation and demand reform, as evident for instance in its rulings on children's status of illegitimacy or the criminalization of consensual same-sex sexual activity.[41] This 'constitutional' dimension of its jurisdiction is now more explicit with the formal notion of the 'pilot judgment'. As Sadurski notes, 'the fiction according to which, before its pilot judgments, the Strasbourg rulings deal with specific cases, and not with the law, was just that: a fiction'.[42]

The ECtHR's jurisdiction over the EU is indirect. While the EU itself is not, as yet, a party to the ECHR, the collective responsibility of the Member States for EU violations is apparent in *Matthews*,[43] where the ECtHR examined a claim against

[40] Art 34 ECHR.

[41] 'Article 25... of the Convention entitles individuals to contend that a law violates their rights by itself, in the absence of an individual measure of implementation, if they run the risk of being directly affected by it.' *Marckx v Belgium* (1979) 2 EHRR 330, paras 26–27. On sexual orientation and identity, see *Dudgeon v UK* (1981) 4 EHRR 149; *Norris v Ireland* (1988) 13 EHRR 186.

[42] W Sadurski, 'Partnering with Strasbourg: Constitutionalization of the European Court of Human Rights, the Accession of Central and East European States to the Council of Europe, and the Idea of Pilot Judgments' (2009) 9 HRLR 397, 421.

[43] *Matthews v UK* (1999) 28 EHRR 361.

the Member States based on an alleged human rights violation rooted in EU Treaty law. A decisive feature of the breach was that there was no remedy against it before the CJEU. Based on *Matthews* and *Bosphorus*,[44] Strasbourg may scrutinize EU acts if there is a lack of judicial protection for fundamental rights within the EU system. Furthermore, in *Bosphorus*, the ECtHR held that a national measure required by EU law (i.e. leaving the implementing Member State no discretion) would also enjoy the presumption of equivalent protection with ECHR standards, unless there was a 'manifest deficiency' in protection. My initial reading of *Bosphorus* argued that 'viewed as part of a process, it [was] a step towards greater control over the EU',[45] stressing that the equivalent protection test was applicable only in cases where the relevant EU measure left the Member States no discretion, as the ECtHR emphasized that 'a State would be fully responsible under the Convention for all acts falling outside its strict international legal obligations'.[46] Subsequent cases indicated that the ECtHR now applies the *Bosphorus* presumption too liberally, giving too much deference to the EU (and other outside bodies to whom it had been extended).[47] If and when the EU eventually accedes to the ECHR (now again stalled by the CJEU), it is doubtful whether the *Bosphorus* presumption will still apply after accession.[48] However, as accession is now stalled, the ECtHR may move to scrutinize EU acts more intensively than before.[49]

To conclude, the jurisdiction of the ECtHR is characterized by the requirement to exhaust domestic remedies. It may also indirectly review EU acts. Officially, it aims to establish violations against individual victims in the case before it, with its legislative review function somewhat tacit. (As will be discussed in Chapter 4, the contestation around the nature of its review functions produced a divergence in the Chamber Decision in *Biao v Denmark*.[50]) This jurisdictional position places constraints on the ECtHR, particularly when contrasted to the CJEU.

[44] *Bosphorus Hava Yollari Turizm Ve Ticaret Anonim Sirketi (Bosphorus Airways) v Ireland* (2006) 42 EHRR 1. See C Costello, 'The Bosphorus Ruling of the European Court of Human Rights: Fundamental Rights and Blurred Boundaries in Europe' (2006) 6 HRLR 87.

[45] Costello (n 38) 90.

[46] *Bosphorus* (n 44), para 147.

[47] Post-*Bosphorus* cases of note include *Coopérative des Agriculteurs de Mayenne Anjou v France* App no 16931/04 (ECHR, 10 October 2006). Most controversial has been the extension of the doctrine in *Behrami and Behrami v France* and *Saramati v France, Germany and Norway* (2007) EHRR 45 SE10. See further T Lock, 'Beyond Bosphorus: the European Court of Human Rights' Case Law on the Responsibility of Member States of International Organisations under the European Convention on Human Rights' (2010) Human Rights Law Review 529; *MSS v Belgium and Greece* (2011) 53 EHRR 2; *Michaud v France* App No 12323/11 (ECHR, 6 December 2012).

[48] While this has been subject to much academic debate, the better view is that its logic is ill-fitting if the EU is a party to the ECHR. But see in contrast de Schutter, who suggests that an expansion of the *Bosphorus* doctrine could redefine a more horizontal relationship between the ECtHR and the States Parties to the Convention. O de Schutter, 'Bosphorus post-Accession: Redefining the Relationships between the European Court of Human Rights and the Parties to the Convention' in V Kosta, N Skoutaris, and V Tzevelekos (eds), *The EU Accession to the ECHR* (Hart Publishing 2014). cf C Timmermans 'The Relationship between the European Court of Justice and the European Court of Human Rights' in A Arnull et al. (eds), *A Constitutional Order of States? Essays in Honour of Alan Dashwood* (Hart Publishing 2011) 155–56.

[49] *Opinion 2/2013* [2015] OJ C65/2.

[50] *Biao v Denmark* App No 38590/10 (ECHR, 25 March 2014), discussed in Chapter 4.

## 2. CJEU jurisdiction

The CJEU's jurisdiction runs wider and deeper than the ECtHR, reflecting its two main constitutional tasks: ensuring Member State compliance with EU law and keeping the EU institutions in check. For many years, the Court's jurisdiction over justice and home affairs (including asylum and immigration) was limited, compromising access to justice.[51] With each successive Treaty revision, its jurisdiction has been extended. With the entry into force of the Treaty of Lisbon, justice and home affairs became largely the same as other areas of EU activity. To understand that normal jurisdiction, it is worth revisiting its genesis and transformation. To keep the Member States in check, the drafters' main innovation was providing for compulsory CJEU jurisdiction for interstate actions, and more dramatically, conferring prosecutorial power on the European Commission under Article 226 EC [now Article 258 TFEU].

However, the real drama came with the domestication of EEC (now EU) obligations via *Van Gend*.[52] As the CJEU recognized from the outset, domestication dramatically increases the compliance pull of EU obligations, by drawing on the 'vigilance' of individual litigants along with the institutional enforcement mechanisms expressly provided for.[53] The CJEU's fundamental rights jurisdiction is an adjunct to its general mandate to ensure Member State compliance with EU norms, and to review the legality of EU acts. As regards Member State acts, it may only review their fundamental rights compatibility if national acts fall 'within the scope of EU law.' Although this settled formulation belies various significant extensions, the CJEU consistently reaffirms that it does not have a general human rights jurisdiction. Nonetheless in the context of the Charter, the remit of which extends only to national acts 'implementing' EU law, a wide construction of that scope has been adopted.[54]

The preliminary reference procedure was the locus for most of the dramatic EU legal developments. In allowing national judges at all levels to refer questions to the CJEU, that jurisdiction was transformed into one whereby the compliance of national laws and practices with superior EU norms could be checked. The doctrines honed in that context (direct effect, supremacy, indirect effect, effective remedies, including the specific EU remedy of damages for States' serious breaches of EU law), all aim to secure Member State compliance with EU law. However, the preliminary reference procedure has some important limits, in particular the CJEU's role is confined to the interpretation and determination of validity of EU acts. The line dividing the CJEU's legitimate task of interpreting EU law and that

[51] S Peers, 'The Jurisdiction of the Court of Justice over EC Immigration and Asylum Law: Time for a Change' in A Baldaccini, E Guild, and H Toner (eds), *Whose Freedom Security and Justice? EU Immigration and Asylum Law and Policy* (Hart Publishing 2007) 85.

[52] Case 26/62 *Van Gend en Loos* [1963] ECR 1.

[53] By Arts 226 and 227 EC [now Arts 258 and 259 TFEU].

[54] See e.g. Case C-617/10 *Akerberg Fransson* [2013] OJ C 114/7; E Hancox, 'The Meaning of "Implementing" EU Law under Article 51(1) of the Charter: Akerberg Fransson' (2013) 50(5) CMLRev 1411.

of the national court of applying the law to the facts may be blurred. However, the CJEU certainly cannot engage in the type of detailed victim-centred revisiting of the factual background we find in Strasbourg, which has gone so far as to send delegates to interview those involved in asylum cases.[55]

Concerning review of EU acts, the TFEU privileges institutional litigants under what is now Article 263 TFEU [ex Article 230 EC], although it was the CJEU initially which included the European Parliament (EP) within the remit of privileged applicants. Later, the Treaty of Nice granted the Parliament full standing. The first case in which it exercised its powers as a human rights litigant was the *FRD Ruling*,[56] examined in Chapter 4. The limited standing of individual litigants seeking to challenge the legality of EU acts of general application has been a constant source of legal intrigue,[57] but the CJEU asserts that effective judicial protection is secured by recourse to the preliminary reference procedure to challenge EU acts.[58]

The CJEU's jurisdiction under what was before Title IV EC was more limited than under the normal EC provisions. The Commission brought numerous infringement proceedings against the Member States for non-implementation,[59] and inter-institutional litigation has also been launched.[60] Substantive questions are arising in the context of litigation between the institutions. When human rights are invoked to impugn the validity of EU legislative acts, as in the *FRD Ruling*, the constitutional nature of the action renders the mechanical application of the Strasbourg standards inappropriate.

Under Title IV EC, the preliminary reference procedure, the main avenue for individuals to hold Member States to their EU legal commitments, which could have been used both to test the validity of EU legislative measures *and* prompt uniform interpretations of EU law, was significantly restricted. Under Article 68 EC (now already repealed), only national courts and tribunals 'against whose decisions there is no judicial remedy under national law' were empowered to refer.[61] Largely due to this restriction, at the outset, there were few preliminary rulings on EU asylum and immigration measures. In the decade before the entry into force of the Treaty of Lisbon, the main preliminary rulings were *Zurita Garcia*[62] on the Schengen Borders Code (SBC), alluded to in Chapter 3; *Elgafaji* on the QD, discussed at length in Chapter 4; and *Petrosian*,[63] on the Dublin Regulation,

[55] See, e.g., *N v Finland* App No 38885/02 (ECHR, 26 July 2005) discussed in Chapter 5.

[56] Case C-540/03 *Parliament v Council (FRD Ruling)* [2006] ECR I-5769.

[57] Leading to a somewhat underwhelming reform in the Treaty of Lisbon. See S Balthasar, 'Locus Standi Rules for Challenges to Regulatory Acts by Private Applicants: The New Art. 263(4) TFEU' (2010) 35(4) European Law Review 542.

[58] Case C-50/00 *UPA* [2002] ECR I-6677.

[59] See Peers, 'The Jurisdiction of the Court of Justice over EC Immigration and Asylum Law' (n 51) 91.

[60] See, e.g., Case C-257/01 *Commission v Council* [2005] ECR I-345.

[61] Indeed, they were obliged to refer if they consider that a decision on the question is necessary to enable them to give judgment. As a result, the first two preliminary references in the immigration field have to date been deemed inadmissible as the references apparently came from lower instances. Case C-51/03 *Georgescu* [2004] ECR I-3203; Case C-45/03 *Dem'Yanenko* [2004] OJ C 106/16.

[62] Joined Cases C-261/08 and C-348/08 *Zurita Garcia and Choque Cabrera* [2009] ECR I-10143.

[63] Case C-19/08 *Migrationsverket v Petrosian* [2009] ECR I-495.

discussed in Chapter 5. Since the entry into force of the Lisbon Treaty, there is a burgeoning case law on asylum and immigration, examined throughout this work. Due to the direct line of communication between national judges and the CJEU, new and challenging questions of asylum and immigration law are being asked of the CJEU.

## 3. Contrasting institutional positions

From these institutional positions, the two courts have honed different relationships with national legal orders. The starting point in drawing this contrast is the different domestic status of EU and ECHR law. As Lawson explains:

> A comparison of *Ireland v UK*[64] with *Van Gend & Loos* immediately shows the differences between Strasbourg and Luxembourg. The Strasbourg Court did *not* speak of 'a new legal order', although the precedent was there. It did *not* oblige Contracting Parties to incorporate its provisions into national law [*McCann v UK*[65]]. Only in 2006—i.e. at the time that the ECHR had finally been incorporated by all Contracting States—did the [Strasbourg] Court state that the Convention 'directly creates rights for private individuals within their jurisdiction.' [*Blečić v Croatia*[66]].[67]

The contrasting domestic statuses both reflect and inform the distinctive institutional positions of the two Courts. The ECtHR's starting point is that it is a subsidiary organ, and the primary guarantors of ECHR rights are the Member States. In contrast, the CJEU stipulates duties for national judges directly, reflecting their shared role as EU law judges. Strasbourg and Luxembourg operate under different institutional constraints. Both courts have successfully staked claims as the authoritative interpreter within their respective domains and both enjoy considerable autonomy, creating an important space for principled decision-making. Nonetheless, as pluralism suggests, national orders continue to exercise influence.

What is crucial to note is that the two supranational courts find themselves in different institutional positions, which means that they enjoy different degrees of decisional autonomy. Like all judicial review courts, they must be mindful of securing compliance with their rulings. In this endeavour, Strasbourg is in a weaker position than Luxembourg, in two respects. First, it lacks the direct line of communication with national judges of the preliminary reference procedure, so must secure the compliance of States, rather than simply domestic judges. Secondly, Strasbourg has a wider and more diverse pool of Contracting States to keep in check.

Sadurski explains the low compliance pull of Strasbourg in institutional terms, noting that 'while States have a strong incentive to *join* the Council of Europe

[64] *Ireland v UK* (1978) 2 EHRR 5, para 239.
[65] *McCann v UK* (1995) 21 EHRR 97, para 153.
[66] *Blečić v Croatia* (2006) 43 EHRR 48, para 90.
[67] R Lawson, 'The Monitoring of Fundamental Rights in the Union as a Contribution to the European Legal Space (III): The Role of the European Court of Human Rights' (2006) REFGOV-FR-7, 9.

and consequently the ECHR system (for its prestige value and as a prerequisite for membership to the EU), once they are *in* they have little incentive to comply with the norms of the ECHR (not to mention the rather nebulous sanctions that the Council of Europe system may impose on them)'.[68] In contrast, he suggests that compliance mechanisms for EU norms are stronger, as they spill into the economic realm. Even sticking to a formal institutional account, there are stronger enforcement mechanisms within the EU system, and the preliminary reference mechanism has succeeded in domesticating EU law more so than the long road to Strasbourg has done for the ECHR. From the outset, the institutional position of the CJEU has been remarkably secure. For Alter, '[t]he CJEU is about the most powerful and influential international court that is realistically possible'.[69] To exaggerate the contrast somewhat, the ECHR tends to operate in an incrementalist, minimalist, fact-specific mode, as it faces more extensive threats of non-compliance, particularly in the greater Europe it services.

On the second difference, Strasbourg's wider, more diverse cohort of Contracting States, it is noteworthy that it has a jurisprudential technique, the doctrine of European consensus, to allow space for gradual developments. As explored further in Chapter 3, in some areas, the CJEU has been mindful of this institutional difference when engaging with the Strasbourg standards.[70]

The overall result is captured in Guiraudon's stylized contrast between the CJEU and the ECtHR:

> We have a bold CJEU and a tamer ECHR. One is a separation-of-powers court with many potential allies (the Commission, economic interest groups, varying member-states, courts asking for preliminary rulings) whose decisions have direct effect [*sic*]. The second is a human rights court that can only rule after all national means of appeal have been exhausted...We can therefore expect that the CJEU will have less fear of increasing its competence and to issue controversial rulings, while the ECHR will adopt a self-limiting approach to slowly gain legitimacy and avoid provoking nation-states.[71]

While this may be a caricature, it points to an institutional difference I contend is particularly influential in the case law on migrants' rights, as explored in the next section.

## V. Contrasting Case Law

When we look at the case law of the two courts on migrant rights, as examined throughout this book, I contend that the statist immigration control

[68] Sadurski (n 42) 405.

[69] K Alter, 'The European Court of Justice's Political Power across Space and Time' (2009) 9 Northwestern University School and Law and Economics Working Paper 3.

[70] e.g. Case C-117/01 *KB v The National Health Service and the Secretary of State for Health* [2004] ECR I-541.

[71] V Guiraudon, 'European Courts and Foreigners' Rights: A Comparative Study of Norm Diffusion' (2000) 34 International Migration Review 1088, 1094.

assumption carries considerable weight in Strasbourg, profoundly shaping the legal analysis. Two general contrasts are set out here, concerning migration status and remedies in migration cases. Then this part identifies some general contrasts in the jurisprudential styles of the two courts, which mean that direct transplantation of the ECtHR rulings to the CJEU context may be inappropriate.

### 1. Migration status

In its case law on migrants' rights, Strasbourg's subsidiary self-inhibition means that it does not demand that States afford any particular migration status to those who are non-removable. In the bulk of its case law, Strasbourg does not require of States that they accord particular migration statuses. Admittedly, as explored further in Chapter 3, there are glimpses of a different approach in some Strasbourg case law, where it acknowledges that precarious migration status may impede the exercise of ECHR rights.[72] But even in this acknowledgement, Strasbourg does not assert that security of residence should be accorded via a particular status. The CJEU takes a different approach, in effect creating status by asserting EU rights to enter and reside, which are not dependent on national authorization. Its assertion reflects basic immanent features of EU law, namely the whole-hearted judicial embrace of the individual, as the 'locus of normative concern' which is 'woven into the fabric of European integration by repeated acts of interpretation on the part of innumerable participants over many years'.[73] As Halberstam explains,

> The individual is both legally freed from the constitutional confines of her Member State and endowed with what Robert Cover would have called an immediate 'jurisgenerative' capacity at the supranational level of governance.[74]

Halberstam's reference to 'her' Member State reveals that the 'individual' is normally an EU Citizen. However, the CJEU's embrace of the individual will also potentially encompass those third-country nationals (TCNs) who derive rights from the EU legal order, as the following chapters illustrate. In each, I demonstrate that EU law provides a distinctive added-value, namely security of residence. That the Strasbourg case law may in turn reinforce these distinctive EU rights is evident in *Mendizabal*,[75] where the ECtHR treated the EU right of residence of a Spanish national in France as an aspect of her Article 8 ECHR legal patrimony, as explored in Chapter 4.

[72] See further, *Sisojeva* et al *v Latvia* App No 60654/00 (ECHR, 16 June 2005), (Grand Chamber, ECHR, 15 January 2007).

[73] D Halberstam, 'The Bride of Messina: Constitutionalism and Democracy in Europe' (2005) 30 ELR 775, 777.

[74] D Halberstam, 'Constitutionalism and Pluralism in *Marbury* and *Van Gend*' (2008) Public Law and Legal Theory Working Paper Series Working Paper No 104, 5 citing R Cover, 'Foreword: Nomos and Narrative' (1983) 97 Harv LR 4.

[75] *Mendizabal v France* App No 51431/99 (ECHR, 17 January 2006).

## 2. Remedies for migrants

The ECtHR, prompted by developments in other international *fora*, gradually established the binding force of its interim measures. In *Mamatkulov*, it held that State failure to comply with interim measures interferes with the right of individual petition under Article 34 ECHR.[76] It is no coincidence that this development emerged in the context of cases challenging illegal deportations, where the ECtHR was faced with non-compliance with non-deportation orders, pending its own examination of the nature of the risks returnees faced. The popularity of the Rule 39 petition reveals the shortcoming of domestic non-removal proceedings. Yet maintaining the ECtHR as a subsidiary, last recourse, instance, means that domestic remedies should match or ideally exceed those available in Strasbourg. Otherwise cases will flow inevitably and too readily to the ECtHR. Accordingly, one can trace a development whereby Strasbourg instructs national courts to do as it does, in order to reduce institutional incentive for litigants to have recourse outside the national system, and overburden the scarce resources of the supranational human rights instance. Thus we see that following *Mamatkulov*, the ECtHR established that Article 13 ECHR similarly requires that domestic remedies have suspensive effect,[77] as explored in Chapter 6. Yet, there is a tension: in the act of instructing national courts how to remedy or avoid human rights violations, the ECtHR may be seen to overstep the line of its subsidiary nature.[78]

Using its direct line of communication with national courts, the preliminary reference procedure, the CJEU has used rhetoric signalling deference to national procedural law (using the masking device of 'national procedural autonomy'), yet imposed requirements of equivalence and effectiveness of national procedures and remedies. Specific entitlements have emerged out of these principles, including interim relief,[79] and an individual right to damages for 'sufficiently serious' state breaches of EU law.[80] The added remedial potential of EU law creates strong incentives to rely thereon and may enhance the compliance pull of EU norms, in contrast to the ECHR.

The interaction between Strasbourg and Luxembourg case law on procedures and remedies in the immigration and asylum context has been extensively examined elsewhere. Suffice to note that both the EUCFR and the CJEU case law clearly offer stronger procedural and remedial protections for migrants' rights that fall within the scope of EU law.[81]

[76] *Mamatkulov v Turkey* (2005) 41 EHRR 25 in this respect overrules *Cruz Varas v Sweden* (1992) 14 EHRR 1. See further, G Letsas, 'International Human Rights and the Binding Force of Interim Measures' (2003) 5 European Human Rights Law Review 527.

[77] Letsas (n 76) 535.

[78] See further, T Spijkerboer, 'Subsidiarity and "Arguability": the European Court of Human Rights' Case Law on Judicial Review in Asylum Cases' (2009) 21 IJRL 1.

[79] Case C-213/89 *Factortame* Ltd [1990] ECR I-243. See Craig and de Búrca (n 15) 312–13.

[80] Cases 6 and 9/90 *Francovich & Bonifaci v Republic of Italy* [1991] ECR I-5357. See Craig and de Búrca (n 15) 328–41.

[81] See further C Costello, 'The Asylum Procedures Directive in Legal Context: Equivocal Standards Meet General Principles' in Baldaccini, Guild, and Toner (n 51) 151; M Reneman, *EU Asylum Procedures and the Right to an Effective Remedy* (Hart Publishing 2014).

## 3. Contrasting jurisprudential styles

The different institutional positions of the CJEU and ECtHR produce different jurisprudential outputs. The ECtHR and the CJEU reason and write differently. The latter's deductive, legalistic, and magisterial style[82] is in sharp contrast with the inductive, fact-specific, casuistic ECtHR. The different jurisprudential output has other features, which need to be appreciated in order to understand the engagement between EU and ECHR norms.

Strasbourg uses distinctive jurisprudential accommodation strategies, in particular the margin of appreciation and European consensus. As is explored further in Chapter 4, the Luxembourg Court should be wary of the margin, as it is ill-fitting in the EU context.

Strasbourg tends to avoid contentious issues in a way that is not open to Luxembourg, as exemplified by the issue of financial limitations on family reunification explored in Chapter 4. In *Haydarie v The Netherlands*,[83] faced for the first time with a claim concerning the application of financial conditions on family reunification, the ECtHR was deferential both as to the principled question and the application of the conditions to the applicant's case, delivering a rather empty judgment. It may plausibly be read as the ECtHR discouraging further applications on the topic, suggesting that it does not wish to engage in a review of these restrictions. It was unsurprising that the first case referred to the CJEU on the FRD, *Chakroun*,[84] concerns the self-same Dutch practices. The overlapping supranational jurisdictions should not converge on this issue. Luxembourg could not legitimately avoid the issue in the manner that Strasbourg has. It is required to give preliminary references in order to provide general guidance on the meaning of EU norms. While it is not unheard of for the CJEU to give underwhelming answers, avoiding a fulsome consideration of all the human rights issues raised,[85] it must at least answer directly relevant questions on the applicable EU measures, the FRD in this case.

Strasbourg and Luxembourg also move their case law along in different ways. Incrementalism is a ubiquitous feature of judicial review. As Shapiro explains, judicial review courts invariably 'choose the time and tempo of their case-by-case policy interventions so as to at least partially avoid, finesse, and obfuscate policy conflict with other politically powerful actors.'[86] Strasbourg and Luxembourg operate in different procedural and institutional settings, so

82 For a general critique of the CJEU's style of reasoning, see JHH Weiler, 'Epilogue: The Judicial Après Nice' in JHH Weiler and G de Búrca (eds), *The European Court of Justice* (OUP 2001) 215.

83 *Haydarie v The Netherlands* App No 8876/04 (ECHR, 20 October 2005). See case note by P Boeles and M Bruins (2006) EJML 364.

84 *Chakroun* (n 39).

85 See further D Sarmiento, 'Half a Case at a Time: Dealing with Judicial Minimalism at the European Court of Justice' in M Claes, M de Visser, P Popelier, and C Van de Heyning (eds), *Constitutional Conversations in Europe* (Intersentia 2012).

86 M Shapiro, 'The European Court of Justice' in P Craig and G de Búrca (eds), *The Evolution of EU Law* (OUP 1999) 321, 324.

display different modes of incrementalism. As mentioned, Strasbourg expressly uses a doctrine of European consensus to track the progressive development of human rights. In addition, for example, in the Article 8 ECHR case law examined in Chapter 3, we see the role of dissenting judgments in prompting change, leading gradually to the recognition that all settled migrants have a privacy right to remain in their host country.[87] The development of the Strasbourg case law on the right to a suspensive appeal under Article 13 ECHR displays similar gradualism.[88] Luxembourg, in contrast, if it does change tack, tends to do so more abruptly, as the overruling of *Akrich*[89] in *Metock*[90] exemplifies. The contrast between evolution by 'creeps' and 'jerks' comes to mind: the ECtHR creeps slowly, while the CJEU sometimes jerkily changes course.[91]

As will be seen, the EU legislature at times incorporates or attempts to codify Strasbourg standards, bringing a further dimension to EU–ECHR relations. In this endeavour, as is explored throughout this book, the style of the ECtHR rulings poses a challenge: their casuistry makes them difficult to codify. Nonetheless, even bearing in mind this difficulty, I have identified examples of EU legislative trimming or even distorting of ECHR case law, in a manner that suggests that ECHR obligations are not being fulsomely translated into EU law.

## VI. Four Flashpoints: Human Rights Pluralism and EU Legislative Re-writing

The argument set out thus far has proceeded at different levels. The EU's constitutional ethos and institutionalization of shared competence over admissions demands a rethink of the statist assumption. Moreover, as the previous section outlines, there are also particular reasons pertaining to the two Courts, which explain different approaches to the fundamental rights of migrants and refugees.

The rest of this book is structured around four substantive flashpoints where EU law deals with entry and residence rights, in interaction with ECHR norms. They reveal both the importance and shortcomings of Strasbourg standards for the EU's admissions rules. This book thus stands out in that it is by its nature more sector-specific and fine-grained than much of the existing scholarship on European human rights pluralism. The literature has focused almost exclusively on

[87] Judge Martens' dissenting opinion in *Beldjoudi v France* (1992) EHRR 801 and *Boughanemi v France* (1996) EHRR 228. The ECtHR finally adopted this position in *Üner v the Netherlands* (2007) 45 EHRR 421.

[88] See Chapter 6.

[89] Case C-109/01 *Akrich* [2003] ECR I-9607.

[90] Case C-127/08 *Metock* [2008] ECR I-6241.

[91] These are terms borrowed from a debate in evolutionary biology. See further, SJ Gould and S Rose (eds), *The Richness of Life: The Essential Stephen Jay Gould* (W W Norton & Co 2007) 6.

the court-to-court, i.e. Luxembourg-to-Strasbourg, interactions. I take this interaction as a given, and also explore EU legislative norms.

Chapter 3 next examines the manner in which EU law constructs migration status and the notion of 'illegal immigration.' While EU law possesses the capacity to authorize residence of certain privileged categories, it also sets up mechanisms for bolstering the statist entry control assumption, in particular by setting up mechanisms of negative mutual recognition and thwarting regularization. Strasbourg case law too is informed by the statist assumption, although there is a nascent recognition in the case law that long-residence, even if irregular, ought to be recognized as creating a right to stay. This chapter illustrates that migration status permeates human rights claims by migrants. I suggest that the interactions across EU and ECHR standards, as well as engagement with other appropriate normative and legal sources, may offer some progressive rights-protective moves.

The four substantive areas are the focus on the remaining chapters. Broadly speaking, Chapter 4 deals with family migration, Chapter 5 with refugees, Chapter 6 with access to protection, and Chapter 7 examines detention.

As Chapter 4 illustrates, EU law has long dealt with the migration of family members of EU Citizens within the EU, irrespective of their nationality, now in the Citizenship Directive (CD).[92] The FRD has set out minimum standards for the entry of family members of TCN migrants who have a 'reasonable prospect' of acquiring a right of permanent residence. The CJEU in the *FRD Ruling* engages with the Strasbourg jurisprudence under Article 8 ECHR. I contend in Chapter 4 that it ought to have developed a distinctive higher EU human right to family reunion, which is now evident in later cases.[93] Since *Bonger v Netherlands*,[94] there is now clear divergence between and within EU and ECHR standards on family migration, although there is a hint of convergence in *Jeunesse v Netherlands*.[95]

Chapter 5 examines the scope of protection from removal under the ECHR and its interaction with the EU QD, in particular its definition of subsidiary protection. Various tensions are identified and explored, contrasting the Strasbourg case law and the QD. Focusing on the CJEU's ruling in *Elgafaji*, I explore the manner in which the CJEU resisted governmental submissions to take a narrow reading of the ECHR, ruling rather that the subsidiary protection definition adds protection beyond the ECHR minimum. In so doing, it carved out an area of refugee protection all its own, beyond the CSR and ECHR. Chapter 6 deals with access to protection for refugees, examining both the barriers to lawful entry in the EU, and the Dublin System, which ostensibly allocates responsibility for processing asylum claims across the EU.

[92] Directive 2004/38/EC of the European Parliament and of the Council of 29 April 2004 on the right of citizens of the Union and their family members to move and reside freely within the territory of the Member States (CD) [2004] OJ L229/45.

[93] *Chakroun* (n 39).

[94] *Bonger v the Netherlands* App No 10154/04 (ECHR, 15 September 2005).

[95] *Jeunesse v the Netherlands* App No 12738/10 (ECHR, 4 December 2012).

Finally, Chapter 7 links back to the issues raised in Chapter 1 when considering detention of asylum seekers. This issue reveals the linkage between authorization of residence and basic rights: Whether asylum seekers and other migrants to the EU may be detained depends largely on their legal status. In *Saadi v UK*,[96] the ECtHR treats authorization as a matter of State discretion. Although it insists that detention not be 'arbitrary', it permits detention on a range of instrumental grounds. Chapter 7 explores EU law's potential to remedy the exposure of migrants to this naked power.

[96] *Saadi v UK* (2008) 47 EHRR 17.

# 3

# Constructing Migration Status

## I. Introduction

The European Union (EU) immigration and asylum competence has as its object the creation of an Area of Freedom, Security and Justice (AFSJ). As explored in Chapter 1, one of the challenges with this constitutional object is its ambiguity: it is open to either an inert or transformative interpretation. The Treaty requires the EU to 'develop a common immigration policy aimed at ensuring, at all stages, the efficient management of migration flows, fair treatment of third-country nationals (TCNs) residing legally in Member States, and the prevention of, and enhanced measures to combat, illegal immigration and trafficking in human beings'.[1] Inherent in the formulation of this aim is a binary between migrants 'legally residing in the Member States' (who are to be treated fairly) and the adoption of measures to 'combat illegal immigration'. The competence seems to assume that the distinction between legal and illegal immigration is primordial, and that EU policy aims to make more 'efficient' the 'management' of 'flows'. We are invited to imagine migrants, pre-constructed with a status (legal or illegal), with only the 'legals' entitled to fair treatment.

This chapter challenges that construction. Rather, the role of national and EU law in constructing migration status is explored, and indeed the notion of a sharp binary between 'legal' and 'illegal' migration is also questioned. This chapter considers the law, institutional practice, and policy discourse around 'illegal immigration' in the EU. Part II sets out the central normative claim of the chapter, that even those who have committed immigration law infractions should have long residence recognized with a right to stable residence, as they have become members of their societies of residence. Part III provides an overview of the various modes of becoming legal and illegal, regular and irregular in terms of immigration status. Part IV explores the highly tentative recognition of a human right to stay in the case law of the European Court of Human Rights (ECtHR), a weak instantiation of the social membership thesis.

While one might expect human rights to be invoked in a manner that 'trumps' immigration control, that move is more feasible under EU law than International Human Rights Law (IHRL), as Part V explores. The EU both creates and cures

[1] Art 79 (1) TFEU (ex Art 63, points 3 and 4, TEC).

illegality in various ways. While EU law is status-generative for those migrants and refugees who are accorded an EU right of residence, it sometimes hinders one of the main modes of admission to legal residence in the Member States—regularization.

## II. Illegal, Unauthorized, or Irregular?

The EU Treaties, as noted above, set a policy frame that treats migration status as a binary (legal or illegal). This section questions that frame not only as an analytical construct, but also as a legal designation. While legal epistemology usually has a 'binary structure', it is an overstatement to say that 'the law can only cognise human behaviour in terms of its legality and illegality'.[2] Legal epistemology *generally* has a binary structure, but other concepts may be employed to capture law's diverse normative stances.[3]

This chapter examines migration status from a dynamic and multilevel perspective. An individual's status may change over time. The change in status or statuses may be effectuated by a range of actors (legislative, executive, or judicial) based on different legal authorities (domestic, EU, or even human rights based, for instance, under the ECHR). In this context, the binary structure of legal and illegal becomes blurred, presenting sites of contestation, and opportunities for status to shift.

Even naming the phenomenon of 'illegal migration' is fraught.[4] Sympathetic observers and activists use the term 'irregular', 'undocumented', 'clandestine', or 'unauthorized' immigration to capture the diversity of forms of migration which may not comply with all domestic legal requirements, and also to avoid 'illegality's' pejorative connotations. I also use the term 'irregular' throughout this chapter for lawyerly reasons, mainly as it forestalls overly hasty determinations of law-breaking or lawfulness. It is also helpfully broad, capturing both illegal and unauthorized conduct. 'Unauthorised' helps to capture presence that has not been given official approval, but in some instances ought to be permitted for overriding legal or moral reasons.

For instance, within the EU context, the migration and presence of EU Citizens and their family members is as of right, with domestic authorization merely declaratory rather than constitutive of those rights.[5] Refugee status too is often conceived of as declaratory rather than constitutive.[6] Accordingly, it no longer makes sense,

[2] H Lindahl, 'Finding a Place for Freedom, Security and Justice: The European Union's Claim to Territorial Unity' (2004) 29 European Law Review 461, 480.

[3] In a more recent work, Lindahl explores a third notion of 'alegality'. See H Lindahl, *Fault Lines of Globalization: Legal Order and the Politics of A-Legality* (OUP 2013).

[4] See further, E Guild, 'Who is an Irregular Migrant?' in B Bogusz, R Cholewiski, A Cygan, and E Szyszczak (eds), *Irregular Migration and Human Rights* (Martinus Nijhoff Publishers 2004) 3.

[5] Case C-48/75 *Procureur du Roi v Royer* [1976] ECR 497; C-60/00 *Carpenter v Secretary of State for the Home Department* [2002] ECR I-6279; Case C-127/08 *Metock* [2008] ECR I-6241.

[6] UN High Commissioner for Refugees (UNHCR), *Note on Determination of Refugee Status under International Instruments*, 24 August 1977, EC/SCP/5, para 5.

save in exceptional cases, even to conceive of EU Citizens exercising their EU rights of movement and residence as 'illegal', whereas they may well find themselves 'unauthorized'. The intuition underlying the term 'unauthorized' extends well beyond the situation of EU Citizens. It also helpfully reminds us that in the discussion of migration, States (in particular but not only governments) also act unlawfully or illegally, and that migrants may have a moral and legal claim to have their presence authorized.

In its most usefully capacious sense, then, 'irregularity' refers to a multiplicity of liminal statuses.[7] A Commission Communication highlights that the EU's 'illegal population' includes both illegal entrants and overstayers.[8] To the Commission's typology, one should add those who lose legal status or breach conditions thereof, in ways that may imperil their right of residence.[9] Many migrants find themselves from time to time in semi-compliance with immigration law.[10] Taking this 'dynamic, processual perspective'[11] reveals that migrants often drift between different statuses.[12] Importantly, they often lack control over their legal status. Rather they may depend on employers or sponsors to ensure the legality of their stay, so are vulnerable to the threat or actual deprivation of legal status at the behest of another.[13] Asylum seekers are another noteworthy category. It would seem right and sensible to regard asylum seekers whose claims for international protection are being processed as temporarily being regular migrants (irrespective of their means of entry).[14] However, that position is contested. While EU law supports that position,[15] for some purposes, governments and the ECtHR accept that they may be regarded as 'unauthorised entrants' and in some cases detained on that basis.[16]

[7] For a survey of diverse national definitions of 'irregular migration', see F Düvell, 'Paths into Irregularity: The Legal and Political Construction of Irregular Migration' (2011) 13 EJML 275, 279–280.

[8] European Commission, *Preparing the next steps in border management in the European Union* COM(2008) 69; European Commission, *Communication on migration*, COM(2011) 248, 10.

[9] Düvell (n 7) 289–90, in which he highlights other paths to illegality, including those of migrants who are unable to switch migration status due to legal or practical impediments, and so overstay; and those unable to comply with cumbersome bureaucratic processes, and those whose status changes due to the frequent changes in domestic immigration laws.

[10] M Ruhs and B Anderson, 'Semi-compliance and Illegality in Migrant Labour Markets: An Analysis of Migrants, Employers and the State in the UK' (2010) 16 Population, Space and Place 195.

[11] A Kraler, 'Regularisation: A Misguided Option or Part and Parcel of a Comprehensive Policy Response to Irregular Migration?' (2009) IMISCOE Working Paper No 24, 9.

[12] M Baldwin-Edwards and A Kraler, *REGINE: Regularisations in Europe. Study on Practices in the Area of Regularisation in the Member States of the EU—Final Report* (ICMPD 2009) 2–4 for a table of the various permutations of legal entry, residence, and informal and formal working.

[13] This may expose some migrants to particular forms of domination, and *in extremis* human rights violations. See further C Costello, 'Migrants and Forced Labour: A Labour Law Response' in A Bogg, C Costello, A Davies, and J Prassl, *The Autonomy of Labour Law* (Hart Publishing 2015).

[14] Convention relating to the Status of Refugees (adopted 28 July 1951) 189 UNTS 137, Art 31. See further Chapter 8.

[15] Directive 2013/32/EU of the European Parliament and of the Council of 26 June 2013 on common procedures for granting and withdrawing international protection (recast) (Asylum Procedures Directive) [2013] OJ L180/60, Art 9.

[16] *Saadi v United Kingdom* (2008) 47 EHRR 17. See further Chapter 8.

Normally, in international fora operating at a distance from the domestic assessment of legal or illegal presence, the term 'irregular' is used. For instance, the Global Commission on International Migration,[17] and International Convention on the Protection of the Rights of All Migrant Workers and Members of their Families,[18] all employ the term 'irregular'. The International Labour Organisation (ILO) tends to employ the term 'irregular migration' in policy documents, although some conventions use the term 'illegal' in particular contexts.[19] The EU, in contrast, employs the term 'illegal immigration' with a vengeance.[20] However, until the adoption of the Returns Directive (RD)[21] in December 2008, and the Employer Sanctions Directive (ESD)[22] in June 2009, there was no EU level definition of 'illegal' or 'irregular' immigration. Indeed, as will be explored in Part V.2, those measures contain mixed EU and national elements, reflecting shared competence over admissions.

Long before the adoption of these instruments, dense EU institutional practice coalesced in the 'fight' against 'illegal immigration', constructing that phenomenon notwithstanding the absence of common legal definition. This EU policy discourse on illegal immigration sets up an institutional practice around 'illegal' migration that is detached from the subtleties of the law. In this way, 'illegal' migration is not simply an epiphenomenon of migration and citizenship law, but rather takes on an institutional life of its own.[23] This feature of the discourse and practice is reflected in the following statement by the European Commission, explaining when visa requirements will be imposed on entrants from any particular country:

> Illegal immigration represents one of the basic criteria for the determination of those third countries whose nationals are subject to visa requirements, besides other criteria such as public policy, security, EU's external relations, regional coherence and reciprocity.[24]

However, in many instances, who counts as an 'illegal' will depend on whether a visa was required to enter. If a visa requirement is imposed, entry to the EU is more likely

[17] See GCIM, 'Migration in an Interconnected World: New Directions for Action—Report of the Global Commission on International Migration', October 2005 (GCIM Report).

[18] See International Convention on the Protection of the Rights of All Migrant Workers and Members of their Families (adopted 18 December 1990, entered into force 1 July 2003) 2220 UNTS 3 (Migrant Workers Convention).

[19] See, e.g., GCIM Report, 32–42; Migrant Workers Convention, Arts 5, 25(3), 28, 30, 69(2).

[20] The term 'illegal' immigration is not unanimously used among EU institutions, however. See, e.g. European Parliament, *Report on the proposal for a regulation of the European Parliament and of the Council establishing the Asylum and Migration Fund* (COM(2011)0751—C7-0443/20011—2011/0366(COD)), PE491.289, 13 January 2014.

[21] Directive 2008/115/EC of the European Parliament and of the Council of 16 December 2008 on common standards and procedures in Member States for returning illegally staying third-country nationals (Return Directive) [2008] OJ L348/98.

[22] Directive 2009/52/EC of the European Parliament and of the Council of 18 June 2009 providing for minimum standards on sanctions and measures against employers of illegally staying third-country nationals (Employer Sanctions Directive) [2009] OJ L168/24.

[23] M Samers, 'An Emerging Geopolitics of "Illegal" Immigration in the European Union' (2004) 6 EJML 23, 25.

[24] European Commission, *Communication on a Common Policy on Illegal Immigration*, COM(2001) 672, 15 November 2011, 4.

to be irregular, given that visas are difficult to procure. Guild argues that illegal migration is accordingly a 'phantom ill.'[25] While that claim may be rhetorically loaded, it aptly captures how 'illegal immigration' is a product of the laws that seek to combat it, not an autonomous phenomenon. When the state or the EU act to prevent 'illegal immigration' by making migration subject to greater legal and practical barriers, those moves may well create further impediments to legal migration, and thus more illegal migration.

This section serves to problematize the notion of 'illegal' as it pertains to migration status. Taking into account both multi-level legality and the temporal shifts in status reveals the complexity of 'illegality'. Nonetheless, there are migrants whose residence is in breach of the domestic migration law of their state of residence. In the next section, I outline a normative argument to the effect that even these migrants, if they have been present for a long time, should be accorded a legal right to stay.

## III. The Social Membership and the Right to Stay

### 1. The social membership thesis

This section outlines the social membership thesis as a moral limit to the statist approach to migration control and migration status. The widely endorsed social membership thesis posits that social connections formed by migrants over a significant time in the host state warrant legal recognition with a right to stay. To remove long-term residents would be to rupture those social ties and so would be unjust. I take the social membership thesis as well-established, and endorse the version thereof defended at length by other scholars. The social membership thesis recognizes the ties formed as time passes. Social membership emerges due to the migrant's subjection to the laws of the host state over time, and the connections he or she develops in the host state. As Rubio-Marín argues,

> People cannot simply be expected to go indefinitely without developing ties and attachments, without engaging in long-term commitments which may come to be essential for them, or without taking from the cultural and social context in which they live the necessary tools for interpreting their meaningfulness.[26]

Similarly, in advocating 'amnesty' for irregular migrants present for over five years, Carens explains that '[t]he moral right of the state to apprehend and deport irregular migrants erodes with the passage of time'.[27] Crucially, as Carens puts it, '[s]ocial membership does not depend on official permission'.[28]

[25] Guild (n 4); House of Lords European Committee Report, *The Hague Programme: A Five Year Agenda for EU Justice and Home Affairs* (HL 2004–05, 84) para 27.

[26] R Rubio-Marín, *Immigration as a Democratic Challenge: Citizenship and Inclusion in Germany and the United States* (Cambridge University Press 2000) 35, and 85–98 on irregular migrants in particular.

[27] J Carens, 'The Case for Amnesty' in J Carens, *Immigrants and the Right to Stay* (Massachusetts Institute of Technology Press 2010).

[28] Carens describes this as 'the crux' of his argument. See further J Carens, *The Ethics of Immigration* (OUP 2013) 150.

## 2. The social membership of irregular migrants

The social membership thesis may be seen as reflecting a settlement model of migration, one which may be palatable if migrants are compliant with domestic migration law. However, my contention is that a right to stay ought to be recognized for all with long residence, irrespective of their migration status. Rights for 'illegals' may seem counter-intuitive: how does persisting in the illegal act remedy it? There are three main responses.

First, at least part of the response in the EU context must be to recall the ad hoc nature of immigration law and the faulty nature of asylum systems in many Member States (as explored in Chapter 5). Both these phenomena in turn feed into the regularization practices outlined in the next section. The 'illegality' of migration itself must be open to question, if the rules and practices governing migration lack the qualities of predictability and stability intrinsic to a meaningful understanding of law. Many EU Member States design immigration laws for non-compliance, creating 'illegality traps'.[29] For instance, in both Italy and Spain, immigration law requires a formal contract of employment in order to obtain a residence permit. However, migrant workers are concentrated in irregular sectors, where formal contracts are rarely used, so this requirement is difficult to meet.[30] In that context, it is arguable that the State is complicit in creating or at least tolerating the large informal sector and designing immigration law to perpetuate the irregular immigration status of immigrants who work in it. Similarly, high fees for processing applications for legal status have been shown to correlate with 'high (or very high) stocks of illegal residents'.[31] It seems plausible that high fees deter poorer migrants from obtaining even the formal statuses to which they are entitled.

Secondly, even if we were to find clear and predictable immigration laws, their non-enforcement over a long period could itself ground a claim to stay. On this second point, there is an evocative analogy between the rights of irregular migrants and the doctrine of adverse possession, drawn in particular by commentators who ground their conception of immigration justice in property theories[32] or duties to grant access to the global patrimony of territory.[33] Adverse possession is the legal mechanism whereby a squatting occupant acquires lawful title to property with the passage of time. Risse, for example, draws an analogy between the 'absent home owner' and the immigration state. His argument, framed in the US context but of general application, goes as follows:

> Like the absent home owner, the [state] underoccupies its claimed space, but it has also created an economic niche for illegal immigrants who know that, often enough, they will

[29] Kraler (n 11) 31. [30] Düvell (n 7) 291.

[31] Baldwin-Edwards and Kraler (n 12) 126.

[32] A Shachar, *The Birthright Lottery: Citizenship and Global Inequality* (Harvard University Press 2009) 185–88.

[33] See in particular M Risse, 'On the Morality of Immigration' (2008) 22 *Ethics and International Affairs*25. The piece develops an argument conceived of in M Risse and M Blake, 'Migration, Territoriality and Culture' in J Ryberg, TS Petersen, C Worf (eds), *New Waves in Applied Ethics* (Palgrave Macmillan 2008) 153.

find employment, including employment in parts of the economy where illegal immigrants are especially welcome. Since, in addition, the [state] falls short of what in principle it *could* do by way of enforcing its immigration law, we can plausibly say that a certain population moves into the country in a rather open manner, and in a manner known to... society.[34]

Shachar similarly draws the analogy with the '[s]tartling means of acquiring property' that is adverse possession.[35] She too grounds the rights of irregular migrants in the State's complicity in 'turn[ing] a blind eye' to the '*millions* of unauthorized migrants who settled in their territory (after crossing the border without permission or overstaying their visas)'.[36] Accordingly:

there must be a point in time when [the authorities] are estopped by their own inaction; in other words, the unauthorized entrants ought to gain immunity from deportation and removal, in addition to being offered an eventual route for legalizing their status.[37]

The adverse possession analogy provides a demonstration of how over time the law may transform the illegal to legal: the trespasser becomes the legitimate holder of title. The analogy suggests that the State is in a position akin to the landlord in two respects. First, the State is likened to the landowner who has been 'sleeping on its rights' for a prolonged period. Just as the landowner in the adverse possession scenario has failed to comply with a duty of stewardship over her land,[38] the State had failed to take action against the irregular immigrant. Secondly, the adverse possession analogy suggests that granting a stable right of residence in the territory is akin to granting title to specific property. Yet, granting stable rights of residence to non-members is not as 'startling' as the move in adverse possession, where the squatter takes directly from the legitimate property owner in a zero-sum transaction. Regularization, in contrast, does not automatically deprive another member of his or her title. While conferring a stable right of residence usually involves the allocation of shares in goods, many of which are public goods, such as security and a functioning legal system, these goods are not normally significantly diminished by their distribution to new members. Indeed, regularization may increase some of those public goods, by preventing exploitation of those with insecure status. Accordingly, while the adverse possession analogy is evocative, if anything, the claim of the irregular migrant is stronger than that of the squatter insofar as the squatter's title extinguishes that of the previous lawful owner. In contrast, 'regularizing' irregular migrants does not necessarily deprive insiders of any specific goods, and may increase enjoyment of public goods overall.

[34] ibid 31–32.

[35] Shachar (n 32) 185, citing J Dwyer and P Menell, *Property Law and Policy: A Comparative Institutional Framework* (NY Foundation Press 1998) 80.

[36] ibid 185. [37] ibid.

[38] This explanation is informed by a reading of L Fox-O'Mahony and N Cobb, 'Taxonomies of Squatting: Unlawful Occupation in a New Legal Order' (2008) 71 MLR 878.

A further variant of the right to regularization also develops on notions of the integrity of the legal system, invoking the rule of law as a basis for regularization in situations where deportation would be arbitrary.[39] The 'integrity of the legal system' is a helpfully broad term, and captures the importance of creating opportunities to live within the law for those who are not amenable to removal. Bosniak identifies a somewhat similar approach in 'administrative reset' as a rationale for 'amnesty'.[40] Under this approach, when the legal system fails to reflect 'realities', a reset mechanism is required to ensure legal integrity.

## 3. Objections to the social membership thesis refuted

The social integration thesis posits that the ties that migrants develop to the host society over time warrant recognition irrespective of their migration status. In contrast, the arguments based on the integrity of the legal system do not purport to set out an individual right to stay per se, but rather provide reasons why creating a right to legal status is a legally appropriate response under many conditions. While the former claim holds irrespective of the nature of the 'illegality' committed by the migrant, the latter depends on an assessment of the States' actions also, and a more context-sensitive appraisal. Accordingly, the counterarguments also need consideration, in particular the countervailing concerns against regularization.

Against regularization, we may raise a specific concern about the dangers of undermining the integrity of immigration law by rewarding law-breaking, in particular egregious flouting of immigration laws. The social membership thesis posits that connections in effect 'trump' turpitude in this context. Alternatively, the integrity of the legal system arguments would take a broader view, and remind us that the presence of a population of irregular migrants also undermines the integrity of immigration law, and in creating a legally vulnerable population, facilitate further illegal acts by insiders. Rubio-Marín thus raises the 'parallel question': 'how much does this credibility suffer from the *de facto* consolidation of a second-class citizenship which is formed by an exploitable labour pool of thousands of people who live and work in the dark?'[41]

A further recurring theme in the debate seeks to downplay the turpitude of irregular migration. Carens, for instance, repeatedly asserts that illegal immigrants 'are not criminals like thieves and murderers'.[42] This appeal turns on the relative harmlessness of irregular migration: there are no victims as such and illegal immigrants do not steal from or injure others. However, some States do use the criminal law to intensify migration controls, and some criminalize

[39] See A Ellerman, 'The Rule of Law and the Right to Stay: The Moral Claims of Undocumented Migrants' (2014) 42 Politics & Society 293.

[40] LS Bosniak, 'Amnesty in Immigration: Forgetting, Forgiving, Freedom' (2013) 16 Critical Review of International Social and Political Philosophy 344.

[41] Rubio-Marín (n 26) 95. [42] Carens (n 27) 4.

certain forms of irregular or clandestine entry or even irregular stay itself.[43] So we must focus on the relative harmlessness of irregular migration. Evidently, there is no direct victim. Nonetheless, some point to the more remote harms of irregular migration, such as the 'harm to state's tax revenue and capacity to enforce decent minimum standards of employment, housing, or health'.[44] In response, advocates of regularization for irregular migrants point out that if irregular migrants commit wrongs such as non-payment of taxes, these are often attributable to their irregular status, and law-abiding behaviour would be encouraged by regularization.

Finally, the pull-factors argument rests on the empirical claim that regularization encourages further irregular migration. The claim is difficult to test empirically, as it would require a counterfactual assessment. Intuitively, it seems that where regularization is a remote or uncertain event, it is unlikely to trigger further irregular migration. Carens, in this vein, emphasizes that as a regularization entitlement takes several years to accrue, it would be unlikely to motivate migrants.[45] In contrast, as Bauböck suggests, where 'amnesties occur more or less predictably every four or five years—as they have in Italy since 1986—they clearly create an incentive for future irregular migration'.[46] Much depends on the mechanisms of regularization and the available modes of regular migration. Bauböck is surely correct that repeated mass regularizations are more likely to encourage further irregular migration. Accordingly, Carens and Rubio-Marín both advocate an individual regularization entitlement based on duration of residence alone. Politically though, some EU States seem to prefer mass regularizations, arguably as they come with the political promise of a subsequent 'crackdown'.[47]

To summarize, this section has not set out the social membership thesis at length, but rather simply endorsed it. This chapter accordingly works from the premise that there are very strong reasons for recognizing the connections forged through long residence with a right to stay. In addition, it has identified various legal reasons why this recognition is not only morally but also legally apt. The integrity of the legal system captures diverse reasons why those who reside in a host state should be permitted to do so if they are not to be removed. Often, on closer examination, States' treatment of migrants may reveal illegalities also, such as under-recognition of international protection needs. Regularization brings law and reality in line in a manner analogous to legal mechanisms in other fields, such as 'adverse possession' or legitimate expectations. Furthermore, irregular migrants are vulnerable to labour and other forms of exploitation, as they often fear recourse to the state will lead to their removal or

[43] For an overview, see E Guild, 'Criminalisation of Migration in Europe: Human Rights Implications' (2010) Council of Europe Issue Paper; FRA, *Criminalisation of Migrants in an Irregular Situation and of Persons Engaging with Them* (European Union Agency for Fundamental Rights Publication Office 2014); M Provera, 'The Criminalisation of Irregular Migration in the European Union' (2015) CEPS Paper in Liberty and Security in Europe No 80.

[44] R Bauböck, 'There is a mismatch between citizens' moral intuitions and their political views' (2009) *Boston Review*.

[45] Carens (n 27) 8, argues that 'it is plausible to suppose that such a long-term consideration as possible regularization years down the road would have little impact'.

[46] Bauböck (n 44). [47] ibid.

detention. Regularization offers a way to avoid or at least mitigate this vulnerability to exploitation.[48]

## IV. Regularization in Practice

The previous section sets out the normative argument in favour of a legal right to stay, that is a secure migration status, for all those who have established ties in a new state. Sometimes, those ties will be recognized as a matter of course under the immigration laws of the host state: Highly skilled migrants for example often have a secure migration status from the outset, and benefit from a clear legal route to permanent settlement. EU Citizens too have a route to secure status, with strong protections for their rights to work and reside. However, for many others, the immigration and asylum laws fail to recognize these connections. In this context, EU Member States frequently use less formal regularizations to effect a transformation of status. This section provides an overview of these practices, and notes their shortcomings.

### 1. Modes of regularization

While 'legal migration' suggests following explicit channels to secure lawful entry and residence, these channels are neither as navigable nor as predictable as the policy rhetoric on 'managed migration' suggests. Indeed, on the other side of 'illegality' is not only regular migration, but also legalization, or regularization. Again here there is a definitional struggle.[49] Regularization usually refers to a discretionary process whereby the presence of a migrant assumed or deemed to be in an irregular position is authorized. Kraler's typology, based on the REGINE study, takes a broader view. Regularization encompasses 'any state procedures by which non-nationals who are illegally residing, or who are otherwise in breach of national immigration rules in the current country of residence are granted a legal status.'[50] He contrasts regularization programmes, mechanisms, and entitlements.[51]

- Regularization programmes are typically large ad hoc 'amnesties' for migrant workers who lack either permission to stay or work in the Member States concerned.

[48] This is not to suggest that regularization is the only way to mitigate the exploitability of irregular migrants. Other mechanisms include establishing firewalls between immigration enforcement and, in particular, labour rights. Moreover, in practice, some regularization mechanisms afford *employers* the right to regularize, increasing the dependency of the migrant on the employer, exacerbating vulnerability in the process.

[49] See A Kraler, 'Fixing, Adjusting, Regulating, Protecting Human Rights—The Shifting Uses of Regularisations in the European Union' (2011) 13 EJML 297.

[50] ibid.

[51] See also the distinction drawn by K Brick, 'Regularizations in the European Union: The Contentious Policy Tool' (2011) Insight 1, 3.

- Regularization mechanisms include various humanitarian statuses, often mere protection against removal in the form of 'toleration' of presence.
- Regularization entitlements connote migrants' securing a new legal status which entails a right to stay, such as via marriage or EU Citizenship.

Before examining each in turn, it is important to note that the line between these different practices is often blurred. In particular, as explored in Chapter 6, asylum systems often are loaded against applicants, producing populations of non-removable rejected asylum seekers. Indeed, there is evidence that many refugees choose to remain in an irregular status rather than risk applying for asylum in those countries where recognition rates are particularly low.[52] Even when protection needs are recognized, States frequently grant ad hoc statuses (a regularization mechanism in Kraler's typology), rather than recognition as a refugee under the 1951 Convention on the Status of Refugees and its 1967 Protocol (Refugee Convention or CRS). The entry into force of the EU Qualification Directive (QD),[53] with its two formal statuses of refugee status and subsidiary protection, does not seem to have reduced States' propensity to grant ad hoc statuses.[54] Rejected asylum seekers may then become irregular workers who in time may benefit from regularization programmes of the first sort.

In addition, normal immigration admissions and regularization practices overlap. Given the ad hoc nature of immigration procedures in some EU Member States, application for a residence permit in the normal way resembles the discretionary assessment one tends to associate with 'regularization'. Studies acknowledge the difficulty. For example, the 2000 Odysseus Study accepted that the discretionary renewal of a residence permit was legally indistinguishable from regularization, the only factual difference being the migrant's presence on the territory in the latter case.[55] The rudimentary immigration law in some EU countries has simply emerged out of ad hoc regularization practice.[56] For instance, Belgium's rules emerged out of the possibility for migrants on the territory to request a right of residence. Gradually executive discretion was circumscribed by ministerial circulars and later enacted rules.[57] In the Netherlands, strategic litigation prompted courts to require the reluctant executive to reveal the written guidance governing the exercise of discretion.[58] This trajectory is also evident in UK law, with some informal concessions later being codified in the binding immigration rules.[59]

[52] Düvell (n 7) 283.

[53] Directive 2011/95/EU of the European Parliament and of the Council of 13 December 2011 on standards for the qualification of third-country nationals or stateless persons as beneficiaries of international protection, for a uniform status for refugees or for persons eligible for subsidiary protection, and for the content of the protection granted (recast) (Qualification Directive) [2011] OJ L337/9.

[54] See European Migration Network (EMN), *The Different National Practices Concerning Granting of Non-EU Harmonised Protection Statuses* (EMN 2010).

[55] J Apap, P de Bruycke, and C Schmitter, 'Regularisation of Illegal Aliens in the European Union. Summary Reports of a Comparative Study' (2000) 2 EJML 263, 264–65. The full study in contained in P De Bruycker (ed), *Regularisations of Illegal Immigrants in the European Union* (Odysseus/Bruylant 2000).

[56] ibid, 271. [57] ibid. [58] ibid.

[59] See Part II.2.iii on the discussion of the UK long-term residence concession.

The broad view of regularization is important for a second reason. It avoids the erroneous assumption that regularization is inevitably an act of executive beneficence. Rather, regularization may occur via legislative or judicial acts, rooted in domestic or supranational authority. It may also emerge out of domestic official recognition of shortcomings in legal processes that warrant a legal response.[60] In this respect, I offer a corrective to Dauvergne, who treats regularization as 'always framed outside the law as an exception rather than a challenge',[61] a 'purification ritual'.[62] Accordingly, I reject her contention that '[t]he law is a necessary site for constructing illegality, but is much less apt for remedying it'.[63] In the legal system of the EU in particular, 'law' is multilevel, and so one level may cure an apparent 'illegality' at the domestic level by having recourse to another level. Indeed, 'regularization' is often legally required, to maintain the integrity of the legal system. It maintains legality in some scenarios, rather than undermining it.

The next section sets out some salient features of each of the three modes of regularization as practised in the Member States of late, drawing on some empirical studies.[64] This sketch is necessary to set the scene for the examination in Part IV of how EU law, institutions, and practices variously support, undermine, and thwart that process of regularization.

### *i. Regularization programmes*

Large-scale regularizations are often associated with Southern European countries, but have been undertaken across Europe in different forms. Several million migrants have been regularized under various programmes over the past decades in the EU. For instance, one estimate is that from 1973 to 2008, EU Member States ran 68 discrete regularization programmes, with a total of about six million migrants regularized.[65] A more recent estimate was that in the EU as whole, at least 3.5 million persons were regularized through regularization programmes in the past two decades.[66] One challenge in measuring regularization is that its sustainability is unclear: some regularization programmes accord a temporary migration status, so regularization leads once again to irregularity. Some programmes

[60] As discussed above, Bosniak uses the term 'administrative reset' to capture this facet of regularization. Bosniak (n 40) 348. 'On this approach, amnesty functions as a response to administrative failure; there is a pragmatic need to bring the law and actual behavior into closer alignment for purposes of effective governance and systemic legitimacy.'

[61] C Dauvergne, *Making People Illegal: What Globalization Means for Migration and Law* (Cambridge University Press 2008) 28.

[62] ibid, 139. [63] ibid, 27.

[64] In particular Baldwin-Edwards and Kraler (n 12); A Levinson, *The Regularisation of Unauthorized Migrants: Literature Survey and Country Case Studies* (COMPAS 2005). See further the work of the Clandestino Network, available at: <http://clandestino.eliamep.gr/>, and Triandafyllidou, 'EU Irregular Migration Policies' in A Triandafyllidou (ed), *Irregular Migration in Europe: Myths and Realities* (Ashgate 2010); A Kraler, D Reichel, A König, M Baldwin-Edwards, and M Şimşek, *Final Report—Feasibility Study on the Labour Market Trajectories of Regularised Immigrants within the European Union* (REGANE I) (ICMPD 2014).

[65] Kraler (n 11) 17. For a more recent study, see Brick (n 51). [66] REGANE I (n 64).

'perpetuate an endogenous cycle of undocumented migration', particularly in Italy and Spain.[67] However, other programmes have sought to address this, by granting a permanent right of residence to those who had repeatedly renewed temporary permits in the past.

The largest programmes are associated with Italy and Spain. Regularization has been dubbed Italy's 'primary strategy to manage irregular migration'.[68] Spain's regularization of 2005 granted legal residence to 578,000 migrants and prompted concern at European level.[69] Greece[70] and Portugal[71] too have implemented repeat programmes. Although large-scale regularization programmes are associated with Southern Europe, they also feature in France,[72] Belgium,[73] and Luxembourg.[74] The Netherlands has undertaken a number of small programmes.[75] Germany has resisted large scale ad hoc regularizations. Instead, it affords individual temporary injunctions against deportation, known as tolerations (*Duldung*), to migrants in an irregular position who are non-deportable for 'humanitarian' reasons. In 2006, the German *Länder* set up a regularization programme aiming to end the practice of *Kettenduldung* whereby toleration orders of short duration are repeatedly renewed over the course of many years.[76] These examples serve to illustrate the prevalence and persistence of regularizations programmes in Europe. What they have in common is that they attempt to mitigate the vagaries of formal migration status.

### *ii. Regularization mechanisms*

Regularization mechanisms include various forms of status granted to those recognized as being non-removable due to the situation in their countries of origin, where States were reluctant or unwilling to recognize the migrants as Convention refugees. There are many alternative statuses of varying degrees of formality and security, including forms of temporary and complementary protection, humanitarian status, formal and informal toleration.[77] While Kraler includes all of these within his taxonomy,[78] the Odysseus Study in contrast only included regularization of rejected asylum seekers in recognition of flaws in the asylum system, rather

[67] Council of Europe Parliamentary Assembly (PACE), *Regularisation Programmes for Irregular Migrants* Report of the Committee on Migration, Refugees and Population, Doc 11350, 6 July 2007, para 94.

[68] ibid, para 34. See also EMN Italy, *Practical Responses to Irregular Migration: The Italian Case* (2012): <http://www.emnitaly.cnr.it/eng/wp-content/uploads/2015/02/Practical-responses-to-irregular-migration.-the-Italian-case-2012-.pdf> accessed 10 April 2015.

[69] ibid, paras 23–32. [70] ibid, paras 36–42. [71] ibid, paras 43–44.

[72] ibid, paras 45–51. [73] ibid, paras 52–53.

[74] ibid, paras 54–55; EMN Luxembourg, *2012 Policy Report on Migration and Asylum* (2013) <https://www.emnluxembourg.lu/sites/default/files/Policy%20report%20on%20migration%20and%20asylum%20WEB.pdf> accessed 10 April 2015.

[75] ibid, paras 60–65; European Policy Centre (EPC), *Event Report: What Future for Amnesties in Europe?* (EPC, 7 October 2008) 2.

[76] F Geyer, 'Germany's Regularisation of November 2006: Committed to an EU Immigration Policy? (CEPS, 9 February 2007).

[77] EMN (n 54). [78] Kraler (n 11).

than the grant of subsidiary protection.[79] These mechanisms are often a response to legal obligations, particularly where people are not deportable under IHRL, but their official framing as regularization tends to downplay legal obligation.

As explored in Chapter 5, the QD has created an EU status of subsidiary protection across the EU, so brings EU legal obligation to this arena. As the Court of Justice of the European Union (CJEU) ruled in *Elgafaji*,[80] this status in some respects goes beyond ECHR obligations. Nonetheless, the QD comes nowhere close to providing a status for all those protection-seekers who are non-removable, so inevitably ad hoc non-removal practices are still prevalent.[81] Studies on the QD implementation demonstrate that States continue to confer ad hoc statuses, rather than those under the QD.[82] Member States' responses to the Syrian refugee crisis also reflect recourse to ad hoc national statuses for some of those fleeing this conflict,[83] notwithstanding UNHCR's well-argued contention that most of those fleeing are Convention refugees with a well-founded fear of persecution by reason of their political opinion or imputed political opinion.[84] Moreover, the inter-linkages between asylum and apparently irregular migration are revealed in the fact that some of the regularization programmes outlined above apply to rejected asylum seekers who frequently slip into irregular working.

### *iii. Regularization by entitlement*

Some Member States have statutory mechanisms that recognize long residence, even if irregular, as creating a right to reside. The examples below illustrate their range: from reactive to stable.

A reactive example was found in France. Following the restrictive Pasqua Laws of 1993, France found that it had created a group of 'legal illegals'.[85] As a corrective, it introduced the Loi Debré of 1997, which granted legal residence to parents of French children, spouses of French nationals, youths aged over eighteen who entered France before the age of ten, and aliens present for more than fifteen years. In a similar vein, the Loi Chevènement of 11 May 1998 regularized those who had resided for over ten years (or three years for families with children and fifteen years for students). Both were of limited duration and the statutory scheme has now changed.[86]

[79] Apap et al. (n 55) 275.

[80] Case C-465/07 *Elgafaji v Staatssecretaris van Justitie* [2009] ECR I-921.

[81] As will be exacerbated by Case C-542/13 *M'Bodj* [2015] OJ C 65/12.

[82] UNHCR, *Safe at Last? Law and Practice in Selected EU Member States with Respect to Asylum Seekers Fleeing Indiscriminate Violence* (UNHCR 2011); EMN (n 54).

[83] P Fargues and C Fandrich, 'The European Response to the Syrian Refugee Crisis What Next? (2012) *MPC Research Report 2012/14*.

[84] UNHCR, *International Protection Considerations with regard to people fleeing the Syrian Arab Republic, Update II* (UNHCR 2013).

[85] Apap et al. (n 55) 275. The term reflects the fact that the law had created a new category of illegally present person, who was on other bases entitled to remain.

[86] ibid.

In Ireland until 2005, the operation of *jus soli* nationality law meant that children born in the territory gained Irish citizenship, irrespective of the migration status of their parents. Their constitutional right to family life in turn provided a mode to regularize residence rights of the parents, which was reflected in a non-statutory scheme.[87] However, this approach proved short-lived. The constitutional jurisprudence shifted away from providing the family with residence as of right: in 2003, in *Lobe and Osayande*,[88] the Supreme Court confirmed that family members of Irish children were deportable, even if this meant that the right of the Irish-born child to reside in Ireland was ineffective (a stance now at odds with the approach of the CJEU as enunciated in *Zambrano*).[89] The domestic citizenship provisions themselves were dramatically altered in 2005, moving decisively away from automatic *jus soli*.[90] This example illustrates the imbrication of nationality, immigration, and EU law.[91]

A relatively stable example of regularization by entitlement was formerly that in the UK, where there was for many years a statutory 'long residency concession'.[92] The terms of the original concession were as follows:

> Where a person has 10 years or more continuous lawful residence or 14 years or more continuous residence (of any legality), indefinite leave to remain should normally be granted in the absence of any strong countervailing factors.

The subsequent codification in the Immigration Rules restricted the rule somewhat, stating that 'indefinite leave to remain' should be granted, if 'having regard to the public interest there are no reasons why it would be undesirable', taking into account factors such as age, connections to the UK, personal history and character, criminal record, or compassionate circumstances.[93] A similar rule permitted children born in the UK (regardless of the legal status of their parents) to apply for citizenship if they lived there for ten years after their birth. As of July 2012, however, the rule of fourteen years of continuous residence under para 276B of the Immigration Rules has been abolished.

87 Known as the 'Irish Born Child Scheme'. See further: <http://www.inis.gov.ie/en/INIS/IBC05Renewal.pdf/Files/IBC05Renewal.pdf> accessed 10 April 2015.

88 *Lobe and Osayande v Minister for Justice, Equality and Law Reform* [2003] IESC 1. See further, B Ryan, 'The Celtic Cubs: The Controversy over Birthright Citizenship in Ireland' (2004) 6 EJML 173; C Costello, 'Child Citizens and *De Facto* Deportation: Tender Years, Fragile Ties and Security of Residence' in K Bradley, A Whelan, and N Travers (eds), *Of Courts and Constitutions: Liber Amicorum in Honour of Nial Fennelly* (Hart Publishing 2014).

89 Case C-34/09 *Ruiz Zambrano v Office national de l'emploi (ONEm)* [2011] ECR I-1117. See discussion in Chapter 4.

90 The Constitution of Ireland was amended so that citizenship is granted to children born on the island of Ireland if they have 'at least one parent who is an Irish citizen or entitled to be an Irish citizen.' For a critique, see C Costello, 'Accidents of Place and Parentage: Birthright Citizenship and Border Crossings' in *The Citizenship Referendum: Implications for the Constitution and Human Rights* (Law School Trinity College Dublin 2004) 5.

91 See further ibid.

92 See G Clayton et al, *Textbook on Immigration and Asylum Law* (6th edn, OUP 2014) 205–06.

93 Immigration Rules 2003, para 276B.

## 2. Rationales for regularization

Whilst there is continuity in the practice of regularization, its rationalization has shifted over time. Regularization was previously often characterized as linked to labour market concerns and the aim of protecting workers (both local and migrant). Indeed, that rationale still figures in European trade union critiques of EU migration policy.[94] However, there has been a shift since the 1990s to frame regularization as a 'human rights' or 'humanitarian' matter.[95]

Unfortunately, official and scholarly discourse has tended to conflate these two labels. A 'human rights' claim should be viewed as creating a duty for the State, whereas a humanitarian one may be more akin to a plea for beneficence or generosity. If an individual can claim a human right to stay, then regularization is as of right, and the State has an obligation to accord a right of residence, or at least protect him or her against removal. By using 'humanitarian' carelessly where there is a *legal* right to stay, governments (and inadvertently some scholars doing policy-motivated research) obscure the existence of a *duty* on the State. This move treats as a matter of generosity that which is a matter of obligation, as least for some migrants.

The Council of Europe Parliamentary Assembly has long endorsed further consideration and use of regularizations, in order to avoid having large numbers of persons living in an irregular situation. It notes the sharply contrasting views for and against regularization, with those against construing it as a reward for lawbreakers, creating a pull effect for further irregular migration,[96] whilst the arguments in favour range from intrinsic values such as those encapsulated by human rights and human dignity, and instrumental ones like encouraging circular migration, decreasing the likelihood of exploitation, reducing the underground economy, and increasing tax revenues and social security contributions.[97] The report singles out the Spanish regularization of 2005 as having been 'welcomed by irregular migrants, civil society, employers and trade unions, as well as by the majority of politicians in Spain'[98] whilst acknowledging that one of its failings was the failure of the Spanish authorities to inform European partners, which '[led] to misunderstandings as to the nature of the programmes and also created a backlash against such programmes in a number of countries across Europe'.[99] As will be explored further below, this Spanish regularization was a catalyst for a restrictive turn at the EU level. The EU Fundamental Rights Agency too has examined the human rights of migrants in an irregular situation and recommends mechanisms (at national or EU level) to avoid situations where migrants live in legal limbo for years.[100]

[94] 'The EU needs a clear strategy for regularisation of migrants and to fight their exploitation within the informal economy.' ETUC position on the new European Commission's five-year programme on migration (EC Communication 'An Open and Secure Europe: Making It Happen'). ETUC Executive Committee on 11–12 June 2014

[95] Kraler (n 49). [96] PACE (n 67), para 7. [97] ibid, para 8.

[98] ibid, para 10. [99] ibid, para 12.

[100] FRA, *The Fundamental Rights of Migrants in an Irregular Situation* (FRA 2011) 11.

At present, human rights law precludes removal of migrants in two main scenarios. Migrants may claim protection from removal in light of their integration into the host State, which may be invoked as an aspect of their family or private life under Article 8 ECHR.[101] In the second, the ECHR protects against removal if there is a real risk of serious human rights violation in another country (explored at length in Chapter 5). The shortcoming of this case law is that it fails to require the State to create a secure status for the non-removable migrant. Nonetheless, the obligation not to return a migrant is tantamount to a duty to let her stay. Both these human rights protections have at least in part been codified and transformed in EU legislation, with protection for long-term migrants in the Long-Term Residents Directive (LTRD)[102] and for those protected against against removal to face serious human rights abuses in the Qualification Directive. Latterly, the protections of the Returns Directive have also become pertinent.[103] The next sections examine those legal protections in detail, and the extent to which these two systems, ECHR and EU, recognize the right to stay of settled migrants.

## V. The ECHR on Irregular Migrants

Thus far, I have endorsed the social membership thesis, and a right to secure migration status for those who are long-term residents. This section examines the extent to which human rights law, in particular the ECHR, creates such a right to stay. Much of the literature on regularization assumes that it is an act of executive discretion, or urges that a right to regularization should be enshrined in legislation. This section turns to human rights law, and with that turns towards the judicial arena. Under the jurisprudence of the ECtHR, we find a strong recognition of the social membership thesis. However, that Court also seeks, somewhat awkwardly, to give leeway to the States' migration control prerogatives.

Article 8 ECHR provides some security of residence for settled migrants.[104] However, that case law reflects the statist assumption. The ECtHR repeatedly asserts that:

> a State is entitled, as a matter of well-established international law and subject to its treaty obligations, to control the entry of aliens into its territory and their residence there. The Convention does not guarantee the right of an alien to enter or to reside in a particular country.[105]

[101] See Chapter 4.

[102] Council Directive 2003/109/EC of 25 November 2003 concerning the status of third-country nationals who are long-term residents (Long-Term Residents Directive) [2004] OJ L16/44.

[103] Case C-562/13 *Abdida*. [2015] OJ C 65/13 discussed in Part V.2.vii.

[104] See Chapter 4. For an overview, see M Bruins and P Boeles, *Case Law on Article 8 of the European Convention on Human Rights: A Survey* (Institute of Immigration Law 2006); MB Dembour, 'Human Rights Law and National Sovereignty in Collusion: The Plight of Quasi-Nationals at Strasbourg' (2003) 21 Netherlands Quarterly of Human Rights 63.

[105] *Omoregie v Norway* [2008] ECHR 761, para 54.

As will be explored further in Chapter 4, that assumption permeates the case law and in general means that irregular migrants face additional hurdles when seeking to vindicate their right to family life under Article 8 ECHR. In particular, where connections emerge while migration status is unsettled, the ECHR protections are often unavailable. For example, in *Omoregie* the ECtHR has stated that Article 8 ECHR protection was not available

> where family life was created at a time when the persons involved were aware that the immigration status of one of them was such that the persistence of that family life within the host State would from the outset be precarious.[106]

In addition, as mentioned in Chapter 1, the ECtHR stance of treating States as the principal guarantors of ECHR rights means that it does not require that even those who are legally protected against removal on human rights grounds are afforded a stable domestic migration status. Instead, it leaves the mode of compliance for the State to determine. In so doing, however, it may feed into the very precariousness the right to stay ought to protect against.

Nonetheless, in a line of cases, the ECtHR has acknowledged that Article 8 ECHR may require the regularization of irregular stay in exceptional cases.[107] In two cases concerning the Russophone minority in the Baltics, which makes up a significant proportion of the populations of Latvia and Estonia, the ECtHR found that irregular status may in and of itself violate the right to privacy under Article 8 ECHR, conceived of as the network of social relations built up over long residence.[108] In *Sisojeva*, the Chamber was bold in asserting that:

> [I]t is not enough for the host State to refrain from deporting the person concerned; it must also, by means of positive measures if necessary, afford him or her the opportunity to exercise the rights in question without interference.[109]

Consequently, the ECtHR considered that the prolonged refusal of the Latvian authorities to grant the applicants the right to reside in Latvia on a permanent basis constituted an interference with their right to respect for their private life.[110] The *Sisojeva* Grand Chamber ruling seems to resile somewhat from the Chamber's assertion of a right to a particular status. While it confirmed that Article 8 ECHR protects those in an irregular situation, it also held the precarious mode of regularization was sufficient to vindicate the right to private and family life, as the applicants did not face a 'real and imminent risk of deportation'.[111] Its reasoning reasserted the orthodox ECHR position that the Convention does not require the grant of a secure migration status.[112]

[106] ibid, para 57. cf *Nunez v Norway* App No 55597/09 (ECHR, 28 June 2011) discussed below.

[107] See further, D Thym, 'Respect for Private and Family Life under Article 8 ECHR in Immigration Cases: A Human Right to Regularize Illegal Stay?' (2008) ICLQ 87.

[108] *Slivenko v Latvia* App No 48321/99 (ECHR, 9 October 2003); *Sisojeva* et al. *v Latvia* App No 60654/00 (ECHR, 16 June 2005) (Grand Chamber ECHR, 15 January 2007).

[109] *Sisojeva* [GC] (n108) para 104.

[110] ibid, para 105.

[111] ibid, para 100.

[112] ibid, para 91.

*Mendizabal*[113] concerned a Spanish national Maria Isabel Aristimuño Mendizabal, resident in France. The government's failure to issue a residence permit was deemed to be not 'in accordance with law' given that it was in breach of EU law. The ECtHR reiterated the orthodox position that Article 8 'does not guarantee the persons concerned the right to a particular type of residence permit (indefinite, temporary or other)', and emphasized that 'as long as the solution proposed by the authorities allows for the effective exercise of their right to respect for private and family life'.[114] However, the Court's consideration went much further, in noting that having a precarious migration status for a long period is a source of hardship, with serious negative 'consequences... in material and psychological terms' namely in that particular case 'precarious and uncertain employment, social and financial difficulties, impossibility to... exercise... the profession she was trained for'.[115]

In *Rodrigues da Silva & Hoogkamer v the Netherlands*,[116] the applicant Ms Solange Da Silva entered the Netherlands from her country of origin, Brazil, in 1994 and overstayed her tourist visa. She subsequently had a daughter, Rachel, with a Dutch man, Mr. Daniël Hoogkamer, the daughter automatically acquiring her father's Dutch nationality. Ms da Silva's two Brazilian children then joined her in the Netherlands, although none of the three ever regularized their residence there. The ECtHR, following its established line, accepted that an 'important consideration' was whether family life was created when migration status was irregular. If so, 'only... in the most exceptional circumstances [would] the removal of the non-national family member... violate Article 8'.[117] The novelty of the judgment was the ECtHR's acknowledgement that illegal residence is just one factor to be taken into account. In particular, the ECtHR laid emphasis on the fact that Ms da Silva had an excuse for not having exercised her entitlement to apply to regularize her stay, being the unavailability of documents concerning Mr Hoogkamer's income. (Of course, EU lawyers would nowadays focus on the daughter with Dutch nationality, and whether *Zambrano*[118] would assist the family.)

In *Nunez v Norway*,[119] the ECtHR held that Article 8 ECHR precluded the deportation of the mother of young children Mirtha Nunez, notwithstanding the fact that Ms Nunez's residence had been irregular throughout her stay. The 'best interests' of the children tilted the balance in favour of the mother's continued residence, in spite of her immigration law infractions. In *Antwi and Others v Norway*,[120] the Court explained *Nunez* as turning on 'the exceptional circumstances pertaining to the applicant's children in that case' which included 'the children's long lasting and close bonds to their mother, the decision in the custody proceedings [to move the children to the father], the disruption and stress that the children had already experienced and the long period that elapsed before the immigration authorities took their decision to order the applicant's

[113] *Mendizabal v France* App No 51431/99 (ECHR, 17 January 2006).
[114] ibid, para 66. [115] ibid, paras 70–71.
[116] *Rodrigues da Silva/Hoogkamer v the Netherlands* App No 50435/99 (ECHR, 31 January 2006).
[117] ibid, para 39. [118] *Zambrano* (n 89). [119] *Nunez* (n 106).
[120] *Antwi and Others v Norway* App No 26940/10 (ECHR, 14 February 2012).

expulsion with a re-entry'.[121] These 'exceptional' facts were not present in *Antwi*, so the Court effectively treated *Omoregie* as the relevant precedent. Most recently in *Jeunesse*,[122] the Court found a violation of Article 8 ECHR in the failure to regularize the presence of a long-term migrant. The case concerned Meriam Jeunesse, a Surinamese national, whose migration status was irregular for most of her long residence in the Netherlands. She had made numerous attempts to regularize her migration status, so she was aware of its 'precariousness'.[123] She had three children, all of whom were Dutch. The Grand Chamber held that the Netherlands was in breach of Article 8 ECHR in failing to regularize her presence.[124]

Some of these rulings have been criticized for 'attribut[ing] too little weight to the necessary effectiveness of immigration law, for which the sanctioning of illegal entry and stay are important foundations to maintain the credibility of the overall system'.[125] However, this chapter has argued in contrast that the social membership thesis ought to prompt recognition of a legal right to stay. Moreover, that claim is *also* supported by an argument concerning legal integrity, as discussed in Part II of this chapter. These cases may also be read as tacit condemnation of the bureaucratic conditions imposed on the family seeking to regularize their status. While these cases share some exceptional features,[126] courts often break new ground in cases where the facts are compelling, or when full ramifications of the cases' novelty may be obscured by another less contentious ground, such as the EU right of residence of Ms Aristimuño Mendizabal, or the former Dutch nationality of Ms Jeunesse.

This phenomenon suggests that we should not underplay the significance of the ECtHR's acknowledgment that precariousness in and of itself undermines Article 8 ECHR. In this recognition, the ECtHR opens the way for other *courts*, in particular national ones, to assert a regularization role. After the Chamber judgment in *Sisojevo*, German courts applied Strasbourg principles to regularize.[127] Perhaps the most significant ramification is that regularization becomes the domain of rights claims and courts' jurisdictions, based on an individual assessment.[128] The position of irregular migrants thereby is no longer the preserve of executive discretion.

[121] ibid, para 100.
[122] *Jeunesse v Netherlands* App No 12738/10 (Grand Chamber, ECHR, 3 October 2014).
[123] ibid, para 113.
[124] Three judges dissented: Judges Villiger, Mahoney, and Silvis expressed a joint dissenting opinion.
[125] Thym (n 107) 102.
[126] ibid, 107. For instance, he suggests exceptionality lay in the fact that *Rodrigues da Silva* was a 'caring mother who may negligently not have regularized her illegal stay during the relationship with the Dutch citizen.'
[127] D Thym, 'Menchenrecht auf Legalisierung des Aufenthalts?' (2006) Europäische Grundrechte-Zeitschrift 541.
[128] Kraler also identifies this phenomenon as the 'judicialisation of regularisation': Kraler (n 49) 316.

These cases reflect a recognition that time and ties matter, and that over time, attachment to the host community continues. Stronger grounds are required for removal as time passes. Moreover, there is also a tentative tendency to look into the workings of the immigration system, and take into account that it may be difficult for migrants to regularize their status as a mitigating factor.[129] These aspects of the case law reflect the integrity of the legal system concerns identified previously. While the Strasbourg case law is far from recognizing fully the duty in justice to recognize the right to stay outlined in the previous section, these two features are significant moves in that direction.

## VI. The EU and 'Illegal Immigration'

This part explores the role of the EU. Section 1 outlines the EU's support for legal migration, by creating legal statuses which diminish the significance of national authorization. The CJEU in this context is much bolder than the ECtHR. Section 2 provides an account of the EU entry control system,[130] and the two key measures attempting to define illegality, the RD and ESD. Taking a systematic view, I identify the restrictive tendencies built into the system, which are likely to increase the phenomenon of 'illegal immigration.' Section 3 then identifies the EU's anti-regularization ethos.

### 1. Rights of entry and residence

#### *i. EU Citizens and their family members*

EU law creates rights of entry and residence which take precedence over national law. Crucially, the legal construction of EU Citizenship is such that migration within the EU is as of right and although EU Citizens may have to comply with certain conditions of residence, and may be amenable to deportation *in extremis*, the right to entry and residence has a particular weightiness which constrains domestic discretion. The rights to entry and residence subsist irrespective of domestic authorization.[131]

The treatment of TCN family members of EU Citizens is highly instructive. In *Commission v Spain*,[132] *MRAX*,[133] and *Metock*,[134] the CJEU insisted that their

[129] On this point, see also *Alim v Russia* App No 39417/07 (ECHR, 27 September 2011), in particular paras 87–89. However, the Court's assessment in this context becomes highly context-sensitive, and if migrants are deemed not to have used due diligence to regularize their status, their Art 8 ECHR claim is weakened.

[130] The phrase is Pastore's. See F Pastore 'Visas, Borders, Immigration: Formation, Structure, and Current Evolution of the EU Entry Control System' in N Walker (ed), *Europe's Area of Freedom, Security and Justice* (OUP 2004) 89.

[131] *Royer*; Case C-413/99 *Baumbast* [2002] ECR I-7091.

[132] Case C-503/03 *Commission v Spain* [2005] ECR I-1097.

[133] Case C-459/99 *MRAX* [2002] ECR I-6591.

[134] *Metock* (n 5).

EU residence rights entailed a right of first entry to join their family member. In *Carpenter* and *Metock*, the effect of the EU right of residence was such that the residence of a TCN spouse was regularized.[135] Similarly, in *Zambrano*, Mr Ruiz Zambrano acquired a right to reside and work in Belgium in order to vindicate the EU Citizenship of two of his children. *Zambrano* illustrates how EU law in effect cures the liminality of the family's migration status under Belgian law. Mr Zambrano and Mrs Moreno López and their first child entered Belgium on short-stay visas from Columbia, and applied for asylum. Although their asylum application was refused, a *non-refoulement* decision was made, meaning that the State accepted it was unsafe to remove them to Columbia. However, this decision did not amount to a stable right of residence. They made repeated attempts to regularize their status in Belgium, but were refused. Nonetheless, Mr Zambrano worked and paid social security contributions, and the family's residence was registered with the municipality. To some commentators, they are clearly 'illegals', who should have been removed pursuant to the RD.[136] However, that perspective is misleading, and obscures the refugee-like features of their predicament, and their bona fide efforts to regularize their status.[137] The impact of the Court's decision to treat the children's claim as falling with the scope of EU law is that Mr Zambrano acquired a stable EU right to reside *and* work in Belgium, in order to vindicate the children's EU Citizenship right to reside in the 'territory of the Union.'

In these EU Citizenship cases concerning TCN family members, the significance of domestic authorization is diminished, although national immigration law is not set at nought. It remains permissible to impose administrative penalties for breaches of immigration law. However, although it is legally conceivable, it is less likely that infractions of immigration law alone would reach the level of turpitude required to restrict residence rights.[138]

### *ii. Association Agreements*

Some migrants also derive residence rights from other EU rules. In this context, a contrast may be drawn between measures that create EU right of entry and residence and, say, the Association Agreement with Turkey where national competence over the authorization of first entry remains. [139]

[135] See (n 5).

[136] K Hailbronner and D Thym 'Annotation of Case C-34/09 *Ruiz Zambrano*' (2010) 48 CMLRev 1253.

[137] M Olivas and D Kochenov, 'Case C- 34/09 Ruiz Zambrano: A Respectful Rejoinder' (2012) University of Houston Public Law and Legal Theory Series 2012-W-1.

[138] As codified in Directive 2004/38/EC of the European Parliament and of the Council of 29 April 2004 on the right of citizens of the Union and their family members to move and reside freely within the territory of the Member States [...] (Citizenship Directive) [2004] OJ L158/77, Art 27.

[139] The Turkish Agreement does not confer a right to first entry, but rather in Art 41(1) of the Additional Protocol of 1970 contains a standstill clause, precluding any additional restrictions on freedom of establishment, which does apply to conditions of entry and residence.

*Panayotova*,[140] *Cetinkaya*,[141] and *Dörr*[142] concern entry rights under Europe Agreements. In *Panayotova*, the general principles necessitated a procedural system which was 'easily accessible and capable of ensuring that the persons concerned will have their applications dealt with objectively and within a reasonable time'.[143] The right to effective judicial protection was also applicable, requiring that refusals 'be capable of being challenged in judicial or quasi-judicial proceedings'.[144] These key cases indicate that once there is an EU right of residence, due process in border crossings is a corollary, reflecting that immanent feature of EU law identified in Chapter 1, its wholehearted embrace of the individual.

Under the Association Agreement with Turkey, Turkish workers do not enjoy a right of first entry to the EU, but have some security of residence. Even in this context, the CJEU's case law curtails migration control. For example, the CJEU has rejected governmental arguments that Turkish workers could not rely on the Agreement if they had committed previous immigration law infractions. (The governments had attempted unsuccessfully to argue that the workers had thereby 'abused their rights'.[145]) The case law suggests that there can be no blanket rules deeming prior immigration law infractions to preclude recourse to rights under the Association Agreements.[146]

*Soysal*[147] makes clear the standstill clause in the Agreement also precludes the imposition of the Schengen Visa requirement, as the EU visa requirement had to be interpreted 'as far as possible' subject to the Agreement.[148] In this respect, it is analogous to Case C-503/03 *Commission v Spain*,[149] where the priority of the admission rights of TCN family members over the Schengen system was established.

140 Case C-327/02 *Panayotova v Minister voor Vreemdelingenzaken en Integratie* [2004] ECR I-11055, para 27.

141 Case 467/02 *Cetinkaya v Land Baden-Wurttemberg* [2004] ECR I-10895.

142 Case C-136/03 *Dörr v Sicherheitsdirektion fur das Bundesland Karnten* [2005] ECR I-4759.

143 *Panayotova* (n 140) para 26.

144 ibid, para 27, citing by analogy, Case C-157/99 *Smits and Peerbooms* [2001] ECR I-5473, para 90.

145 Case C-285/95 *Suat Kol v Land Berlin* [1997] ECR I-3079; Case C-36/96 *Faik Günaydin v Freistaat Bayern* [1997] ECR I-5143. See further Case C-294/06 *The Queen on the application of Payir, Akyuz, Ozturk v Secretary of State for the Home Department* [2008] ECR I; Case C-16/05 *R (on the application of Veli Tum and Mehmet Dari) v Secretary of State for the Home Department* [2007] ECR I-7415.

146 See further C Costello, 'Citizenship of the Union: Above Abuse?' in R de la Feria and S Vogenauer (eds), *Prohibition of Abuse of Law: A New General Principle of EU Law* (Hart Publishing 2011) 321.

147 Case C-288/06 *Soysal* [2009] ECR I-1031. See further S Peers, 'EC Immigration Law and EC Association Agreements: Fragmentation or Integration?' (2009) 34 ELRev 628.

148 ibid, para 59. 149 Case C-503/03 *Commission v Spain* [2005] ECR I-1097.

### iii. Other TCNs with EU residence rights

The EU has also set minimum standards for some TCNs' entry into and residence in the EU, in particular that of Students,[150] Researchers,[151] Seasonal Workers,[152] and Intra-Corporate Transferees.[153] At first glance, it would appear that what these sectoral Directives have in common is that they do not create a right to first entry to the EU for TCNs, but rather set out conditions under which Member States ought to afford this particular migration status. However, the CJEU has asserted that, where EU law sets out exhaustive clear admissions criteria, national authorities must accord a right to enter, not merely unsettling, but effectively inverting the statist assumption.[154] As well as these sectoral measures, there is also the wider Blue Card Directive[155] on highly skilled immigration. The Blue Card Directive lays down the conditions of entry and residence for third-country nationals (and their family members) who will be present in the territory of a Member State for more than three months for the purpose of engaging in highly qualified employment.[156] The Directive creates a fast-track procedure for issuing the special residence and work permit to such 'highly qualified' third-country workers who have been offered a job in the EU. Again, while Member States retain control over the issuing of Blue Cards, they can also introduce their own schemes offering better conditions than the Blue Card.[157]

[150] Council Directive 2004/114/EC of 13 December 2004 on the conditions of admission of third-country nationals for the purposes of studies, pupil exchange, unremunerated training or voluntary service (Students Directive) [2004] OJ L375/12. Note that a recast version of this Directive is currently under negotiations between Council and Parliament. European Commission, *Proposal for a Directive of the European Parliament and of the Council on the conditions of entry and residence of third-country nationals for the purposes of research, studies, pupil exchange, remunerated and unremunerated training, voluntary service and au pairing (recast)*, COM(2013) 151.

[151] Council Directive 2005/71/EC of 12 October 2005 on a specific procedure for admitting third-country nationals for the purposes of scientific research (Researchers Directive) [2005] OJ L289/15. Note that a recast version of this Directive is currently under negotiations between Council and Parliament: European Commission, *Proposal for a Directive on the conditions of entry and residence of third-country nationals* (n 150).

[152] Council Directive 2014/36/EU of 26 February 2014 on the conditions of entry and stay of third-country nationals for the purpose of employment as seasonal workers (Seasonal Workers Directive) [2014] OJ L94/375. See also J Hunt, 'Making the CAP Fit: Responding to the Exploitation of Migrant Agricultural Workers in the EU' (2014) 30(2) IJCLLIR 131.

[153] Council Directive 2014/66/EU of 15 May 2014 on the conditions of entry and residence of third-country nationals in the framework of an intra-corporate transfer (Intra-Corporate Transferees Directive) [2104] OJ L157/1.

[154] On Students' Directive see Case C-491/13 *Ben Alaya* [2014] OJ C 409/18. See further D Kostakopoulou, D Acosta Arcarazo and T Munk, 'EU Migration Law: The Opportunities and Challenges Ahead' in D Acosta Arcarazo and C Murphy (eds), *EU Security and Justice Law after Lisbon and Stockholm* (Hart Publishing 2014) 129–45.

[155] Council Directive 2009/50 on the conditions of entry and residence of third-country nationals for the purposes of highly qualified employment (Blue Card Directive) [2009] OJ L155/17. See also K Eisele, 'Why Come Here if I Can Go There? Assessing the "Attractiveness" of the EU's Blue Card Directive for "Highly Qualified" Immigrants' (2013) CEPS Liberty and Security in Europe Paper No. 60.

[156] Blue Card Directive Art 1.

[157] ibid, Arts 4(2) and 6.

The conditions for obtaining a Blue Card are laid out in Article 5. Applicants must have a valid work contract or a binding job offer; demonstrate that they are appropriately qualified for the position under national law; possess a valid travel document; and present evidence that they have, or have applied for, health insurance for periods when coverage is not provided under the applicant's employment contract. Applicants must not be considered a threat to public policy, public security, or public health.[158] Member States may also determine the duration of the Blue Card, from one to four years renewable.[159] While the first issuance of the Blue Card is subject to broad Member State discretion, once the Card has been issued, other legal consequences ensue. The card holder is entitled to progressive access to the labour market of the Member State concerned. For the first two years of employment, a card holder can only engage in paid employment that meets the conditions outlined in Article 5, and any change in employer must be authorized in advance by the relevant Member State authorities.[160] After that time, Member States may grant the card holder 'equal treatment with nationals as regards access to highly qualified employment'. If the Member State does not choose to grant equal treatment in accordance with Article 12(1) after this time, a card holder is required to communicate any changes that affect the conditions in Article 5 to the competent Member State authorities.

Additionally, a card holder's right of residence in unaffected by temporary periods of unemployment.[161] There is an extensive right to equal treatment with home nationals, which extends to: working conditions, including pay and dismissal;[162] freedom of association;[163] education and vocational training;[164] recognition of diplomas and professional qualifications in accordance with national procedures;[165] provisions in national law regarding social security, subject to the relevant EEC and EC Regulations;[166] payment of income related pensions, without prejudice to existing bilateral agreements;[167] access to goods and services generally available to the public;[168] and free access to the entire territory of the relevant Member State in accordance with national law.[169] The right to family reunification is linked to the Family Reunification Directive (FRD),[170] but not subject to the integration requirements foreseen in the other measure.[171] Periods of residence as a card holder may be added together for the purposes of acquiring rights under the LTRD.[172] Blue Card holders may, subject to conditions, move to another Member State after eighteen months for the purpose of highly qualified employment[173] with family reunification rights.[174]

The two other EU measures which create rights of entry and residence are the FRD and QD. The FRD is examined in Chapter 4, while the focus of Chapter 5 is the QD, the basis for admission of those seeking international protection.

[158] ibid, Art 5(1)(a)–(f). [159] ibid, Art 7(2). [160] ibid, Art 12(1)–(2).
[161] ibid, Art 13. [162] ibid, Art 14(1)(a). [163] ibid, Art 14(1)(b).
[164] ibid, Art 14(1)(c). [165] ibid, Art14(1)(d). [166] ibid, Art 14(1)(e).
[167] ibid, Art 14(1)(f). [168] ibid, Art 14(1)(g). [169] ibid, Art 14(1)(h).
[170] Council Directive 2003/86/EC of 22 September 2003 on the right to family reunification (Family Reunification Directive) [2003] OJ L251/12.
[171] Blue Card Directive Art 15. [172] ibid, Art 16. [173] ibid, Art 18.
[174] ibid, Art 19.

Moreover, the Single Permit Directive[175] lays down a common set of rights for third-country workers legally residing in the EU. Accordingly, while the authorization of residence of TCNs remains significantly a matter of national law and competence, EU measures do create a right to reside for certain privileged categories, thereby constraining the Member States' immigration discretion, expunging the statist assumption. Yet, they do not demand that those who fail to meet the criteria set out therein are denied entry. The Member States' residual discretion to admit remains, embodying an appropriate mode of sharing competence.

This patchwork of legislative measures in the Union's immigration *acquis* reveals an overall hesitation on the part of the EU to introduce a general migration status for labour migrants. Rather, EU law creates carefully circumscribed rights of entry and residence for specific categories of TCNs. The rights attaching to different statuses vary considerably: the privileged Blue Card holder has a more secure migration status than the Seasonal Worker. Nonetheless, a migration status regulated by EU law is in itself a differently constituted status, with greater judicial protection to limit migration control, as *Ben Alaya* on the Students' Directive exemplifies.

## 2. The EU's amplification of illegality

While the previous discussion highlights the importance of secure migration status created by EU law, the EU also bolsters the Member States' migration control prerogatives. This section provides a somewhat stylized overview of the EU's entry control system.[176] Space precludes a full exposition of the migration control apparatus of the EU, but suffice to note that it operates not just through law, but also practical coordination and surveillance.[177] The primary legal instruments of the entry control system are the Visa Code,[178] the Visa Information System (VIS),[179] carrier sanctions,[180] and the Schengen Information System (SIS),[181] and Schengen Borders

[175] Directive 2011/98/EU of the European Parliament and of the Council of 13 December 2011 on a single application procedure for a single permit for third-country nationals to reside and work in the territory of a Member State and on a common set of rights for third-country workers legally residing in a Member State (Single Permit Directive) [2011] OJ L343/1.

[176] This term is borrowed from Pastore (n 130).

[177] e.g. Regulation No 1052/2013 of 22 October 2013 establishing the European Border Surveillance System (Eurosur) [2013] L 295/11. See generally G Feldman, *The Migration Apparatus: Security, Labor, and Policymaking in the European Union* (Stanford University Press 2012).

[178] Regulation (EC) No 810/2009 of the European Parliament and of the Council of 13 July 2009 establishing a Community Code on Visas (Visa Code) [2009] OJ L 243/1.

[179] Regulation (EC) No 767/2008 of the European Parliament and of the Council of 9 July 2008 concerning the Visa Information System (VIS) and the exchange of data between Member States on short-stay visas (VIS Regulation) [2008] OJ L218/60.

[180] Council Directive 2001/51/EC of 28 June 2001 supplementing the provisions of Article 26 of the Convention implementing the Schengen Agreement of 14 June 1985 [2001] OJ L187/45. For a thorough analysis, see S Peers, E Guild, D Acosta Acaro, K Groenendijk, and V Moreno-Lax, 'Carrier Sanctions' in *EU Asylum and Immigration Law (Text and Commentary)* (2nd rev edn, Martinus Nijhoff Publishers 2012) chapter 12.

[181] Regulation (EC) No 1987/2006 of the European Parliament and of the Council of 20 December 2006 on the establishment, operation and use of the second-generation Schengen Information System (SIS II) [2006] OJ L381/4.

Code (SBC).[182] Three key systematic features are built into the system, which together demonstrate the EU's construction and indeed amplification of the phenomenon of 'illegality'. These features include (i) the institutionalization of discretion, (ii) negative mutual recognition, and (iii) the enduring consequences of refusals of entry.

### *i. The institutionalization of discretion*

Whether a visa is required to enter the EU depends on whether a country appears on an EU agreed list. That determination is political, agreed by the Council and Parliament with few criteria governing the exercise of that political decision.[183] The EU Visa Code sets out the procedures and conditions for issuing visas for the purpose of short stays and airport transit. A common feature of visa systems is that they mainly establish powers and discretions, rather than rules and standards. The obligation to get a visa subjects the admission seeker to the exercise of discretionary power. The would-be migrant who is subject to a visa requirement is required to apply for a visa when outside the EU, the granting of which remains largely subject to administrative discretion.[184] Without a visa, regular means of travel will usually be blocked, due to carrier sanctions.

### *ii. Negative mutual recognition*

As explored in Chapter 1, prevalent in these interrelated sets of measures is 'negative mutual recognition', which amplifies the notion of illegality in the EU. Negative mutual recognition deems one Member State's determination of 'illegality' to be binding throughout the EU, precluding entry to the entire territory. Many of the instruments discussed bind national administrations to recognize one another's decisions in the immigration and asylum field. Those regarded as 'illegal' or 'unwanted' in one Member State must be so regarded by all the others. Under the SIS, a migrant may find himself or herself unwanted throughout *Schengenland* on the basis of a decision of one national administration, based on a minor infraction of national immigration procedures. As now exemplified

[182] Regulation (EC) No 562/2006 of the European Parliament and of the Council of 15 March 2006 establishing a Community Code on the rules governing the movement of persons across borders (Schengen Borders Code) [2006] OJ L105/1. For detailed analysis, see S Peers 'Key Legislative Developments on Migration in the European Union' (2006) 8 EJML 321, 324–50. See also Regulation (EU) No 1051/2013 of the European Parliament and of the Council of 22 October 2013 amending [SBC] in order to provide for common rules on the temporary reintroduction of border control at internal borders in exceptional circumstances [2013] OJ L295/1.

[183] See Regulation (EC) No 539/2001 of 15 March 2001 listing the third countries whose nationals must be in possession of visas when crossing the external borders and those whose nationals are exempt from that requirement [2001] OJ L81/1 and its successive amendments.

[184] Visa Code Arts 19 and 21. See also Case C-84/12 *Koushkaki* [2013] OJ C 52/7, para 61: '[T]he competent authorities...have, when examining visa applications, a wide discretion which relates to the conditions of application.'

under the RD, a migrant subject to a national expulsion order must in principle be treated as unlawfully present by the other Member States, subject to certain exceptions.

To illustrate, the SIS permits the exchange of information on migration status, and biodata, such as fingerprints and photographs. The EU has expanded the SIS in its move to the SIS II.[185] From its inception, national authorities entered six types of 'alert' into the system. Under the Schengen Implementing Convention (SIC), it is for each authority to determine whether the matter is 'important enough' to warrant inclusion,[186] in light of the system's stated purposes of 'maintaining public policy and public security, including national security'.[187] Alerts concern the following matters:

- Those wanted for arrest and extradition (Article 95)
- Those to be refused entry into *Schengenland* (Article 96)
- Missing and dangerous persons (Article 97)
- People wanted to appear in court (Article 98)
- People to be placed under surveillance (Article 99)
- Lost and stolen objects (Article 100)

These grounds are ambiguous, particularly Article 96 on 'refusal of entry'. Two main categories of alerts are prevalent: first, those who are refused entry on public order or national security grounds and secondly, those who have not complied with national immigration law. The impact of entry into the system is considerable. The person subject to the alert will not be able to enter any of the other Contracting States.[188] Again, we see negative mutual recognition. Clearly, prohibition on future entry into the entire EU territory is an extreme sanction for 'what in some cases may have resulted from an indiscretion on the individual's part rather than a premeditated attempt to evade immigration controls'.[189] Member States interpret these criteria very differently.[190] Some Member States appear to make routine use of Article 96 alerts, with Germany and Italy accounting for over

[185] J Parkin, 'The Difficult Road to the Schengen Information System II: The Legacy of "Laboratories" and the Cost for Fundamental Rights and the Rule of Law' (4 April 2011) CEPS Paper in Liberty and Security in Europe; European Commission (2013) Questions and answers: Schengen Information System (SIS II). MEMO/13/309, 9 April.

[186] Convention implementing the Schengen Agreement of 14 June 1985 between the Governments of the States of the Benelux Economic Union, the Federal Republic of Germany and the French Republic on the gradual abolition of checks at their common borders [2000] OJ L239/19, Art 94.

[187] ibid, Art 93 SIC.

[188] ibid, Art 5(1)(d) [now Art 5(1)(d) SBC] and Art 15 SIC.

[189] R Cholewinksi, 'Preventing Irregular Migration' in F Julien-Laferriere, H Labaye, and O Erdström (eds), *The European Immigration and Asylum Policy: Critical Assessment Five Years after the Amsterdam Treaty* (Bruylant 2005) 107.

[190] E Brouwer, 'Data surveillance and border control in the EU: Balancing efficiency and legal protection of third country nationals' (Challenge Project, 14 June 2005) <http://www.libertysecurity.org/article289.html> accessed 11 April 2015.

three-quarters of the entries.[191] The Schengen Joint Supervisory Authority has highlighted the lack of controls and inconsistencies of national use of Article 96.[192]

### *iii. The enduring consequences of refusals of entry*

A further feature of the SIS, VIS, and RD is the tendency to create enduring legal consequences for a refusal of entry. In contrast, one of the key features of the CJEU's case law explored above is the refusal to allow States to draw blanket enduring negative consequences from immigration law infractions, when committed by TCNs who derive rights from particular EU instruments.

This section has sketched three key institutional features of EU law and practice in this field, namely (i) discretionary power; (ii) negative mutual recognition; and (iii) the enduring consequences of rejection. Together, I suggest that these signal an amplification and expansion of irregularity, in particular combined with the externalization of controls and their intensification via privatization in the form of Carrier Sanctions and Employers Sanctions. The next section identifies the diverse tools of EU migration control. The purpose is not to provide a detailed analysis of these complex measures, but rather to sketch the key policy trends of externalization, privatization, and deportation rather than regularization as a solution to irregularity.

## 3. Externalization: Visas

The key instrument of remote entry control is the visa, a tool for prior certification for entry. The EU has had a competence in the area of visas for some time, but this was originally limited to setting out the list of States whose nationals are required to have visas in order to enter the EU. The most recent measure was adopted in 2001.[193] The incorporation of the Schengen *acquis* has put visa politics at the centre of the EU entry control system. Schengen established a dividing line between long-stay and short-stay visas. Long-stay visas are 'national visas issued by one of the Contracting Parties in accordance with its national law'.[194] At present, there is no EU practice of granting humanitarian visas to those in need of international protection, although arguably there is an EU legal duty to operationalize such a system.[195]

191 Statewatch, 'Three quarters of a million "illegal aliens" banned from the Schengen area' *Statewatch News Online* (April 2005) <http://www.statewatch.org/news/2005/apr/08SISart96.htm> accessed 11 April 2015.

192 Schengen Joint Supervisory Authority, *Report on an Inspection of the Use of Article 96 Alerts in the Schengen Information System* (Schengen Joint Supervisory Authority 2005).

193 Council Regulation (EC) No 539/2001 of 15 March 2001 listing the third countries whose nationals must be in possession of visas when crossing the external borders and those whose nationals are exempt from that requirement, [2001] OJ L81/1, as amended by Regulation (EU) No 259/2014 of the European Parliament and the Council of 3 April 2014 [2014] OJ L105/9.

194 Art 18(1) SIC.

195 U Iben Jensen, 'Humanitarian Visas: Option or Obligation?' (2014) Study for the LIBE Committee, PE 509.986.

Concerning the common short-stay visas, the system operates in an ad hoc, politicized manner. At the general level, whether an individual requires a visa depends on whether her country is on the EU 'black list' of such countries. Irregular migration is one reason for transferring a country from the white to the black list for short-term visas.[196] Changes in listing are generally prompted by the third country's response to the EU's pressure to preclude irregular migration. For example, Bulgaria and Romania (in the pre-accession period) were placed on the White List:

only after these countries made commitments to apply draconian restrictions in respect of their own nationals apprehended in EU Member States for irregular entry or stay, which involve the possibility of confiscating their passports in both countries and even imprisonment for up to five years in Romania.[197]

As mentioned in Part II.1, the process of defining illegal immigration becomes self-perpetuating. Visa requirements are imposed when irregular migration is perceived, leading to further layers of control and mutual recognition of negative decisions, which in turn produces further illegality.

There are some common criteria for the issue of short-stay visas, now contained in the Visa Code. Previously, these conditions were set out in the Common Consular Instructions and the Common Manual, 'a body of law of uncertain legal standing and highly restricted contents'.[198] With the Treaty of Amsterdam's integration of the Schengen *acquis* into EU law, the Luxembourg court's jurisdiction over that instrument was secured.[199] The SBC marks a further legalization of the Schengen arrangements. The EP's amendments thereto signal a clear improvement in border practices, as indeed does the access to the CJEU to interpret the SBC. The Visa Code also increases transparency around the procedures for issuing short-stay visas by including, among others, procedures for appeal against a refusal of visa.[200]

The Visa Code replaces the former Common Consular Instructions. It clarifies which Member State is responsible for processing a visa application, defines the different phases for examination and decision-taking, harmonizes the fees that can be charged, and sets common standards for the service provided which include rules on non-discrimination,[201] and on deciding on applications within fifteen calendar days.[202] The position of visa applicants is strengthened by newly defined obligations for the Member States to give refused applicants the reasons for their decision and to inform them about their rights of appeal.[203] Yet the Schengen visa regime overall is toughened by the new Code as biometric identifiers (including the ten fingerprints of the applicants) have now to be collected,[204] new defined conditions (including 'integrity and reliability') apply to the issuing of multiple entry visas,[205] and former CCI provisions on group visas have not been retained.

[196] Recital 5 Regulation 539/2001. [197] Cholewinksi (n 188) 95, 103.
[198] Pastore (n 130) 106. [199] See Case C-241/05 *Bot* [2006] ECR I-9627.
[200] Visa Code Art 32(3). [201] ibid, Art 39. [202] ibid, Art 23.
[203] ibid, Art 32(3) and Annex VI. [204] ibid, Art 13. [205] ibid, Art 24(2).

The CJEU's first case on the SBC, *Zurita Garcia*,[206] concerned Spanish legislation which allowed the Spanish authorities to impose a fine rather than expulsion, in cases of individuals no longer in compliance with their SBC conditions of entry. The Spanish text of the SBC suggested that expulsion was compulsory if the conditions of stay were no longer fulfilled.[207] The CJEU confirmed that expulsion in those circumstances was not compulsory, but discretionary. In other words, Member State competence to authorize presence remains. I contend that this is an appropriate reflection of shared competence. As will be seen, there are attempts in the RD to establish an EU duty to remove, which I contend in contrast is inappropriate. Furthermore, the CJEU has also taken a stricter stance towards national discretion with regard to the issuing of visas in recent cases. In *Zakaria*,[208] the Court found that the SBC obliges Member States to establish a means of obtaining redress only against decisions to refuse entry. Moreover, in *Air Baltic*,[209] it found that an appropriate reading of the SBC precludes Member States from refusing entry on the ground that visas are not affixed to a valid travel document.

## 4. Privatization: Carrier sanctions, smuggling prohibitions, and employer sanctions

Those who facilitate irregular entry into the EU are increasingly subject to repressive measures. Carriers' liability in particular represents a significant transformation of border control mechanisms. In effect, it represents a privatization of border control, creating incentives for carriers to check migration status and refuse to transport individuals whose right to enter is in doubt. The difficulty here is that the private party is not in a position to make that discretionary assessment, so the restrictive tendencies in the legal regime are amplified. As Kritzman-Amir explains: 'While carriers are threatened with sanctions if they err and allow entry to undocumented migrants, they are not subject to any sanctions if they effectively deny entry and admission of asylum seekers. There are thus incentives to err on the side of caution which in this case means to refuse to transport asylum seekers [and others] who wish to enter clandestinely.'[210]

As well as civil carrier sanctions, the EU also supports the criminalization of smuggling, broadly defined. The main EU measure on facilitation of irregular migration[211] is wider in scope than the UN Smuggling Protocol.[212]

206 Joined Cases C-261/08 and C-348/08 *Zurita Garcia* and *Choque Cabrera* [2009] ECR I-10143.

207 SBC Art 13.

208 Case C-23/12 *Zakaria* [2013] OJ C 63/6, para 42.

209 Case C-575/12 *Air Baltic Corporation* [2014] OJ C 395/8.

210 T Kritzman-Amir, 'Privatization and Delegation of State Authority in Asylum Systems' (2011) 5 Law and Ethics of Human Rights 203.

211 Council Directive 2002/90/EC of 28 November 2002 defining the facilitation of unauthorized entry, transit, and residence [2002] OJ L328/17; Council Framework Decision 2002/946/JHA of 28 November 2002 on the strengthening of the penal framework to prevent the facilitation of unauthorized entry, transit, and residence [2002] OJ L328/1.

212 UN Protocol on the Smuggling of Migrants by Land, Sea and Air. The Protocol was ratified by the (then) EC. See [2001] OJ L30/44. See further Peers et al. (n 180) 389–91.

The Employer Sanctions Directive embodies a further element in the privatization of border controls, requiring employers to check migration status, and prohibiting their employment of irregular migrants. The core obligation under the ESD is to prohibit the employment of any 'illegally-staying' TCN,[213] defined as a TCN 'present on the territory of a Member State who does not fulfil, or no longer fulfils, the conditions for stay or residence in that Member State'.[214] However, Member States are allowed not to apply the prohibition 'to illegally staying third-country nationals whose removal has been postponed and who are allowed to work in accordance with national law'.[215] This addition reflects the ambiguity of the notion of 'illegality': it seems to refer to migrants, in particular rejected asylum seekers, who are non-removable, but deemed to be illegal in their residence, though not in their labour market participation. Although the ESD appears to introduce a sweeping prohibition on employment, the definition of illegally staying appears to be, at least according to the Preamble, 'without prejudice to national law prohibiting the employment of legally staying third-country nationals who work in breach of their residence status'.[216] Therefore, those who are in semi-compliance with immigration law, in particular those who are lawfully present but illegally working, may not be covered. Thus we see two significant potential exclusions: the legally present, but illegally working, and the illegally present, but legally working. As national authorities for the most part retain the power of definition over all four axes, the complexities of the notion of 'illegal presence' are revealed.

The ESD obliges employers to require that TCNs demonstrate, as a condition of employment, their valid residence permit or other authorization for his or her stay.[217] The ESD envisages financial sanctions for general non-compliance, including bearing the costs of the return.[218] Criminal sanctions are required for the most serious offences.[219] The ESD also contains some worker-protective provisions. In particular, Article 6 requires employers to pay outstanding remuneration, at least at the level of the legal minimum wage, irrespective of the illegality of the contract of employment. In some Member States, that illegality would preclude recovery of outstanding wages.[220]

Yet, the ESD remains of great significance in signalling strong resistance to irregular working and the attendant labour market regularization practices currently prevalent across the EU. The Commission's Explanatory Memorandum to the ESD mentions various economic benefits of the irregular labour market.[221]

213 ESD Art 3(1).

214 ibid, Art 2(b).

215 ibid, Art 3(3).

216 ibid, Recital 5.

217 ibid, Art 4(1)(a).

218 ibid, Art 5.

219 ibid, Arts 9 and 10.

220 E Dewhurst, 'The Right of Irregular Immigrants to Outstanding Remuneration under the EU Sanctions Directive: Rethinking Domestic Labour Policy in a Globalised World' (2011) 13 EJML 389; E Dewhurst, 'The Right of Irregular Immigrants to Back Pay: The Spectrum of Protection in International, Regional and National Legal Systems' in C Costello and M Freedland (eds), *Migrants at Work* (OUP 2014).

221 European Commission, Staff Working Document accompanying the Proposal for a Parliament and Council Directive providing for minimum standards on sanctions and measures against employers of illegally staying third-country nationals—Impact assessment, SEC(2007) 603, 7.

Yet, it hastily dismisses the regularization option, on grounds that it is to be subject to a separate study later and might also constitute a pull factor.[222] Dismissing the regularization option is in tension with its main conclusion on the obduracy of irregular working:

Most Member States have high numbers of illegally staying [TCNs] in work despite having employers' sanctions in place and this does not seem to be linked with types and levels of employer sanctions, but rather geographical location and possibilities to find work in certain sectors. This leads to the conclusion that the fact that Member States have adopted certain sanctions or other means to combat illegal employment of third-country nationals does not mean they are effective.[223]

## 5. Deportation vs. regularization

### *i. The Returns Directive (RD)*

The Directive on the mutual recognition of expulsion decisions[224] applies to broad categories of expulsion decisions, including those issued for 'failure to comply with national rules on the entry and residence of aliens.'

The RD builds on the previous measure. It is the first major piece of EU immigration legislation to be adopted by co-decision.[225] Unsurprisingly in light of the institutional context, human rights sensitivities and the RD's potential to thwart regularization, it was immensely controversial.[226] During the legislative process, the UN Human Rights Commission expressed concern about the human rights impact of the measure, in particular the rules on detention,[227] which are analysed in Chapter 8. Governments of several migrant sending countries entered the debate, to highlight the potential restrictive turn it signalled. Amongst these, notable were governments of several Latin American countries, whose nationals were the main beneficiaries of the Spanish regularization of 2005. This section does not provide an exhaustive analysis of the Directive,[228] but rather seeks to examine how it contributes to the EU construction of 'illegality'.

222 ibid, 13. 223 ibid, 9.

224 Council Directive 2001/40 of 28 May 2001 on the mutual recognition of decisions on expulsion of third country nationals [2001] OJ L149/34. See further K Groenendijk, 'The Directive on Mutual Recognition of Expulsion Decisions: Symbolic or Unbalanced Politics?' in P De Bruycker (ed), *The Emergence of a European Immigration Policy* (Bruylant 2003) 447.

225 D Acosta, 'The Good, the Bad and the Ugly in EU Migration Law: Is the European Parliament Becoming Bad and Ugly? (The Adoption of Directive 2008/15: The Returns Directive)' (2009) 11 EJML 19; A Ripoll Servent, 'Co-decision in the European Parliament: Comparing Rationalist and Constructivist Explanations of the Returns Directive' (2011) 7 Journal of Contemporary European Research 3.

226 See, 'No to the Outrageous Directive', Document prepared by 14 European pro-migrant NGOs, subsequently supported by 400 European organizations and more than 8000 citizens. <http://www.statewatch.org/news/2007/dec/eu-returns-ngo-compilation.pdf> accessed 12 April 2015.

227 United Nations Press Release, 'UN experts express concern about the proposed EU Return Directive' (UN 18 July 2008).

228 See generally, ECRE, *ECRE Information Note on Directive 2008/115/EC of the European Parliament and Council of 16 December 2008* (ECRE 2008); A Baldaccini, 'The Return and Removal of Irregular Migrants under EU law: An Analysis of the Returns Directive' (2009) 11 EJML 1.

For the first time, a binding piece of EU legislation attempts to define 'illegal presence'. As mentioned in Part II.1, a common phenomenon amongst migrant populations is semi-compliance with conditions of residence.[229] Whether semi-compliance nullifies residence rights would normally be a matter for adjudication. However, Article 3(2) RD defines 'illegal stay' as:

> the presence on the territory of the Member State of a third-country national who does not fulfil, or no longer fulfils the conditions of entry as set out in Article 5 of the [SBC] or other conditions for entry, stay or residence in that Member State.

On one reading, to be deemed illegal requires that the migrant no longer fulfils all the conditions of 'entry, stay or residence'. Alternatively, it could connote that the migrant is in breach of any one condition. The latter reading would clearly expand the notion of illegality significantly. In contrast, domestic laws often treat different categories of migrants who may have precarious residence rights differently. For instance, Germany does not consider tolerated persons as illegally staying whereas the Netherlands does.[230]

The RD amplifies negative mutual recognition. The core obligation in Chapter 11, entitled 'termination of illegal stay', requires Member States to issue a return decision to every TCN staying illegally on their territory, subject to certain exceptions.[231] This duty is subject to the discretion acknowledged, that Member States may 'at any moment decide to grant an autonomous residence permit or other authorisation offering a right to stay for compassionate, humanitarian or other reasons'.[232] Member States shall also 'consider refraining from issuing a return decision' to persons whose applications for renewal of a permit are pending.[233] The RD seems to build in arbitrariness.[234] Moreover, it may plausibly be read as an anti-regularization measure, in that it would seem to require individual assessment before regularization. Mass regularizations thus appear to be in tension with the RD, a reading that is entirely consonant with the thrust of EU political commitments in the European Pact on Immigration and Asylum, discussed in the next section.

The RD sets out 'common standards and procedures to be applied in Member States for returning illegally staying third-country nationals in accordance with fundamental rights as general principles of EU law as well as international law, including refugee protection and human rights obligations'.[235] The RD applies to third-country nationals 'staying illegally' in the territory of a Member State,[236] although Member States may exclude from the Directive's scope those 'subject to a refusal of entry' or 'who are apprehended or intercepted by the competent authorities in connection with the irregular crossing by land, sea or air of the external border of a Member States and who have not subsequently obtained an authorisation

[229] Ruhs and Anderson (n 10).
[230] Baldwin-Edwards and Kraler (n 12) 2.
[231] RD Art 6(1).
[232] ibid, Art 6(3).
[233] ibid, Art 6(4).
[234] Baldwin-Edwards and Kraler (n 12) 133.
[235] RD Art 1.
[236] ibid, Art 2(1).

of a right to stay in that Member State'.[237] In excluding those 'turned away' at the border, the RD has the capacity to be employed as 'a non-entry tool'.[238] Family members of EU Citizens are excluded,[239] as are those being removed for criminal law reasons.[240] As discussed at length in Chapter 8, the CJEU has interpreted this provision on two occasions, in *El Dridi*[241] and *Achughbabian*.[242] In both cases, the Court held that Member States' criminal laws had to confirm with the Directive, and in particular that where the criminal law was brought to bear solely for reasons relating to irregular migration, the RD processes precluded the imposition of criminal sanctions which were liable to hinder the removal process foreseen by the RD. Member States may maintain or adopt more favourable measures 'provided that such provisions are compatible with this Directive'.[243] The RD is also 'without prejudice' to more favourable EU immigration and asylum provisions.[244]

Also potentially exacerbating illegality is the provision on re-entry bans,[245] which provides that such bans must be issued where a return decision was issued without a period for voluntary departure being granted or where an obligation for return was not complied with. Given the breadth of these provisions, the RD appears to licence 'systematic imposition of entry bans'.[246]

The RD does not elaborate on the human rights standards concerning removal. Instead, it contains bald references to human rights compliance. Article 1 asserts that the RD creates removal rules and procedures 'in accordance with fundamental rights as general principles of Community law as well as international law, including refugee protection and human rights obligations'.[247] Article 5 sets out that Member States are to take 'due account' of (a) the best interests of the child; (b) family life; (c) the state of health of the TCN concerned; and respect the principle of *non-refoulement*. Preambular provisions contain more detail. For instance, para 22 of the Preamble states that the 'best interests of the child' are to be a 'primary consideration', in keeping with the formulation in the UN Convention on the Rights of the Child (CRC).[248] The RD's procedural guarantees are noteworthy, in particular the entitlement to legal aid, albeit couched in tentative terms.[249] The most significant ruling on the non-return obligation is in *Abdida*,[250] which needs to be read in conjunction with *M'Bodj*,[251] decided on the same day, on the Qualification Directive. *M'Bodj* held that some of those who could not be returned to their countries of origin for extreme health reasons such as to warrant protection

[237] ibid, Art 2(2)(a). However, Art 4(a) and (b) set out constraints on turning back.
[238] ECRE (n 228) 8.
[239] RD Art 2(3) refers to persons enjoying the EU right of free movement as defined in SBC Art 2(5).
[240] ibid, Art 2(2)(b).
[241] Case C-61/11 PPU *Hassen El-Dridi alias Karim Soufi* [2011] ECR I-3015.
[242] Case C-329/11 *Alexandre Achughbabian v Préfet du Val-de-Marne* [2011] ECR I-12695.
[243] RD Art 4. [244] ibid, Art 4(2). [245] ibid, Art 11.
[246] ECRE (n 228) 16. [247] RD Art 1.
[248] Convention on the Rights of the Child (adopted 20 November 1989) 1577 UNTS 3, Art 3(1).
[249] See RD Chapter III on Procedural safeguards.
[250] *Abdida* (n 103).
[251] Case C-542/13 *M'Bodj* [2015] OJ C65/12.

under Article 3 ECHR, do not warrant formal subsidiary protection status under the QD. However, *Abdida* adds a form of protection, of sorts, noting that the state of health has to be given due regard in deportation decisions. Importantly, in *Abdida*, the Court added that social rights protections would have to be accorded to the non-removable migrant.

### *ii. The EU's anti-regularization ethos*

**The Council as venue for intergovernmental tensions**

The EU provides the venue where Member States increasingly bemoan one another's regularization practices. The transnational dimension is emphasized: if one Member State provides lawful residence to migrants, those migrants may in time naturalize and move to other EU Member States in reliance on their rights as EU Citizens. Alternatively, over time they may gain a secure right of residence under the LTRD and also avail of the (much more tentatively constructed) right to reside elsewhere in the EU. The scope of this argument should be noted. It applies equally to all decisions of the Member States which may lead to naturalization or free movement, including granting citizenship to children of natives. The selective invocation against *regularized* migrants is evidence not of an anti-immigration sentiment generally, but of hostility towards the type of migrants who are perceived to benefit from regularization programmes. As regularization should be a matter of right for long-term residents, reliance on spill-over effects to thwart recognition of the duties of justice other Member States owe to those resident in their territory is to perpetuate injustice.

The anti-regularization ethos is most evident in the RD, under which there is an obligation (albeit subject to exceptions) to remove 'illegally' present migrants. The adoption of this measure should be seen against the background of EU responses to the Spanish regularization of 2005. Immediately thereafter, the Council called for the sharing of information on planned regularizations. The tenor of that call suggests that the aim of the information exchange would be to discourage regularization.[252] The resultant decision is cast, however, in more neutral terms.[253] Yet, it is premised on the same spill-over logic: information is to be shared on national asylum and immigration measures that are likely to have a significant impact on several Member States or on the EU as a whole. As outlined in Part II above, there have been regularizations in EU Member States since 2005, interestingly in both the Netherlands and Germany, neither of which have a strong tradition of regularizations. In both instances, too, the impetus came from municipal and provincial

[252] Press Release PRES 05/74 Council of Ministers meeting on Justice and Home Affairs, Luxembourg, 14 April 2005.

[253] Council Decision 2006/688 of 5 October 2006 on the establishment of a mutual information mechanism (MIM) concerning Member States' measures in the areas of asylum and immigration [2006] OJ L283/40.

level, concerned with on-the-ground conditions for irregular migrants, in particular rejected asylum seekers.

The French Presidency of 2008 displayed a condemnatory attitude to regularization, in keeping with the domestic restrictive turn. The resultant European Council Conclusions, containing the European Pact on Immigration and Asylum, reflect that stance. The central commitment on illegal immigration is to 'control illegal immigration in particular by ensuring that illegal immigrants return to their countries of origin or to a transit country'.[254] Member States commit to use 'only case-by-case regularisation, rather than generalised regularisation, under national law, for humanitarian or economic reasons'.[255] The RD in turn seems to embody a latent recognition of this position.

**The Commission's changing attitude**

In 1994, the Commission supported the ratification of the International Convention on the Protection of the Rights of All Migrant Workers and Members of their Families,[256] which supports regularizations where removal is not possible.[257] In its 2000 *Communication on a Community Immigration Policy*, the Commission deemed Member States' policies of zero immigration as 'no longer ... appropriate', 'given the economic opportunities now available in the EU', and drew attention to the prevalence of regularization programmes as evidence of substantial illegal immigration, 'driven by' the absence of legal immigration channels.[258] The Commission advocated a 'coordinated approach' 'to regulate migrant flows successfully, therefore, and to reduce illegal immigration', meaning one which took into account 'all the various interlinked aspects of the migratory system and to work in close partnership with the countries of origin and transit'.[259] Its 2001 *Communication on a Common Policy on Illegal Immigration*[260] struck an ambivalent note on regularizations, stating that '[i]llegal entry should not lead to the desired stable form of residence.' The focus on return rather than regularization emerged in the 2002 *Communication on a Community Return Policy on Illegal Residents*,[261] with return conceived of as a 'vital and integral component' of EC immigration and asylum policy, leading to the 2002 *Commission Green Paper on a Community Return Policy*, followed by the 2002 *Council Action Plans on Illegal Immigration, External Borders and Return.*

254 European Council, *European Pact on Immigration and Asylum*, Council Doc 13440,08 (24 September 2008) 7.

255 ibid, 7.

256 For the rights of irregular migrants, see particularly Arts 25(3), 28, 30, and 69(2).

257 European Commission, *Communication on Immigration and Asylum Policies*, COM(1994) 23, 23 February 1994.

258 European Commission, *Communication on a Community Immigration Policy* COM(2000) 757, 13, citing Apap et al. (n 55).

259 ibid, 13–14.

260 European Commission, *Communication on a Common Policy on Illegal Immigration* COM(2001) 672, 6.

261 European Commission, *Communication on a Community Return Policy on Illegal Residents* COM(2002) 564.

A positive Commission statement on regularization emerged in its 2003 *Communication on Immigration, Integration and Employment*.[262] Whilst acknowledging that the 'only coherent approach to dealing with illegal residents is to ensure that they return to their country of origin', it also accepted that 'in a considerable number of cases it is not possible to implement such a policy for legal, humanitarian or practical reasons'.[263] Regularization was desirable for 'pragmatic reasons', and to combat social exclusion and marginalization. In a similar vein, the 2004 *Communication on the Links between Legal and Illegal Immigration*,[264] took a more balanced view, exploring both the negative and positive effects of regularization programmes. Benefits for the State included population management and increases in government revenue, whilst on the negative side, regularization risked encouraging further irregular migration and becoming self-perpetuating. The Commission's stance reflects the 2005 turning point. The 2006 *Communication on Policy Priorities in the Fight against Illegal Immigration of TCNs*[265] noted the 'concern and interest' in Member States when one of them implements large scale regularization, but does not condemn the practice.[266]

The strong intergovernmental message embodied in the European Pact on Immigration and Asylum has unsurprisingly permeated the Commission's current thinking. Its 2008 *Communication on a Common Immigration Policy for Europe: Principles, Actions and Tools* states that 'indiscriminate and large-scale mass regularisations of immigrants in an illegal situation do not constitute a lasting and effective tool for migration management and should be prevented.'[267] The Commission has largely refrained from addressing the issue of regularization in its more recent pronouncements on irregular immigration,[268] save for a commitment to review national practice on 'non-removable returnees'.[269]

### The European Parliament

In contrast, while the European Parliament is critical of regularization practices, the basis for the critique is different. Its comments on the Commission Communication of 2006 on *Policy priorities in the fight against illegal immigration of third-country nationals* reflect ambivalence on regularization practices. For

[262] European Commission, *Communication on Immigration, Integration and Employment* COM(2003) 336, 26.

[263] ibid.

[264] European Commission, *Communication on the Links between Legal and Illegal Immigration* COM(2004) 412 final.

[265] European Commission, *Communication on Policy Priorities in the Fight against Illegal Immigration of Third-Country Nationals* COM (2006) 402, 7–8.

[266] ibid, para 33.

[267] European Commission, *Communication on a Common Immigration Policy for Europe: Principles, Actions and Tools*, COM(2008) 359, 11. This is pronounced despite the finding in the REGINE study that EU rules should at least encourage regularization in some cases.

[268] European Commission, *Action Plan implementing the Stockholm Programme*, COM(2010) 171, 20 April 2010; European Commission, *Communication on migration* (n 8); European Commission, *An Open and Secure Europe: Making it happen*, COM(2014) 154, 11 March 2014; European Commission, *On EU Return Policy* COM(2014) 199.

[269] European Commission, *On EU Return Policy*, (n 268), 8.

the Civil Liberties, Justice and Home Affairs (LIBE) Committee, regularization signals a 'lack of appropriate measures in place to deal with a phenomenon which forms part of societies in most Member States',[270] namely migration. Accordingly, '*en masse* regularization of illegal immigrants should be a one-off event since such a measure does not resolve the real underlying problems'.[271] The Foreign Affairs Committee report is starker, urging that 'Member States should not adopt national measures regularising the situation of illegal immigrants because this creates a suction effect.'[272] Hopes were high that the Parliament would use its powers of co-decision to assert a less statist view of immigration control. However, the RD in contrast suggests the institution is keen to be seen as the Council's partner in migration control, in contrast to its rhetorical commitment to a more open EU immigration policy when its powers were limited to consultation.[273]

## VII. Conclusions

To condemn migration as 'illegal', there should be some meaningful notion of 'legal' migration. In many instances, illegal immigration emerges out of illegality traps, 'excessive formalism' (to use the words of the ECtHR in *Mendizabal*) and, as will be shown in Chapters 4–6, failings in asylum systems. In that context, to deem a migrant 'illegal', and expose her to punitive measures and stigma, is objectionable. Regularization remains a key corrective, which ought to be seen as a requirement of justice, rather than an act of executive beneficence. This chapter endorses the social integration thesis and the moral significance of long-term residence: long-term residence leads to social membership, and States have duties in justice to include those who have become social members, irrespective of legal status. As was seen in Part IV, the jurisprudence of the ever-tentative ECtHR lends some support to this contention, although Strasbourg's endorsement of the statist assumption prompts high deference to States' authorization of residence.

The EU adopts two strikingly different approaches to irregular migration. Both the EU and ECHR systems, however, envisage a role for courts in regularization, that is, in making individual rights-based assessments of entitlement to stay. However, unlike the ECtHR, the CJEU case law on the residence rights of EU

270 European Parliament, *Report on policy priorities in the fight against illegal immigration of third-country* nationals, (2006/2250(INI)), Doc PE380/872, 17 September 2007, para 58.

271 ibid.

272 European Parliament, *Report on policy priorities in the fight against illegal immigration of third-country nationals, (2006/2250(INI))*, Doc PE384.302, 17 April 2007, para 16.

273 Acosta (n 225); A Héritier, 'Institutional Change in Europe: Co-decision and Comitology Transformed' (2012) 50(S1) JCMS 38; E Lopatin, 'The Changing Position of the European Parliament on Irregular Migration and Asylum under Co-decision' (2013) 51(4) JCMS 740; A Ripoll Servent, 'The European Parliament and the Returns Directive: The End of Radical Contestation; The Start of Consensual Constraints' in B Anderson, MJ Gibney, and E Paoletti (eds), *The Social, Political and Historical Contours of Deportation* (Springer 2013); cf SA Espinoza and C Moraes, 'The Law and Politics of Migration and Asylum: The Lisbon Treaty and the EU' in D Ashiagbor, N Countouris, and I Lianos (eds), *The European Union after the Treaty of Lisbon* (Cambridge University Press 2012).

Citizens, and in particular their TCN family members, exemplifies migration as of right, with the significance of national authorization downplayed. Even where individuals have no right to enter the EU as such (like Turkish workers), but have protection against removal, we find a sensitivity to the challenges posed by compliance with immigration law, and a willingness to assert EU rights over executive discretion. I explore this particular EU–ECHR divergence further in Chapter 4.

In contrast though, the EU also serves to support national executives in restricting entry and effectuating removals. The EU visa system exports control over entry to officials in far-away consulates, with few reliable criteria to guide the exercise of their discretion. Carrier sanctions privatize control over entry. In these circumstances, securing a lawful entry to the territory of the EU becomes less likely. Duties of 'negative mutual recognition' amplify the notion of illegality in the EU, by deeming one Member State's determination of 'illegality' to be binding throughout the EU, precluding entry to the entire territory. A further feature of the SIS, VIS, and RD is the tendency to create enduring legal consequences for a refusal of entry. The EU seems in this vein to create the problem of illegal immigration, as much as cure it. Against this background, the EU's anti-regularization ethos thwarts the recognition of the duties in justice the Member States have to those migrants resident in their territory.

It may be recalled that the EU's commitment to creating an AFSJ has been understood as entailing:

> Freedom to live in a law-abiding environment in the knowledge that public authorities are using everything in their individual and collective power... to combat and contain those who seek to deny or abuse that freedom.[274]

Admission-seekers to the EU face considerable challenges if they seek 'freedom to live in a law-abiding environment'. Their legal environment is replete with booby traps that increase the likelihood that they may find themselves liable to be deemed 'illegal'. To determine whether the public authorities of the EU are doing 'everything in their individual and collective power... to combat and contain those who seek to deny or abuse' the freedom of migrants to live in a law-abiding manner, we need to identify the actors who construct illegality. This chapter reveals that in large measure the EU bolsters national authorities in their discretion and *ad-hocery* in deeming people 'illegal'.

[274] European Commission, *Towards an area of freedom, security and justice*, COM (98) 459 final, 5.

# 4

# Human Rights to Family Life and Family Migration

## I. Introduction

The human right to family life provides the basis for national and supranational judicial scrutiny of restrictions on migration of families, in particular family reunification. Family migration includes families reunifying after one family member has migrated, families migrating together, and family formation migration where couples and children migrate to be together. Given complex life courses and blended families, there are often no sharp distinctions between these different forms, so they are treated together in this chapter, although much of the discussion focuses on family reunification. Importantly, migration status and migration controls often dictate family decisions about where to live and when and whether to reunite, a phenomenon this chapter seekers to elucidate. Family reunification in particular is usually portrayed as concerning both the rights of insiders (sponsors) and the more contentious notion of a claim for admission of their family members. It thus touches directly on admissions, the focus of this entire book.

Part II sets out a framework to understand family reunification in particular, which turns on the recognition of the connections between the sponsor and the host State, and the sponsor and her family members. As will be seen, this means there are two sources of stratification: one concerned with how the sponsor is categorized and the other as to the diverse sets of conditions governing being joined or accompanied by family members.[1] European Convention on Human Rights (ECHR) and European Union (EU) law recognize (and indeed fail to recognize) these connections in different ways, interacting in various permutations, providing a complex yet fruitful field for exploration of human rights pluralism.[2]

1 'Stratification' captures the phenomenon whereby law-makers tend to create several migration statuses, with different rights attaching. See further L Morris, 'Stratified Rights and the Management of Migration' (2001) 3 European Societies 387 and, L Morris, *Asylum, Welfare and the Cosmopolitan Ideal: A Sociology of Rights* (Routledge 2010). See further R Schweitzer, 'A Stratified Right to Family Life? Patterns and Rationales behind Differential Access to Family Reunification for Third-Country Nationals Living within the EU' (2014) *Sussex Centre for Migration Research Working Paper No 70*.

2 The focus is on these two sources, although other IHRL instruments do play a role. See further, OHCHR, *Migration Paper: Family Reunification* (OHCHR November 2005).

Part III sets out the ECHR jurisprudence on family migration, while Part IV sets out the EU rules pertaining to family members of EU Citizens and under the Family Reunification Directive (FRD),[3] the EU Directive which regulates family reunification for some third-country nationals (TCNs) in the EU.[4] The European Court of Human Rights (ECtHR) endorses the statist assumption, so while Article 8 ECHR provides some stability of residence for long-settled migrants, rights to enter for family members are precarious. In contrast, as Part IV explores, EU law has long provided for migration of family members of EU Citizens as of right, irrespective of their nationality,[5] now enshrined in the Citizenship Directive.[6] While governments resisted the application of these provisions to first admissions of TCNs to the EU, the Court of Justice of the European Union (CJEU) confirmed that the Citizenship Directive provides a right to enter and reside in the EU for TCN family members of EU Citizens.[7] By expanding the scope of protection of EU Citizenship to at least some scenarios concerning 'static EU Citizens'[8] in *Zambrano*,[9] the CJEU has created a new route to protect residence rights of EU Citizens and their TCN families. Yet normally it remains the case that stronger protections are available for migrant EU Citizens who have exercised free movement rights.

In contrast, if the sponsor is not an EU Citizen, the FRD has set out minimum standards for the entry of family members of TCN migrants who have a 'reasonable prospect' of acquiring a right of permanent residence. Agreed unanimously by the then ministers comprising the EU Council, the FRD seems to

[3] Council Directive 2003/86/EC of 22 September 2003 on the right to family reunification (Family Reunification Directive or 'FRD') [2003] OJ L251/12.

[4] I do not consider the implications of association agreements for family migration.

[5] Regulation (EEC) No 1612/68 of the Council of 15 October 1968 on freedom of movement for workers within the Community [1968] OJ SpEd L257/2, Art 10.

[6] Directive 2004/38/EC of the European Parliament and of the Council of 29 April 2004 on the right of citizens of the Union and their family members to move and reside freely within the territory of the Member States [...] (Citizenship Directive or 'CD') [2004] OJ L158/77. See generally, see E Guild, S Peers, and J Tomkin, *The EU Citizenship Directive: A Commentary* (OUP 2014).

[7] Case C-127/08 *Metock* [2008] ECR I-6241. See further, C Costello, '*Metock*: Free Movement and "Normal Family Life" in the Union' (2009) 46 CMLRev 587.

[8] That is, where EU Citizens remain in their country of nationality without exercising EU free movement rights. I use the term throughout, although it suggests (inaccurately) a sedentary population, less dynamic than those who exercise transnational free movement rights.

[9] Case C-34/09 *Gerardo Ruiz Zambrano v Office national de l'emploi (ONEM)* [2011] ECR I-1177. The case has been the subject of an outpouring of scholarly comment: K Hailbronner and D Thym, 'Annotation of Case C-34/09 *Ruiz Zambrano*' (2010) 48 CMLRev 1253 and the reply thereto: M Olivas and D Kochenov, 'Case C- 34/09 *Ruiz Zambrano*: A Respectful Rejoinder' (2012) 1 University of Houston Public Law and Legal Theory Series; A Wiesbrock, 'Union Citizenship and the Redefinition of the "Internal Situations" Rule: The Implications of *Zambrano*' (2011) 12 German Law Journal 2077; N Nic Shuibhne, 'Seven Questions for Seven Paragraphs' (2011) 36 ELRev 162; D Kochenov, 'A Real European Citizenship, A New Jurisdiction Test, A Novel Chapter of the Development of the Union in Europe' (2011) 18 CJEL 56; A Lansbergen and N Miller, 'European Citizenship Rights in Internal Situations: An Ambiguous Revolution?' (2011) 7 Eur Const LR 287; P Van Elsuwege and D Kochenov, 'On the Limits of Judicial Intervention: EU Citizenship and Family Reunification Rights' (2011) 4 EJML 443; I Solanke, 'Using the Citizen to Bring the Refugee In: *Gerardo Ruiz Zambrano* v *Office national de l'emploi (ONEM)*' (2012) 75 MLR 101.

permit all manner of restrictions on family reunification. Yet, as will be seen, it also creates an EU right to reunification, which sets up important constraints and justificatory requirements for any restrictions thereto. While this chapter confirms the disparity in treatment between the family rights of EU Citizens and TCNs, it also reveals a more complex picture than any sharp insider-outsider dichotomy would suggest.

As explained in Chapter 2, the EU literature on pluralism is preoccupied with jurisdictional conflict. In this field, the danger of outright jurisdictional conflict happens to be minimal. The FRD allows Member States much leeway, so Member States may set higher domestic standards. They may protect migrants' rights well beyond the ECHR minimum, allowing them to comply with higher domestic human rights standards, where these exist. Moreover, as they have broad discretion, they are, according to both Luxembourg and Strasbourg jurisprudence,[10] bound to respect Strasbourg norms, and cannot claim that their decisions are immune from scrutiny for being required by EU law. Nonetheless, there are profound human rights challenges in this field. In particular, I contend in Part IV that the EU legal context demands the articulation of a distinctive human right to family reunification, moving above the Strasbourg minimum, under both the Citizenship Directive and FRD. Showcasing the CJEU's *FRD Ruling*[11] I illustrate some of the disadvantages when Luxembourg imports Strasbourg jurisprudence *in toto*. Subsequent case law illustrates the episodic and fitful character of judicial developments, with the bold ruling in *Chakroun*,[12] followed by cautious, even perhaps evasive rulings, in particular in *Noorzia*.[13]

Engaging with the human right to family life inevitably implicates contentious value judgments. The law tends to privilege the family based on heterosexual marriage, with a male breadwinner and mother tending exclusively to their offspring. That this privilege reflects patriarchal, hetero-normative, and ethnocentric value judgments is self-evident. As will be seen, the most significant contemporary trend is to restrict family migration in the name of 'integration', with particular marriage patterns of ethnic minority insiders (often naturalized or second generation citizens of the Member States concerned) being restricted, as these patterns have been labelled as a failure of integration in themselves. The very notion of 'marriage pattern' suggests stereotyping, although as will be seen, the

[10] *Bosphorus Hava Yollari Turizm v Ireland* (2006) 42 EHRR 1. See C Costello, 'The Bosphorus Ruling of the European Court of Human Rights: Fundamental Rights and Blurred Boundaries in Europe' (2006) 6 HRLRev 87.

[11] Case C-540/03 *Parliament v Council (Family Reunification)* [2006] ECR I-5769. For comments, see A Arnull, 'Family Reunification and Fundamental Rights' (2006) 31 ELRev 611; R Lawson, 'Family Reunification and the Union's Charter of Fundamental Rights, Judgment of 27 June 2006, Case C-540/03 *Parliament v Council*' (2007) European Constitutional Law Review 342; M Bulterman, 'Casenote on Case C-540/03 *Parliament v Council*' (2008) 45 CMLRev 245.

[12] C-578/08 *Rhimou Chakroun v Minister van Buitenlandse Zaken* [2010] ECR I-01839. See further A Wiesbrock, 'Court of Justice of the European Union: The Right to Family Reunification of Third-Country Nationals under EU Law' (2010) 6 European Constitutional Law Review 462.

[13] Case C-338/13 *Marjan Noorzia v Bundesministerin für Inneres* [2014] OJ C 315/18.

two supranational courts have, as yet, failed to scrutinize properly this restrictive turn and the peculiar notion of 'integration' it institutionalizes.[14] The use of integration and other restrictions on family migration has nonetheless proliferated, as well as other more banal, but no less effective restrictions, such as high fees, age, and time limits.[15]

This chapter must of necessity bracket out some other contentious questions on the construction of family life,[16] as its main focus is not on the meaning of family per se, but rather how migration and family life intersect in law. Yet, as will be seen, this intersection reproduces, indeed in many respects further reifies, the traditional family paradigm. On the potentially productive side, though, Part V examines an inclusive dynamic that may result from overlapping Strasbourg/Luxembourg jurisdiction. EU law's bright lines may compensate for the ECtHR's casuistry, while the ECtHR's case-specifity and gradualism may temper EU law's rigidity in defining family life.

## II. A Framework for Family Reunification

Normatively, family reunification is often treated as necessary to vindicate the rights of insiders ('sponsors') who have already established themselves in the host country or are citizens thereof. According to the 'insider privilege' account, the sponsor's right to be joined by her family emerges in recognition of the sponsor's insider status. As Carens explains:

> family reunification is primarily about the moral claims of insiders, not outsiders. The state's obligation is derived not so much from the claims of those seeking to enter as the claims of those they seek to join: citizens, residents and those who have been admitted for an extended period.[17]

Family reunification thus turns on the recognition of two sets of connections, first between the sponsor and host State and the second between the sponsor and family. While the 'insider privilege' account is a useful heuristic, as will be seen, recognition of these two sets of connections varies under different legal regimes, bringing complexity and stratification. This is particularly so when we appreciate that family reunification often comes after family separation structured by migration law.

[14] See the discussion in Part IV.

[15] See generally E Guild, K Groenendijk, and S Carrera (eds), *Illiberal Liberal States* (Ashgate 2009); A Kraler and others (eds), *Gender, Generation and the Family in International Migration* (Amsterdam University Press 2011); T Strik, B de Hart, and E Nissen, *Family Reunification: A Barrier or Facilitator of Integration: A Comparative Study* (Wolf Legal Publishers 2013).

[16] In particular the issue of polygamous households.

[17] JH Carens, 'Who Should Get In? The Ethics of Immigration Admissions' (2003) Ethics and International Affairs 95, 96. Thus, he acknowledges that a cosmopolitan view of immigration, where strangers are acknowledged as having a right to immigrate, may require a rethinking of any priority attached to family reunification.

## 1. Connection between sponsor and host community: The complex concept of 'insider'

The notion of 'insider' in the EU is not as straightforward as it might seem at first glance. The social membership thesis endorsed in Chapter 3 demands that links with the host society established through long residence be legally recognized. Indeed, as that Chapter demonstrates, the argument for the recognition of long residence also holds in the case of irregular migrants. In practice, in the absence of such recognition, nationality, human rights and EU law, as well as States' regularization practices, will determine whether and if so how recognition of the connection between the sponsor and the host community takes place.

The main 'mode of admission' to the EU is by acquiring nationality of a Member State, an accident of birth for most. Nationality brings with it EU Citizenship, and so, provided the EU Citizen can bring herself within the scope of EU law (and the law on this is in some flux, as will be seen), stronger family rights are available under EU law. In the absence of accessible routes to naturalization, constitutional courts in several Member States intervened to secure rights to reside for settled migrants, with attention to the second generation in particular.[18] The domestic constitutional developments were later reflected in Strasbourg jurisprudence under Article 8 ECHR, as discussed later in this chapter.

The EU Long-Term Residents Directive (LTRD) is a potentially significant legal basis for greater security of residence for settled migrants in the EU.[19] It applies to those lawfully resident for over five years, and crucially has been extended to recognized refugees and holders of subsidiary protection.[20] Yet, given the range of exceptions and restrictions it permits, it remains to be seen whether a robust right of residence will emerge.[21] In a familiar pattern, EU case law has firmed up the right to long-term resident (LTR) status somewhat, although many issues remain contested. In *Tahir*,[22] the Court established that Member States were not permitted to exempt family members from the qualifying period for long-term resident status. In other words, five years was a pan-EU minimum standard for the EU LTR status. In *Iida*,[23] the Court noted that while

[18] See, e.g. the landmark 1978 ruling of the BVerfG holding that repeated renewal of residence permits created a legitimate expectation of on-going renewal, 26 September 1978, 1 BvR 525/77.

[19] Council Directive 2003/109/EC of 25 November 2003 concerning the status of third-country nationals who are long-term residents (Long-Term Residents Directive or LTRD) [2003] OJ L16/33.

[20] Directive 2011/51/EU of the European Parliament and of the Council of 11 May 2011 amending Council Directive 2003/109/EC to extend its scope to beneficiaries of international protection [2011] OJ L123/1. See also S Peers, 'Transfer of international protection and European Union law' (2012) 24 IJRL 527.

[21] See further, D Kostakopolou, '"Integrating" Non-EU Migrants in the European Union: Ambivalent Legacies and Mutating Paradigms' (2002) 8 Columbia Journal of European Law 187; K Groenendijk, 'The Long-Term Residents Directive, Denizenship and Integration' in A Baldaccini, E Guild, and H Toner (eds), *Whose Freedom, Security and Justice? EU Immigration and Asylum Law and Policy* (Hart Publishing 2007) 429; D Acosta, *The Long-Term Residence Status as a Subsidiary Form of EU Citizenship. An Analysis of Directive 2003/109* (Martinus Nijhoff Publishers 2011).

[22] Case C-469/13 *Shamim Tahir* [2014] OJ C 315/22.

[23] Case C-40/11 *Iida* [2013] OJ C9/10.

national law determined who was lawfully resident for the purposes of acquiring status under the LTRD, Member States were obliged to grant the status to those who met the conditions under that measure.[24] Although the Court seemed to be of the view that the applicant met the requirements of the LTRD, it noted that he had withdrawn his application for that status. Application was a requirement for the grant of that permit.[25] The most important ruling to date on the personal scope of the LTRD is *Singh*.[26] Some Member States took the view that migrants with temporary residence permits, even if renewable, fell outside the Directive.[27] In this, they relied on the Directive's provision concerning residence permits that were 'formally limited'.[28] The Court confirmed this term warranted an autonomous EU interpretation.[29] It was a 'strong indication' that the permit in question fell within the LTRD if it was renewable for successive periods, including beyond a five-year period,[30] although this was not decisive. This ruling is crucially important given that precarious temporary migration statuses are commonplace across the EU.

Together, these cases suggest that LTR status must be accorded once the criteria in the Directive are met and the applicant applies. The Court has also condemned any additional hurdles to that status: In *Commission v Netherlands*,[31] the Court found that the Netherlands was in breach of the LTRD in levying excessive and disproportionate administrative charges for the acquisition of LTR status. Yet to be litigated are questions about the application of integration conditions and measures as hurdles for the acquisition of LTR status and onward movement within the EU.[32] Given the conditions set out in the LTRD, and the Member States' interpretations thereof, it is perhaps unsurprising that LTR status is accorded only rarely. In its 2011 LTRD Implementation Report, the Commission 'deplored' the weak impact of the Directive, as evidenced by the few permits issued by most Member States.[33] As the report noted, in many instances, the advantages of LTR status may

[24] ibid, paras 36–37. [25] ibid, para 48.

[26] Case C-502/10 *Staatssecretaris van Justitie v Mangat Singh* [2012] OJ C 379/4. See further, S Peers, 'Case C-571/10, *Servet Kamberaj v Istituto per l'Edilizia sociale della Provincia autonoma di Bolzano (IPES) and Others*, Judgment of the Court (Grand Chamber) of 24 April 2012, nyr; Case C-508/10 *Commission v Netherlands*, Judgment of the Court of 26 April 2012; Case C-502/10, *Staatssecretaris van Justitie v Mangat Singh*, Judgment of the Court of 18 October 2012' (2013) 50 CMLRev 529.

[27] European Commission, *Report on the application of Directive 203/109/EC concerning the status of third-country nationals who are long-term residents* (LTRD Implementation Report), COM(2011)585, section 3.1.

[28] Art 3(2)(e) LTRD. [29] *Mangat Singh* (n 26) paras 42–43. [30] ibid, para 54.

[31] Case C-508/10 *Commission v Netherlands* [2012] OJ C 174/7.

[32] Articles 5(2) and 15(3) LTRD. The Opinion of AG Mengozzi in Case C-138/13 *Naime Dogan v Bundesrepublik Deutschland* [2014] OJ C 315/11, examined 'integration measures' under the FRD. However, he contrasted that term with 'integration conditions' under the LTRD, giving some important guidance on that concept. However, the Court ruled on other grounds.

[33] European Commission, *LTRD Implementation Report* (n 27) 10–11. It noted that in 2009, around four-fifths of these third-country nationals having LTR status were living in four Member States: Estonia (187 400), Austria (166,600), Czech Republic (49,200), and Italy (45,200). In France and Germany, only 2,000 third-country residents had acquired the LTR permit.

not be apparent, or migrants may prefer to seek to naturalize if that is possible in their Member State of residence. As regards family reunion though, as will be seen, naturalizing and remaining in one's Member State of nationality as a static EU citizen may diminish the rights to family reunion available, as some States treat their own nationals less favourably than TCNs under the FRD.

This interplay between nationality and migration is a longstanding one. Take spousal migration, for example, meaning a sponsor being re-joined by a trailing spouse, or a sponsor seeking to have a fiancé or spouse enter for the purpose of residency together. Spousal migration is increasingly of the latter variety, in other words it is for the purpose of family formation rather than reunification. Traditionally, States applied more 'generous' rules for spousal migration if the sponsor was a citizen, than if not. Indeed, automatic citizenship by way of declaration was commonplace, although often in patriarchal form: husbands could transfer citizenship to their wives but not vice versa.[34] However, over the past decades nationality laws across Europe have moved decisively away from this mode of *ex lege* attribution of nationality to spouses.[35] The erosion of the right to be joined by a spouse represents a serious devaluation of nationality. In Joppke's account, citizenship upon marriage:

> became a concern once the 'citizens' involved...were the descendants of immigrants whose choice for marriage partners from their countries of origin are deemed to aggravate the problem of ethnically segregated and marginalized communities.[36]

He represents the resulting changes as:

> [m]ore than just a tinkering with a miniscule aspect of citizenship.... [T]he entire citizenship construct, which had once been kept strictly separate from the exigencies of migration control, has in effect been fused with and subordinated to migration control, with the...rights of citizens [becoming] downwardly approximated to the rights of legal immigrants.[37]

This account suggests that recourse to human rights may be prompted by a background diminution of rights of citizens. In Joppke's account, the rights of citizens have been downgraded uniformly. In addition, we are also witnessing a differential downgrading of citizens' family rights in some instances. For instance, the Danish restrictions at issue in *Biao v Denmark*[38] differentiate between naturalized and 'Danish-born' citizens. These developments unsettle the 'insider privilege' account of family reunification, as the ostensible insider, the citizen, is now less

[34] *Abdulaziz, Cabales and Balkandalo v UK* (1985) 7 EHRR 471. While, as discussed below, the ECtHR found no violation of Art 8 ECHR, it did find that the sex discrimination violated Articles 14 and 8 ECHR. The UK responded by levelling down, removing the right of spousal nationality by declaration from men. See further B de Hart, 'Love Thy Neighbour: Family Reunification and the Rights of Insiders' (2009) 11 EJML 235, 239.

[35] See further H Waldrauch, 'Acquisition of Nationality' in R Bauböck, E Ersboll, K Groenendijk, and H Waldrauch (eds), *Acquisition and Loss of Nationality*, vol 1 (Amsterdam University Press 2006) 121, 159–67.

[36] C Joppke, 'Comparative Citizenship: A restrictive turn in Europe?' (2008) 2(1) Law and Ethics of Human Rights 1, 7.

[37] ibid, 11.

[38] *Biao v Denmark* App No 38590/10 (ECHR, 25 March 2014).

privileged than that account assumes, having lost previous privileges. Moreover, as is explored further below, the Strasbourg jurisprudence does not vindicate the right of residence of insiders as it permits States to require even their own citizens and long-settled denizens to live elsewhere in order to enjoy family life with foreigners.

To illustrate this approach, consider the early case of *Sorabjee v UK*,[39] the former European Commission of Human Rights declared the applicant's Article 8 complaint inadmissible. The mother of a three-year-old was facing deportation from the UK to Kenya. Given the applicant's young age, it was found that she could move with her mother and be expected to adapt to the change in environment. Her British citizenship was irrelevant. In recent cases, the nationality of children has played a role, but only as a part of an all-things-considered assessment. Consider the Grand Chamber ruling in *Jeunesse v Netherlands*,[40] discussed in Chapter 3. The case concerned Meriam Jeunesse, a Surinamese national, whose presence in the Netherlands had been irregular since she outstayed the forty-five-day tourist visa granted to her in 1997. She had made many attempts to regularize her migration status, so she was aware, as the ECtHR put it, of its 'precariousness'.[41] She had married a Dutch national and they had three children, all of whom were Dutch. The family had lived together in the Netherlands for sixteen years, and the children had never been to Suriname. Nonetheless, the Dutch government argued they could relocate to Suriname without any exceptional hardship, as they were of an adaptable age (13, 8, and 3).[42] The central issue concerned the positive obligations under Article 8 ECHR to regularize Meriam's presence in the Netherlands.[43] In assessing whether a 'fair balance' had been struck between the right to family life, the Court took into account nationality, best interests, and the impact on family life of moving to Suriname. On nationality, emphasis was placed not only to the nationality of the children, but also that Meriam was Dutch at birth.[44] It was also noted that the Netherlands 'tolerated her presence for a long time', that she was a homemaker and primary caregiver, and that the children had never been to Suriname. Based on this 'all things considered' assessment, the Court found a violation of Article 8.[45]

The ECtHR approach contrasts sharply with that of EU law, which assumes that in general the EU Citizen's right of residence entails rights of residence for the family in the self-same territory. Yet, EU rights are enjoyed by 'insiders' (EU Citizens) only under certain circumstances, namely when they fall within the material scope of EU protections. Formerly, this scope was defined mainly by the exercise of transnational free movement rights within the EU, leaving static EU Citizens' family reunion regulated by domestic law. The background of domestic restriction

[39] *Sorabjee v UK* [1996].

[40] *Jeunesse v Netherlands* App No 12738/10 (Grand Chamber, ECHR, 3 October 2014).

[41] ibid, para 113. [42] ibid, para 92.

[43] ibid, para 105, citing *Ahmut v the Netherlands* App No 21702/93 (ECHR, 28 November 1996) and *Butt v Norway* App no 47017/09 (ECHR, 4 December 2012).

[44] ibid, para 115. The Court stated that as a result her position was not 'on a par with that of other potential immigrants who have never held Netherlands nationality.'

[45] ibid. Three judges dissented: Judges Villiger, Mahoney, and Silvis expressed a joint dissenting opinion.

helps explain EU governments' reluctance to include static EU Citizens as sponsors under the FRD, and their resistance to the application of the Citizenship Directive to first admissions and internal situations, as exemplified in the jurisprudential wrangles from *Akrich*[46] to *Metock* and from *Zambrano*,[47] *McCarthy*,[48] and *Dereci*[49] explored below. It is noteworthy that in *Jeunesse v Netherlands*, the EU material was considered, and *Zambrano* cited. Indeed, one of the interveners explicitly argued that the ECHR protections should be interpreted to reach the same level as EU law.[50] However, the Court rejected this argument, maintaining its less protective 'all things considered' method.

## 2. Connection between sponsor and family members: The role of immigration law in producing family separation

Migration of family members takes many forms, with different entitlements granted to different categories of sponsors. Any generalization about immigration laws immediately runs up against their complex stratified nature. Bracketing out this complexity for purposes of exposition, a contrast may be drawn between approaches to family migration under temporary and settlement migration systems.

Under temporary migration systems, the migrant is usually expected to be single and child-free, or leave her family behind and return to her country of origin at the expiry of the temporary stay. European countries run mainly temporary migration systems, with few initial family rights for the migrant.[51] If at all, temporary migrants may only seek to have their 'trailing family' join them after a significant period. Migration status tends to vary according to skills levels, a stratification also reflected in EU law. The highly skilled Blue Card holder may bring her family with her to the EU, the Seasonal Worker not.[52] Family reunification emerges as an epiphenomenon, not only of other forms of migration but of migration law itself.[53] In contrast, legal admission of the entire family unit from the outset is a rarity, as few EU countries offer settlement migration programmes even for the highest skilled

46 Case C-109/01 *Secretary of State for the Home Department v Hacene Akrich* [2003] ECR I-09607.
47 *Zambrano* (n 9).
48 Case C-434/09 *McCarthy v Secretary of State for the Home Department* [2011] ECR I-03375.
49 Case C-256/11 *Murat Dereci and Others v Bundesministerium für Inneres* [2011] ECR I-11315.
50 In its intervention, the Immigrant Council of Ireland advocated for coherence on European family reunification principles, arguing that the Court should ensure that the level of human rights protection under the Convention was at least equal to the level of protection afforded by EU law without preventing the Court from giving a more extensive human rights protection than was guaranteed under EU law. See *Jeunesse* (n 40) para 99.
51 S Castles, 'Guestworkers in Europe: A Resurrection?' (2006) 40 International Migration Review 741.
52 Council Directive 2009/50/EC of 25 May 2009 on the conditions of entry and residence of third-country nationals for the purposes of highly qualified employment (Blue Card Directive) [2009] OJ L155/17; Council Directive 2014/36/EU of 26 February 2014 on the conditions of entry and stay of third-country nationals for the purpose of employment as seasonal workers (Seasonal Workers Directive) [2014] OJ L94/375.
53 See further, E Kofman, 'Female "Birds of passage" a decade later: gender and immigration in the European Union' (1999) 33 International Migration Review 269.

immigrants. Settlement migration typically offers entire families residency status. In traditional countries of immigration, Australia, Canada, and the US, such migration has been encouraged and a wider range of family members accepted.[54]

As will be seen, the Strasbourg Court generally assumes the voluntary nature of migrants' family separation, obscuring the role of immigration laws in producing family separation. In the earlier case law in particular, even refugees and those protected from removal for refugee-like reasons found their claims to be joined by minor children rejected on the basis that they were responsible for the initial separation. In sharp contrast, EU Citizens' residence rights are relatively secure and they may have their families join them at any stage. Family formation and reunification are in effect treated as equivalent rights under the EU free movement law, as seen in the case law on the Citizenship Directive. However, for TCN sponsors, the FRD permits various waiting periods and the like which in effect require family members to be left behind. Notably, family members of EU Blue Card holders are exempted from some of the restrictive requirements of the FRD, reflecting the privileged status of those highly-skilled migrants.[55]

## III. ECHR on Family Migration

### 1. Strasbourg's statist assumption

Strasbourg's case law is informed by the statist assumption. The ECtHR repeatedly asserts that:

> a State is entitled, as a matter of well-established international law and subject to its treaty obligations, to control the entry of aliens into its territory and their residence there. The Convention does not guarantee the right of an alien to enter or to reside in a particular country.[56]

The statist assumption, it will be recalled, treats immigration control as the State's right. In the Strasbourg formulation, the State's right is 'subject to its treaty obligations', which presumably include the ECHR itself. However, rather than simply assert that human rights obligations thereby limit immigration control, the ECtHR attempts to reconcile the two (immigration control and human rights obligations) using various devices, which, I suggest, obscure rather than reveal the manner in which migration control bears down both on migrants and insiders.

As Section 2 explores, Article 8(1) permits settled migrants to resist removal, or seek regularization in recognition of their *de facto* ties with host countries.

[54] See further E Kofman, 'Family-Related Migration: A Critical Review of European Studies' (2004) 30 Journal of Ethnic and Migration Studies 243.

[55] Blue Card Directive, Art 15.

[56] See, e.g., *Omoregie v Norway* [2008] ECHR 761, para 54, citing 'among many other authorities'; *Abdulaziz* (n 34) para 67; *Boujlifa v France* (1997) 25 EHRR 686, para 42.

This recognition of connection between the migrant and the host State remains precarious though. Section 3 illustrates the State's justification of removal under Article 8(2), wherein the ECtHR employs a multi-factor balancing test, rather than its typical mode of proportionality assessment. As Section 4 explains, the statist assumption means that some family migration issues, particular family formation migration, do not even raise infringements under Article 8(1), the ECtHR rather finding that refusing admission is the State's permitted default position. Refusal to admit, particularly of spouses, is regarded as an interference with human rights only exceptionally if families cannot relocate together to enjoy family life elsewhere. This feature of the case law I refer to as the 'elsewhere' test or approach.[57]

The cases considered deal variously with first admissions, refusals to renew residence permits, requests for readmission of family members who have temporarily left the host country, and actual removals. While we might expect to find a difference in treatment between admission and removal, in *Gül*,[58] the ECtHR refused to draw a sharp distinction between the negative obligation not to deport, and the positive obligation to admit.[59] It stated that:

> the boundaries between the State's positive and negative obligations under [Article 8] do not lend themselves to precise definition. The applicable principles are nonetheless similar. In both cases, regard must be had to the fair balance that has to be struck between the competing interests of the individual and of the community as a whole; and in both contexts the State enjoys a certain margin of appreciation.[60]

This approach seems to explain the assessment of the entire issue under Article 8(1), rather than raising distinct issues of interference (8(1)) and justification (8(2)) in turn. It reflects the statist assumption that refusing admission does not normally require justification. In addition, Spijkerboer suggests that this integration of positive and negative obligations means the Court avoids having to articulate clear principles, with the result of its 'anti-formal attitude' that it tends to 'assess the facts of each case separately, and minimise the precedential value of its judgments'.[61]

The following sections provide what is, of necessity, a fact-laden account of the Strasbourg jurisprudence, highlighting both the fault-lines in the structure of analysis and the inconsistent outcomes.

[57] For an overview, see S Peers, 'Family Reunion and Community Law' in N Walker (ed), *Towards an Area of Freedom, Security and Justice* (OUP 2004) 143.

[58] *Gül v Switzerland* (1996) 22 EHRR 93.

[59] It is notable that the UK Supreme Court in *Quila* (Lord Wilson, giving the leading judgment) concluded that the distinction between a State's positive obligation to allow applicants to reunite with their British spouses and its negative obligation not to expel a foreign national was 'elusive' and should be abandoned. *R (Quila and Others) v Secretary of State for the Home Department* [2011] UKSC 45, para 43.

[60] *Gül*, para 38, reiterated in *Dragi and Martina Pejcinoski v Austria* App No 33500/96 (ECHR, 23 March 1999; *Yash Priya v Denmark* App No 13594/03 (ECHR, 6 July 2006).

[61] T Spijkerboer, 'Structural Instability: Strasbourg Case Law on Children's Family Reunion' (2009) 11 EJML 271, 291.

## 2. Article 8 ECHR: Connection between migrant and host state—A recapitulation

The Strasbourg case law embodies an uneasy tension between acknowledging the State's rights to set the terms of admission, and recognizing the moral significance of enduring presence. Article 8 ECHR permits settled migrants to resist removal, or seek a form of regularization in recognition of the *de facto* ties with host countries. Initially, the ECtHR only recognized the rupturing of family ties in the country of residence as preventing removal. However, it recently recognized that the various connections and relationships of long-term residents in the country of residence warrant protection as 'private life' irrespective of whether family ties have been developed.[62] The Grand Chamber confirmed in *Üner* that in assessing the impact of removal, or refusal to renew residence permission, 'the totality of social ties between settled migrants and the community in which they are living constitute part of the concept of "private life" within the meaning of Article 8.'[63]

As was explored in Chapter 2, a further recent development is acknowledgement that a State's failure to provide a secure right of residence may itself violate Article 8 ECHR,[64] in effect meaning that irregular migrants may invoke Article 8 ECHR to regularize their stay. These cases seem to suggest a new approach, in particular when children are involved. However, children are not a trump card. While their best interests may tilt the balance decisively against removal of a parent (as may be seen in *Nunez v Norway*[65] and *Kaplan v Norway*[66]), in other cases, in particular where the parent's residence has always been irregular, and there are no exceptional circumstances, migration control will trump the rights of the child. This deference to the State's prerogative to authorize entry and presence remains the dominant theme, as exemplified in *Omoregie v Norway* and *Antwi v Norway*,[67] cases discussed at length in Section 4.

There is a body of case law concerning migrants who commit criminal offences, in particular assessing whether deportation is permitted in order to 'prevent disorder or crime'. The ECtHR set out criteria in *Boultif v Switzerland* for assessing the justifiability of removal under Article 8(2) where the migrant has committed criminal offences.[68] The criteria are:

- the nature and seriousness of the offence committed by the applicant;
- the length of the applicant's stay in the country from which he or she is to be expelled;

[62] *Slivenko v Latvia* App No 48321/99 (ECHR, 9 October 2003).

[63] *Üner v the Netherlands* (2007) 45 EHRR 421, para 59. For comments, see P Boeles and M Bruins, (2005) 7 EJML 321; C Steinorth, '*Üner v the Netherlands:* Expulsion of Long-Term Immigrants and the Right to Respect for Private and Family Life' (2008) 8 HRLRev 185.

[64] See the discussion in Chapter 2 of *Mendizabal v France* App No 51431/99 (ECHR, 17 January 2006); *Rodrigues da Silva/Hoogkamer v the Netherlands* App No 50435/99 (ECHR, 31 January 2006); *Sisojeva* et al *v Latvia* App No 60654/00 (ECHR, 16 June 2005), (Grand Chamber, ECHR, 15 January 2007); *Jeunesse v the Netherlands* (n 40).

[65] *Nunez v Norway* App No 55597/09 (ECHR, 28 June 2011).

[66] *Kaplan and others v Norway* App No 32504/11 (ECHR, 24 July 2014).

[67] *Antwi and others v Norway* App No 26940/10 (ECHR, 14 February 2012).

[68] *Boultif v Switzerland* App No 54273/00 (ECHR, 2 August 2001) para 40.

- the time elapsed since the offence was committed and the applicant's conduct during that period;
- the nationalities of the various persons concerned;
- the applicant's family situation, such as the length of the marriage, and other factors expressing the effectiveness of a couple's family life;
- whether the spouse knew about the offence at the time when he or she entered into a family relationship;
- whether there are children of the marriage, and if so, their age; and
- the seriousness of the difficulties which the spouse is likely to encounter in the country to which the applicant is to be expelled.

In *Üner*, the ECtHR added two more:

- the best interests and well-being of the children, in particular the seriousness of the difficulties which any children of the applicant are likely to encounter in the country to which the applicant is to be expelled; and
- the solidity of social, cultural, and family ties with the host country and with the country of destination.[69]

These criteria reflect the 'family life elsewhere' approach we have already seen under Article 8(1). In practice, the criteria require the home spouse to demonstrate that she would not easily adapt to life in her spouse's country of origin. *Boultif* concerned Abdelouahab Boultif, the Algerian husband of a Swiss woman. After three years of living in Switzerland, Mr Boultif was sentenced to two years' imprisonment for criminal offences but released early for good behaviour and then found a job. The immigration authorities refused to renew his permit and later ordered him to leave the country. The ECtHR found that his wife could not be expected to follow her husband, as she did not speak Arabic, did not know her in-laws, and had never been to Algeria, so Mr Boultif's removal was held to violate Article 8 ECHR. In *Amrollahi*,[70] when applying the *Boultif* criteria, although the offence in question (drug trafficking) was accepted as serious,[71] the ECtHR also took into account that the Danish wife was not a Muslim and did not speak Persian,[72] where return to Iran was at issue.

The position of long-settled and second generation immigrants has long been of concern to the ECtHR.[73] However, despite a prompt from the Council of Europe's political institutions,[74] the ECtHR has resisted endorsing any bright-line

[69] *Üner* (n 63) para 58.

[70] *Amrollahi v Denmark* App No 56811/00 (ECHR, 11 July 2002).

[71] ibid, para 37.

[72] ibid, para 39.

[73] See, e,g, *Moustaquim v Belgium* (1991) EHRR 802 (the applicant had lived in Belgium since the age of 2); *Mehemi v France No 1* App No 85/1996/704/896 (ECHR, 26 September 1997); *Beldjoudi v France* (1992) EHRR 801 (the applicant argued that he was *de facto* French, not Algerian, being born in France of parents who too regarded themselves as French).

[74] Council of Europe Committee of Ministers, *Recommendation concerning the security of residence of long-term migrants*, Rec(2000)15; Council of Europe Parliamentary Assembly, *Non-expulsion of long-term immigrants*, Recommendation 1504 (2001).

proposition precluding their removal. In *Üner*, the ECtHR clarified that Article 8 '[did] not confer to persons who were born in a member State an absolute right not to be expelled from the territory of that State'.[75] Accordingly, protection from expulsion remains somewhat attenuated. Post-*Üner*, the ECtHR has permitted the removal of second generation immigrants, as exemplified by *Kilic*[76] and *Kaya*.[77]

Hizir Kilic was born and lived his entire life in Denmark. However, the ECtHR also emphasized that he had strong ties with his ancestral home, Turkey, as he spoke Turkish, had some extended family there, and visited every two years.[78] In light of the serious offences he had committed, removal was permitted. Erkan Kaya was born and lived his entire life in Germany, visiting his ancestral home in Turkey only two or three times during his holidays. The ECtHR accepted that the offences he committed were sufficiently grave to justify his removal from Germany. The ECtHR's assessment of the solidity of Mr Kaya's ties with Germany also warrants particular attention. Despite living, studying, and working in Germany for all of his life, he was not fully integrated. In particular, the ECtHR mentioned that 'in spite of having completed his vocational training as a car-mechanic, had not integrated into the labour market, but lived for a certain period of time from the earnings he had forcefully extorted from his former partner.[79] The ECtHR also observed that the applicant had not applied for naturalization.[80] The separate Concurring Opinion of Judge Rozakis emphasized that the intention of *Üner* was to acknowledge that 'a long-term immigrant who was born in a State Party has the *right* not to be expelled from that State, a right which is part and parcel of the more general right to private and family life enshrined in Article 8 of the Convention.'[81]

*Üner, Kilic, Kaya*, and *Chair v Germany*[82] suggest that the gravity of the offences seems to be a decisive criterion, capable of justifying removal of even the most settled migrant pursuant to Article 8(2). If the offence is sufficiently serious, the ECtHR is likely to downplay the connections between the migrant and the host State. Two notable cases in which removal was precluded are *Sezen v The Netherlands*[83] and *Maslov v Austria*.[84] In *Sezen*, the ECtHR refuted the Dutch authority's factual assessment, including its assessment of the father's misconduct. In the four-year period since committing the offence and the decision to remove, the applicant had not reoffended. Yuri Maslov's infractions were characterized as 'acts of juvenile delinquency',[85] so the Grand Chamber found that the 'very serious reasons... required to justify expulsion' of a 'settled migrant who has lawfully spent all or the major part of his or her childhood and youth in the host country' were not met.[86] In addition, Maslov had only visited his country of origin, Bulgaria,

[75] *Üner* (n 63) paras 55–56.
[76] *Kilic v Denmark* App No 20277/05 (ECHR, 22 January 2007).
[77] *Kaya v Germany* App No 31753/02 (ECHR, 28 June 2007).
[78] *Kilic* (n 76) para 6. [79] *Kaya* (n 77) para 64. [80] ibid.
[81] ibid. Separate Concurring Opinion, para 3, citing *Üner* (n 63) para 55.
[82] *Chair v Germany* App No 69735/01 (ECHR, 6 December 2007).
[83] *Sezen v The Netherlands* App No 50252/99 (ECHR, 31 January 2006). See further, P Boeles and M Bruins, 'Case Reports of the European Court of Human Rights' (2006) 8 EJML 357, 367–70.
[84] *Maslov v Austria* (2008) 47 EHRR 20. [85] ibid, para 81.
[86] ibid, para 75.

twice. The divided Grand Chamber (4:3) found removal to be a disproportionate interference. The Court has also found removal incompatible with Article 8 in *Omojudi v UK*[87] and *Khan v UK*.[88]

## 3. Article 8 ECHR: Connection between sponsor and family members

### *i. Cases concerning couples and spouses*

Concerning spouses, the case law explicitly privileges the State's admission control prerogatives over individual autonomy in the choice of life-partner. The case of *Abdulaziz* remains the leading authority in spite of subsequent developments in other areas of ECHR case law that could open it up to question. The ECtHR expressly rejected any 'general obligation…to respect the choice by married couples of the country of their matrimonial residence and to accept the non-national spouses for settlement in that country'.[89] This proposition applied even though the sponsors were clearly 'insiders', nationals, or long-settled denizens of the UK. In effect, the responsibility to develop family life together falls on the sponsor rather than on the State. In a trope that remains dominant in spousal cases today, the ECtHR held that their awareness that the State might refuse admission to the husbands undermined any claim to family life together in the UK. The applicants in *Abdulaziz* were three lawfully and permanently settled residents of the UK who were precluded under the Immigration Rules in force at the time from having their husbands join them in the UK. In contrast, men were permitted to have their wives join them. The government described the policy as aiming to protect the domestic labour market and maintain 'public tranquillity'. As well as rejecting the claim based on Article 8 alone, the Court also rejected the argument that the rules discriminated on racial grounds. Before exploring these discrimination arguments, it is important to identify one of the particular consequences of the 'elsewhere approach' in practice.

Under the 'elsewhere approach', divorced or separated parents tended to find it easier to show that both parents' moving to one parent's country of origin is impossible.[90] *Berrehab* illustrates this phenomenon: given the divorce, there was no consideration of whether the entire family could relocate.[91] However, later similar cases have played out differently, revealing unexplained gendered assumptions concerning caring obligations. Contrast *Rodrigues da Silva* and *Useinov*,[92] decided only months apart.[93] The former case concerned a non-custodial mother actively caring for her child, the latter a non-custodial father

[87] *Omojudi v UK* (2009) 51 EHRR 10.
[88] *A W Khan v UK* App No 474/86/06 (ECHR, 12 January 2010).
[89] *Abdulaziz* (n 34) para 68.
[90] See S van Walsum, 'Against All Odds: How Single and Divorced Migrant Mothers were Eventually Able to Claim Their Right to Respect for Family Life' (2009) 11 EJML 295.
[91] *Berrehab v the Netherlands* (1988) EHRR 322.
[92] *Useinov v the Netherlands* App No 61292/00 (ECHR, 11 April 2006).
[93] Albeit by different chambers, Second cf Third.

taking care of his child four days a week. The mother was allowed to stay, while the father was amenable to deportation. The underlying assumption seems to be that the mother in *Useinov* would be expected to follow the father to his home in the FYR of Macedonia, whereas no such expectation would be imposed on the father in *da Silva*.[94] Similarly in *Nunez*, the mother gets to stay, in spite of her various immigration law infractions. In addition, the ECtHR emphasized that Useinov could return to the FYR of Macedonia and the distance between it and the Netherlands 'was not so great as to render contacts between the applicant and his children virtually impossible'.[95] The care of the father is characterized as adequately provided from a distance, in contrast to that of the mother. *Nunez* reinforces this impression. Although the ECtHR in *Abdulaziz* condemned sex discrimination in family admissions policies, it seems tacitly to license different treatment of mothers and fathers.

Returning to *Abdulaziz*, the alleged race discrimination was based on the fact that the rules contained an exemption where the wife or fiancée of the intending entrant was born or had a parent born in the United Kingdom, or met the 'United Kingdom ancestry rule', which applied to Commonwealth citizens having a grandparent born in the British Islands.[96] The background to these changes was the status of 'patrial' which permeated UK immigration law since the Commonwealth Immigration Act 1962 removed the right of abode in the UK from most Commonwealth citizens. Instead, it used the notion of 'patriality' to delimit those with a right of abode in the UK, based on their and their immediate antecedents' birth in the British Islands. The Court regarded these provisions as being exceptions designed for the benefit of persons having close links with the United Kingdom, which did not affect the general tenor of the rules. Excluding would-be migrants entailed inherent distinctions, and any indirect discrimination arising out of that differentiation was treated as acceptable. The fact that the rules had an impact mainly on New Commonwealth and Pakistani migrants was deemed not to flow from the rules, but rather from the composition of the population wishing to migrate. However, missing from the analysis is indirect discrimination. The race discrimination analysis in *Abdulaziz* predates the development of a proper indirect discrimination jurisprudence in Strasbourg.

Nonetheless, *Abdulaziz* remains the leading authority, and was relied upon in the reasoning in *Biao v Denmark*.[97] *Biao* concerns the highly restrictive Danish family reunification policies.[98] The Court, in a 4:3 Chamber judgment, which will go the Grand Chamber,[99] found that the Danish authorities had struck a fair balance between the immigration control and the applicants' interests under Article

[94] de Hart (n 34) 245.

[95] *Useinov* (n 92) para 9.

[96] Being the United Kingdom, the Channel Islands, and the Isle of Man.

[97] *Biao* (n 38).

[98] According to MIPEX III, Denmark is second only to Ireland in terms of the restrictiveness of its family reunification policies. See T Huddleston, J Niessen, E Chaoimh, and E White, *Migrant Integration Policy Index III (MIPEX III)* (British Council and Migration Policy Group 2011) 14–15.

[99] ECtHR, 'Grand Chamber Panel's Decisions' *ECHR Press Release 250* (9 September 2014).

8 ECHR, and that there was no unlawful discrimination under Article 14 ECHR. Ousmane Biao was a naturalized Danish citizen of Ghanaian origin. Seeking a residence permit in Denmark on family grounds was his wife, Asia, also Ghanaian. The Danish authorities refused the application, on the basis that they did not meet the requirement set out in Danish law that they must not have stronger ties with another country, Ghana in the applicants' case, than with Denmark, the so-called 'attachment requirement'. They argued that this requirement violated their Article 8 ECHR right and, in addition, argued they were discriminated against on grounds of race, ethnicity, and 'other status', as this requirement was not imposed on Danish citizens by birth or those who had held Danish citizenship for at least twenty-eight years.

The Court characterized the refusal to grant admission to Asia as an alleged breach a positive obligation.[100] The Court summarized its previous case law, reiterating the 'insurmountable obstacles' aspect of the 'elsewhere approach'; immigration control factors; and considerations of public order. It also treated as 'another important consideration' 'whether family life was created at a time when the persons involved were aware that the immigration status of one of them was such that the persistence of that family life within the host State would from the outset be precarious', confirming that in these circumstances, only in 'exceptional circumstances' will the right to live together prevail.[101] The Court noted the first applicant's enduring ties with Togo (his previous country of nationality) and Ghana, where he resided for fifteen years from the age of six to twenty-one, and where he attended school for ten years. It was on one of his four visits back to Ghana that he met and married Asia.[102] She was born and raised in Ghana, and had never visited Denmark before her marriage. After her spousal visa application was refused, Asia entered Denmark on a tourist visa, and subsequently moved to Sweden (presumably to secure the EU rights to reside together in another EU Member State, and that of their later born Danish son).[103] In this case, the issue of the applicants' awareness of migration control was also operative, and the Court emphasized that they must have been aware of the 'attachment requirement' when they married.[104] Accordingly, the Court found no violation of Article 8.

Concerning the discrimination arguments, the Court pointed out that as Ousmane acquired Danish citizenship when he was 31, according to the twenty-eight-year rule, he would not gain the right to family reunification until he turned 59. The Danish Supreme Court was divided over this issue, as was the ECtHR. Following the effective lead of the Danish Supreme Court, the ECtHR held that the distinction between Danish-born and naturalized citizens was not indirect discrimination on grounds of ethnic origin, citing *Abdulaziz*. However, the distinction based on the length of time since naturalization was accepted as discrimination on the basis of 'other status' under Article 14 ECHR. As to whether that difference in treatment was objectively and reasonably justified, the Court again referred to

100 *Biao* (n 38) para 52. 101 ibid, para 53. 102 ibid, para 55.
103 ibid, para 56. 104 ibid, para 57.

*Abdulaziz*, accepting that there were 'in general persuasive social reasons for giving special treatment to those who have strong ties with a country, whether stemming from birth within it or from being a national or a long-term resident'.[105] On this basis alone, it accepted that the twenty-eight-year rule pursued a legitimate aim. As to proportionality, the Court appeared to take the view that twenty-eight years might be excessively strict, making the chances of reunification 'almost illusory' for some. However, it pulled its punch at this point and refused to 'review the legislation in the abstract' instead (as the dissenters put it) engaging in a double legal fiction by only examining its impact on the couple in question and only in 2004.

The separate opinions reveal the split within the Court turns on different views of its judicial review functions. While the concurring opinion of Judges Raimondi and Spano maintains that the majority has gone too far in criticizing the law in the abstract, even opining that that the three paragraphs noting the discriminatory impact of the law should not have been included.[106] In contrast, the powerful Dissenting Opinion of Judges Sajó, Vučinič, and Kūris, starts with the assertion that the majority had 'confined' its analysis excessively.[107] In particular, they recall the breakthrough analysis on indirect discrimination in *DH and Others*,[108] a case where Strasbourg was influenced by the EU's highly evolved jurisprudence on that topic. The dissenters noted that the majority treats the twenty-eight-year rule as an exception, rather than one of the only two ways in which family reunion for naturalized citizens may be achieved.[109] The essence of indirect discrimination analysis was that it looks at the impact of laws and policies on groups, not just individuals,[110] and seeks to scrutinize the impact of stereotypes on minority groups.[111] When distinctions between citizens are at issue, the Court raises the spectre of 'second-class citizenship', a phenomenon it describes as 'impossible' for Article 14 ECHR to permit.[112] In this move, it treats discrimination between citizens as a presumptively suspicious form of differentiation. As to the grounds of that indirect discrimination, the Court noted that while justification was normally permissible, indirect discrimination based to a 'decisive extent'[113] on ethnic or national origin is not open to justification.[114] In the main substantive point of divergence from the majority, the dissenters took the view that the twenty-eight-year rule was in effect indirect discrimination on ethnic grounds, in that 'naturalised immigrants who are, predominantly, of different ethnic or national origin or belong to ethnic groups different from ethnic Danes, are treated differently from the latter'.[115] They note the silence of the majority on this point. As regards the differentiation between citizens, they noted that the *Gaygusuz*[116]

[105] ibid, para 94. [106] ibid, paras 99–102.
[107] ibid. Dissenting Opinion of Judges Sajó, Vučinič, and Kūris, para 1.
[108] *DH and Others v the Czech Republic* (2008) 47 EHRR 3.
[109] *Biao* (n 38). Dissenting Opinion of Judges Sajó, Vučinič, and Kūris, para 4.
[110] ibid, para 7. [111] ibid, para 8. [112] ibid, para 9. [113] ibid, para 13.
[114] ibid, paras 8–9.
[115] ibid, para 11. [116] *Gaygusuz v Austria* (1996) 23 EHRR 364.

ruling and the European Convention on Nationality (ECN)[117] do not allow for different treatment between citizens. National origin was an '"ethnic criterion" in the non-racist sense' so justification was possible,[118] so everything turned on whether there was a 'reasonable and objective justification' for the requirement.

As regards the aim of the measure, the dissenters probed much more deeply than the majority, noting the aim was to discourage the 'widespread marriage pattern [of recently naturalized Danes and other settled migrants] to marry a person from their countries of origin'.[119] The Danish policy reflected an assumption that this reflected a 'lack of integration.' Accordingly, 'the policy reflects and reinforces, albeit indirectly, a negative stereotype',[120] to be treated with the same degree of scepticism as stereotypes based on sex attracted.[121] The policy was deemed to have been based on 'fictional assumptions' about which citizens will have stronger ties to Denmark.

The minority too stated that the Court does not engage in 'constitutional review' of legislation,[122] but rather looks to the application of legislation in individual cases. On that point, too, they find the majority has engaged in a fiction, which they characterize as treating '2004 as "the end of time"', when the final Supreme Court decision was in 2010, and the decision was in 2014. The couple and their son continue to live in Sweden as they cannot live in Denmark. Under the Danish law, that state of affairs would continue until 2030, at which point the father would be assumed to have sufficiently strong connections with Denmark! Their Danish son also, if he married a non-Dane, would also be effectively precluded from returning to Denmark until he was twenty-eight. The palpable incredulity of the minority is put like this: '[i]magine the level of attachment of that Danish national to Denmark, should he decide to return to Denmark as an adult. This tells us a lot about the "appropriateness" of the means chosen by the legislature to generate attachment.'[123] The conclusion is worth reproducing in full:

> Fictions can prove things otherwise unprovable in a lawyer's writings. As a matter of common sense, however, for a citizen, even if naturalised, to have to wait twenty-eight years for permission to reunite in his country of citizenship is disproportionately, drastically and unjustly far too long and amounts for that human being, and for his spouse, to deprivation of their right to pursuit of happiness. We do not believe that the Convention was meant to endorse such deprivation.[124]

As Ersbøll emphasizes, *Abdulaziz* concerned differences in treatment based on the applicants' birthplace (within or outside the State's borders), while *Biao* concerned

[117] European Convention on Nationality, European Treaty Series No 166, Strasbourg, 6 November 1997. This is a Council of Europe convention, which has been ratified by 20 states (as of 17 September 2014), including Denmark on 24 July 2002.

[118] *Biao* (n 38). Dissenting Opinion of Judges Sajó, Vučinič, and Kūris, para 15.

[119] ibid, see para 29 concerning the preparatory work in respect of the Amendment, and also the Supreme Court minority opinion in para 25.

[120] ibid, para 16. [121] *Konstantin Markin v Russia* (2013) 56 EHRR 8, para 127.

[122] *Biao* (n 38). Dissenting Opinion of Judges Sajó, Vučinič, and Kūris, para 24.

[123] ibid, para 30.

[124] ibid, para 34.

different treatment of citizens based on how and when they have acquired their citizenship status. Article 5(2) ECN specifically establishes that States shall be guided by the principle of non-discrimination between their citizens, whether they are citizens by birth or have acquired their citizenship subsequently.[125] So the centrality of *Abdulaziz* to the reasoning in *Biao* could be seen as inappropriate. Moreover, *Abdulaziz* predates the Strasbourg case law on indirect discrimination. Furthermore, the majority's characterization of the aim of the measure as to privilege those with 'close ties' to Denmark is odd given that the exceptions were designed to cater for Danish expatriates.

It is to be hoped that the Grand Chamber will seize the opportunity to give a more coherent ruling on these policies. Denmark, as Annex 1 explains, is not bound by the FRD. Static Danish citizens, as will be seen, may attempt to invoke EU law via the *Zambrano* route, or fall under the EU Citizenship provisions if they are returning to Denmark from another EU Member State. So if the Biao family chose to return from Sweden, they may invoke EU protections. In the meantime, Strasbourg remains the main port of call.

We see that Article 8 ECHR will only protect spousal rights to live together in exceptional cases. Moreover, procedural barriers to reunion, which are all too common now, have not attracted condemnation in Strasbourg either. In *GR v the Netherlands*, the Court examined allegedly excessively high fees for the regularization of the immigration situation of a foreign spouse under Article 13 ECHR, the right to an effective remedy for breach of ECHR rights.[126] In effect, this means the fees are only challengeable if there is an 'arguable case' that Article 8 ECHR can be established.

### *ii. Cases concerning children—The impact of the 'best interests' standard*

The ECtHR has explicitly tempered the elsewhere test in cases on the admission of children. Initially it required applicants to demonstrate that admission was the 'only way' they could enjoy family life together, but after *Sen v the Netherlands* the requirement was lowered to showing that admission was the 'most adequate way' of developing family life.[127] The early approach is evident in *Gül v Switzerland* and *Ahmut v the Netherlands*.[128] In *Gül*, the fact that a Turkish father had attained a residence permit on humanitarian grounds in Switzerland was not enough to persuade the ECtHR that there were obstacles to him and his wife returning to Turkey in order to enjoy family life with their 12-year-old son. Moreover, the ECtHR stressed that the father had left Turkey, leaving his son behind. The refusal to grant the son permission to join them in Switzerland was thus not an interference with family life. *Ahmut* concerned the treatment of a family of Moroccan origin by the

[125] E Ersbøll, '*Biao v Denmark*: discrimination among citizens' (2014) 79 *EUI Working Paper RSCAS* 14.

[126] *GR v the Netherlands* App No 22251/07 (ECHR, 10 January 2012).

[127] *Sen v the Netherlands* 21 December 2001 (2003) 36 EHRR 7.

[128] *Ahmut v the Netherlands* 28 November 1996 (1997) EHRR 62.

Netherlands. Mr Ahmut left his ex-wife and their children in Morocco in 1986. She died in 1987. At that time, two of the children came to live with Mr Ahmut while two others were entrusted to the care of their paternal grandmother. In 1990, Mr Ahmut, by then a Dutch citizen, applied for permission for the latter two children to come to live in the Netherlands. The Dutch authorities refused, applying the 'effective family bond' criterion, the then Dutch legal requirement (as explored further in Part V below). In 1996, the ECtHR held (5:4) that the refusal had not violated Article 8. The ECtHR took into account the fact that Mr Ahmut's divorce had influenced his decision to move to the Netherlands, that the children had lived in Morocco all their lives, and that Mr Ahmut had not relinquished his Moroccan nationality and so could return there. The powerful dissent of Judge Martens (joined by Judge Lohmus) argued that the father's settled status and Dutch nationality should have been decisive, rendering the availability of alternative care arrangements in Morocco largely irrelevant. The other separate dissents (of Judges Morenilla and Valticos) also stressed his Dutch nationality.

In *Sen v the Netherlands*, a more accommodating approach seemed emergent. The case concerned the admission of a 12-year-old child of Turkish parents who were legally resident in the Netherlands. Mr Sen had lived in the Netherlands since he was 12, returning in 1982 to Turkey to get married there and then returning to the Netherlands leaving his wife in Turkey. In 1986 Mrs Sen moved to the Netherlands also, leaving their 3-year-old daughter with family members. The couple had two further children who were born in the Netherlands. The authorities refused the eldest child's entry on the basis that there was no longer an 'effective family bond' between them. The decisive transformative element in the reasoning was the Strasbourg Court's refusal to draw negative inferences from the parents' decision to leave their eldest child in Turkey. It concluded that the 'best way of developing family life with the family as it existed' would be for that child to be admitted, unanimously finding an Article 8 violation. The decision is unanimous, but ambiguous.[129] While citing *Gül* and *Ahmut* with approval, it nonetheless adopts the position of Judge Marten's dissent in the latter case in distinguishing *Abdulaziz*, by treating family reunification more generously than family formation migration. A key factor seems to have been the fact that the two younger Sen children were born in the Netherlands and had never lived anywhere else. Yet, in *Gül*, there was also a Swiss sibling, whose existence did not figure in the reasoning. The post-*Sen* cases reflect rather than resolve these contradictions.

In *IM*,[130] a Cape Verdean migrant to the Netherlands sought to have her daughter join her after six and a half years.[131] The ECtHR held that there was no obstacle to establishing family life together in Cape Verde, and that as the daughter was at

[129] For discussion, see S van Walsum, 'Comment on the *Sen* Case. How Wide is the Margin of Appreciation Regarding the Admission of Children for Purposes of Family Reunification?' (2002) 4 EJML 1.

[130] *IM v the Netherlands* App No 41226/98 (ECHR, 25 March 2003).

[131] She also had a son in the Netherlands. However, she had not mentioned him during the Dutch proceedings, so the ECtHR held it could not take this into account. See S van Walsum (n 90), 307.

the time of the decision 12, she was no longer 'in need of care as a young child' and could be cared for by relatives in Cape Verde. The ECtHR returned to the tacitly condemnatory trope, regarding the mother's decision to leave her young child behind as a basis for the later refusal of reunification. The ECtHR rejected several similar claims as inadmissible for lack of distinguishing features,[132] suggesting that *Sen* did not herald any significant change, until it found an Article 8 violation in *Tuquabo-Tekle*.[133] The child in question who remained in Eritrea, Mehret, was aged 15 when her parents applied for her to join them in the Netherlands. By that time, she had had been withdrawn from school by her carer, her grandmother, and was vulnerable to being 'married off', although the ECtHR did not regard these protection issues as decisive.[134] Strasbourg decided *Tuquabo-Tekle* when the *FRD Ruling* was pending before the CJEU. The FRD, as will be seen, seemed to allow refusal of family reunification where children were over 15. The Strasbourg ruling seems to have been addressed not only to the Dutch authorities but also to a wider European audience, serving as a reminder that human rights law may require the admission of older children, notwithstanding the minimal rules set out in EU legislation.

A clear fault line in the cases is the ECtHR's characterization of the decision to leave children behind. In *Gül* and *Ahmut*, the ECtHR treats the separation as 'caused' by the parents' decisions to leave.[135] The complex interplay of social forces and the immigration laws of the respondent State is thereby obscured from examination. In contrast in *Sen*, the family's decisions were not held against them and the initial decision to leave children behind was not taken to preclude later reunification.[136] In *Tuquabo-Tekle*, it emphasized that:

> parents who leave children behind while they settle abroad cannot be assumed to have irrevocably decided that those children are to remain in the country of origin permanently and to have abandoned any idea of a future family reunion.[137]

*Omoregie* illustrates that the States' migration control prerogatives will outweigh family life in many instances. Louis Osaze Darren Omoregie was a rejected Nigerian asylum seeker, married to a Norwegian woman, Elisabeth Darren. Together they had a young child, Selma, who had Norwegian nationality. The ECtHR had no difficulty recognizing that his proposed deportation was an interference with family life. Citing *Üner*, the ECtHR stated that the interference had to be necessary in a democratic society, that is, 'justified by a pressing social need and, in particular, proportionate to the aims pursued'.[138] Mr Omoregie had not committed any criminal offences. The state simply relied on its migration control prerogative as

[132] *Ebrahim and Ebrahim v the Netherlands* App No 59186/00 (ECHR, 18 March 2003); *Chandra v the Netherlands*, App No 53102/99 (ECHR, 13 May 2003); *Andradev v the Netherlands* App No 53675/00 (ECHR, 6 July 2004).

[133] *Tuquabo-Tekle v the Netherlands* App No 60665/00 (ECHR, 1 December 2005). See case note by Boeles and Bruins (n 83) 372.

[134] ibid, para 50.

[135] *Gül*, para 41; *Ahmut* (n 128) para 70.

[136] *Sen* (n 127), paras 39–41.

[137] ibid, para 45.

[138] *Omoregie* (n 56) para 56.

embodying a 'pressing social need' justifying removal. The crux of the matter was the ECtHR's view that where family life was created when the persons involved knew of one partner's insecure migration status, no right to family life in the host state arose.[139] The Court accepted the governments' argument that they should not be presented with family life as a '*fait accompli*'[140] that overrides migration control prerogatives.

In contrast, *Nunez v Norway* heralds a further move to vindicate the 'best interests' of children even where this involved precluding the removal of a parent in breach of migration law. Mirtha Nunez was a Dominican national, who first entered Norway in 1996 on a tourist visa. She was deported having been convicted of theft, and re-entered on a different passport in defiance of a two-year ban. She then promptly married a Norwegian national and obtained a residence permit, stating in her application that she had not previously entered Norway. After their divorce, she had two daughters with a settled immigrant of Dominican origin in Norway. The Norwegian government sought to distinguish *Rodriguez da Silva* on the basis that in that case, the applicant would have received a residence permit had she applied for one.[141] They, too, felt that contact between the applicant and her children would remain possible 'for example by the father's arranging for visits in the Dominican Republic during summer and Christmas holidays'.[142] The applicant argued that her violations of immigration law ought not to be treated as of similar gravity to criminal offences.[143] The Court found that at no time had her residence in Norway been lawful,[144] and the expulsion was an appropriate remedy for breach of immigration law, in particular given the aggravated character of the applicant's breaches.[145] She also did not have any reasonable expectation of being able to remain in the country.[146] Nonetheless, the Court held that as expulsion would deprive the children of contact with their mother for two years,[147] and that Norway had not acted promptly in removing her,[148] expulsion with a two-year re-entry ban was disproportionate.

In *Antwi and Others v Norway*,[149] the father Henry was a Ghanaian national facing removal from Norway, where his residence had always been irregular, having been based on forged EU documents. His wife was born and raised in Ghana and now held Norwegian nationality, as did their daughter Nadia by birth. At the time of the decision, Nadia was 10 years old. The ECtHR held that expelling Henry did not violate Article 8 ECHR, nor did the five-year re-entry ban since both he and his wife maintained strong links with Ghana. Nadia, in contrast, spoke Norwegian and had little contact with Ghana. To distinguish *Nunez* from *Antwi*, the Court emphasized the lack of exceptional circumstances in Nadia's case. The Court admitted that while it would be difficult for her to adapt to life in Ghana,[150] it endorsed the assessment of the

[139] ibid, para 57. [140] ibid, para 64.
[141] *Nunez* (n 65), para 37. [142] ibid, para 41. [143] ibid, para 59.
[144] ibid, para 67. [145] ibid, paras 71–72. [146] ibid, para 67.
[147] ibid, para 81. [148] ibid, para 82.
[149] *Antwi and Others v Norway* App No 26940/10 (ECHR, 14 February 2012).
[150] ibid, para 96.

Norwegian High Court in emphasizing that she had no special needs and that her mother would be able to care for her in the event of her father's removal.[151] Recall that in Nunez the mother was facing removal, and the children in question had already experienced the upheaval of moving to the father's primary custody.[152] In addition, there had been no delay on the part of the authorities in *Antwi*, in contrast to *Nunez*.[153] *Antwi* was likened to *Omorogie*, in particular on the duration of the re-entry ban (five years).[154]

In contrast, exceptional circumstances were found in *Kaplan v Norway*. In that case, the youngest child's autism and consequent need for special care was decisive.[155] It was also noted that the authorities had been dilatory in enforcing removal and that the father's infractions of immigration law had not been as egregious as in *Nunez*, although he also had a criminal conviction for aggravated assault which weighed in favour of removal. This case law, turning as it does on findings of 'exceptional circumstances', is inevitably casuistic and unpreditable.

In contrast to cases where children are left in the home country when parents migrate, the Court has also considered cases where children leave the host country and seek readmission. *Osman v Denmark* concerned a teenage Somali girl, Sahro Osman, who was a long-term lawful resident with her family in Denmark.[156] Her father had arranged for her to move from Denmark to care for her elderly grandmother in a refugee camp in Kenya. (She alleged she had effectively been trafficked but this allegation was not properly argued or considered.) After two years, she applied to re-join her family in Denmark but her application was rejected. The Court held that Denmark had breached Article 8. The Court noted that she had spent her formative years in Denmark (from the age of seven to fifteen years old), that she spoke Danish, that she had received schooling there until August 2002, and that all her close family remained there. Accordingly, very serious reasons would be needed to justify the authorities' refusal to restore Sahro's residence permit, which were lacking.

In these cases, much turns on the facts, with often divergent evaluation of the surrounding context. While in *Gül*, the ECtHR treated the father's failed asylum claim as evidence of his voluntary departure, in *Tuquabo-Tekle* the surrounding general conditions were taken into account to explain the mother's decision to leave the child behind, notwithstanding that the mother's asylum claim was also rejected.

## 4. Article 8(2) ECHR and migration control: A scrutinized public interest?

By declining to distinguish between positive and negative duties under Article 8 ECHR, the Court often makes an 'all things considered' assessment of the situation, rather than clearly analyzing the interference with the right under

[151] ibid, para 99.
[152] ibid, para 100, citing *Nunez*, paras 78–81. [153] ibid, para 102.
[154] ibid, para 104. [155] *Kaplan* (n 66) para 98.
[156] *Osman v Denmark* App No 38058/09 (ECHR, 14 June 2011).

Article 8(1), and the State's justification for such interference under Article 8(2). Article 8(2) lists various justificatory grounds: 'national security, public safety or the economic well-being of the country, for the prevention of disorder or crime, for the protection of health or morals, or for the protection of the rights and freedoms of others.'

The ECtHR tends to assume that States pursue a legitimate aim when refusing admission or deporting. Although the ECtHR will not accept bare assertions that removal is necessary for 'national security' reasons,[157] migration control per se is assumed to amount to a legitimate aim. For instance, in *Berrehab*, the ECtHR equated a general immigration law enforcement prerogative with concern for population density and labour market regulation, which in turn fell under the aim of the 'preservation of the country's economic well-being'.[158] In cases where migrants have never been afforded a stable right of residence, the ECtHR seems to treat migration control as a 'pressing social need' in itself. When the State is not required to articulate the aim of its actions clearly, the proportionality assessment is weakened. One of the difficulties is that deportation is sometimes viewed as the inevitable requirement for immigration laws to be meaningful. However, as discussed in Chapter 2, it cannot be assumed in all cases of irregular or insecure migration status that deportation is the legally appropriate response. Rather, rule of law arguments may militate in favour of regularization of migrants with insecure statuses.[159]

*Omoregie* exemplifies the migration control approach. Although Mr Omoregie was a rejected asylum seeker, the Court emphasized that when family life was created, the persons involved knew of one partner's unstable migration status.[160] The asylum seeker is treated not as someone who might be recognized as a refugee but rather as someone whose right to stay should be acknowledged as temporary from the outset. On the facts, the ECtHR found that the couple were aware of his precarious status, although when the couple met and later started to live together, the applicant was awaiting a first instance decision on his asylum claim. They married later when his claim had been definitively rejected.[161] The ECtHR defers to the statist assumption here and rejects such claims where they appear to amount to presenting the State with a '*fait accompli*'.[162] The assessment of whether family life could be continued in Nigeria appears almost as an addendum. The decisiveness of the issue of migration status is revealed in the diametrically opposing separate opinions. The Concurring Opinion of Judge Jebens is even harsher than the majority in that he argues that no rights accrue to asylum seekers: due to their 'unlawful residence' they have no 'reasonable or legitimate expectations that they could enjoy family life in Norway'. In sharp contrast, the Dissenting Opinion of

[157] *CG and Others v Bulgaria* App No 1365/07 (ECHR, 24 April 2008) para 49.

[158] *Berrehab* (n 91) para 26. Concerning divorced couples, see further *Ciliz v the Netherlands* App No 29192/95 (ECHR, 11 July 2000).

[159] See, discussion in Chapter 2 of A Ellerman, 'The Rule of Law and The Right to Stay: The Moral Claims of Undocumented Migrants' (2014) 42 Politics & Society 293.

[160] *Omoregie* (n 56) para 57. [161] ibid, para 59. [162] ibid, para 64.

Judge Malinverni (joined by Judge Kovler) stressed the issue of proportionality. The applicant had not committed a criminal offence but merely breached immigration law. For the dissenting judges this act was 'purely administrative and in no sense criminal', so the State's justification was weak. *Antwi* also reflects the primacy of migration control, in that instance under very different circumstances. There, it will be recalled that the father had always resided irregularly, based on a forged EU passport. In contrast, in *Omoregie*, the rejected asylum-seeker is treated similarly to the person who has evaded migration control by deceptive means from the outset.

In contrast, in *Nunez, Kaplan,* and *Jeunesse*, exceptional circumstances were identified. In all three cases, the States' delay in acting to remove irregular migrants weighed against ultimate removal. Most important though was the identified distinguishing circumstances of the children: in *Nunez*, that they had already experienced upheaval in moving to the father's custody; in *Kaplan*, the child's autism and consequent special needs. Again, the cases turn on distinguishing facts, rather than principles. The multi-factor approach produces much uncertainty.

## 5. Comments on the Strasbourg jurisprudence

With the *Üner* recognition that all migrants develop a private life in the host State over time, some of the vagaries of the previous Article 8 case law pertaining to settled migrants have been addressed. However, in refusing to draw any bright line propositions, security of residence remains elusive. The multifactor test under Article 8 fails to provide an appropriate metric for the evaluation of the gravity of the interference with individual autonomy entailed in removal. A particular drawback is the ECtHR's tendency to treat connections between the home and host country as zero-sum, 'privileging unidirectional migration and exclusive forms of belonging'.[163] The migrant who retains links with her ancestral or home country will be deemed not to be enduring much of a rights-interference in being removed, a factual assumption that belies increasing migrant transnationalism.[164]

Even if the sponsor can establish his or her connections with the host State, the Article 8(1) case law reveals that refusal of entry for family members is usually regarded as the acceptable default position under the 'elsewhere approach'. The State is not required to offer any particular, individual justification for its refusal. The admission-seeker is treated as placing herself subject to the State's beneficence. One resultant strand of cases treats migrants as if they were consenting to being mere objects of the State's control, rather than autonomous subjects. Evidently, this approach sits uneasily in a human rights context, so other cases tend to accept migrants' agency and scrutinize the State's prerogatives more closely. *Abdulaziz*

[163] A Farahat, 'The Exclusiveness of Inclusion: On the Boundaries of Human Rights in Protecting Transnational and Second Generation Migrants' (2009) 11 EJML 253, 258.

[164] The European Commission has long acknowledged that the 'Changing nature of migration itself which has become a much more flexible process of movement between countries rather than simply a one-way flow. Globally, migratory movements change direction, rise and fall depending on the evolution of the economic and demographic situations both in receiving and sending countries.' See European Commission, *Communication on a Community Immigration Policy*, COM(2000) 757, 13.

remains the decisive ruling on the admission of spouses of insiders: there is no duty to admit, and couples cannot generally rely on family life created when migration status was irregular or precarious. In assessing the viability of family life elsewhere, as *Boultif* and *Amrollahi* illustrate, the insider spouse must 'exoticize' or 'orientalize' the spouse's country of origin in order to demonstrate that there are obstacles to establishing family life there. The settled spouse's connection with his or her home State tends to be obscured in this assessment, and consequently the gravity of interfering with his or her choice of country of residence diminished.[165]

*Abdulaziz* avoided difficult questions concerning when the differentiation intrinsic in migration control should be regarded as indirectly on grounds of race, ethnicity, or national origin. As the sex discrimination was overt in that case, the focus on attention on that ground seems understandable. Moreover the ruling predates the relatively recent development of an indirect discrimination case law by the ECtHR. Therefore, the 4:3 ruling in *Biao* is all the more disappointing, for its failure to question the discriminatory impact of the rules in question. Moreover, the majority did not properly identify or interrogate the aim of the measure. We await the Grand Chamber ruling.

Concerning admission of children, the shift from *Ahmut* and *Gül* to *Sen* and *Tuquabo-Tekle* turns on the Strasbourg Court's acceptance that migration decisions in the later cases are treated as worthy of recognition as part of family autonomy, whereas in the earlier jurisprudence they are treated as tantamount to voluntary subjugation to the receiving State's immigration control *dictat*.

*Omoregie* and *Antwi* suggested that migration status is sometimes decisive, yet *Nunez, Kaplan,* and *Jeunesse* demonstrate a strong commitment to ensure that the children's best interests are vindicated. Recall that in *Omoregie*, the migrant had committed no crime, yet the State's generic migration control prerogatives were taken to amount to a 'pressing social need.' Although proportionality takes many guises under the ECHR, its typical structure builds on the textual reference to necessity, often amounting to a less or even least restrictive means test. However, if enforcement of immigration law is taken as both the means and an end in itself, the proportionality test loses traction, and fails to restrict the State's writ. Certainly the *fait accompli* rationale in *Omoregie* requires migrants to play along with immigration law. In contrast *Nunez v Norway* suggests that the 'best interests' standard is gaining additional weight in cases concerning young children. Moreover, as Chapter 2 explores, in *Mendizabal, Sisojeva, Rodrigues da Silva,* and *Jeunesse v Netherlands*, the ECtHR treated the State's failure to recognize stay as lawful as itself violating the Convention. Implicitly, we see that total compliance with the State's migration control whims is not required. Yet, the position of asylum seekers emerges as particularly precarious, as *Omoregie* illustrates. In Chapter 7, I examine the 2008 Grand Chamber ruling in *Saadi v UK*,[166] where the ECtHR accepted that States were permitted to regard asylum seekers as 'unauthorised entrants' even while their

[165] See further de Hart (n 34).
[166] *Saadi v UK* (2008) 47 EHRR 17.

claims were being assessed. *Omoregie* and *Saadi* cohere in that both allow States immense leeway to limit the rights of those on their territory for the purposes of seeking protection, notwithstanding the duration of that residence or the intimate connections they may have formed with insiders.

Yet, as *Nunez, Kaplan*, and *Jeunesse* illustrate, the Court struggles to find a metric to assess the turpitude of immigration law infractions and clearly the best interests of the child may outweigh any immigration infractions of the parents, however egregious. While the fact patterns of these cases differ somewhat, they have in common (with the exception of *Nunez)* that the families often include children of Norwegian and other nationalities, with parents of Norwegian and another nationality. Had these families been resident in EU Member States, EU law would have been applicable, either through *Zambrano* protections for the child-citizens, or *Carpenter* if the EU parent could bring him or herself within the scope of EU free movement protections. Recourse to the ECHR is had in the absence of EU protections.

The proportionality assessment is distorted by the statist assumption. Proportionality normally requires a balancing of the interference with individuals' rights and the collective interest. In contrast, the multifactor balancing approach in family migration cases does not reflect a clear cut proportionality standard. The assessment of justifications assumes that migration control amounts to a general 'pressing social need'. Policies are not closely scrutinized and they are assumed to pursue legitimate aims, as *Biao* exemplifies, thereby masking policy assumptions that courts ought to be open to examine. Accordingly, the proportionality review is diluted to a non-arbitrariness standard.[167] The State's interest in migration control permeates the ECtHR's entire approach. It is assumed that both refusal of entry and removal in themselves pursue legitimate aims, which are approximated to the express Article 8(2) grounds. Without wishing to detract from the importance of the case law as a factor which tempers some migration control practices, it is evidently unstable. As Spijkerboer puts it, 'identical or comparable factors may turn up on each side of the scale, facts are reframed so as to fits [*sic*] the Court's arguments.'[168] In this context, the preference for recourse to the clearer rights and more rigorous proportionality assessments characteristic of EU law is understandable, as the next part explores.

## IV. EU Law on Family Migration

TCN family members derive residence rights from EU law in various ways. Again, the first step is to clarify the sponsor's status. This chapter focuses on EU Citizens and settled TCN migrants falling under the FRD. Note also that other

[167] *Omoregie* (n 56) para 68: '[T]he Court does not find that the national authorities... acted arbitrarily or otherwise transgressed the margin of appreciation'.
[168] *Tuquabo-Tekle* (n 133) 280.

EU instruments create different rights of family reunification. For instance, family members of EU Blue Card holders are exempted from some of the restrictive requirements of the FRD, reflecting the privileged status of those highly-skilled migrants.[169] In contrast, the Students Directive (SD)[170] and the Seasonal Workers Directive (SWD)[171] contain no provisions on family reunification, whereas the Researchers Directive (RD)[172] and the Intra-Corporate Transferees Directive (ICTD)[173] do not require admission of family members, but if Member States do admit them, the duration of their residence permit must be the same as for the sponsor. Convention refugees are covered by special rules under the FRD,[174] but it does not cover beneficiaries of subsidiary protection,[175] a shocking omission given their analogous needs and situation.

The privileged status of EU Citizens is consonant with an insider privilege account, but as we have seen, European States often draw distinctions between their citizens, ostensibly for migration control and 'integration'-related reasons. So, the equality intrinsic in the status of EU Citizenship becomes a valuable recourse for families of migrant background. However, as will be seen, there are instances when EU Citizens cannot bring their situations within the scope of EU law (which at present requires a transnational element to trigger the free movement provisions, or since *Zambrano*, establishing an interference with the 'genuine enjoyment of the substance of the rights of EU Citizenship'), and so find themselves peculiarly unprotected by EU law. As Davies suggests, this means that EU Citizens' right

[169] Art 15 Blue Card Directive. See K Eisele, 'Why Come Here If I Can Go There? Assessing the "Attractiveness" of the EU's Blue Card Directive for "Highly Qualified" Immigrants' (2013) *CEPS Liberty and Security in Europe Paper No. 60*, 11–12.

[170] Council Directive 2004/114/EC of 13 December 2004 on the conditions of admission of third-country nationals for the purposes of studies, pupil exchange, unremunerated training or voluntary service (Students Directive) [2004] OJ L375/12. Note that a recast version of this Directive is currently under negotiations between Council and Parliament. European Commission, *Proposal for a Directive of the European Parliament and of the Council on the conditions of entry and residence of third-country nationals for the purposes of research, studies, pupil exchange, remunerated and unremunerated training, voluntary service and au pairing (recast)*, COM(2013) 151.

[171] Directive 2014/36/EU of the European Parliament and of the Council of 26 February 2014 on the conditions of entry and stay of third-country nationals for the purpose of employment as seasonal workers (Seasonal Workers Directive) [2014] OJ L94/375, Recital 46.

[172] Council Directive 2005/71/EC of 1 October 2005 on a specific procedure for admitting third-country nationals for the purposes of scientific research (Researchers Directive) [2005] OJ L289/15, Art 9. Note that a recast version of this Directive is currently under negotiations between Council and Parliament. European Commission (n 170).

[173] Directive 2014/66/EU of the European Parliament and of the Council of 15 May 2014 on the conditions of entry and residence of third-country nationals in the framework of an intra-corporate transfer (Intra-Corporate Transferees Directive) [2014] OJ L157/1, Art 19.

[174] Chapter V FRD; Art 9 and 2(b) FRD. On the position of both Convention refugees and those enjoying subsidiary protection, see further, S Peers, 'EC Law on Family Members of Persons Seeking or Receiving International Protection' in P Shah (ed), *The Challenge of Asylum to Legal Systems* (Cavendish 2005) 83. For the position in international law, see K Jastram and K Newland, 'Family Unity and Refugee Protection' in E Feller, V Turk, and F Nicholson (eds), *Refugee Protection in International Law: UNHCR's Global Consultations on International Protection* (Cambridge University Press 2003).

[175] Art 3(2)(c) FRD.

to stay at home is impaired.[176] The couple at the centre of one of the UK cases, *Quila*, she British, he Chilean, moved first to Chile and then to Ireland (to avail of EU protections) as UK law did not afford them reunification. Ms Amber Aguilar stated that she felt 'as if [she] had been exiled from [her] country.'[177] Indeed, the language employed to describe the situation of EU Citizens residing in their own State of nationality never having exercised free movement rights, namely 'static EU Citizens' suggests a sedentary population of less concern to EU law than their active transnational comparators.

## 1. TCN family members of EU citizens

EU law has long provided economic migration rights for EU nationals. From its earliest case law, the approach of the CJEU to transborder movement within the EU for EU nationals has been rights-based. Individuals derive judicially enforceable residence rights directly from the Treaty. Limitations are no longer insulated from scrutiny through assertions of sovereign discretion, and the significance of national authorization is downplayed, being treated as declarative rather than constitutive of rights.[178] Citizenship of the EU has served to amplify the rights-based tenor. Originally, families of migrant workers were entitled to accompany the migrant worker when he or she moved to another Member State.[179] Family reunification for migrant EU Citizens is a right, not a privilege.[180] The EU Citizenship case law goes beyond the letter of the legislation, permitting EU Citizens, even in infancy,[181] to be accompanied or joined by family members. In *Carpenter*,[182] *Baumbast*,[183] and *Chen*, the CJEU recognized as bearers of an EU right to reside various TCN family members of migrant EU Citizens. The residence rights were rationalized as necessary to avoid barriers to free movement for the EU Citizen, which required that the EU Citizen be able to live a 'normal family life.'

The Court has clarified in 2014 that family members may acquire an EU right to permanent residence under certain circumstances.[184] In *Metock* it stated that 'if Union citizens were not allowed to lead a normal family life in the host Member State, the exercise of the freedoms they are guaranteed by the

[176] G Davies, 'The Right to Stay at Home: A Basis for Expanding European Family Rights' in D Kochenov (ed), *EU Citizenship and Federalism: The Role of Rights* (Cambridge University Press 2016, Forthcoming).

[177] BBC, '"Unlawful" marriage ruling: "I felt like I'd been exiled"' *BBC* (12 October 2011) <http://www.bbc.co.uk/news/uk-15270198> accessed 11 April 2015.

[178] See, e.g., Case 48/75 *Royer* [1976] ECR 497.

[179] Art 10 Regulation 1612/68.

[180] The original legislation imposed a condition that workers must possess accommodation considered as normal by national standards. This potential limitation has been interpreted restrictively, as only applying a condition at the time of initial entry. Case 249/86 *Commission v Germany* [1989] ECR 1263.

[181] Case C-200/02 *Chen* [2004] ECR I-9925.

[182] Case C-60/00 *Carpenter* [2002] ECR I-6279.

[183] Case C-413/99 *Baumbast* [2002] ECR I-7091.

[184] Case C-244/13 *Ogieriakhi v Minister for Justice and Equality* [2014] OJ C 315/15.

Treaty would be seriously obstructed.'[185] In that case, the CJEU interpreted the Citizenship Directive's reference to family members who 'accompany or join' the EU Citizens so as to create a right to enter the territory of the EU for TCN family members, confirming that both entry and residence rights for TCN family members were amongst 'the necessary measures to bring about freedom of movement for Union citizens'.[186] The purpose of these family migration rights remains, for now, tied to the internal market and economic activity or the genuine enjoyment of EU Citizenship. While Article 7 of the Charter of Fundamental Rights of the European Union (EUCFR) contains a right to family and private life analogous to Article 8 ECHR, this provision, like all in the Charter, may only be invoked within the scope of EU law.

*Carpenter* and *Metock* illustrate the added value of EU rights over and above the ECHR standards. As illustrated in Part III above, the ECHR approach is informed by the statist assumption, resulting in the 'elsewhere approach'. In contrast, EU Citizenship entails a stable right of residence for the sponsor, with family reunification as of right. Had the *Carpenter* family sought protection under the ECHR, the decision would have turned on whether the entire family could relocate to Mrs Carpenter's country of origin, the Philippines. Perhaps on the facts the UK authorities would have deemed relocation overly burdensome. However, the focus of EU law is the effectiveness of Mr Carpenter's economic freedoms, his transborder provision of services in particular, which create a stable right to reside within the EU. Consequently, denial of Mrs Carpenter's right of residence would have created an 'obstacle' (broadly defined) to living in the UK. Absent strong justification, this obstacle would be a violation of Mr Carpenter's Citizenship *and* human rights.[187]

In *Metock*, the CJEU stated that the Citizenship right to 'normal family life' precluded Member States even from encouraging a blended TCN/EU Citizen family to make their home elsewhere. This passing statement invites interpretation as a tacit criticism of the approach of the ECHR to family reunification matters.[188] Yet, rather than explicitly engage with the Strasbourg case law, in *Metock* the CJEU was curiously reticent on the issue of the human right to family reunification, confining its analysis to EU Citizenship and free movement. The strict separation of human rights and EU Citizenship rights is also evident in the Opinion of AG Kokott in the *FRD Ruling*. She drew a sharp distinction between the two, her starting premise being that 'protection of the family as a *human right* [was] something distinct from the fundamental rights of citizens of the Union, that is to say is typically less extensive than citizens' rights'.[189]As discussed in Section 3, a sharp dichotomy between EU Citizenship and human rights is untenable, at least where TCN sponsors enjoy EU rights of residence.

185 *Metock* (n 7) para 62. 186 ibid, para 61. 187 *Carpenter* (n 182) paras 39–45.

188 Costello, '*Metock*' (n 7) 603–04. Cited in agreement by S Peers 'Free Movement, Immigration Control and Constitutional Conflict' (2009) European Constitutional Law Review 173, 191.

189 *FRD Ruling* (n 11) Opinion of AG Kokott, para 63.

Whether the law on Citizenship of the Union is applicable to a given situation depends on whether that scenario falls within the personal *and* material scope of EU law. Traditionally, there were three key requirements: The sponsor had to be (1) a national of a Member State; (2) exercising an economic activity; and (3) in a transborder context. Nationality law remains predominantly national, as discussed in the preceding sections. Exercise of an economic activity remains relevant to assessing the rights of migrant EU citizens, but the right to reside no longer depends exclusively on economic activity.[190] The third requirement created much-litigated anomalies in the family reunification context, which national governments systematically sustained. In response, individuals sought to find ways to rely on EU law, sometimes deliberately engaging in transborder activity for that purpose, because, to paraphrase the applicants in *Akrich*, they had heard about EU rights.[191]

Various forms of transborder movement are sufficient. For instance, leaving the home State and returning after a period is sufficient, and EU rights endure on return.[192] In *Akrich*, the TCN family member had avoided the impact of a UK deportation order by moving to Ireland with his British spouse. On return to the UK, the authorities resisted the application of the *Surinder Singh* principle. The CJEU attempted an awkward reconciliation of domestic immigration law prerogatives and EU rights by deeming the right to move to another Member State to be dependent on 'prior lawful residence' in a first EU State. However, that criterion proved unworkable, and the CJEU unequivocally overruled that aspect of *Akrich* in *Metock*.[193] Important clarification of the *Surinder Singh* ruling was given in Joined Cases *O* and *S (O/S)*.[194] The nature of the residence in the second Member State was clarified, with the emphasis placed on the requirements of Article 7 Citizenship Directive, which then applied by analogy on return to the home States. 'Genuine residence' was required under the Citizenship Directive.[195] The movement to the other Member State had to be such as to facilitate or strengthen family life, so the requisite threshold of 'genuine residence' would not be satisfied by a movement shorter than three months, or even cumulative movements of such duration.[196] Having lived in another EU Member State prior to family formation had no bearing on the matter, being irrelevant to whether the scenario at issue would be regarded as falling within the scope of the Citizenship Directive.

[190] Art 21 TFEU; Art 7(1)(b)–(c) CD. See, *Chen* (n 181); *Baumbast* (n 183); Case C-209/03 *Bidar* [2005] ECR I-2119; Case C-73/08 *Bressol Chaverot* [2010] ECR I-2735.

[191] *Akrich* (n 46) para 36.

[192] Case C-370/90 *Surinder Singh* [1992] ECR I-4265; Case C-291/05 *Minister voor Vreemdelingenzaken en Integratie v Eind* [2007] ECR I-10719.

[193] *Metock* (n 7) para 58.

[194] Joined Cases C-456/12 *O v Minister voor Immigratie en Asiel* and C-457/12 *S v Minister voor Immigratie en Asiel* [2014] OJ C 135/6.

[195] ibid, para 56.

[196] ibid, para 52. See also N Cambien, 'Cases C-456/12 *O. and B.* and C-457/12 *S. and G.*: Clarifying the Inter-State Requirement for EU Citizens?' (*European Law Blog*, 11 April 2014) <http://europeanlawblog.eu/?p=2301> accessed 11 April 2015.

In some contexts, a transborder element may emerge through the interaction of national systems, without actual transborder movement. In *Chen*, baby Chen had not moved from one Member State to another at all, her entire life having been spent in the UK. However, due to her birth in Northern Ireland, she was an Irish citizen. The CJEU accepted that there was a sufficient transborder element in the case. Dual citizenship can also create transborder issues, as is evident in *Garcia Avello*,[197] although is not *per se* sufficient to bring a case within the scope of EU law.[198] *Carpenter* remains the ruling where the CJEU's finding of cross-border activity seems most tenuous, with Mr Carpenter's occasional service-provision outside the UK sufficient to allow him to rely on EU law. The Opinion of AG Sharpston in *O/S* and the Judgment have provided guidance on the meaning of the *Carpenter* ruling, emphasizing that it depended on the demonstration that family life supported the cross-border economic activity in question.[199]

These tenuously cross-border cases make the legal position of static EU Citizens look even more troubling. Given the evident inconsistencies in the case law, there was growing scholarly support for a rethink of the approach to 'purely internal situations' in light of the Citizenship provisions.[200] Some AGs suggested an interim approach, allowing EU scrutiny of the anomalies that result from the rule in individual cases.[201] I argued that TCN family residence rights provide an example where the rationale underlying the concept of 'purely internal situations' is not borne out, so that in this particular context at least, EU law should embrace internal situations.[202] The Grand Chamber ruling in *Zambrano* is a response to these criticisms, heralding a new era in EU Citizenship law.

### *i. Zambrano and its progeny*

The Zambranos and their child fled violence in Columbia and sought asylum in Belgium. Their asylum application was refused, but a *non-refoulement* clause granted them a precarious right of residence there. They remained in Belgium and had two further children, Diego and Jessica, who had Belgian nationality by operation of law. They sought to assert their rights as EU Citizens, in order to establish a derivative right of residence for their father, Ruiz. The masterful Opinion of AG

197 Case C-148/02 *Garcia Avello v Belgian State* [2003] ECR I-11613.

198 *McCarthy* (n 48).

199 *O/S* (n 194). Opinion of AG Sharpston, paras 114–31.

200 For a detailed examination in the context of family reunification, see A Walter, *Reverse Discrimination and Family Reunification* (Wolf Legal Publishers 2008). For general criticisms of the 'purely internal rule' see N Nic Shuibhne, 'Free Movement of Persons and the Wholly Internal Rule: Time to Move On?' (2002) 39 CMLRev 731; E Spaventa, 'Seeing the Wood Despite the Trees? On the Scope of Union Citizenship and its Constitutional Effects' (2008) 45 CMLRev 13.

201 Case C-72/03 *Carbonati* [2004] ECR I-8027 Opinion of AG Maduro. The Opinion reflects his position in 'The Scope of European Remedies: The Case of Purely Internal Situations and Reverse Discrimination' in C Fitzpatrick, T Novitz, and P Skidmore, *The Future of Remedies in Europe* (Hart Publishing 2000) 117. See also, Opinion of AG Sharpston in Case C-212/06 *Government of the French Community and Walloon Government* [2007] ECR I-5305.

202 Costello '*Metock*' (n 7) 619–21.

Sharpston sets out various options for the Court to overcome the strictures and inconsistencies of its previous case law in order to vindicate the promise of EU Citizenship as the 'fundamental status of nationals of the Member States'.[203]

The Opinion clearly influenced the Court, but the latter's terse, elliptical ruling left much to be clarified. It held that deprivation of the father's right to reside and right to work was such as to deprive the EU Citizen children 'of the genuine enjoyment of the substance of the rights conferred by virtue of their status as citizens of the Union'.[204] The reason for this characterization was the Court's assumption that denying the father a right to reside and work would lead to a situation where the children 'would have to leave the territory of the Union in order to accompany their parents'.[205] This is not tested on the facts, but rather built into the legal analysis as embodying a measure which undermines 'the genuine enjoyment of the substance of the rights'.

In *McCarthy*, Shirley McCarthy held dual UK and Irish nationality, but had always lived in the UK. She sought to rely on her EU Citizenship, in light of *Zambrano*, in order to establish an EU right of residence for her TCN husband. The Opinion of AG Kokott, in sharp contrast to that of AG Sharpston in *Zambrano*, is a reassertion of the orthodoxies of EU law on internal situations. Perhaps in light thereof, the Court (Third Chamber) held that, in contrast to *Zambrano*, the denial of a right of residence to Mrs McCarthy's husband did not have the effect of obliging her to leave the territory of the European Union.[206] This is assumed rather than analysed, with the Court simply noting that as a British national she enjoyed 'an unconditional right of residence in the United Kingdom'.[207] However, the same could have been said of the Belgian Zambrano children, at least in law. In *McCarthy*, the Court seems to conceive of the obligation to leave as a legally enforceable one, while in *Zambrano*, and as will be seen in *Dereci*, the underlying assumption seems to be that without the support of the TCN family member, the EU Citizen would be compelled to leave for practical reasons, but not necessarily legal ones.

The next reference, *Dereci*, was a joint case concerning five different TCN applicants, each with a distinctive family relationship with an Austrian national resident in Austria.[208] The Court interpreted *Zambrano* as only applying where the effect of

[203] Case C-184/99 *Grzelczyk* [2001] ECR I-6193, para 31.

[204] *Zambrano* (n 9) para 42, citing Case C-135/08 *Rottmann* [2010] ECR I-1449, para 42.

[205] ibid, para 44. [206] *McCarthy* (n 48) para 50. [207] ibid.

[208] *Dereci* (n 49) paras 24–26. Mr Dereci was a Turkish national, who entered Austria illegally and married an Austrian national with whom he had three children who are also Austrian nationals. Mr Maduike was a Nigerian national, who entered Austria illegally and married an Austrian national with whom he currently resides in Austria. Mrs Heiml is Sri Lankan, married an Austrian national before entering Austria legally where she currently lives with her husband, although her residence permit has expired. Mr Kokollari entered Austria legally at the age of two with his parents who possessed Yugoslav nationality at the time. At 29, he described himself as maintained by his mother who is now an Austrian national. Mrs Stevic is a Serbian national, residing in Serbia with her husband and three adult children, and has applied for family reunification to join her father, an Austrian national since 2007. She has regularly received monthly support from her father and claims that he would continue to support her if she resided in Austria.

the impugned national measure was to oblige the EU Citizen 'in fact, to leave not only the territory of the Member State of which he is a national but also the territory of the Union as a whole'.[209] This 'exceptional' protection was to ensure the effectiveness of EU Citizenship.[210] In contrast, 'the mere fact that it might appear desirable to a national of a Member State, for economic reasons or in order to keep his family together in the territory of the Union, for the members of his family who do not have nationality of a Member State to be able to reside with him in the territory of the Union, is not sufficient in itself to support the view that the Union citizen will be forced to leave Union territory if such a right is not granted.'[211] The CJEU left this to the national court to verify.[212] The Court reiterated the orthodox position (which *Zambrano* did not purport to alter) that EU fundamental rights would only be applicable if the matter fell within the scope of EU law, which was dependent on finding a prior infringement of EU law.[213]

*Dereci* appears to limit *Zambrano* in two ways. First, it emphasizes the 'exceptional' nature of the *Zambrano* residence rights. Second, it states that the 'genuine enjoyment' test will be met only when the Citizen is in effect obliged to leave the territory of the Union as a whole, not only his or her own Member State, by the denial of the family member's residence rights. This is somewhat puzzling, as the novel reference in *Zambrano* to the 'territory of the Union' had the purpose of diminishing the importance of cross-border movement. If the EU Citizen moves to another Member State, he or she brings himself or herself within the protections of the Citizenship Directive, so in that way he or she can secure a right of residence for his or her TCN family member, provided the conditions in the Citizenship Directive are fulfilled. Even if not, the Citizenship case law offers additional protections in this transnational context. By implicitly suggesting that the 'hop' to another Member State should be exercised, the Court seems to reassert the importance of the transnational dimension of Union Citizenship.

In another respect though, *Dereci* confirms that breadth of *Zambrano* as a residual protection for residence rights. While *McCarthy* was read by some as suggesting that the *Zambrano* ruling would only come to the assistance of minors, the, admittedly terse, ruling in *Dereci* lends no support to that view. In contrast, whether the EU Citizen would have to leave 'territory of the Union' is open for assessment in all situations. The Opinion of AG Mengozzi casts some light on the scenarios when it would be accepted that residence in the territory of the Union was imperilled. AG Mengozzi opined that in none of the five applicants' cases was the EU Citizen being compelled to leave the territory of the Union (the trigger for the *Zambrano* genuine enjoyment tests) or experiencing an impediment to his or her free movement (as under the traditional test).[214] Yet, he also admitted that examining the possibility of moving to another EU Member State may put families with one EU Citizen parent at a disadvantage in contrast to the Zambranos, as the option to move to another Member State would be open in their case. However, if that were

[209] ibid, para 66. [210] ibid, para 67. [211] ibid, para 68. [212] ibid, para 74.
[213] ibid, paras 70–74. [214] Opinion of AG Mengozzi in *Dereci* (n 49) paras 33–37.

not possible, for instance if the EU Citizen parent was for whatever reason, 'unable to work and thus to provide for the needs of her children', then the TCN parent's residence might be protected in order to maintain the children's residence in the EU.[215] The notion of dependency informing the Opinion is broad, encompassing 'legal, administrative or emotional dependency'.[216] Accordingly, the Opinion also countenances the situation whereby a TCN child derives a *Zambrano* right of residence in order to maintain the residence rights of a dependent EU Citizen parent.[217]

Thus far, the 'genuine enjoyment' test protects nationality itself (as in *Rottmann*) and rights of residence (as in *Zambrano*). The difficulty with *McCarthy* and *Dereci* is that, while in *Zambrano* the Court establishes an assumption that the family would have to leave Belgium were Mr Zambrano not to be accorded a right to reside and work, in *McCarthy* the Court assumes the converse: that Mrs McCarthy will not be compelled to leave the UK to be with her husband. In *Zambrano*, the Court effectively stipulates that the family would have to leave as a matter of law, obviating the need to examine the facts. Of course, whether they would actually leave remained to be seen—perhaps the family could have muddled along in the shadows of the irregular economy, like so many others in their situation? In contrast, in *McCarthy*, the opposite was assumed, that Mrs McCarthy would not in practice have to leave the UK. There was no examination of the consequences of the UK action on Mrs McCarthy's right to reside in the UK. In contrast, in *Dereci*, the Court delegates the assessment of the 'genuine enjoyment' test to the national courts; a significant transformation, in that it treats the matter as a question of fact for national courts to assess. As AG Mengozzi admits, the 'genuine enjoyment' test leaves much to be desired from a legal certainty point of view. Yet, in focusing on the severity of interference with Citizenship rights, it establishes a form of corrective jurisdiction, to be exercised by national courts and the CJEU in tandem. Accordingly Kochenov's analogy with the 'equivalence' and 'effectiveness' test for national remedies is apt.[218] In general, Member States are left to legislate for domestic scenarios, but their nationals are also EU Citizens, and so a residual EU jurisdiction is suitable, even for internal situations.

To conclude, there are now two distinct ways to trigger the family rights of EU Citizens. The first and more legally straightforward one is to move to another Member State to trigger the application of the Citizenship Directive, or otherwise come within the protection of the free movement rules. The second involves meeting the high threshold of *Zambrano*, which requires demonstration that one would have to leave the territory of the EU if the family members' residence is not permitted in order to meet the current interpretation of the 'genuine enjoyment' test. Each approach has its own internal logic, but the result is great differentiation between and across families, depending on their means and appetite for transborder movement and indeed, all too often, litigation. For some, a previous decision to naturalize may bring legal disadvantage—in some Member States.

[215] ibid, para 47. [216] ibid, para 48. [217] ibid. [218] Kochenov (n 9).

### *ii. The meaning of family under the Citizenship Directive*

Under the Citizenship Directive, a 'family member' is a (a) spouse; (b) partner under a registered partnership treated as equivalent to marriage by the host Member State's legislation; (c) direct descendant under the age of 21 or a dependant, including one of the spouse or partner; (d) a dependent parent, including one of the spouse or partners.[219] In *Rahman*, the Court clarified that, concerning other family members, the Citizenship Directive creates an obligation to facilitate admission.[220]

## 2. The FRD and *FRD ruling*

The FRD was adopted in 2003, following tortuous negotiations, during which time the Commission revised its proposal twice, as concessions were made to restrictive practices of many national governments.[221] Like the other immigration and asylum measures of this era, it was adopted by unanimity in the Council comprising fifteen national governments. It creates a *right* to family reunification, itself a significant legal innovation, in particular when compared with the ECHR approach. However, it also reflects the restrictive turn in national policies at the time of its adoption. It thus sets up on-going legally mediated friction between a rights-based approach to family migration and an approach which subjugates family choices about migration to various policy concerns subsumed under the broad amorphous heading of migration control. In particular, it reflects the highly contested notion that certain marriage patterns and forms of family migration warranted restriction in the name of migrant integration. The Preamble affirms the FRD's fundamental rights credentials,[222] and Article 5(5) states that '[w]hen examining an application, the Member States shall have due regard to the best interests of minor children.' However, the Preamble also reflects the ambiguities surrounding 'integration'.[223]

A quick overview of the FRD illustrates these tensions: Chapter I sets out the General Provisions, identifying as the purpose of the Directive 'to determine the conditions for the exercise of the right to family reunification by third country nationals residing lawfully in the territory of the Member States.' It is a minimum standards Directive, as Article 3(5) makes clear. Chapter II defines family

[219] Art 2(2) CD.

[220] Case C-83/11 *Secretary of State for the Home Department v Rahman and Others* [2012].

[221] European Commission, *Proposal for a Council Directive on the right to family reunification*, COM(1999) 638; European Commission, *Amended Proposal for a Council Directive on the right to family reunification*, COM(2000) 624; European Commission, *Amended Proposal for a Council Directive on the right to family reunification*, COM(2002) 225. On the negotiations, see P Boeles, 'Directive on Family Reunification: are the dilemmas resolved?' (2001) 3 EJML 61; R Cholewinski, 'Family Reunification and Conditions Placed on Family Members: Dismantling a Fundamental Human Right' (2002) 4 EJML 271.

[222] FRD Recital 2 refers to ECHR and EUCFR, while Recital 5 refers to non-discrimination.

[223] ibid, cf Recital 4, Recital 12, and Recital 15.

members, mainly spouses and minor children.[224] Others may be admitted,[225] including unmarried partners.[226] The issue of polygamy is dealt with by only allowing one wife in a polygamous family to enter.[227] Article 4 contains three controversial derogations. Concerning children, if they are over twelve and arrive independently from the family, Member States may 'by way of derogation':

> before authorising entry and residence under this Directive, verify whether he or she meets a condition for integration provided for by its existing legislation on the date of implementation of this Directive.[228]

The concept of 'integration condition' is not defined. In contrast, under Article 7(2), there is a general discretion to require TCNs to 'comply with integration measures, in accordance with national law.' Furthermore, Member States may limit entry of children over fifteen. Somewhat ambiguously, Article 4(6) states:

> By way of derogation, Member States may request that the applications concerning family reunification of minor children have to be submitted before the age of 15, as provided for by its existing legislation on the date of the implementation of this Directive. If the application is submitted after the age of 15, the Member States which decide to apply this derogation shall authorise the entry and residence of such children on grounds other than family reunification.

For spousal reunification, Article 4(5), interpreted in the 2014 ruling in *Noorzia*,[229] states that:

> In order to ensure better integration and to prevent forced marriages Member States may require the sponsor and his/her spouse to be of a minimum age, and at maximum 21 years, before the spouse is able to join him/her.

Chapter III deals with the process, generally requiring applications to be made when the family is outside the EU (although by derogation they may be made in country),[230] with decisions to be taken normally within nine months.[231] Chapter IV sets out various 'requirements for the exercise of the right to family reunification' including the aforementioned integration measures under Article 7(2) and various material conditions including adequate housing, sickness insurance and 'stable and regular resources'.[232] Member States are permitted to impose a waiting period of two years (or exceptionally three) before family reunification.[233] Chapter V deals with refugees specifically, with SP beneficiaries excluded as mentioned at the outset.[234] Chapter VI deals with entry and residence. Member States are to grant family migrants who meet the conditions 'every facility for obtaining visas'[235] and

[224] ibid, Art 4(1). [225] ibid, Art 4(2). [226] ibid, Art 4(3).
[227] ibid, Art 4(4). [228] ibid, Art 4(1).
[229] n 13. See further also G Milios, 'The CJEU's approach on the minimum age requirement for spouses in an application for family reunification' (*EU Law Analysis*, 25 July 2014) <http://eulawanalysis.blogspot.ie/2014/07/the-cjeus-approach-on-minimum-age.html> accessed 11 April 2015.
[230] FRD Art 5(3). [231] ibid, Art 5(4). [232] ibid, Art 7(1)(a)–(c).
[233] ibid, Art 8 provides: 'Member States may require the sponsor to have stayed lawfully in their territory for a period not exceeding two years, before having his/her family members join him/her.'
[234] ibid, Art 3(2)(c). [235] ibid, Art 13(1).

normally a one-year renewable residence permit.[236] After no later than five years, family members are normally to be granted an 'autonomous residence permit'.[237] The rights of admitted family members include the right to education[238] and work (in both employed and self-employed capacity).[239] However, a one-year waiting period may be imposed on this entitlement.[240] Chapter VII is entitled 'Penalties and redress', and sets out general conditions for the rejection and non-renewal of permits, emphasizing the ongoing application of the FRD's requirements, and the right to check the genuine and on-going nature of the family relationship.[241]

Article 17 sneaks in a provision reflecting some of the Strasbourg-type assessments:

> Member States shall take due account of the nature and solidity of the person's family relationships and the duration of his residence in the Member State and of the existence of family, cultural and social ties with his/her country of origin where they reject an application, withdraw or refuse to renew a residence permit or decide to order the removal of the sponsor or members of his family.

As regards remedies against removal, Article 18 refers to the 'right to mount a legal challenge.' Although unusually worded, there is no avoiding the EU right to an effective remedy in this context in any event.

Having set out this brief snapshot of the Directive's text, it is apparent that some of the derogations seem liable to undermine seriously the right to family reunification. As mentioned previously, the Parliament was not involved as co-legislator for the FRD, but chose to exercise its legal entitlement to challenge the legality of some of the Directive's more restrictive provisions. It chose to challenge three of the most controversial restrictions in the Directive: Articles 4(1)(final indent), and 4(6) limiting reunification with minor children, and Article 8 on waiting periods. The ruling embodied two firsts: it was the first time the Parliament used its enhanced post-Nice *locus standi* to challenge a legal act on fundamental rights grounds, and the CJEU made its first express reference to the EUCFR.[242] The following account interweaves the key features of the FRD and the CJEU's ruling.

### *i. Legal base and normative force*

The FRD's legal base, Article 63(3)(a) EC, now replaced by Article 79(2)(a) TFEU, appears to allow Member States to enact both higher and lower domestic standards. Textually, the FRD only permits higher ones.[243] As discussed in Chapter 1, the Opinion of AG Kokott in the *FRD Ruling* explores the implications of the legal base. She concludes that the base was to be read not as 'limiting the legal effect of legislation' but rather 'enjoining the Community legislature... to leave Member States an appropriate degree of latitude,' as it had done in the 'range of options' left to Member States.[244]

[236] ibid, Art 13(2). [237] ibid, Art 15. [238] ibid, Art 14(1)(a) and (c).
[239] ibid, Art 14(1). [240] ibid, Art 14(2). [241] ibid, Art 16.
[242] *FRD Ruling* (n 11) para 38. [243] FRD Art 3(5).
[244] *FRD Ruling* (n 11); Opinion of AG Kokott, para 41.

The CJEU did not engage directly with the legal base issue, but its interpretation of the FRD refutes any contention that the legal base precludes binding, or even directly effective, EU rights. In particular, the CJEU stated that Article 4(1) imposed:

> precise positive obligations, with corresponding clearly defined individual rights, on the Member States, since it requires them, in the cases determined by the Directive, to authorise family reunification of certain members of the sponsor's family, without being left a margin of appreciation.[245]

The case raised another jurisdictional conundrum. Challenges to the validity of Directives require allocation of responsibility for fundamental rights violations between the EU and the Member States. By their nature, Directives require national implementation and application, leaving discretion to the Member States. The Council argued that any fundamental rights violation would be attributable to the Member States rather than the EU. Accordingly, it disputed the CJEU's jurisdiction to hear the case. The CJEU disagreed, stating that 'a provision of a Community act could, in itself, not respect fundamental rights if it required, or expressly or impliedly authorized, the Member States to adopt or retain national legislation not respecting those rights.'[246]

### *ii. The sponsor's connection with the host State*

The Commission originally proposed that the Directive would also apply to TCNs and all EU nationals who had not exercised their free movement rights.[247] The national governments in the Council ultimately rejected inclusion of static EU Citizens, reflecting their resistance to exposing their practices in this area to EU law's rights-based scrutiny. Family members of EU citizens are excluded, whether or not the family member has moved within the EU or not,[248] as are persons applying for or receiving subsidiary protection status,[249] although recognized Convention refugees *are* included.[250]

An important issue is whether the FRD applies to dual EU citizens/ TCNs.[251] Its text is ambivalent on this point.[252] If dual nationals are excluded, the likelihood is that on naturalization, their rights may deteriorate, as several Member States have less favourable rules for their own citizens than the FRD.[253] Drawing on the Association Agreement case law, Member States

[245] ibid, para 60. [246] ibid, para 23. See also, Opinion of AG Kokott, para 45.

[247] European Commission, *1999 FRD Proposal* (n 221) Art 2(d).

[248] FRD Art 3(3). [249] ibid, Art 3(2)(c).

[250] Peers 'EC Law on Family Members of Persons Seeking or receiving International Protection' (n 174).

[251] For an extensive discussion, see K Groenendijk, 'Family Reunification as a Right under Community Law' (2006) 8 EJML 215, 227–29. For an overview of the current practices, see K Groenendijk, R Fernhout, D van Dam, R van Oers, and T Strik, *The Family Reunification Directive in EU Member States: The First Year of Implementation* (Centre for Migration Law 2007) 11–12.

[252] FRD Art 1, cf Art 3(3).

[253] European Commission, *Communication on the application of Directive 2003/86 on the right to family reunification* (FRD Implementation Report), COM(2008) 160, 4. This is the case in Cyprus, Lithuania, Germany, and the Netherlands.

should not normally disregard the 'external' nationality of the sponsor if she had naturalized in the host state.[254] The alternative would be inappropriate in a legal order which otherwise encourages the holding of dual EU nationalities.[255]

**'Reasonable prospect of permanent residence'**

The FRD applies to TCN sponsors residing lawfully in a Member State, holding a residence permit of at least one year's validity, and with a 'reasonable prospect' of attaining 'permanent resident' status.[256] This phrase is undoubtedly uncertain in scope.[257] Rather than providing a phrase that would demand uniform EU interpretation, the language reflects divided competence over authorization of residence. Unsurprisingly, the Member States have implemented the provision in divergent ways.[258] Most allow family reunification for migrants with a temporary residence permit, although applying a residence requirement of eighteen months in France, or at least once renewed in Spain. The laws of Cyprus, Malta, Lithuania, and Luxembourg appear to use the FRD phrase 'reasonable prospects of obtaining the right of permanent residence'. In the Cypriot case, as migrants are legally precluded from gaining a right to permanent residence, the right to family reunification is rendered illusory. Regrettably, the Commission's recent guidance seems to reaffirm the Directive's ambiguity, as it deems that 'it is for [Member States] to determine what kind of residence permits they accept as sufficient to consider that there are reasonable prospects', although this is in tension with the CJEU ruling on the LTRD in *Singh*.[259]

**Further waiting periods**

In addition to this prior residence requirement, the FRD permits further waiting periods, allowing States to require further passage of time to demonstrate the sponsor's connection with the host state. Article 8 allows Member States to require that the 'sponsor' has stayed lawfully in the Member States for two years before family reunification may be permitted. As the Commission notes, this wording precludes the imposition of a delay of two years from the date of application, casting doubt on the implementation in some Member States.[260] However, the consideration of the implementation of a similar provision of the FRD in *Noorzia* suggests that the CJEU might take an indulgent approach to Member States' expansive readings of their discretion under the FRD on this issue.[261] Article 8, second indent, permits

[254] C-179/98 *Mesbah* [1999] ECR I-7955 cf Joined Cases C-7/10 and C-9/10 *Kahveci and Inan*, [2012] OJ C 151/3.

[255] Note that no reference to dual nationality is made in the Commission's latest guidelines on the FRD. European Commission, *Communication on guidance for application of Directive 2003/86/EC on the right to family reunification* (FRD Guidance), COM(2014) 210.

[256] FRD Art 3(1).

[257] Peers describes it as violating 'the principle of clear and precise drafting.' S Peers, *EU Justice and Home Affairs Law* (2nd edn, OUP 2006) 216. See also Peers 'Family Reunion and Community Law' (n 57) 179–80.

[258] European Commission, *FRD Implementation Report* (n 253) 4 and *Singh* (n 26).

[259] European Commission, *FRD Guidance* (n 255) 4.

[260] European Commission, *FRD Implementation Report* (n 253) 8.

[261] *Noorzia* (n 13) on FRD Art 4(5). See analysis at Part IV.2.iii.

a longer waiting period of three years in the name of 'reception capacity' if this is provided for in existing national legislation. This provision was inserted at Austria's insistence, which still had a quota system when the Directive was adopted.

The AG and CJEU disagreed in their assessments of Article 8 FRD. AG Kokott found that it was liable to violate human rights. If Member States implemented the provision 'one-dimensionally', that is, taking it at its face value, its application would lead to a rights violation.[262] Article 8 was:

> at least liable to be misunderstood. This ambiguity on account of the failure to take into account hardship situations increases the risk that human rights will be infringed. Should that occur, responsibility would lie not only with the national legislature which implemented the Directive, but also with the Community legislature. Since human rights must be protected effectively, and the law has to be clear, Article 8 of the Directive is contrary to Community law.[263]

The CJEU, in an argument demanding a modicum of doublethink, rationalized waiting periods as ensuring 'effective integration' of the members of the family in the host community, by ensuring that family reunification does not take place until the sponsor has found in the host State a solid base, both economic and domestic, for settling a family there.[264] One could just as easily argue that depriving the sponsor of her family could make establishing that 'solid base' more difficult. In any event, the Court treated the time limit as merely preserving 'a limited margin of appreciation' for the States so they could ensure family reunification would 'take place in favourable conditions'. The CJEU endorsed the legislature's factual assumption that 'after the sponsor has been residing in the host State for a period sufficiently long... the family members will settle down well and display a certain level of integration'.[265] Duration of residence was just one factor to be taken into account in granting family reunification,[266] as was the notion of 'reception capacity'.[267] In applying these factors, the CJEU emphasized the duty to comply with Article 17 and, in cases involving children, Article 5(5) on the 'best interests' principle.

Articles 5(5) and 17 are both general requirements to be applied in cases concerning first entry, renewal and withdrawal of permits. The 2002 Commission proposal referred explicitly to the UN Convention on the Rights of the Child (CRC) in this article,[268] but Article 5(5) no longer makes an express reference, simply providing that '[w]hen examining an application, Member States shall have due regard to the best interests of minor children'. As mentioned above, Article 17 is redolent of the Strasbourg *Boultif/Üner* criteria.

These considerations operate in tandem with the grounds of public policy, public security, or public health in Article 6 FRD. For the CJEU then, human rights law simply requires that there is a process for consideration of family reunification

[262] *FRD Ruling* (n 11). Opinion of AG Kokott, para 103. [263] ibid, para 105.
[264] ibid, para 93. [265] ibid, para 98.
[266] ibid, para 99. [267] ibid, para 100
[268] European Commission, *2002 FRD Proposal* (n 221) 19.

applications. Once the FRD permits a process that will comply with ECHR standards, it too complies with fundamental rights. In interpreting each of the impugned restrictions, the CJEU emphasizes that the measure's human rights compatibility depended on the assessment of individual applications in light of human rights criteria.

### *iii. The sponsor's connection with family members*

The definition of family members is found in Article 4. The Directive permits Member States to restrict the definition of 'spouse' to those over twenty-one years old, an option exercised by Belgium, Cyprus, Lithuania, Malta, and the Netherlands.[269] The rationale for this age limit is to help foster integration and combat forced marriages. In practice, age limits may function as additional time limits, although this was not considered in the ruling.

The ruling in *Noorzia* concerned Article 4(5) FRD, which provides that:

> in order to ensure better integration and to prevent forced marriages Member States may require the sponsor and his/her spouse to be of a minimum age, and at maximum 21 years, before the spouse is able to join him/her.

Austria chose to implement this provision by requiring applicants to be twenty-one when the application was submitted, rather than when the envisaged reunification would take place. The Court held that this was permitted, focusing on the importance of the aim of Article 4(5), which it characterized as to prevent forced marriage and ensure that migration was voluntary. Notably, the measure was framed more in these terms, than in relation to facilitating integration. By focusing on the narrower aim, we might expect the Court would find a narrower measure was more suitable. That approach was taken by the UK Supreme Court in 2011 when it found a similar UK restriction a disproportionate interference with human rights.[270] However, the CJEU avoided strict proportionality, by laying emphasis on the 'margin of discretion' afforded to the Member States.[271] The ruling also conflicts with the Commission's guidance on the implementation of the Directive, according to which 'the minimum age requirement needs to be fulfilled at the moment of the effective family reunion and not when the application is submitted'.[272] In contrast, AG Mengozzi took the opposite view, based on a broader reading of the purposes of the FRD more in keeping with *Chakroun*.[273] In *Chakroun*, the Court emphasized the FRD creates a right to family reunification. AG Mengozzi opined in *Noorzia* that an interpretation of Article 4(5), applying the minimum age requirement at the moment when the application is submitted, would undermine rather than promote the right to family reunification.[274]

269 European Commission, *FRD Implementation Report* (n 253) 5.
270 *R (Quila and another) v Secretary of State for the Home Department* [2011] UKSC 45.
271 *Noorzia* (n 13) para 14. 272 European Commission, *FRD Guidance* (n 255) 8.
273 Case C-578/08 *Chakroun v Minister van Buitenlandse Zaken* [2010] ECR I-1839.
274 *Noorzia* (n 13), Opinion of AG Mengozzi, paras 37–50.

'Family' includes minor children of the sponsor and his/her spouse, including adopted children.[275] The definition of 'minor children' refers to the unmarried child 'below the age of majority set by the law of the Member State concerned'. For the other family members covered by the Directive, admission appears to be restricted. Member States may admit first-degree dependent relatives in the ascending line 'if they do not enjoy proper family support in the country of origin',[276] and adult unmarried children if they 'do not enjoy proper family support in the country of origin'[277] or are 'objectively unable to provide for their own needs on account of their state of health'.[278] On one reading, these provisions may be otiose. A minimum standards Directive could not prevent Member States from admitting relatives, and the 'may' clause cannot constrain the Member States to only admit relatives if they meet these strict conditions.

### *iv. The impugned restrictions on reunification with children: Integration tests and age limits*

Under the impugned Article 4(1) FRD derogation, it will be recalled that:

> By way of derogation, where a child is aged over 12 years and arrives independently from the rest of his/her family, the Member State may, before authorising entry and residence under this Directive, verify whether he or she meets a condition for integration provided for by its existing legislation on the date of implementation of this Directive.

Recital 12 elaborates:

> The possibility of limiting the right of family reunification of children over the age of 12, whose primary residence is not with the sponsor, is intended to reflect the children's capacity for integration at early ages and shall ensure that they acquire the necessary education and language skills in school.

Germany insisted on the inclusion of this exception in the Directive, although did not finally include such a restriction in its domestic law.[279] The AG and CJEU's assessments of the provision in the *FRD Ruling* provide important guidance on the widespread practice of imposing 'integration conditions'. The Parliament argued that the underlying reasoning was unconvincing, since family reunification was itself an aspect of integration. Accordingly, it was 'incongruous' to impose a condition for integration before granting this right. It 'render[ed] family reunification unachievable and negates this right'.[280] The CJEU disagreed, treating the notion

[275] FRD Art 4(1)(a) and (b) refers to 'children adopted in accordance with a decision taken by the competent authority in the Member State concerned or a decision which is automatically enforceable due to international obligations of that Member State or must be recognized in accordance with international obligations'.

[276] ibid, Art 4(2)(a). [277] ibid, Art 4(2)(b). [278] ibid, Art 4(3).

[279] Groenendijk, 'Family Reunification as a Right under Community Law' (n 251) 218.

[280] *FRD Ruling* (n 11) para 40.

of 'integration' as amongst the legitimate State concerns under Article 8 ECHR. Again it emphasized Articles 17 and 5(5). Article 4(1) was valid, as it allowed account to be taken also of the exceptional cases where human rights required family reunification and did not act as an absolute bar.

The Court had an opportunity in the *FRD Ruling* to set some constraints, inject a modicum of rationality even, to these practices. However, the AG and CJEU rejected outright the Parliament's contention that the integration derogation was perverse,[281] merely setting out some generic stipulations: Member States were not permitted 'to employ [the integration concept] in a manner contrary to general principles of Community law, in particular to fundamental rights' and they were not permitted to use an 'unspecified concept of integration'.[282]

Article 4(1) permits Member States to treat applications of children over twelve less favourably than others. The second impugned restriction in Article 4(6) is even broader, allowing Member States to request that applications concerning family reunification of minor children be submitted before the age of fifteen. The Commission reports that no Member State has implemented this restriction, and as the article contains a standstill clause, the facility to do so has now been extinguished.[283] Nonetheless, its assessment remains pertinent to understanding the CJEU's conception of the applicable standards. Although Article 4(6) seems to preclude family reunification with children over fifteen, the CJEU insisted it could not 'be interpreted as prohibiting the Member States from taking account of an application relating to a child over 15 years of age or as authorising them not to do so'.[284] Strasbourg required the admission of the fifteen-year-old girl in *Tuquabo-Tekle* just the previous year, it will be recalled.[285] The CJEU did not cite this particular ruling, although the Opinion does mention the Strasbourg admissibility decision.[286] The timeline suggests that Strasbourg's ruling may have had the EU audience in mind, both the CJEU and national jurisdictions contemporaneously reviewing the application of the FRD. AG Kokott's Opinion of 8 September 2005 predates the Strasbourg Court's substantive ruling of 1 December that year by less than three months. Knowing that the CJEU was about to rule on the legality of an EU provision which might all too easily have been read to confer on Member States wide scope to refuse admission of children over fifteen may have contributed to the *Tuquabo-Tekle* ruling.

The CJEU also held that these age limits were not age discriminatory, as it was objectively justifiable to treat children over twelve arriving independently as a distinct group, as that age corresponded 'to a stage in the life of a minor child when the latter has already lived for a relatively long period in a third country without the members of his or her family, so that integration in another environment is

[281] ibid, Opinion of AG Kokott, para 85; *FRD Ruling*, para 68. [282] ibid, para 70.

[283] European Commission, *FRD Implementation Report* (n 253) 5–6.

[284] *FRD Ruling* (n 11) para 85. [285] See Section III above.

[286] *FRD Ruling* (n 11) Opinion of AG Kokott, para 53, citing the admissibility decision of 19 October 2004 in *Tuquabo-Tekle*.

liable to give rise to more difficulties'.[287] '*A fortiori*', the limit of fifteen was justified on similar grounds.[288] The finding of objective justification seems based on dubious factual assumptions.

### *v. Further derogations*

The public policy derogation in the FRD requires consideration of the 'severity or type of offence of public policy or public security committed by the family member, or the dangers that are emanating from this person'.[289] The FRD contains a preambular statement that the notion of public policy and public security covers 'also cases in which a third country national belongs to an association which supports international terrorism, supports such an association or has extremist aspirations'.[290] This preambular assertion is in tension with the interpretation of the public policy derogation in the Citizenship context.[291] It remains to be seen whether the grounds of derogation will be interpreted similarly to the analogous grounds under EU Citizenship law;[292] the Commission, for its part, supports such an analogy in its 2014 guidance.[293] As will be seen, while the CJEU in *Chakroun* drew on EU Citizenship principles, the more recent *Noorzia* ruling is more indulgent of Member State discretion.[294]

Family members of migrant EU Citizens enjoy a right to work. In contrast, Article 14(2) FRD confers discretion on the host Member State as to whether to allow family members to engage in 'employed or self-employed activity' for the first twelve months of residence. Procedural requirements may also be imposed. Member States may require applications to be submitted whilst family members are outside the relevant Member State, which is required to make a decision usually within nine months of the application.[295] In contrast, TCN family members of EU Citizens are not subject to any such requirements, provided their sponsors are in a transborder situation.

## 3. Towards a distinctive EU human right to family reunification

The *FRD ruling* has been praised as providing an 'elegant middle way' to protect fundamental rights and allow for national diversity.[296] Two contrasting perspectives

[287] ibid, para 74. [288] ibid, para 89. [289] FRD Arts 6(2) and 17.

[290] ibid, Recital 14. [291] See Arts 27–33 CD.

[292] Notably in *Ziebell* the Court rejected equality between Turkish nationals under the EU-Turkey Association Agreement and EU Citizens, rather assimilating their rights to those of long-term resident TCNs under the LTRD. It stated that 'It follows from the substantial differences to be found not only in their wording but also in their object and purpose between the rules relating to the EEC-Turkey Association and European Union law concerning citizenship that the two legal schemes in question cannot be considered equivalent, with the result that the scheme providing for protection against expulsion enjoyed by Union citizens under [the Citizenship Directive] cannot be applied mutatis mutandis for the purpose of determining the meaning and scope of [Association Agreement]. Case C-371/08 *Ziebell* [2011] ECRI-12735, para 74.

[293] European Commission, *FRD Guidance* (n 255) 11. [294] See Part IV.2.ii.

[295] FRD Art 5(4). [296] Lawson (n 11), 341–42.

may be adopted: On one view, focusing on the constraints placed on the EU legislature, the ruling is underwhelming. Apparently sweeping, perverse restrictions are permitted, without much constraint at the EU level. However, in stipulating that the FRD creates a directly effective right, the CJEU opens the way for domestic litigation challenging national restrictions, and hints at various national practices which would be incompatible with that right. In addition, although not stated, the orthodox interpretative stance in EU law demands that restrictions to rights be read narrowly, and subjected to a fairly strict proportionality standard. This stance suggests a jurisprudential trajectory towards a more robust EU right than the rhetoric of the ruling suggests. In the event of individual refusals, the FRD requires that the individual concerned is entitled to 'mount a legal challenge',[297] a provision reflecting the EU right to effective judicial protection. The CJEU emphasizes that access to domestic courts to challenge refusals will be key to securing the right to family reunification provided for. In so doing, it reminds us that its review of the Directive's validity is but a first step in abstract review, to be complemented by interpretations in later, concrete cases. In this section, I set out an approach to a distinctive EU human right to family migration, and identify whether the subsequent case law, in particular in the cases of *Chakroun*[298] and *Noorzia*,[299] fits this approach.

As well as citing the usual sources of inspiration for EU fundamental rights law,[300] and the International Covenant on Civil and Political Rights (ICCPR),[301] the CJEU also referred to the CRC[302] and, as mentioned, the EUCFR.[303] It noted that the CRC and the Charter enshrine the 'best interests' standard, and the latter instrument also contains a right for a child to maintain on a regular basis a personal relationship with both of his or her parents.[304] Taking a somewhat minimalist view, the CJEU characterized the IHRL position as follows:

> [V]arious instruments stress the importance to a child of family life and *recommend* that States have regard to the child's interests but they do not create for the members of a family an individual right to be allowed to enter the territory of a State and cannot be interpreted as denying Member States a certain margin of appreciation when they examine applications for family reunification.[305]

In contrast, the CJEU characterized the FRD as enshrining a right to family reunification,[306] referring to the 'right to live with one's close family',[307] and so regarded the core provision in Article 4, which 'imposes precise positive obligations' as going beyond IHRL, since it required family reunification and deprived Member States of any 'margin of appreciation' in this context.[308]

The main shortcoming of this approach is its failure to articulate a distinct standard of human rights protection, going beyond the IHRL minimum. As

[297] FRD Art 18. [298] *Chakroun* (n 12).
[299] *Noorzia* (n 13). [300] *FRD Ruling* (n 11) paras 35–36.
[301] ibid, para 37. [302] ibid. [303] ibid, para 38. [304] Art 24(3) EUCFR.
[305] *FRD Ruling* (n 11) para 59 (emphasis added). [306] ibid, para 60.
[307] ibid, para 52. [308] ibid, para 60.

Chapter 1 explains, generally speaking, wholesale incorporation of Strasbourg's case law is rarely suitable in Luxembourg, as the former operates under particular institutional constraints that do not apply to the latter. Luxembourg's application of EU human rights should not ossify around the ECHR minimum. The CJEU should articulate a distinct EU standard.

Three aspects of the *FRD Ruling* in particular warrant criticism: First, the CJEU's focus on international standards to the exclusion of the 'common constitutional traditions'; secondly, the CJEU's employment of the 'margin of appreciation'; and thirdly, the failure to engage with the values and principles immanent in EU law. Were the CJEU to take the alternative route advocated here, a transformative shift could be accomplished. We see a step in that direction in *Chakroun*, but a retreat in *Noorzia*.

### *i. The 'common constitutional traditions'*

The CJEU fails to engage with the 'common constitutional traditions of the Member States.' If we take *Hauer*[309] as an archetypal case on review of EU acts,[310] the CJEU starts with the ECHR, but then goes on to examine also 'the indications provided by the constitutional rules and practices of the nine [as there were then] Member States'.[311] Whilst there is no thorough examination of constitutional jurisprudence in *Hauer*,[312] the space for its examination is staked out, and in some cases, allows domestic conceptions to influence the content of the general principles.[313] The failure to engage in meaningful consideration of the domestic constitutional jurisprudence in the *FRD Ruling* is not unusual, but it has a troubling aspect in this instance, as the Council argued that a waiting period was not akin to refusal and was 'a classical element of immigration policy which exists in most Member States and has not been held unlawful by the competent courts'.[314] The Council's argument seems to present a partial account of the constitutional jurisprudence. Litigants in several EU Member States have invoked the right to family life to challenge removals and limitations on entry of family members. Soysal describes the process whereby '[t]hroughout the 1970s, constitutional and administrative courts in many European countries repealed [*sic*] limitations on [family] reunification'.[315] In particular, there is ample constitutional jurisprudence

[309] Case 44/79 *Liselotte Hauer v Land Rheinland-Pfalz* [1979] ECR 3727.

[310] JHH Weiler, 'Fundamental Rights and Fundamental Boundaries: On the Conflict of Standards and Values in the Protection of Human Rights in the European Legal Space' in *The Constitution of Europe* (Cambridge University Press 1999).

[311] *Hauer* (n 309) para 20.

[312] The CJEU in *Hauer* (n 309) merely cites the provisions of the German, Italian, and Irish constitutions.

[313] See further, F Bignami, 'Creating European Rights: National Values and Supranational Interests' (2005) 11 Columbia Journal of European Law 241.

[314] *FRD Ruling* (n 11) para 93.

[315] Y Soysal, *Limits of Citizenship: Migrants and Postnational Membership in Europe* (University of Chicago Press 1994) 121.

limiting States' use of waiting periods.[316] For instance, in 1983, the BVerfG struck down the three-year waiting period proposed by Bavaria and Baden-Württemberg, although it accepted a one-year period.[317] Following on from key rulings of the Conseil d'Etat on the right to normal family life,[318] in 1993, the Conseil Constitutionnel constrained the legislature's imposition of a two-year waiting period, stipulating that it would be permissible only in cases when the application was submitted before the sponsor had been resident for that long.[319] Lack of space precludes an exhaustive analysis, but my suggestion is merely that the shift to the EU level seems to have been a way to legitimate waiting periods that had been constitutionally constrained at the national level.

In contrast, the CJEU only considers the 2003 Austrian Verfassungsgerichtshof (Constitutional Court of Austria, 'VfGH') ruling, cited by the Parliament in support of its arguments against the reception capacity criterion and waiting periods. In October 2003, the VfGH held that the restrictive annual quota system was contrary to the Austrian Constitution.[320] The VfGH objected to the system of operation of the quota for family reunification, on the basis that when the authorities refuse an application for lack of quota-place, they have no criteria to guide their discretion. In the absence of criteria, the applicant cannot legally challenge the refusal, so there was a violation of the rule of law ('Rechtsstaatsprinzip'). In addition, the VfGH found that the legislature's failure to establish criteria created an objectionable lack of legal certainty. While the VfGH accepted that the legislature enjoyed a margin of discretion[321] as to the system of family reunification established, the system imposed was nonetheless unconstitutional.

As Chapter 2 acknowledges, engagement with domestic constitutional jurisprudence raises many quandaries for the CJEU, not least of which is how to avoid getting tied to some sort of maximum standard. My contention is simply that the comparative distillation method allows the rich resource of constitutional discourse to be tapped into. In the *FRD Ruling*, we see that the Council's account thins out the constitutional practice. Indeed, given that domestic constitutional developments often lead Strasbourg, it seems even more troubling that the Luxembourg

[316] See further A John, 'Family Reunification for Migrants and Refugees: A Forgotten Human Right? A Comparative Analysis of Family Reunification under Domestic Law and Jurisprudence, International and Regional Instruments, ECHR Caselaw and the EU 2003 Family Reunification Directive' (2003) *University of Coimbra Human Rights Center Working Paper*. He considers constitutional case law in Belgium, France, and Germany.

[317] 76 BVerfG 1, 12 May 1987. See further G Neuman, 'Immigration and Judicial Review in the Federal Republic of Germany' (1990) NYU J Int'l L & P 35, 57–63.

[318] Arrêt *GISTI*, CE Ass. 8 December 1978; Arrêt *GISTI II*, CE 26 September 1986.

[319] Decision 93-325, 13 August 1993. See further, C Joppke and E Marzal, 'Courts, the New Constitutionalism and Immigrant Rights: The Case of the French Conseil Constitutionnel' (2004) 43 European Journal of Political Research 823.

[320] Case G 119, 120/03-13, 8 October 2003.

[321] 'Ermessensspielraum' cf the ECtHR concept of 'margin of appreciation' is usually translated as 'Einschätzungsspielraum.' With thanks to Dr Kai Möller for this clarification and assistance with translation.

Court, which expressly undertakes to take them into account, accepts such a distorted account.

### *ii. The margin of appreciation*

The crucial feature of the impugned derogations, in the CJEU's assessment, was that they could be seen as 'partially preserving' the margin of appreciation Strasbourg permits.[322] The margin of appreciation is one of the most controversial aspects of the Strasbourg case law. It is invoked in a variety of circumstances, defining the scope of protected rights as in the Article 8(1) ECHR case law examined above, and informing the appraisal of justifications under Article 8(2) ECHR. To consider whether it is appropriate to transplant the margin of appreciation from the ECHR to the EU context, we must distinguish between its structural and substantive roles.

The structural concept relates to 'the limits or intensity of the review of the [ECtHR] in view of its status as an international tribunal'.[323] The structural margin of appreciation has no place when the CJEU reviews EU acts. The structural margin of appreciation reflects an accommodation of diversity across the Council of Europe, and the distance between an international court and the States Parties. When domestic courts apply the Convention, the structural margin of appreciation should not play a role, for its rationale is tied to the construction of pan-European minimum standards. We expect domestic courts to apply the Convention in a more robust manner. While they may temper their assessments in order to accord appropriate deference to democratically accountable institutions, that deference is distinct from the margin of appreciation. By analogy, when the CJEU reviews the validity of an EU legislative measure, the margin should not apply. Normally, we expect legislative review to be undertaken using a distinct EU standard of fundamental rights protection. Again referring to *Hauer*, we see that compliance with the ECHR was merely the starting point in the process of the construction of the distinct EU standard. Although reviewing a Directive may raise more complex jurisdictional issues than reviewing a Regulation, as explored in the next section, nonetheless, we would expect more rigorous human rights standards when scrutinizing an act of the EU institutions. The CJEU, in that context, interrogates its own political institutions, and must assess interferences with rights against the EU general interest. The substantive concept of the margin is embodied in the balancing approach used to assess the proportionality of interferences with rights.[324] One difficulty with this substantive notion of the margin of appreciation is that it is liable to be circular.[325] Balancing is demanded by the right to family life, but cannot be equated

[322] *FRD Ruling* (n 11) paras 61–62.

[323] G Letsas, *A Theory of Interpretation of the European Convention on Human Rights* (OUP 2007) 81.

[324] ibid, 80–81. [325] ibid, 88.

with it. Luxembourg reads the Strasbourg case law as only exceptionally requiring family reunification as of right, but in so doing it conflates the outcome of the Strasbourg cases with the balancing process Article 8 demands. Regrettably, Luxembourg imbibes the Strasbourg approach *in toto*. In their reading of the Strasbourg case law, both AG and CJEU in the *FRD Ruling* emphasize that family reunification is only 'exceptionally' required under the ECHR. For Luxembourg to treat as the permitted 'margin' all the leeway to refuse admission in the routine cases where there are no 'exceptional' factors, is to follow Strasbourg in granting heavy weight to the State's migration control interests. In other words, Luxembourg thereby endorses the statist assumption, unsurprising when in the Article 8 case law the margin provides the rhetorical space to normalize it. In endorsing this assumption, the CJEU dilutes the principle of proportionality in EU law, and potentially diminishes its status as a ubiquitous, robust EU general principle.

For these reasons, I contend that the CJEU should avoid this uncritical embrace of the Strasbourg device of the margin of appreciation.

### *iii. Elements in the construction of the distinctive EU right to family reunification*

**Security of residence in the European condominium**

In the Citizenship context, family rights emerge as necessary for effective mobility and residence rights of EU Citizens. In her *FRD Opinion*, AG Kokott emphasized that as TCNs did not enjoy a right of residence in the EU, the rationale of the Citizenship cases was inapplicable to the FRD context. However, that sharp dichotomy needs reconsideration. Many TCNs do acquire a right to permanent residence, as the personal scope of that Directive envisages.

As Chapter 1 explains, where TCNs enjoy independent rights of residence under EU law, as under the Europe Agreements, the CJEU has adopted a Citizenship-style analysis to ensure the effectiveness of those rights.[326] The LTRD also provides an EU basis of the right to reside within the territory of the Union for TCNs.[327]

In addition, in the Citizenship context, the CJEU has decoupled residence and other rights. Migrant EU Citizens whose residence rights derive from national law are nonetheless protected under EU law.[328] The result is that family members of EU Citizens enjoy an EU right to residence, even if they were initially irregularly present under national law. The contrast between the CJEU case of *Metock* and the ECtHR ruling in *Omoregie* could not be starker. In the former case, the spouses' statuses as rejected asylum seekers was irrelevant to their EU rights, while in the latter case, the ECtHR held that Article 8 ECHR did not afford any protection to the family life in Norway as the couple could have had no expectation of the asylum seeker's continued residence there.

[326] Case C-327/02 *Panayotova* [2004] ECR I-11055, para 27.
[327] Opinion of AG Bot in *Commission v Netherlands*, para 58.
[328] A trend with its origins in Case C-85/96 *Martinez Sala* [1998] ECR 1-2691.

These developments suggest that EU law should develop a more general notion of security of residence than the Article 8 ECHR case law. However, the CJEU's assessment in the *FRD Ruling* is entirely insensitive to the personal scope of the FRD. The FRD provides that the sponsor must have a 'reasonable prospect' of acquiring a right of permanent residence, so the EU legislature has created a right for sponsors who in likelihood will remain in the EU. Accordingly, the FRD itself is in tension with the Strasbourg 'elsewhere approach', which turns on the legitimacy of requiring the sponsor to return to her country of origin. Under the FRD, the vindication of the rights of sponsors requires that their rootedness in the Member State be respected, which the 'elsewhere approach' does not. We need more than mere reiteration of the ECHR minimum standards.

It would have been open to the CJEU (and this approach is more evident in the subsequent ruling in *Chakroun*)[329] to interpret the right to family reunification under Article 4(1) as itself embodying a distinct EU fundamental right to family reunification, which is both reflective and constitutive of the sponsor's stability of residence. As the sponsor is likely to be afforded a right to stay, family reunification as of right should follow.

Where the EU legislates on fundamental rights, for example in the equality arena, we do not expect the CJEU to confine its conception of fundamental rights to the ECHR minimum. More commonly, the CJEU takes the EU legislative standards as informing the content of the general principles of EU law. Indeed, in the equality arena, as mentioned in Chapter 2, the CJEU has led the ECtHR in providing a more sophisticated concept of discrimination to tackle deep-rooted societal divisions. Admittedly, too hasty constitutionalization of EU legislative enactments as general principles may be inappropriate. For instance in *Mangold*,[330] the CJEU's derivation of a general principle of non-discrimination on grounds of age drew criticism, given that that particular ground is not as well-recognized in human rights and constitutional law as others. Nonetheless, it reflects the fact that EU legislation contributes to the judicial conception of fundamental rights.

**Justification: Replacing statism with the articulation of a general EU interest**

The premise underlying the statist assumption, operative in Strasbourg, is that excluding aliens needs no justification. It is simply a corollary of statehood. As argued in Chapter 1, when admission decisions come to be taken on the basis of EU law, Member States can no longer rely on *ipso facto* justifications for their acts *qua* States. At the very least, the EU adjudicatory context opens up space for, and requires, reasoned argument, not pre-emptive assertions. Hence, we should expect that the troublesome 'weightiness' attached to migration control does not distort appraisal. Transferring competences once conceived of as integral to statehood to the EU level is not to confer statehood on the EU, even by stealth. Nor does it entail simply a shift in venue. The EU is a transformative political space, and in

[329] *Chakroun* (n 12).
[330] Case C-144/04 *Mangold* [2005] ECR 1-9981.

taking decisions out of the exclusive domain of the State, the underlying assumption (in this case, the confluence of territory, authority, and rights) is undone in a way that destabilizes statist migration control assumptions. The FRD represents a sharing of competence between the EU and the Member States as to who may lawfully enter and reside in the EU. As such, the States no longer come to this issue as plenipotentiaries. Accordingly, exclusion, to be justified, should pursue a common legitimate interest. That EU interest should be articulated in terms not of creation of a State with common (State-like) frontiers, but rather, as explained in Chapter 1, an Area of Freedom, Security and Justice which puts citizens, residents, and admission seekers at the centre of attention.

**A concession to the peculiarities of judicial review of Directives: Legislative review and national deference?**

The *FRD Ruling* belongs in that cohort of cases where the CJEU has upheld the validity of Directives, whilst interpreting their provisions in a human rights compliant manner, and emphasizing the duty of Member States to respect the general principles of EU law in their implementation.[331] For Bignami, these cases are laudable for expressly leaving the balancing to national authorities and courts.[332] Arnull similarly praises the *FRD Ruling* for its:

> welcome degree of confidence in the capacity of national legislatures and courts to strike the right balance between individual and collective interests. That confidence was also apparent in *Schmidberger* and *Omega Spielhallen* where the Court declined to interfere with the level of protection applied by the national authorities even though it involved interference with fundamental freedoms laid down in the EC Treaty... Underlying these decisions... is a recognition of the threat that excessive interference by the Union with national authorities' assessments of the requirements of fundamental rights would pose to its already enfeebled legitimacy.[333]

*Schmidberger*[334] and *Omega*[335] are both rulings where Member States invoked human rights to justify national measures that restricted EU economic freedoms. In the former case, Austria established that its ECHR obligations to permit protests in effect took precedence over its internal market obligations to facilitate trade. In contrast, *Omega* concerned a German internal market restriction based on the German constitutional conception of human dignity. The CJEU accepted that the EU general principles would also incorporate this notion of dignity, reflecting an openness to domestic constitutional standards in this context, albeit couched in more tentative terms than the incorporation of the Strasbourg minimum in

[331] Case C-377/98 *Netherlands v Parliament and Council (Biotechnology)* [2001] ECR I-7079; Joined Case C-101/01 *Lindqvist* [2003] ECR I-12971; Cases C-465/00, C-138/01, C-139/01 *Rechnungshof* [2003] ECR I-4989.

[332] F Bignami, 'The Case for Tolerant Constitutional Patriotism: The Right to Privacy Before the European Courts' (2008) 41 Cornell International Law Journal 211.

[333] Arnull (n 11) 611.

[334] Case C-112/00 *Schmidberger* [2003] ECR I-5659.

[335] Case C-36/02 *Omega Spielhallen* [2004] ECR I-9609.

*Schmidberger*. *Omega* and *Schmidberger*, however, both concern defining the permissible outer limits of human rights. In so doing, the CJEU must leave great leeway to ensure that intrinsically valuable human rights are not undermined by instrumentally valuable economic freedoms. The *FRD Ruling* in contrast, is concerned with the validity of an EU minimum standard. The Member States are permitted to set higher standards themselves, but, at the same time, there is no reason to celebrate the CJEU's setting the bar low for the EU minimum. Arnull misses this crucial distinguishing feature when lauding the *FRD Ruling* in the same vein as *Omega* and *Schmidberger*.

There is admittedly one important difference between the CJEU's role in legislative review and that of strong constitutional review in a State context. In the latter context, if a supreme or constitutional court decides legislation violates human rights, it has limited means to ensure that the impugned legislation is revised to meet the fundamental rights standards. However, it still controls the exercise of administrative action in that field, and may review the executive's actions, thereby vindicating its vision of the constitutional rights. In the EU context, annulling a Directive takes away the powers of review of the CJEU, as the field may then fall outside the scope of EU law altogether. This institutional observation suggests a careful calibration of the CJEU's standard of review in assessing the validity of EU legislation, employing reinterpretation more readily than annulment. However, the judicial standard of review should not be conflated with the substantive human rights standards themselves. My contention goes to the content of the standards of fundamental rights protection EU law should develop.

To conclude on a distinct EU approach, my suggestion is that a better fit with the EU legal order would come by treating the 'margin of appreciation' with caution, and rather focusing on the sponsor's security of residence and the right to family life in the context of that secure residence right. On this basis, admitting family members of those who have or will make their home in the EU should be as of right. Strong justification ought to be needed for refusing admission, which requires more than general notions of 'integration'. This approach does not purport to be a radical departure, but rather one that befits the structure of both the EU legal order, and indeed the FRD. It simply takes seriously the usual added-value of EU rights, namely that they create bright-line rules with derogations assessed under the proportionality standard.

## 4. Testing the distinctive EU approach to family reunification

### *i. The demise of the 'effective family bond' criterion*

An excellent illustration of the added-value of EU norms is provided by the demise of the 'effective family bond' criterion in Dutch law. As is evident in the accounts of *Ahmut, Gül, Sen,* and *Tuquabo-Tekle,* the criterion was employed in the Netherlands to deem family life to have been ruptured, where parents left their children in the care of others whilst they established themselves in the Netherlands. Given the ambiguities inherent in the Strasbourg case law, even after

*Tuquabo-Tekle*, it was still arguable that the 'effective family bond' criterion was acceptable. The Dutch government also maintained its compatibility with the FRD, based on Article 16 thereof, which refers to 'real marital or family relationship.' The matter was promptly litigated before the Dutch courts, but the case before the *Raad van State* deemed unripe, as the FRD was not in force.[336] As Van Walsum explains, although official explanations for the reform of the 'effective family bond' criterion cited *Tuquabo-Tekle*, it was the threat of CJEU litigation that prompted the official change.[337] It was not the letter of the FRD, but EU law's stronger review and proportionality and the CJEU's propensity to employ bright lines that seems to have been decisive.

However, this early policy adjustment was not entirely typical. In the 2008 FRD Implementation Report, the Commission identified that some Member States lowered standards when implementing the FRD, citing in particular the implementation rules on waiting periods, minimum age of the sponsor, income requirements, and integration measures.[338] These restrictions in turn have set up two new litigation fronts, one in relation to financial restrictions on family reunification, on which the CJEU has decisively ruled in *Chakroun*, and the other on integration measures and conditions, where governmental and judicial moves have thus far not yielded decisive outcomes.[339] The next two sections examine each of these topics in turn.

### *ii. Financial restrictions on family reunification*

As discussed above, the ECtHR stated in *GR v the Netherlands* that excessively high fees for the regularization of the migration status of a spouse could be challengeable under Article 13 ECHR only if there is an 'arguable case' that Article 8 ECHR has been violated. In *Haydarie v The Netherlands*,[340] Strasbourg for the first time examined income requirements for family reunification under the Dutch immigration rules. With scanty reasoning, the ECtHR asserted that it:

> did not consider unreasonable a requirement that an alien who seeks family reunion must demonstrate that he/she has sufficient independent and lasting income, not being welfare benefits, to provide for the basic costs of subsistence of his or her family members with whom reunion is sought.[341]

[336] *Raad Van State* Decision 200510214/1, 29 March 2006.

[337] S Van Walsum, 'Transnational Mothering, National Immigration Policy, and European Law: The Experience of the Netherlands' in S Benhabib and J Resnik (eds), *Migrations and Mobilities: Citizenship, Borders, and Gender* (New York University Press 2009) 228, 243–45.

[338] European Commission, *FRD Implementation Report* (n 253). For further details on implementation, see Groenendijk and others (n 251).

[339] Two pending cases will be important: Case C-579/13 *P, S*, lodged 15 November 2013 (on the LTRD); Case C-153/14 *K & A*, lodged 3 April 2014.

[340] *Haydarie v The Netherlands* App No 8876/04 (ECHR, 20 October 2005). See case note by P Boeles and M Bruins (2006) 8 EJML364.

[341] ibid, 13.

As regards the application of the requirement to the individual, it noted that the applicant cared for her wheelchair-bound sister at home, but accepted that it had not been demonstrated that it would be impossible for her to engage an agency to do this, allowing her to get paid employment. The ECtHR's review seems far too light-touch. First of all, if return to Afghanistan was impossible for human rights reasons (which the ECtHR did not assess), then it would seem that the family could have demonstrated that it would only have been possible for them to live together in the Netherlands. Secondly, concerning the assessment of the applicant's efforts to gain employment, the approach seems to permit excessive bureaucratic discretion. Such a ruling is not atypical for Strasbourg: the most plausible interpretation is to see it as the ECtHR discouraging further applicants on the topic, suggesting that it does not wish to engage in a review of these restrictions. The CJEU could not legitimately avoid the issue in this way. It is required to give preliminary rulings in order to provide general guidance on the meaning of EU norms.

In contrast, the FRD contains a specific, relatively clear provision on financial requirements. As mentioned above, Article 7 FRD permits various material preconditions for family reunification, requiring the sponsor to have 'normal' accommodation;[342] sickness insurance;[343] and 'stable and regular resources'.[344] The Commission's FRD Implementation Report shows that the Netherlands imposes the highest income requirement, being 120% (for family formation) of the legal minimum wage of a twenty-three-year-old worker, irrespective of the age of the sponsor, which the Commission suggests may be age discriminatory.[345] It is unsurprising then that the first case referred to the CJEU on the FRD, *Chakroun*, concerns just this issue.

The *Raad van State* referred two questions to the CJEU, the first concerning the phrase 'recourse to the social assistance system' under Article 7(1)(c) FRD and the second concerning the permissibility of distinguishing between family formation and family reunification, as the Dutch legislation had done. AG Sharpston opined that in the circumstances, the latter distinction violated the general principle of equal treatment, 'to the extent that it is not based on any objective factor related to the level of resources required to maintain the sponsor and his or her family and applies without regard to the circumstances of each case'.[346] Concerning the Dutch income threshold, the AG rejected the Dutch government's submission that it was set at a level to ensure that 'recourse to the social assistance system' would not occur,[347] given that the threshold reflected a level of income at which some discretionary support was available. Accordingly the threshold precluded the individual assessment required by the FRD.[348] The Court followed the Opinion, emphasizing that the FRD creates a precise positive obligation to authorize family migration as a general rule, such that the restrictions thereto must be interpreted

[342] FRD Art 7(1)(a). [343] ibid, Art 7(1)(b).
[344] ibid, Art 7(1)(c).
[345] European Commission, *FRD Implementation Report* (n 253) 7.
[346] *Chakroun*, (n 12) Opinion of AG Sharpston, para 55. [347] ibid, para 69.
[348] ibid, para 70.

strictly.[349] Two crucial features of the reasoning are to be noted: the CJEU emphasizes the centrality of individual assessment, and draws on its case law on EU Citizenship in rejecting a distinction between family formation and family reunification,[350] and in impugning the income thresholds.[351]

The Commission also reports a variety of other requirements imposed under this heading.[352] It expressed concern in particular about the fees levied in Spain, Finland, and the Netherlands. Spain doubles the required amount for each additional family member. In Finland, the amount increased by €450 for each reunited child. Indeed, the Commission is, if anything, too tentative. It may be argued that such entrance fees are *per se* prohibited under the FRD, as they amount to an additional condition, not expressly provided for.[353] In infringement proceedings against the Netherlands, the Court condemned excessive fees under the LTRD.[354] *Chakroun* suggests that the Court would examine these conditions using the right/restriction dichotomy and strict proportionality assessment.

### *iii. Integration measures and conditions*

As noted in the analysis of the *FRD Ruling* above, the CJEU had the opportunity to set out some principled guidance on integration measures and conditions in that ruling, but did not do so. In *Noorzia*, the Court examined Article 4(5) FRD, which permits spousal migration to be restricted to those over twenty-one, in the name of 'better integration' and 'prevention of forced marriages'. As discussed above, the Court focused on the more specific aim of preventing forced marriage, rather than 'integration', thereby avoiding having to explain how delaying family reunification facilitates integration, which would have required an assessment of the exclusionary invocation of 'integration'.

There have been other near misses: in March 2011, the Dutch integration test was the subject of a preliminary reference to the CJEU, but the case was deemed inadmissible as it became hypothetical.[355] The Commission's submission in that case had been critical of the test, so it is surmised that the Dutch authorities granted the applicant a residence permit in order to avoid the matter coming to judgment. We should recall the political context in order to understand the reluctance of both the governmental innovators and the CJEU to subject integration measures and conditions to supranational judicial scrutiny.

Over a decade ago, Groenendijk noted this new restrictive concept of 'integration' where migrants were required to demonstrate their capacity for integrating in host societies before admission.[356] The means used included testing knowledge

[349] ibid, paras 41–43.

[350] ibid, para 64, citing *Metock*, para 93.

[351] ibid, para 46, citing *Eind*, para 29.

[352] European Commission, *FRD Implementation Report* (n 253) 7.

[353] Groenendijk 'Family Reunification as a Right under Community Law' (n 251) 222.

[354] Case Case C-508/10 *Commission v Netherlands*.

[355] Case C-155/11 *Bibi Mohammad Imran v De Minister van Buitenlandse Zaken*, [2011] ECR I-05095. See also withdrawn case C-513/12 *Ayalti* [2013] OJ C63.

[356] K Groenendijk, 'Legal Concepts of Integration in EU Migration Law' (2004) 6 EJML 111. See further, K Groenendijk, 'Pre-departure Integration Strategies in the European Union: Integration or Immigration Policy?' (2011) 13(1) EJML 1.

of language and host society before admission. Family migrants in particular were subject to these requirements as the particular marriage patterns of some settled migrants in EU Member States were regarded as in themselves a manifestation of lack of integration, particularly if migrants chose to marry someone from the country of origin of their parents. The policies are generally regarded as a Dutch innovation. Then a process of horizontal policy transfer took place, with integration measures and conditions being adopted by Austria, Denmark, France, Germany, and the UK. Goodman argues that the FRD set 'a supranational precedent that created the political opportunity for national implementation' and 'created a legitimacy that makes it possible for member states to link integration requirements to immigration'.[357] The EU level provided the platform for this policy transfer across the Member States. While the FRD is not binding on either Denmark or the UK, the negotiations leading to the adoption of the FRD facilitated the dissemination of the Dutch practices to the other national officials.[358]

Bonjour also identifies a further subsequent transnational dimension, whereby Member States sought to confer legitimacy on pre-departure integration measures by referring to their prevalence across Europe, in part because the 'top-down' legitimacy from the FRD and LTRD is now under question under EU law.[359] In this context, while the policies spread and become more institutionalized across the EU, there is growing awareness that they may be in tension with EU law. The European Commission in particular in its guidance on the FRD comes out against them, and its stance in the aborted preliminary reference on the Dutch integration measures and conditions made its position even more explicit.[360] The battle-lines have been drawn, but the ultimate arbiter, the CJEU, has thus far avoided the fray.

The closest it has come is in *Dogan*.[361] Again here, the Court declined to interpret the integration requirements in the LTRD, leaving legal uncertainty surrounding this matter, choosing instead to resolve the case by interpreting special rights for the families of Turkish residents covered by the Association Agreement between the EU and Turkey.[362] In contrast, AG Mengozzi also examined Article

[357] S Goodman, 'Controlling Immigration through Language and Country Knowledge Requirements' (2011) 34(2) West European Politics 235, 242.

[358] S Bonjour, 'The Transfer of Pre-Departure Integration Requirements for Family Migrants among Member States of the European Union' (2014) 2(2) Comparative Migration Studies 203.

[359] ibid.

[360] European Commission (n 255) 15–16; European Commission, *Written Declaration submitted on 4 May 2011 to the EU Court of Justice in the case C-155/11*, Sj.g(2011) 540657. As Bonjour notes, this opinion was unequivocal: the Commission advised the Court to rule that 'the directive does not allow for a family member…to be denied entry and stay only because this family member has not passed the integration exam abroad'. In May 2013, the Commission sent a Letter of Formal Notice to the German government about its pre-departure language requirement, thus initiating the first phase of infringement proceedings. Bonjour (n 358) 215.

[361] Dogan (n 32). See S Peers, 'The CJEU Transforms Family Reunion for Turkish Citizens' (*EU Law Analysis*, 12 July 2014) <http://eulawanalysis.blogspot.gr/2014/07/the-cjeu-transforms-family-reunion-for.html> accessed 11 April 2015.

[362] In particular, the ruling focused on the standstill clause under Article 41(1) of the Additional Protocol to the Association Agreement [1972] OJ L293/4. For an analysis of this aspect of the case, see Peers (n 361).

7(2) FRD on 'integration measures'. In the particular case, Germany imposed a requirement that family migrants demonstrate proof of basic knowledge of German before admission. While the AG confirmed that 'integration measures' could be imposed before admission to the Member States concerned,[363] he purported to give effect to the guiding interpretative principles derived from *Chakroun*. These he characterized, first, that authorization of family reunification is the 'general rule' and the provisions enabling restrictions to be placed on it must be interpreted strictly and, secondly, that Member State discretion must not be used in a manner which would undermine the objective of the FRD, namely the promotion of family reunification.[364]

He also provided important guidance on the distinction between 'integration measures' and 'integration conditions' in the LTRD.[365] Under the latter Directive, Member States may make acquisition of LTR status conditional on meeting 'integration conditions', while residence thereafter in another Member State is conditional only on 'integration measures', the same term as used in the FRD. Accordingly, AG Mengozzi regarded the two notions as 'quite separate and are certainly not synonymous', with measures being less onerous than conditions.[366] Article 7 FRD sets out specific conditions in Article 7(1), and refers to 'integration measures' additionally in Article 7(2). Accordingly, Article 7(2) cannot pursue the aim of *selecting* the persons who may exercise their right of reunification, as such selection is the aim of the criteria and conditions laid down in Article 7(1). On the contrary, the integration measures in Article 7(2) must essentially be intended to facilitate integration in the Member States.[367] A condition was a 'prerequisite which must be proven by the interested party', in contrast to a measure.[368]

Nonetheless, as it is permissible to impose 'integration measures' before admission, they may be obligations to achieve a particular result, provided that they are proportionate to the objective of integration laid down in Article 7(2) FRD and that the effectiveness of the FRD was not undermined.[369] Individual assessment was always required under Article 17 FRD, in particular to allow consideration of any 'possible material or personal difficulties which the person concerned may encounter in order to comply with the integration measures imposed' including accessibility of training, materials, and cost issues.[370] In the instant case, only evidence relating to 'physical, mental or psychological illness or disability' could lead to an exemption, whereas Mrs Dogan had literacy problems.[371] Accordingly, AG Mengozzi concluded that:

> Making authorisation of family reunification for a spouse conditional on his/her literacy may, therefore, depending on the circumstances, be disproportionate to the objective of integration pursued by the measures adopted under Article 7(2) [FRD] and frustrate the effectiveness of that directive.[372]

[363] Opinion of AG Mengozzi in *Dogan* (n 32) para 48.
[364] ibid, para 50, citing *Chakroun*, paragraph 43. See also *O/S* (n 194) para 74.
[365] ibid, para 51. [366] ibid, para 52. [367] ibid, para 53. [368] ibid, para 54.
[369] ibid, para 56. [370] ibid, para 59. [371] ibid, para 60. [372] ibid.

The Opinion contains sound EU law analysis, yet the CJEU has thus far not addressed the issue directly. That stance is disappointing as the efficacy, rationality, and fairness of these policies are open to question.

These practices have now been the subject of many scholarly studies, noting their illiberal nature.[373] This approach to 'integration' is potentially a mask for discrimination and exclusion. Goodman suggests they have been devised to employ politically acceptable language of integration and inclusion to achieve potentially objectionable and discriminatory outcomes of exclusion.[374] Some national practices have been condemned as discriminatory, due to the fact that they do not apply to all TCNs, with applicants from Canada, the United States, Japan, and South Korea often exempt.[375] Indeed, the practices underpinning the new integration discourse often seem, on one view, patently irrational, being based on the premise that would-be migrants can imbibe and adapt to national cultures from a distance.[376]

Two notable empirical studies provide important evidence to inform the political and legal debate, Integration and Naturalisation tests, the new way to European Citizenship (INTEC),[377] and Promoting Sustainable Policies for Integration (PROSINT).[378] The International Organization for Migration (IOM) notes that:

> In practice, the recent transnational projects such as INTEC and PROSINT have found no indications of the long-term effectiveness of pre-entry tests for immigrant integration. In fact, integration is a long-term process that is influenced by a wide range of individual migrant characteristics, but also systemic conditions in the country of destination. The

[373] Guild et al. (n 15); R van Oers, E Ersbøll, D Kostakopoulou (eds), *A Re-definition of Belonging? Language and Integration Tests in Europe* (Martinus Nijhoff Publishers 2010); S Bonjour, 'Between Integration Provision and Selection Mechanism. Party Politics, Judicial Constraints, and the Making of French and Dutch Policies of Civic Integration Abroad' (2010) 12(3) EJML 299.

[374] Goodman (n 357).

[375] See further, HRW, *The Netherlands: Discrimination in the Name of Integration* (HRW, 13 May 2008); ECRI (European Commission against Racism and Intolerance), *Third periodical report on the Netherlands*. The UN Committee on the Elimination of Racial Discrimination (CERD) found that the exemption led to discrimination on the basis of nationality, particularly between 'Western' and 'non-Western' state nationals, and recommended that the Netherlands review its legislation. CERD, *Report on the Netherlands—Seventy-sixth session 15 February to 12 March 2010* (2010), CERD/C/NLD/CO/1718.

[376] See further D Kostakopolou 'The Area of Freedom, Security and Justice and the Political Morality of Migration and Integration' in H Lindahl (ed), *A Right to Inclusion and Exclusion? Normative Fault Lines of the EU's Area of Freedom, Security and Justice* (Hart Publishing 2009) 185, 204.

[377] T Strik, A Böcker, M Luiten, and R van Oers, *The INTEC Project: Synthesis Report - Integration and Naturalisation tests: the new way to European Citizenship, A Comparative study in nine Member States on the national policies concerning integration and naturalisation tests and their effects on integration* (2011).

[378] International Centre for Migration Policy Development (ICMPD), *Research Project on Promoting Sustainable Policies for Integration*. PROSINT ran from 2009 to 2011 and evaluated the main target groups of compulsory and voluntary integration measures, as well as the different logics underlying integration policies in eight EU Member States (Austria, Czech Republic, Denmark, Spain, Italy, the Netherlands, Sweden, UK) and Switzerland.

success or failure to pass a pre-entry test is not a representative indicator of the subsequent integration outcomes.[379]

Although the preceding section has critiqued the *FRD Ruling* for over-reliance on the ECHR minimum in terms of the human rights standard used to review the Directive, the CJEU is explicit in interpreting the FRD as setting higher standards than the ECHR. Indeed, EU law's propensity to establish bright lines and strict proportionality is in marked contrast to the casuistry and multi-factor balancing of the ECtHR. *Chakroun* is a ruling typical of and befitting the EU legal context, while *Noorzia* is indulgent of national discretion in an anomalous manner. To date, the CJEU has avoided the integration challenge, so we await sound EU interpretation of the FRD (and LTRD) provisions on these practices.

## V. Back to Strasbourg? Casuistry, Gradualism, and Universalism

In *Biao v Denmark*,[380] the Second Chamber of the ECtHR accepted highly contestable integration-based claims to limit family migration. Thankfully, that case will now be examined by the Grand Chamber. Before concluding this chapter, it is worth recalling some of the added-value of the ECtHR.

### 1. The meaning of 'family'

The meaning of family life unfurls in the Strasbourg internal case law, untainted by the statist assumption. Although we find the typical accommodation strategies, the margin of appreciation and European consensus in particular, there is potential for Strasbourg to improve the EU approach to the meaning of family, particularly as the ECtHR takes a *de facto* approach to family life, in contrast to EU law's focus on formal status.[381] The productive engagement between Luxembourg and Strasbourg is reflected in the CJEU's use of human rights principles to secure residence rights for family members, even if EU legislation is silent. In *Chen, Carpenter*, and *Baumbast* in particular, the CJEU employed the (admittedly latently patriarchal) notion of the 'primary caregiver' to vindicate the residence rights of mothers, deemed necessary to realize the residence rights of their EU Citizen infant children in *Chen* and *Baumbast*, and to facilitate the economic activities of the EU Citizen husband in *Carpenter*.

379 IOM, *Contribution to the Consultation on the Right to Family Reunification of Third-Country Nationals Living in the EU (Directive 2003/86/EC)* (2012), 6 <http://ec.europa.eu/dgs/home-affairs/what-is-new/public-consultation/2012/pdf/0023/famreun/internationalorganisationssocialpartnersngos/international_organization_for_migration_-_iom.pdf> accessed 11 April 2015.

380 *Biao* (n 38).

381 See further, H Stalford 'Concepts of Family under EU Law: Lessons from the ECHR' (2002) 16 International Journal of Law, Policy and the Family 410.

The notion of family life under Article 8(1) ECHR depends on the existence of close, continuing, and practical ties.[382] However, the legal status of marriage is also indicative of family life[383] and a child born of wedlock is *ipso jure* part of the family from birth, even if the parents are not living together.[384] It is long established that whether children are born within or outside wedlock is irrelevant to the existence of family ties.[385] Indeed the ECtHR assumes the existence of family relationship between parent and child regardless of the family's living arrangements[386] or apparent lack of commitment to the child,[387] although events may break that family tie between a child and a non-resident parent. Relationships between siblings are also protected.[388] However, as regards relationships between adult siblings, the ECtHR requires 'further elements of dependency involving more than the normal emotional ties' in order for family life to be recognized.[389] Similarly, relationships within the extended family may attract protection under Article 8.[390] However, in *Slivenko* the ECtHR held that the relationship between an adult child and a non-dependent parent was not family life, but rather covered as an aspect of the right to privacy.[391]

In *X, Y, and Z v UK*,[392] the relationship between a female-to-male transsexual, his female partner and her child was recognized as constituting a family. More recently in *Goodwin v UK*,[393] a unanimous ECtHR departed from its earlier case law and found a violation of Article 12 ECHR (the right to marry) in the UK's bar on transsexuals' marrying in their new/assigned gender. The ECtHR noted that in the analogous Article 9 EUCFR, the reference to marriage as between 'men and women' had been removed. The CJEU applied *Goodwin* in *KB*.[394] AG Ruiz-Jarabo in *KB* took account of a comparative study of the then EU Member States revealing that the marriage of transsexuals in their acquired gender was generally accepted, except in Ireland and the UK. He considered that the Irish and UK positions alone were not capable of preventing the identification of a 'sufficiently uniform tradition capable of being a source of general principle of Community law'.[395] The *KB* approach is laudable in that in incorporating the Strasbourg standards, the CJEU was mindful that it was developing a standard based on a consensus amongst a narrower, less diverse group of States than the EU. Moreover, when the CJEU is called on to articulate fundamental rights to guide the EU legislature, it may well need

[382] The following account draws on the summary of the Strasbourg case law in *Al-Nashif v Bulgaria* (2003) 36 EHRR 37, para 112.

[383] *Abdulaziz* (n 34) para 62.

[384] *Berrehab* (n 91) para 21.

[385] *Marckx v Belgium* (1979) 2 EHRR 330; *Johnston v Ireland* (1986) 9 EHRR 203; *Boughanemi v France* (1996) 22 EHRR 228.

[386] *Berrehab* (n 91).

[387] *Ahmut* (n 128).

[388] *Moustaquim* (n 73); *Olsson v Sweden* (1989) 11 EHRR 259; *Boughanemi* (n 385).

[389] *Javeed v the Netherlands* App No 47390/99 (ECHR, 3 July 2001); *Ezzoudhi v France* App No 47160/99 (ECHR, 13 February 2001).

[390] See, e.g. *Boyle v UK* (1994) 19 EHRR 179 concerning the uncle-nephew relationship.

[391] *Slivenko* (n 62).

[392] (1997) 24 EHRR 143.

[393] (2002) 35 EHRR 18.

[394] Case C-117/01 *KB v The National Health Service and the Secretary of State for Health* [2004] ECR I-541.

[395] *KB* (n 394) Opinion of AG Ruiz-Jarabo, paras 27–28.

to do more than assess evolving consensus as reflected in national practices. The commitments and values in the EU Treaties and legislation may also legitimately inform the Luxembourg human rights standards.

Strasbourg's engagement with same-sex relationships reflects its evolutionary approach, with the right to privacy providing its initial basis for impugning criminalization of consensual same-sex sexual activity, and later sexual orientation recognized as a prohibited ground of discrimination. However, the ECtHR is moving towards requiring some form of public recognition of same-sex relationships,[396] although its case law is evolving. Originally, the European Commission on Human Rights refused to accept that family life existed between same-sex couples who were being separated by an immigration decision.[397] However, the treatment of same-sex relationships has evolved considerably. For example, in *Karner v Austria*,[398] the ECtHR found a violation of Article 14 (in conjunction with Article 8) in the failure to allow inheritance rights for a gay partner, although it expressly refused to determine whether private life or family life was at stake. Change is coming, though. In 2008, the Grand Chamber in *EB v France*[399] found the refusal of adoption on the basis of sexual orientation violated Articles 14 (and 8), marking a shift from the 2002 ruling in *Fretté v France*.[400] *Schalk and Kopf v Austria* takes a further step towards recognition of same-sex relationships.[401] The ECtHR took account of the evolving State practice on this issue,[402] under its consensus approach, and held that same-sex couples enjoy family life together, and that failure to afford formal recognition to such relationships may violate Articles 8 and 14 ECHR, although it stopped short of recognizing a right to same-sex marriage under Article 12 ECHR. Strasbourg will be called to revisit the issue in the pending cases of *Chapin & Carpentier v France*[403] and *Orlandi v Italy*.[404]

In EU law, family of EU Citizens originally comprised only spouses and descendants under twenty-one years of age or dependent[405] and dependent relatives in the ascending line of the worker and/or spouse. 'Spouse' meant married spouse only[406] and the status of ex-spouses was uncertain.[407] The Citizenship Directive

[396] See JM Scherpe 'The Legal Recognition of Same-Sex Couples in Europe and the Role of the European Court of Human Rights' (2013) 10 Equal Rights Review 83.

[397] *X and Y v UK* (1983) 32 DR 220; *WP and DP v UK* (1986) EHRR 49.

[398] *Karner v Austria* (2004) 38 EHRR 24. cf *Mata Estevez v Spain* App No 56501/00 (ECHR, 10 May 2001) where the ECtHR held that provision of a survivor's pension only for a spouse was permissible in order to protect the family based on marriage.

[399] *EB v France*, App No 43546/02 (Grand Chamber, ECHR, 22 January 2008).

[400] *Fretté v France*, App No 36515/97 (ECHR, 26 February 2002).

[401] *Schalk and Kopf v Austria* (2011) 53 EHRR 20. See further R Wintemute, *Written Comments (Shalck and Kopf v Austria) for FIDH, ICJ, Aire Centre & ILGA-Europe*, 26 June 2007; L Hodson, 'A Marriage by Any Other Name? *Schalk and Kopf v Austria*' (2011) 11 HRLRev 170. See further Application No XXXX/ XX *Vallianatos and Others v Greece* 7 November 2013 (Grand Chamber).

[402] On which, see K Boele-Woelki and A Fuchs (eds), *Legal Recognition of Same-Sex Relationships in Europe: National, Cross-Border and European Perspectives* (2nd edn, Intersentia 2012).

[403] App No 40183/07.

[404] App No 26431/12.

[405] On the definition of dependency, see Case 316/85 *Lebon* [1987] ECR 2811; *Chen* (n 181).

[406] Case 59/85 *Netherlands v Reed* [1986] ECR 1283.

[407] Case 267/83 *Diatta v Land Berlin* [1985] ECR 567.

now clarifies that in the event of the termination of the marriage, EU ex-spouses/partners retain their right to reside,[408] while the right of residence of TCN family members in these circumstances is subject to conditions.[409] Although it has never been considered in relation to Article 10 Citizenship Directive, in another context, the CJEU held that the term 'spouse' did not include a non-married registered life partner, be that relationship homosexual or heterosexual.[410] The Citizenship Directive now extends the concept of family member to include non-married partners with whom EU Citizens have 'contracted a registered partnership, on the basis of the legislation of a Member State, if the legislation of the host Member States treats registered partnerships as equivalent to marriage and in accordance with the conditions laid down in the relevant legislation of the host Member State'.[411] Although this provision depends on such a status existing in the laws of the home and host State, it goes some way to closing a long-recognized gap in EU protection.[412] In addition, Member States are under an obligation 'in accordance with…national legislation' to facilitate the rights to reside of other family members[413] and non-married partners 'with whom the Union citizen has a durable stable relationship'.[414] The FRD contains a narrower definition of 'family member' than the Citizenship Directive, as explored above.

EU law has limited competence over family law, so cannot take the lead on the creation of a status for same-sex couples, yet has a broad legal base in Article 19 TFEU to 'combat discrimination'. In *Maruko*,[415] the CJEU took a nuanced position on the issue of same-sex partnerships and sexual orientation discrimination, moving beyond its previous position in *D and Sweden v Council*.[416] In *D and Sweden*, a case which concerned an EU civil servant and the confinement of staff entitlements to spouses, the CJEU held that it was for the Community legislature to change the rules to accord benefits also to same-sex partners, refusing to regard differentiation on ground of marital status as indirect sexual orientation discrimination. In *Maruko*, an employment case,[417] the CJEU held that where national law created two separate statuses of heterosexual marriage and same-sex partnership, couples should be treated equally.[418] It was not only for national legislatures, but also national judges to assess the equality of the two statuses, thus establishing a mode of shared judicial competence over this issue. A similar approach is seen

[408] Art 13(1) CD. [409] Art 13(2) CD.

[410] Joined Cases C-122/99P and C-125/99P *D and Sweden v Council of the European Union* [2001] ECR I-4319.

[411] Art 2(2)(b) CD.

[412] See further H Toner, *Partnership Rights, Free Movement and EU Law* (Hart Publishing 2004).

[413] Art 3(2)(a) CD. See Opinion of AG Bot in *Rahman* (n 220). [414] Art 3(2)(b) CD.

[415] Case C-267/06 *Maruko* [2008] ECR I-1757.

[416] See also the later staff case of Case F-86/09 *W v Commission* [2010] OJ C 32861 for an interpretation of the revised Staff Rules, which do provide for household allowances for same-sex couples in formalized relationships.

[417] So Council Directive 2000/78/EC establishing a general framework for equal treatment in employment and occupation [2000] OJ L303/16 applied.

[418] *Maruko* (n 415) paras 72–73.

in *Römer* concerning pensions.[419] For family reunification purposes, this line of cases suggests that the EU general principle of non-discrimination could be used to prompt recognition of formalized same-sex relationships. The Charter, after all, contains a broad non-discrimination clause in Article 21:

> Any discrimination based on any ground such as sex, race, colour, ethnic or social origin, genetic features, language, religion or belief, political or any other opinion, membership of a national minority, property, birth, disability, age or sexual orientation shall be prohibited.

## 2. Questioning the privileged position of EU citizens

On occasion, the ECtHR is confronted with applications from TCNs whose family connection with EU Citizens would have provided them with enhanced protection under EU law. *Mehemi v France*[420] concerned an Algerian national, married to an Italian resident in France. The 'elsewhere' analysis in the case involved examining the possibility of family life in Italy as well as Algeria, making family life in France even more precarious.[421] There was no mention of the EU context. Nowadays, post-*Mendizabal*, we would expect the ECtHR not simply to take the EU right to live in Italy into account, but also to assess the lawfulness of France's conduct in light of its EU obligations. Indeed, that such litigants find themselves relying on the ECHR suggests lack of awareness of the EU protections, or a serious deficit in national compliance with EU norms.

A deeper problem is whether the privileged status of EU Citizens (and their family members) in EU law ought to be scrutinized under Article 14 ECHR. To date, the ECtHR has given EU Citizenship a wide berth, accepting that as the EU has created a 'special legal order', there is an 'objective and reasonable justification' for treating EU Citizens more favourably than others.[422] However, as the position of high deference to the EU is no longer appropriate, and as the Article 14 ECHR jurisprudence has evolved, this is another area where Strasbourg should interrogate EU practices more thoroughly. Peers has long been highly critical of this deferential approach. As he puts it:

> it is hard to see why the 'special legal order' criterion exists at all, unless it simply refers to the enhanced immigration status of EC national sponsors. Otherwise EU Member States would have carte blanche to justify any form of unequal treatment between EU and non-EU nationals as regards any of the rights in the Convention, including such matters as detention, fair trials and freedom of religion. It may even be questioned whether this concept is now implicitly overruled by the more recent judgment bringing the activity of the EU Member States implementing EC law within the scope of the Convention.[423]

Peers's citation of *Bosphorus* is apposite. A Strasbourg shot across the bows even hinting at questioning the anomalies created by the privileged status of EU Citizens could provide further impetus for Luxembourg to level up the protections of TCN

[419] Case C-147/08 *Römer* [2011] ECR I-3591.
[420] *Mehemi v France No 1* (n 73). [421] ibid, para 36.
[422] *Moustaquim* (n 73) para 43.
[423] S Peers 'EU Law and Family Reunification: A Human Rights Critique' *ECLN Essays no 16*, 2005, 1.

families to those of EU Citizens. At present, the CJEU has privileged migrant EU Citizens, and by analogy, those sponsors who fall within the FRD.[424] Yet the claims of others may be equally compelling. The ECtHR ought to question the privileges attached to EU Citizenship, rather than insulate them from scrutiny as the current approach does.

## VI. Conclusions

The contrast between the ECtHR and CJEU on family reunification is striking. Strasbourg's adherence to the statist assumption shapes its jurisprudence. The contrast between *Metock* and *Omoregie* could not be starker. In the former case, the spouses' statuses as failed asylum seekers was irrelevant to their EU rights as TCN spouses of EU Citizens, while in the latter case, Strasbourg held that Article 8 ECHR did not afford any protection to the family life in Norway, as the couple could have had no expectation of the asylum seeker's continued residence there. Given that many TCN migrants to the EU have temporary migration status (like asylum seekers), the implications of refusing protection as family life was created where the couple knew that one of them had no right to stay has potentially sweeping ramifications. Yet, the very strength of the EU protections leads to contention about their scope. Migrant EU Citizens fall under the Citizenship Directive. Static ones, even post-*Zambrano* and its progeny, must demonstrate that failure to grant residence rights to family members will impair the 'genuine enjoyment of the substance of their rights as EU Citizens.' This new test opens up a new litigation front, but early indications are that it only provides a form of residual protection for residence rights, where otherwise entire families would have to leave the 'territory of the Union'.

Interaction between Luxembourg and Strasbourg is stultifying when the CJEU ignores its own institutional advantages, in particular when, as in the *FRD Ruling*, it is reviewing an act of its own legislature. This context demands the articulation of a distinctive human rights approach to family reunification, moving above the Strasbourg minimum, under both the Citizenship Directive and FRD. As explained, the building blocks for a distinctive EU right to family reunification are in place. It remains open to the CJEU to interpret the right to family reunification under the FRD as itself embodying a distinct EU human right to family reunification, which is both reflective and constitutive of the sponsor's stability of residence. As the sponsor is likely to be afforded a right to stay, family reunification as of right should follow as a matter of human right—the 'elsewhere approach' has no place in EU law. *Chakroun* clearly indicates that the FRD establishes higher standards than the Strasbourg case law, although the Court arrives at its conclusions by analogizing between the FRD and EU Citizenship, rather than by using the language of EU fundamental rights. EU law's propensity to establish bright lines

[424] Assuming that such sponsors fall within its personal scope, Art 11 LTRD supports this contention.

and strict proportionality is in marked contrast to the casuistry and multi-factor balancing of the ECtHR, and is thereby apt to offer a more secure right to family reunification, as *Chakroun* and the case law on EU Citizens' TCN family members illustrate. Strasbourg has the capacity to offer a corrective to the privileged status of EU Citizens, but as yet, has maintained its position of high deference to the peculiarities of the EU system.

In contrast, Luxembourg/Strasbourg interaction may be fertile when Luxembourg draws on the rich internal Strasbourg case law concerning family life. The latter's gradualism and casuistry may temper the EU's narrow, rigid, legislative definition of 'family member'.

The indications are that governments continue to seek greater restrictions on family reunification. For instance, the European Pact on Immigration and Asylum states that:

> The European Council agrees to regulate family migration more effectively by inviting each Member State, in compliance with the European Convention for the Protection of Human Rights and Fundamental Freedoms, to take into consideration in its national legislation, except for certain specific categories, its own reception capacities and families' capacity to integrate, as evaluated by their resources and accommodation in the country of destination and, for example, their knowledge of that country's language.[425]

The European Commission issued a Green Paper on the FRD in November 2011.[426] Notably, several respondents urged that the FRD not be reformed, as standards were likely to be lowered in any new legislative process, but rather that the Commission focus its energies on the proper implementation of the current legislation. In the meantime, the productive engagement between CJEU and ECtHR may offer the best way to contest restrictions and vindicate the right to family life. The pending Grand Chamber ruling in *Biao v Denmark* and the pending CJEU rulings on integration measures offer the opportunity to question this insidious form of restriction on family migration in the EU. *Jeunesse v Netherlands* illustrates that while EU and ECHR protections are distinct, mutual reinforcement and cross-fertilization can be productive and progressive, under the right conditions.

[425] European Council, *European Pact on Immigration and Asylum*, 13440/08 ASIM 72. See further, European Commission, *Tracking method for monitoring the implementation of the European Pact on Immigration and Asylum*, COM(2009) 266.

[426] European Commission, *Green Paper on the right to family reunification of third-country nationals living in the European Union (Directive 2003/86/EC)*, COM(2011) 735. The consultation period was until 1 March 2012. Submissions are available at: <http://ec.europa.eu/dgs/home-affairs/what-is-new/public-consultation/2012/consulting_0023_en.htm> accessed 11 April 2015.

# 5

# Defining Protection: Refugeehood, *Non-refoulement*, and Human Rights

## I. Introduction

This chapter deals with those who seek protection in Europe, refugees in the broad sense. The Convention on the Status of Refugees 1951 and its 1967 Protocol (referred to together as the 'Refugee Convention' or 'CSR') is the pre-eminent global protection instrument.[1] Its *non-refoulement* guarantee in particular has been supplemented and extended by International Human Rights Law (IHRL),[2] in particular by the European Court of Human Rights (ECtHR).[3] Part II sets the scene by exploring the concept of the refugee and the role of human rights in informing basic concepts in refugee law and supplementing protection against *refoulement* thereunder. Some contrasts are drawn between the Refugee Convention and the protections under the ECHR.

Part III sets the contours of the ECtHR non-removal case law. In 2000, Noll predicted that future battles concerning access to and the scope of protection in Europe were 'to be fought in the arena provided by the ECHR' as 'a potentially broader protection package [was] at stake [than under the CSR], coupled with a rather impressive inherent right to access'.[4] This chapter takes up Noll's prediction, examining the Strasbourg case law in the intervening years. The jurisprudence continues to centre on Article 3 ECHR, although the ECtHR has accepted that a 'flagrant breach' of many other rights may preclude removal.[5] However, there have

[1] Convention relating to the Status of Refugees (28 July 1951) 189 UNTS 137; Protocol relating to the Status of Refugees (4 October 1967) 606 UNTS 267.

[2] Both the International Covenant on Civil and Political Rights (ICCPR) and the United Nations Convention against Torture (UNCAT) protect against *refoulement*, but are not examined in this chapter. For an extensive analysis and comparison of these norms and the ECHR, see K Wouters, *International Legal Standards for the Protection from Refoulement* (Intersentia 2009). Article 3(1) UNCAT provides: 'No State party shall expel, return (refouler) or extradite a person to another State where there are substantial grounds for believing that he would be in danger of being subjected to torture.' For analysis, see M Nowak and E McArthur, *The United Nations Convention against Torture* (OUP 2008) Part I, Article 3: Principle of Non-Refoulement, 126–228.

[3] See E Lauterpacht and D Bethlehem, 'The Scope and Content of the Principle of Non-*Refoulement*' in E Feller, V Türk, and F Nicholson (eds), *Refugee Protection in International Law: UNHCR's Global Consultations on International Protection* (Cambridge University Press 2003) 78.

[4] G Noll, *Negotiating Asylum* (Martinus Nijhoff Publishers 2000) 454.

[5] Finding for the first time in *Othman (Abu Qatada) v United Kingdom* App No 8139/09 (ECHR, 17 January 2012) a 'flagrant breach' of Art 6 ECHR on the facts.

been significant shifts in the Article 3 case law, and it now potentially protects those fleeing the death penalty,[6] general situations of conflict[7] and, *in extremis*, material deprivation and poverty.[8]

Part IV turns to the Qualification Directive (QD)—both in its 2004 Original and 2011 Recast forms—the EU's codification of the standards of international protection, encompassing both refugee status and subsidiary protection (SP).[9] For sake of clarity, the Original is referred to as such or as the QD, and the Recast as the RQD. Part IV.2 explains the place of the CSR in EU law. While the ECHR has worked around the Refugee Convention, it has no jurisdiction to enforce it. In contrast, EU policy is expressly required to be in accordance with the Refugee Convention,[10] as is reflected in the text of the QD,[11] so core refugee law concepts are now amenable to the jurisdiction of the Court of Justice of the European Union (CJEU). It has interpreted EU provisions that mirror the Refugee Convention on several occasions to date. The first three cases concerned the outer edges of refugee protection, examining cessation (*Abdulla*);[12] Palestinian refugees under Article 1D (*Bolbol*,[13] later followed by *El Kott*);[14]

[6] See the development from *Öcalan v Turkey* [GC] (2005) 41 EHRR 45 to *Al-Saadoon and Mufdhi v United Kingdom* (2011) 53 EHRR 9, discussed in Part III.3.

[7] *NA v UK* (2009) 48 EHRR 15; *Sufi and Elmi v UK* (2012) 54 EHRR 9.

[8] *MSS v Belgium and Greece* [GC] (2011) 53 EHRR 2. For commentary, see P Mallia, 'Case of *M.S.S. v. Belgium and Greece*: A Catalyst in the Re-thinking of the Dublin II Regulation' (2011) 30 RSQ 107; F Maiani and C Hruschka, 'Le partage des responsabilités dans l'espace Dublin, entre confiance mutuelle et sécurité des demandeurs d'asile' (2011) 2 Revue suisse pour la pratique et le droit d'asile *(ASYL)* 12; J Carlier and S Sarolea, 'Le Droit d'Asile dans l'Union européenne contrôlé par la Cour européenne des droits de l'homme' (2011) 6436 Journal des Tribunaux 353; V Moreno-Lax, 'Dismantling the Dublin System: *MSS v Belgium and Greece*' (2011) 13(4) EJML 1; G Clayton, 'Asylum Seekers in Europe: *MSS v Belgium and Greece*' (2011) 11 HRLRev 758; *Sufi and Elmi v UK* (n 7).

[9] Council Directive 2004/83/EC of 29 April 2004 (QD); Directive 2011/95/EU of the European Parliament and of the Council of 13 December 2011 on standards for the qualification of third-country nationals or stateless persons as beneficiaries of international protection, for a uniform status for refugees or for persons eligible for subsidiary protection, and for the content of the protection granted (recast) (RQD) [2011] OJ L337/9, Article 2(a) QD. On the implementation of the Original QD, see UNHCR [UN High Commissioner for Refugees], *Asylum in the European Union: A Study on the Implementation of the Qualification Directive* (UNHCR November 2007) ('UNHCR QD Study'); European Commission, *Report on the Application of Directive 2004/83/EC* COM(2010) 314; UNHCR, *Safe at Last?* Law and Practice in Selected EU Member States with Respect to Asylum-Seekers Fleeing Indiscriminate Violence' (UNHCR July 2011).

[10] Art 78(1) TFEU provides that 'The Union shall develop a common policy on asylum, subsidiary protection and temporary protection with a view to offering appropriate status to any third-country national requiring international protection and ensuring compliance with the principle of *non-refoulement*. This policy must be in accordance with the Geneva Convention of 28 July 1951 and the Protocol of 31 January 1967 relating to the status of refugees, and other relevant treaties.'

[11] See, in particular, Recitals 2, 3, 8, 15, 16, 17, and 24 QD, as well as Arts 9(1) and 12(1)(R)QD.

[12] Joined Cases C-175/08, C-176/08, C-178/08, and C-179/08 *Aydin Salahadin Abdulla and others* [2010] ECR I-1493. See R Errera, 'Cessation and Assessment of New Circumstances: A Comment on *Abdulla*, CJEU, 2 March 2010' (2011) 23 IJRL 521.

[13] Case C-31/09 *Bolbol* [2010] ECR I-5539.

[14] Case C-364/11 *El Kott* [2013] OJ C 46/8.

and exclusion under Article 1F (*Germany v B* and *D*).[15] Two cases have now addressed the central issue in refugee law that is the meaning of persecution. *Y and Z*[16] addressed religious persecution, while *X, Y, and Z*[17] addressed persecution on grounds of sexual orientation. The CJEU repeats that the Refugee Convention is the 'the cornerstone of the international legal regime for the protection of refugees and that [the QD was] adopted to guide the competent authorities of the Member States in the application of [the Refugee Convention] on the basis of common concepts and criteria'.[18]

Part IV.4 examines SP under the QD. There are now two CJEU cases on the interactions between refugee status and SP (*MM*[19] and *HN*[20]), while two dealt with the scope of SP: *Elgafaji*,[21] and *Diakité*.[22] The ECtHR case law played a decisive role in informing the EU definition of SP in the QD. In some respects, the QD simply codifies the Strasbourg case law, in particular in its Article 15(1)(b) limb on torture, inhuman and degrading treatment. However, there are also points of tension, unsurprising given the case law's instability and national governments' desire to limit their protection obligations. As I will illustrate, the EU legislature seems to have attempted to trim the ragged edges of the Strasbourg case law in its SP definition, as is now apparent in *M'Bodj*.[23] In the CJEU's first substantive case on SP, *Elgafaji*, some intervening governments invited Luxembourg to adopt a restrictive interpretation of the QD, going so far as to encourage it to adopt a narrow construction of Article 3 ECHR itself. The CJEU resisted this line of argument, ruling that the SP definition adds protection beyond the ECHR minimum, in particular in protecting some of those fleeing indiscriminate violence under Article 15(c). In so doing, it seemed to carve out an area of refugee protection all of its own, beyond the Refugee Convention and ECHR, although that move has met resistance from national courts and indeed from the ECtHR.[24] To date, as is discussed further in Chapter 6, the CJEU seems to be taking a limited view of *non-refoulement*, at least in the context of deportations under the Dublin Regulation. Thus far, it has focused on risks of torture, inhuman or degrading treatment.[25] Meanwhile,

[15] Joined Cases C-57/09 and C-101/09 *Germany v B* and *D* [2010] ECR I-10979. See further G Gilbert, 'Exclusion under the Qualification Directive and the German Reference' (2009) Paper presented at the IARLJ Conference, Berlin, 19–20 October 2009.

[16] Joined Cases C-71/11 and C-99/11 *Germany v Y and Z* [2012] OJ C 331/5.

[17] Joined Cases C-199/12, C-200/12 and C-201/12 *X, Y, and Z v Minister voor Immigratie en Asiel* [2014] OJ C 9/8. See further S Chelvan, 'Case Comment: *X, Y, and Z v Minister voor Immigratie en Asiel*: A Missed Opportunity or a New Dawn?' (2013) No5 Chambers Newsletter; M Mouzourakis, 'Case Comment: *X, Y, and Z v Minister voor Immigratie en Asiel*' (*Rights in Exile*, 1 December 2013).

[18] Case C-604/12 *HN* [2014] OJ C 202/6, para 27, citing *X, Y, and Z*, para 39 and the case law cited.

[19] Case C-277/11 *MM* [2013] OJ C 26/9.

[20] *HN* (n 18).

[21] C-465/07 *Elgafaji v Saatssecreteris van Justitie* [2009] ECR I-921.

[22] Case C-285/12 *Diakité* [2014] OJ C 93/6.

[23] Case C-542/13 *M'Bodj* [2015] OJ C 65/12.

[24] *Sufi and Elmi* (n 7).

[25] Joined Cases C-411/10 and C-493/10 *NS v Secretary of State for the Home Department and ME v Refugee Applications Commissioner & Minister for Justice, Equality and Law Reform* [2011] ECR I-13905, references from the UK Court of Appeal and Irish High Court respectively.

as outlined in Part V, the EU legislature has revisited this matter, and the Recast QD was agreed by Parliament and Council in late 2011.

A chapter of this length cannot do justice to every nuance of the case law, but appraises, in somewhat broad brush, the new and far-reaching role of the CJEU as a refugee law court. However, that role has its limits, and not all questions of refugee law are deemed to fall within its jurisdiction. In 2014, it declined to interpret the non-penalization provision in Article 31 CSR in *Qurbani*,[26] as will be discussed further in Chapter 6. While in 2000 Noll cast the ECtHR as 'a singular, and indeed revolutionary forum',[27] the ECtHR is no longer a singular supranational instance. It is now part of a duality of human rights jurisdictions. Indeed, given the manner in which the core refugee law concepts are now incorporated into EU law, Luxembourg can truly be characterized as a refugee law court. Whilst the pluralistic interaction between Luxembourg and Strasbourg is generally seen as beneficial for human rights protection, some potential pitfalls are revealed in this Chapter.

## II. The Refugee Convention and ECHR

### 1. Definition, status, and human rights

The twentieth-century history of refugee law in Europe can be traced in terms of moving from ad hoc responses to particular groups fleeing persecution, oppression, and war to legalization around a general definition in the Refugee Convention.[28] Thereafter, refugee law has been characterized by dynamic, evolutive interpretation, yet also contorted by pressures to maintain a limited sphere of protection in order to control numbers entitled to protection. Governments frequently resist recognition of compelling claims for international protection, in order to avoid having to accord formal status to potentially numerous similar claimants (the 'precedential pull'). The refugee definition in Europe is usually applied by governmental adjudicators in the first instance, with appellate bodies and domestic courts often only exercising a supervisory jurisdiction. States' distortion of the refugee definition meets some resistance from courts[29] and ethicists,[30] yet the tendency remains all too evident in practice. Throughout, I identify the impact of governmental restrictiveness on the process of elaborating EU norms.

[26] Case C-481/13 *Qurbani* [2014] OJ C 31/24. [27] Noll (n 4) 562.

[28] See further, G Goodwin-Gill and J McAdam, *The Refugee in International Law* (3rd edn, OUP 2007) 13–37.

[29] As Foster puts it, 'the senior courts in the common law world have emphasized repeatedly [that] the floodgates argument is not a valid legal argument'. M Foster, *International Refugee Law and Socioeconomic Rights: Refuge from Deprivation* (Cambridge University Press 2007) 79.

[30] As Shacknove puts it, 'states reason in reverse from their fear that they will be forced to shoulder the burden of refugees unilaterally to a narrow conception of refugeehood which limits the numbers of claimants. In so doing, they are attempting to resolve what is in fact a procedural and institutional problem by a legalistic sleight of hand.' A Shacknove, 'Who is a Refugee?' (1985) 95 Ethics 274, 277.

There is no dedicated court of international refugee law,[31] so in the absence of a single authoritative interpretative body, notwithstanding the international law on Treaty interpretation, a plurality of interpretative voices emerge, with UNHCR syntheses, State practice, national court rulings, and scholarly views all claiming some authoritative status.[32] In this context, various national approaches to the refugee definition have emerged, and unsurprisingly, idiosyncratic interpretations became commonplace. A vivid divergence across Europe concerned the treatment of claims by victims of non-State persecution,[33] an issue now resolved within the EU by the QD.[34] However, typical of the inclusive-exclusive dynamic in refugee law, incorporating non-State persecution has also been accompanied by the development of the concept of internal protection alternative, which permits examination of whether a claimant could have received protection elsewhere in the State of origin. Notwithstanding its lack of clear foundation in the Refugee Convention,[35] this notion has now been institutionalized in State practice and UNHCR guidance.[36] It is also the site of contestation between the EU and ECHR protections, with significant revisions in the RQD in light of the ECtHR case law.[37]

While the Refugee Convention's virtually global reach and institutionalization in the UNHCR mandate[38] ensure its pre-eminence, governments often display reluctance to afford refugees the status due to them under the Refugee Convention, due to the precedential pull and the range of rights attendant on that status.[39] The practice of European States when faced with large numbers of asylum claims in the 1990s was increasingly to award *ad hoc* status, under a variety of diverse nomenclatures, including 'B status', 'humanitarian status', 'temporary protection', and

[31] Under the CSR, States parties may, under Art 38 CSR, accord the ICJ jurisdiction over that instrument. However, this jurisdiction has never been invoked, leading to what is known as the 'Article 38 deficit'.

[32] For systematic accounts, see J McAdam, 'Interpretation of the Refugee Convention' in A Zimmermann (ed), *Commentary on the Refugee Convention* (OUP 2011) 75; G Goodwin-Gill, 'The search for the one, true meaning…' in G Goodwin-Gill and H Lambert (eds), *The Limits of Transnational Law: Refugee Law, Policy Harmonization and Judicial Dialogue in the European Union* (Cambridge University Press 2010) 204.

[33] ELENA, *Research Paper on Non-State Agents of Persecution and Inability of the State to Protect—the German Interpretation* (ELENA September 2000).

[34] Art 6 QD; Art 6 RQD.

[35] J Hathaway and M Foster, 'Internal Protection/Relocation/Flight Alternative' in E Feller, V Türk, and F Nicholson (eds), *Refugee Protection in International Law: UNHCR's Global Consultations on International Protection* (Cambridge University Press 2003) 357.

[36] UNHCR, *Guidelines on International Protection No. 4: 'Internal Flight or Relocation Alternative' Within the Context of Article 1A(2) of the 1951 Convention and/or 1967 Protocol Relating to the Status of Refugees*, 23 July 2003, HCR/GIP/03/04.

[37] See J Eaton 'The Internal Protection Alternative under European Union Law: Examining the Recast Qualification Directive' (2012) 24 IJRL 765, 777.

[38] Of course, the UNHCR mandate extends beyond Convention Refugees. See Goodwin-Gill and McAdam (n 28) 23–32.

[39] See generally, ECRE, *Complementary/Subsidiary Forms of Protection in the EU Member States* (ECRE 2004); R Piotrowicz and C van Eck, 'Subsidiary Protection and Primary Rights' (2004) ICLQ 107; R Mandal, *Protection Mechanisms Outside of the 1951 Convention ('Complementary Protection')*, (UNHCR, Department of International Protection, Doc. PPLA/2005/02, June 2005); J McAdam, *Complementary Protection in International Refugee Law* (OUP 2007).

'exceptional leave to remain'. In eleven of the old fifteen Member States, alternative statuses were granted more frequently than refugee status.[40] By their nature, these statuses were *ad hoc*, particularly in content and duration. In responding to the current Syrian refugee crisis, EU harmonization notwithstanding, *ad hoc* national statuses and responses are also prevalent.[41]

The move to other statuses has not only been an escape from law, but also a response to additional *non-refoulement* obligations in human rights law, in particular the ECHR, as explored in Part III below. Recourse to the ECtHR became commonplace for rejected asylum seekers, with the Strasbourg system offering 'comparative enforcement advantages' over the Refugee Convention,[42] in particular as the ECtHR developed its interim jurisdiction to preclude removals.[43] However, in contrast to the Refugee Convention, which specifies a status and attendant rights, the ECHR does not require a particular status to be granted to asylum seekers, merely that they not be imperilled by removal.[44] In this respect, as will be seen in Part IV, the QD's outstanding contribution is to create an SP status, with a defined set of rights attaching thereto.

There are other important contrasts between the Refugee Convention and ECHR protection against removal. Three key contrasts are set out in the following sections, concerning persecution on Convention grounds, risk assessment, and exclusions from protection.

## 2. Three contrasts between the Refugee Convention and ECHR protections

### *i. Persecution on a Convention ground cf 'flagrant' human rights violation*

The Refugee Convention protects those with a 'well-founded fear of being persecuted' for reasons of a Convention ground,[45] whilst the ECHR precludes removal where there are substantial grounds to believe there is a real risk of treatment contrary to Articles 2 or 3, and, as explored in Part III.4, certain exceptionally serious 'flagrant breaches' of other rights. There is no need to show a link with any particular ground under the ECHR: the harm threatened is *per se* sufficient to preclude removal, while the Refugee Convention additionally requires that persecution be on a Convention ground.

'Persecution' is a distinct yet elusive concept, therein lies its utility for refugee protection. As the UNHCR Handbook puts it, '[t]here is no universally accepted

[40] J McAdam, 'The European Union Qualification Directive: The Creation of a Subsidiary Protection Regime' (2005) 17 IJRL 461, 464.

[41] P Fargues and C Fandrich, 'The European Response to the Syrian Refugee Crisis What Next?' (2012) MPC Research Report 2012/14.

[42] H Lambert, 'Protection against *Refoulement* from Europe: Human Rights Law Comes to the Rescue' (1999) 48 ICLQ 543.

[43] See discussion in Chapter 1 of Strasbourg's Rule 39 jurisdiction.

[44] As reiterated in *Bonger v The Netherlands* App No 10154/04 (ECHR, 15 September 2005).

[45] Art 1A(2) CSR.

definition of 'persecution', and various attempts to formulate such a definition have met with little success.'[46] Read in conjunction with the Convention grounds, it tends to reflect a political conception of asylum, rather than a humanitarian one.[47] Yet, there is a symbiotic relationship between persecution and human rights law in contemporary practice. As Foster explains:

> one of the most significant developments in refugee law jurisprudence in recent years has been the well-documented move towards an understanding of 'being persecuted', as well as other elements of the definition, that is informed and understood in the context of international human rights standards.[48]

Goodwin-Gill's 1983 study framed persecution against the background of international human rights law.[49] Hathaway's 1991 analysis conceived of persecution as 'sustained or systemic violation of basic human rights demonstrative of a failure of state protection'.[50] While the human rights approach to persecution has not gone unchallenged,[51] the overwhelming lawyerly response has been laudatory. Anker, for example, characterizes it as refugee law's 'coming of age' in 'claiming its international human rights roots'.[52]

Not every human rights violation will amount to persecution, but then again, nor will it amount to a ground to preclude removal under the ECHR as explored in Part III. Hathaway's original account was based on a formal hierarchy between different human rights and violations of varying gravity. Foster's account of persecution, in contrast, focuses on the core of all human rights, animated by her project to elucidate that persecution is also entailed in violations of socio-economic rights.[53] Reviewing the practice of predominantly common law courts, she argues that '[a]lthough they do not always use the precise words, the approach of these decision-makers could be characterised as an attempt to ascertain whether the *core* of a relevant right has been violated.'[54] Their latest joint work reflects a flexible approach, open to recognizing all sustained and systematic denials of broadly accepted international human rights (bar *de minimis* ones) as persecution. They examine these across three categories (physical security, liberty and freedom, and

[46] UNHCR *Handbook on Procedures and Criteria for Determining Refugee Status* (UNHCR 1979) para 51.

[47] See further M Price, *Rethinking Asylum: History, Purpose and Limits* (Cambridge University Press 2009) 103–36.

[48] Foster (n 29) 27. See also Goodwin-Gill and McAdam (n 28) 91: 'Comprehensive analysis requires the general notion of persecution to be related to developments within the broad field of human rights.'

[49] G Goodwin-Gill, *The Refugee in International Law* (Clarendon Press 1983).

[50] J Hathaway, *The Law of Refugee Status* (Butterworths 1991) 104–05.

[51] See further Price (n 47).

[52] D Anker, 'Refugee Law, Gender and the Human Rights Paradigm' (2002) 15 Harvard Human Rights Law Journal 133, 135–36. It has been suggested, however, that this approach has been adopted less widely in civilian than common law countries. See further, D Vanheule, 'A Comparison of the Judicial Interpretation of the Notion of Refugee' in JY Carlier and D Vanheule (eds), *Europe and Refugees: A Challenge?* (Kluwer Law International 1997) 91.

[53] Foster (n 29) 194–201. [54] ibid, 195.

autonomy and self-realization), obviating any bifurcation between civil and political and social and economic rights.[55]

As explored in Part IV.2, the QD attempts to codify an EU definition of persecution, stated to be 'within the meaning of Article 1A of the [CSR]'.[56] The central notion of persecution encompasses acts which are 'sufficiently serious by their nature or repetition as to constitute a severe violation of basic human rights, in particular the rights from which derogation cannot be made under Article 15(2) [ECHR]', introducing the notion of hierarchy of rights and violations into the concept of persecution. While the Recast QD introduces some changes and clarifications,[57] it does not alter this core definition of persecution. Notwithstanding its express human rights content, persecution and 'serious harm'[58] (the threshold concept for SP) remain distinct under the QD, so human rights law continues to inform the two statuses in different ways.

### *ii. Risk assessment and individuation*

The Refugee Convention uses the 'well-founded fear' standard, while the ECtHR speaks of 'substantial grounds' for believing there is a 'real risk'.[59] The real risk criterion arguably sets a stricter standard than well-founded fear.[60] McAdam stresses the importance of the additional subjective in the CSR definition as 'captur[ing] a need for protection that is outside the realm of a pure human rights assessment and which cautions against tying the concept of persecution exclusively to human rights law'.[61]

Regarding the fraught question of the degree of individuation or singling out required for a protection claim, there is some common, if shifting and contested, ground between the Refugee Convention and ECHR. Under the Refugee Convention, refugeehood turns on group membership (linked to the Convention grounds), but the well-founded fear requirement suggests an individual assessment of how the threat is experienced. In a distortion of the refugee law requirement, States sometimes require applicants to demonstrate that the risks they face go

[55] J Hathaway and M Foster, *The Law of Refugee Status* (2nd edn, Cambridge University Press 2014) 193–208.

[56] Art 9(1)(a) QD. See also Art 9(1)(b) QD, which provides that persecution may also stem from 'an accumulation of various measures, including violations of human rights which is sufficiently severe as to affect an individual in a similar manner' as an act of persecution.

[57] The Recast QD brought about, *inter alia*, an approximation of the rights of refugees and SP beneficiaries with regard to residence permits, access to employment, and healthcare (Art 23 et seq. QD), clarification on the application of the 'internal flight alternative' in Art 8, as well as clearer guidance on the 'particular social group' ground in Art 10(1)(d).

[58] Art 15 QD.

[59] While Article 19(2) EUCFR refers to 'serious risk', the Charter may not provide lower protection than the ECHR, so 'serious' must be equated with 'real'.

[60] H Battjes, *European Asylum Law and International Law* (Martinus Nijhoff Publishers 2006) 225, and copious references therein.

[61] McAdam (n 40) 471.

beyond those generally faced by their cohort, irrespective of whether the claim is for refugee status or protection from removal under the ECHR. This is one of the more insidious forms of governmental restrictiveness. Hathaway rightly points out that to demand individuation or 'singling out' 'confuses the requirement to assess risk on the basis of the claimant's particular circumstances with some erroneous notion that refugeehood must be based on a completely personalized set of facts'.[62]

The Strasbourg case law embodies significant shifts of late, from *Vilvarajah v UK*[63] to *Salah Sheekh v the Netherlands*,[64] *NA v UK*,[65] *MSS v Belgium and Greece*,[66] and *Sufi and Elmi v UK*.[67] The earlier cases tended to demand a high degree of individuation. As Durieux explains:

> the coexistence of the two systems [CSR and ECHR] appears to have aggravated the restrictive tendencies of both—in other words, competition between the two systems has resulted in constraining the protection opportunities of asylum seekers, instead of amplifying them.[68]

The enforcement apparatus of the ECtHR means it has the capacity to back up and expand *non-refoulement* in the Refugee Convention, albeit indirectly. Yet, that same feature makes a pull to its standards more likely, thereby undermining the Refugee Convention. The issue of individuation also reappears in the QD, both in the persecution and serious harm definitions, taking centre stage in the CJEU's *Elgafaji* ruling, explored in Part IV.5.

### *iii. Absolute protection under Article 3 ECHR*

Article 33(2) CSR envisages an exception to *non-refoulement* for those refugees who pose a serious security threat to the country of asylum.[69] Article 1F CSR also permits exclusion from refugee status on various grounds. In contrast, as analyzed at length in Part III.2.v., *non-refoulement* under Article 3 ECHR is not open to derogation. Accordingly, the absolute ECHR protection under Article 3,[70] and indeed the UNCAT provision precluding removal to face risks of torture,[71] are important supplements to the CSR. As Part III.2.v. explores, the ECtHR has maintained a consistent position that the protection against removal under Article 3 ECHR is absolute, ruling out any 'balancing' with national security concerns. That protection under Article 3 ECHR is accordingly wider than under the CSR is evident in

[62] Hathaway (n 50) 91–92. [63] *Vilvarajah and Others v UK* (1992) 14 EHRR 248.

[64] *Salah Sheekh v the Netherlands* (2007) 45 EHRR 50. See case note by P Boeles and M Bruins (2007) EJML 265.

[65] *NA* (n 7). [66] *MSS* (n 8). [67] *Sufi and Elmi* (n 7).

[68] JF Durieux, 'Salah Sheekh is a Refugee: New Insights into Primary and Subsidiary Forms of Protection' (2008) RSC Working Paper No 49, 9.

[69] Art 33(2) CSR provides that refugees 'whom there are reasonable grounds for regarding as a danger to the security of the country in which he is, or who, having been convicted by a final judgement of a particularly serious crime, constitutes a danger to the community of that country'.

[70] *Chahal v UK* (1997) 23 EHRR 413; reaffirmed in *Saadi v Italy* (2009) 49 EHRR 439.

[71] Art 3(1) UNCAT.

*Ahmed v Austria*.[72] The applicant had been excluded from refugee status due to his criminal convictions, but nonetheless was granted protection from removal under Article 3 ECHR.

## III. The ECHR and *Non-refoulement*

### 1. The Origins of *non-refoulement* under the ECHR: *Soering* and its progeny

Since 1989, the ECtHR has developed a line of case law constraining removal of aliens from the respondent's territory.[73] While UNCAT contains an express provision prohibiting removal to face torture,[74] the extension of the ECHR to removal issues emerged *via* judicial innovation in *Soering*. The *Soering* reasoning has been repeated in all the subsequent cases, so warrants particular attention.[75] The ECtHR emphasized that States were not absolved 'from responsibility under Article 3…for all and any foreseeable consequences of extradition[76] suffered outside their jurisdiction'.[77] Where removal had 'as a direct consequence the exposure of an individual to proscribed ill-treatment',[78] it was prohibited under Article 3 ECHR. In support of its conclusion, the ECtHR additionally invoked the ubiquitous requirement that Convention rights must be 'practical and effective'.[79]

From the 'absolute and non-derogable' nature of Article 3, the ECtHR concluded that Article 3 'enshrine[d] one of the fundamental values of the democratic societies making up the Council of Europe'.[80] The ECtHR also emphasized the universality of these provisions, noting that similar prohibitions were enshrined in other IHRL instruments, such as the ICCPR. Article 3 accordingly reflected 'an internationally accepted standard.'[81] In addition, the ECtHR characterized the harm faced as 'serious and irreparable.'[82] In light of all of these factors, removal was precluded.

The ECtHR in *Soering* immediately ruled out the imposition of a requirement that protection of human rights in the receiving State must meet the ECHR standards in all respects,[83] instead establishing distinctive standards for internal and removal cases. An individual would be removable even in cases of real risk of breaches of Article 6, unless 'exceptionally' the individual 'has suffered or risks

[72] *Ahmed v Austria* (1996) 24 EHRR 278.

[73] The seminal study is that of N Mole and C Meredith, *Asylum and the European Convention on Human Rights* (Council of Europe 2010).

[74] Art 3(1) UNCAT.

[75] For example, Battjes notes that in no later case has the ECtHR 'elaborated in such detail *why* Article 3 applies to expulsion cases.' H Battjes, 'Landmarks: Soering's Legacy' (2008) 1 Amsterdam Law Forum 139.

[76] *Soering v UK* (1989) 11 EHRR 439 concerned extradition, but the same principles now apply to all forms of removal. See *Cruz Varas v Sweden* (1991) 14 EHRR 1, para 70.

[77] *Soering* (n 59) para 86. [78] ibid, para 91. [79] ibid, para 88. [80] ibid.

[81] ibid. [82] ibid, para 90. [83] ibid, para 86.

suffering a flagrant denial of a fair trial in the requesting country'.[84] In so doing, the ECtHR established a hierarchy between Articles 3 and 6. While the former provision enshrined a 'fundamental value', the latter enjoyed a 'prominent place in a democratic society'.[85] We see that from the outset in *Soering* the jurisprudence entails a divergence in the approach to internal and removal protections.

'Flagrant breaches' of Convention rights other than Article 3 may prevent removal. The ECtHR has explicitly recognized this possibility as regards 4,[86] 5,[87] 6,[88] 7,[89] 8,[90] and 9.[91] Yet, the central case remains removal to face risks of treatment contrary to Article 3 ECHR. In practice, the ECtHR maintains Article 3's centrality by often treating severe infringements of other Convention rights as 'inhuman treatment' contrary to Article 3 ECHR. For example, where applicants argued that their right to life would be threatened on return, the ECtHR has usually treated the risk as amounting to one of inhuman treatment.[92] In a rare case, *Bader*, the ECtHR found a stand-alone Article 2 violation in a removal scenario.[93] In its inadmissibility decision in *Z and T v UK*, the ECtHR endorsed the view of the House of Lords in *Ullah*,[94] 'that it would be difficult to visualise a case in which a sufficiently flagrant violation of Article 9 would not also involve treatment in violation of Article 3 of the Convention'.[95]

In 2005 in *Öcalan v Turkey*, the ECtHR held that until Protocol No 13 ECHR[96] was widely ratified, the ECtHR would not consider the death penalty per se as contrary to Article 3 ECHR.[97] By 2010, that wide ratification had taken place.[98] In *Al-Saadoon*, the Court noted that Article 1 of Protocol 13, as regards

[84] ibid, para 113. [85] ibid, para 113.

[86] *Ould Barar v Sweden* (1999) 28 EHRR CD 213 illustrates that the ECtHR is open to claims under Art 4 ECHR, but found no risk of treatment contrary to Art 4 ECHR on return in the particular case.

[87] *Tomic v UK* App No 17387/03 (ECHR, 14 October 2003).

[88] *Soering* (n 59); *Drozd and Janousek v France and Spain* (1992) 14 EHRR 745; *Einhorn v France* App No 71555/01 (ECHR, 16 October 2001); *Mamatkulov v Turkey* (2005) 41 EHRR 25; *Al-Moayad v Germany* (2007) 44 EHRR SE22; *Stapleton v Ireland* (2010) 51 EHRR SE1; *Othman* (n 5).

[89] *Gabarri Moreno v Spain* (2004) 39 EHRR 40. For discussion, see N Mole and C Meredith (n 73) 98–99.

[90] *F v UK* [2004] ECHR 723.

[91] *Z and T v UK* App No 27034/05 (ECHR, 28 February 2006).

[92] *HLR v France* (1998) 26 EHRR 29; *D v UK* (1997) 24 EHRR 425. Cited with approval by UNCAT in *Njamba and Balikosa v Sweden*, CAT/C/41/D/322/2007, 11 June 2007.

[93] *Bader v Sweden* App No 13284/04 (ECHR, 8 November 2005).

[94] *R v Special Adjudicator (Respondent) ex parte Ullah v SSHD* [2004] UKHL 26.

[95] *Z and T* (n 91) 7. But see, for an illustration to the contrary, *EM (Lebanon) (FC) v Secretary of State for the Home Department* [2008] UKHL 64, in particular *per* Lord Hope, para 16.

[96] Protocol No 6 to the ECHR prohibits the death penalty in peace time. It has been strengthened by Protocol No 13, prohibiting the death penalty in all circumstances. The EU Member States have ratified Protocol No 13, with the exceptions of Latvia, Poland, and Spain, which have signed but not yet ratified.

[97] *Öcalan* (n 6) para 165. For an examination of this apparent paradox, see J Yorke, 'The right to life and abolition of the death penalty in the Council of Europe' (2009) 34 ELRev 205.

[98] See Council of Europe Treaty Office, 'Protocol No. 13 to the Convention for the Protection of Human Rights and Fundamental Freedoms, concerning the abolition of the death penalty in all circumstances' CETS No.: 187. As of 25 May 2011, 42 States have ratfied or acceded to the Protocol.

the States bound by it, 'ranks alongside the rights in Articles 2 and 3 as a fundamental right, enshrining one of the basic values of the democratic societies making up the Council of Europe'.[99] The reasoning differs from *Soering*, in that the *Soering* invocation of universality refers to Article 3-like prohibitions across the globe. In contrast, in *Al-Saadoon*, the death penalty prohibition is acknowledged as fundamental based on its position in European law and values, and accordingly provides the basis for a non-removal obligation. Given the wide ratification of that provision by Council of Europe States, the Court took the view that it could make the interpretative leap that it had previously resisted, and regarded the death penalty as included in the prohibition of 'inhuman or degrading treatment or punishment' under Article 3 ECHR.[100] As is discussed below, Article 15(a) QD prohibits return to face real risks of 'death penalty or execution', according SP status in these circumstances.

As will be discussed in Part IV.4, the drafters of the QD decided against inclusion of a general human rights non-removal clause to track the Strasbourg 'flagrant breach' case law. The further development of this line of case law is principally for Strasbourg alone, its own remaining province of *non-refoulement* jurisprudence. In *NS/ME*, Luxembourg's ruling on non-removal obligations under the Dublin System, it only had regard to Article 4 EUCFR (the analogous provision to Article 3 ECHR). In contrast, AG Trstenjak had considered fundamental rights more broadly as a basis for protection against deportation.

## 2. Prohibition of torture, inhuman or degrading treatment: Article 3 ECHR

### *i. The proscribed ill-treatment and positive duties*

Article 3 ECHR states that '[n]o one shall be subjected to torture or to inhuman or degrading treatment or punishment.'

This is not the place for a comprehensive examination of these terms, now well-defined and understood in their focal meanings in IHRL.[101] Strasbourg's foundational rulings on torture arose in highly-politicized interstate disputes, in the *Greek Case*[102] and *Ireland v UK*,[103] when the institutional underpinnings of the European human rights system were weaker than today.[104] Indeed, it has been

[99] *Al-Saadoon and Mufdhi v UK*, (n 6) para 118. [100] ibid, para 120.

[101] See Nowak and McArthur (n 2) Part I, Art 1, 25–86 and Part I, Art 16, 538–76. Of course, we live in an era where the international meaning has been challenged. On these 'disturbing definitional shenanigans', see J Waldron, 'Torture and Positive Law: Jurisprudence for the White House' (2005) 105 Columbia Law Review 1681, 1709; reproduced as Chapter 7 of J Waldron, *Torture, Terror and Trade-offs: Philosophy for the White House* (OUP 2010).

[102] *Denmark, Norway, Sweden and the Netherlands v Greece* ('*Greek Case*') (1969) Yearbook XII, 186.

[103] *Ireland v UK* (1979–1980) 2 EHRR 25.

[104] On the *Greek Case*, see T Hammarberg, *Human Rights in Europe: No Ground for Complacency* (Council of Europe 2008) 15–19.

suggested that the interrogation techniques deemed 'inhuman' in the former case would be deemed to be 'torture' today, in light of raised human rights standards.[105]

According to the ECtHR, the difference between the three forms of mistreatment identified in Article 3 ECHR 'derives principally from a difference in the intensity of the suffering inflicted'.[106] In addition, there are other important differences. Torture usually has 'a purpose, such as the obtaining of information or confessions, or the infliction of punishment, and it is generally an aggravated form of inhuman treatment'.[107] Torture connotes a distinct set of practices, while inhuman and degrading are predominantly evaluative standards, demanding an assessment of any impugned treatment in light of those value-laden terms.[108] Inhuman treatment is the most capacious notion, capturing 'at least such treatment as deliberately causes severe suffering, mental or physical, which, in the particular situation, is unjustifiable'.[109] The hallmark of degrading treatment and punishment is that it 'grossly humiliates [the individual] before others or drives him to act against his will of conscience', or in a more recent formulation, it:

> humiliates or debases an individual showing lack of respect for, or diminishing, his or her human dignity or arouses feelings of fear, anguish or inferiority capable of breaking an individual's moral and physical resistance.[110]

There is no need to show a specific intent to degrade.[111]

As Waldron eloquently puts it, the Article 3 prohibition reflects a choice that:

> [i]n a world where people were locked up and interrogated and in general made vulnerable to the sharp end of official action, it was better to have such practices shadowed by a debate about cruelty, inhumanity and degradation—a debate sponsored and focused by the law—than to leave these practices unregulated.[112]

In its focal meaning then, Article 3 is concerned with deliberate ill-treatment by State actors. However, it also provides important protection against exposure to suffering. Consider this example: the State deprives an individual of electricity supplies, leading to extreme suffering in the form of substandard living conditions.[113] Whether this scenario amounts to an Article 3 ECHR violation depends not only on the severity of the suffering, but crucially on the attribution of responsibility to the State for those living conditions. There must be some 'treatment' (be it

[105] *Selmouni v France* (1999) 29 EHRR 403, para 101, cited by Goodwin-Gill and McAdam (n 28) 313.

[106] *Ireland v UK* (n 103). [107] *Greek Case* (n 102).

[108] See further, J Waldron, 'Cruel, Inhuman and Degrading Treatment: The Words Themselves' (2008) *NYU School of Law Public Law & Legal Theory Research Paper Series No 08-36*; reproduced as Chapter 9 of J Waldron, *Torture, Terror and Trade-offs: Philosophy for the White House* (OUP 2010).

[109] *Greek Case* (n 102). [110] *Pretty v UK* (2002) 35 EHRR 1, para 52.

[111] *Kalashnikov v Russia* App No 47095/99 (ECHR, 15 July 2002) paras 102–03; *Peers v Greece* App No 28524/95 (ECHR, 19 April 2001) para 74.

[112] Waldron 'Cruel, Inhuman and Degrading Treatment: The Words Themselves' (n 108) 46–47.

[113] This scenario evokes *van Volsem v Belgium* App No 14641/89 (ECHR, 9 May 1990). See further, A Cassese, 'Can the Notion of Inhuman and Degrading Treatment be applied to Socio-Economic Conditions?' (1991) 2 EJIL 141.

act or omission) attributable to the State. In general, the failure to meet positive obligations is actionable only where the individual is in a particular position of vulnerability or dependency on the State. In prison conditions cases, a situation of comprehensive State responsibility for the individual's well-being, that vulnerability is readily apparent.[114] The State has particular responsibilities for prisoners' well-being, given that they are deprived of normal means of self-care. Going even further, in *Z v UK*, where the State failed in its duty to prevent 'serious long-term neglect and abuse' of children, an Article 3 ECHR violation was found.[115] The ECtHR has made the following statement of principle in *Pretty v UK*:

> [S]uffering which flows from naturally occurring illness, physical or mental, may be covered by Article 3 ECHR, where it is, or risks being, exacerbated by treatment, whether flowing from conditions of detention, expulsion or other measures, for which the authorities can be held responsible.[116]

The UK House of Lords (as it then was) ruling in *Limbuela* is a good example.[117] The House of Lords accepted that, where a statutory regime provides support for asylum seekers, withdrawal of support from some as a punishment for non-compliance with administrative deadlines amounts to actionable 'treatment'. The surrounding legal context meant that there was actionable treatment directed at asylum seekers. As is explored further below, in *MSS v Belgium and Greece*, the Court deemed asylum seekers to be a vulnerable category, such as to render the State responsible for their inhuman and degrading living conditions.

### *ii. The non-removal obligation*

In several cases, the ECtHR found substantial grounds for believing there was a real risk of treatment contrary to Article 3 ECHR where individuals faced inhuman punishment, such as death by stoning[118] or corporal punishment.[119] In the latter case, the ECtHR also held that the non-removal duty extended to the applicant's husband and daughter, given their fear resulting from her prospective ill-treatment.[120] In *Said v the Netherlands*,[121] a deserter from the Ethiopian army was protected from removal, where he faced a real risk of being tied up and left exposed under high temperatures, treatment deemed 'inhuman.' It has been

[114] See, e.g. *Keenan v UK* 3 (2001) 33 EHRR 38.
[115] *Z v UK* App No 29392/95 (ECHR, 10 May 2001).
[116] *Pretty* (n 110) para 52; *Keenan v UK* (n 114) para 116. See further, C O'Cinnéide, 'A Modest Proposal: Destitution, State Responsibility and the European Convention on Human Rights' (2008) EHRLRev 583.
[117] *R (on the applications of Adam, Tesema, and Limbuela) v Secretary of State for the Home Department* [2005] UKHL 66. See further, S Fredman, 'Human Rights Transformed: Positive Duties and Positive Rights' (2006) PL 498, 520, arguing that *Limbuela* marks 'the first step in an important new development.' For a critique of an aspect of the reasoning, see S Palmer 'A Wrong Turning: Article 3 ECHR and Proportionality' (2006) 65 CLJ 438.
[118] *Jabari v Turkey* [2000] ECHR 368.
[119] *D and others v Turkey* App No 24245/03 (ECHR, 22 June 2006).
[120] ibid, para 56, citing *Bader v Sweden* (n 93).
[121] (2006) 43 EHRR 14.

observed that the case law precluding removal tends to focus on the two more serious wrongs under Article 3, being torture and inhuman treatment.[122]

Strasbourg made an important contribution to refugee protection in Europe in clarifying that the non-removal obligation may arise irrespective of whether the threat emanates from State or private actors. This principle was successfully invoked in *Ahmed v Austria* concerning return to Somalia, where at the time there was no functioning State.[123] In *HLR v France*, although finding no violation on the facts, the ECtHR accepted that ill-treatment caused by private actors would fall within the scope of Article 3 ECHR, if the authorities of the receiving State were not able to obviate the risk by providing adequate protection.[124] In *Ammari v Sweden*,[125] the ECtHR accepted that threats from a private militia group could trigger protection under Article 3 ECHR, again if the authorities of the receiving State were not able to provide adequate protection. The ECtHR conception of internal protection has developed apace, setting out some important constraints.[126]

### iii. *The health cases*

In *D v UK* the ECtHR held that the expulsion of the applicant (identified only as 'D'), an AIDS sufferer nearing the end of his life, to St Kitts where he had no prospect of medical care or family support, would be inhuman treatment.[127] Removal would expose him to the 'real risk of dying under most distressing circumstances'.[128] The crucial legal innovation was extending Article 3 to scenarios where the suffering arose through a state of affairs that could not in itself be regarded as 'treatment or punishment'. Removal was the actionable State act, and if the resultant suffering would be severe enough, Article 3 was applicable 'notwithstanding that the source of the proscribed treatment in the receiving country stem[med] from factors which [could not] engage either directly or indirectly the responsibility of the public authorities of that country, or which, taken alone, [did] not in themselves infringe the standards of that Article.'[129]

However, the ECtHR deemed later applications concerning removal of the sick inadmissible for lack of exceptionality.[130] For example, in *SCC v Sweden*,[131] the

[122] Goodwin-Gill and McAdam note in no case has the threat of degrading treatment alone given rise to a protection obligation. Goodwin-Gill and McAdam (n 28) 349, n 437.

[123] *Ahmed* (n 72).

[124] *HLR* (n 92).

[125] App No 60959/00 (ECHR, 22 October 2002).

[126] See *Salah Sheekh* (n 64); *Collins and Akaziebie v Sweden*, (8 March 2007); *Sufi and Elmi* (n 7); *KAB v Sweden* App No 886/11, 5 September 2013; *AAM v Sweden* App No 68519/10 (3 April 2014) (but see the Dissenting Judgment of Judge Power-Forde). See J Schultz 'The European Court of Human Rights and the Internal Flight Alternative: An "Unduly Harsh" Standard?' in J-P Gauci, M Giuffré, and E Tsourdi (eds), *Exploring the Boundaries of Refugee Law: Current Protection Challenges*, (Brill 2015) 31.

[127] *D v UK* (n 92) para 54.

[128] ibid, para 53.

[129] ibid, para 49.

[130] See, e.g. *Karara v Finland*, App No 40900/98 (ECHR, 29 May 1998); *Ndangoya v Sweden* App No 17868/03 (ECHR, 22 June 2004); *Amegnigan v the Netherlands* App No 25629/04 (ECHR, 25 November 2004); *Hukić v Sweden* App No 17416/05 (ECHR, 27 September 2005).

[131] App No 46553/99 (ECHR, 15 February 2000).

application was deemed inadmissible where treatment was available in the country of origin, the applicant was relatively well-off, in the early stage of illness, and had close relatives residing in her homeland. In the more difficult case of *Bensaid*,[132] the high threshold was not met in a case concerning the deportation of an individual suffering from psychotic illness, where some treatment was available in the country of destination. The applicant was also unable to establish that his moral integrity would be 'substantially affected to a degree falling within the scope of Article 8 ECHR'.[133] Three judges (Bratza, joined by Costa and Greve) agreed that there was no Article 3 violation for lack of exceptional circumstances akin to *D v UK*, but urged the UK Government to take account of the 'powerful and compelling humanitarian considerations' in the applicant's favour.[134] In *Arcila Henao v the Netherlands* the ECtHR similarly found that the required treatment was 'in principle' available in the receiving State, Colombia.[135] A rare successful claim emerged in *BB v France*,[136] where the Commission found an Article 3 violation where the deportation of a citizen of the Congo suffering from AIDS would have a high probability of leaving him without medical treatment, and accordingly susceptible to multiple further conditions. In addition, like in *D v UK*, he would have been without family support in the advanced stages of that fatal condition.[137]

The Grand Chamber ruling in 2008 in *N v UK*[138] concerned a rejected asylum seeker from Uganda, who argued that her removal from the UK would violate Article 3, as it would expose her to a high risk of extreme suffering and death due to the absence of appropriate medical treatment there. The House of Lords rejected her Article 3 claim as she failed to meet the test of exceptional circumstances set in *D v UK*. The majority of the ECHR (Judges Tulkens, Bonello, and Spielmann dissenting) held that removal was permissible. On one reading, the ruling is a straightforward application of *D*.[139] D's case was compelling because he was nearing the end of his life and would die quickly and alone on return. In contrast, N was not close to death and would have family with her in Uganda when her condition deteriorated. D 'wins', N 'loses'. However, the ECtHR also attempted to establish some limits around the 'health' cases, stating that:

> [I]nherent in the whole of the Convention is a search of a fair balance between the demands of the general interest of the community and the requirement of the protection of the

[132] *Bensaid v UK* (2001) 33 EHRR 205. [133] ibid, para 48.

[134] ibid, 17. Judge Bratza, in regretful terms: 'It is with considerable hesitation that I have voted in favour of a finding that the return of the applicant to Algeria would not violate Article 3 of the Convention.'

[135] *Arcila Henao v the Netherlands* App No 13669/03 (ECHR, 24 June 2003) para 8.

[136] *BB v France* Commission App No 30930/96 (ECHR, 9 March 1998). In response to the Commission decision, France issued a residence permit, on the basis of which the ECtHR struck the matter off the list on 7 September 1998.

[137] ibid, para 55.

[138] *N v UK* App No 26565/05 (ECHR, 27 May 2008). This came after the House of Lords ruling in *N v Secretary of State for the Home Office* [2005] UKHL 31.

[139] *N v UK* (n 138), para 24. Indeed, the dissenting judges agreed that 'Without interpreting the scope of Article 3 of the Convention differently from our Court in the case of *D v the UK*, a violation could therefore have been found in the light of the very extreme facts of this case. In other words, finding a potential violation of Article 3 in this case would not have been an extension of the exceptional category of cases which is represented by *D v the UK*.' Dissenting Opinion of Judges Tuklens, Bonello, and Spielmann.

individual's human rights...Article 3 does not place an obligation on the Contracting States to... [provide] free and unlimited health care to all aliens without a right to stay in the jurisdiction. A finding to the contrary would place too great a burden on the Contracting States.[140]

The ECtHR appeared to resile from the *D v UK* approach, i.e. focusing on the act of removal and its consequences, instead emphasizing that 'the alleged future harm would emanate not from the intentional acts or omissions of public authorities or non-State bodies, but instead from a naturally occurring illness and the lack of sufficient resources to deal with it in the receiving country.'[141] Secondly, it emphasized that 'although many of the rights [the ECHR] contains have implications of a social or economic nature, the Convention is essentially directed at the protection of civil and political rights.'[142]

Does *N* overrule *D*? Not expressly. However, some uncertainty remains as the ECtHR in *N* is departing from its central assertion in *D*, that Article 3 may include scenarios where the source of the proscribed treatment in the receiving country stems from factors which cannot engage the responsibility of the authorities of that country. In *N*, in contrast, in focusing on 'intentional acts or omissions of public authorities or non-State bodies', the question shifts to whether the situation in the receiving State would *per se* amount to a rights violation. That change is significant. Normally, expulsion is itself the actionable 'treatment' which, if liable to exacerbate the individual's suffering to the requisite degree of severity, may be assessed under Article 3 ECHR. On this view, the intentional State act is removal. Once that intentional act has as its reasonably foreseeable consequence suffering of sufficient gravity, it should be precluded. However, *N* suggests that removal must lead not just to suffering of sufficient gravity, but to treatment that would in itself violate Article 3 ECHR.[143]

The ECtHR's second point in *N v UK* was to emphasize that although many of the ECHR rights 'have implications of a social or economic nature', as an instrument it is 'essentially directed at the protection of civil and political rights'.[144] The Dissenting Opinions of Judges Tulkens, Bonello, and Spielmann took issue with this stance, arguing instead for an 'integrated approach',[145] where the 'social dimension' of Convention rights is acknowledged. The dissenters' rhetoric is certainly more in keeping with the emblematic Strasbourg assertion that 'there is no watertight division' between civil and political and social and economic rights.[146]

In a later Chamber judgment, several judges have called on the Grand Chamber to revisit the *N v UK* case law. In *Yoh-Ekale v Belgium*,[147] the Second Section noted that the facts of the case were similar to *N v UK*, and so rejected the

[140] ibid, para 44. [141] ibid, para 43. [142] ibid, para 44.

[143] See further V Mantouvalou, '*N v UK*: No Duty to Rescue the Nearby Needy?' (2009) 72 MLR 815, 819–20.

[144] *N v UK* (n 138) para 44.

[145] ibid, para 6. Dissenting Opinion of Judges Tuklens, Bonello, and Spielmann.

[146] *Airey v Ireland* (1979) 2 EHRR 305, para 26.

[147] *Yoh-Ekale v Belgium*, App No 10486/10 (ECHR, 20 December 2011).

Article 3 ECHR claim.[148] Six (of the seven) judges[149] noted the extremity of the exceptionality threshold set in *N v UK*, requiring the applicant to be 'almost dying' ('quasi-mourant'). This standard, in their view, was hard to reconcile with the letter and spirit of Article 3 ECHR: To accord protection to someone on her deathbed over someone who would reach that state shortly seemed to lack humanity. The judges invited the Court to revisit its judgment on this matter.

As outlined in Part IV.4.ii, the CJEU has held that these health-based protections against removal fall outside the definition of SP under the QD.[150] The EU legislature, in a rather opaque and oblique manner (by adding the phrase 'in the country of origin' to qualify the treatment contrary to Article 3 ECHR in the 'serious harm' definition) was held to have excluded those non-removal in the 'health cases' from SP. Accordingly, the capacity for the CJEU to influence the development of Strasbourg case law on this topic is limited.

### *iv. Inhuman living conditions*

The assessment of the living conditions in Greece in *MSS* broke new legal ground.[151] The ECtHR reasoned that while there was no general duty 'to give refugees financial assistance to enable them to maintain a certain standard of living,'[152] two factors distinguished the case at hand. First, the duty to provide for asylum seekers had 'entered into positive law' in the RCD, and Greece was obliged to comply with these standards. MSS alleged that Greece has deliberately rendered it impossible for him to avail of these rights 'and provide for his essential needs.' Secondly, the Court for the first time recognized asylum seekers themselves as a vulnerable group to whom States may have heightened positive duties, citing a case concerning the Roma.[153] The finding of vulnerability was grounded in the 'broad consensus at the international and European level concerning this need for special protection, as evidenced by the [Refugee] Convention, the remit and activities of the UNHCR and the standards set out in the [RCD]'.[154] Having established the State had a specific duty towards asylum seekers, the Court then found that the situation of 'extreme material poverty' raised an issue under Article 3 ECHR.[155] MSS endured such extremes whilst homeless in Athens. The applicant's allegations were supported by the various reports, so the Court did not hesitate in accepting his account.[156] The Greek Government argued that MSS was responsible for his own

[148] Judgment, paras 80–83.
[149] Judges Tulkens, Jočienė, Popović, Karakaş, Raimondi, and Pinto de Albuquerque.
[150] *M'Bodj* (n 23). [151] *MSS* (n 8), paras 167–72 and 247–64.
[152] ibid, para 249, citing *Müslim v Turkey* App No 53566/99 (ECHR, 26 April 2005).
[153] ibid, para 251, citing *Oršuš and others v Croatia* [GC] (2011) 52 EHRR 7 concerning a Croatian policy of placing Roma children in Roma-only classrooms. In a subsequent case, the Court has again employed this notion of vulnerability, to identify unaccompanied minors as a particularly vulnerable subcategory of asylum seekers. See also *Affaire Rahimi v Greece* App No 8687/08 (ECHR, 5 April 2011) para 86–87.
[154] ibid.
[155] ibid, paras 252–53, citing *Budina v Russia* App No 45603/05 (ECHR, 18 June 2009).
[156] ibid, para 255.

predicament, in that he had failed to report to the authorities. The Court stated that the 'weight' of that claim was reduced by the fact of the lack of places in reception centres for adult male asylum seekers: it noted UNHCR's statement that such asylum seekers had 'virtually no chance' of being accommodated in a State reception centre.[157] Unlike under the UK system at issue in *Limbuela*, in Greece asylum seekers are *de jure* entitled to work once they are in possession of the appropriate residence permit (the 'pink card'). However, the Court relied on various reports in the public domain in reaching its finding that 'in practice access to the job market is so riddled with administrative obstacles that this cannot be considered a realistic alternative'.[158] The Court's conclusion on this point warrants setting out in full:

> the Court considers that the Greek authorities have not had due regard to the applicant's vulnerability as an asylum seeker and must be held responsible, because of their inaction, for the situation in which he has found himself for several months, living in the street, with no resources or access to sanitary facilities, and without any means of providing for his essential needs. The Court considers that the applicant has been the victim of humiliating treatment showing a lack of respect for his dignity and that this situation has, without doubt, aroused in him feelings of fear, anguish or inferiority capable of inducing desperation. It considers that such living conditions, combined with the prolonged uncertainty in which he has remained and the total lack of any prospects of his situation improving, have attained the level of severity required to fall within the scope of Article 3.[159]

The impact of this jurisprudential development is evident in *Sufi and Elmi*, concerning return to Somalia. The Court distinguished between dire humanitarian conditions 'solely or even predominantly attributable to poverty or to the State's lack of resources to deal with a naturally occurring phenomenon, such as a drought' and humanitarian crisis due to the 'direct and indirect actions of the parties to the conflict'.[160] In the former situation, the test in *N v UK* would be applicable, while in the latter the *MSS* approach would. The former test is extremely difficult to meet, as it requires applicants to show the humanitarian conditions are 'very exceptional', and that, if returned, it was 'highly probable' that the applicant would not have access to the basic necessities of life, and that these deficiencies would result in an immediate threat to life or the impossibility of maintaining human dignity. The line between humanitarian conditions which are due to direct or indirect State action, and those which are simply natural misfortune, will no doubt be tested in subsequent cases.

The workability of the distinction is doubtful, as is evident in the case of *SHH*.[161] In a 4:3 Chamber judgment, the Court rejected the contention that the expulsion of a severely disabled person to Afghanistan would violate Article 3 ECHR. A key question was the applicable standard under which to assess the expulsion, that under *N v UK* or that under *MSS*. SHH argued that his disability rendered him particularly vulnerable in a situation of indiscriminate violence, and that he would be particularly vulnerable to material deprivations given scarce resources

[157] ibid, paras 258–59. [158] ibid, para 261. [159] ibid, para 263.
[160] *Sufi and Elmi v UK* (n 7) para 282. [161] *SHH v UK* (2013) 57 EHRR 18.

and discrimination against persons with disabilities. Accordingly, he sought to rely on *MSS* rather than *N v UK*. However, accepting the UK's arguments, the majority held that *N* was applicable, as the source of the harm was lack of resources, rather than deliberate acts and omissions on the part of the receiving State.[162] So the distinction between *MSS* and *N* is the responsibility of the receiving State. In *MSS*, the Greek authorities' inaction with regard to their positive obligations under European and domestic legislation to provide reception facilities to asylum seekers had created an Article 3 violation. On the other hand, Afghanistan, 'a non-Contracting State...cannot be held accountable under the Convention for failures to provide adequate welfare assistance to persons with disabilities'.[163] If the distinction is between Contracting and non-Contracting States, however, what of *Sufi and Elmi*? The Court also distinguished its ruling from *Sufi and Elmi* on the basis that the suffering there was 'predominantly due to the direct and indirect actions of all parties to the conflict.'[164] The dissenting judges, in contrast, opined that the case raised substantively new issues, in particular taking into account the applicant's disabilities.

### *v. Article 3 ECHR as an absolute right*

As outlined in Part II, in contrast to the CSR *non-refoulement* guarantee, the prohibition in Article 3 is absolute, in the sense that the rights enshrined therein 'cannot be overridden in any circumstances, so that it can never justifiably be infringed and it must be fulfilled without any exceptions'.[165] While treating the negative dimension of Article 3 as an absolute prohibition is conceptually unchallenging, the notion that the non-removal obligations are similarly absolute has been challenged.

Before the absolute nature of the non-removal obligation is explored, two general features of Article 3 ECHR, which apparently call into question the absolute character of its prohibition, must quickly be rebuffed.

**Relativity**

Treatment must reach a 'minimum level of severity' before Article 3 protection is triggered.[166] The assessment of severity is contextual, taking into account all the circumstances of the case.[167] In this sense, it is relative, in that whether the treatment is deemed to be inhuman or degrading takes into account not only 'the duration of the treatment, its physical and mental effects [but also]...in some cases, the sex, age and state of health of the victim.'[168] Relativity does not amount

[162] ibid, para 89. [163] ibid, para 90. [164] ibid, para 91.

[165] A Gewith, 'Are There any Absolute Rights?' in J Waldron (ed), *Theories of Rights* (OUP 1984) 91, 92.

[166] *Greek Case* (n 102) para 11; *Ireland v UK* (n 103) para 162; *Soering* (n 88) para 100.

[167] *Cruz Varas* (n 76) para 83: 'Ill-treatment must attain a minimum level of severity if it is to fall within the scope of Article 3 ECHR. The assessment of this minimum is, in the nature of things, relative.'

[168] *Soering* (n 88) para 100.

to a qualification on the absolute nature of Article 3, but rather it is an appropriate feature of any victim-centred understanding of those terms. For instance, detention of a young child in adult conditions will in likelihood be inhuman treatment.[169] While torture may be understood principally (although not exclusively) in agent-centred terms, focusing on the perpetrator's actions and intentions, inhuman and degrading treatment demands a victim-centred approach, and so is necessarily relative in this sense. This relativity, and the contextual assessment it demands, in no way undermines the absolute nature of the right, indeed it supports it.

**Reasons cf justifications**

In some cases, the ECtHR examines the reasons for particular forms of treatment in order to determine whether it is 'inhuman'. For instance, in deciding whether the use of restraints is inhuman or degrading, it considers the reasons for their use.[170] Does this consideration of the reasons mean that Article 3 mistreatment is tacitly open to justification just like infringements of qualified ECHR rights? If it is permissible, say, to restrain a prisoner to prevent her from harming others, how is this to be distinguished from shackling to make her talk?

There is an important difference.[171] Reasons and justifications are not the same, and an assessment of the reasons does not amount to countenancing justification of inhuman or degrading treatment. In the first case, the justification makes the degradation 'evaporate'—it does not degrade a prisoner to be restrained if it is necessary to protect others. The degradation in shackling lies in treating the prisoner like an animal, incapacitating her more than necessary, inducing 'feelings of fear and inferiority' (to use the ECtHR's phrase). It is present in the case of shackling to break the prisoner's will, but not where it is a proportionate method to protect others. While this distinction may be fine, it is intelligible and does important work in underpinning the nature of absolute rights.

**Absolute rights and *non-refoulement***

The ECtHR in *Soering* lays emphasis on the absolute and non-derogable nature of Article 3 ECHR. However, the duty of non-removal seems at odds with this characterization, as it entails various positive duties to assess the risk posed to the individual on removal. As explained in Chapter 3, the ECtHR does not draw a sharp distinction between positive and negative obligations in this field. The more illuminating view is that the non-removal case law entails the identification of a variety of different types of obligations, including duties of effort and of result.[172]

[169] *Mayeka and Mitunga v Belgium* (2008) 46 EHRR 449.

[170] Contrast *Herczegfalvy v Austria* (1992) 15 EHRR 437, and *Hénaf v France* (2003) 40 EHRR 44.

[171] The following account draws on Waldron (n 108) 25. For an example of the flawed argument, see H Battjes, 'In Search of a Fair Balance: The Absolute Character of the Prohibition of *Refoulement* under Article 3 ECHR Reassessed' (2009) 22 Leiden Journal of International Law 583, in particular 614–15.

[172] M Den Heijer, 'Whose Rights and Which Rights? The Continuing Story of *Non-refoulement* under the European Convention on Human Rights' (2008) 10 EJML 277, 291, citing R Lawson

The non-removal case law is centrally concerned with the risk assessment States must undertake pre-removal, a positive duty of effort. A duty of result, to secure a certain state of affairs, may be absolute, once exposure to the defined level of risk is revealed. In that context, the duty of non-removal is aptly characterized as absolute.

Despite some suggestions in *Soering* that the right not to be removed could be balanced against the general interest of the returning State,[173] in *Chahal*, the ECtHR clarified that as Article 3 ECHR is absolute, the activities of the individual in question, however undesirable or dangerous, could never be a material consideration.[174]

In the heightened anti-terrorist climate post 9/11, this proposition has come under increasing governmental resistance. In a clear attempt to argue for a dilution of human rights standards, the UK and, at its urging,[175] several other States intervened in cases before the Strasbourg court, inviting it to reconsider its ruling in *Chahal*.[176] The notion that deporting suspected or convicted terrorists is a sensible policy response to global terrorism is evidently dubious.[177] Yet, the governments argued that national security concerns justified removal, even where there was a real risk of torture. Their intervention nonetheless purported to respect the absolute prohibition on torture: first, they argued that when national security concerns were at stake, the 'real risk' test should be raised to a requirement that the applicant resisting removal demonstrate that he or she would 'more likely than not' face torture. Secondly, they supported reliance on diplomatic assurances from receiving States not to torture the deportee to meet this risk assessment burden.[178] Unsurprisingly the governmental interventions

'Positieve verplichtingen onder het EVRM: opkomst en ondergang van de 'fair balance'- test' (1995) NJCM-Bulletin, 558 and 727, in particular 740–50.

[173] *Soering* (n 88) para 89. [174] *Chahal* (n 70) para 79.

[175] The UK Government sought support for its intervention by raising the 'problem' of the absolute nature of Art 3 ECHR in the EU JHA Council. See Council of the European Union, *Conclusions of the JHA Council*, 12645/05, 12 October 2005, cited in MT Gil-Bazo, 'Refugee Status and Subsidiary Protection under EC law: The EC Qualifications Directive and the Right to be Granted Asylum' in A Baldaccini, E Guild, and H Toner (eds), *Whose Freedom, Security and Justice? EU Immigration and Asylum Law after 1999* (Hart Publishing 2007) 229, 255.

[176] Observations of the Government of Lithuania, Portugal, Slovakia, and the UK intervening in *Ramzy v the Netherlands* App No 25424/05 (ECHR, 27 May 2008). When *Saadi* leapfrogged *Ramzy* in the ECtHR's list, the interveners requested that their interventions be considered in *Saadi v Italy* instead. See further H Duffy, 'Human Rights Litigation and the "War on Terror"' (2008) 90 International Review of the Red Cross 573, 585–86.

[177] As Macklin puts it, '[m]igration law is least apt for resolving global terrorist threats because its remedy—transfer from the territory of one state to another—presumes the very parochialism that global terrorism renders dangerously obsolete.' A Macklin, 'Transjudicial Conversations about Security and Human Rights' *CEPS Special Report* (CEPS March 2009) 3.

[178] On diplomatic assurances, see further, HRW, *Not the Way Forward: The UK's Dangerous Reliance on Diplomatic Assurances* (HRW, New York, 2008); G Noll, 'Diplomatic Assurances and the Silence of Human Rights Law' (2006) 7 Melbourne Journal of International Law 104. The ECtHR has repeatedly found such assurances insufficient to obviate the risks faced by returnees. See further *Ismoilov v Russia* (2009) 49 EHRR 42; *Ryabikin v Russia* (2009) 48 EHRR 55; *NA v UK* (n 7); *Othman* (n 5).

provoked counter-interventions, although notably by NGOs rather than other governments.[179]

In response, in *Saadi v Italy*,[180] the ECtHR reasserted *Chahal*, ruling out the possibility of 'balancing' national security concerns against the absolute prohibition on removal to face torture. The ECtHR responded unequivocally that:

> [T]he argument based on the balancing of the risk of harm if the person is sent back against the dangerousness he or she represents to the community if not sent back is misconceived. The concepts of 'risk' and 'dangerousness' in this context do not lend themselves to a balancing test because they are notions that can only be assessed independently of each other. Either the evidence adduced before the Court reveals that there is a substantial risk if the person is sent back or it does not. The prospect that he may pose a serious threat to the community if not returned does not reduce in any way the degree of risk of ill treatment that the person may be subject to on return. For that reason it would be incorrect to require a higher standard of proof, as submitted by the intervener, where the person is considered to represent a serious danger to the community, since assessment of the level of risk is independent of such a test.[181]

Judge Zupančič's concurring opinion was scathing in rejecting the balancing approach. To permit balancing in non-removal cases, where the right is acknowledged as otherwise absolute, amounts to diminishing the humanity of foreigners. In his words:

> the only way to avoid the logical necessity flowing from the categorical imperative flowing from the rights of the individual would be to maintain that such individuals do not deserve human rights... because they are less human.[182]

The governmental submissions demonstrate that European executives are anxious to secure greater leeway to deport suspected terrorists to countries where they face risk of torture. As will be seen, the QD strikes a worryingly ambivalent note on this point, again an example of the governmental restrictiveness permeating the EU legislation.

### *vi. Burden of proof and risk assessment*

Article 3 ECHR prohibits removal whenever substantial grounds have been shown for believing that an individual would face a real risk of being subjected to treatment contrary to Article 3 if removed to another country. The threshold is explained as appropriate to removal cases as they do not concern the direct responsibility of the Contracting State for the infliction of harm.[183] The 'substantial grounds' test

[179] See Written Comments by Amnesty International, Association for the Prevention of Torture, Human Rights Watch, Interights, International Commission of Jurists, Open Society Justice Initiative and Redress, pursuant to Article 36(2) of the ECHR and Rule 44(2) of the Rules of the ECHR, 22 November 2005.

[180] See further, D Moeckli, 'The Rules of the Game Have *Not* Changed' (2008) HRLRev 534.

[181] *Saadi v Italy* (n 70) para 139.

[182] Concurring Opinion of Judge Zupančič in *Saadi v Italy* (n 70) para 2.

[183] *Bensaid* (n 132) para 40.

establishes an onerous burden of proof. Real risk, in contrast, is not so demanding. It means a 'foreseeable risk,'[184] going beyond a mere possibility of ill-treatment. It appears the same standards apply to other rights.[185]

In *Vilvarajah v UK*, the ECtHR set out the general approach to the appraisal of risk in the context of removals. On the particular facts of the case, the ECtHR held that the UK's removal of young male Tamil asylum seekers to Sri Lanka did not breach Article 3. Although there was a possibility of ill-treatment, this was not sufficient to give rise to a breach of Article 3. The ECtHR noted that there were 'no special distinguishing features in their cases'[186] that could or ought to have enabled the authorities to foresee that they would be ill-treated on return. Governments tended to apply this individuation requirement, derived from a particular fact-specific finding in *Vilvarajah*, in a rigid manner, requiring asylum seekers to demonstrate that they would be singled out for mistreatment on return. In the worst cases, the individuation requirement has been divorced from the assessment of the intensity of the generalized risks faced by returnees, facilitating the rejection of otherwise compelling claims. The requirement all too easily becomes that elusive 'something extra' claims are found to lack.[187]

A shift in emphasis on the individuation requirement is evident in the 2007 case of *Salah Sheekh*. Mr Abdirizaq Salah Sheekh was a Somali asylum seeker belonging to the Ashraf ethnic minority. By the time he fled Somalia in 2003, majority clan militia had shot his father and brother, raped his sister, and repeatedly beaten him. The ECtHR held that there was a risk of violation of Article 3 ECHR on return. Crucially, on the issue of individuation, the ECtHR signalled its dissatisfaction with the rigid imposition of such a requirement:

> It cannot be required from the applicant that he establishes that further special distinguishing features, concerning him personally, exist in order to show that he was, and continues to be, personally at risk... [I]t might render the protection offered [by Article 3] illusory if, in addition to the fact that he belongs to the Ashraf [minority clan]... the applicant be required to show the existence of further distinguishing features.[188]

*Salah Sheekh* was applied in *NA v UK*. In *NA v UK*, given the surrounding circumstances, there were substantial grounds for finding a violation of Article 3 ECHR.

*Sufi and Elmi* is a landmark ruling concerning removal to Somalia. The Court examined the general risks posed in the country, as well as in particular IDP camps. Concerning the risk emanating from the situation of generalized violence, it noted that only in extreme cases would it be of sufficient intensity to create a risk of ill treatment simply on account of an individual's presence there.[189] The Court noted that Article 15(c) QD and Article 3 ECHR were 'comparable.'[190] It determined, based on various human rights reports and press coverage, that the 'level of violence in Mogadishu is of sufficient intensity to pose a real risk of treatment reaching the Article 3 threshold to anyone in the capital.'[191]

[184] *Soering* (n 88) para 100.
[185] *Bader* (n 93); *Z and T v UK* (n 91).
[186] *Vilvarajah* (n 63) para 112.
[187] See previous discussion in Part II.3.
[188] *Salah Sheekh* (n 64).
[189] *Sufi and Elmi* (n 7) para 218.
[190] ibid, para 226.
[191] ibid, para 248.

As will be seen in Part IV.4 below, this clarification means that those fleeing conflict are more likely to have claims falling under both Article 15(b) QD (which tracks Article 3 ECHR in effect) and 15(c) QD (concerning flight from indiscriminate violence). In turn, it has led some national courts, erroneously in my view, to hold that 15(c) adds little, despite the CJEU's ruling in *Elgafaji*.

## 3. Right to life: Article 2 ECHR

The 'death-row phenomenon' may itself constitute inhuman treatment, as held in *Soering*. In *Bader v Sweden*, the ECtHR found an Article 2 violation in a removal case, where following a flagrantly unfair trial, the death penalty had been imposed. In those circumstances, applying *Öcalan*,[192] the ECtHR held that both Articles 2 and 3 would be violated if Bader were returned to face this punishment.[193]

The internal Strasbourg right to life jurisprudence demonstrates that vindication of the right to life entails positive obligations for States. For example, in *Öneryildiz v Turkey*[194] the ECtHR found an Article 2 ECHR violation in the State's failure to take action to prevent loss of life due to explosions from methane gas. In *Budayeva and Others v Russia*,[195] the ECtHR found that Russia had violated its positive obligation under Article 2 ECHR in failing to take action to mitigate the damage caused by a mudslide, of which the authorities had ample warning. The ECtHR described the positive obligation under Article 2 ECHR as 'to take appropriate steps to safeguard the lives of those within their jurisdiction'.[196] In these cases on positive rights, the ECtHR often emphasizes that the State's first duty is to establish a functioning legal system.[197] Thereafter, different rights may be institutionalized in different ways, leaving a wide margin of appreciation.[198]

Sending State governments may resist imposition of a non-removal duty to vindicate a positive obligation of the receiving State. Nonetheless, following *Soering*, we should focus on removal as a deliberate State act with foreseeable consequences. This approach suggests that the internal positive obligations case law ought to inform the scope of the non-removal protections, as explored further in Part III.2.iv.

Neither the QD definition of persecution nor that of 'serious harm' captures the full potential of ECHR protections, as they extend to other life-threatening scenarios where States may breach the right to life by their omissions. The QD definition of serious harm includes 'death penalty or execution',[199] reflecting Protocols 6 and 13 ECHR. Accordingly, Article 15(a) enhanced Member States'

[192] *Öcalan* (n 6) in particular paras 166–69. [193] *Bader* (n 93) para 48.

[194] *Öneryildiz v Turkey* [GC] (2004) 39 EHRR 12.

[195] *Budayeva and Others v Russia* App No 15339/02 (ECHR, 20 March 2008). See also *Kolyadenko and Others v Russia* App No 17423/05 (ECHR, 28 February 2012).

[196] *Budayeva and Others v Russia* (n 195), para 128.

[197] States are required to 'put in place a legislative and administrative framework designed to provide effective deterrence against threats to the right to life.' ibid, para 129, references omitted.

[198] ibid, para 134. [199] Art 15(a) QD.

obligations, going beyond the ECHR minimum at the time of its drafting. Strasbourg has since caught up, in *Al-Saadoon*. However, in referring to these forms of highly individualized, targeted killing, the EU legislature has failed to reflect the Article 2 ECHR positive duties case law. Admittedly, the QD definition of persecution refers to 'severe violations' of 'basic rights' which presumably could include violation of the right to life due to breach of positive obligations. Threats to 'life or person' in conflict situations may also constitute serious harm under Article 15(c) QD, leading to quite some debate as to its interrelation with Article 3 ECHR.[200]

## 4. The 'flagrant breach' case law

As mentioned, in *Soering*, the ECtHR introduced the notion that only 'a flagrant denial of a fair trial in the requesting country' would preclude removal.[201] The ECtHR has since given further guidance, demonstrating that although the nature of a 'flagrant breach' is difficult to determine, it is a meaningful constraint on removal.[202] Three key Strasbourg non-removal rulings on the 'flagrant breach' test are *F v UK, Z and T v UK*, and *Othman (Abu Quatada) v UK*.[203]

In *F*, it was uncontested that the threatened treatment of the receiving State would violate Article 8 standards. The ECtHR has long condemned the criminalization of 'homosexual adult consensual relations' as a violation of the right to privacy.[204] Yet, F's removal was permitted as the treatment in the country of origin Iran, although it would be a breach of Article 8 ECHR, did not amount to a 'flagrant breach' as there was some evidence he would be able to conduct his private life covertly. Note in contrast that such conditions may warrant recognition as persecution on grounds of membership of a particular social group. The dynamism of refugee law in this context contrasts with the cautious, unprincipled approach of the ECtHR. The CJEU, interpreting the QD's provisions on the CSR definition of refugeehood, has since also rejected this approach where the avoidability of persecution by acting discreetly would be decisive.[205]

In *Z and T*, the applicants argued that the conditions in Pakistan would require them to 'modify their conduct, conceal their adherence to Christianity, and [forgo] the possibility of talking about their faith and bearing witness to others, in order to avoid hostile attention'.[206] Again, the ECtHR found that the limited remaining scope for religious freedom meant that any Article 9 breach was not 'flagrant'. On these issues too it seems that a refugee claim based on religious persecution may be more likely to succeed than one under the ECHR, an important reminder that refugee law can offer better protection than the ECHR in important respects.[207]

200 See Part IV.4.

201 *Soering* (n 88) para 113.

202 *Othman* (n 5).

203 *F v UK* (n 90); *Z & T v UK* (n 91); *Othman* (n 5).

204 *Dudgeon v UK* (1982) 4 EHRR 149.

205 See the discussion at Part IV.3.i.

206 *Z and T* (n 91) 7.

207 *Germany v Y and Z* (n 16). See further UNHCR, *UNHCR statement on religious persecution and the interpretation of Article 9(1) of the EU Qualification Directive* (UNHCR 17 June 2011).

In both cases, the ECtHR reiterated the *Soering* proposition concerning a hierarchy between ECHR rights.[208] Yet, it also sought to explain the specificities of the removal case law more fulsomely than before. The standards in internal case law, the ECtHR stated, were 'first and foremost the standard applied within the Contracting States, which are committed to democratic ideals, the rule of law and human rights'.[209] The ECtHR is making two different claims here: one for the regional limits of the Convention and the other for its normative underpinning in shared commitments to 'democratic ideals, the rule of law and human rights.' Rather than explore either line of argumentation, both judgments then shift in tenor, with the ECtHR asserting that:

> On a purely pragmatic basis, it cannot be required that an expelling Contracting State only return an alien to a country which is in full and effective enforcement of all the rights and freedoms set out in the Convention.[210]

The ECtHR's concern not to impose its standards on third countries seems more plausibly understood as a concession to its own Contracting States' migration control prerogatives. After all, the actions of the Contracting State are principally under scrutiny and its official action liable to be constrained. This real concern for migration control is articulated in *Z and T*, where the ECtHR seems to accept that a right not to be removed entails an analogous right to enter the territory of the Contracting States. The ECtHR expresses the difficulty as follows:

> If for example, a country outside the umbrella of the Convention were to ban a religion but not impose any measure of persecution, prosecution, deprivation of liberty or ill-treatment, the Court doubts that the Convention could be interpreted as requiring a Contracting State to provide the adherents of that banned sect with the possibility of pursuing that religion freely and openly on their own territories.[211]

The workings of the 'flagrant breach' test can be seen by contrasting *Stapleton v Ireland* and *Othman (Abu Quatada) v UK*. In the former case, an Irish national sought to resist transfer to the UK under the European Arrest Warrant (EAW).[212] His claim was dismissed as inadmissible: as the UK had ratified and incorporated the ECHR, and the UK courts were better placed to assess any possible unfairness in the trial, transfer raised no question under the ECHR. In contrast, for the first time in January 2012, the Court found that the 'flagrant breach' standard had been met in relation to Article 6 ECHR in *Othman*, where there were substantial grounds to believe that there was a real risk the applicant's trial in Jordan would use evidence obtained by means of torture. The Court stated that:

> the admission of torture evidence is manifestly contrary [to Article 6] ... It would make the whole trial not only immoral and illegal, but also entirely unreliable in its outcome.

[208] *F v UK* (n 90) 12, citing *Soering* (n 88) para 88; *Z and T v UK* (n 91) 6. [209] ibid.
[210] *Z and T v UK* (n 91) 6; *F v UK* (n 90) 12. [211] *Z and T* (n 91) 7.
[212] Council Framework Decision of 13 June 2002 on the European arrest warrant and the surrender procedures between Member States (2002/584/JHA) [2002] OJ L190/1.

It would, therefore, be a flagrant denial of justice if such evidence were admitted in a criminal trial.[213]

The Court clarified the meaning of the flagrant breach or 'flagrant denial of justice.' It went 'beyond mere irregularities or lack of safeguards in the trial procedures such as might result in a breach of Article 6 if occurring within the Contracting State itself. What is required is a breach of the principles of fair trial guaranteed by Article 6 which is so fundamental as to amount to a nullification, or destruction of the very essence, of the right guaranteed by that Article.[214]

While it remains arguable that 'flagrant breaches' of ECHR rights should preclude removal, *Z and T v UK, F v UK* and indeed *Othman*, suggest that Article 3 ECHR will remain the mainstay of Strasbourg's *non-refoulement* jurisprudence. The 'flagrant breach' test reflects a hierarchy between Article 3 ECHR and other qualified ECHR rights, but nonetheless illustrates that when the legality of deportation is being assessed, there will be instances when serious breaches of qualified rights under the ECHR will preclude removal. It is all the more revealing then that when faced with cases on Dublin deportations within Europe, the CJEU has focused only on the right to be free from torture, inhuman or degrading treatment (Article 4 EUCFR—Article 3 ECHR).[215] The AG in that case, AG Trstenjak, in sharp contrast, seemed to set an undifferentiated test for breaches of all fundamental rights.[216] Had that path been taken, which as I discuss in Chapter 6 would have been appropriate in the EU context, EU law would have underpinned the Dublin system with higher standards than the ECHR minimum, which distinguishes between Articles 2 and 3, and other rights where the 'flagrant breach' standard is applicable.

## IV. The Qualification Directive (QD)

### 1. Two statuses under the QD

The Original QD has as its main objectives:

on the one hand, to ensure that Member States apply common criteria for the identification of persons genuinely in need of international protection, and, on the other hand, to ensure that a minimum level of benefits is available for these persons in all Member States.[217]

The Recast QD (or 'RQD') goes further in order 'to achieve a higher level of approximation of the rules on the recognition and content of international protection on the basis of higher standards'.[218]

213 *Othman* (n 5) para 237. 214 ibid, para 260.

215 *NS/ME* (n 25) para 94; see also Case C-394/12 *Abdullahi v Bundesasylamt* [2013] OJ C 45/12, para 62.

216 ibid, para 178. Opinion of AG Trstenjak.

217 Recital 6. 218 Recital 10 QD.

The Original QD had three legal bases, Article 63(1)(c) EC on qualification as a refugee, 63(2)(a) on SP, and 63(3)(a) on conditions of entry and residence. As explored in Chapter 1, Article 63(1) EC [now found in Article 78 TFEU] requires the measures thereunder to be 'in accordance with the [CSR] and other relevant treaties'. Despite various appeals from the EP, the definition of SP contains no express references to the specific treaties.[219] The relevant recital also refers to its basis in 'practices existing in Member States'.[220] Accordingly, the CJEU confirmed in *Elgafaji* that the QD goes beyond the ECHR and Refugee Convention minima.

This chapter focuses on how the QD interfaces with the protections of the Refugee Convention and ECHR, in particular as regards the established criteria for recognition as a refugee or beneficiary of subsidiary protection. Evidently, the Refugee Convention, as its title makes clear, creates a distinct status for refugees. However, although the Strasbourg case law provides additional protection from removal, beyond the CSR, it does not require States to grant a status to the non-removable persons it protects. Nor are its protections easily established, given the high standard of proof involved. In light of this background, the EU codification of SP is remarkable for affording a status to those who are non-removable.[221]

The interaction between refugee status, SP, and other *ad hoc* statuses is of concern, as it may side-line the CSR, undermining its primacy. Spijkerboer has argued that if the CSR were interpreted correctly, i.e. more capaciously, the need for subsidiary status would be obviated. Indeed, he suggests that the development of other statuses has been to reinvent the CSR unnecessarily.[222] In a convincing countermove to the prevalence of alternative statuses, McAdam has argued that refugee status should attach to *all* those protected against *refoulement* under IHRL. Her argument turns on viewing the CSR as a specialist human rights instrument, whose protections should be liable to extension by developments in human rights law.[223] Moreover, she sees this move as apt to maintain the CSR's primacy:

> Simply entrenching the [CSR] as the pinnacle of protection does not engage with the underlying protection principles it reflects, and may in fact undermine its primacy by siphoning refugees into complementary strategies. Conceptually, the affirmation of the

[219] See further, McAdam, (n 40) 467–68.

[220] Recital 34 QD. [221] McAdam (n 40).

[222] T Spijkerboer, 'Subsidiarity in Asylum Law. The Personal Scope of International Protection' in D Bouteillet-Paquet (ed), *Subsidiary Protection of Refugees in the European Union: Complementing the Geneva Convention?* (Bruylant 2002) 28–29. See also Durieux (n 68) 13.

[223] J McAdam 'The Refugee Convention as a Rights Blueprint for Persons in Need of International Protection' in J McAdam (ed), *Forced Migration, Human Rights and Security* (Hart Publishing 2008) 263. Judge Pinto du Albuqueque in his Concurring Opinion in *Hirsi v Italy* App No 27765/09 (ECHR, 23 February 2012) para 65 seems to support this view.

[CSR]'s primacy is, in effect, a commitment to respect its protection principles and refrain from diluting its scope by developing the law *outside* its boundaries.[224]

The QD creates a clear status hierarchy between refugee status and SP, so it fails to meet McAdam's prescription.[225] Gil-Bazo has critiqued the Original QD for institutionalizing two separate statuses.[226] The rights attaching to SP are fewer, a phenomenon the RQD has considerably reduced, but not removed. Notably the duration of the residence permit attaching to SP may be shorter than that for refugee status.[227] As Chapter 4 discusses, the absence of family reunification rights for SP holders, in contrast to Convention refugees, is an egregious differentiation. However, the types of threats relevant to SP set out in Article 15 indicate a strong presumption of persecution.[228] Thus arises the challenge of ensuring that SP does not siphon off those who warrant recognition as Convention refugees into the lesser status, as is reflected throughout UNHCR's comments.[229] The QD provides that SP is to be 'complementary and additional' thereto.[230] The SP definition seeks to ensure that the Convention is not sidelined, by stipulating that only those who do not qualify as refugees are to be considered for SP. In addition, as the two statuses are distinct, cessation of one does not preclude the availability of the other, as the Court has clarified in *Abdulla*.[231] As both *MM* and *HN* illustrate, States may have two separate procedures for refugee status and SP,[232] but the requirement of effective remedies and good administration entailing a right to a decision within a reasonable time constrains how the two procedures should interact.[233]

As seen in Part IV.4, the QD does not grant a status to all those who are non-removable under even the ECHR (as *M'Bodj* now confirms), so it cannot be taken to have defined the field exhaustively. In light of this fact, Recital 15 RQD [Recital 9 of the Original] is unfortunate, as is assumes that those not covered under the QD are only allowed to stay 'on a discretionary basis on compassionate or humanitarian grounds', rather than that they may be protected by other provisions of IHRL. As explained in Chapter 1, the minimum standards nature of the competence means that Member States may afford greater protection, so there is no question of any clash between the QD and their other human rights obligations. Nonetheless, the mere fact that the Council Legal Service sought to argue that affording protection beyond the minimum set out in the QD would

[224] ibid, 279–80. [225] See further, McAdam (n 40).

[226] Gil-Bazo (n 175) 243–45. [227] Art 24 QD. See also Part V.

[228] UNHCR, *Annotated Comments on the EC Council Directive 2004/83/EC of 29 April 2004 on Minimum Standards for the Qualification and Status of Third Country Nationals or Stateless Persons as Refugees or as Persons who otherwise need International Protection and the Content of the Protection granted (OJ L 304/12 of 30.9.2004)* (UNHCR January 2005) 31.

[229] ibid. [230] Recital 24 QD. [231] *Abdulla* (n 12) para 78.

[232] *MM* (n 19) para 95; *HN* (n 18) paras 30 and 32. Note, however, that the recast Asylum Procedures Directive (PD) envisages a single procedure now. Directive 2013/32/EU of the European Parliament and of the Council of 26 June 2013 on common procedures for granting and withdrawing international protection (recast) (Asylum Procedures Directive) [2013] OJ L180/60, Recital 11.

[233] *HN* (n 18) para 45.

undermine its purpose displays a worrying tendency to treat the QD as embodying a ceiling rather than a floor of rights.[234]

## 2. The refugee under the QD

Article 2(c) QD provides an EU definition of refugee. This section highlights some of the key features of the codificatory exercise. While there are many welcome points of clarification, the QD also sets up tensions with the Refugee Convention, as has been analysed exhaustively elsewhere.[235]

The QD sets out detailed rules on the two key concepts under the refugee definition: Acts of persecution in Article 9, and the Convention grounds or 'reasons for persecution' in Article 10. As previously mentioned, the elaborate definition of persecution is stated to be 'within the meaning of article 1A of the [CSR]'.[236] As already discussed, one of the sharpest divergences in the interpretation of the CSR (and indeed in the practice of national authorities in granting SP prior to the QD) concerned the issue of non-State persecutors. The text of Article 1A(2) CSR supports the view that fears of persecution by State and non-State actors are both sufficient for refugeehood,[237] so this divergence is properly characterized as a misapplication of the CSR by some EU States. Article 6 QD responds with an appropriate definition of 'actors of persecution and serious harm' which includes State entities[238] and non-State actors, 'if it can be demonstrated that [the State entities]...are unable or unwilling to provide protection against persecution or serious harm as defined in Article 7'.[239]

However, Article 7, on actors of protection, modifies our rapture about Article 6. Most controversially, not only States, but also 'parties or organisations, including international organisations, controlling the State or a substantial part of the territory of the State' may be deemed to provide protection.[240] The RQD contains important amendments to this provision on non-State agents of protection,[241] a compromise outcome, as the Parliament would have deleted it altogether.[242]

Article 8 QD on the 'internal protection alternative' seems to further dilute protection. It omits the legally essential requirement that 'the proposed location is practically, safely and legally accessible to the applicant'.[243] The Strasbourg Court's Article 3 jurisprudence has dealt with this issue, as it is a frequent ground

234 See discussion in Chapter 1. 235 See further UNHCR (n 228).

236 Art 9(1) QD. 237 Goodwin-Gill and McAdam (n 28) 98–100; Noll (n 4) 519–20.

238 It refers to (a) the State and (b) parties or organizations controlling the State or a substantial part of the territory of the State.

239 Art 7(1)(c) QD. 240 Art 7(1)(f) QD.

241 Art 7(2) QD cf Art 7(2) RQD. 242 See discussion in Part VI.

243 UNHCR, *Asylum in the European Union: A Study on the Implementation of the Qualification Directive* (UNHCR November 2007) ('UNHCR QD Study') 10. For an authoritative treatment of the topic in general, see J Hathaway and M Foster (n 35).

for refusal of protection. In *Salah Sheekh*, the ECtHR read this requirement into its Article 3 ECHR assessment,[244] in a manner which has influenced the Recast QD.[245]

Concerning Convention grounds, the notion of 'particular social group' is crucial to understanding the systematic and evolving nature of persecution. As the UNHCR Handbook explains,

> membership of a particular social group may be at the root of persecution because there is no confidence in the group's loyalty to the government or because the political outlook, antecedents or economic activity or its members, or the very existence of the social group as such, is held to be an obstacle to the Government's policies.[246]

The notion of particular social group has been the locus for developments around gender and sexual-identity based persecution, two of the most important late twentieth-century global developments in refugee law. The definition of social group proffered in Article 10(1)(d) QD, while not necessarily undermining the international developments, certainly takes a rather tentative view. As Goodwin-Gill and McAdam put it:

> [t]he axiomatic linkage of innate characteristics *and* social perception is somewhat dogmatic and out of touch with much of the doctrine described...while the accompanying language on gender and sexual orientation ('might include', 'might be considered') is equivocal, to say the least.[247]

The QD's equivocal language on gender and sexual orientation has, however, been rectified to a large extent by the recast QD, mainly at the EP's insistence.[248]

Moreover, the QD defines the requisite link between the persecutory act and the Convention ground in a manner that may be an 'overly restrictive interpretation of the CSR.'[249] Under the CSR, there must be a causal link between the Convention ground and the refugee predicament, while the QD foresaw a connection between the persecutory act and the ground, a more restrictive formulation.[250] As is discussed in Part V, the RQD addresses this deficit, allowing either connection between the persecution and the Convention ground, 'or the absence of protection against such acts'.[251]

Along with the SP definition, refugee status under the QD has been confined to third-country nationals (TCNs), in line with Protocol 29 to the TEC on asylum for nationals of Member States of the European Union [the so-called 'Spanish Protocol'—now in essence Protocol 24 to the TEU and the TFEU]. This restriction has been widely criticized, so those criticisms will not be rehearsed here.[252]

[244] *Salah Sheekh* (n 64) para 141.
[245] See Eaton (n 37).
[246] UNHCR Handbook (n 46) para 78.
[247] Goodwin-Gill and McAdam (n 28) 86, n 164. The fears that the EU approach to PSG might prompt a restrictive turn seem to have been borne out in the UK at least. See C Querton 'The Interpretation of the Convention Ground of "Membership of a Particular Social Group" in the Context of Gender-related Claims for Asylum', (2013) RLI Working Paper No 3.
[248] See Part VI.
[249] Battjes, *European Asylum Law and International Law* (n 60) 260.
[250] Art 9(3).
[251] Art 9(3) QD.
[252] See, e.g. Noll (n 4) 540–56. See also F Ippolito and S Velluti, 'The Recast Process of the EC Asylum System: A Balancing Act between Efficiency and Fairness' (2011) 30 RSQ 24, 41–43; G Gilbert, 'Is Europe Living up to its Obligations to Refugees?' (2004) 15 EJIL 963, 975.

Article 351 TFEU [ex Article 307 EC] also plays a role as regards Member States' prior Treaty obligations. On the basis of this provision, Member States arguably remain bound by their prior obligations under the [CSR] when dealing with applications for asylum from EU nationals.[253]

## 3. The CJEU on Refugee Law

The first Luxembourg rulings on refugee law concerned not the grant of protection, but its end, with references from courts on cessation due to changed circumstances in *Abdulla*; exclusion from refugee status in *B and D*; and the position of Palestinian refugees under Article 1D in *Bolbol* and *El Kott*. These were followed by the two rulings on persecution, *Y and Z* and *X, Y, and Z*.

### *i. The meaning of persecution*

The CJEU's interpretation of persecution under Article 9 QD reveals that it is informed by an interplay between the Refugee Convention and human rights. As discussed in Part III.4, the Strasbourg flagrant breach case law seems less protective than the CSR, as there are many instances of persecution which do not reach the threshold of inhuman and degrading treatment under Article 3 ECHR, or the flagrant breach standard under the qualified ECHR rights. In contrast, the CJEU's two rulings on the meaning of persecution, *Y and Z* on religion and *X, Y, and Z* on sexual orientation, illustrate how the Convention refugee includes some who would not be protected from removal under the ECHR. This is a salutary reminder of the importance of maintaining the primacy and centrality of the CSR.

In *Germany v Y and Z*, the applicants fled Pakistan after having experienced past incidents of persecution for reasons of their membership of the Ahmadiyya religious community. Under the criminal law of Pakistan, members of that community may face imprisonment of up to three years or a fine 'if they claim to be Muslim, describe their faith as Islam, preach or propagate their faith or invite others to accept it.' Furthermore, 'any person who defiles the name of the Prophet Mohammed may be punished by death or life imprisonment and a fine'.[254] The question referred effectively asked the CJEU to assess prevailing interpretation of the CSR by the German courts, which tended only to regard violations of the 'core' of religious freedom as persecution. The core was equated with the private or internal sphere. Public manifestation of religion was thus not its 'core'.

The CJEU in effect rejected this approach, noting that the broad definition of religion under Article 10(1) EUCFR (Article 9 ECHR) did not support this distinction between core areas ('*forum internum*') of the right to religious freedom,

[253] K Lenaerts and E de Smijter, 'The European Union as an Actor under International Law' (1999–2000) 9 Yearbook of European Law 117.

[254] *Y and Z* (n 16) para 31.

which exclude religious activities in public (*forum externum*).[255] The CJEU held that:

> acts which, on account of their intrinsic severity as well as the severity of their consequences for the person concerned, may be regarded as constituting persecution must be identified, not on the basis of the particular aspect of religious freedom that is being interfered with but on the basis of the nature of the repression inflicted on the individual and its consequences.[256]

As Tsourdi and Leboeuf note, the CJEU reasoning 'is not free of ambiguity.' In particular, the Court treats as the decisive question regarding whether prosecution would amount to persecution, the severity of the consequences.[257] However, the CJEU did explicitly reject the German Government's submission that the applicants would not face persecution in their home country if they abstained from religious practice by stressing that the QD did not require any consideration of whether there was a 'possibility open to the applicant of avoiding the risk of persecution by abstaining from the religious practice in question.'[258] In rejecting this so-called 'discretion' requirement, the ruling paved the way for examination of a case on sexual orientation, given the prevalence of that approach in cases concerning claims in relation to persecution of sexual minorities.

*X, Y, and Z v Minister voor Immigratie en Asiel* concerned three asylum seekers in the Netherlands who feared persecution on account of their sexual orientation in their respective countries of origin: Sierra Leone, Uganda, and Senegal. Consensual same-sex sexual acts are a criminal offence in all three countries and are punishable by a term of imprisonment of ten years to life sentence, maximum life sentence, and one to five years respectively.[259] As in the previous ruling, the Court treated persecution as turning on the severity of the consequences, and stated that:

> the mere existence of legislation criminalising homosexual acts cannot be regarded as an act affecting the applicant in a manner so significant that it reaches the level of seriousness necessary for…persecution.[260]

However, the term of imprisonment accompanying a criminal provision was deemed to amount to an act of persecution, 'provided that it is actually applied in the country of origin which adopted such legislation'.[261] The CJEU's approach has been criticized for failing to consider the case where criminal laws are not formally enforced, but rather set the content for other repressive actions, such as extortion or blackmail.[262] However, the CJEU answered the question referred, which focused on whether the criminalization and threat of imprisonment could

[255] ibid, para 62. [256] ibid, para 65, citing Opinion of AG Sharpston, para 52.
[257] E Tsourdi and L Leboeuf, 'Towards a Redefinition of Persecution? Assessing the Potential Impact of Y and Z' (2013) 13(2) HRLR 402.
[258] *Y and Z* (n 16) para 78. [259] ibid, para 25. [260] ibid, para 55.
[261] ibid, para 56. [262] Chelvan (n 17) 5.

amount to persecution under Article 9(2)(c) QD. It did not rule on whether they could set up an accumulation of discriminatory 'legal measures' under Article 9(2)(b). Article 9(2)(b) provides the appropriate context in which to assess persecution claims where criminalization creates a hostile persecutory environment.[263]

Crucially, building on *X and Y*, the CJEU held that an asylum seeker 'cannot be expected to conceal his homosexuality in his country of origin in order to avoid persecution'.[264] 'Persecution' clearly encompasses rights violations that do not seem to meet the Strasbourg flagrant breach standard (if we take *Z and T v UK* and *F v UK* as definitive rulings), and rightly so. The enduring vitality and dynamism of the CSR is illustrated in developments on protections for sexual minorities facing persecution. The vigorous debate about how the CSR should be interpreted to best protect sexual minorities[265] contrasts sharply with how the ECtHR effectively thwarted these claims with its blunt, unprincipled 'flagrant breach' case law.

Following on from *X, Y, and Z* a question was referred to the CJEU on credibility assessment in the context of refugee claims where persecution relates to sexual orientation. In the background were many deeply disturbing governmental practices concerning credibility assessment in asylum procedures, in some Member States including pseudo-medical testing to 'prove' sexual orientation and focusing exclusively or excessively on past sexual conduct as the only manifestation of sexual identity.[266] The question referred related to the limits imposed by Article 4 QD and the EUCFR—Articles 1 (human dignity), 3 (right to integrity), and 7 (right to respect to private and family life in particular—on the method of assessing the credibility of a declared sexual orientation in the context of asylum proceedings. The Opinion of AG Sharpston was a tour de force, ruling out a range of approaches to credibility assessment as violating these human rights, and lacking probative value. These were medical and pseudo-medical examinations, intrusive questioning, and using explicit evidence of sexual practices. Indeed, she clarified that even if an applicant consented to any of these three practices, they would still be prohibited. Her Opinion draws on the August 2013 written observations of the UNHCR. The Judgment takes a similar approach, also ruling out 'questions based only on stereotyped notions concerning homosexuals'; 'detailed questioning

[263] Mouzourakis (n 17) 5. [264] *Y and Z* (n 16), para 71.

[265] See for example the symposium prompted by the UK Supreme Court ruling in *HJ (Iran) and HT (Cameroon) v Secretary of State for the Home Department* [2010] UKSC 31. The lead contribution is that of J Hathaway and J Pobjoy, 'Queer Cases Make Bad Law' (2012) 44(2) NYU Journal of International Law & Policy 315; see also UNHCR, *Guidance Note on Refugee Claims Relating to Sexual Orientation and Gender Identity* (UNHCR, 21 November 2008); N LaViolette,'UNHCR Guidance Note on Refugee Claims Relating to Sexual Orientation and Gender Identity': a Critical Commentary (2010) 22(2) IJRL 173; UNHCR, *Guidelines on International Protection No. 9: Claims to Refugee Status based on Sexual Orientation and/or Gender Identity within the context of Article 1A(2) of the 1951 Convention and/or its 1967 Protocol relating to the Status of Refugees* (UNHCR, 23 October 2012); T Spijkerboer (ed), *Fleeing Homophobia: Sexual Orientation, Gender Identity and Asylum* (Routledge 2013).

[266] See for instance UNHCR's *Comments on the Practice of Phallometry in the Czech Republic to Determine the Credibility of Asylum Claims based on Persecution due to Sexual Orientation* (UNHCR 2011).

as to the sexual practices of an applicant for asylum'; 'evidence such as the performance by the applicant for asylum concerned of homosexual acts, 'his submission to "tests" with a view to establishing his homosexuality or, yet, the production by him of films of such acts' and 'delay in disclosing sexual orientation'.[267] This is one of the few cases where the impact of the Charter is palpable, including its dignity guarantee.

### *ii. Cessation of refugee status in cases of changed circumstances*

Article 11 QD deals with cessation of refugee status, reproducing the grounds under Article 1C CSR.[268] Concerning changed circumstances, Article 11(1)(e) QD provides for cessation where the refugee:

> can no longer, because the circumstances in connection with which he or she has been recognised as a refugee have ceased to exist, continue to refuse to avail himself or herself of the protection of the country of nationality.

In its original 2004 drafting, the QD did not reflect the 'compelling reasons' proviso in the second sentence of the CSR provision,[269] although the Recast QD contains a new Article 11(3) which does.[270] Article 11(2) QD provides that in making this assessment, Member States must assess 'whether the change of circumstances is of such a significant and non-temporary nature that the refugee's fear of persecution can no longer be regarded as well-founded.' Article 16(2) QD contains a similar provision relating to the cessation of SP.

The CJEU ruling in *Abdulla v Germany* concerns these provisions. The applicants were Iraqi nationals whose refugee status Germany purported to revoke. They were recognized as refugees in 2001 and 2002, their original asylum applications being motivated by fear of persecution by Saddam Hussein's Baath Party.[271] Due to change of circumstances, the German authorities revoked their refugee status in 2005. Following a series of challenges in domestic court proceedings, the applicants' case came before the *Bundesverwaltungsgericht* (Federal Administrative Court) on point of law.[272] That Court in turn referred detailed questions to the CJEU. The first question asked whether cessation should follow once the underlying reasons for the grant of refugee status ceased, in other words whether there was symmetry between the ground for grant and cessation of refugee status. If the answer to that

[267] Joined cases C-148/13 to C-150/13 *A, B and C* [2015] OJ C 46/4, para 72.

[268] See generally, J Fitzpatrick and R Bonoan, 'Cessation of Refugee Protection' in E Feller, V Türk, and F Nicholson (eds), *Refugee Protection in International Law: UNHCR's Global Consultations on International Protection* (Cambridge University Press 2003) 491 and 501; UNHCR, *Guidelines on International Protection: Cessation of Refugee Status under Article 1(C)(5) and (6) of the 1951 Convention Relating to the Status of Refugees (the "Ceased Circumstances" Clause)* (UNHCR 10 February 2003).

[269] 'Provided that this paragraph shall not apply to a refugee falling under section A(1) of this article who is able to invoke compelling reasons arising out of previous persecution for refusing to avail himself of the protection of the country of nationality.' See further, D Milner, 'Exemption from Cessation of Refugee Status in the Second Sentence of Art. 1C(5)/(6) of the 1951 Refugee Convention' (2004) 16 IJRL 91.

[270] See Part V.

[271] *Abdulla* (n 12) paras 30–31.

[272] ibid, paras 32–37.

question was in the negative, the next question asked which other factors were to be assessed, and by which standards. The German, Italian, Cypriot, and UK governments intervened, as well as the Commission.

Although the referring court leaned towards the symmetrical view, in light of the German law and practice, it had doubts as to the correctness of this position due to the Commission's QD legislative proposal[273] and the UNCHR Guidelines on cessation.[274] The appellants and the Commission argued that the conditions to obtain refugee status and those necessary for cessation differed.[275] Germany, Italy, Cyprus, and the UK (with some minor variations) also supported this symmetrical view, with the UK reminding the Court that 'UNHCR Guidelines are not binding on Member States as a matter of international law and have not been incorporated into Community law.'[276] While UNHCR was not a formal intervener, it did issue a statement aiming to influence the proceedings.[277] UNHCR interprets Article 1C(5) CSR restrictively, in light of its potentially onerous impact on refugees and their families who have settled in countries of refuge. It rejects the symmetrical view, emphasizing instead that the absence of the fear of persecution is necessary, but insufficient. In addition, as Article 11(2) QD reflects, the change in circumstances must be 'significant' and 'non-temporary', terms which UNHCR interprets in light of the aim of securing durable solutions for refugees. UNHCR characterized Germany's invocation of the cessation clause as premature, 'in view of the highly volatile security situation [in Iraq], as well as of the continuing internal and external displacement due to violence and serious human rights violations'.[278]

AG Mazák rejected the symmetrical view, emphasizing the importance of a cautious approach to cessation, 'fully respecting human dignity'.[279] The assessment of the availability of 'protection' under Article 11(1)(e) QD required that an actor of protection was capable of preventing acts of persecution.[280] A 'significant and non-temporary' change of circumstances entailed 'that a lasting solution free from persecution [was] available for the refugee in his country of nationality'.[281] Concerning the role of multinational troops, the AG opined that 'in order to comply with the terms of Article 7 [QD], a State may only rely on the assistance of multinational troops provided such troops operate under the mandate of the international community, for example under the auspices of the United Nations.'[282] However, the need for multinational troops did not indicate that protection was

[273] European Commission, *Proposal for a Council Directive on minimum standards for the qualification and status of third country nationals and stateless persons as refugees or as persons who otherwise need international protection* (QD Proposal) COM(2001) 510, 26.

[274] *Abdulla* (n 12) para 20, Opinion of AG Mazák, para 45.

[275] ibid, para 32.

[276] ibid, paras 34–36.

[277] UNHCR, *UNHCR Statement on the "Ceased Circumstances" Clause of the EC Qualification Directive*, August 2008. UNHCR reiterated the position in its UNHCR Guidelines on International Protection: Cessation of Refugee Status under Article 1(C)(5) and (6) of the 1951 Convention relating to the Status of Refugees (UNHCR, 10 February 2003).

[278] ibid, 11.

[279] *Abdulla* (n 12) para 45. Opinion of AG Mazák.

[280] ibid, para 54.

[281] ibid, para 56.

[282] ibid, para 58.

ineffective—it was one fact among many to be assessed.[283] The next question concerned the stability of the security situation and the general living conditions. The former was an integral part of the protection assessment.[284] Although the latter was not an 'independent relevant criterion', it ought to be 'taken into consideration as part of the assessment of whether the change in circumstances there can be considered significant and non-temporary in nature'.[285] The AG took a narrow view of the relaxation of the rules of assessment contained in Article 4(4) QD, as requiring 'a link, if only partial' between past persecution and the new, different circumstances founding persecution.[286]

The Court's ruling is terser, answering only the first question in full. The Court acknowledged the CSR as 'the cornerstone of the international legal regime for the protection of refugees'.[287] Yet, its focus was on the general scheme and purpose of the QD, to be interpreted 'while respecting the [CSR] and other relevant treaties'.[288] While it regarded the grant and cessation of refugee status as based on similar considerations, suggesting adherence to the symmetrical view, it required assessment not only of whether the original ground for grant of refugee status has lapsed, but also whether the person had *any other* reason to fear being persecuted. The availability of 'protection' was to be assessed in light of Article 7(1) QD, 'having regard to the refugee's individual situation'.[289] Crucially, the change of circumstances must be of a 'significant and non-temporary' nature (under Article 11(2) QD), meaning that the factors grounding the fear must be 'permanently eradicated'.[290]

As regards the relevant actors of protection, the Court merely noted the license in Article 7(1) to include non-State actors of protection.[291] AG Mazák had inferred that such actors were pertinent 'only when the requisite level of control over the State [was] exercised and the objective standard of protection imposed by Article 7(2) ...was fulfilled'.[292] The Court, unlike the AG, did not answer the precise question posed as it related to 'multinational troops'. The Court thus failed to grasp the opportunity to limit this most problematic of provisions in the QD.

While the Court took the view that there was no need to answer the second question, the Court did point out that refugee status and SP were two distinct 'systems of protection'.[293] Cessation of refugee status was not dependent on cessation of SP, nor did it preclude the grant of SP. [294] The third question went to the standard for assessing any remaining protection needs, even when the circumstances on the basis of which refugee status was granted have ceased to exist. The Court acknowledged that while there may be practical differences in the assessment of risk at the time of initial grant of status, and thereafter, nonetheless:

> At both of those stages of the examination, the assessment relates to the same question of whether or not the established circumstances constitute such a threat that the person

[283] ibid, para 59. [284] ibid, para 62. [285] ibid, para 63. [286] ibid, para 75.
[287] Recital 3 QD. [288] *Abdulla* (n 12) para 53. [289] ibid, para 70.
[290] ibid, para 73. [291] ibid, para 75. [292] ibid, para 58. Opinion of AG Mazák.
[293] ibid, para 78. [294] ibid, paras 79–80.

concerned may reasonably fear, in the light of his individual situation, that he will in fact be subjected to acts of persecution.

That assessment of the extent of the risk must, in all cases, be carried out with vigilance and care, since what are at issue are issues relating to the integrity of the person and to individual liberties, issues which relate to the fundamental values of the Union.[295]

Article 4(4) QD on the salience of past persecution was applicable where there was a connection between the past persecution and the particular circumstances under examination.[296]

### *iii. Exclusion from refugee status*

Article 12(2) QD reflects the grounds of exclusion under Article 1F CSR. The interpretation of these exclusion clauses in the CSR is highly contentious. A comprehensive examination of the grounds of exclusion is outside the scope of this chapter.[297] One contentious feature of the QD warrants mention, in light of the previous discussion of the impact of the 'war on terror' on the QD's terms.[298] One ground of exclusion, mirroring Article 1F(c) CSR, is where the refugee 'is guilty of acts contrary to the purposes and principles of the United Nations' as set out in the Preamble and Articles 1 and 2 of the Charter of the United Nations.[299] The QD Preamble appears to expand the notion of terrorism, thereby seeming to expand the EU basis for exclusion, placing the CSR's narrow conception under strain.[300] Again, we see governmental restrictiveness and desire for greater discretion to exclude influencing the text. Unsurprisingly, national courts sought guidance on this question from the CJEU.

*Germany v B and D* concerned the asylum applications of two Turkish nationals of Kurdish origin. B was a supporter of DHKP/C (Revolutionary People's Liberation Party-Front), whereas D had been a guerrilla fighter with the PKK (Kurdistan

[295] ibid, paras 89–90.

[296] ibid, para 98: 'By contrast, where the refugee, relying on the same reason for persecution as that accepted at the time when refugee status was granted, submits to the competent authorities that the cessation of the facts which gave rise to the granting of that status was followed by the occurrence of other facts which gave rise to a fear of persecution for that same reason, the assessment to be carried out will normally be covered, not by Article 4(4) of the Directive, but by Article 11(2) thereof.'

[297] See, G Gilbert, 'Current Issues in the Application of Exclusion Clauses' in E Feller, V Türk, and F Nicholson (eds), *Refugee Protection in International Law* (Cambridge University Press, 2003) 425.

[298] See further, E Guild and M Garlick, 'Refugee Protection, Counter-Terrorism, and Exclusion in the European Union' (2011) 29 RSQ 63.

[299] Art 12(2)(c) QD.

[300] Recital 22 QD states that acts contrary to the purposes and principles of the United Nations are 'set out in the Preamble and Articles 1 and 2 of the Charter' and also set out in the United Nations Resolutions relating to measures combating terrorism, which declare that 'acts, methods and practices of terrorism are contrary to the purposes and principles of the United Nations' and that 'knowingly financing, planning and inciting terrorist acts are also contrary to the purposes and principles of the United Nations.' See further, B Saul, 'Exclusion of Suspected Terrorists from Asylum: Trends in International and European Refugee Law' IIIS Discussion Paper No 26/July 2004, 4.

Workers' Party). At issue was their exclusion from refugee status in Germany. After a series of domestic appeals, their cases came to the *Bundesverwaltungsgericht*, which in turn referred questions to the CJEU on the meaning of Article 12(2) QD. The detailed questions sought interpretative guidance on whether 'serious non-political crime' under Article 12(2)(b) or 'act contrary to the purposes and principles of the UN' under Article 12(2)(c) encompassed membership of recognized terrorist organizations.[301] The referring court also asked whether exclusion required a proportionality assessment, and if so, whether in this context the protection against removal under Article 3 ECHR was to be taken into account. Finally the court probed the minimum standards nature of the Directive, as per Article 3 QD, asking about the compatibility with the QD of asylum under national constitutional law. The referring court pointed out that exclusion from refugee status would not thereby exclude from applicants asylum under the German Constitution,[302] nor would it necessarily remove the right to remain in Germany.[303]

The CJEU reiterated the incantation concerning the CSR as a 'cornerstone of the international legal regime for the protection of refugees', and that the QD was to be interpreted accordingly. In response to the first question, the Court stated that 'terrorist acts, which are characterised by their violence towards civilian populations, even if committed with a purportedly political objective, fall to be regarded as serious non-political crimes.'[304] International terrorism was also to be regarded as 'contrary to the purposes and principles of the United Nations'.[305] The Court accepted (in line with the submissions of all the intervening governments) that those 'involved in terrorist acts with an international dimension' were liable to exclusion under Article 12(2)(c) QD.[306] However, to warrant exclusion, there had to be commission of or culpability for particular acts,[307] a matter requiring individual assessment.[308] Accordingly, membership alone did not automatically warrant exclusion.[309] The facts behind the EU's listing of an organization as 'terrorist' were to be taken into account,[310] but were not a substitute for individual assessment.[311] In particular, that assessment must allow attribution to the refugee of 'a share of the responsibility for the acts committed by the organisation in question while that person was a member'.[312] The Court came uncharacteristically close to determining the facts of D's case when it stated that when a person 'like D—occupied a prominent position within an organisation which uses terrorist methods' the State was entitled to presume his 'individual responsibility for acts

[301] As listed in the Council Common Position of 27 December 2001 on the application of specific measures to combat terrorism (2001/931/CFSP) [2001] OJ L344/93.

[302] *B and D* (n 15) para 65. [303] ibid, para 66. [304] ibid, para 81.

[305] ibid, paras 82–83. [306] ibid, para 84. [307] ibid, para 86.

[308] ibid, para 87. [309] ibid, para 88. [310] ibid, para 90. [311] ibid, para 91.

[312] ibid, para 95. The Court noted further: 'That individual responsibility must be assessed in the light of both objective and subjective criteria. To that end, the competent authority must, inter alia, assess the true role played by the person concerned in the perpetration of the acts in question; his position within the organisation; the extent of the knowledge he had, or was deemed to have, of its activities; any pressure to which he was exposed; or other factors likely to have influenced his conduct.' ibid, paras 96–97.

committed by that organisation during the relevant period, but it nevertheless remain[ed] necessary to examine all the relevant circumstances.'[313]

In response to the second question, the Court rejected the notion of exclusion as conditional upon the person concerned continuing to represent a danger for the host Member State. A literal interpretation revealed that exclusion was 'a penalty for acts committed in the past.'[314] It identified those who were undeserving of refugee status and ought not to be sheltered from punishment.[315]

In response to the third question, the Court rejected an explicit proportionality test.[316] Evaluating the seriousness of the acts concerned was inherent in the exclusion assessment, so the Court accepted the arguments of the German, French, Netherlands, and UK governments that a proportionality test would add an inappropriate layer of assessment.[317] In so doing, it rejected the submissions of UNHCR, the Commission, and the Swedish Government, and also departed markedly from the Opinion of AG Mengozzi.[318] *B and D* thus implicitly endorsed the notion that exclusion from refugee status may come before the inclusion assessment.[319] However, in emphasizing the need for individualized assessment of the gravity of the actions and the degree of individual culpability, its approach could be seen as quite close to proportionality in all but name.[320]

### *iv. Palestinian refugees under Article 1D CSR*

The CJEU has ruled on two references concerning the Article 12(1)(a) QD, which reflects Article 1D CSR.[321] The references were made by the same Hungarian judge, keen for guidance on this particularly contested provision of the CSR. Article 1D CSR provides:

> This Convention shall not apply to persons who are at present receiving from organs or agencies of the United Nations other than the United Nations High Commissioner for Refugees protection or assistance.
>
> When such protection or assistance has ceased for any reason, without the position of such persons being definitively settled in accordance with the relevant resolutions adopted

[313] ibid, para 98. [314] ibid, para 103. [315] ibid, para 104.

[316] ibid, para 107. For a discussion on proportionality, see Goodwin-Gill and McAdam (n 28) 178–84; J Bond, 'Excluding Justice: The Dangerous Intersection between Refugee Claims, Criminal Law, and "Guilty" Asylum Seekers' (2012) 24(1) IJRL 37.

[317] ibid, para 109.

[318] ibid, paras 89–98. Opinion of AG Mengozzi. The AG noted [para 95] that it is 'essential to retain...the flexibility needed both to take account of the progress made by the international community in the protection of human rights and to facilitate an approach based on consideration of all the circumstances of the individual case, even if this requires the application of a system under which a balance has to be struck twice (when assessing whether the conduct is serious enough for the purposes of exclusion and when weighing the seriousness of that conduct against the consequences of exclusion).

[319] See D Kosař, 'Inclusion before Exclusion or Vice Versa: What the Qualification Directive and the Court of Justice Do (Not) Say' (2013) 25(1) IJRL 87, 109.

[320] ibid, 117.

[321] For a comprehensive analysis of Art 1D CSR, see Goodwin-Gill and McAdam (n 28) 151–61.

by the General Assembly of the United Nations, these persons shall *ipso facto* be entitled to the benefits of this Convention.

The first sentence excludes from the protection of the CSR, while the second re-includes some Palestinian refugees. Palestinians are the only group to which this ambiguous Article applies at present, given the role of the United Nations Relief and Works Agency for Palestine Refugees in the Near East (UNRWA). UNRWA provides assistance to around five million registered Palestinian refugees in Jordan, Lebanon, Syria, the West Bank (including Jerusalem East), and Gaza.[322]

In *Bolbol,* Budapest Municipal Court referred questions to the CJEU, asking (1) whether the provisions of the first paragraph covered those who had actually availed of protection from UNRWA or more broadly whether it also covered those entitled to such protection; (2) the meaning of cessation of protection or assistance; and (3) the meaning of *ipso facto* entitlement. The reference was, in effect, an invitation to the CJEU to clarify Article 1D CSR.[323]

Some background may be illuminating: in a study of the practices in seventeen countries,[324] Hungary (and Norway) stood out as reversing previous practices that had been favourable to Palestinian refugees. It had granted 'a few Palestinians asylum based on Article 1D' in 2003, but later reversed the practice, apparently because the Hungarian authorities became aware that other States took a more limited reading of Article 1D CSR.[325]

*Bolbol* concerned Ms Nawras Bolbol, a Palestinian, who arrived in Hungary in 2007 from the Gaza Strip and applied for asylum. The Hungarian authorities rejected her asylum application, and on appeal she invoked Article 1D. UNHCR has put forth a persuasive contextual interpretation of Article 1D, which it reiterated specifically in the context of the *Bolbol* reference.[326] Also persuasive in the litigation was the opinion of leading scholars on Article 1D.[327] However, none of the five governments that intervened before the Luxembourg Court (Belgium,

[322] See generally S Akram, 'UNRWA and Palestinian Refugees' in E Fiddian-Qasmiyeh, G Loescher, K Long, and N Sigona (eds), *Oxford Handbook of Refugee and Forced Migration Studies* (OUP 2014).

[323] *Bolbol* (n 13) para 34. The CJEU noted that '[a]ccording to the referring court, Article 1D . . . is open to a number of interpretations. [The 2002 UNHCR Note] fails to provide sufficiently clear and unequivocal guidance to guarantee consistent application of that provision with regard to Palestinians. As the Directive includes a reference to Article 1D of the Geneva Convention, the Court has jurisdiction to interpret the meaning of that article of the Convention.'

[324] Australia, Belgium, Canada, Denmark, France, Hungary, Ireland, Italy, Netherlands, New Zealand, Norway, Poland, Spain, Sweden, Switzerland, United Kingdom, and United States.

[325] BADIL Resource Center for Palestinian Residency and Refugee Rights, *Closing Protection Gaps: A Handbook on Protection of Palestinian Refugees in States Signatories to the 1951 Refugee Convention. Jurisprudence Regarding Article 1D 2005-2010* (BADIL 2010 Update) 10–11.

[326] UNHCR, *UNHCR Revised Statement on Article 1D of the 1951 Convention: Issued in the context of the preliminary ruling reference to the Court of Justice of the European Communities from the Budapest Municipal Court regarding the interpretation of Article 12(1)(a) of the Qualification Directive* (UNHCR, October 2009).

[327] See, e.g. S Akram and G Goodwin-Gill, 'Brief *Amicus Curiae* on the Status of Palestinian Refugees under International Law' (2000–2001) 11 Pal. YIL 185.

Germany, France, Hungary, and the United Kingdom) supported the UNHCR line, nor did the European Commission.

AG Sharpston's Opinion in *Bolbol* expressly took into account the UNHCR statement, which she treated as 'an unofficial *amicus curiae* brief'.[328] However, the Opinion departs from the UNHCR position in two respects. While UNHCR defines the scope of Article 1D by reference to two groups of Palestinians who are *entitled* to receive assistance, the AG confined it to those who had actually received assistance.[329] Secondly, she interpreted 'ceased' in the second sentence of Article 1D as meaning that the person who was within the scope of the first paragraph was no longer able to benefit from protection or assistance from UNRWA, excluding those who had 'of their own volition' forsaken UNRWA assistance.[330] However, the AG also rejected the UK's arguments for a restrictive temporal scope of Article 1D, thereby departing from the interpretation of Article 1D that prevailed in the UK Court of Appeal, confining Article 1D to those receiving protection in 1951.[331] She also agreed that the effect of the '*ipso facto* entitlement' was that those relevant Palestinians were entitled to the 'automatic grant of refugee status, without further individual assessment'.[332] The Opinion articulated the value of rationing special rights for Palestinians, as these rights would come at the expense of protection for other refugees.[333] This stance led her to read the two parts of Article 1D 'consecutively, not disjunctively' in order to arrive at an interpretation which '[struck] a reasonable balance between caring for displaced Palestinians (under Article 1D) and caring for other potential refugees (under the 1951 Convention as a whole).'[334]

The Court followed the Opinion, but only answered the first question referred, prompting the *El Kott* reference asking the two remaining questions again.[335] It too explicitly rejected the UK's argument to restrict the temporal scope.[336] However, it took a literal interpretation of the first part of Article 1D, noting that the 'clear wording' of Article 1D meant that it only applied to those 'who have actually availed themselves of the assistance provided by UNRWA'.[337] Article 1D was an exclusion clause and so was to be interpreted narrowly.[338] Actual registration with UNRWA was sufficient, but not necessary. Other evidence could also demonstrate

[328] *Bolbol* (n 13) para 16. Opinion of AG Sharpston. [329] ibid, paras 71–76.

[330] ibid, para 75, see also paras 77–84.

[331] *El-Ali v Secretary of State for the Home Department* [2002] EWCA Civ 1103. For criticism, see Goodwin-Gill and McAdam (n 28) 157–59. In contrast, Hathaway and Foster support this 'historically bounded interpretation'. See Hathaway and Foster, *The Law of Refugee Status* (n 55) 513–14. For detailed analysis and contrasting authority from other jurisdictions, see M Symes and P Jorro, *Asylum Law and Practice* (2nd edn, Bloomsbury Professional 2010) 378–84. Since *Bolbol*, the UK Asylum and Immigration Tribunal has applied *Bolbol* rather than *El-Ali*. See *Said* [2012] UKUT 00413.

[332] *Bolbol* (n 13) para 89. Opinion of AG Sharpston.

[333] ibid, para 50: 'the historical intention behind Article 1D was clearly to give some form of *special treatment and consideration* to displaced Palestinians.' Nevertheless, the AG found that an interpretation enabling every displaced Palestinian to automatically claim refugee status 'would provide disproportionately favourable treatment for displaced Palestinians at the expense of other genuine applicants.' ibid, para 55.

[334] ibid, para 56. [335] *El Kott* (n 14). [336] *Bolbol* (n 13) para 47.

[337] ibid, para 51. [338] ibid.

assistance.[339] UNHCR continues to urge for a broader reading, keen to ensure the mandates of UNHCR and UNRWA are kept distinct.[340]

Hathaway characterizes *Bolbol* as 'a highly decontextualised understanding of the exclusion from refugee status of persons in receipt of UN protection'.[341] I disagree. Read together with *El Kott*, an important protective interpretation has emerged.

In *El Kott*, the Court responded to the questions about the second paragraph of Article 1D. It interpreted 'cessation of protection or assistance' as encompassing the situation of a person who, after actually availing herself of such protection or assistance, ceases to receive it for a reason beyond their control and independent of their volition.[342] The objective of Article 1D CSR must be taken into account and, in light of that, a Palestinian refugee must be regarded as having been forced to leave UNRWA's area of operations if 'his personal safety is at serious risk and if it is impossible for that agency to guarantee that his living conditions in that area will be commensurate with the mission entrusted to that agency'.[343] This interpretation has important protection consequences for Palestinian refugees who flee UNRWA areas of operations (which, after all, include Gaza and Syria).

As to the meaning of 'be entitled to the benefits of [the QD]', the Court interpreted this phrase as an entitlement only to refugee status, since that clause was based on Article 1D and the QD must be interpreted in the light of that provision. While '*ipso facto*' meant 'as of right', the second sentence of Article 1D did not provide an 'unconditional right to refugee status'.[344] Rather, an individual assessment should be carried out in which Article 4(3) QD may be applicable by analogy.[345] Such a process should be employed to verify whether the applicant actually sought assistance from UNRWA; whether that assistance had ceased; and importantly, whether any other ground of exclusion (such as under Article 1F) was applicable.[346] Refugee status would cease if the individual is able to return to the UNRWA area of operations where he or she was formerly habitually resident.[347]

After the *El Kott* ruling, UNHCR provided an updated position on the proper interpretation of Article 1D CSR, taking into account *Bolbol* and *El Kott*, and its own note issued ahead of *El Kott*.[348] In particular, the UNHCR position sets out a range of indicative situations which in UNHCR's view would constitute objective reasons why the applicant is unable to return or re-avail herself of the protection or assistance of UNRWA, which would include, but are not limited to threats to life, physical security, or freedom, or other serious protection-related reasons. Practical,

[339] ibid, para 52.

[340] UNHCR, *Note on UNHCR's Interpretation of Article 1D of the 1951 Convention relating to the Status of Refugees and Article 12(1)(a) of the EU Qualification Directive in the context of Palestinian refugees seeking international protection* (UNHCR, May 2013).

[341] J Hathaway, 'EU Accountability to International Law: The Case of Asylum' (2011) 33 Mich. JIL 1, 5.

[342] *El Kott* (n 14) para 74. [343] ibid, para 63. [344] ibid, para 75.

[345] ibid, para 64. [346] ibid, para 76. [347] ibid, para 77.

[348] UNHCR (n 340) and *UNHCR Observations in the case C-364/11 and Others regarding the interpretation of Article 1D of the 1951 Convention and Article 12(2)(a) of the Qualification Directive* (UNHCR, October 2011).

legal, and safety barriers to return could impede re-availment of protection or assistance, such as 'mine fields, factional fighting, shifting war fronts, banditry or the threat of other forms of harassment, violence or exploitation'.[349] No doubt this statement anticipates the fact that many Palestinian refugees are being displaced from the region, and may seek to rely on the important *El Kott* innovation.[350]

### *v. Conclusion on the CJEU refugee law cases*

As is invariably the case in the preliminary reference procedure, much is in the hands of national judges. The references analyzed show national judges keen for CJEU guidance, sending detailed, carefully crafted questions on those terms in the QD that mirror the CSR. The *Bolbol* reference, from the Budapest municipal court, and its subsequent re-referral of the outstanding questions in *El Kott*, as well as the narrowly framed questions in *X, Y, and Z*, demonstrate the centrality of the role of national judges. The German *Bundesverwaltungsgericht* is already a repeat EU refugee law player.

The CJEU's responses display some common features. While the Court acknowledges that the CSR is the cornerstone of the international legal regime for the protection of refugees, its interpretations avoid the interpretative methodology familiar to refugee lawyers, focusing rather on systematic readings of the QD itself. A leitmotif is the centrality of individualized assessment both in the context of persecution (*Y and Z, X, Y, and Z*) and across all limitation issues: cessation (*Abdulla*), exclusion (*B and D*), and Article 1D (*El Kott*). It attempts to steer a middle course between eccentric national interpretations of the CSR (such as the German 'core' approach to religious freedom in *X and Y*, and the UK interpretation of Article 1D as temporally limited in *El-Ali*) and according UNHCR guidance, however legally well-constructed, definitive status, particularly when governmental resistance is apparent in the interventions.

## 4. SP under the QD

### *i. The omission of a general human rights clause*

Recital 34 QD makes clear that the definition of SP draws on both international law and State practice. Article 2(e) QD defines 'person eligible for SP' as:

> a third country national or a stateless person who does not qualify as a refugee but in respect of whom substantial grounds have been shown for believing that the person concerned, if returned to his or her country of origin, or in the case of a stateless person, to his or her country of former habitual residence, would face a real risk of suffering serious harm as

[349] UNHCR (n 340) 5.

[350] See, e.g., *Decisions No 04020557 and 04020558* (*Cour nationale du droit d'asile*, 24 May 2013), in which the French National Court of Asylum applied Article 12(1)(a) QD to grant refugee status to Palestinians who were forced to leave a refugee camp in Jordan due to a conflict with a local family.

defined in Article 15, and to whom Article 17(1) and (2) [on exclusion] do not apply, and is unable, or, owing to such risk, unwilling to avail himself or herself of the protection of that country.

Article 15 QD in turn defines 'serious harm' as:

(a) death penalty or execution; or
(b) torture or inhuman or degrading treatment or punishment of an applicant in the country of origin; or
(c) serious and individual threat to a civilian's life or person by reason of indiscriminate violence in situations of international or internal armed conflict.

The drafting history of the 'serious harm' definition reveals the abandonment of a general human rights guarantee. In the original Commission proposal, serious harm included 'a violation of a human right, sufficiently severe to engage the Member State's international obligations'.[351] As explored in Part III.4, the ECtHR will preclude removal in cases of 'flagrant breach' of articles other than 2 and 3 ECHR. The abandoned formulation provided a neat device to track developments in Strasbourg and other international *fora*. Noll had argued that the inclusion of such a provision was imperative to maintain congruence between the two systems of protection, ECHR and EU.[352] McAdam similarly argued that:

the deletion of this broader human rights provision has dramatically reduced the scope of the QD. It was the provision which allowed for the greatest development of the human rights–refugee law nexus, providing flexibility for addressing new situations arising in international law and relevant developments in the jurisprudence of the [ECtHR]. [353]

As will be seen, in the absence of such a clause, the interaction between Luxembourg, Strasbourg, and national courts continues, with much attention focusing on whether Article 15(c) QD adds protections beyond the ECHR.

### *ii. Overview of 'serious harm'*

**Article 15(a) QD: Death penalty or execution**

Prior to *Al-Saadoon*, the ECtHR did not regard the removal to face the death penalty per se as contrary to Article 3 ECHR. Accordingly, at the time of drafting, Article 15(a) QD enhanced Member States' obligations, going beyond the ECHR minimum. Since *Al-Saadoon*, the Strasbourg case law has effectively caught up, in light of the widespread ratification of Protocol 13.[354] However, the QD does not include other forms of targeted killing, assassinations, and the like, or the other actionable deprivations of life that arise in breach of positive duties under Article 2 ECHR.[355]

[351] European Commission, *QD Proposal* (n 273) Art 15(b).

[352] G Noll, 'Fixed Definitions or Framework Legislation? The Delimitation of Subsidiary Protection *Ratione Personae*' (2002) *UNHCR New Issues in Refugee Research Working Paper No 55*.

[353] McAdam (n 40) 492.

[354] See Part III.3.

[355] An omission described as 'surprising' by Sedley LJ in *QD (Iraq) and AH (Iraq) v Secretary of State for the Home Department* [2009] EWCA Civ 620, para 13, referring to 'targeted deprivation of life in breach of ECHR article 2'.

**Article 15 (b) QD: Torture or inhuman or degrading treatment or punishment of an applicant in the country of origin**

This limb, reflecting the text of Article 3 ECHR, was apparently the easiest to agree upon. Its main significance lies in according a status, rather than simply rendering non-removable, persons in these circumstances.

The phrase 'in the country of origin' was added at a late stage in the negotiations, with the apparent intention of preventing health cases, explored in Section III.2, coming under the QD. Battjes takes the view that these cases are thereby excluded, as the impugned treatment does not take place in the country of origin, but rather arises out of a failure to fulfil a positive obligation in the host state.[356] However, when a sick person is expelled in a manner contrary to Article 3 ECHR, it is conditions in the country of origin (concerning the absence of treatment, support, and the like) which make that expulsion impermissible. As such, the issue may turn more on the meaning of 'treatment' in the definition, than the reference to 'in the country of origin'.[357] The CJEU in *M'Bodj* has now ruled on this matter.[358] The Court interpreted the scope of Article 15(b) in light of the fact that actors of serious harm are defined in Article 6 QD. It held that this definition 'supported the view' that:

> [S]uch harm must take the form of conduct on the part of a third party and that it cannot therefore simply be the result of general shortcomings in the health system of the country of origin.[359]

The Court also noted the 'in his country of origin' addendum, so that subsidiary protection should be granted only in those cases in which such treatment occurred in the applicant's country of origin.[360] It noted the Strasbourg health cases,[361] and simply asserted that the fact that individuals might exceptionally be protected against *refoulement* under Article 3 ECHR did not mean they were entitled to subsidiary protection. In this way, the Court distanced Article 15(b) QD from the Strasbourg jurisprudence. Moreover, its reasoning as regards 'intentional acts' potentially undermines protection in a wider range of cases than the medical ones directly at issue. Also of concern was that the Court held that Member States could not grant subsidiary protection beyond the ceiling set by the case itself.

In contrast, in *Elgafaji* the CJEU had described Article 15(b) as corresponding 'in essence, to Article 3 … ECHR'.[362] We should recall also that *Sufi and Elmi* introduces a distinction between conditions in the country of origin which are attributable to conflict (to which the normal standards of assessment under Article 3 ECHR apply), and those 'solely or even predominantly attributable to poverty

[356] Battjes (n 60) 235–36, where he argues that 'The requirement in Article 15(b) QD that the ill-treatment occur "in" the country of origin however excludes "humanitarian grounds" [ie cases like *D v UK*] cases from the scope of SP.'

[357] See further, H Storey, 'EU Refugee Qualification Directive: A Brave New World?' (2008) 20 IJRL 1, 31.

[358] *M'Bodj* (n 23).

[359] ibid, para 35.

[360] ibid, para 34.

[361] ibid, para 39, citing *N v UK* (n 138).

[362] *Elgafaji* (n 21) para 28.

or to the State's lack of resources to deal with a naturally occurring phenomena' (to which the more onerous standards of exceptionality in *N v UK* are applicable).[363] *SHH* demonstrates the difficulty of determining which standards apply in which context, suggesting that the current ECtHR approach is unworkable.

**Article 15(c) QD: Serious and individual threat to a civilian's life or person by reason of indiscriminate violence in situations of international or internal armed conflict**

Article 15(c) was the most challenging aspect of the definition to agree on, and its interpretation has been the most contentious also. The provision underwent several amendments during the drafting process. The original Commission proposal referred to:

> A threat to his or her life, safety or freedom as a result of indiscriminate violence arising in situations of armed conflict, or as a result of systematic or generalised violence in situations of armed conflict, or as a result of systematic or generalised violations of their human rights.[364]

This drew inspiration from the Temporary Protection Directive (TPD).[365] The national governments in the Council were willing to commit to the expansive formulation in the latter measure, as it only becomes effective on a Council decision (taken by qualified majority) if a situation of 'mass influx' is deemed to arise. Unsurprisingly, it has never been used. The final Article 15(c) wording is evidently more restrictive than the original proposal.

Several terms in Article 15(c) are redolent of international humanitarian law (IHL).[366] Express reference to this body of law in an early draft was dropped. Nonetheless, some commentators argued that this body of law should determine the meaning of Article 15(c)'s terms, in particular the notions of 'indiscriminate violence', 'civilian', 'international armed conflict', and 'internal armed conflict.'[367] The UK Court of Appeal, prompted by strong submissions from the UNHCR,

[363] *Sufi and Elmi* (n 7) paras 280–83.

[364] European Commission, *QD Proposal* (n 273) Art 15(c). See McAdam (n 40) 479–80 for a detailed account of the drafting history.

[365] Council Directive 2001/55/EC of 20 July 2001 on minimum standards for giving temporary protection in the event of a mass influx of displaced persons and on measures promoting a balance of efforts between Member States in receiving such persons and bearing the consequences thereof (Temporary Protection Directive) [2001] OJ L212/12, Article 2(c).

[366] IHL is used to describe the Geneva Conventions of 12 August 1949—Geneva Convention for the amelioration of the condition of the wounded and sick in armed forces in the field (Convention I), Geneva Convention for the amelioration of the condition of the wounded, sick and shipwrecked members of the armed forces at sea (Convention II), Geneva Convention relative to the treatment of prisoners of war (Convention III), and Geneva Convention relative to the protection of civilian persons in time of war (Convention IV); Protocol Additional to the Geneva Conventions of 12 August 1949, and relating to the Protection of Victims of International Armed Conflicts (Protocol I), 8 June 1977; Protocol Additional to the Geneva Conventions of 12 August 1949, and relating to the Protection of Victims of Non-International Armed Conflicts (Protocol II), 8 June 1977. See also Protocol Additional to the Geneva Conventions of 12 August 1949, and relating to the adoption of an additional distinctive emblem (Protocol III), 8 December 2005; and doctrine of the International Committee of the Red Cross (ICRC).

[367] e.g. Storey (n 357).

has now held that the use of international humanitarian law is not an appropriate prism through which to interpret the QD, as it does not meet the objective of securing protection and is liable to create gaps and anomalies.[368]

The CJEU in *Diakité* has now followed suit, establishing that IHL and the QD's subsidiary protection regime 'pursue different aims and establish quite different protection mechanisms'.[369] Accordingly, the term 'internal armed conflict' in Article 15(c) QD is to be understood independently from IHL, as meaning a situation where 'a State's armed forces confront one or more armed groups or [where] two or more armed groups confront each other'.[370] This is not to suggest there are no productive interactions between IHL and international refugee law.[371] However, in the particular context of SP, IHL terminology would not be fit for the protective purposes envisaged. In *Elgafaji*, the CJEU also gave the notion of 'indiscriminate' violence an autonomous EU reading, suggesting that IHL was not a useful guide.

Previous drafts referred to 'life, safety or freedom' and 'life or physical integrity.' 'Life or person' is more open-textured. Clearly, the notion of personhood is broad, and invites a contextual assessment in light of the reference to 'indiscriminate violence'. As the CJEU noted in *Elgafaji*, 15(c) 'covers a more general risk of harm' than the other limbs of Article 15.[372] Battjes fears that:

> [i]f we understand 'person' as physical integrity, this element is covered by Article 15(b) to a large extent. If 'person' should be attributed the meaning of 'personal' (as opposed to physical) integrity, Article 15(c) would potentially cover any violation of any human right, which would be an unreasonable interpretation.[373]

He does not explain why a broad view would be unreasonable, but again seeks doctrinal security in IHL, a body of law whose applicability I dispute. In contrast, UNHCR argues that 'all forms of physical and psychological harm are capable of falling within the definition if they are sufficiently serious.'[374]

SP requires that the applicant show 'substantial grounds' that he or she faces a 'real risk' of the serious harm on return. In this respect, the definition adopts the ECHR risk assessment criteria. However, Article 15(c) appears to dilute the risk assessment criterion, as it refers not to specific ill-treatment, but rather exposure to a 'threat.' McAdam had suggested that 15(c) thereby sets up a 'circular, if not

[368] *QD (Iraq)* in particular Sedley LJ (n 355) paras 15–16. He accepted that the international humanitarian law gloss led the Asylum and Immigration Tribunal to construe the notion of 'indiscriminate violence' and 'life or person' too narrowly, and to construe the qualification of 'individual' threat too broadly, and set the threshold of risk too high.

[369] *Diakité* (n 22) para 24, citing the Opinion of AG Mengozzi, paras 66–67.

[370] ibid, para 35.

[371] See generally, D Cantor and JF Durieux (eds), *Refuge from Humanity? War Refugees and International Humanitarian Law* (Brill—Nijhoff 2014).

[372] *Elgafaji* (n 21) para 33.

[373] Battjes (n 60) 238.

[374] UNHCR, *Submission in QD (Iraq) and AH (Iraq) v Secretary of State for the Home Department [2009] EWCA Civ 620* (UNHCR, May 2009), para 50, citing by analogy *R (Razgar) v Secretary of State for the Home Department* [2004] 2 AC 368.

double threshold' in that it in effect requires a 'foreseeable, real and personal risk of a real risk'.[375] Some domestic courts have taken the view that the risk assessment under 15(c) is the same as under the other limbs of the Article.[376] As will be seen, the AG in *Elgafaji* deals with this issue, while the CJEU skirts around it.

The reference to 'individual threat' was inserted at a late stage in the negotiations, evidently in order to prevent 'an undesired opening of the scope of this subparagraph'.[377] As previously mentioned, individuation criteria are often used insidiously to limit those entitled to protection, allowing adjudicators to deem claims to lack that elusive something extra that would differentiate the applicant from others sharing her predicament. Read in the context of a provision on 'indiscriminate violence', it is particularly problematic. Logically, it cannot mean 'singled out' as this would negate the 'indiscriminate' nature of the violence. Recital 35 QD is particularly unhelpful in this regard as it stipulates that:

> Risks to which a population of a country or a section of the population is generally exposed do normally not create in themselves an individual threat which would qualify as serious harm.[378]

Even throughout the implementation process, Member States contested whether the serious harm covered by Article 15(c) was broader than Article 15(b).[379] The CJEU was quickly drawn into this controversy in *Elgafaji*, as explored in the next section.

## 5. The CJEU on SP: *Elgafaji* in focus

The first reference on the QD came from the *Raad van State* (Dutch Council of State), arising out of the refusal of the asylum applications of two Iraqi nationals, Mr and Mrs Elgafaji, a Shiite and a Sunni Muslim respectively. Mr Elgafaji worked for approximately two years as a security officer in Baghdad for a British company. His uncle, who worked for the same undertaking, was targeted by militia, his death certificate stating that his death followed a terrorist attack. Some days after the uncle's death, the couple received a threatening letter, stating 'death to collaborators'. They fled Iraq and sought asylum in the Netherlands, where Mr Elgafaji's father, mother, and sisters were resident.[380] From the brief account of the facts, they may have been Convention refugees, or at risk of targeted killing, which would fall under Article 15(a) or (b). However, the first instance Dutch court had decided the case on the basis of 15(c),[381] so the reference was posed solely on the meaning of that provision.

[375] McAdam (n 40) 473.

[376] Sedley LJ in *QD (Iraq)* (n 355) para 19 describes the 'ostensibly cumulative' test as 'logically intractable'. He therefore holds that they should not be read cumulatively, but rather '"risk" in 2(e) overlaps with "threat" in Article 15(c), so that the latter reiterates but does not qualify or dilute the former.' ibid, para 27.

[377] Storey (n 357) 33.

[378] Recital 35 QD (former Recital 26 Directive 2004/83).

[379] Durieux (n 68) 15.

[380] Opinion of AG Maduro in *Elgafaji* (n 21) para 6.

[381] R Errera, 'The CJEU and Subsidiary Protection: Reflections on *Elgafaji*—And After' (2009) Paper presented at the IARLJ conference, Berlin, 19–20 October 2009, 3.

The questions referred were as follows:

(1) Is Article 15(c) [QD] to be interpreted as offering protection only in a situation in which Article 3 [ECHR], as interpreted in the case-law of the European Court of Human Rights, also has a bearing, or does Article 15(c), in comparison with Article 3 [ECHR], offer supplementary or other protection?

(2) If Article 15(c) [QD], in comparison with Article 3 [ECHR], offers supplementary or other protection, what are the criteria in that case for determining whether a person who claims to be eligible for SP status runs a real risk of serious and individual threat by reason of indiscriminate violence within the terms of Article 15(c) [QD], read in conjunction with Article 2(e) thereof?[382]

Eight national governments intervened: the Netherlands, Belgium, Greece, France, Italy, Finland, Sweden, and the UK.

EU law's axiomatic interpretative stance of *effet utile* demands that Article 15(c) mean something over and above the other provisions. In addition, there is no textual indication that 15(c) is intended to be an instantiation of or a subset of 15(b). Unsurprisingly then, in *Elgafaji*, the CJEU held that Article 15(c) was substantively different to that of Article 3 ECHR so 'the interpretation [thereof] must…be carried out independently although with due regard for fundamental rights, as they are guaranteed under the ECHR.'[383] Moreover, as AG Maduro reminded the CJEU, Article 15 must bear an autonomous EU meaning:

> [EU] provisions, irrespective of which provisions are concerned, are given an independent interpretation which cannot therefore vary according to and/or be dependent on developments in the case-law of the ECtHR.[384]

### *i. Opinion of AG Maduro*

AG Maduro's Opinion began by clarifying the interaction between Article 3 ECHR and Article 15 QD. While the submissions displayed 'above all the differences between the Member States concerning the interpretation of Article 3 and of the case-law of the [ECtHR] which stems from it',[385] the 'real heart' of the dispute was Article 15(c) itself.[386] Given the dynamic, 'non-linear'[387] development of the Strasbourg Article 3 case law, it could not set the meaning of the EU provisions, although it was 'a starting point' for interpreting the EU rights and 'essential to ensure that the Union…[would] contribute to extending the protection of those rights in the European area'.[388] Setting the terms for constructive human rights pluralism, as previously discussed in Chapter 2, he stated that while the EU, ECHR, and national systems were distinct, they should:

> seek to understand how the other systems interpret and develop those same fundamental rights in order not only to minimise the risk of conflicts, but also to begin

382 *Elgafaji* (n 21) para 26. 383 ibid, para 28.
384 ibid, para 19. Opinion of AG Maduro. 385 ibid, para 16. 386 ibid, para 17.
387 ibid, para 20, citing *Vilvarajah* (n 63) and *Salah Sheekh* (n 64). 388 ibid, para 23.

a process of informal construction of a European area of protection of fundamental rights. The European area thus created will, largely, be the product of the various individual contributions from the different protection systems existing at European level.[389]

On the substance of the dispute, AG Maduro noted the depth of the interpretative controversy, as evident in the 'diametrically opposed' governmental submissions.[390] In the view of the restrictive governments (France, Netherlands, UK), the individuation requirement was paramount. For them, Article 15(c) was 'modelled on' Article 3 ECHR, and Article 15(c) was not intended to 'burden the Member States with new obligations'.[391] In contrast, for those governments urging a broader construction (Belgium, Greece, Sweden), the individuation requirement was barely pertinent. In urging a wide interpretation of 15(c), they arguably seek, indirectly, to distribute that burden (or more accurately, responsibility).

AG Maduro admitted that there was 'weight on both sides', so proceeded to outline an interpretative method suitable 'to guarantee the fundamental right to asylum'.[392] International protection, he explained, aimed to protect those at risk of breach of 'the most fundamental rights', such as 'the right to life, the right not to be tortured, and so on'.[393] Both RS and SP then were instruments to make it possible to 'evaluate whether that risk and harm to fundamental rights are likely to arise'.[394] Article 15(c) had to add something to the protections of 15(a) and (b),[395] and had to give due weight to its central term 'indiscriminate violence'.[396]

Maduro's melding of the apparently contradictory notions of 'individual threat' from 'indiscriminate violence' reads 'individual threat' as going to the risk assessment. 'Individual threat' under 15(c) could not mean 'threat directed at a person by reason of circumstances concerning him individually or specifically (or a social group to which he belongs)' as this would undo its application to situations of indiscriminate violence.[397] Clearly aware of the problematic practices based on the Strasbourg 'special distinguishing characteristic' case law,[398] Maduro reiterated that:

> [t]he distinction between a high degree of individual risk and a risk which is based on individual features is of defining importance. Although a person is not covered by reason of features concerning him particularly, that person is no less individually affected when indiscriminate violence substantially increases the risk of serious harm to his life or person, in other words to his fundamental rights.[399]

On the other hand, not all situations of indiscriminate violence could be covered, as this would be to read down the requirement of individual threat.[400] While Article 15(c) reflected an acknowledgement that breaches of fundamental rights

[389] ibid, para 22. [390] ibid, para 26. [391] ibid, para 27. [392] ibid, para 30.
[393] ibid, para 33. [394] ibid. [395] ibid, para 32. [396] ibid, para 31.
[397] ibid, para 32. [398] See Part III.2.vi.
[399] *Elgafaji* (n 21), Opinion of AG Maduro, para 35. [400] ibid, para 32.

can arise 'even in the absence of any discrimination',[401] this arises only when the violence in question is of sufficient intensity:

Article 15(c) [was] intended to cover... situations of indiscriminate violence which are so serious that, as the case may be, any individual within the ambit of that violence may be subject to a risk of serious harm to his person or life.[402]

Accordingly, the burden of proof in respect of the individual link required was less under Article 15(c) than under Article 15(a) and (b), which define targeted punishments and treatment. However, it was higher as regards the degree of violence contemplated under 15(c).[403] To capture this empirical supposition, AG Maduro set up an evidential presumption, referred to as the 'sliding scale',[404] whereby:

the more the person is individually affected (for example, by reason of his membership of a given social group), the less it will be necessary to show that he faces indiscriminate violence in his country or a part of the territory which is so serious that there is a serious risk that he will be a victim of it himself. Likewise, the less the person is able to show that he is individually affected, the more the violence must be serious and indiscriminate for him to be eligible for the SP claimed.[405]

That interpretation was apt to fulfil the purpose of the QD and to avoid the 'absurd result' that 'the more indiscriminate the violence and, consequently, the greater the number of persons likely to suffer harm to their life or person, the weaker the Community protection'.[406]

### *ii. The CJEU*

The Judgment largely reflects the Opinion, but takes a broader, more systematic view of the QD. The CJEU specifically stated that Article 15(b) 'correspond[ed], in essence, to Article 3 ECHR', so Article 15(c) bore a different meaning.[407] Comparing the three limbs of Article 15 revealed that while Article 15(a) and (b) 'cover[ed] situations in which the applicant for SP [was] specifically exposed to the risk of a particular type of harm,'[408] Article 15(c) covered a more general risk,[409] apparent in particular in the reference to 'indiscriminate violence' which the CJEU interpreted as implying that it may 'extend to people irrespective of their personal circumstances.'[410] The problematic term 'individual' then, the CJEU read as:

covering harm to civilians irrespective of their identity, where the degree of indiscriminate violence characterising the armed conflict taking place—assessed by the competent national authorities before which an application for SP is made, or by the courts of a Member State to which a decision refusing such an application is referred—reaches such a high level that substantial grounds are shown for believing that a civilian, returned to the relevant country or, as the case may be, to the relevant region, would, solely on account of his presence on

401 ibid, para 34. 402 ibid. 403 ibid, para 36.
404 See discussion of the presumption in UNHCR, *Safe at Last?* (n 9) 49–54.
405 *Elgafaji* (n 21), Opinion of AG Maduro, para 37. 406 ibid, para 38.
407 *Elagfaji* (n 21), Judgment, para 28. 408 ibid, para 32.
409 ibid, para 33. 410 ibid, para 34.

the territory of that country or region, face a real risk of being subject to the serious threat referred to in Article 15(c) of the Directive.[411]

Recital 26 [now Recital 35] did not 'invalidate' this reasoning,[412] as the use of the word 'normally' allowed for the 'exceptional situation' where the above circumstances would arise.[413] At this point, the judgment seems to take on a different tenor, suggesting a somewhat different take on 'individuation'. The CJEU assumed that 'the harm defined in paragraphs (a) and (b) of that article requires a clear degree of individualisation', such that Article 15(c) should be regarded as exceptional. However, while it was characterized by 'collective factors' in that:

the person concerned belongs, like other people, to a circle of potential victims of indiscriminate violence in situations of international or internal armed conflict, it is nevertheless the case that that provision must be subject to a coherent interpretation in relation to the other two situations referred to in Article 15 of the Directive and must, therefore, be interpreted by close reference to that individualisation.[414]

The CJEU helpfully goes on to adopt AG Maduro's sliding scale approach, such that 'the more the applicant is able to show that he is specifically affected by reason of factors particular to his personal circumstances, the lower the level of indiscriminate violence required for him to be eligible for SP.'[415] The CJEU also linked the risk assessment with the rules of evidential assessment set out in Article 4(3) QD.[416] A final addendum to the operative part notes that the preferred interpretation of Article 15(c) was 'fully compatible with the ECHR, including the case law of the [ECtHR] relating to [Article 3 ECHR]' .[417] This final stipulation seems strongly to suggest a divergence of opinion within the CJEU, given its previous, clear statement that Article 15(c) had different content to Article 3 ECHR.

### *Back to the* Raad van State

The Dutch *Raad van State* took the view that the field of application of Article 15(c) QD and Article 3 ECHR post-*NA v UK* were both catered for in the same domestic provision which referred to the Article 3 ECHR risks.[418] This assertion is hard to square with the CJEU's clear assertion that 15(c) went further than Article 3 ECHR.[419] In so finding, the *Raad van State* seems to have taken an unduly narrow reading of the CJEU's ruling, seeing Article 15(c) as dealing only with the situation where the level of armed conflict was so high as to be regarded as threatening all individuals simply by virtue of their presence.[420] Strasbourg in *Sufi and Elmi* also regarded Article 15(c) QD and Article 3 ECHR as 'comparable'[421] in light of its acceptance of the risks from intense conflict as sufficient, in that instance, to warrant protection under Article 3 ECHR.

[411] ibid, paras 35.
[412] ibid, para 36.
[413] ibid, para 37.
[414] ibid, para 38.
[415] ibid, para 39.
[416] ibid, para 40.
[417] ibid, para 44, citing 'inter alia, *NA v UK*, paras 115–17 and the case law cited therein.'
[418] Case Number 200702174/2/V2, 25 May 2009, para 2.3.8.
[419] *Elgafaji* Judgment (n 21) para 28.
[420] Case Number 200702174/2/V2, para 2.3.9.
[421] *Sufi and Elmi* (n 7) para 226.

As is all too often the case in judicial review proceedings, the applicants were unable to dislodge the previous findings that their submissions lacked credibility, so the *Raad van State* simply reaffirmed that there was no real risk in their case in any event.[422] Moreover, the *Raad van State* also affirmed the country of origin report provided by the Dutch Ministry of Foreign Affairs of December 2006 that the degree of indiscriminate violence at that time did not mean that mere presence in the relevant area was such as to pose a 'real risk of a serious and individual threat to life or person'.[423] The facts of the case revealed ample individuating factors, in particular Mr Elgafaji's work as a security guard for the British company and the assassination of his uncle for his similar links with the UK occupying forces. Nonetheless, the Dutch authorities found that the evidence was insufficient, particularly due to the absence of official corroborating documents.[424]

## 6. Exclusion from SP

In the negotiations, a divergence of opinion was apparent on the appropriate standard for exclusion from SP.[425] The resulting article is such that that exclusion from SP is far broader than exclusion from refugee status. Article 17(1) appears to be mandatory. Persons falling within these provisions are excluded from SP. In contrast, Member States may exclude those falling within Article 17(3).[426] Article 1F CSR sets out much more limited grounds than exclusion under Article 17 QD. One illustration will suffice. The broadest ground of SP exclusion is Article 17(1)(d) QD, which requires exclusion from SP if the individual 'constitutes a danger to the community or to the security of the Member State in which he or she is present.' This provision allows an apparently open-ended security-based exclusion. In addition, Recital 37 QD suggests a broad construction of the security exception. It provides that:

> The notion of national security and public order also covers cases in which a third country national belongs to an association which supports international terrorism or supports such an association.

As Gilbert notes, 'the worst aspect of Article 17 is that it undermines the absolute prohibition on surrender to face torture'.[427] As outlined above, and as the ECtHR reiterated in *Saadi v Italy*, the Article 3 ECHR non-removal protections are absolute, and no considerations pertaining to the individual's behaviour can weigh in favour of removal. On one reading, there is no tension between Article 17 and this principle. Article 17 only deals with exclusion from SP, a particular status under the QD. Member States' obligations under the ECHR (and Article 3 UNCAT)

[422] Case Number 200702174/2/V2, para 2.5.2. [423] ibid, para 2.5.3.

[424] Opinion of AG Maduro in *Elgafaji* (n 21) para 7.

[425] For a full account of the drafting history of the provisions on exclusion, revocation, and non-refoulement, see Gil-Bazo (n 175) 246–52.

[426] Art 17(3) QD.

[427] Gilbert, 'Is Europe Living up to its Obligations to Refugees?' (n 252) 979–80.

remain, and will prevent removal to face risk of torture or inhuman and degrading treatment. However, Recital 15 QD suggests a different picture. As set out, it suggests that while such persons may still be allowed to remain, they simply fall outside the remit of the QD[428] and indeed, the realm of legal obligation. The original Commission proposal included the crucial caveat to the effect that the application of exclusion did not 'in any manner affect obligations that Member States have under international law'.[429]

Member States' obligations under the ECHR and other international instruments remain when implementing the QD. Indeed, as it only establishes minimum standards, Member States may always argue that it does not impact on their ECHR obligations, where these are higher than those in the Directive. Member State discretion would by definition remain, and hence ECHR obligations would have to be respected. Nonetheless, Article 17 looks ominous in light of the governmental resistance to the Strasbourg line of cases.

## V. The 2011 Recast QD

As explored in Chapter 1, the EU's development of a 'Common European Asylum System' was envisaged as progressive. The Original QD was a 'first phase' legislative measure, aiming to establish minimum standards. The Commission proposed the Recast in 2009,[430] acknowledging that:

> [T]he cumulative effect of all [the QD's] restrictive provisions, ambiguities, deliberate 'gaps' and derogation possibilities is that the current Directive does not guarantee the full compatibility of national implementation measures with [the CSR and IHRL].[431]

The aim of the Recast was to achieve greater harmonization and ensure consistency with international standards. Nonetheless, the recast proposal left much of the Original QD intact, in particular Article 15 on 'serious harm'. The Recast was agreed in late 2011 at first reading, following an intensive series of trialogues between the three institutions, Commission, Council, and Parliament.

Article 7 QD on actors of protection has been tightened up, with a new Article 7(2) making express the requirement that protection be of an 'effective and

[428] Cf. Battjes (n 171) 6 argues this places such individuals outside EU law.

[429] European Commission, *QD Proposal* (n 273) Recital 9.

[430] European Commission, *Proposal for a Directive of the European Parliament and of the Council on minimum standards for the qualification and status of third country nationals or stateless persons as beneficiaries of international protection and the content of the protection granted (recast)* (Recast QD Proposal), COM(2009) 551. For detailed comments, see UNHCR, *Comments on the European Commission's proposal for a Directive of the European Parliament and of the Council on minimum standards for the qualification and status of third country nationals or stateless persons as beneficiaries of international protection and the content of the protection granted (COM(2009) 551, 21 October 2009)* (UNHCR, July 2010).

[431] European Commission, *Staff Working Document Accompanying the Proposal for a Directive of the European Parliament and of the Council on minimum standards for the qualification and status of third country nationals or stateless persons as beneficiaries of international protection and the content of the protection granted (Recast)—Impact Assessment*, SEC(2009) 1371, 11.

non-temporary' nature. The Parliament's Committee on Civil Liberties, Justice and Home Affairs (LIBE) would have removed the notion of non-State actors of protection altogether.[432] Article 8 QD on 'internal protection' has also been revised, to bring coherence with the Strasbourg ruling in *Salah Sheekh*. Article 8(1) now requires that the applicant 'can safely and legally travel to and gain admittance to that part of the country and can reasonably be expected to settle there'. Article 8(2) imposes an express obligation to consider precise and up-to-date country information. Article 8 is complemented by a Recital 27, which provides that where the State is the agent of persecution or serious harm, there should be a presumption against the availability of internal protection. Article 9 QD on acts of persecution has been amended to bring coherence with the CSR, in that it is also sufficient if protection is withheld on such Convention grounds, even if the persecutory act in question is not. Article 10(d) QD on 'particular social group' has been altered; the provision on gender-based persecution has been strengthened.[433] Additional preambular references to the best interests of children, unaccompanied minors in particular, have also been added.[434]

The cessation provisions as regards refugee status and SP have been amended to incorporate the CSR's 'compelling reasons' proviso.[435] Other amendments bring greater (but not complete) consistency between the rights attendant on refugee status and SP. Beneficiaries are to get the same rights to access to employment and employment related education opportunities,[436] access to health care,[437] and access to integration facilities, but not as regards the duration of the residence permit[438] and access to welfare benefits.[439] The definition of 'family member' has been expanded to include the parent/caregiver of unmarried minor refugees.[440]

## VI. Conclusions

The chapter has attempt to sketch the interactions between the Refugee Convention, ECHR, and EU law which go to protect refugees from removal, and (in the case of the Refugee Convention and QD) afford them a status in their countries of refuge.

[432] European Parliament, *Report of the Committee on Civil Liberties, Justice and Home Affairs (LIBE) on the proposal for a directive of the European Parliament and of the Council on minimum standards for the qualification and status of third country nationals or stateless persons as beneficiaries of international protection and the content of the protection granted (recast) (COM(2009)0551—C7-0250/2009—2009/0164(COD)*, 14 July 2011.

[433] QD Art 10(1)(d) provided that 'Gender related aspects *might* be considered...' In contrast, RQD (n 9) Art 10(d) provides: 'Gender related aspects, including gender identity, *shall be given due consideration* for the purposes of determining membership of a particular social group or identifying a characteristic of such a group' (emphasis added). See also Recital 30 RQD which elaborates on gender-based persecution, mentioning 'genital mutilation, forced sterilisation and forced abortions.'

[434] RQD (n 9) Recitals 27 and 38.

[435] ibid, Arts 11(3) and 16(3).

[436] ibid, Art 26.

[437] ibid, Art 30.

[438] ibid, Art 24 provides that the permit shall be at least three years for RS, and at least one year and in case of renewal at least two years for SP.

[439] ibid, Art 29.

[440] ibid, Art 2(j).

Despite significant developments in the case law, Noll's conclusion still holds. There is 'no simple and objective criterion [that] can be found which would determine *non-refoulement* obligations under the ECHR and its Protocols'.[441] The ECtHR has reiterated the Article 3 protections against removal. That provision has been interpreted as an important bolstering of refugee protection, with significant developments concerning removal to face the death penalty (*Al-Saadoon*) and removal to face deprivation (*MSS v Belgium and Greece; Sufi and Elmi v UK*) and conflict (*NA v UK; Sufi and Elmi*). It has also incorporated and tempered the notion of internal protection. Yet, its case law on other Convention rights begs more questions than it answers, and it risks being seen as adopting a 'purely pragmatic' (to quote *F* and *Z and T*) compromise between human rights and migration control. That refugee law needs human rights standards to flesh out the notion of persecution is widely acknowledged. That human rights law needs to be informed by the concept of persecution is less widely appreciated, yet the ambiguous edges of the 'flagrant breach' test suggest that this is so. The two CJEU rulings on persecution, *Y and Z* and *X, Y, and Z*, show the vitality and centrality of the concept of persecution under the CSR. *ABC* on assessment of claims shows that EU human rights law's dignitary foundations can have real legal impact.

There is much to welcome in the QD and its Recast, and the EU's incorporation and elaboration of key CSR concepts is no doubt important. Perhaps the greatest transformation of refugee law is that Luxembourg can truly be characterized as a refugee law court. Central terms of refugee law appear in the QD. In its two persecution readings, *Y and Z* and *X, Y, and Z*, the CJEU showcases its ability to interpret the CSR in such ways as to offer innovative avenues for protection, to bring within the ambit of refugee status, applicants who not long ago might have been rejected as unmeritorious due to the possibility of avoiding persecution risks by exercising discretion. Admittedly, the CJEU is mirroring domestic case law and UNHCR guidelines in its move.[442] Yet, a binding supranational ruling is of wider significance.

Its other four refugee law rulings, *Abdulla, B and D*, and *Bolbol*, and *El Kott*, show fidelity to the CSR, yet also adherence to the QD text and structure. In *El Kott* in particular, the Court adopted a middle course of its own in its interpretation of Article 1D CSR, in spite of the international legal controversy surrounding that provision. The main success of the QD recast process was ironing out some of the discrepancies between the CSR and QD.

Concerning SP, as my analysis of the meaning of 'serious harm' demonstrates, the EU legislature has attempted to tidy up the Strasbourg case law, to avoid having to grant an EU status to all those who benefit from ECHR protection from removal. The tensions include, first, the rights violations that create obligations of *non-refoulement*: The QD does not contain a general human rights clause to track the Strasbourg case law on 'flagrant breaches.' Secondly, the QD only covers certain types of targeted killing, rather than the full potential of the Article 2 ECHR

[441] Noll (n 4) 467. [442] Hathaway and Pobjoy (n 265).

jurisprudence. Thirdly, its re-formulation of the Article 3 ECHR protection and the sweeping exclusion in *M'Bodj* of 'health cases' and other possible cases concerning socio-economic conditions under Article 3 ECHR. Fourthly, although the ECtHR has unequivocally reiterated the absolute nature of the Article 3 ECHR protections, the QD allows for exclusion from SP on wide grounds.

The wording of Article 15(c) QD on 'indiscriminate violence' is of great ambiguity, even by EU standards. The UNHCR QD Study found that SP has not been granted to significant numbers, due to the impact of procedural flaws and the narrow interpretation of the provision.[443] In general, Article 15(c) was undermined by a 'highly restrictive interpretation of "individual threat" in line with Recital 26 of the Directive,' rendering SP 'illusory' in cases of flight from violent conflict.[444] A further UNHCR Study identified a variety of interpretative controversies and practical divergences in approaches to Article 15(c).[445] The ambiguous provisions in turn cast unenviable interpretative dilemmas to the CJEU, as exemplified in *Elgafaji*. The AG set up some useful principles of human rights pluralism, and the CJEU too has carved out a distinct EU terrain of refugee protection, although that move has been resisted by Strasbourg and some national courts and judges writing extra-curially.[446] The Commission's decision not to propose amendments to Article 15 is a choice to leave these developments in the multi-level judicial arena, rather than engage in what could have been a futile or even regressive attempt to reform them through the legislative process. As its ruling in *Diakité* illustrates, the CJEU has taken up the invitation to clarify the scope of Article 15 QD by developing an independent EU meaning to the provision.

The ECtHR case law displays Strasbourg's usual tendencies to focus on the specificities of the individual case before it, often producing rulings of contestable precedential value. In refugee-like cases, though, the ability to delve deep into the facts has become a key feature of the case law. As will be explored further in Chapter 6, this ability has allowed the ECtHR not only to correct various faulty evidential assessments in individual cases, but also thereby condemn many dubious domestic procedural practices. Strasbourg's appellate jurisdiction in this respect has a clear advantage over the preliminary reference mechanism. In contrast, the CJEU's main asylum jurisdiction is one based on law rather than fact. The inherent limits of the mechanism are evident in *Elgafaji* and *Abdulla*, where the CJEU is not capable of making any assessment which would deem the situation in Iraq to generally amount to one of 'indiscriminate violence', or to be such as to preclude cessation of refugee status.

Preliminary references begin and end in the national court. That is a source of strength (CJEU rulings gain traction in the national system) but also a source of fragility (they may be distorted to fit the national context or judicial predilections). *Elgafaji* is revealing in this respect. The *Raad van State* seems to have undermined

[443] UNHCR *QD Study* (n 9) 11. [444] ibid. [445] UNHCR, *Safe at Last?* (n 9).

[446] See P Tiedemann, 'Subsidiary Protection and the Function of Article 15(c) of the Qualification Directive' (2012) 31 RSQ 123, 138, arguing that Article 15(c) is 'superfluous' as Article 15(b) and Article 3 ECHR are sufficient.

some of the CJEU's ruling, asserting that Article 3 ECHR and the orthodoxy on individuation still hold. Admittedly, despite the CJEU's finding that Article 15(c) QD has a scope of application beyond Article 3 ECHR, post-*NA v UK* and *Sufi and Elmi*, we see that the QD and Article 3 ECHR will increasingly overlap. The added-value of 15(c) principally rests in the diluted risk assessment threshold it presupposes. We can see clearly a process of mutual backup, correction and support between the ECHR and EU protections, culminating in *Sufi and Elmi*.

The ECtHR has reiterated the absolute nature of the guarantee in *Saadi v Italy*. The governmental interventions in the case reveal the tensions between this proposition and the security concerns of some national governments. Those same concerns have influenced the text of the QD, in particular the broad and in some instances mandatory provisions on exclusion. The CJEU may be called on to reaffirm the absolute nature of the prohibition on return to face torture, inhuman and degrading treatment.

The chapter reveals greater complexity and an increase in the grounds of protection. The following chapter will examine the impact of the other EU measures which go to access and allocation of protection. Having compared and contrasted the CSR, ECHR, and EU law protections, we see that there are three different, partially overlapping legal sources of protection. Nonetheless, the suspicion is that these do not lead to an overall increase in those likely to receive actual protection from removal. More labels, more grounds, yet perhaps, fewer refugees?[447]

[447] Here I evoke R Zetter, 'More Labels, Fewer Refugees: Remaking the Refugee Label in an Era of Globalization' (2007) 20(2) Journal of Refugee Studies 172.

# 6

# Access to Protection

## I. Introduction

This chapter explores issues of access to protection.[1] The extension of the scope of protection against *refoulement* and status in the Qualification Directive (QD) and Recast QD (RQD) could be seen as reflecting a strong regional commitment to refugee protection.[2] However, that impression is incomplete without an account of the barriers to access refugee protection in the EU. Refugee protection depends, in practice, on access to a place of refuge. A practically effective right to seek asylum remains elusive: Even the *non-refoulement* principle presupposes some kind of contact between the State and the protection-seeker. However, the EU and its Member States employ many means to preclude that contact. As has been noted for some time, '[l]iberal democratic states publicly avow the principle of asylum but use fair means and foul to prevent as many asylum seekers as possible from arriving on their territory where they could claim its protections.'[3] Border controls have been 'offshored and outsourced', to use Gammeltoft-Hansen's memorable phrase,[4] meaning that they have been extended beyond the territory of the State, and privatized. At first glance, it might be assumed that precluding access to territory would successfully limit States' legal obligations. However, that is not so, as has been ably demonstrated in recent exemplary scholarship on this topic.[5]

[1] This chapter contains an updated and extended version of a previous article, C Costello 'Courting Access to Asylum in Europe: Recent Supranational Jurisprudence Explored' (2012) 12 HRLR 287. That article acknowledged in particular Dr Violeta Moreno-Lax, Dr Irini Papanicolopulu, Aaron Rathmell, and Dr Bernard Ryan for most helpful comments and Ms Emma Dunlop for invaluable research assistance. The new material in this chapter has benefitted greatly from the input of Minos Mouzourakis. The usual disclaimer of course applies.

[2] Directive 2011/95/EU of the European Parliament and of the Council of 13 December 2011 on standards for the qualification of third-country nationals or stateless persons as beneficiaries of international protection, for a uniform status for refugees or for persons eligible for subsidiary protection, and for the content of the protection granted (recast) (Qualification Directive) [2011] OJ L337/9.

[3] MJ Gibney, *The Ethics and Politics of Asylum: Liberal Democracy and the Politics of Asylum* (Cambridge University Press 2004) 229. See also J Hathaway, 'The Emerging Politics of Non-Entrée' (1992) 91 Refugees 40.

[4] T Gammeltoft-Hansen, *Access to Asylum: International Refugee Law and the Globalization of Migration Control* (Cambridge University Press 2011) 2.

[5] See in particular Gammeltoft-Hansen (n 4); B Ryan and V Mitsilegas (eds), *Extraterritorial Immigration Control: Legal Challenges* (Martinus Nijhoff Publishers 2010); M den Heijer, *Europe and Extratterritorial Asylum* (Hart Publishing 2012); J Hathaway and T Gammeltoft-Hansen,

Depending on the means used, the deflection activity may amount to an exercise of jurisdiction by the State concerned. The developments in the concept of 'jurisdiction' in international human rights law (IHRL) and EU law are promising in this respect.[6] Yet, real access for most refugees will not be assured by litigation. The EU could develop protected entry procedures and have Member States issue humanitarian visas.[7] The failure to do so is all the more striking in light of the human rights case law examined here.

Part II sets the scene by briefly outlining some offshore border control practices. The chapter then recaps the extent to which the legal obligation of *non-refoulement*, in particular under the Convention relating to the Status of Refugees (the 'Refugee Convention' or 'CSR'),[8] the European Convention on Human Rights (ECHR), and EU law,[9] track this extension of border practices.[10] The chapter opens by recalling the geographical scope of the CSR *non-refoulement* provision, Article 33. It then outlines the evolving position in IHRL on extraterritorial jurisdiction, in particular that under ECHR[11] in light of the Grand Chamber ruling in *Al-Skeini v United Kingdom*,[12] concerning UK jurisdiction in Iraq, and *Hirsi v Italy*,[13] concerning Italy's push-backs of migrants intercepted in international waters to Libya. EU law may provide means to enhance access to asylum, given the express commitments to respect *non-refoulement* in EU primary and secondary law, including the Schengen Borders Code (SBC).[14]

Part III follows the journey of the protection seeker further in her attempt to reach a place of refuge. On reaching the jurisdiction of an EU (or Dublin)[15] State,

'Non-Refoulement in a World of Cooperative Deterrence' (2014) U Mich. Law & Econ. Research Paper No. 14-016.

[6] See, C Costello and V Moreno-Lax, 'The Extraterritorial Application of the EU Charter of Fundamental Rights: From Territoriality to Facticity, the Effectiveness Model' in S Peers, T Hervey, J Kenner, and A Ward (eds), *Commentary on the EU Charter of Fundamental Rights* (Hart Publishing 2013) 1658.

[7] G Noll, J Fagerlund, and F Liebaut, 'Study on the Feasibility of Processing Asylum Claims outside the EU' (2002) The Danish Centre for Human Rights, European Commission; U Iben Jensen, 'Humanitarian Visas: Option or Obligation?' 2014 Study for the LIBE Committee, PE 509.986

[8] Convention relating to the Status of Refugees (adopted 28 July 1951) 189 UNTS 137.

[9] *Non-refoulement* is also a principle of customary international law, perhaps also *jus cogens*, but that fact is not determinative of its scope of application. For endorsements of the customary status of *non-refoulement*, see G Goodwin-Gill and J McAdam, *The Refugee in International Law* (3rd edn, OUP 2007) 346, fn 421 ('Although a sound case can be made for the customary international law status of the principle of *non-refoulement*, its claim to be part of *jus cogens* is much less certain'). See also the Separate Concurring Opinion of Judge Pinto de Albuquerque in *Hirsi Jamaa and Others v Italy* (2012) 55 EHRR 21, para 67.

[10] I examine only the 'offshoring angle'. For assessment of the accountability of States for private border control actions, see Gammeltoft-Hansen (n 4) Chapter 5.

[11] See generally, O De Schutter, *International Human Rights Law* (Cambridge University Press 2010) 123; M Milanovich, *Extraterritorial Application of Human Rights Treaties: Law, Principles, and Policy* (OUP 2011).

[12] *Al-Skeini v United Kingdom* (2011) 53 EHRR 18. See P Ronchi, 'The Borders of Human Rights' (2012) 128 LQR 20; M Milanovic '*Al-Skeini* and *Al-Jedda* in Strasbourg' (2012) 23 EJIL 121.

[13] *Hirsi v Italy* (2012) 55 EHRR 21.

[14] Regulation (EC) No 562/2006 of the European Parliament and of the Council of 15 March 2006 establishing a Community Code on the rules governing the movement of persons across borders (Schengen Borders Code) [2006] OJ L105/1.

[15] The EU Member States with Norway, Iceland, Switzerland, and Liechtenstein.

she will encounter an additional layer of legal deflection, namely the mechanisms for allocation of responsibility for asylum claims, under 'safe third country' (STC) rules as embodied in the Asylum Procedures Directive (PD),[16] left largely unchanged by the Recast PD,[17] and the Dublin System for allocation of responsibility between European States.[18] The CSR seems to allow at least some STC practices, subject to conditions. Examining the case law on extraterritorial border controls and transfers of asylum seekers together reveals instrumental manipulation of jurisdiction. When States extend their borders abroad, they often attempt to rely on constrained territorial constructions of jurisdiction to avoid responsibilities. Yet, when it comes to Dublin cases, we see States attempting to rely on further legal fictions that they form a uniform expanded area of protection, such that transfers of asylum seekers may be assumed to be safe. The ECtHR has, over time, come to insist on the responsibility of transferring States. This chapter traces the development of the Strasbourg case law from *TI v UK*[19] to *KRS v UK*[20] and to the 2011 Grand Chamber ruling in *MSS v Belgium and Greece*.[21] In December 2011, in *NS and ME*,[22] the CJEU finally ruled

[16] Council Directive 2005/85/EC of 1 December 2005 on minimum standards on procedures in Member States for granting and withdrawing refugee status (PD) [2005] OJ L326/13, Article 27. See, in particular, C Costello, 'The Asylum Procedures Directive and the Proliferation of Safe Country Practices: Deterrence, Deflection and the Dismantling of International Protection' (2005) 7 EJML 35.

[17] Directive 2013/32/EU of the European Parliament and of the Council of 26 June 2013 on common procedures for granting and withdrawing international protection (Recast PD) [2013] OJ L180/60, Articles 38–39.

[18] The Dublin System comprises Regulation (EU) No 604/2013 of the European Parliament and of the Council of 26 June 2013 establishing the criteria and mechanisms for determining the Member State responsible for examining an application for international protection lodged in one of the Member States by a third-country national or stateless person (recast) (Dublin III Regulation) [2013] OJ L180/31 and Regulation (EU) No 603/2013 of the European Parliament and of the Council on the establishment of 'Eurodac' [...] (recast) (EURODAC Regulation) [2013] OJ L180/1. The Dublin III Regulation is a recast of Council Regulation (EC) No 343/2003 of 18 February 2003 establishing the criteria and mechanisms for determining the Member State responsible for examining an asylum application lodged in one of the Member States by a third-country national [2003] OJ L50) (Dublin II Regulation), which had replaced the Convention Determining the State responsible for Examining Applications for Asylum Lodged in one of the Member States of the European Communities (Dublin Convention) [1997] OJ C254/1. Dublin III entered into force on 1 January 2014.

[19] *TI v United Kingdom* [2000] INLR 211.

[20] *KRS v United Kingdom* Application (2009) 48 EHRR SE8.

[21] *MSS v Belgium and Greece* Application (2011) 53 EHRR 2. For commentary, see P Mallia, 'Case of *M.S.S. v. Belgium and Greece*: A Catalyst in the Re-thinking of the Dublin II Regulation' (2011) 30 RSQ 107; F Maiani and C Hruschka, 'Le partage des responsabilités dans l'espace Dublin, entre confiance mutuelle et sécurité des demandeurs d'asile' (2011) 2 Revue suisse pour la pratique et le droit d'asile (ASYL) 12; JY Carlier and S Sarolea, 'Le Droit d'Asile dans l'Union européenne contrôlé par la Cour européenne des droits de l'homme' (2011) 6436 Journal des Tribunaux 353; V Moreno Lax, 'Dismantling the Dublin System: *MSS v Belgium and Greece*' (2012) 14(1) EJML 1; G Clayton, 'Asylum Seekers in Europe: *MSS v Belgium and Greece*' (2011) 11 HRLRev 758.

[22] Joined Cases C-411/10 and C-493/10 *NS v Secretary of State for the Home Department and ME v Refugee Applications Commissioner and Minister for Justice, Equality and Law Reform* [2011] ECR I-13905. For an analysis by lawyers in the former case, see M Henderson and A Pickup, 'The Saeedi/NS Judgment: Using the EU Charter of Fundamental Rights in Dublin Cases and More Widely' (2012) paper presented at ILPA / Doughty Street Seminar, 25 January 2012. My comments here reflect my previous note C Costello, 'The Ruling of the Court of Justice in *NS/ME* on the Fundamental Rights of Asylum Seekers under the Dublin Regulation: Finally, An End to Blind Trust across the EU?' (2012) 2 Asiel & Migrantenrecht 83.

for the first time on States' EU law responsibilities under the Dublin Regulation, following Strasbourg's strong lead rather than developing any distinctive EU principles. Rather than signalling clarity and finality on access to asylum in the EU, these rulings have had limited influence on legislative developments (in particular the Dublin III regulation), inevitably prompting further litigation, with a further Grand Chamber from the ECtHR on Dublin deportations to Italy in *Tarakhel v Switzerland*[23] offering a riposte to the CJEU in *NS/ME*.[24]

## II. Access to Asylum

### 1. The migration of border controls

The EU and its Member States employ an array of means to control their borders, extending well beyond the territory of the Member States. States deflect would-be migrants, often protection seekers, in territorial and international waters. The marine context brings with it a complex interplay of legal regimes, including international law of the sea,[25] and international criminal law on smuggling[26] and trafficking,[27] a comprehensive analysis of which is beyond the scope of this chapter.[28] The EU co-operates with countries of transit and origin and engages in joint border control missions under the auspices of the EU Borders Agency, Frontex.[29] Frontex activities frequently involve patrols in international waters and in the territorial waters of third

[23] App No 29217/12 (ECHR, 4 November 2014).

[24] The discussion of *Tarakhel* is informed by C Costello and M Mouzourakis, 'Reflections on Reading *Tarakhel*: Is "How Bad is Bad Enough" Good Enough?' (2014) 10 Asiel & Migrantenrecht 404.

[25] Concerning obligations at sea, see A Fischer-Loscano and T Löhr, *Border Control at Sea: Requirements under International Human Rights and Refugee Law* (European Centre for Constitutional and Human Rights 2007); E Papastavridis, '"Fortress Europe and FRONTEX": Within or without International Law?' (2010) 79 Nord. JIL 75; V Moreno-Lax, 'Seeking Asylum in the Mediterranean: Against a Fragmentary Reading of EU Member States' Obligations Accruing at Sea' (2011) 23 IJRL 174; G Goodwin-Gill, 'Opinion: The Right to Seek Asylum: Interception at Sea and the Principle of *Non-refoulement*' (2011) 23 IJRL 443; Barnes, 'The International Law of the Sea and Migration Control' in Ryan and Mitsilegas (n 5), 103.

[26] Protocol against the Smuggling of Migrants by Land, Sea and Air, supplementing the United Nations Convention against Transnational Organized Crime (adopted 15 November 2000, entered into force 28 January 2004) 2241 UNTS 507. Note Article 19 on *non-refoulement.*

[27] Protocol to Prevent, Suppress and Punish Trafficking in Persons, Especially Women and Children, supplementing the United Nations Convention against Transnational Organized Crime (adopted 15 November 2000, entered into force 2003) 2237 UNTS 319. Note Article 14 on *non-refoulement.*

[28] Ryan and Mitsilegas (n 5); Moreno-Lax (n 25).

[29] Council Regulation 2007/2004 establishing a European Agency for the Management of Operational Cooperation at the External Borders of the Member States of the European Union (Frontex Regulation) [2004] OJ L349/1, as amended by Council Regulation 863/2007 establishing a mechanism for the creation of Rapid Border Intervention Teams and amending Council Regulation (EC) No 2007/2004 as regards that mechanism and regulating the tasks and powers of guest officers [2007] OJ L 199/30, and Council Regulation 1168/2011 amending Council Regulation (EC) 2007/2004 establishing a European Agency for the Management of Operational Cooperation at the External Borders of the Member States of the European Union [2011] OJ L304/1.

countries.[30] The legal underpinnings of patrols in foreign waters are often informal memoranda of understanding between individual EU Member States and the third country in question.[31]

States also often extend their borders by stationing their officials in other countries, under various guises. The EU Network of Immigration Liaison Officers posts officials to transit and sending countries,[32] although they do not purport to exercise official border control functions abroad. In contrast, the UK's juxtaposed controls in France purport to place the UK border in France, in that the underlying bilateral agreement stipulates that the UK officials in France are enforcing UK immigration law.[33] Distant consulates and embassies process visa applications, and may be faced with more direct pleas for refuge.

In any of these scenarios, State actors may encounter protection seekers. The key legal question is the extent to which legal obligations, in particular *non-refoulement*, apply irrespective of the location of the activities in question.

## 2. Access to asylum under UDHR, CSR, and IHRL

Article 14(1) of the Universal Declaration of Human Rights (UDHR)[34] states that 'everyone has the right to seek and to enjoy... asylum from persecution'. The formulation was controversial, reflecting States' unease at inclusion of a right to be granted asylum lest it create a subjective right to enter their territory.[35] However,

[30] Relevant Frontex operations include Operation Nautilus (now Operation Chronos) in the Mediterranean and Operation Hera off the Canary Islands. For an overview, see Moreno-Lax (n 25). See also Human Rights Watch, 'Pushed Back, Pushed Around: Italy's Forced Return of Boat Migrants and Asylum Seekers, Libya's Mistreatment of Migrants and Asylum Seekers.' (Human Rights Watch, September 2009); S Klepp, 'A Contested Asylum System: The European Union between Refugee Protection and Border Control in the Mediterranean Sea' (2010) 12 EJML 1; R Andrijasevic, *How to Balance Rights and Responsibilities on Asylum at the EU's Southern Border of Italy and Libya* (2006) Compas Working Paper No 27; S Carrera, 'The EU Border Management Strategy: Frontex and the Challenges of Irregular Immigration in the Canary Islands' (2007) CEPS Working Document No 261. More recently, Frontex has expanded Operation Triton in the Central Meditteranean. See European Commission Statement 'Frontex Joint Operation 'Triton'—Concerted efforts to manage migration in the Central Mediterranean' Brussels, 7 October 2014.

Note also that sea operations coordinated by Frontex are now subject to the rules laid down in Regulation (EU) No 656/2014 of the European Parliament and of the Council of 15 May 2014 establishing rules for the surveillance of the external sea borders in the context of operational cooperation coordinated by [Frontex] (Sea Operations Regulation) [2014] OJ L189/93.

[31] Papastavridis (n 25) 87–92; J Rijpma, 'Frontex: Successful Blame Shifting of the Member States?' (2010) 68 Análisis del Real Instituto Elcano (ARI), 4. See, for example, Agreement between Spain and Mauritania of 1 July 2003 (*BOE* 185, 4.08.03); Agreement between Spain and Senegal of 5 December 2006 (*BOE* 173, 18.7.2008).

[32] Council Regulation (EC) No 377/2004 of 19 February 2004 on the creation of an immigration liaison officers network [2004] OJ L64/1; Regulation (EU) No 493/2011 of the European Parliament and of the Council of 5 April 2011 amending Council Regulation (EC) No 377/2004 on the creation of an immigration liaison officers network [2011] OJ L141/13.

[33] Le Touquet Treaty (signed 4 February 2003); Nationality, Immigration and Asylum Act 2002 (Juxtaposed Controls) Order 2003. See further G Clayton, 'The UK and Extraterritorial Immigration Control: Entry Clearance and Juxtaposed Control' in Ryan and Mitsilegas (n 5) 397.

[34] Universal Declaration of Human Rights 1948.

[35] Goodwin-Gill and McAdam (n 9) 358–61.

Article 14 UDHR does seem to necessitate a right to an asylum procedure of some sort in order to be meaningful.[36] However, the CSR does not create a right of admission to the territory per se. As Goodwin-Gill and McAdam put it:

> States were not prepared to include in the [CSR] any article on admission of refugees; *non-refoulement* in the sense of even a limited obligation to allow entry may well have been seen as coming too close to the unwished-for duty to grant asylum.[37]

The CSR duty of *non-refoulement* clearly protects those within the State's territory. The weight of authority is now that it also applies to rejection at the frontier.[38] Analysis of the ordinary meaning of the text, its purpose and object, and the subsidiary interpretative material provided by its drafting history support a reading inclusive of 'at least border situations and possibly an even wider application'.[39] To determine the width of this 'wider application' requires recourse to general developments in IHRL on the meaning of 'jurisdiction'. In other words, Article 33 CSR ought to be read constructively in light of evolving IHRL precepts on jurisdiction.[40] Although the text of the International Covenant on Civil and Political Rights (ICCPR) is ambiguous,[41] the Human Rights Committee, displaying considerable creativity, interprets it as applying 'to anyone within the power or effective control of that State party, even if not situated within the territory of the State party'.[42] Article 3 of the Convention against Torture and Other Cruel, Inhuman or Degrading Treatment or Punishment (CAT) contains no geographical limitation, leading to a broad construction of its scope of application.[43] The CAT Committee has confirmed that jurisdiction may arise *de jure* (i.e. where the State is entitled to act under traditional precepts of public international law) or

[36] T Gammeltoft-Hansen and H Gammeltoft-Hansen, 'The Right to Seek – Revisited. On the UN Human Rights Declaration Article 14 and Access to Asylum Procedures in the EU' (2008) 10 EJML 439.

[37] Goodwin-Gill and McAdam (n 9), 206–07.

[38] E Lauterpacht and D Bethlehem, 'The Scope and Content of the Principle of Non-refoulement', in E Feller, V Türk, and F Nicholson (eds), *Refugee Protection in International Law: UNHCR's Global Consultations on International Protection* (Cambridge University Press 2003) 87, 113–15.

[39] Gammeltoft-Hansen (n 4), 68; G Noll, *Negotiating Asylum* (Martinus Nijhoff Publishers 2000) 427. See generally Goodwin-Gill and McAdam (n 9) 244–57.

[40] UNHCR, *Advisory Opinion on the Extraterritorial Application of Non-refoulement Obligations under the 1951 Convention relating to the Status of Refugees and its 1967 Protocol*, (UNHCR January 2007); Lauterpacht and Bethlehem (n 38) 110–11; A Klug and T Howe, 'The Concept of State Jurisdiction and the Applicability of the *Non-refoulement* principle to Extraterritorial Interception Measures' in Ryan and Mitsilegas (n 5) 69.

[41] International Covenant on Civil and Political Rights (adopted 16 December 1966) 999 UNTS 171, Article 2(1) states that the rights apply to all individuals within a State's 'territory and subject to its jurisdiction.' To read this phrase cumulatively would exclude extraterritorial effects.

[42] Human Rights Committee, *General Comment No 31*: The Nature of the General Legal Obligation Imposed on States Parties to the Covenant, 12 May 2004, UN Doc. HRI/GEN/1/Rev.7, 195. The ICJ subsequently confirmed this view in its Advisory Opinion on the *Legal Consequences of the Construction of a Wall in the Occupied Palestinian Territory* (Advisory Opinion) [2004] ICJ Reports 136, 179. cf G Noll, 'Seeking Asylum at Embassies: A Right to Entry under International Law? (2005) 17 IJRL 542, 557 for a more sceptical assessment of the Human Rights Committee's attempt 'to rework the cumulative criteria' in Article 2(1) ICCPR.

[43] Goodwin-Gill and McAdam (n 9) 248.

*de facto* where there is control over persons or territory.[44] In the *Marine I* case, that Committee held that Spain maintained such control over migrants rescued at sea and brought to Mauritania and detained there, 'from the time [their] vessel was rescued and throughout the identification and repatriation process that took place at Nouadhibou [Mauritania's second city]. In particular, the State party exercised, by virtue of a diplomatic agreement concluded with Mauritania, constant *de facto* control over the alleged victims during their detention in Nouadhibou.'[45] As will be seen in the next section, while the ECtHR is at the vanguard of developments on the meaning of 'jurisdiction' in that it has been confronted with a variety of extraterritorial scenarios, it has tended to emphasize a high threshold of 'control' to determine jurisdiction under Article 1 ECHR, in contrast to the apparently looser approach of the HRC and CAT.

The importance of anchoring the CSR in regional human rights protection mechanisms may be illustrated by reference to the legal controversy surrounding the US Supreme Court ruling in the *Sale* case.[46] The US Supreme Court held that Article 33 CSR did not apply to the US naval interdiction of protection-seekers from Haiti in international waters. When a case concerning the same interdiction practices came before the Inter-American Commission of Human Rights some time later, it expressly disagreed with the US Supreme Court's interpretation of Article 33 CSR, rather endorsing the view of UNHCR that Article 33 'had no geographical limitation'.[47] Nonetheless, the US insists on its interpretation of the CSR.[48] Australian courts too take this mischievously restrictive view of the scope of *non-refoulement*,[49] and again, the views of international human rights monitoring bodies have little impact internally, so these domestic mis-interpretations largely persist.[50] In the European context, national and supranational courts are more closely enmeshed, so we expect aberrant national practices and decisions to be challenged before supranational courts more promptly, routinely, and effectively than in other regions.

[44] UN Committee Against Torture, *General Comment No 2*, 23 November 2007, CAT/C/GC/2/CRP.1/Rev.4, para 16.

[45] UN Committee Against Torture, *JHA v Spain*, Communication No 323/2007, 10 November 2008 at para 8.2. For analysis, see K Wouters and M Den Heijer, 'The *Marine I* Case: A Comment' (2010) 22 IJRL 1.

[46] *Sale v Haitian Center Council*, 11 SCt 2549, 509 US 155 (1993), 21 June 1993. See though the powerful dissenting opinion of Justice Blackmun. See also H Hongju Koh, 'YLS Sale Symposium: Sale's Legacies' (*Opinio Juris*, 17 May 2014).

[47] Haitian Centre for Human Rights et al v United States (Haitian Interdiction Case), Case 10675, Report 51/96, (IACHR 13 March 1997).

[48] US Observations on UNHCR Advisory Opinion on Extraterritorial Application of *Non-refoulement* Obligations (28 December 2007).

[49] See *Minister for Immigration and Multicultural Affairs v Haji Ibrahim* [2000] 204 CLR 1, 45 (per Gummow J); *Minister for Immigration and Multicultural Affairs v Khawar* [2002] 210 CLR 1, 42 (per McHugh and Gummow JJ).

[50] See, e.g. Human Rights Committee, *A v Australia*, Communication No 563/1993, 3 April 1997 CCPR/C/59/D/560/1993 (finding Australia in breach of article 9, paragraphs 1 and 4, and article 2, paragraph 3 of the Covenant); Human Rights Committee, *Baban v Australia*, Communication No 1014/2001, 6 August 2003, CCPR/C/78/D/1014/2001 (finding Australia in breach of article 9, paragraphs 1 and 4 of the Covenant).

Even if we accept that *non-refoulement* applies whenever the State exercises jurisdiction, there is a further in-built limitation to the notion of 'refugee' under the CSR, namely that refugeehood is premised on the refugee being outside her home State. If likely receiving States move their borders all the way to sending States, this exilic bias of refugee law seems to preclude applicability of the CSR. So held the UK House of Lords (now the Supreme Court) in the *Roma Rights Case*.[51] However, a different interpretation was put forward in a powerful UNHCR Intervention, written by Goodwin-Gill, emphasizing legal duties of good faith and the applicability of *non-refoulement* at the border.[52] The House of Lords held that the CSR *non-refoulement* obligations did not extend to the 'virtual UK frontier' that had been set up in the Czech Republic. As will be seen, the House of Lords accepted that other international human rights protections, namely those prohibiting racial discrimination, were applicable.[53] As is argued in Section II.3 below, Strasbourg jurisprudential developments suggest that the ECHR would be applicable to UK actions in the Czech Republic now.

## 3. The ECHR

### *i. Reinforcing territorial conceptions of jurisdiction*

The ECtHR has provided a forum in which to contest States' attempts to designate zones as beyond their territorial jurisdiction in order to evade legal obligation. For instance *Amuur v France*,[54] concerned France's deeming the 'international zone' of a Paris airport to be extra-territorial. The ECtHR rejected this legal fiction, and held it was on French territory, so the ECHR obligations were applicable. Even if *de facto* effective control is in dispute, the Court holds the formal territorial sovereign to have jurisdiction, as may be seen in *Ilaşcu and Others v Moldova and Russia*.[55] The ECtHR has also rejected fictions of non-presence. For example, in *D v United Kingdom*, the ECtHR stated that '[r]egardless of whether [the applicant] ever entered the UK in the technical sense it is to be noted that he has been physically present there and thus within the jurisdiction within the meaning of Article 1'.[56] These cases are important in clarifying that States cannot excise territory in

[51] *R (European Roma Rights Centre) v Immigration Officer at Prague Airport* ('Roma Rights Case') [2004] UKHL 55. For detailed analysis, see AG Kesby, 'The Shifting and Multiple Border and International Law' (2007) 27 OJLS 101.

[52] G Goodwin-Gill, 'Document, *R (ex parte European Roma Rights Centre* et al*) v Immigration Officer at Prague Airport and another (UNHCR intervening)*' (2005) 17 IJRL 427.

[53] The applicants succeeded in their discrimination claim, as the checks treated Roma less favourably on racial grounds.

[54] *Amuur v France* (1996) 22 EHRR 533.

[55] *Ilaşcu and Others v Moldova and Russia* (2005) 40 EHRR 46. The Court held that both Moldova and Russia had jurisdiction, Moldova as the *de jure* territorial sovereign over the territory of the 'Moldovan Republic of Transnistria', Russia as having 'effective control.' Although Moldova lacked effective control, it was under a positive obligation under Article 1 ECHR to 'take the diplomatic, economic, judicial or other measures that it is in its power to take and are in accordance with international law to secure to the applicants the rights guaranteed by the Convention'. Para 331.

[56] *D v United Kingdom* (1997) 24 EHRR 423, para 48.

order to escape responsibility under the ECHR. The concept of territory includes the territorial waters of the State, usually twelve nautical miles from the shore.[57]

### *ii. Beyond territorial conceptions of jurisdiction*

The ECtHR has been confronted with various extra-territorial scenarios. The jurisprudence has evolved significantly from the Court's falter on the ill-conceived *espace juridique* notion in *Banković v Belgium*[58] to the 2011 Grand Chamber ruling in *Al-Skeini v United Kingdom*.

*Banković* concerned victims of the NATO bombing of Belgrade in 1999. The Court's starting premise was that one State's jurisdiction is normally 'defined and limited by the sovereign territorial rights of...other relevant States',[59] so that Article 1 ECHR should be interpreted 'to reflect this ordinary and essentially territorial notion of jurisdiction'.[60] Accordingly, extraterritorial jurisdiction only arose in 'exceptional cases'.[61] Citing its case law on Turkish jurisdiction over Northern Cyprus,[62] it stated that only where the respondent State 'through the effective control of the relevant territory and its inhabitants abroad as a consequence of military occupation or through the consent, invitation or acquiescence of the Government of that territory, exercise[d] all or some of the public powers normally to be exercised by that Government'[63] would that State be deemed to have jurisdiction under Article 1 ECHR. The other extraterritorial scenarios mentioned concerned acts of consular agents abroad and their activities on board vessels of that State's flag.[64] The applicants in *Banković* did not fall within the NATO States' jurisdiction, mainly as the Federal Republic of Yugoslavia (FRY) was not within the Convention's 'espace juridique'.[65] The Court added this gloss in a manner that suggested a further limitation on jurisdiction, confining it to the Council of Europe States. It also rejected the applicant's contention that jurisdiction for the purposes of the claim could be established by the rights violation in question, on the basis that this 'cause and effect' approach would render the notion of 'jurisdiction' superfluous.[66] It also objected on the basis that 'dividing and tailoring' the notion of jurisdiction was inappropriate.[67] A conceptualization of jurisdiction as unitary and exclusive clearly informs the reasoning.

In the intervening years, the Court moved away from the 'espace juridique' notion, and found jurisdiction in several cases not dissimilar to *Banković*.[68] Finally in *Al-Skeini*, the Grand Chamber expressly abandoned both the 'espace juridique' notion[69] and its

[57] UN Convention on the Law of the Sea (10 December 1982) 1833 UNTS 3, Article 2(1).
[58] *Banković and Others v Belgium and Others* Application (2007) 44 EHRR SE5, para 80.
[59] ibid, para 59. [60] ibid, para 61. [61] ibid, para 67.
[62] ibid, para 70-1, citing *Loizidou v Turkey* (1995) 20 EHRR 99 and *Cyprus v Turkey* (2002) 35 EHRR 30.
[63] ibid, para 71. [64] ibid, para 73. [65] ibid, para 80.
[66] ibid, para 75. [67] ibid.
[68] *Issa v Turkey* (2004) 41 EHRR 568; *Pad v Turkey* App No 60167/00 (ECHR, 28 June 2007); *Isaak and others v Turkey* App No 44587/98 (ECHR, 28 September 2007).
[69] *Al-Skeini* (n 12), para 142. The concept had been powerfully criticized. See, e.g., O Ben-Naftali and Y Shany, 'Living in Denial: The Co-application of Humanitarian Law and Human Rights Law to

objection to 'dividing and tailoring' jurisdiction.[70] The case concerned the killing of six Iraqi nationals by British troops in Iraq. The UK House of Lords relied on an overblown version of the 'espace juridique' concept of *Banković*, and particularly stringent approaches to both territorial and personal control.[71] On the former, it held that although the UK was the occupying power, it did not have effective overall control in Southern Iraq. On the latter, it found the requisite degree of control only in the case of one applicant, Baha Mousa, who was held in UK detention in Iraq. It rejected the argument for UK jurisdiction in the cases of the other applicants, shot in separate incidents in the course of activities conducted by UK forces in Iraq. In contrast, the ECtHR held that all the applicants were under UK jurisdiction, not based on control over the territory of Southern Iraq, but rather focused on the UK's exercise of 'public powers normally to be exercised by a sovereign government'[72] based on the pertinent UN Security Council Resolutions and regulations of the Coalition Provisional Authority in Iraq.[73] The British soldiers 'exercised authority and control over individuals killed in the course of...security operations' such as to establish UK jurisdiction.[74] The result is that killing per se does not trigger jurisdiction, but instead there must be a background exercise of governmental authority. The UK was the occupying power in the areas concerned, yet the Court did not determine whether that fact alone would establish jurisdiction under Article 1 ECHR. Rather, it emphasized both the personal and territorial dimensions of control. Although the reasoning in *Banković* no longer stands, it is arguable that the outcome would be the same if the same facts came before the Court today, as the NATO forces were not exercising 'public powers' in the FRY at the time of the airstrikes.[75] Of course, this turns on the assumption that the planning and execution of the airstrikes was not the exercise of 'public powers' in the pertinent sense, which may be contested by those who wish to expand the *Al-Skeini* reasoning. The Court's subsequent explanation in *Hirsi* was that there was no jurisdiction in *Banković* as the act in question was 'instantaneous'.[76] However, this seems unconvincing, given that the airstrikes were part of a prepared and concerted military action.

Judge Bonello, in his separate Concurring Opinion in *Al-Skeini*, criticized the Court for failing to articulate a 'coherent and axiomatic regime.'[77] He urged a move away from territorial fixation to a functional approach focusing on the capability of the State to fulfil the human rights obligations in question.[78] In the absence of any such overarching unifying principle, we must instead fall back on a casuistic method and identify from the case law the various scenarios where the ECHR applies extraterritorially. The case law acknowledges that either *de jure* and *de facto* jurisdiction may arise. The latter notion is important as it reflects

the Occupied Territories' (2004) 37 Israel LRev 17; R Wilde, 'The "legal space" or "espace juridique" of the European Convention on Human Rights: is it relevant to extraterritorial State action?' (2005) EHRLRev 115.

[70] ibid, para 137.

[71] *Al-Skeini v Secretary of State for Defence* [2007] UKHL 26. For a critique, see Milanovic (n 12) 125–27.

[72] *Al-Skeini* (n 12) para 149. [73] ibid, paras 143–48. [74] ibid.

[75] For a similar view, see Milanovic (n 12) 130. [76] *Hirsi v Italy* (n 13) para 73.

[77] Concurring Opinion of Judge Bonello in *Al-Skeini* para 4. [78] ibid, paras 11–20.

the fact that human rights obligations do not simply track the State's traditional scope of entitlement to act under public international law, but establish distinct forms of accountability for human rights violations.[79] Either *de facto* or *de jure* jurisdiction will do to trigger the application of the ECHR. The former refers to recognized lawful exercises of authority extraterritorially, such as acts of consular or diplomatic agents abroad and their activities on board vessels of that State's flag.[80] *De facto* jurisdiction can arise in at least three ways. The first is a territorial conception, based on the occupying power-type scenario. The second scenario is personal, and involves individuals subject to the State's physical power or control. The third reflects a combination of the territorial and personal elements of the first two, with an emphasis on the background exercise of governmental authority.[81] Its scope depends on our reading of the *Al-Skeini* notion of public powers.

Examples of the first scenario arise where the State is deemed to have 'effective control' over the territory in question as seen in *Loizidou v Turkey* and *Cyprus v Turkey*. An example of the second is seen in *Medvedyev v France*,[82] where the Court found France to have exercised jurisdiction when its military personnel intercepted and boarded a boat (of Cambodian flag) in international waters, and brought it to a French port. The '*de facto* continued and uninterrupted control exercised by France over the [vessel] and its crew' was decisive.[83] In *Al-Skeini*, the Court explained that the decisive factor in *Medvedyev* was the 'exercise of physical power and control over the person in question'.[84] In this, the Grand Chamber implicitly admits that it is 'dividing and tailoring' jurisdiction in a manner it had rejected in *Banković*.[85] Similarly the Court held in *Al-Saadoon and Mufdhi v United Kingdom* that the UK had exercised jurisdiction when it held the applicants in custody in Iraq and handed them over to the Iraqi authorities. The Court held that 'given the total and exclusive *de facto,* and subsequently also *de jure,* control exercised by the UK authorities over the premises in question, the individuals detained there, including the applicants, were within the UK's jurisdiction'.[86] The Court rejected the UK's argument that it lacked jurisdiction as it had a legal obligation under its bilateral agreement with Iraq to hand over the detainees.[87] The

[79] See, e.g. Klug and Howe (n 40) in particular 98–99. [80] *Banković* (n 58) para 73.

[81] This tripartite typology resembles that put forward by Milanovich (n 12), to the extent that his first heading is 'a spatial model of jurisdiction' and his second 'a personal model of jurisdiction.' However, my third heading differs from his. He reads the third heading a mix of the first two, under which the distinction between positive and negative obligations is decisive. While illuminating, I do not endorse a sharp distinction between positive and negative obligations in this context.

[82] (2010) 51 EHRR 39.

[83] As per the Grand Chamber in *Hirsi v Italy* (n 13) para 80. See also *Medvedyev v France* (n 82), para 67.

[84] *Al-Skeini* (n 12) para 136, citing also *Öcalan v Turkey* Application (2005) 41 EHRR 45, *Issa v Turkey* (n 68) and *Al-Saadoon and Mufdhi v United Kingdom* (2011) 53 EHRR 9. The inclusion of *Issa v Turkey* in this category is noteworthy. Some commentators had interpreted the decision as reflective of a broader anti-circumvention principle whereby the ECHR precludes states from taking action in the territory of another Statewhich it is prohibited from doing on its own. A Fischer-Lescano, T Löhr and T Tohidipur, 'Border Controls at Sea: Requirements under International Human Rights and Refugee Law' (2009) 21 IJRL 256, 276.

[85] *Al-Skeini* (n 12) para 137; cf *Banković* (n 58) para 75.

[86] ibid, para 88. [87] ibid, paras 126–28.

puzzle with this notion of control over the person as the basis for jurisdiction is how to delimit it. The Court rejects the notion of a cause-and-effect jurisdiction, as liable to render the notion of jurisdiction coterminous with the victim requirement. However, it is hard to justify the distinction between custody (which will trigger jurisdiction) and capacity to kill (which will not).[88]

*Al-Skeini* illustrates the combined personal and territorial elements. It also emphasizes the issue of the exercise of public powers that are normally those of a territorial State. The ECtHR has yet to elucidate the meaning of 'public powers' in this context,[89] and much will turn on whether this is conceived as a general basis for jurisdiction, or merely a gloss on the notion of territorial or personal control. The earlier case of *Drozd and Janousek v France and Spain*[90] illustrates that not all exercises of authority will be treated as exercises of official authority by the respondent State. The case concerned the particular situation of French and Spanish judges seconded to courts in Andorra. In that context, the Court held that neither France nor Spain was answerable under the ECHR. Admittedly, the scenario is an atypical one, as the judges were not purporting to exercise official authority on behalf of France or Spain, but rather only Andorra. Nonetheless the Court did countenance jurisdiction arising where acts of the State authorities 'produce effects' outside the State's territory.[91]

### *iii. The ECtHR on migration control activities*

Applying these principles, the ECtHR has considered the migration control actions of naval vessels in international waters in two rulings. In the admissibility decision in *Xhavara* et al *v Italy and Albania*,[92] the ECtHR assumed that Italy was subject to the Convention when its naval vessel, in an attempt to intercept an Albanian boat, collided with it, resulting in the death of irregular migrants on board. The 2012 Grand Chamber decision in *Hirsi v Italy* concerned migrants intercepted in international waters, thirty-five miles south of Lampedusa, as part of Italy's official 'push-back' policy. The migrants were taken on board an Italian military vessel and brought to Libya, apparently against their protests. UNHCR intervened, arguing that by taking the migrants onto its Italian-flagged vessels, Italy was exercising jurisdiction as it had 'full and effective control of the persons throughout the "push-back" operations'.[93] The Grand Chamber ruling is a resounding endorsement of the responsibility of States for their migration control activities at sea. The Italian government sought to distinguish *Medvedyev*, on the basis that in *Hirsi* they

88 For an insightful analysis, see Den Heijer (n 5) 41–51.

89 Ronchi (n 12) 22.

90 *Drozd and Janousek v France and Spain* (1992) 14 EHRR 745.

91 ibid, para 91, cited in Klug and Howe (n 40) 88.

92 *Xhavara* et al *v Italy and Albania* App No 39473/98 (ECHR, 11 January 2001), cited by J Rijpma and M Cremona, 'The Extra-Territorialisation of EU Migration Policies and the Rule of Law' (2007) EUI Working Papers Law 2007/1, 22. The application was declared inadmissible on other grounds.

93 UNHCR, *Submission in the Case of Hirsi v Italy (Application No 277765/09)* (UNHCR, March 2010) para 4.3.2.

were engaged in a search and rescue, 'had not boarded the boats and had not used weapons'.[94] The Court, unsurprisingly, rejected this argument, basing its conclusion on two distinct bases: first, there was *de jure* jurisdiction as the Italian flagged vessel was in international waters.[95] Secondly, the individuals were under the *de facto* control of Italy as the events took place on Italian armed forces' vessels, 'the crews of which were composed exclusively of Italian military personnel'[96] such that the applicants were under the both '*de jure* and *de facto* control of the Italian authorities'.[97] In *Medvedyev*, it will be recalled, the vessel in question was flying the flag of a third State, but the French troops had seized it and taken control of the crew, exercising *de facto* control.[98] In *Hirsi*, both *de facto* and *de jure* jurisdiction was found.

While the conclusion in *Hirsi* on Article 1 ECHR is unimpeachable, the Court's reasoning suggests perhaps an over-synthesis of the previous cases. It cites *Al-Skeini* as an example of a case where exceptionally the facts led to the conclusion that there was extraterritorial jurisdiction, based on 'full and exclusive control over a prison or a ship'.[99] However, the operative reasoning in *Al-Skeini* clearly went beyond the notion of control over a place of detention as decisive. Recall that the UK House of Lords had focused on control over the detainee as decisive, but the ECtHR employed a broader construction when finding that all of the applicants, not merely the one in detention, fell within the UK's jurisdiction.[100]

To recapitulate, the jurisprudence indicates that either *de jure* or *de facto* jurisdiction will trigger application of the ECHR. There are three approaches to *de facto* jurisdiction, one based on control over territory (as in *Loizidou*), a second based on control over persons (as in *Medvedyev*), and a third based on a combination of the territorial and personal factors and a background exercise of public powers (as in *Al-Skeini*). The thresholds of 'control' in the first two scenarios are high, such that Klug and Howe argue that the ECtHR standard 'seems to be much higher than that adopted by other supervisory bodies.'[101] With this in mind, we can turn to examine whether some common extraterritorial migration-control practices fall within the ECHR notion of jurisdiction.

**Consulates and embassies**

Consulates and embassies embody a well-established scenario of *de jure* extraterritorial jurisdiction. They have a range of migration control functions, from dealing with direct pleas for refuge from those physically present to dealing with visa requests. Writing in 2005, Noll suggested that while the Refugee Convention and ICCPR did not require protection requests to be examined at embassies, the ECHR and CRC did.[102] Writing more recently, Ogg has suggested that the conception of jurisdiction has evolved generally, such that embassies and consulates

[94] *Hirsi v Italy* (n 13) para 66. [95] ibid, para 77. [96] ibid, para 81.
[97] ibid. [98] ibid, para 80. [99] ibid, para 73. [100] See Section III.3.ii.
[101] Klug and Howe (n 40) 99.
[102] G Noll (n 42).

are, in certain circumstances, obligated to consider a claim for asylum and, if the requirements are met, grant protection.[103]

The UK Court of Appeal considered the particular issue of diplomatic asylum[104] in *B v Secretary of State for the Foreign and Commonwealth Office.*[105] The Court of Appeal was willing to assume, based on the Strasbourg interpretation of Article 1 ECHR, that Convention rights were applicable to the actions of officials in a British consulate in Australia.[106] The officials had returned asylum seeker children to asylum detention in that country, in spite of evidence of the detention's indefinite duration and inhuman conditions. However, the particular context of a consulate, which is by definition located on the territory of a foreign country by its consent, prompted the Court to alter the legal standards: rather than applying the normal *Soering* test,[107] it took into account the legal duty of non-intervention in the affairs of the host State, holding that only if 'the receiving State intends to subject the fugitive to treatment so harsh as to constitute a crime against humanity' or if it was 'clearly necessary in order to protect them from the immediate likelihood of experiencing serious injury', would a duty to afford diplomatic asylum arise.[108]

The UK relied on *B* in *Al-Saadoon and Mufdhi,*[109] but the ECtHR distinguished between embassies and the scenario at issue in *Al-Saadoon*, where the UK authorities had taken the applicants into custody. In contrast, it acknowledged that '[d]iplomatic and consular premises have a particular status under international law' so that when an individual seeks refuge at an embassy, the duties owed to the territorial State are 'known and apply *ab initio*'.[110] It chose not to comment on the standards applicable to diplomatic asylum (as it was not at issue in the case), but cited a previous decision of the European Commission of Human Rights in *M*, which applied the *Soering* standard.[111]

Visa processing raises more difficult questions given its remoteness from the impact on access to protection. It has been suggested that where there is a causal link between the rejection of a visa application and the appropriate level of risk to trigger an Article 3 ECHR violation, the responsibility of the State should be engaged.[112] An even wider view is endorsed by the Concurring Opinion of

[103] K Ogg, 'Protection Closer to Home? A Legal Case for Claiming Asylum at Embassies and Consulates' (2014) 33(4) Refugee Survey Quarterly 1.

[104] Diplomatic asylum, as opposed to the commonly used concept of territorial asylum, refers to asylum granted by a State outside its territory. See *Colombian-Peruvian Asylum Case,* Judgment of 20 November 1950, ICJ Reports 1950, 266; UNHCR, *Question of Diplomatic Asylum—Report of the Secretary-General* (UNHCR 1975).

[105] [2004] EWCA Civ 1344.

[106] ibid, para 66.

[107] *Soering v UK* (1989) 11 EHRR 439.

[108] *B*, at para 88–89. For a cogent critique, see V Moreno-Lax, '(Extraterritorial) Entry Controls and (Extraterritorial) Non-*Refoulement* in EU Law' in M Maes, MC Foblets, and P De Bruycker (eds), *External Dimensions of EU Migration and Asylum Law and Policy* (Bruylant 2011) 385, in particular at 429–34.

[109] *Al-Saadoon* (n 84) paras 139–43.

[110] ibid, para 140.

[111] *M v Denmark* App No 17392/90 (ECHR, 14 October 1992). See further Moreno-Lax (n 108) 347–48.

[112] Noll (n 42) 564–70.

Judge Pinto de Albuquerque in *Hirsi*, subjecting the State's entire 'visa policy' to IHRL.[113] However, strictly speaking, the Court has only examined visa issuance where there is a pre-existing link between the applicant and the State in question, such as its case law on family reunification under Article 8 ECHR.[114] A more particular argument has been made in relation to humanitarian visas under the Visa Code.[115] It has been cogently argued that there is an EU law obligation to issue humanitarian visas, since they are provided for under Articles 19 and 25 of the Visa Code.[116] Were the EU to commence this practice,[117] some of the barriers to access to protection for refugees could be lowered.

**Border controls abroad**

Formal border controls abroad, particularly juxtaposed controls, may involve exclusive control over small portions of foreign territory, with the consent of the territorial State. While the ECtHR has tended to find this form of jurisdiction in the occupying power scenario, there are some examples where smaller zones were at issue.[118] It is arguable that a juxtaposed border zone could be treated as within the jurisdiction of the border State on the basis of territorial control. Arrest and detention at border checks would amount to the taking control of persons, such as to trigger the second head of *de facto* jurisdiction. However, routine border controls do not seem to amount to taking control over the person, so it would be more difficult to establish jurisdiction on the basis of person control in this context.[119] Aside from these *de facto* bases of jurisdiction, we can also consider whether some border controls abroad are a straightforward *de jure* exercise of jurisdiction, falling squarely within the notion of activities 'in accordance with custom, treaty or other agreement, [whereby] authorities of the [respondent State] carry out executive or judicial functions on the territory of another State'.[120] The most promising approach is to apply the *Al-Skeini* reasoning, emphasizing elements of territorial and personal control, as well as the exercise of official authority. On this basis, the operations of some formalized border controls abroad would clearly trigger Article 1 ECHR. In contrast, the APD envisages the juxtaposed control scenario, and places the territorial State firmly in control. So even if any asylum seeker approaches a UK border guard in Calais and seeks asylum, EU legislation deems that request to have been made to the French authorities.[121] However, that

[113] Concurring Opinion of Judge Pinto de Albuquerque in *Hirsi v Italy* (n 13) 73: '[A] country's visa policy is subject to its obligations under [IHRL].'

[114] *Haydarie v the Netherlands* App No 8876/04 (ECHR, 20 October 2005) (failure to issue a visa to an applicant in Pakistan); *Tuquabo-Tekle v the Netherlands* App No 60665/00 (ECHR, 1 December 2005).

[115] Regulation (EC) No 810/2009 of the European Parliament and of the Council of 13 July 2009 establishing a Community Code on Visas (Visa Code) [2009] OJ L243/1.

[116] Iben Jensen (n 7) 51.

[117] Note that a proposal for a recast Visa Code is currently under negotiation. European Commission, *Proposal for a Regulation of the European Parliament and of the Council on a Union Code on Visas (Visa Code) (recast)*, COM(2014) 164.

[118] *Issa v Turkey* (n 68).

[119] cf *Women on Waves v Portugal*, discussed Part II.3.iv.

[120] *Al-Skeini* (n 12) para 135.

[121] Article 4(5) PD.

position in EU secondary law does not definitely address the question of whether the UK could also have IHRL duties in that context.

Admittedly, the previously mentioned *Roma Rights Case* sets an ambivalent precedent as regards border controls abroad. It will be recalled that the UK House of Lords held that, while the CSR *non-refoulement* guarantee was inapplicable in the migrants' country of origin, IHRL on non-discrimination was applicable to the exercise of UK border controls in Prague Airport.[122] Yet, concerning the ECHR, Lord Bingham expressed 'the very greatest doubt' as to whether the functions performed by UK immigration officers at Prague 'could possibly be said to be an exercise of jurisdiction in any relevant sense over non-UK nationals such as the appellants'.[123] However, the matter was not given extensive consideration, so the ruling does not detract from the cogency of the arguments set out in the preceding paragraph.

Juxtaposed controls are at the more formal end of the co-operative spectrum. States also employ less overt forms of border co-operation, which are more difficult to fit within current conceptions of jurisdiction under the ECHR.[124] Consider, say, the fact that Italy agreed to provide boats and staff for border controls conducted under the Libyan flag, often in Libyan waters. Would the resulting border control activities then fall within Italy's obligations under the ECHR?[125] The thresholds of control over territory or persons would be difficult to meet in these circumstances. However, building on *Al-Skeini* and depending on the role of its officers on board the Libyan boats, there may be some exercise of official authority in international waters or on the Libyan territory such as to warrant a determination that jurisdiction in being exercised. Another avenue of argumentation would look to general international legal principles on State responsibility. State responsibility may be incurred for complicity when aiding and abetting another State in committing an international wrong.[126] The ECtHR has not yet explored these principles carefully, possibly as it would in some cases require it to determine the wrongfulness of the

[122] *Roma Rights Case* (n 51) see in particular the judgment of Lord Steyn, paras 44–45, and that of Baroness Hale, paras 98–103, with whom the other judges agreed.

[123] ibid, per Lord Bingham, para 21. He went on to state that in any event the facts did not raise any issues on Articles 2 or 3 ECHR, which he implicitly treated as exhausting the relevant ECHR articles.

[124] See Hathaway and Gammeltoft-Hansen (n 5), referring to various forms of co-operative *non-entrée*, including diplomatic relations (including development assistance, trade agreements, visa facilitation, and immigration quotas), financial incentives, direct provision of equipment, and training. They argue that 'these new trends of non-entrée call for modern understandings of jurisdiction, which reject the "all or nothing" view and come more closely into line with the dominant position in public international law that two or more States responsible for the same wrongful act may both be held liable on the basis of their own conduct and international obligations', 48–49.

[125] See further C Costello 'Courting Access to Asylum in Europe: Recent Supranational Jurisprudence Explored' (2012) 12 HRLR 287, 303–04.

[126] Article 16, *Draft Articles on Responsibility of States for internationally wrongful acts*. Article 17 deals with the situation where a State incurs responsibility when it 'directs and controls' the acts of another; Article 18 when it 'coerces' another State. See also Hathaway and Gammeltoft-Hansen (n 5), 49.

third State's conduct. Nonetheless, it should do so. In addition, it has developed various techniques to capture the wrongs involved in joint conduct.[127]

The more attenuated a State's role on the border control practices in question, the more impediments will emerge to establishing legal accountability. For instance, applying the 'victim' requirement may be tricky. In some cases, the Court has dismissed actions for lack of proximity between the victim and the underlying policy of the Contracting State.[128] While intensified border controls may imperil human life, in that tighter border controls seem to encourage use of more dangerous migration routes, establishing legal accountability is another matter. It is well-established that Article 2 ECHR creates positive obligations for States, yet it may be difficult to show cause and effect between intensified border controls and deaths of irregular migrants, particularly at sea.[129] Establishing jurisdiction under Article 1 ECHR, it should be recalled, is but the first step in establishing legal accountability. Yet, the case law also reveals the Court's creativity in identifying discrete breaches contributing to the wrongs committed to a particular victim, as in *Rantsev v Cyprus and Russia*,[130] where both States were found in breach of distinct positive obligations under the ECHR to prevent human trafficking.

There are many examples of the EU's involvement in expansive border practices. For example, in June 2010, the European Commission and Libya signed a Memorandum of Understanding, with the Commission undertaking to provide EU technical assistance and co-operation for managing migration.[131] When the EU gets involved, this brings an additional hurdle to establishing jurisdiction under the ECHR. Pending EU access to the ECHR, bringing action against the EU Member States for EU actions faces an additional jurisdictional hurdle, as the ECtHR presumes that the EU system provides 'equivalent protection' to human rights. A litigant seeking to take action against the EU (via an action against the Member States collectively) must rebut the presumption by demonstrating a 'manifest deficiency' in EU protection.[132] While the EU and its Member States collectively engage with third States such as Libya in seeking to deny access to asylum in the EU, establishing legal accountability under the ECHR faces considerable

[127] For an overview, see M Den Heijer, 'Issues of Shared Responsibility before the European Court of Human Rights' (2012) ACIL Research Paper No 2012-04 SHARES Series.

[128] See, e.g. *Segi v 15 States of the European Union* App Nos 6422/02 and 9916/02 (ECHR, 23 May 2002).

[129] See further, T Spijkerboer 'The Human Costs of Border Control' (2007) 9 EJML 137; T Spijkerboer, 'Moving Migrants, States, and Rights: Human Rights and Border Deaths' (2013) 7(2) The Law & Ethics of Human Rights 213.

[130] *Rantsev v Cyprus and Russia* (2010) 51 EHRR 1.

[131] European External Action Service (EEAS), *European Neighbourhood and Partnership Instrument, Libya: Strategic Paper and National Indicative Programme 2011–2013.*

[132] *Bosphorus v Ireland* (2006) 42 EHRR 1; See also C Costello, 'The *Bosphorus* Ruling of the European Court of Human Rights: Fundamental Rights and Blurred Boundaries in Europe' (2006) 6(1) HRLRev 87; P De Hert and F Korenica, 'The Doctrine of Equivalent Protection: Its Life and Legitimacy Before and After the European Union's Accession to the European Convention on Human Rights' (2012) 13(7) German Law Journal 874.

hurdles. However, as will be explored further below in Part II.4 below, EU law potentially provides greater access to protection than the ECHR.

### *iv. Conclusion on the ECHR*

A move to a broad, more encompassing construction of State jurisdiction is supported by the powerful Concurring Opinion of Judge Pinto de Albuquerque in *Hirsi*, which aimed to encompass all official border control-related activities, irrespective of where they were carried out.[133] He stated that:

> the full range of conceivable immigration and border policies, including denial of entry to territorial waters, denial of visa, denial of pre-clearance embarkation or provision of funds, equipment or staff to immigration control operations performed by other States or international organisations on behalf of the Contracting Party, remain subject to the Convention standard. They all constitute forms of exercise of the State function of border control and a manifestation of State jurisdiction, wherever they take place and whoever carries them out.[134]

The litmus test under this conception of jurisdiction was simply whether the border control is carried out 'on behalf of' the ECHR state. The case law on extraterritorial jurisdiction may not yet have evolved to support such a broad reading, but it is noteworthy that in some contexts, once an identifiable State act is seen to violate a human right, the jurisdictional objection is not raised. For example, in *Women on Waves v Portugal*,[135] Portugal was found to have violated the rights of the Dutch applicant organization, which seeks to raise awareness of reproductive rights issues, by refusing its entry to Portuguese waters. The government adopted an express edict prohibiting the entry of the Women on Waves boat, and sent a warship to prevent such entry. The applicants sought relief in the Portuguese courts, alleging breaches *inter alia* of their rights to freedom of expression and association. Having exhausted their domestic remedies, they brought proceedings to the ECtHR, which deemed the case admissible and found an Article 10 ECHR violation, although it declined to examine the pleas under Articles 5, 6, and 11 ECHR and Article 2 of Protocol 4. Notably, Portugal did not contest the existence of its jurisdiction. Clearly its edict and policy had an impact on the applicant organization, as did the dispatch of the warship. In this context, no attempt was made to argue that the acts were extraterritorial because their impact was felt on a foreign would-be entrant to the territory. In contrast, when migration is at issue, States tend to invoke constrained territorial conceptions of their jurisdiction.

Overall, the ECHR tracks many extra-territorial State activities. The potential of the ECHR as an instrument for securing access to protection is evident. In 2000, Noll

[133] Concurring Opinion of Judge Pinto de Albuquerque in *Hirsi v Italy* (n 13) 79.

[134] ibid, 79–80.

[135] *Women on Waves v Portugal* App No 31276/05 (ECHR, 3 February 2009). For analysis, see, I Papanicolopulu, 'Donne sulle onde: libertà di espressione, libertà di navigazione o libertà di circolazione?' (2010) 4 Diritti Umani e Diritto Internazionale 205.

identified the ECHR as providing 'a rather impressive inherent right to access'.[136] Since then, the case law on Article 1 ECHR has opened up further possibilities for extraterritorial applications. Nonetheless, these duties have not been institutionalized in the migration context, in spite of practical suggestions to that effect.[137] Without such institutionalization, for example through making humanitarian visas accessible, the legal principles in the case law may have limited impact beyond the particular cases. Bringing legal challenges against opaque and distant border practices faces considerable practical obstacles. Recall, in this respect, the significant efforts which brought the *Roma Rights Case* and *Hirsi v Italy* to judicial determination. A pioneering NGO brought the *Roma Rights Case*, having gathered data to reveal the systematic discriminatory practices at the UK border in Prague.[138] Italian lawyers in *Hirsi* went to great efforts to ensure contact with those who had been pushed back to Libya. The ECtHR had deemed a previous similar case inadmissible for lack of proper authority.[139] This background is a reminder that while extraterritorial border controls do not take place in a legal vacuum, the practical impediments to ensuring legal accountability are many, obscuring the processes whereby lives are lost and access to protection precluded.

## 4. EU law

As discussed in Chapter 2, EU human rights law has several interrelated sources. The Charter of Fundamental Rights of the European Union (EUCFR) is now binding and the general principles of EU law remain in place.[140] The ECHR is the principal source of the general principles, and forms a floor below which the protection of rights under the EUCFR must not fall.[141] Accordingly, the intriguing question is not whether EU law meets the standards of the ECHR, for it must, but rather to what extent it offers additional protections or at least the possibility to overcome some of the statist constraints in the Strasbourg jurisprudence.

EU law seems to provide an ideal context to move to a functional approach to jurisdiction.[142] In addition, the EUCFR contains a right to asylum, which suggests further potential for innovative legal developments.[143] A minimum requirement would have EU fundamental rights track the notion of 'jurisdiction' under Article 1 ECHR. Alternatively, EU law may develop its own autonomous notion of jurisdiction. If

136 Noll (n 39) 454. 137 See, e.g. Noll, Fagerlund, and Liebaut (n 7).

138 See *Roma Rights Case* (n 51) paras 92–94.

139 *Hussun and Others v Italy* App Nos 10171/05, 10601/05, 11593/05 and 17165/05 (ECHR, 19 January 2010) was struck out. A similar case against Spain was also rejected by the UN Committee Against Torture: *J.H.A v Spain*, Application No 323/2007, CAT/C/41/D/323/2007, 11 November 2008, in particular paras 8.2–8.3.

140 Article 6(1) Treaty on European Union (TEU) [2010] OJ C83/13; Art 6(3) TEU. Art 6(2) TEU requires EU accession to the ECHR.

141 Art 53 EUCFR.

142 For a thorough exposition of this argument, see Costello and Moreno-Lax (n 6).

143 Art 18 EUCFR states that 'The right to asylum shall be guaranteed with due respect for the rules of the Geneva Convention of 28 July 1951 and the Protocol of 31 January 1967 relating to the status of refugees and in accordance with the Treaty on European Union and the Treaty on the Functioning of the European Union.'

we look into the organizing premises of the Strasbourg case law, we see that even in *Al-Skeini*, it takes territorial jurisdiction as the norm. It also originally assumed that jurisdiction was unitary and exclusive, rather than divisible and shared. Both ontological organizing premises are ill-fitting in the EU context. The EU's approach to jurisdiction, across a range of fields, is functional rather than territorial. Moreover, the EU is the embodiment of divisible and shared jurisdiction. EU fundamental rights obligations apply to the Member States whenever they act within the scope of EU law.[144] There is no territorial component. The EU itself has no territory in law, so it would be particularly inapt for its Court to absolve it from fundamental rights obligations when it acts extraterritorially.

The CJEU took a functional view of jurisdiction in the *Airport Transit Visas* case.[145] At the time, the EC Treaty contained a legal base for adopting rules concerning 'crossing the external borders of the Member States'.[146] However, the Council argued successfully that airport transit did not amount to such a border crossing, so the measure was lawfully adopted under the EU (rather than EC) base. The CJEU took a legalistic view of border crossing, deeming the EC base only applicable in cases where TCNs were 'not only present on the territory of a Member State but...also duly authorised to move within that territory'.[147] This holding seems to go against the grain of the ECtHR in *Amuur v France*. However, the case is concerned with an inter-pillar EU competence dispute, and reflects peculiar EU institutional concerns, so it should not be accorded general significance.

It has been argued that Article 18 EUCFR indicates that 'the right to be granted asylum has become a subjective right of individuals under the Union's legal order'.[148] Irrespective of the inevitable interpretative controversies surrounding the Charter, the QD indisputably creates a 'subjective right to be granted asylum'.[149] As AG Maduro stated in *Elgafaji*, the QD aims to vindicate 'the fundamental right to asylum'.[150] As of yet, the CJEU has not been drawn on the implications of the right to asylum. In *NS and ME*, it instead focused on the orthodox obligations of *non-refoulement*, as it could resolve the case by reference to Article 4 EUCFR, which reflects Article 3 ECHR. Whether this right to asylum will secure greater access depends on further doctrinal and institutional questions.

[144] Art 51 EUCFR. [145] Case C-170/96, *Commission v Council* [1998] ECR I–2763.

[146] Art 100c EC [repealed by the Treaty of Amsterdam].

[147] Case C-170/96 *Commission v Council (Airport Transit Visas Case)* [1998] ECR I-2768, para 23.

[148] MT Gil-Bazo, 'The Charter of Fundamental Rights of the European Union and the Right to be Granted Asylum in the Union's Law' (2008) 27 RSQ 33, 34. cf C Harvey, 'The Right to Seek Asylum in the European Union' (2004) 1 EHRLRev 17.

[149] Gil-Bazo (n 148) 231, referring to both Articles 13 and 18 QD. Although both provisions speak of access to particular statuses, as UNHCR observes 'the [QD] appears to use the term "refugee status" to mean the set of rights, benefits, and obligations that flow from the recognition of a person as a refugee. This second meaning, is, in UNHCR's view, better described by the use of the word "asylum".' UNHCR, *Annotated Comments on the EC Council Directive 2004/83/EC of 29 April 2004 on Minimum Standards for the Qualification and Status of Third Country Nationals or Stateless Persons as Refugees or as Persons who otherwise need International Protection and the Content of the Protection granted (OJ L 304/12 of 30.9.2004)* (UNHCR January 2005) 10–11.

[150] Case C-465/07, *Elgafaji v Saatssecreteris van Justitie* [2009] ECR I-921, Opinion of AG Maduro, para 30.

Space precludes an exhaustive review of EU secondary norms on border controls. Suffice to note that they contain preambular endorsements of adherence to fundamental rights and textual references to *non-refoulement* in particular.[151] Regarding the reach of the SBC, it defines borders both territorially[152] and functionally, in that it contains explicit rules on extraterritorial border controls.[153] Den Heijer identifies 'a certain discrepancy between the definitional provisions of the Borders Code—which may be seen to reflect a narrow geographical understanding of the external border—and the scope of activities covered by the Code—which are much broader and extend to measures of extraterritorial control'.[154] To resolve this discrepancy and avoid legal protection gaps, he urges a functional interpretation of border controls, to ensure that those that take place at a distance from the formal external border are nonetheless subject to the SBC.[155] If this approach is adopted, we have an additional basis for the application of *non-refoulement* extraterritorially. Article 3(b) SBC states that the regulation is 'without prejudice to . . . the rights of refugees and persons requesting international protection, in particular as regards non-refoulement'. Accordingly, it is contended that Schengen States may not contest the applicability of *non-refoulement* to those of their extraterritorial border practices that are subject to the SBC.[156] Similarly, the Frontex Regulation and its surrounding mandates for extraterritorial border controls affirm the applicability of *non-refoulement*.[157]

The EU asylum *acquis*, in contrast, is remarkably silent on its application beyond the EU borders. The key EU asylum instruments (PD, Dublin Regulation) all apply to those who apply at the borders or within the territory of the Member States,[158] with the recast PD now also referring to applications made within the territorial waters.[159] Battjes asserts that '[t]here is no reason to assume that the [QD] serves to harmonise the disparate domestic legislation on [extra-territorial processing].'[160] The scope of the QD, on this reading, are determined by the PD.[161] However, this reading is open to question.[162] It is noteworthy in this respect that the recast QD still leaves this question as to the QD's geographical scope open, evidently leaving the matter ultimately for the CJEU to resolve. In

151 See, Moreno-Lax (n 25) 439–447; V Moreno-Lax, 'Must EU Borders have Doors for Refugees?' (2008) 10 EJML 315.

152 Art 2(2) SBC. 153 Annex VI SBC. 154 Den Heijer (n 5) 178–79.

155 ibid, 180.

156 Moreno-Lax (n 25) 445. This reading is supported by the analysis of the European Commission. See Letter from Mr Jacques Barrot, Vice-President of the European Commission to the Parliament's Committee on Civil Liberties, Justice and Home Affairs, cited in *Hirsi v Italy* (n 13) para 34. See also UNHCR (n 93), para 2.

157 Art 1(2) Frontex Regulation, as amended by Regulation 1168/2011. Following Case C-355/10 *Parliament v Council* [2012] OJ C331/12, where the CJEU annulled Council Decision 2010/252/EU on the ground that a co-decision procedure should have been used rather than comitology, the Sea Operations Regulation (SOR) also mandates compliance with *non-refoulement* in extraterritorial border controls at sea. See Recital 10, 12, 13, 19, and Art 4 SOR.

158 H Battjes, *European Asylum Law and International Law* (Martinus Nijhoff Publishers 2006) 208–09. See also Letter from Mr Jacques Barrot, Vice-President of the European Commission to the Parliament's Committee on Civil Liberties, Justice and Home Affairs (n 156).

159 Art 3(1) APD. 160 Battjes (n 158) 210. 161 ibid, 211.

162 Den Heijer (n 5) 173–74.

so doing, the legislation, like all EU measures, must be interpreted in conformity with *non-refoulement* and other EU human rights norms and principles.[163]

## III. Allocating Responsibility for Protection

### 1. The 'safe country' concepts

The preceding part reveals that some contact between the protection seeker and State authorities is needed to trigger the *non-refoulement* guarantee. However, even triggering this guarantee does not guarantee access to a full asylum procedure. Rather, it precludes States from returning asylum seekers to their countries of origin, but not necessarily elsewhere. States assert a right to allocate responsibility to process asylum claims by forcibly removing asylum seekers to so-called 'safe third countries' (STCs).[164] While there is no explicit basis for these practices in the CSR, that instrument has not prevented their widespread proliferation.[165]

STC practices shift responsibility for asylum seekers back to countries in which they could have claimed asylum in the course of their flight. These practices were originally conceived of by individual states, but their logic is extraterritorial, so they spread across the EU,[166] and were eventually reflected in non-binding EU resolutions.[167] STC practices are now embedded in the PD and Dublin System.[168] As Lavenex characterizes them, Member States' STC practices 'unilaterally incorporated third countries outside their legal and political domain... into their system of redistribution for handling asylum claims'.[169]

From initial unilateral incorporation, Member States and then the EU have come to use readmission agreements to underpin STC practices,[170] some of which raise serious *refoulement* concerns. For example, a 2004 study of the Greek-Turkish readmission agreement revealed that all those returned to Turkey under the period

[163] As is evident from Art 51 EUCFR.

[164] Various terms are used, but throughout I use the term STC (safe third country). The PD also refers to 'First Country of Asylum', but STC rules are more common. See further Costello (n 16); S Legomsky, 'Secondary Refugee Movements and the Return of Asylum Seekers to Third Countries: The Meaning of Effective Protection' (2003) 15 IJRL 567.

[165] This is not to defend their legality under the CSR. Indeed, as V Moreno-Lax has recently argued, STC practices appear to violate the CSR. V Moreno-Lax, 'The Legality of the "Safe Third Country" Notion Reconsidered: An Appraisal in Light of General International Rules on the Law of Treaties' in G Goodwin-Gill (ed), *International Migrations* (Martinus Nijhoff Publishers 2014).

[166] For an account of their origins and spread, see R Byrne, G Noll, and J Vedsted-Hansen, 'Understanding Refugee Law in an Enlarged European Union' (2004) 6 EJIL 355.

[167] Council of the European Communities, *Conclusions of the Ministers Responsible for Immigration (London, 30 November–1 December 1992). Resolution on a Harmonized Approach to Questions Concerning Host Third Countries; Resolution on Manifestly Unfounded Applications for Asylum; Conclusions on Countries in which there is Generally no Risk of Persecution.*

[168] Arts 38–39 PD; Art 3(3) Dublin III Regulation.

[169] S Lavenex, *Safe Third Countries: Extending the EU Asylum and Immigration Policies to Central and Eastern Europe* (Central European University Press 1999) 76.

[170] For a survey of the dense web of bilateral readmission agreements between EU Member States and transit and sending countries, see MIREM, *Inventory of Agreements Linked to Readmission*, available at: <http://rsc.eui.eu/RDP/research/analyses/ra/>, accessed 11 April 2015.

of the study were Iranian or Iraqi, and all were subsequently returned to their home countries.[171] The Italy-Libya push-back condemned in *Hirsi* is a powerful illustration of the continuing abuse of the STC notion by EU Member States. As the ECtHR determined in *Hirsi*, Libya does not meet even basic protections against inhuman and degrading treatment and *refoulement*.

## 2. The PD and Recast PD on STC

The PD and Recast PD not only permit the maintenance of STC rules, but create the notion of 'super-STC' in the European region. The generalized assessment of safety inherent in safe country practices is always likely to be controversial. Moreover, no matter how rigorous this general assessment is, in all instances human rights law demands assessment of whether the third country is safe for the individual applicant, usually conceived of in terms of whether the third country will provide 'effective protection'.[172] Concerning the basic STC rule in the original PD, the generalized assessment of safety is based on minimal criteria, firstly that 'life and liberty are not threatened on account of race, religion, nationality, membership of a particular social group or political opinion'; secondly, respect of the principle of *non-refoulement*; and, thirdly, the possibility to request refugee status and, if found to be a refugee, 'to receive protection in accordance with the [CSR].'[173] To that, the Recast PD has added a further criterion: that 'there is no risk of serious harm as defined in the [QD].'[174] This threshold requirement would clearly not be met by some of the States with whom EU Member States (and the EU itself) have readmission agreements.

There is thus no explicit requirement to demonstrate that the protection standards under the CSR are actually adhered to, merely that the possibility exists to seek and be accorded such protection. The original proposal for the PD [Directive 2005/85] provided that a country could be regarded as safe for an individual application only if 'there are no grounds for considering that the country is not a [STC] in [the applicant's] particular circumstances'.[175] No agreement could be reached on this text, and Directive 2005/85 requires Member States to set out 'rules on the methodology' used by authorities to determine whether the

[171] J Apap, S Carrera, and K Kirişci, 'Turkey in the European Area of Freedom, Security and Justice' *CEPS EU-Turkey Working Papers No 3* (CEPS 2004) 22–23. Note that the EU-Turkey readmission agreement was signed in 2014. See Council Decision of 14 April 2014 on the conclusion of the Agreement between the European Union and the Republic of Turkey on the readmission of persons residing without authorisation (2014/252/EU) [2014] OJ L134/1.

[172] See further Costello (n 16) 57–59.

[173] Art 27(1)(a)–(d) Directive 2005/85.

[174] Art 38(1)(a)–(e) PD.

[175] European Commission, *Proposal for a Council Directive on minimum standards on procedures in Member States for granting and withdrawing refugee status* (2000 Proposal), COM(2000) 578, 24 October 2000, Article 22; European Commission, *Amended Proposal for a Council Directive on minimum standards on procedures in Member States for granting and withdrawing refugee status* (2002 Amended Proposal), COM(2002) 249, Article 28.

rule is applicable to 'a particular country or to a particular applicant'.[176] These rules must be:

> [I]n accordance with international law, allowing an individual examination of whether the third country concerned is safe for a particular applicant which, as a minimum, shall permit the applicant to challenge the application of the [STC] concept on the grounds that he/she would be subjected to torture, cruel, inhuman or degrading treatment or punishment.[177]

This clause was inserted in the April 2004 draft, in order to avoid the violation of international law inherent in the previous draft, which denied access to the asylum procedure altogether.[178] However, that clause does not seem to go far enough, requiring only an assessment of Article 3 ECHR concerns, rather than wider human rights and effective protection issues. On that point, the Recast PD has slightly broadened the reviewability of STC rules, as it provides that the aforementioned rules:

> as a minimum, shall permit the applicant to challenge the application of the safe third country concept on the grounds that the third country is not safe in his or her particular circumstances. The applicant shall also be allowed to challenge the existence of a connection between him or her and the third country in accordance with point (a).[179]

The 'super-STC' provision allows Member States to deny access to the procedure to all asylum seekers who arrive 'illegally' from designated countries.[180] Not only does the Recast PD contain no significant improvements on this device, but it now enables broader use of 'super-STC' provisions without prior designation from the Council.[181] The underlying assumption is that these European countries 'observe particularly high human rights and refugee protection standards'.[182] The countries potentially at issue, neighbouring the enlarged European Union, include Albania, Belarus, Croatia, FYR Macedonia, the Russian Federation, Serbia and Montenegro, Norway, Turkey, Ukraine, and Switzerland. Many of these countries, although they may have adopted asylum laws, implement them only in a very limited fashion and in effect cannot provide access to a proper procedure. There is

[176] Art 27(2)(b) Directive 2005/85. [177] Art 27(2)(c) Directive 2005/85.

[178] G Gilbert, 'Is Europe Living Up to Its Obligations to Refugees?' (2004) 15 EJIL 963, 981.

[179] Art 38(2)(c) Recast PD. Article 38(2)(a) Recast PD refers to 'rules requiring a connection between the applicant and the third country concerned on the basis of which it would be reasonable for that person to go to that country'.

[180] Art 36 Directive 2005/85. The practice may be applied either where the Council has agreed a common list of such super-safe European countries (Art 36(3) Directive 2005/85) or, in the absence of such a list, Member States may maintain their own in national legislation in force on 1 December 2005 (Art 36(7) Directive 2005/85).

[181] Art 39 APD. See also Recital 45 Recast PD cf Recital 24 PD (The new Recital no longer contains the following provision: 'Given the potential consequences for the applicant of a restricted or omitted examination, this application of the safe third country concept should be restricted to cases involving third countries with respect to which the Council has satisfied itself that the high standards for the safety of the third country concerned, as set out in this Directive, are fulfilled. The Council should take decisions in this matter after consultation of the European Parliament').

[182] Recital 45 Recast PD.

much evidence to rebut any generalized assumption of safety in relation to these countries.[183]

These STC rules permit transfer to countries outside the EU. They operate in conjunction with the Dublin System, which allocates responsibility for asylum seekers across the EU. In addition, some Member States continue to use bilateral arrangements to transfer asylum seekers, evading the Dublin safeguards.[184]

## 3. The Dublin System

### *i. Recapping the Dublin System*

The Dublin System purports to establish an allocation mechanism for processing asylum claims across its contracting parties (the EU Member States with Norway, Iceland, Switzerland, and Liechtenstein). Its core obligation as between participating States requires responsible countries to take back asylum seekers and process their claims. The allocation mechanism across the Member States is based on the following considerations. In order of priority and in outline, the State responsible is the one where,

- A family member of an unaccompanied minor is legally present,[185] or if there is no such State, where the unaccompanied minor makes her most recent application;[186]
- A family member has been recognized as a refugee or has an outstanding asylum application.[187] Note the narrow definition of family under the Dublin II Regulation has been broadened by the Dublin III Regulation;[188]
- A visa or residence permit has been issued;[189]

[183] For recent reports on Turkey as a STC, see Human Rights Watch, *'Containment Plan': Bulgaria's Pushbacks and Detention of Syrian and Other Asylum Seekers and Migrants* (HRW, April 2014) 27 et seq. On Ukraine, see UNHCR, *Observations on the situation of asylum seekers and refugees in Ukraine* (UNHCR, July 2013) para 133.

[184] *Sharifi and Others v Italy and Greece* App No 16643/07 (ECHR, 21 October 2014). It concerns transfers of asylum seekers from Italy to Greece under the Readmission Agreement signed between the Italian and the Greek Governments on 30 March 1999. UNHCR reports that Italy does not apply the Dublin II Regulation to asylum seekers it wishes to return to Greece, invoking instead the Readmission Agreement as its basis for such returns. UNHCR, *Written Submission by the Office of the United Nations High Commissioner for Refugees in the Case of Sharifi and others v Italy and Greece (Application No. 16643/09)* (UNHCR, October 2009) 7.

[185] Art 8(1)–(3) Dublin III Regulation.

[186] Art 8(4) Dublin III Regulation, as interpreted by the CJEU in Case C-648/11 *MA v Secretary of State for the Home Department* [2013] OJ C255/1838. Note that a proposal by the Commission clarifying this provision is currently under negotiation. European Commission, *Proposal for a Regulation of the European Parliament and of the Council amending Regulation (EU) No 604/2013 as regards determining the Member State responsible for examining the application for international protection of unaccompanied minors with no family member, sibling or relative legally present in a Member State*, COM(2014) 382.

[187] Arts 9–11 Dublin III Regulation.

[188] Art 2(h) Dublin III Regulation now includes a new definition of 'relative', distinct from that of 'family members' under Article 2(g).

[189] Art 12 Dublin III Regulation.

- The first irregular external border crossing took place;[190]
- Visa requirements have been waived for the particular applicant;[191]
- The application was first lodged.[192]

In practice, the allocation criteria are so often ignored that they are characterized as 'unworkable and dysfunctional',[193] in that 'responsibility ultimately lies, in the vast majority of cases, with the State where the application was first filed'.[194] Nonetheless, an unlucky minority of asylum seekers find themselves at the sharp end of the Dublin System, often detained and facing return to Dublin States where their fundamental rights are imperilled. While there is a duty on the responsible State to take back asylum seekers, transfer is subject to such extensive exceptions as to be more akin to a privilege than a duty. Under the so-called 'sovereignty clause',[195] Member States may process claims, irrespective of the other rules in the DR. In *NS and ME*, the CJEU confirmed that the exercise of the sovereignty clause falls within the scope of EU law. Accordingly EU human rights law will sometimes *require* Member States to refuse to transfer the asylum seeker. The CJEU has held that this duty is triggered if the transferring Member State authorities cannot be unaware that systemic deficiencies amount to substantial grounds for believing that there is a real risk of treatment contrary to Article 4 EUCFR (Article 3 ECHR),[196] as discussed later.

Dublin III also permits transfer outside the EU under STC rules, as did the Dublin Convention.[197] Article 3(3) of the Regulation provides that '[a]ny Member State shall retain the right, pursuant to its national laws, to send an applicant for asylum to a third State, in compliance with the provisions of the [CSR].'

The Dublin Regulation does not simply allocate responsibility for processing asylum claims, but in effect determines in which Member State the refugee will have to make her home. As discussed in Chapter 1, there is no duty of mutual recognition of positive determinations, in other words recognition as a refugee or subsidiary protection beneficiary still leaves the refugee confined to one Member State.[198] An amendment to the Long Term Residents Directive (LTRD)[199] to include beneficiaries of international protection gives some rights to cross-border

[190] Art 13 Dublin III Regulation. [191] Art 14 Dublin III Regulation

[192] Arts 15 and 3(2) Dublin III Regulation.

[193] F Maiani and V Vevstad, 'Reflection Note on the Evaluation of the Dublin System and the Dublin III Proposal' (2009) European Parliament, PE 410.690.

[194] ibid, 2. See also European Asylum Support Office (EASO), *Annual Report on the Situation of Asylum in the European Union 2013*, 30: 'Dublin transfers were made in the case of only about 3% of those making an asylum claim in the EU.'

[195] Art 3(2) Dublin II Regulation; Art 17(1) Dublin III Regulation.

[196] *NS and ME* (n 22) para 94; see also para 106 where this test is stated as a requirement of Art 4 EUCFR.

[197] Art 3(5) Dublin Convention.

[198] Admittedly, the CSR does provide some rights to onward movement, but these are couched in tentative terms. See further, JC Hathaway, *The Law of Refugee Status* (Butterworths 1991) 840–74.

[199] Council Directive 2003/109/EC of 25 November 2003 concerning the status of third-country nationals who are long-term residents (Long-Term Residents Directive) [2004] OJ L16/44.

movement and residence after five years.[200] However, rejection of an asylum claim does have consequences beyond the particular deciding State, and the rejected asylum seeker becomes legally unwanted across the EU. The asymmetry in treatment between recognition and rejection of asylum claims is perhaps the most vivid example of negative mutual recognition in the EU system. From the point of view of the protection seeker therefore, the incentives to avoid detection and seek asylum in the Member State of choice are strong. For example, the UNHCR QD Study noted that 67% of asylum applications in the Slovak Republic were closed as the asylum seekers were no longer present, presumably having travelled further west as irregular migrants, rather than risk rejection (or even recognition) there.[201]

The Dublin System presupposes a degree of similarity between protection standards, procedures, and most importantly outcomes that simply does not exist. Divergent recognition rates across the EU have been evident for years. Neumayer's study stands out, being based on recognition rates for asylum seekers from different countries from 1980 to 1999 across Western Europe.[202] He finds substantial variation across the countries examined, with a lack of convergence, such that he describes the situation as a 'frontal assault on the ethical standards of fairness and non-discrimination supposedly underlying the process of granting asylum'.[203] The divergences in treatment of Iraqi asylum seekers are another case in point, with recognition rates varying from 0% to 90% across different EU Member States.[204] Similar discrepancies are seen in protection rates for Syrian refugees.[205] This empirical evidence remains, against the backdrop of which the CJEU's assertion in *Abdullahi*—that 'rules applicable to asylum applications having been accepted to a large extent, harmonized at EU level, most recently by Directives 2011/95 and 2013/32'[206]—suggests uniformity where there is none.

While the Asylum Directives may gradually contribute a degree of convergence, evidence suggests that they have brought their own interpretative discrepancies. Studies of the QD's implementation demonstrate its diverse interpretation and application, attributable both to ingrained local interpretative and institutional

[200] Directive 2011/51/EU of the European Parliament and of the Council of 11 May 2011 amending Council Directive 2003/109/EC to extend its scope to beneficiaries of international protection [2011] OJ L132/1.

[201] UNHCR, *Asylum in the European Union: A Study on the Implementation of the Qualification Directive* (UNHCR QD Study) (UNHCR 2007) 24.

[202] Being Norway, Switzerland, and the fourteen countries (excluding Luxembourg) that formed the EU in 1999.

[203] E Neumayer, 'Asylum Recognition Rates in Western Europe: Their Determinants, Variation and Lack of Convergence' (2005) 49 Journal of Conflict Resolution 43, 44.

[204] See ECRE, *Five Years on Europe is Still Ignoring its Responsibilities towards Iraqi Refugees* (2008) AD1/03/2008/ext/ADC. The rates concern first instance decisions. See further M Sperl, 'Fortress Europe and the Iraqi "Intrudersto": Iraqi Asylum-Seekers and the EU, 2003–2007' (2007) UNHCR Working Paper No 144, 6. A 2011 UNHCR study examined the treatment of Iraqi, Somali, and Afghan asylum seekers, finding significant divergences in the treatment of all three. See UNHCR, *Safe at Last? Law and Practice in Selected EU Member States with Respect to Asylum-Seekers Fleeing Indiscriminate Violence* (UNHCR 2011).

[205] See EASO, *Annual Report on the Situation of Asylum in the European Union*, 28.

[206] Case C-394/12 *Abdullahi v Bundesasylamt* [2013] OJ C 45/12, para 54.

peculiarities, and to the textual novelties and strained drafting of the QD itself.[207] The PD also has facilitated, probably encouraged, disparate procedural practices.[208] The Dublin System presupposes sufficient similarities across the EU (and beyond) to engender the requisite trust for the system to work. However, the diverse empirical reality stands in tension with the institutionalization of mutual recognition.

## 4. The ECHR response

### i. *From* TI v United Kingdom *to* KRS v United Kingdom

Systems of mutual recognition are premised on trust in spite of diversity. However, blind trust is simply unacceptable in this human rights-sensitive field, as is reflected in the Strasbourg case of *TI v United Kingdom*. In *TI,* the ECtHR held that:

> [I]ndirect removal . . . to an intermediary country, which is also a Contracting State, [did] not affect the responsibility of the [transferring State] to ensure that the applicant is not, as a result of its decision to expel, exposed to treatment contrary to Article 3 [ECHR].[209]

The UK sought to remove the applicant, a Sri Lankan asylum seeker, to Germany under Dublin. However, there was a risk of chain *refoulement*, as Germany had already issued a deportation order against the applicant, having refused him asylum there. In determining that the UK was permitted to send the applicant to Germany, the ECtHR relied on the fact that he would be entitled to make a fresh domestic asylum application there, and that these proceedings would provide effective protection of the applicant's Article 3 rights. In addition, in assessing the applicant's Article 13 claim, the ECtHR noted the practice of the English courts to carefully review Dublin Convention removals in light of divergences in national asylum laws and practices. In light of the existence of this safeguard, the ECtHR found compliance with Article 13. The ruling clearly implies that transfers to third countries are only permissible under the ECHR where such safeguards are in place.

In the background was the fact that although the ECtHR had clarified that Article 3 ECHR protected against risks from non-State actors,[210] this case law was not reflected in German asylum practice. Noll expresses discomfort that 'the ECtHR seems to endorse *de facto* a situation by which the German organs interpret their obligations under Article 3 ECHR in a way which is at loggerheads with the ECtHR's own case-law'.[211] The ECtHR permitted removal on the basis of the

[207] K Zwaan (ed), *The Qualification Directive: Central Themes, Problem Issues, and Implementation in Selected Member States* (Wolf Legal Publishers 2007); UNHCR QD Study, 13; ECRE, *The Impact of the Qualification Directive on International Protection* (ECRE October 2008); UNHCR (n 204).

[208] UNHCR, *Improving Asylum Procedures Comparative Analysis and Recommendations for Law and Practice: A UNHCR Research Project on the Application of Key Provisions of the Asylum Procedures Directive in Selected Member States* (UNHCR APD Study) (UNHCR 2010).

[209] *TI v UK* (n 19) para 15.

[210] As recently reiterated in *Salah Sheekh v the Netherlands* (2007) 45 EHRR 50.

[211] G Noll, 'Formalism v Empiricism: Some Reflections on the Dublin Convention on the Occasion of Recent European Case-law' (2001) 70 Nordic Journal of International Law 161, 180.

German assurances that protection was available under domestic law, despite admitting that the provision in question had never been used to reopen an asylum case.[212] Shockingly, as Mole reports of a similar case '[d]espite the assurances given to the Court in *TI* by the Government of Germany, the individual was permitted neither to submit a fresh claim nor to access the discretionary procedure and was sent by the border guards onward to his own country where he was arrested and ill-treated.'[213]

Following *TI*, and despite its somewhat equivocal message, some national courts took Strasbourg's prompt and refused removal under Dublin on the basis of their ECHR obligations. The UK experience is particularly instructive as it reveals a tension between governmental and judicial readings of *TI*.

In *Ex p Adan and Aitseguer*,[214] the applicants had (to borrow Endicott's characterization) 'fled to Germany to escape persecution by a rival clan [in Somalia]; then…fled to Britain to escape the German interpretation of the [CSR]'.[215] Previous domestic authority had required cooperation with other judiciaries unless their standards were 'outside the range of tolerance'.[216] In contrast, the House of Lords in *Adan* applied *TI* and refused removal. The UK Government's response was to introduce legislation containing an irrebuttable statutory presumption that EU Member States were 'safe' for the purposes of return, thus precluding judicial enquiry into whether those States would provide effective protection.[217]

In 2007, the UK High Court in *Nasseri*[218] precluded the return of a seventeen-year-old Afghan to Greece, although he had previously claimed asylum there. As the statutory presumption rendered it impossible for him to challenge the safety of Greece in his case, and there was considerable evidence that Greece would not be 'safe', the High Court declared the provision incompatible with Article 3 ECHR. A 'declaration of incompatibility' is the most extreme remedy under the Human Rights Act 1998, connoting that it is not possible for courts to reinterpret the impugned provision in line with the UK's ECHR obligations.[219] However, the Court of Appeal and the House of Lords overruled the High Court, and upheld

212 'It is true that the Government have not provided any example of Section 53(6) being applied to a failed asylum seeker in a second asylum procedure. [….] While it may be that on any re-examination of the applicant's case the German authorities might still reject it, this is largely a matter of speculation and conjecture.' *TI v UK* (n 19) 18.

213 N Mole and C Meredith, *Asylum and the European Convention on Human Rights* (Council of Europe 2010) 79.

214 *R v Secretary of State for the Home Department ex parte Adan and Aitseguer* [2001] 2 AC 477. See further, Noll (n 211); A Nicol and S Harrison, 'The Law and Practice of the Application of the Dublin Convention in the UK' (1999) 1 EJML 465.

215 T Endicott, '"International Meaning": Comity in Fundamental Rights Adjudication' (2002) IJRL 280.

216 *Kerrouche v Secretary of State for the Home Department* [1997] Imm AR 610, per Lord Woolf, cited in Endicott (n 215) 285.

217 Immigration and Asylum Act 1999, section 11(1). As Thomas notes, 'The effect of the 1999 Act has been to nullify the effect of *Adan*': R Thomas, 'The Impact of Judicial Review on Asylum' (2003) PL 479, 496–97. The presumption is now contained in Paragraph 3 of Schedule 3 to the Asylum and Immigration (Treatment of Claimants, etc.) Act 2004.

218 *Nasseri v Secretary of Statefor the Home Department* [2007] EWHC 1548 (Admin).

219 Sections 2 and 3 Human Rights Act 1998.

the irrebuttable presumption of safety. In the Court of Appeal, Laws LJ accepted that the Greek asylum procedures were 'to say the least shaky' yet noted that there were no deportations or removals to Afghanistan.[220] In 2009, the House of Lords upheld the Court of Appeal's ruling largely on the basis of the Strasbourg ruling in *KRS*, discussed later in this section.[221] (Nasseri brought new judicial review proceedings later that year, and for reasons specific to the case, he was replaced as lead applicant by *Saeedi (NS)*, the applicant in the case with the reference to Luxembourg.)[222]

Before discussing *KRS*, a brief account of the then growing concerns about conditions in Greece is helpful to illustrate the absence of common standards in the EU. For some time, there were concerns about Dublin returns to Greece, not only due to the detention and reception conditions there, but also as Dublin returnees were deemed to have abandoned their claims in Greece and so denied access to procedures.[223] In April 2008, the UNHCR advised EU Member States to suspend returns to Greece, due to the reception conditions for Dublin returnees; treatment of 'interrupted' claims; and the dubious adjudication practices.[224] At the European level, in July 2007, the European Parliament urged the Member States not to transfer people to another State under the Dublin Regulation if it was known that that country does not properly consider Iraqi asylum claims.[225] In early 2008, the European Commission brought infringement proceedings against Greece for failure to readmit asylum seekers returned under the Dublin Regulation to the procedure. The infringement mechanism proceeds softly, aiming to achieve a settlement with the offending State. Greece did introduce a new refugee law in July 2008 to comply with the basic Dublin obligation to process claims of those returned, apparently in response to the Commission's infringement action. However, the UNHCR has expressed qualms about other aspects of the procedure and in 2009 announced it would not cooperate with it.[226] A coalition of NGOs has submitted a voluminous complaint to the European Commission alleging Greece's ongoing violation of all the EU asylum measures.[227]

In the meantime, concerns about the Greek practices led to an increasing volume of emergency applications to the ECtHR to preclude transfers.[228] Of these,

[220] *R (Nasseri) v Secretary of State for the Home Department* [2008] EWCA Civ 464, para 41.

[221] *R (Nasseri) v Secretary of State for the Home Department* [2009] UKHL 23; [2009] WLR (D) 148.

[222] Henderson and Pickup (n 22) para 6.

[223] UNHCR, *The Return to Greece of Asylum-Seekers with 'Interrupted' Claims* (UNHCR 9 July 2007).

[224] UNHCR, *Position on the Return of Asylum-Seekers to Greece under the 'Dublin Regulation'* (UNHCR 15 April 2008).

[225] European Parliament, *Resolution of 12 July 2007 on the humanitarian situation of Iraqi refugees Member States*, P6_TA-PROV(2007)0357.

[226] UNHCR will not participate in the new asylum procedure in Greece unless structural changes are made. See UNHCR Press Release No 32/09, 17 July 2009.

[227] Dutch Council for Refugees, ProAsyl, Refugee Advice Centre, Refugee and Migrant Justice (endorsed by 19 other NGOs) *Complaint to the Commission of the European Communities Concerning Failure to Comply with Community Law Against Greece* (10 November 2009).

[228] See further, ECRE, *Information Note ECtHR Interim Measures (Rule 39) to stop Dublin transfers* (ECRE 19 June 2009).

one unexpectedly came to a full ruling, being *KRS v United Kingdom. KRS* concerned an Iranian asylum seeker resisting transfer from the UK back to Greece. The Court granted a Rule 39 order suspending his removal to Greece, on the basis of the April 2008 UNHCR intervention.[229] Nonetheless, the Chamber took an entirely different view. Whilst accepting the 'independence, reliability and objectivity' of UNHCR, and the genuineness of its concerns about the standards of asylum reception and adjudication in Greece,[230] the ECtHR nonetheless 'consider[ed] that they cannot be relied upon to prevent the UK from removing the present applicant to Greece'.[231] The reasoning is open to criticism on three main grounds. Firstly, Strasbourg only considered removal practices, rather than the Greek asylum system more generally. Secondly, the supposition that Article 3 ECHR violations would be adequately dealt with in the Greek domestic system is open to empirical challenge. Thirdly, and most disturbingly, the Chamber judgment was premised on a presumption that the entire EU asylum system protected fundamental rights 'as regards both the substantive guarantees offered and the mechanisms controlling their observance'[232] and complied with the EU Asylum Directives.[233] In effect, no individual assessment of the risks posed to the applicant was carried out.

*KRS*, in this respect, represents a significant shift from *TI*. In *TI*, the ECtHR simply ignored the UK's submission that it was sufficient that the applicant could make a fresh application to Strasbourg under Rule 39 on return to Germany if any risk of onward *refoulement* emerged. Instead, the Court emphasized the importance of a domestic remedy in the German system of submitting a fresh asylum application.[234] This aspect of *KRS* is particularly troubling as *Soering* was at least in part motivated by the irreparability of harm threatened. If there are substantial grounds for believing that there is a real risk of treatment contrary to Article 3 ECHR, non-removal, admittedly a somewhat ill-fitting response, is required, as any other remedy may result in subjecting the individual to inhuman treatment. Even if we were to accept the empirical plausibility of an effective *post-facto* remedy in a country that does mete out inhuman treatment, that remedy would always be, at least in some respects, inadequate, due to the nature of the harms. *TI v United Kingdom* asserted States' duties to consider all the likely risks on removal of an asylum seeker. In contrast, *KRS* evidences the abandonment of scrutiny to blind trust. The ECtHR Chamber erred in its conceptualization of the Dublin mechanism, which creates a discretionary power, rather than a duty to transfer. Moreover, it erred in treating the mere existence of the EU Directives as raising such a strong presumption of compliance by one of its own Contracting Parties, in the face of ample empirical evidence to the contrary.

Post-*KRS,* domestic courts and indeed governments across the Dublin System took divergent views of their EU and ECHR obligations in the context of Dublin returns.[235] As a result, the Strasbourg Court's Rule 39 jurisdiction came under

229 *KRS v UK* (n 20) 3. 230 ibid, 16–17. 231 ibid, 17. 232 ibid, 16.

233 ibid, 17. 234 Noll (n 211) 179.

235 See, e.g. UNHCR, *Information Note on National Practice in the Application of Article 3(2) of the Dublin II Regulation in particular in the context of intended transfers to Greece* (UNHCR 16 June 2010).

immense strain, as thousands of asylum seekers resisting Dublin transfer sought a supranational judicial remedy.[236]

## *ii.* MSS v Belgium and Greece

*MSS v Belgium and Greece* provided the much needed opportunity for the Grand Chamber to revisit the *KRS* ruling. It distinguished *KRS* on the facts, without overruling it, attaching 'critical importance' to the UNHCR letter of April 2009 requesting Belgium to suspend transfers to Greece in light of the deteriorating situation there.[237] The judgment is a resounding reassertion of each State's responsibility to ensure that the ECHR guarantees were practical and effective. It held unanimously that the detention conditions in Greece violated Article 3 ECHR, and by a majority (16:1), that the living conditions in Greece violated Article 3 ECHR. The finding on living conditions is legally ground-breaking, being based on an acknowledgement that the legal commitments to provide reception conditions, in particular under the EU Reception Conditions Directive (RCD),[238] together with asylum seekers' particular vulnerability, create specific positive obligations under Article 3 ECHR, as discussed in Chapter 5.[239]

The Grand Chamber in *MSS* also held unanimously that the Greek asylum procedures violated Article 13 ECHR. For our purposes, of greatest interest is the finding that Belgium violated Article 3 ECHR, in exposing the applicant to risks linked to the deficiencies both in the asylum procedure and in the detention and living conditions in Greece (15:2). Of note is that the ECtHR applied its standard test concerning Article 3 risks, and found Belgium in breach as it 'knowingly' exposed the applicant to conditions which violated Article 3 ECHR.[240] The Court also held that Belgium violated Article 13 ECHR in failing to provide an adequate remedy to prevent the transfer to Greece.

As one separate Concurring Opinion noted, the focus is entirely on the conditions in Greece, rather than on the specific risks posed if removed to Afghanistan.[241] The ECtHR laid great emphasis on a series of reports published since 2006 by the Council of Europe, EU, UNHCR, and respected NGO sources.[242] Its assessment of the detention conditions was premised on the reports' evidence of the 'systematic' practice of detaining asylum seekers on arrival for periods from a few days to a few months.[243] Similarly generalized findings were accepted in relation to

[236] Statement of the President of the European Court of Human Rights concerning requests for interim measures (Rule 39 of the Rules of the Court), 11 February 2011.

[237] *MSS v Belgium and Greece* (n 21) para 344.

[238] Council Directive 2003/9/EC laying down minimum standards for the reception of asylum seekers [2003] OJ L31/18, now recast as Directive 2013/33/EU of the European Parliament and of the Council of 26 June 2013 laying down standards for the reception of applicants for international protection (recast) (RCD) [2013] OJ L108/96.

[239] See further, Chapter 4, Part III.2.

[240] *MSS v Belgium and Greece* (n 21) paras 365–67.

[241] Concurring Opinion of Judge Villiger in *MSS v Belgium and Greece*, 93–99.

[242] ibid, para 160 lists.

[243] ibid, para 167.

the poor detention conditions.[244] Also pertinent was the fact that the Court had in the previous two years found degrading detention conditions in three cases against Greece.[245] Whether the applicant had been subjected to the prevailing practices was in dispute, but the Court treated the general information as supporting the applicant's allegations. Even Judge Sajó, who otherwise dissented, shared this finding in spite of his hesitancy to ground the finding relating to the particular applicant in general information 'relating to conditions at *other* premises at times *other* than the material one'.[246] Decisive for him was the failure of the Greek Government to prove that the detention did not take place in an 'overcrowded place in appalling conditions of hygiene and cleanliness'.[247]

### *iii.* Hirsi v Italy *on 'unsafe' third countries*

*Hirsi v Italy* also contains important safeguards concerning returns to third countries. The Court found an Article 3 violation due to the conditions in Libya and the risk of onward *refoulement*. Concerning the conditions in Libya, like in *MSS*, the applicants relied on general evidence, being various IGO and NGO reports,[248] in particular of the Council of Europe's Committee for the Prevention of Torture (CPT) evidencing the inhuman and degrading conditions for irregular migrants in Libya, particularly those of Somali and Eritrean origin.[249] On this basis, they argued that Italy 'could not have been unaware of [the] increasingly worsening situation when it signed bilateral agreements with Libya and carried out the push-back operations at issue'.[250] The Court found that those returned to Libya were 'systematically arrested and detained in conditions that outside visitors, such as the delegations from the UNHCR, Human Rights Watch, and Amnesty International, could only describe as inhuman'.[251] Italy was not entitled to rely on assurances from Libya or the terms of the Italy–Libya Friendship Treaty (2008) in the face of evidence from 'reliable sources' of 'practices...manifestly contrary to the principles of the Convention'.[252] (In the face of this finding, it is troubling that the Court's proposed remedy was to seek assurances from the Libyan authorities.)[253] As in *MSS*, the Court was willing to impute knowledge to the transferring State.

[244] *MSS v Belgium and Greece* (n 21) para 230.

[245] *SD v Greece* App No 53541/07 (ECHR, 11 June 2009); *Tabesh v Greece* App No 8256/07 (ECHR, 26 November 2009); *AA v Greece* App No 12186/08 (ECHR, 22 July 2010).

[246] Dissenting Opinion of Judge Sajó in *MSS v Belgium and Greece* (n 21) 100.

[247] ibid, 101.

[248] *Hirsi v Italy* (n 13). These include a UNHCR press release of 7 May 2009 (ibid, para 33); a letter of 15 July 2009 of Jacques Barrot, Vice-President of the European Commission (ibid, para 34); Report of the Council of Europe's Committee for the Prevention of Torture (28 April 2010) (ibid, paras 34–35); Human Rights Watch Report of 21 September 2009 (ibid, paras 37–39); report of a visit of Amnesty International from 15-23 May 2009 (ibid, paras 40–41) and other international material (ibid, para 42).

[249] *Hirsi v Italy* (n 13) para 88, citing the CPT Report of 28 April 2010, which in turn is outlined at paras 35–36.

[250] ibid, para 89.

[251] ibid, para 125.

[252] ibid, para 128.

[253] ibid, para 211.

Italy argued that the applicants had not applied for asylum. To this, the Court responded that it was for the Italian authorities, who faced a situation which involved systematic violations of human rights, to 'find out about the treatment to which the applicants would be exposed after their return,' irrespective of whether the applicants had expressly requested asylum.[254]

The Court also found an Article 3 violation due to the risk of arbitrary repatriation to Eritrea and Somalia. Here again the evidence was damning: UNHCR reported that Libya frequently conducted collective expulsions, such that there was a high risk of 'chain *refoulements*'.[255] Libya had not ratified the CSR, and the Court unsurprisingly rejected the Italian government's argument that UNHCR presence in Tripoli was sufficient to ensure protection against arbitrary repatriation. Accordingly, it held that Italy breached Article 3 ECHR as it 'knew or should have known' of the lack of protection in Libya.[256]

While the Article 3 analysis is orthodox and unsurprising given the brutality of the then Libyan regime, *Hirsi v Italy* established important new legal principles on collective expulsions under Article 4, Protocol 4.[257] Italy argued that the provision was inapplicable, as the applicants were refused entry, rather than expelled.[258] The Court, for the first time, gave effect to this provision extraterritorially. It noted that its purpose was to 'prevent States being able to remove certain aliens without examining their personal circumstances' and so without affording them the opportunity to put forward their arguments against expulsion.[259] As the ECHR was to be a 'living instrument', its meaning should track the changing nature of border controls.[260] In addition, effectiveness demanded that the prohibition apply also to migrants who encounter their destination State at sea, as well as by land.[261] Coherence across Convention articles was one further reason weighing in favour of its extraterritorial scope. Accordingly, its scope should track all exercises of jurisdiction under Article 1 ECHR.[262] The absence of any individual examination of the applicants' situation was sufficient to lead to the conclusion that Article 4, Protocol 4 ECHR had been violated.[263] The application of the prohibition of collective expulsion at the borders has significant procedural implications. To avoid findings of collective expulsion requires individual procedures. Border controls must involve screening, not deflecting.

The complete absence of screening procedures also amounted to an Article 13 violation. The Court reiterated its Article 13 case law, in particular on suspensive effect.[264] On the facts, Italy had violated Article 13 due to the absence of information provided on how to access asylum procedures.[265] The applicants had no way

[254] ibid, para 133. [255] ibid, para 143. [256] ibid, paras 156–57.

[257] Protocol No 4 to the ECHR, Strasbourg, 16 November 1963, Article 4: 'Collective expulsion of aliens is prohibited.'

[258] *Hirsi v Italy* (n 13) para 160. Notably, this interpretation is also supported by Den Heijer (n 5) 131.

[259] ibid, para 177. [260] ibid, paras 175–76. [261] ibid, para 177.

[262] ibid, para 180. [263] ibid, paras 185–86.

[264] ibid, para 200, citing *Gebremedhin v France* (2007) 50 EHRR 745, para 66; and *MSS v Belgium and Greece*, para 293.

[265] ibid, para 204.

to access any domestic remedy in order to have a 'thorough and rigorous assessment of their requests before the removal measure was enforced'.[266] The Court ordered a specific remedy, namely that the Italian Government take 'all possible steps to obtain assurances from the Libyan authorities that the applicants will not be subjected to treatment incompatible with Article 3 of the Convention or arbitrarily repatriated'.[267] In contrast, the separate Concurring Opinion of Judge Pinto de Albuquerque went further, suggesting that the remedy required by the Court was insufficient. He urged that the Italian Government should also have a positive obligation to provide the applicants with practical and effective access to an asylum procedure in Italy. [268]

On the issue of jurisdiction, recall that in *Banković*, the Court rejected the idea of partial application of the ECHR. The objection to 'dividing and tailoring' was a manifestation of the notion that Convention obligations were indivisible. While the Court resiled from this position in *Al-Skeini*, the *Hirsi* approach is nonetheless noteworthy, in that we see the Court asking whether particular rights should apply in given extraterritorial scenarios. While the Court ultimately holds that Article 4, Protocol 4 has the same extraterritorial scope as Article 3 ECHR,[269] that conclusion follows an examination of the specificities of the right to protection against collective expulsion, reflective of the tailoring of ECHR obligations to the extraterritorial context.

## 5. The CJEU on Dublin transfers: The *NS and ME* ruling

From the account above, it can be seen that thousands of cases were going through the national courts and to the ECtHR on the workings of the EU's creation, the Dublin System. However, it was not until 2010 that a case came to the CJEU on Dublin[270]. The applicant in *NS* was an Afghan asylum seeker resisting removal from the UK to Greece under the Dublin Regulation. His domestic appeal rights were precluded by the previously mentioned UK irrebuttable statutory presumption.[271] On this basis, the High Court in London dismissed his claim, but allowed the appeal to the Court of Appeal, which in turn referred seven detailed questions to Luxembourg. The applicants in *ME* were five asylum seekers variously from Afghanistan, Iran, and Algeria, similarly resisting removal to Greece. The Irish High Court referred two questions on the transferring Member States' obligations to assess the receiving States' compliance with Article 18 EUCFR, the Asylum Directives, and the Dublin Regulation, and the consequences of finding the receiving State in breach. The Irish authorities had applied *KRS* and assumed that there was no breach of Article 3 ECHR.

[266] ibid, para 205. [267] ibid, para 211.
[268] ibid, 82. Concurring Opinion of Judge Pinto de Albuquerque. [269] ibid, para 178.
[270] This section draws on my note, Costello (n 22).
[271] *NS and ME* (n 22) Opinion of AG Trstenjak, para 47.

Both references predated *MSS*,[272] so at the time Strasbourg's guidance to national courts, in the form of contradictory Rule 39 rulings[273] and *KRS*, was unclear. However, the Luxembourg ruling post-dates *MSS*, and as will be seen, follows it closely.

Twelve Member States[274] intervened, together with Switzerland (a participant in the Dublin System) and the European Commission. In addition, due to their interventions in the domestic proceedings, UNHCR, the AIRE (Advice on Individual Rights in Europe) Centre, Amnesty International, and the UK Equality and Human Rights Commission (in *NS* only) also made submissions. The contribution of the interveners is noteworthy. Although the cases were joined and there is a single judgment, AG Trstenjak gave two Opinions.[275] The *NS* Opinion is the more comprehensive, with that in *ME* citing the former extensively.

The legal issues examined were as follows:

### *i. Does the exercise of the 'sovereignty clause' fall within the scope of EU law?*

The first *NS* question was whether decisions under Article 3(2) fall within the scope of EU law. The governments of Ireland, the UK, Belgium, and Italy argued that they did not. The *NS* Opinion noted that the EUCFR binds the Member States when 'implementing EU law', which, as the Explanations to the Charter clarify,[276] is to be read as co-extensive with the pre-existing case law, covering both cases where Member States 'implement' and 'derogate from' EU norms.[277] As to the Dublin Regulation, the AG noted that it established 'exhaustive rules' on the allocation of responsibility for the processing of asylum claims, and rules governing the consequences of decisions under Article 3(2). Accordingly, these decisions do amount to 'implementing EU law'.[278] The Court followed this conclusion.[279]

### *ii. When is transfer under the Dublin Regulation prohibited?*

**The opinions**

The AG opined that if there was a 'serious risk' of violations of human dignity (Article 1 EUCFR) or of 'inhuman or degrading treatment' (Article 4 EUCFR), removal should be precluded, as well as in cases where Article 19(2) EUCFR applied.[280] The duty not to return derived from the positive protective function

[272] *ME* (n 22) Opinion of AG Trstenjak, paras 53, 55, 76-8.

[273] ECRE-ELENA, *Research on ECHR Rule 39 Interim Measures* (ECRE April 2012) 44.

[274] Belgium, Germany, Finland, France, Greece, Ireland, Italy, the Netherlands, Austria, Poland, the United Kingdom, and the Czech Republic.

[275] For analysis, see S Peers, 'Court of Justice: The *NS* and *ME* Opinions – The Death of "Mutual Trust"?' (Statewatch Analysis 2011) <http://www.statewatch.org/analyses/no-148-dublin-mutual-trust.pdf> accessed 11 April 2015.

[276] Article 52(7) EUCFR. The Explanations are found at [2007] OJ C303/17.

[277] *NS* (n 22) para 76–8. Opinion of AG Trstenjak.

[278] ibid, para 80. In paras 81–2, the AG drew an analogy with the seminal case of Case 5/88 *Wachauf* [1989] ECR 2609.

[279] ibid, paras 64–9.

[280] ibid, para 112. Opinion of AG Trstenjak, *ME* (n 22) para 64. 'If there were a serious risk...of a violation of the asylum seekers' fundamental rights, as enshrined in Articles 1, 4 or 18 of the [EUCFR],

inherent in Articles 1 and 4.[281] In addition, the right to asylum under Article 18 EUCFR precluded both direct and indirect *refoulement*,[282] so if transferees were 'at risk' of indirect *refoulement*, Dublin transfer would also be prohibited.[283] While the reasoning focuses on these particular Articles, the AG's conclusions envisage breaches of *any* fundamental right enshrined in the Charter as precluding transfer.[284] Article 4 EUCFR risks should be assessed first, with Article 1 being regarded as inapplicable if a violation of the more specific rights were identified.[285] In contrast, not all breaches of the Asylum Directives would prevent transfer. Only where breaches of the Directives also entail breaches of fundamental rights would these be pertinent.[286]

In that respect, it is worth noting that AG Trstenjak already took a narrower approach to the prohibition of Dublin transfers than that proposed by the Commission in the Regulation's recast proposal:

> When the Commission considers that the circumstances prevailing in a Member State may lead to a level of protection for applicants for international protection which is not in conformity with Community legislation, in particular with [RCD] and with [APD], it may decide...that all transfers of applicants in accordance with this Regulation to the Member State concerned be suspended.[287]

### The judgment

The Court emphasized that the Dublin System was a product of 'the principle of mutual confidence' between all the participating States (EU and non-EU), that all observe fundamental rights, leading to a presumption that the treatment of asylum seekers in all Member States complies with the requirements of the CSR, the EUCFR, and the ECHR.[288] For the Court, the '*raison d'être*' of the EU was at issue. In a remarkably unclear paragraph, it stated that:

> At issue here is the raison d'être of the European Union and the creation of an area of freedom, security and justice and, in particular, the Common European Asylum System, based on mutual confidence and a presumption of compliance, by other Member States, with European Union law and, in particular, fundamental rights.[289]

As discussed further in Part 8, the reasoning seems to confuse the ends and means, the processes and products of European integration.

the other Member States may not transfer asylum seekers...but are obliged, in principle, to exercise the right to assume responsibility for the examination under Article 3(2) [Dublin Regulation].'

[281] *NS* (n 22) Opinion of AG Trstenjak; *ME* (n 22) n 17.

[282] *NS* (n 22) Opinion of AG Trstenjak, para 115. [283] ibid, para 115.

[284] ibid, para 127, 178(2); *ME* (n 22) para 79(1). Opinion of AG Trstenjak.

[285] ibid, footnote 44.

[286] ibid, paras 123–26; *ME* (n 22) para 66. Opinion of AG Trstenjak.

[287] European Commission, *Proposal for a Regulation of the European Parliament and of the Council establishing the criteria and mechanisms for determining the Member State responsible for examining an application for international protection lodged in one of the Member States by a third-country national or a stateless person (Recast)* (Dublin III Proposal), COM(2008) 820, Article 31(2).

[288] *NS* (n 22) para 80. [289] ibid, para 83.

In sharp contrast to the Opinions, the Court held that not every infringement of fundamental rights would affect the obligations under the Dublin Regulation.[290] Nor would infringement of just any aspect of the Asylum Directives preclude transfer.[291] Apparently due to the importance attributed to mutual confidence and the presumption of compliance, the Court established a significantly higher threshold than that suggested by AG Trstenjak for precluding Dublin transfers. Member States, including national courts, may not transfer asylum seekers to the responsible State where they:

> cannot be unaware that systemic deficiencies in the asylum procedure and in the reception conditions of asylum seekers in that Member State amount to substantial grounds for believing that the asylum seeker would face a real risk of being subjected to inhuman and degrading treatment within the meaning of Article 4 of the Charter.[292]

### *iii. Is protection against removal under the EUCFR more extensive than under the ECHR?*

The next issue concerned whether Articles 1, 18, and 47 of the EUCFR, and the general principles of EU law, were wider in scope than Article 3 ECHR. The salience of the question was high at the time when *KRS* was the governing Strasbourg ruling. If there was no Article 3 ECHR issue (as was held in *KRS*), could removal nonetheless breach the EUCFR? *MSS* made this question less important, so the AG chose not to answer it, instead clarifying the status of the *MSS* ruling in EU law.[293] In light of Article 52(3) EUCFR, Strasbourg case law, although not 'a source of interpretation with full validity,' had 'particular significance and high importance'[294] in the areas of overlap. The *NS* Opinion noted the *de facto*, but not *de jure*, parallel between the CSR, ECHR, and rights under EU law in this context.[295]

The Court emphasized that the ECtHR in *MSS* had 'reviewed its position [in *KRS*] in the light of new evidence'.[296] Following the AG, the Court simply stated that Articles 1, 18, and 47 EUCFR did not lead to a different response to the questions posed.[297] This statement clearly only applies to the case at hand, and does not exclude the possibility that these rights may provide more extensive protection against return in an appropriate case. In particular, the Court has yet to examine whether the right to asylum under the Charter was a free-standing right which prevented removal, or the extent to which the right to dignity added protection above the Strasbourg minimum.

### *iv. How are the risks posed by transfer to be assessed?*

The Court integrated its response to the questions on the threshold to prevent removal and the evidential assessment.[298] Although it is not for the CJEU on a

290 ibid, para 82. 291 ibid, para 84.

292 ibid, para 94. See also para 86 where the test is identified, and para 106 where this test is stated as a requirement of Article 4 EUCFR.

293 ibid, paras 141–42. Opinion of AG Trstenjak. 294 ibid, para 146.

295 ibid, para 153. 296 ibid, para 112.

297 ibid, paras 113–15. 298 ibid, para 74.

preliminary reference to assess the facts, it incorporated the Strasbourg finding in *MSS* that there was a 'systemic deficiency' in the Greek asylum system.[299] It noted that Strasbourg had taken into account the 'regular and unanimous reports' of NGOs, the input of the UNHCR, and Commission Reports on Dublin as well as the proposals for a Recast Dublin Regulation.[300] Accordingly, it rejected the arguments of the Belgian, Italian, and Polish Governments that they lacked the 'instruments necessary' to assess other Member States' fundamental rights compliance.[301] Following the Opinion, the Court held that conclusive presumptions of compliance were incompatible with EU law,[302] and so were 'precluded' by EU law.[303]

*v. If removal is prohibited, is there a duty to process the claim?*

The Opinion frames the entire case as if the prohibition of transfer implies a duty to process the claim.[304] In contrast, the Court held that even if transfer was prevented on fundamental rights grounds, this did not create an automatic duty to examine the application. Instead, the Member State could use the Dublin criteria to find yet another State responsible, subject only to the requirement that that process should not 'worsen a situation where the fundamental rights of the applicant have been infringed by using a procedure for determining the Member State responsible which takes an unreasonable length of time'.[305]

This difference between the Opinion and Judgment, which could be highly significant in individual cases, has been resolved by the Court after *NS & ME*. In *Puid*, the CJEU clarified that the Member State must 'continue to examine the criteria . . . in order to establish whether another Member State can be identified as responsible.'[306]

*vi. Protocol No 30 on the position of the UK and Poland under the EUCFR*

The seventh question in *NS* relates to Protocol No 30 on the application of the EUCFR to Poland and to the United Kingdom. The Opinion confirms that Article 1(1) thereof is merely an 'express confirmation' of Article 51 EUCFR.[307] In contrast, Article 1(2) did seem to 'rule out new EU rights and entitlements being derived from Articles 27 to 38 [EUCFR]' against the UK or Poland.[308] These are the 'solidarity rights' in the Charter, including the right to family and professional life[309] and the right to healthcare.[310] As these rights were not at issue in the case, the AG declined to go any further in her analysis.[311] Article 2 was also of limited effect,[312] so all in all, Protocol 30 did not alter the findings vis-à-vis the UK. The Court too affirmed that Article 1(1) of Protocol No 30 merely 'explains' Article 51

[299] ibid, para 87. [300] ibid, para 90. [301] ibid, para 91. [302] ibid, para 99.
[303] ibid, para 105. [304] ibid, para 3. Opinion of AG Trstenjak.
[305] ibid, para 108. [306] Case C-4/11 *Puid* [2014] 2 WLR 98, paras 33–36.
[307] *NS* (n 22) para 171. Opinion of AG Trstenjak. [308] ibid, para 173.
[309] Art 33 EUCFR. [310] Art 35 EUCFR.
[311] *NS* (n 22) para 174. Opinion of AG Trstenjak.
[312] ibid, para 176. It was not a 'general opt-out' as it only related to those provisions which refer to 'national laws and practices.'

EUCFR, and does not exempt the Member States concerned.[313] This is an important clarification for there was some confusion about whether the Protocol was an opt-out.[314]

However, it remains to be seen how the solidarity rights limitation in Article 1(2) will evolve. The CJEU was able to avoid this issue. Strasbourg had made the legal innovation in *MSS* using Article 3 ECHR to impugn the reception conditions in Greece, so the question of using these Charter provisions to prevent return to face extreme suffering from destitution or homelessness did not need examination.

## 6. Back to Strasbourg—From *MSS* to *Tarakhel*

*Tarakhel v Switzerland*[315] comes in the wake of *NS/ME* and the confusion surrounding the issue of 'systemic breaches', which led to many incorrect rulings on Dublin transfers.[316] As discussed, in *NS/ME*, while endorsing the Strasbourg approach in *MSS*, the CJEU, on one reading, seemed to treat 'systemic breaches' as a legal requirement.[317] Furthermore, in its most troubling ruling on Dublin II, *Abdullahi*, the CJEU ruled that asylum seekers could only challenge Dublin deportations by 'pleading systemic deficiencies in the asylum procedure and in the conditions for the reception of applicants for asylum' amounting to a violation of Article 4 EUCFR (Article 3 ECHR).[318] *Abdullahi*, even on its own terms, is a ruling of limited application: it only concerned Article 19 of the Dublin II Regulation, so is best read as confined to cases where there is no question of using the sovereignty clause given that the receiving State has agreed to take charge of an applicant.[319] Not only does it set up tensions with ECHR standards, but it also runs counter to another current in the CJEU case law which cuts against removals, and establishes clear duties on States to take charge of claims in order to ensure swift processing and obviate hardship. *MA* exemplifies this approach.[320] Admittedly, it concerns unaccompanied minors, so it is not explicitly of general application. However, giving due weight to the 'best interests' of children, the CJEU held that due to their vulnerability, 'as a rule, unaccompanied minors should not be transferred to another Member State.'[321] The Dublin III Regulation is currently being revised to make *MA* explicit.[322]

313 ibid, para 120.

314 See further, C Barnard, 'The "Opt-Out" for the UK and Poland from the Charter of Fundamental Rights: Triumph of Rhetoric over Reality?' in S Griller and J Ziller (eds), *The Lisbon Treaty, EU Constitutionalism without a Constitutional Treaty?* (Springer 2008) 257–83.

315 App No 29217/12 (ECHR, 4 November 2014).

316 This section draws on Costello and Mouzourakis (n 24).

317 *NS/ME* (n 22) para 94.

318 *Abdullahi* (n 206) para 60. For a cogent critique, see M Hennessy, 'The Dublin system and the Right to an Effective Remedy– The case of C-394/12 *Abdullahi*' (*EDAL* 2013) <http://www.asylumlawdatabase.eu/en/journal/dublin-system-and-right-effective-remedy--case-c-39412-abdullahi> accessed 11 April 2015.

319 ibid.

320 Case C-648/11 *MA v Secretary of State for the Home Department* [2013] OJ C 225/18.

321 ibid, para 55.

322 European Commission, *Proposal for a Regulation of the European Parliament and of the Council amending Regulation (EU) No 604/2013 as regards determining the Member State responsible for*

Cases attempting to halt Dublin deportations to Italy and other Dublin States continued after *MSS* and *NS/ME*. After *MSS*, the ECtHR issued several Rule 39 orders to halt returns, but when it came to the admissibility stage, rejected applications on the basis that Article 3 ECHR did not preclude returns to Italy, as the evidence did not make out 'substantial grounds' of a 'real risk' of treatment contrary to Article 3 ECHR. Italy was a particularly critical case, where reception conditions meant removals are often strongly resisted, and onward movement of asylum seekers appears to have been subject, at least in some cases, to official acquiescence.[323] However, the Italian narrative was framed differently to that of Greece: while the Greek system was portrayed as being in total breakdown, the official accounts on Italy focused on the fact that some measures were being taken to deal with the increasing numbers of applicants in the wake of the Arab Spring. While the most relevant UNHCR submission was highly critical of the protection gaps and inconsistent conditions in Italy,[324] as was highlighted by all the government interveners, UNHCR had not issued a request to suspend transfers to Italy.

In this context, some national courts did halt transfers to Italy, applying *MSS* and *NS/ME*.[325] The Strasbourg litigation tended to emphasize the particular vulnerabilities of the individuals, in the face of uneven and unreliable reception conditions. In *Mohammed Hussein v the Netherlands and Italy*,[326] the ECtHR rejected as inadmissible a claim that return to Italy would amount to a violation of Article 3 ECHR on the ground that the reception conditions in the country did not meet the exceptional *MSS* threshold. The ECtHR also permitted transfer in *Daytbegova and Magomedova v Austria*,[327] where it was held that Italy was aware and prepared to cater for the applicant's special reception needs. *Halimi v Austria*[328] and *Abubeker v Austria*[329] followed a similar pattern. Beyond Italy, the ECtHR rejected the application of *MSS* to suspend a transfer to Hungary in *Mohammed v Austria*.[330]

While these cases mainly turned on factual analysis, legal uncertainty prevailed also as to the significance of the reference to 'systemic breaches', and what sorts of evidence was required to rebut the presumption of safety accorded to Dublin

*examining the application for international protection of unaccompanied minors with no family member, sibling or relative legally present in a Member State*, COM(2014) 382.

[323] In 2014, many asylum seekers declined to be fingerprinted upon first entry in Italy, which did not have the legal or practical means to compel them to provide them involuntarily. See Italian Refugee Council, *AIDA Country Report: Italy* (2014) 26–27.

[324] UNHCR, *Recommendations on important aspects of protection in Italy* (UNHCR, July 2012) 9–12.

[325] See, e.g. Magdeburg Admin Court 9 A 346/10 MD of 26 July 2011 (Syrian applicant with five children); Karlsruhe Admin Court A 3 K3069/11 of 6 March 2012 (risk of homelessness); Administrative Court Cologne 8L 794/13.A of 28 June 2013. See further AIRE, ECRE, and Amnesty International, *Third Party Intervention in Tarakhel v Switzerland: Relevant Extracts from Selected ECRE Research on Practice and Caselaw on Dublin II Regulation Transfers in Europe* (2014), 14–27.

[326] App No 27725/10 (ECHR, 2 April 2013).

[327] App No 6198/12 (ECHR, 4 June 2013), para 66, citing *Mohammed Hussein v Austria*, paras 43–49.

[328] App No 53852/11 (ECHR, 18 June 2013).

[329] App No 73874/11 (ECHR, 18 June 2013).

[330] App No 2283/12 (ECHR, 4 October 2013).

States. *Tarakhel* is the case where these issues came to the Grand Chamber to resolve. The case concerned Mr Golajan Tarakhel, born in 1971, his wife Mrs Maryam Habibi, born in 1981, and their six children, Arezoo, born in 1999, Mohammad, born in 2001, Nazanin, born in 2003, Shiba, born in 2005, Zeynab, born in 2008, and Amir Hassan, born in 2012. In January 2012, the Swiss Federal Office for Migration (FOM) made an order for their removal to Italy.

Having exhausted their domestic remedies, the applicants appealed to the ECtHR. The assigned Chamber relinquished it upwards to the Grand Chamber.[331] The interveners sought to broaden out the assessment to consider Article 8 ECHR issues, but the Court confined its assessment to Article 3 ECHR. The key point of the ruling is to reject any notion of 'systemic breaches' as an additional requirement of the Article 3 assessment. Rather, concerning its ground-breaking finding in *MSS* on the living conditions in Greece, the ECtHR explained its previous ruling in terms of the key factors relied on in that previous ruling, including both the fact that the RCD[332] obliged Greece to provide 'reception conditions' and that the legal vulnerability of asylum seekers created particular positive obligations towards them. Whilst citing *NS/ME,* it also endorses the ruling of the UK Supreme Court in *EM (Eritrea)*,[333] which explicitly rejected 'systemic breaches' as an additional threshold or test.[334] It should be recalled that in *EM (Eritrea)*, the UK Supreme Court held that:

> Violation of article 3 does not require (or, at least, does not necessarily require) that the complained of conditions said to constitute inhuman or degrading conditions are the product of systemic shortcomings.[335]

Applying the principles to the facts, it required that:

> It [was] therefore incumbent on the Swiss authorities to obtain assurances from their Italian counterparts that on their arrival in Italy the applicants will be received in facilities and in conditions adapted to the age of the children, and that the family will be kept together.[336]

While the Swiss authorities had some indications concerning where the family would be accommodated, it did not have 'detailed and reliable information concerning the specific facility, the physical reception conditions and the preservation of the family unit'.[337] The ECtHR concluded, by fourteen votes to three, that:

> [W]ere the applicants to be returned to Italy without the Swiss authorities having first obtained individual guarantees from the Italian authorities that the applicants would be taken charge of in a manner adapted to the age of the children and that the family would be kept together, there would be a violation of Article 3 of the Convention.[338]

[331] *Tarakhel* (n 24) para 5.

[332] Council Directive 2003/9/EC laying down minimum standards for the reception of asylum seekers [2003] OJ L31/18.

[333] *EM (Eritrea) v Secretary of State for the Home Department* [2014] UKSC 12.

[334] *Tarakhel* (n 24) para 104.

[335] *EM (Eritrea)* (n 333) para 42, *per* Lord Kerr.

[336] ibid, para 120. [337] ibid, para 121. [338] ibid, para 122.

*Tarakhel* therefore makes the legality of the sending State's decision to transfer conditional upon a thorough and individualized assessment of the applicant's situation in the receiving State, and the receipt of individualized guarantees from the receiving State.[339]

## 7. After *Tarakhel*

For all the praise for judicial dialogue as a fundamental rights protective phenomenon in Europe, this litigation saga reveals pitfalls as well as benefits. Some asylum decision-makers and lower courts had applied the erroneous systemic breaches notion in a rigid manner, undermining Article 3 ECHR. That this spurious legal approach required great legal minds and energies to rebut, took up public resources to litigate to the highest courts across Europe, and determined the rights of asylum seekers post *NS/ME*, is deeply troubling. The phenomenon is testament to the capacity of some governments to limit human rights principles from within, requiring vigilance to maintain the integrity of even apparently basic principles. Indeed, reviewing the ebb and flow of the case law suggests that when Strasbourg has permitted generalized assumptions of safety to operate (as in say *KRS*), it has been forced to resile and reassert individual scrutiny as the only robust way to ensure that returns do not violate Article 3 ECHR.

The EU Charter of Fundamental Rights requires that the EU interpretation of the protections offered against torture and inhuman and degrading treatment should be at least as strong as under the ECHR.[340] To the extent that *NS/ME* and *Abdullahi* have interpreted Article 4 EUCFR in a manner that is in tension with *Tarakhel*, the CJEU should take the opportunity as soon as possible to bring its case law in line with the Strasbourg minimum. No doubt, a reference to the CJEU to allow it to bring its case law explicitly in line with the ECtHR would be appropriate. *Abdullahi* in particular cannot be reconciled with *Tarakhel*, and does not fit Dublin III, so should be abandoned. The rationale underlying *Abdullahi*, that the Dublin System is principally about inter-state cooperation, with only a residual role for asylum seekers' agency and voice, needs revisiting.

Indeed, the conditions may be ripe to develop stronger duties under EU law, in light of the EUCFR, to take charge of asylum cases in a wider range of cases than the Strasbourg minimum would require. *MA* could lead the way in this regard. Elsewhere, it has been argued that a move to a reconceptualization of 'Dublin with coercion' is necessary and timely.[341] This could be achieved by a reinterpretation of the sovereignty clause case law in light of the new context of Dublin III. In this context, Opinion 2 of 2013 is particularly worrying. As discussed in Chapter 1, in

[339] ibid, para 104. This is also confirmed in *Sharifi v Italy and Greece* App No 16643/09 (ECHR, 21 October 2014), para 223.

[340] Art 52(3) EUCFR.

[341] E Guild, C Costello, M Garlick, V Moreno-Lax, and M Mouzourakis, 'New Approaches, Alternative Avenues and Means of Access to Asylum Procedures for Persons Seeking International Protection' (2014) Study for the LIBE Committee, PE509.989, 84–87.

that Opinion, the CJEU held that the proposed mechanisms for EU accession to the ECHR were not in keeping with the autonomy of the EU legal order. Amongst the principles treated as embodying this autonomy was mutual trust:

> [T]he principle of mutual trust between the Member States is of fundamental importance in EU law, given that it allows an area without internal borders to be created and maintained. That principle requires, particularly with regard to the area of freedom, security and justice, each of those States, save in exceptional circumstances, to consider all the other Member States to be complying with EU law and particularly with the fundamental rights recognised by EU law.[342]

However, the Treaty does not treat mutual trust as constitutive of the AFSJ, but rather states in Article 67(1) TFEU that the EU must 'constitute an area of freedom, security and justice *with respect for fundamental rights*'.

In contrast, for the CJEU, the 'principle of mutual trust' necessitated duties (implicitly under some circumstances, through a 'may' clause)

> to presume that fundamental rights have been observed by the other Member States, so that not only may they not demand a higher level of national protection of fundamental rights from another Member State than that provided by EU law, but, save in exceptional cases, they may not check whether that other Member State has actually, in a specific case, observed the fundamental rights guaranteed by the EU.[343]

Accordingly, the Court opined that the Protocol had failed to reflect the fact that in the relations between each other, Member States should not be treated as subject to the same relations as if they were acting with third States. This seems to elevate the duty of mutual recognition to a necessary feature of the EU legal order. One may question this move, which elevates mutual recognition from an adaptable tool in certain areas of EU policy to a constitutional necessity. Moreover, it seems to overstate what mutual recognition requires: Already in *NS/ME*, the Court has accepted that mutual recognition is subject to human rights compatibility (admittedly prompted by *MSS v Belgium and Greece*).[344] Indeed, in light of this statement in the Protocol, it is difficult not to read *NS/ME* as a reluctant move motivated by the ECtHR, and one on which the CJEU may seek to row back.[345]

### *i. Dublin III*

The Dublin III Regulation is now in force, and applies to all applications for asylum lodged after 1 January 2014.[346] Yet following *Tarakhel*, the narrowly drafted

[342] *Opinion 2/13*, para 191, citing *NS/ME*, paras 78–80, and *Melloni*, paras 37 and 63.
[343] *Opinion 2/13*, para 192.
[344] MSS (n 22).
[345] Peers suggests that 'One can infer that the CJEU is seething about the ECtHR's recent judgment in *Tarakhel*, which conspicuously failed to defer to the [CJEU's] poorly reasoned defence of the Dublin system in last year's *Abdullahi* judgment.' S Peers 'The CJEU and the EU's accession to the ECHR: a clear and present danger to human Human rights protection' available at <http://eulawanalysis.blogspot.com.tr/2014/12/the-cjeu-and-eus-accession-to-echr.html> accessed 20 December 2014.
[346] Art 49 Dublin III Regulation.

new Article 3(2) of the Regulation, a *verbatim* codification of the *NS/ME* ratio on 'systemic deficiencies', is undoubtedly an ill-fitting provision to reflect the necessary legal standards to suspending transfers.

Given the enhanced procedural rights under Dublin III,[347] it seems there is greater scope to argue that a full consideration of the rights of the asylum-seeker pre-transfer is appropriate, not just consideration of the right to be free from torture, inhuman and degrading treatment. Indeed, the CJEU should seize the legal issue of the full range of rights (not just Article 3 ECHR/Article 4 EUCFR), on an appropriate reference. The 'best interests' standard has already done some important work in *MA,* and its application cannot be confined to unaccompanied children. In that light, the scope afforded by the original Commission proposal for the Dublin III Regulation, which called for suspension of transfers when the level of protection in the receiving Member State does not reflect EU standards,[348] seems a more suitable test for rebutting the presumption of safety than Article 3(2).

### *ii. An end to Dublin?*

Discussions of an alternative to Dublin in terms of allocation are gaining ground in Europe, with a range of governmental and NGO proposals for different allocation keys being discussed.[349] Even if political agreement could be reached on alternatives to Dublin in terms of allocation criteria, the central question as to the operability and sustainability of any system will be its capacity to gain the trust and cooperation of asylum seekers, who at present have very good reasons to continue their journeys seeking protection once they reach the EU. Without their trust and cooperation, any system to allocate responsibility for persons will become as complex, coercive, and costly as Dublin. In this context *Tarakhel* is important for signalling the importance of a 'thorough and individualised' assessment in all cases, and a duty not to deport anyone to a place where the relevant risk of inhuman and degrading treatment is established.[350]

## IV. Conclusions

Access to asylum depends practically on access to a place of refuge. Securing access to territory means overcoming both physical and legal barriers. The CSR's *non-refoulement* guarantee applies at the border and beyond. The ECtHR provides a forum to scrutinize extra-territorial border controls, and vindicate the right to

[347] These include the right to a personal interview under Article 5 and the right to appeal in fact and law under Article 27.

[348] European Commission, *Proposal for a Regulation of the European Parliament and of the Council establishing the criteria and mechanisms for determining the Member State responsible for examining an application for international protection lodged in one of the Member States by a third-country national or a stateless person (Recast)*, COM(2008) 820, 52.

[349] ibid, 50–59.

[350] *Tarakhel* (n 24) para 105.

seek protection. In light of the evolving jurisprudence on the meaning of 'jurisdiction' under Article 1 ECHR, the potential to subject many extraterritorial border control activities to Strasbourg standards is evident. *Hirsi v Italy* breaks new legal ground in finding the prohibition of collective expulsions applicable extraterritorially. Screening migrants and providing information about asylum procedures is required under Article 13 ECHR. We may speculate that the EU right to asylum in Article 18 EUCFR, if read together with the evolving ECHR jurisdictional scope (or an autonomous EU functional criterion), has potentially dramatic implications for access to protection. After *Hirsi*, the need to formalize safe access is urgent.

Nonetheless, EU Member States continue to engage in a further layer of deflection activities, employing STC concepts in the PD and Dublin. These concepts turn on generalized assessments of safety of the State to which the asylum seeker is to be transferred. The role of courts here has generally been to question these generalized assessments, and insist that the rights of asylum seekers be protected when there is evidence of a real risk of human rights violation, either due to the conditions in the third country or due to a risk of onward *refoulement*. Court rulings have sometimes met official resistance, leading to legislative change to bolster States' rights to presume safety and transfer, as the UK example shows. Asylum seekers attempting to resist transfer under the Dublin System have turned to the Strasbourg Court for salvation, with thousands of applications for provisional measures received.

Strasbourg at first established clear duties on the transferring State, albeit ones that were easy to discharge in practice (*TI v United Kingdom*). In *MSS v Belgium and Greece*, the Grand Chamber asserted strong duties to protect human rights on all transferring States. Luxembourg's subsequent ruling in *NS and ME* follows the contours of the Strasbourg case law closely, but the added gloss of apparently requiring a 'systemic breach' of Article 4 EUCFR (Article 3 ECHR) standards to resist removal has set off a further raft of litigation in domestic courts and again before the ECtHR. The CJEU ruling in *Abdullahi* seems to privilege the 'efficient' working of Dublin over refugee rights. The Grand Chamber ruling from Strasbourg in *Tarakhel v Switzerland* reasserted the orthodox position concerning risk assessment in Dublin deportation cases. In *MSS, Hirsi v Italy* and *Tarakhel v Switzerland*, the ECtHR makes it abundantly clear that States may not rely on cooperative arrangements in the face of evidence of real risk of human rights violations. When will the EU learn?

Opinion 2 of 2013 suggests that the CJEU regards mutual recognition not as a flexible policy tool, but as an aim in itself. In the context of asylum, that characterization is inapt. The EU and its Member States have sought to hinder access to protection by manipulating conceptions of jurisdiction and responsibility. They excise parts of their own territory using legal fictions, and continue to insist on the exceptionality of border zones and procedures, in spite of clear and longstanding ECtHR authority in *Amuur v France* reinforcing jurisdiction. They extend their borders abroad, and attempt to rely on constrained territorial constructions of jurisdiction to avoid responsibilities. Yet, when it comes to Dublin cases, we see States attempting to rely on further legal fictions that they form a uniform expanded area of protection, such that transfers of asylum seekers may be assumed to be safe. In all instances, the response of the Strasbourg Court has been to reinforce States' responsibility, in the face of these manipulations. Luxembourg in *NS and ME* has similarly insisted on the duties of individual Member States under the Dublin System. These endorsements of individual State responsibility are a hugely important corrective in the face of States' deflection practices.

Yet, real solutions to access must be collective ones. The Strasbourg cases reveal the chasm between EU legal standards and the reality for asylum seekers in many EU Member States. Meanwhile, the EU legislative reform process continues, without engaging in the fundamental re-think required, particularly of Dublin and STC practices. The Recast APD even seems to diminish the procedural protections available in cases of transfer to super-STC. The CEAS reform process seems to have failed to translate the Court rulings into collective, institutional commitments. *Tarakhel* rules out automatic transfers, thus creating further incentives for States to just get on with the job of processing claims, without trying to enforce Dublin deportations. This happens in most cases anyway, with Dublin transfers occurring, it appears from European Asylum Support Office (EASO) data, in only about 3% of asylum cases.[351] When we get to the point that Dublin proceedings become 'lengthier and more cumbersome than ordinary asylum procedures,'[352] a fundamental rethink is required. It is doubtful whether any allocation system that is coercive will succeed in being *both* human rights protective and efficient.

[351] EASO, *Annual Report on the Situation of Asylum in the European Union 2013* (EASO 2014) 30.

[352] M Mouzourakis, '"We Need to Talk about Dublin": Responsibility under the Dublin System as a Blockage to Asylum Burden-Sharing in the European Union' (2014) RSC Working Paper Series 105, 16.

# 7

# Immigration Detention

## I. Introduction

The right to liberty is ubiquitous in human rights instruments, in essence protecting all individuals from arbitrary arrest and detention.[1] It should go without saying that deprivations of liberty require the strongest possible justification. Yet, in practice, immigration detention[2] is increasingly routine, even automatic, across Europe.[3] This detention is linked to immigration law enforcement—usually tied to refusals of admission or deportation. In this way, immigration detention reflects the vagaries of migration control and migration status. We should recall that migration status is often precarious, so if migrants are vulnerable to irregularity (sometimes through little fault of their own, as discussed in Chapter 2), they become vulnerable to detention. Asylum seekers too are liable to detention, and the Dublin System creates a class of deportable asylum seekers. With deportability comes detainability.[4] This remains notwithstanding the fact that asylum seekers, once they have made their claim, have a temporary right of residence at least in EU law.[5]

This chapter examines how international human rights law (IHRL) confronts immigration detention. The protections against immigration detention are weaker than against other forms of detention.[6] The State's migration control powers seem

[1] As reflected in Article 9 ICCPR, Article 5 ECHR, and Article 6 EUCFR.

[2] 'Immigration detention' is understood as referring to the detention of migrants (in the broadest sense, to include all individuals entering the territory of a State other than their own, be it as refugees, asylum seekers, stateless persons, irregular migrants, or regular migrants) either upon seeking entry to a territory or pending deportation, removal, or return from a territory.

[3] See generally Council of Europe Parliamentary Assembly (PACE), 'The detention of asylum seekers and irregular migrants in Europe' Doc No 12105 (2010); AC Mendonça, *'Explanatory Memorandum* to *The Detention of Asylum Seekers and Irregular Migrants in Europe'*; M Flynn and C Cannon, *Detention at the Borders of Europe: Report on the Joint Global Detention Project – International Detention Coalition Workshop* Geneva, Switzerland, 2–3 October 2010 (Global Detention Project 2010).

[4] JRS, *Protection Interrupted: The Dublin Regulation's Impact on Asylum Seekers' Protection* (JRS June 2013).

[5] See generally M Welsh and L Schuster, 'Detention of Asylum Seekers in the US, UK, France, Germany and Italy: A Critical View of the Globalizing Culture of Control' (2005) 5 Criminology & Criminal Justice 331; M Bosworth, *Inside Immigration Detention* (OUP 2014).

[6] See generally A Edwards, *Back to Basics: The Right to Liberty and Security of Person and 'Alternatives to Detention' of Refugees, Asylum-Seekers, Stateless Persons and Other Migrants* (UNHCR 2011); International Detention Coalition, *Legal frameworks and standards relating to the detention of refugees, asylum seekers and migrants: A Guide* (The International Detention Coalition 2011); International

to be given greater sway than even its penal powers. Again, we find the problematic statist assumption, and its tendency to limit human rights, even those as basic as the right to liberty. Yet, as cases challenging immigration detention come before courts and human rights bodies, that tension between the right to liberty and migration control prerogatives has been mediated both before the European Court of Human Rights (ECtHR), which has a specific provision on immigration detention in the European Convention on Human Rights—Article 5(1)(f) ECHR—and in EU law, which now contains detailed provisions on detention of asylum seekers (in the Reception Conditions Directive (RCD)[7] and more elaborately the Recast Reception Conditions Directive (RRCD))[8], and of those facing deportation under the Returns Directive (RD).[9] The Dublin III Regulation too contains provisions on detention.[10] The Court of Justice of the European Union (CJEU) has become part of the apparatus of supranational human rights adjudication over the bulk of immigration detention by EU Member States.[11] The principal focus of this chapter is on the permissibility of detention *per se*, rather than detention conditions, although the latter also raise serious human rights concerns, usually scrutinized under guarantees against inhuman and degrading detention conditions.[12]

As well as the usual focus on the ECtHR and CJEU, I also allude to the position of the UN Human Rights Committee (HRC) in passing. Its recent General Comment on the Right to Liberty contains a useful synthesis of its position on immigration detention.[13] In the background is the increasing attention afforded to immigration detention in international human rights fora. Within the UN system, the Working Group on Arbitrary Detention (WGAD) has considered immigration

Commission of Jurists, *Migration and International Human Rights Law, Practitioners' Guide No 6* (International Commission of Jurists 2011) 147–90.

[7] Council Directive 2003/9/EC laying down minimum standards for the reception of asylum seekers [2003] OJ L31/18.

[8] Directive 2013/33/EU of the European Parliament and of the Council of 26 June 2013 laying down standards for the reception of applicants for international protection (recast) (RRCD) [2013] OJ L108/96, Art 8.

[9] Directive 2008/115/EC of the European Parliament and of the Council of 16 December 2008 on common standards and procedures in Member States for returning illegally staying third-country nationals (RD) [2008] OJ L348/98, Art 15.

[10] Regulation (EU) No 604/2013 of the European Parliament and of the Council of 26 June 2013 establishing the criteria and mechanisms for determining the Member State responsible for examining an application for international protection lodged in one of the Member States by a third-country national or stateless person (recast) (Dublin III Regulation) [2013] OJ L180/31, Art 28.

[11] This chapter focuses on those fields where Member States implement these directives in detaining TCNs and are therefore subject to EU norms. Of course, detention of EU Citizens on migration law grounds requires particularly strong justification in EU law, as does restricting their mobility within the EU. See Case 48/75 *Royer* [1976] ECR 497, and in particular Case C-215/03 *Oulane* [2005] ECR I-1215, para 40.

[12] See, e.g., Art 3, ECHR. Particular concerns are also raised in relation to the detention of children. See, e.g., *Mayeka and Mitunga v Belgium* (2008) 46 EHRR 449. As will be seen, though, the two issues are intertwined, as detention conditions do bear on the permissibility of detention, in particular under the case law of the ECtHR, discussed in Section III.

[13] Human Rights Committee, General Comment No 35 on Article 9 (Liberty and Security of Person), CCPR/C/GC/35 (16 December 2014).

detention since 1997.[14] The UN Special Rapporteur on the Human Rights of Migrants[15] and the UN High Commissioner for Human Rights (OHCHR) have also engaged with this issue.[16] Within the Council of Europe, the Committee of Ministers adopted the *Twenty Guidelines on Forced Return* in 2005,[17] while its Parliamentary Assembly adopted an important resolution and recommendation in early 2010 specifically on immigration detention.[18] Significantly, a UNHCR–OHCHR Global Roundtable on Alternatives to Immigration Detention was held in May 2011 in Geneva,[19] leading to new UNHCR Guidelines on detention.[20] Additionally, the EU's Fundamental Rights Agency (FRA) has reported on pre-removal detention.[21] These political initiatives, and the soft law principles espoused therein, form an important backdrop to this chapter. Indeed, the Council of Europe Guidelines on Forced Return were influential on the content of the EU RD.

## II. International Covenant on Civil and Political Rights (ICCPR)

While one might expect the weak institutional framework of the ICCPR to produce tentative rulings on immigration detention, the HRC has developed a relatively robust line of jurisprudence.[22] Detention must be lawful and non-arbitrary

[14] Human Rights Commission, Resolution 1997/5 (15 April 1997); UN Docs E/CN.4/1999/63 (1998), E/CN.4/2004/3 (2003), E/CN.4/2006/7 (2005), A/HRC/10/21 (2008) and A/HRC/13/30 (2010). A specific recent report on Italy deals extensively with immigration detention. See Report of the Working Group on Arbitrary Detention (WGAD) on its Mission to Italy, UN Docs A/HRC/10/21/Add.5 (2009).

[15] UN Human Rights Council, 'Report of the Special Rapporteur, Ms Gabriela Rodríguez Pizarro, submitted pursuant to Commission on Human Rights resolution 2002/62' UN Doc E/CN.4/2003/85 (30 December 2002); 'Promotion and Protection of All Human Rights, Civil, Political, Economic, Social and Cultural Rights, Including the Right to Development: Report of the Special Rapporteur on the human rights of migrants, Jorge Bustamante' UN Doc A/HRC/11/7 (14 May 2009).

[16] See OHCHR, 'Immigration Control Must Not Compromise Human Rights', (22 September 2009) < http://www.ohchr.org/EN/NewsEvents/Pages/MigrationPanel.aspx > accessed 12 April 2015.

[17] Council of Europe Committee of Ministers, *Twenty Guidelines on Forced Return*, 925th Meeting of the Ministers' Deputies, 4 May 2005. The Parliamentary Assembly prompted the compilation of these guidelines. See PACE Recommendation 1547(2002) *Expulsion procedures in conformity with human rights and enforced with respect for safety and dignity*, 22 January 2002.

[18] See PACE (n 3).

[19] UNHCR and OHCHR, *Concept Note for the Global Roundtable on Alternatives to Immigration Detention* (2011), <http://www.ohchr.org/Documents/Issues/Migration/Events/FinalConceptNote.pdf > accessed 12 April 2015.

[20] UNHCR, *Guidelines on the Applicable Criteria and Standards relating to the Detention of Asylum seekers and Alternatives to Detention* (UNHCR 2012), <http://www.refworld.org/docid/503489533b8.html> accessed 12 April 2015.

[21] See FRA, *Detention of third-country nationals in return procedures* (FRA 2014) 80–81.

[22] For an extensive analysis, see generally G Cornelisse, *Immigration Detention and Human Rights: Rethinking Territorial Sovereignty* (Martinus Nijhoff Publishers 2010) Ch 7.

in order to meet the Article 9 standards.[23] While the notion of lawfulness is similar to that employed by the ECtHR, as will be seen, the HRC notion of arbitrariness is thicker, connoting 'elements of inappropriateness, injustice and lack of predictability' as well as reasonableness and necessity 'in all the circumstances for a specific purpose'.[24] In this context, the HRC also applies the principle of proportionality.[25] The imposition of a proportionality and necessity test may seem unremarkable in a human rights context, but as will be seen it is glaringly absent in the ECHR approach.[26]

Article 9 does not expressly limit the legitimate purposes of detention, unlike Article 5 of the ECHR. However, the HRC has clarified that detention must pursue a specific purpose. Crucially, for immigration detention purposes, illegal entry alone does not justify detention.[27] In this respect too, the HRC has set a more demanding standard than the ECtHR in its case law on 'detention to prevent unauthorised entry.'[28] The HRC demands that there are other additional factors particular to the individual, 'such as the likelihood of absconding and lack of cooperation, which may justify detention for a period.'[29]

Not only must detention pursue a narrow specific aim, it must be necessary and proportionate in the individual circumstances.[30] On this basis, the HRC repeatedly condemned Australia's detention practices, for example, for failure to provide individual justifications.[31] Detention may not be justified on the basis of the country's 'general experience that asylum seekers abscond if not retained in custody',[32] an assumption that does not appear grounded in empirical reality in any event.[33]

[23] Art 9(1) ICCPR: 'Everyone has the right to liberty and security of person. No one shall be subjected to arbitrary arrest or detention. No one shall be deprived of his liberty except on such grounds and in accordance with such procedures as are established by law.'

[24] *Van Alphen v the Netherlands* Communication No 305/1988 (HRC, 23 July 1990) para 5.8.

[25] *A v Australia* Communication No 560/1993 (HRC, 30 April 1997), para 9.2.

[26] See Parts IV.2–IV.4. [27] *A v Australia* (n 25) para 9.4. [28] See Part II.2.

[29] *A v Australia* (n 25) para 9.2, See also HRC, *Communication No 2094/2011* (2013) CCPR/C/108/D/2094/2011, para 9.3.

[30] ibid, para 9.2.

[31] ibid. See also *Saed Shams v Australia* Communication No 1225/2004 (HRC, 11 September 2007); *D and E and their two children v Australia*, Communication No 1050/2002 (HRC, 9 August 2006); *Shafiq v Australia* Communication No 1324/2004 (HRC, 13 November 2006); *Baban v Australia*, Communication No 1014/2001 (HRC, 18 September 2003); *Bakhtiyari v Australia*, Communication No 1069/2002 (HRC, 6 November 2003); *C v Australia* Communication No 900/1999 (HRC, 13 November 2002). In spite of these views, Australia continues its practice of automatic detention. See Australian Human Rights Commission, 'Submission to the Joint Select Committee on Australia's Immigration Detention Network' August 2011, 11–27, <https://www.humanrights.gov.au/australian-human-rights-commission-submission-joint-select-committee-australia-s-immigration> accessed 12 April 2015.

[32] *Shafiq v Australia* (n 31) para 7.3.

[33] See O Field and A Edwards, 'Alternatives to Detention of Asylum Seekers and Refugees' (2006) UNHCR Legal and Protection Policy Research Series POLAS/2006/03.

## III. Convention on the Status of Refugees 1951 (CSR)

The CSR is also relevant here, in particular given the declaratory character of refugee status determination. Refugees who are yet to be recognized (as some asylum seekers and migrants are) have rights under the CSR, which are all too often ignored given their mislabelling as 'irregular migrants'. The CSR establishes a spectrum of rights allocated according to the degree of attachment between the refugee and the State in question.[34] Article 26 CSR on freedom of movement applies to those 'lawfully in' the territory.[35] While Article 26 clearly applies to recognized refugees, there is debate as to whether it applies to asylum seekers too. One view holds that Article 26 should apply to asylum seekers whose applications have been presented.[36] In this view, then, asylum seekers should generally enjoy a right to free movement once formally in the asylum process, although their movement may be restricted under the same conditions as are 'applicable to aliens generally in the same circumstances'.[37] On this basis, of course, they remain vulnerable to 'normal' immigration detention, which may be very vulnerable indeed. Moreover, several European governments still contest the applicability of Article 26 to asylum seekers.[38] Such contestation reflects a general governmental tendency to distort the scope of the CSR, by seeking to limit the rights attaching to the category of 'asylum seeker'. In contrast, as mentioned, the CSR is based on the premise that asylum seekers are presumptive refugees, and should be treated accordingly, particularly in light of the declaratory character of refugee status.[39]

Article 31 CSR prohibits States parties from imposing penalties on refugees who, 'when coming directly from a territory where their life or freedom was threatened, enter or are present in their territory without authorisation, provided they present themselves without delay to the authorities and can show good cause for their illegal entry or presence.' Those falling within this provision are to be immune from penalties and subject only to such restrictions on free movement as are necessary. As to the meaning of 'penalties,' while some take the view that only criminal

[34] Hathaway describes this as the 'structure of entitlement' under the RC: J Hathaway, *The Rights of Refugees under International Law* (Cambridge University Press 2005) 154. See G Goodwin-Gill and J McAdam, *The Refugee in International Law* (3rd edn, OUP 2007) 524–28, who described it as 'criteria of entitlement'.

[35] Art 26 CSR: 'Each Contracting State shall accord to refugees lawfully in its territory the right to choose their place of residence to move freely within its territory, subject to any regulations applicable to aliens generally in the same circumstances.'

[36] See Hathaway (n 34) 173, for extensive consideration of the meaning of 'lawful stay'.

[37] Art 26 CSR.

[38] See R Marx, 'Article 26 (Freedom of Movement/Liberté de Circulation)' in A Zimmermann (ed), *The 1951 Convention Relating to the Status of Refugees and Its 1967 Protocol: A Commentary* (OUP 2011) 1161–64.

[39] See UNHCR, *Handbook on Procedures and Criteria for Determining Refugee Status under the 1951 Convention and the 1967 Protocol Relating to the Status of Refugees*, HCR/IP/4/Eng/REV.1 (UNHCR, Geneva, 1979, reedited January 1992) para 28, cited in J Hathaway, 'What's in a *Label*?' (2003) 5 EJML 1, 9–10.

sanctions are precluded,[40] several authoritative commentators take the view that at least some forms of detention should be precluded as punitive.[41] Alternatively, even if detention is not always regarded as a 'penalty,' Article 31(2) provides that the asylum seeker may be subjected only to such restrictions as are necessary.[42] Regrettably, the CJEU refused to interpret Article 31 CSR in *Qurbani*, on the basis that it fell outside EU law.[43] This is difficult to square with the commitment in the Treaty on the Functioning of the European Union (TFEU) and various EU legislative measures that the Common European Asylum System (CEAS) shall be 'in accordance with the [CSR]'.[44] Regrettably, as Goodwin-Gill notes:

> Comparatively few states have taken any formal steps to incorporate the exemption from penalties required by Article 31 . . . Even where legislative provisions exist, however, refugees and asylum seekers can still face loss of liberty. They are subject to the same law as is applied to non-nationals generally, and are thus exposed to prosecution, punishment, and/or detention, on account of illegal entry, entry without documents, or entry without falsified documents.[45]

The failure of the CJEU to consider Article 31 CSR in *Qurbani,* and the approach of the ECtHR in *Saadi v UK*,[46] as critiqued in Part I.4, mean that the provision has not received an adequate foothold via regional systems either.

The UNHCR's *2012 Revised Guidelines on Detention of Asylum Seekers* confirm that as a general principle, asylum seekers should not be detained solely for the reason of seeking asylum, and that detention is only permissible in exceptional circumstances, when it is reasonable, proportional, and necessary in order to attain a limited range of objectives.[47] However, the range of purposes contemplated by UNHCR is broad: detention is permissible when aimed at protecting public order,

[40] Cornelisse (n 22) 262. Cornelisse simply asserts that '[i]t is not plausible that this provision would be violated when a refugee is detained on account of his illegal entry, if the deprivation of liberty is an administrative measure and is not categorized as a criminal sanction as such.' She assumes that only Article 31(2) limits detention, requiring it to be 'proportional in view of the individual circumstances of each and every individual'.

[41] G Goodwin-Gill, 'Article 31 of the 1951 Convention Relating to the Status of Refugees: Non-penalization, Detention and Protection' in E Feller, V Türk, and F Nicholson, *Refugee Protection in International Law: UNHCR's Global Consultations on International Protection* (Cambridge University Press 2003) 185, 195–96. See also Edwards (n 6) 11, citing G Noll, 'Article 31 (Refugees Unlawfully in the Country of Refuge/Réfugés en Situation Irrégulière dans le Pays d' Accueil)' in A Zimmermann (n 38), 1243, 1263–64.

[42] Hathaway (n 34) 414, 418–19. Hathaway explains the 'strictly provisional' nature of the detention power under Article 31(2), with Article 26 of the CSR as the general provision applicable to most asylum seekers who have been admitted to the asylum procedure. Hathaway also discusses 'necessity.' ibid, 423–39.

[43] Case C-481/13 *Qurbani* [2014] OJ C 31/24.

[44] Art 78(1) TFEU; Directive 2011/95/EU of the European Parliament and of the Council of 13 December 2011 on standards for the qualification of third-country nationals or stateless persons as beneficiaries of international protection, for a uniform status for refugees or for persons eligible for subsidiary protection, and for the content of the protection granted (recast) (Qualification Directive) [2011] OJ L337/9, Recitals 2, 3, 8, 15, 16, 17, and 24.

[45] Goodwin-Gill (n 41) 226.

[46] (2008) 47 EHRR 17

[47] UNHCR (n 20) Guidelines 4.1 and 4.2.

public health, or national security.[48] The breadth of the grounds seems liable to undermine the commitment to ensuring that detention is an exceptional practice.

Another legal route to insulate refugees from immigration detention would be to focus on their permission to enter and stay, albeit temporarily. As will be discussed further below, a significant addition in EU law is confirming the temporary right of residence of asylum seekers.[49] While their claims are being examined, asylum seekers cannot accordingly be treated as awaiting deportation. Both the ECtHR and the CJEU have now confirmed this point.[50] However, the fact that they are not 'unauthorised entrants' either has yet to be accepted.

## IV. European Convention on Human Rights (ECHR)

In contrast to the ICCPR, the ECHR enumerates a finite list of specific grounds of permitted detention, including two forms of immigration detention.[51] Article 5(1)(f) ECHR permits detention 'to prevent... unauthorised entry into the country' and 'of a person against whom action is being taken with a view to deportation or extradition'.[52] Both forms of detention must be 'in accordance with a procedure prescribed by law'.[53]

### 1. The requirement of legality

The requirement of legality, as is commonly the case under the ECHR, refers not only to conformity with enacted domestic law, but also entails rule of law criteria,

[48] ibid, para 21.

[49] Directive 2013/32/EU of the European Parliament and of the Council of 26 June 2013 on common procedures for granting and withdrawing international protection (Recast PD) [2013] L180/60, Art 9(1).

[50] *SD v Greece* App No 53541/07 (ECHR, 11 June 2009); *RU v Greece* App No 2237/08 (ECHR, 7 June 2011), paras 95–96; Case C-534/11 *Arslan* [2013] OJ C 225/13.

[51] Art 5(1), ECHR provides: 'No one shall be deprived of his liberty save in the following cases and in accordance with a procedure prescribed by law:

(a) the lawful detention of a person after conviction by a competent court;
(b) the lawful arrest or detention of a person for non-compliance with the lawful order of a court or in order to secure the fulfilment of any obligation prescribed by law;
(c) the lawful arrest or detention of a person effected for the purpose of bringing him before the competent legal authority on reasonable suspicion of having committed an offence or when it is reasonably considered necessary to prevent his committing an offence or fleeing after having done so;
(d) the detention of a minor by lawful order for the purpose of educational supervision or his lawful detention for the purpose of bringing him before the competent legal authority;
(e) the lawful detention of persons for the prevention of the spreading of infectious diseases, of persons of unsound mind, alcoholics or drug addicts, or vagrants;
(f) the lawful arrest or detention of a person to prevent his effecting an unauthorized entry into the country or of a person against whom action is being taken with a view to deportation or extradition.'

[52] ibid.

[53] Arts 5(4) and (5) ECHR set out the right to have the lawfulness of detention tested 'speedily by a court' and to compensation for unlawful detention, respectively. The procedural safeguard in Art 5(3) applies to those arrested or detained under Art 5(1)(c), but not to those detained under Art 5(1)(f).

particularly relating to the accessibility, precision, and foreseeability of the standards and procedures governing detention.[54] On occasion, the requirement of legality encompasses more general concerns relating to detention conditions, such as when detention of vulnerable individuals or children is at issue.[55] 'In accordance with law' has a further, somewhat latent significance under the ECHR: where the State has additional obligations under EU law and potentially other international legal norms, these are liable to be incorporated into the notion of 'in accordance with law'.[56] Accordingly, there is much potential to read other legal standards into the ECtHR's rule of law conception.

The ECtHR frequently finds violations of Article 5(1) for lack of adherence to rule of law criteria.[57] Some cases concern egregious breaches of domestic law: in *Riad and Idiab v Belgium*, the respondent State kept the applicants in detention despite two domestic court rulings to release them, rendering the detention unlawful under the ECHR also.[58] The ECtHR has found repeated serious infractions of the requirement of legality by Turkey,[59] Malta,[60] and Russia.[61] The ECtHR also scrutinizes conformity with domestic law with increasing intensity, at times effectively finding that the domestic courts have erred in their application of domestic law. In *Rusu v Austria*,[62] the Court ensured strict adherence with the necessity

[54] *Amuur v France* (1996) 22 EHRR 533, para 10.

[55] *Muskhadzhiyeva v Belgium* App No 41442/07 (ECHR, 19 January 2010); *Mayeka v Belgium* (n 12).

[56] In *Mendizabal v France* App No 51431/99 (ECHR, 17 January 2006), the ECtHR treated the EU right of residence of a Spanish national in France as an aspect of its Article 8 ECHR legal patrimony.

[57] See *Shamsa v Poland* App No 45355/99 (ECHR, 27 November 2003); *John v Greece* App No 199/05 (ECHR, 10 May 2007); *Soldatenko v Ukraine* App No 2440/07 (ECHR, 23 October 2008); *Al-Agha v Romania* App No 40933/02 (ECHR, 12 January 2010).

[58] *Riad and Idiab v Belgium* App No 29787/03 & 29810/03 (ECHR, 24 January 2008), paras 74–76.

[59] See *Abdolkhani and Karimnia v Turkey* App No 30471/08 (ECHR, 22 September 2009); *ZNS v Turkey* App No 21896/08 (ECHR, 19 January 2010); *Dbouba v Turkey* App No 15916/09 (ECHR, 13 July 2010); *Tehrani v Turkey* App No 32940/08 (ECHR, 13 April 2010). Flynn reports that 'Turkey has refused to acknowledge, despite successive legal rulings against it, that its systematic confinement of irregular migrants in so-called guesthouses amounts to deprivation of liberty'. M Flynn, 'Immigration Detention and Proportionality' (2011) Global Detention Project Working Paper No 4, 8.

[60] See *Ali v Malta* (2002) 34 EHRR 26; *Kadem v Malta* App No 55263/00 (ECHR, 9 January 2003); *Massoud v Malta* App No 24340/08 (ECHR, 27 July 2010). It appears that Malta continued to detain asylum seekers automatically, notwithstanding these rulings. See Council of Europe, *Report by Thomas Hammarberg, Commissioner for Human Rights of the Council of Europe, following his visit to Malta from 23 to 25 March 2011*, CommDH(2011)17 (Council of Europe 9 June 2011).

[61] See *Garabayev v Russia* App No 38411/02 (ECHR, 7 June 2007); *Nasrulloyev v Russia* App No 656/06 (ECHR, 11 October 2007); *Muminov v Russia* App No 42502/06 (ECHR, 11 December 2008); *Nolan v Russia* App No 2512/04 (ECHR, 12 February 2009); *Yuldashev v Russia* App No 1248/09 (ECHR, 8 July 2010); *Isakov v Russia* App No 14049/08 (ECHR, 8 July 2010); *Iskandarov v Russia* App No 17185/05 (ECHR, 23 September 2010); *Sultanov v Russia* App No 15303/09 (ECHR, 4 November 2010).

[62] *Rusu v Austria* App No 34082/02 (ECHR, 2 October 2008), para 48. For a discussion, see N Mole and C Meredith, *Asylum and the European Convention on Human Rights* (Council of Europe 2010) 158–61. For an intense review of the application of domestic law, see *Jusic v Switzerland* App No 4691/06 (ECHR, 2 December 2010).

test in the applicable domestic law, although the Court does not incorporate this standard into its own requirements for Article 5(1)(f) detention.[63] Other cases push the notion of 'lawfulness' even further. For instance, in a case in which the decision to detain was ostensibly based on national security concerns, the Court deemed the detention to be unlawful as no specific allegations or charges were brought against the applicants, notwithstanding that the detention was authorized under published law.[64] In *Lokpo & Touré v Hungary*,[65] the detention of asylum seekers was deemed unlawful due to the authority's failure to make a reasoned decision to continue detention: Mere acquiescence ('non-action'[66] or 'mere silence'[67]) in the continued detention was deemed insufficient to meet the requirement of legality.[68] Although the legislation in question was adopted to give effect to the EU Asylum Procedures Directive (PD),[69] the ECtHR did not take the opportunity to condemn the detention as unlawful even though it appeared to violate the EU measure's requirement that detention not be for the 'sole reason'[70] that the applicants were asylum seekers. This failure is regrettable, as one of the most straightforward interfaces between EU and ECHR norms is that where they bind the State concerned, they form part of its legal patrimony that should be enforced under the ECHR's legality criteria.

## 2. Deportation to prevent unauthorized entry: Statism writ large

Article 5(1)(f) ECHR permits detention to prevent unauthorized entry. The leading case is *Saadi v UK*.[71] The applicant was an Iraqi doctor who claimed asylum on arrival to the UK at Heathrow Airport. At that point, he was temporarily released

[63] See Section 3.

[64] See *Al-Agha v Romania* App No 40933/02 (ECHR, 12 January 2010); *Ahmed v Romania* App No 34621/03 (ECHR, 13 July 2010). In both rulings, the Court emphasized that national security grounds needed particular safeguards against abuse, in particular to ensure effective judicial protection, lest '*sous le couvert de défendre la démocratie, de telles mesures risquent de la saper, voire de la détruire*' ('under the guise of defending democracy, these measures risk undermine it, even destroying it'). *Al-Agha*, para 90 and *Ahmed* para 33, quoting *Rotaru v Romania* (2000) 8 BHRC 449.

[65] *Lokpo & Touré v Hungary* App No 10816/10 (ECHR, 20 September 2011) paras 16–24.

[66] ibid, para 23. [67] ibid, para 24.

[68] *Lokpo* (n 65). But cf Jočienė and Björgvinsson JJ, dissenting, arguing that the Court had strayed too far into the interpretation of national law, and that the continued detention should be assumed to be on the same grounds as the initial one—and if there was a deficit of judicial scrutiny, this might have been raised as an issue under Art 5(4) ECHR, but had not been.

[69] Council Directive 2005/85/EC of 1 December 2005 on minimum standards on procedures in Member States for granting and withdrawing refugee status (APD) [2005] OJ L326/13. This directive has been recast by Directive 2013/32/EU of the European Parliament and of the Council of 26 June 2013 on common procedures for granting and withdrawing international protection (RAPD) [2013] L180/60.

[70] Art 26(1) Recast PD.

[71] *Saadi v United Kingdom* [GC] (2008) 47 EHRR 17. See generally V Moreno-Lax, 'Beyond *Saadi v UK*: The "Necessity" Requirement for Administrative Detention of Asylum Seekers in the EU' (2010) Reflexive Governance in the Pub. Interest, Working Paper No. REFGOV-FR-31; H O'Nions 'No Right to Liberty: The Detention of Asylum Seekers for Administrative Convenience' (2008) 10 EJML 149.

and requested to return to the airport immigration authorities. He complied with the request, and four days later was detained and transferred to a detention centre. The real reason for detention, in fact the entire institutional rationale for the particular detention centre, was to facilitate fast-track processing of claims.[72]

The central premise of the majority in the Grand Chamber was that detention of those whose entry had not been authorized was a 'necessary adjunct' to the 'undeniable sovereign right to control aliens' entry into and residence in their territory.'[73] This 'necessary adjunct' imports the statist assumption into detention practices. The Court also imported the rejection of a necessity test from the case law on pre-deportation detention, in particular *Chahal* discussed in the next section. The next move in the reasoning places asylum seekers and other migrants in a legally naked position: until a State has formally authorized entry, 'any entry [was] "unauthorized" '.[74] Accordingly, the detention of anyone seeking entry who did not yet have the requisite authorization fell under Article 5(1)(f) ECHR.[75] However, the Court was at pains to stress that the State did not dispose of an open-ended right to detain, and so it tailored four context-specific requirements to avoid arbitrariness. Detention must be (1) carried out in good faith; (2) closely connected to the purpose of preventing unauthorized entry of the person; (3) in an appropriate place and under appropriate conditions bearing in mind that the detainee has not 'committed criminal offences' but rather may have fled fearing for his life; and (4) the length of the detention should not exceed that reasonably required for the purpose pursued.[76] Applying these criteria to the facts, the majority held that seven days in a 'specifically adapted' place of detention was not arbitrary, in light of the difficult administrative problems that confronted the UK during the period in question.[77]

The partly dissenting opinion of Judges Rozakis, Tulkens, Kovler, Hajiyev, Spielmann, and Hirvelä set out powerful counterarguments, urging greater fidelity to other IHRL standards. First, they noted that the majority failed to distinguish between different categories of migrants, subjecting them all to the 'States unlimited sovereignty'.[78] The dissenters viewed the majority's treatment of detention as the adjunct of sovereign entry control as sitting 'uncomfortably with the principle that asylum seekers who have presented a claim for international protection are *ipso facto* lawfully within the territory of a State…'[79] It should be noted that the majority and the minority cite the HRC for authority of this proposition.[80] Dismissing the notion of a statist *carte blanche* to deem any entry unauthorized, they found that in the particular case it had 'in no sense been

[72] Saadi (n 71), paras 23–25.

[73] ibid, para 64; citing *Amuur v France*, para 43; *Abdulaziz, Cabales and Balkandali v United Kingdom* (1985) 7 EHRR 471, paras 67–68; *Chahal v United Kingdom* [GC] (1997) 23 EHRR 413, para 73.

[74] ibid, para 65. [75] ibid. [76] ibid, para 74. [77] ibid, para 80.

[78] ibid, Dissenting Opinion of Judges Rozakis, Tulkens, Kovler, Hajiyev, Spielmann, and Hirvelä, 32.

[79] ibid, 31.

[80] ibid, Dissenting Opinion of Judges Rozakis, Tulkens, Kovler, Hajiyev, Spielmann, and Hirvelä, 32, 35 citing HRC, *Celepli v Sweden*, Communcation No 456/1991 (HRC, 26 July 1994).

established in the present case, as the applicant did not enter or attempt to enter the country unlawfully.'[81] On this point, the dissenters were in a difficult position, because if they deemed *all* asylum seekers to be lawful entrants in all circumstances, then the State would have little power to detain them under Article 5(1)(f). In a deft move then, the suggestion is that asylum seekers be treated as having a purpose-specific temporary admission. Accordingly, while it is not permissible to detain 'refugees on the sole ground that they have made a claim for asylum', where evidence exists that they may abscond before the claim is determined, then detention would be permissible. In contrast, the UK's detention of Saadi was explicitly for the purpose of making the asylum determination process more efficient. The dissenters deemed that rationale improper, in terms worth setting out in full:

> [N]ot just in the context of asylum but also in other situations involving deprivation of liberty, to maintain that detention is in the interests of the person concerned appears to us an exceedingly dangerous stance to adopt. Furthermore, to contend in the present case that detention is in the interests not merely of the asylum seekers themselves 'but of those increasingly in the queue' is equally unacceptable. In no circumstances can the end justify the means; no person, no human being may be used as a means towards an end.[82]

Under the majority's approach, the asylum seeker 'becomes an object rather than a subject of law'.[83]

On the application of the test to the facts, they further questioned how to determine how long detention might last: if seven days was reasonable, 'where and how do we draw the line for what is unacceptable?'[84] The dissenters also took issue with the failure to examine alternatives to detention as part of the non-arbitrariness assessment.[85]

Of central interest for present purposes is the approach of the minority to IHRL more generally. The minority also noted that the ECHR '[does] not apply in a vacuum',[86] setting out the key HRC jurisprudence[87] and EU norms, noting that Article 18(1) of the PD [Article 26(1) Recast PD], precluding detention for the 'sole reason' of being a refugee, should be regarded as 'the minimum guarantee'.[88] On the majority's lack of fidelity to the other international standards, described as the 'crux of the matter,' the minority opinion ends with the following stinging rebuke:

> Ultimately, are we now also to accept that Article 5 [of the ECHR], which has played a major role in ensuring controls of arbitrary detention, should afford a lower level of protection as regards asylum and immigration which, in social and human terms, are the most crucial issues facing us in the years to come? Is it a crime to be a foreigner? We do not think so.[89]

The Council of Europe's Parliamentary Assembly criticized the *Saadi* judgment. First, the interpretation of 'unauthorized entry' meant that the State could detain

[81] ibid, Dissenting Opinion of Judges Rozakis, Tulkens, Kovler, Hajiyev, Spielmann, and Hirvelä in *Saadi*, 33.
[82] ibid. [83] ibid, 34. [84] ibid. [85] ibid. [86] ibid.
[87] ibid, 34–35. [88] ibid, 35. [89] ibid.

'ad infinitum'.[90] Secondly, it was in 'blatant conflict' with the UNHCR guidelines on detention in allowing detention throughout the entire asylum process.[91] The PACE Rapporteur called on the Court to re-examine its case law 'taking fully into account other international sources of law and views of the international community'.[92] There is an alternative: in *Mariel Cubans,*[93] the Inter-American Commission on Human Rights held that the US approach in that instance, which treated 'aliens' as 'paroled' in the country, was to implement a system where they are legally constructed as 'always at the border seeking admission... never having entered the USA'. This was found to lead to a 'presumption of detention rather than a presumption of liberty... fundamentally antithetical' to Article I (liberty), XXV (protection against arbitrary arrest and detention) of the ADHR. The *Saadi* approach to 'unauthorized' entry has the same structure, and is vulnerable to this same critique.

Since *Saadi*, the Court has come back to the issue of detention to prevent unauthorized entry in *Rusu v Austria*. As outlined, in *Rusu* the detention was deemed arbitrary mainly due to the failure to adhere to the Austrian domestic legal standards, in particular its necessity test. However, the Court also emphasized that it was implausible on the facts to treat the applicant as attempting to effectuate an unauthorized entry, when she was in fact trying to leave Austria. This ruling may signal a more intense judicial review of both adherence to domestic standards and the factual matrix surrounding the claim of unauthorized entry.[94] Crucially, if 'unauthorized entry' is a mixed issue of fact and law, doesn't that open it up for full scrutiny?

In *Musa v Malta,*[95] the Court applied *Saadi v UK*, and condemned the Maltese detention practices as 'arbitrary',[96] mainly due to the unsuitable place and conditions of detention. So far, so orthodox. In addition, though, it stated that there was 'some merit' to the applicants' argument that if asylum seekers are authorized in their stay (either under national or EU law), then there is no lawful basis for their detention under Article 5(1)(f).[97] This move seems irresistible under EU law, given the PD and Recast PD's clear statement of the right to reside of the asylum seeker. Indeed, the CJEU has emphasized this right of residence in *Arslan,* in distinguishing the scope of application of the RD and the RRCD.[98] If my reading is correct, asylum seekers should not be regarded as 'effectuating unauthorized entry' once they have entered the asylum process.

[90] Mendonça (n 3) 19. [91] ibid. [92] ibid, 21.

[93] Report No 51/01, Case 9903 Rafael Ferrer-Mazorra et al (Mariel Cubans), (IACHR 4 April 2001).

[94] See Mole and Meredith (n 62) 151, pointing out that *Rusu* is a Chamber judgment delivered by seven judges, four of whom had been dissenters in *Saadi v United Kingdom*, and two of whom had voted with the majority; see also Cornelisse (n 22) 312, suggesting that this 'one case' where the court closely analysed the proportionality of the detention was striking in that it concerned 'a person who was not at all "out of place" in the global territorial ideal, but instead on her way back to the country where she "belonged"'.

[95] [2013] ECHR 721. [96] ibid, para 105. [97] ibid, para 97.

[98] Case C-534/11 *Arslan* [2013] OJ C 225/13. See Part V.2.i.

This would mean either that there is no power at all to detain asylum seekers as a category (a conclusion which admittedly many governments might baulk at), or that the only detention power would have to be justified under the stricter conditions of Article 5(1)(b) ECHR, which permits detention 'to secure the fulfilment of any obligation prescribed by law'. The case law on that provision is highly instructive, given that it illustrates how detention is only permissible (indeed rational) to induce compliance with legal requirements in carefully defined situations.[99]

## 3. Pre-deportation detention: The rejection of a test of 'reasonable necessity'

The leading case on pre-deportation detention is *Chahal v UK*. The Court stated in *Chahal*, and has reiterated since, that Article 5(1)(f) ECHR 'does not demand that the detention of a person against whom action is being taken with a view to deportation be reasonably considered necessary, for example to prevent his committing an offence or fleeing…'[100] The only requirement was that the individual face deportation. Whether the underlying decision to expel could be justified under national or ECHR law was even deemed immaterial for the purposes of Article 5(1)(f).[101] Having rejected the criterion of 'reasonable necessity,' the Court asserted that detention was only lawful as long as deportation proceedings were in progress and prosecuted with 'due diligence'.[102] Strikingly, the Court held that detention while the asylum claim was still being assessed fell under Article 5(1)(f),[103] a position from which it has now resiled, as discussed later. By thirteen votes to six, it found no violation of Article 5(1), but unanimously found a violation of Article 5(4), as the domestic courts were unable to conduct a proper review due to the national security constraints on them.

The Court is increasingly insistent that States demonstrate that deportation must be a realistic prospect. If removal is not feasible due to the absence of travel documents, for example, detention will not be justified.[104] The Grand Chamber ruled in *A v UK* on the detention of foreign terrorist suspects.[105] The Court accepted that they were non-removable under the ECHR standards, due to human rights concerns in their countries of origin. Nonetheless, the UK sought to justify their detention under Article 5(1)(f) as it was keeping the possibility of removal 'under active review'.[106] The Court rejected the UK's argument, as this review was not

[99] See, e.g. *Vasileva v Denmark* (2005) 40 EHRR 27; *Ostendorf v Germany* [2013] ECHR 197. This is an argument I develop in C Costello, 'Immigration Detention: The Grounds Beneath our Feet' (2015) 68(1) Current Legal Problems 143.

[100] *Chahal* (n 73) para 112.

[101] ibid.

[102] ibid, para 113. See also *Quinn v France* [1995] ECHR 9, para 48; *Singh v Czech Republic* App No 60538/00 (ECHR, 25 January 2005), para 61.

[103] *Chahal* (n 73) paras 115–16.

[104] See *Ali v Switzerland* (1998) 28 EHRR 304, para 12; *Mikolenko v Estonia*, 8 October 2009 [2009] ECHR 1471, para 10; *Raza v Bulgaria* App No 31465/08 (ECHR, 11 February 2010), paras 11 and 16.

[105] *A and others v UK* [GC] (2009) 49 EHRR 29.

[106] ibid, para 167.

'sufficiently certain or determinative to amount to 'action…being taken with a view to deportation'.[107] The Grand Chamber distinguished *Chahal,* stating that in the earlier case proceedings were being 'actively and diligently pursued' in order to determine whether removal would violate Article 3 ECHR.[108] In contrast, in *A and Others*, the proceedings concerned the legality of detention, the prohibition of deportation having been conceded.[109]

The position of asylum seekers is precarious. It is arguable that in order to comply with the CSR and the ECHR *non-refoulement* guarantees, they cannot be removed until their claims have been fully examined, and so should be regarded as temporarily lawfully present. Where domestic law reflects this position, the Court has held that asylum seekers are not lawfully in pre-deportation detention, as is seen in *SD v Greece* and *RU v Greece.* These cases are in tension with *Chahal* because, in the earlier case, the period in detention as an asylum seeker was deemed to be lawful pre-deportation detention.[110] That position seems to no longer hold, as the ECtHR in the later cases took into account Greece's obligations under Articles 31 to 33 CSR, in interpreting Article 5(1)(f) ECHR.[111]

## 4. Assessment of the Strasbourg case law

Overall, the bulk of the cases are decided on legality criteria, reflecting at least in part the types of violations coming before the ECtHR, wherein States have internalized the statist assumption, and erroneously regarded their own prerogatives as not requiring legal authority in the normal sense. Yet, it also reflects a choice on the part of the ECtHR to emphasize the domestic protection of rights. However, without clear ECtHR review of the purposes and necessity of detention, domestic law and rule of law criteria may offer little protection in practice.

The two weak points in the Strasbourg case law are the approach to the determination of 'unauthorised entry' under *Saadi* and the loose nexus required between deportation and detention in *Chahal* (which admittedly has been tightened up of late, as evidenced in its influence on the View of AG Szpunar in CJEU ruling in *Mahdi).* On unauthorized entry, the notion of the State's *carte blanche* to authorize entry is also ill fitting when legal authority is exercised at different levels. The CSR, and the EU law giving effect to it, clearly envisages asylum seekers as temporarily authorized entrants, as are many other categories of individuals who enjoy rights of entry and residence under EU and domestic law. For a court of IHRL to ignore these obligations is to treat States as plenipotentiaries over a matter that they have already ceded discretion. Strasbourg moved in the right direction in *RU v Greece*

[107] ibid. [108] ibid, para 169. [109] ibid, paras 169–70.

[110] *Lokpo & Touré v Hungary* (n 65) para 16, noting that it was common ground between the parties that the applicants, albeit asylum seekers, were being detained with a view to deportation.

[111] *SD v Greece* App No 53541/07 (ECHR, 11 June 2009), referring specifically to the fact that *national law* precluded detention unless the deportation was executable; see also *RU v Greece* App No 2237/08 (ECHR, 7 June 2011), paras 95–96, noting that both national law and the CSR prevented removal and that, accordingly, the detention was not lawful under domestic law.

and *SD v Greece,* but regrettably did not engage with the question of EU standards in *Lokpo & Touré v Hungary*. In *Muso v Malta*, it indicated, importantly, that this argument about the authorized status of asylum seekers had 'some merit', but the case was decided on other grounds. Indeed, given that it is often faced with blatant breaches of domestic law and inhuman detention conditions, it decides most detention cases without breaking any new legal ground, understandable given its minimalist reflexes.

On the deportation-detention nexus, by rejecting the necessity test, the Court explicitly sets a lower standard of protection for immigration detention than for other forms.[112] The 'necessary adjunct' construct in fact allowed States to transplant the degree of discretion they (putatively) disposed of over admission to the territory to another domain, detention. It would be appropriate for the ECtHR to take a prompt from the HRC jurisprudence and EU norms, and read requirements of necessity and proportionality into Article 5(1)(f) ECHR. Normally under the ECHR, rights restrictions must be proportionate,[113] meaning that the restriction must be suitable to achieve the particular legitimate aim. Thus necessary and proportionate are used in the strict sense, which involves examining alternative less rights-intrusive means. Such is the 'ubiquity of proportionality analysis'[114] that some defend as *the* central principle of human rights adjudication.[115] Without necessarily endorsing that view, for the ECtHR to be textually faithful to Article 5, the ECHR requires it to insist on finite permissible grounds for detention. But the failure to insist on the appropriate demonstrable link between the detention in question and the ground in question (be it to effectuate deportation *or* to prevent unauthorized entry) renders the limitation on legitimate grounds of detention hollow.

Constructive human rights pluralism is evident in the minority opinion in *Saadi*. The minority opinion shows that appropriate engagement with the external standards of the HRC and CSR, would have led to a different result. Strasbourg's failure to engage with the ICCPR standards in all of its immigration detention cases is striking.[116]

[112] See Cornelisse (n 22) 279, 305–08, comparing case law under Art 5(1)(e), which concerns 'the lawful detention of persons for the prevention of the spreading of infectious diseases, of persons of unsound mind, alcoholics or drug addicts, or vagrants', with that of Art 5(1)(f)).

[113] Art 8-11 ECHR. Admittedly, there is often a textual basis, as the restrictions in question must be 'necessary in a democratic society' under the relevant Convention articles. However, the principle is built into the structure of analysis beyond those provisions as well.

[114] M Kumm, 'The Idea of Socratic Contestation and the Right to Justification: The Point of Rights-Based Proportionality Review' (2010) 4 Law & Ethics of Human Rights 140, 142.

[115] See D Beatty, *The Ultimate Rule of Law* (OUP 2004) 187. See generally R Alexy, *A Theory of Constitutional Rights* (OUP 2002).

[116] See I Bryan and P Langford, 'The Lawful Detention of Unauthorised Aliens under the European System for the Protection of Human Rights' (2011) 80 Nordic Journal of International Law 193, 203–04.

## V. EU Law

This section examines the two types of immigration detention covered expressly by EU Directives, that of asylum seekers and that of TCNs facing deportation.

### 1. Detention of asylum seekers

The original RCD and PD made references to detention.[117] The Recast RCD contains much more detailed detention provisions[118]. In addition, the Dublin III Regulation, the latest revision of the Dublin Regulation, contains a detailed detention provision.[119] At present, the Regulation does not contain any provisions on detention, but in practice it is seen to have contributed to the increase in detention of asylum seekers across Europe, as it increases the cohort of asylum seekers who are amenable to removal before the claims have been processed.[120]

The original proposal for the RCD contained a detailed provision on detention,[121] largely modelled on UNHCR ExCom Committee Conclusion No 44.[122] However, negotiating wrangles produced oblique, piecemeal provisions instead. Article 7 of the RCD provides that '[a]sylum seekers may move freely within the territory of the host Member States'. However, Member States may decide on 'the residence of the asylum seeker for reasons of public interest, public order, or, when necessary, for the swift processing and effective monitoring of his or her application'.[123] This provision seems to fall far short of Article 26 CSR.[124]

On detention *stricto sensu*, Article 26(1) Recast PD states plainly that detention should not be for the sole reason that the individual is an applicant for asylum. Article 7(3) RCD states that '[w]hen it proves necessary, for example for legal reasons or reasons of public order, Member States may confine an applicant to a particular place in accordance with their national law.' Here we find the necessity criterion that is absent in the Strasbourg case law.[125] However, the guarantee is

[117] For analysis of both, see D Wilsher, 'Immigration Detention and the Common European Asylum Policy' in A Baldaccini, E Guild, and H Toner (eds), *Whose Freedom, Security and Justice? EU Immigration and Asylum Law after 1999* (Hart Publishing 2007) 418–25; K Hailbronner, 'Detention of Asylum Seekers' (2007) 9 EJML 159, 169.

[118] Arts 8–11 RRCD.

[119] Regulation (EU) No 604/2013 of the European Parliament and of the Council of 26 June 2013 establishing the criteria and mechanisms for determining the Member State responsible for examining an application for international protection lodged in one of the Member States by a third-country national or stateless person (recast) (Dublin III Regulation) [2013] OJ L180/31, Art 28.

[120] For some qualitative evidence, see Jesuit Refugee Services, *Dublin II: A Summary of JRS Experiences in Europe* (JRS October 2008); JRS, *Protection Interrupted: The Dublin Regulation's Impact on Asylum Seekers' Protection* (JRS June 2013).

[121] European Commission, *Proposal for a Council Directive laying down minimum standards for the reception of asylum seekers*, COM(2001) 181, Art 7(2).

[122] See generally UNHCR, ExCom Conclusion No 44 (XXXVII) 1986. See also Wilsher (n 117) 422.

[123] Art 7(2) RCD.

[124] Marx (n 38) 1163–64.

[125] See generally Moreno-Lax (n 71).

undermined by the vague open-ended grounds expressed as, 'for example for legal reasons or reasons of public order'. The vagueness of these grounds sits uneasily with the approach of the HRC, in particular. The border procedures provision in Article 43 Recast PD seems to envisage confinement of asylum seekers at the border for a prolonged period of up to four weeks, detention in all but name.

The provisions were terse, and so in some ways, replete with transformative potential. The RAPD recognizes the right of the asylum seeker to be on the territory of the Member States,[126] subject to exceptions for persons who make subsequent applications[127] and for certain categories of appeals.[128] On this basis alone, it seems difficult for an EU Member State to treat asylum seekers' presence as unauthorized; at the very least the approach of the minority in *Saadi* would have to be applied. Similarly, asylum seekers could not be normally regarded as in pre-deportation detention, following the approach in *RU v Greece* and *SD v Greece*. The remaining leeway to detain asylum seekers is accordingly diminished, and would require some infraction on the part of the individual asylum seeker in order to render his or her stay unauthorized. Even in that instance, the detention would need to be demonstrated as a necessary means to achieve the particular legitimate aim in view. Proportionality, encompassing the three elements of suitability, necessity, and least restrictive means, is a ubiquitous feature of EU law.[129] The building blocks for a new, more rigorous adjudicatory framework are contained in these terse rules. Before that potential could be exploited, which would have depended on suitably crafted references from national courts coming before the CJEU, the process of legislative revision intervened.

The RRCD contains more elaborate rules on the detention of asylum seekers. Article 8(1) RRCD reiterates the prohibition on detaining an asylum seeker 'for the sole reason' of applying for international protection, referring to Article 26(1) RAPD. Detention is permissible only 'when it proves necessary and on the basis of an individual assessment of each case', and if less coercive alternatives cannot be applied.[130] Member States are required by the RRCD to lay down in their

[126] Art 9(1) Recast PD: 'Applicants shall be allowed to remain in the Member State, for the sole purpose of the procedure, until the determining authority has made a decision in accordance with the procedures at first instance set out in Chapter III. This right to remain shall not constitute an entitlement to a residence permit.' See also Recital 9 RD: 'In accordance with [APD] a third-country national who has applied for asylum in a Member State should not be regarded as staying illegally on the territory of that Member State until a negative decision on the application, or a decision ending his or her right of stay as asylum seeker has entered into force'.

[127] Arts 9(2) and 41 Recast PD.

[128] Art 46(6) Recast PD. However, the case law of the ECtHR requires suspensive effect of appeals to vindicate Articles 3 (where such risks pertain) and 13 ECHR. See *Gebremedhin v France* App No 25389/05 (ECHR, 26 April 2007), para 34. See also T Spijkerboer, 'Subsidiarity and "Arguability": the European Court of Human Rights' Case Law on Judicial Review in Asylum Cases' (2009) 21 IJRL 48, 69–73.

[129] Proportionality is a general principle of EU law. In addition, the EUCFR contains a general limitation clause in Art 52(1). See Art 52(1) EUCFR, which states '[a]ny limitation on the exercise of the rights and freedoms recognised by this Charter must be provided for by law and respect the essence of those rights and freedoms. Subject to the *principle of proportionality*, limitations may be made only if they are *necessary* and genuinely meet objectives of general interest recognised by the Union or the need to protect the rights and freedoms of others.' (emphasis added).

[130] Art 8(2) Recast RCD.

national law rules concerning alternatives to detention such as 'regular reporting to the authorities, the deposit of a financial guarantee, or an obligation to stay at an assigned place.'[131] Moreover, Article 8(3) sets out six exhaustive grounds for detention: (a) determining the applicant's identity or nationality; (b) determining elements of the claim, particularly where there is a risk of absconding, (c) determining the applicant's right to enter, (d) preventing an applicant from delaying or frustrating a return procedure under the RD, (e) on national security or public order considerations, or (f) under a Dublin procedure, where detention is only permissible to prevent a 'significant risk of absconding'.[132] While specifying grounds, together with the necessity and ATD requirement, seems likely to constrain detention, much will depend on the standard of review and institutional practice. The most problematic ground is '(c) determining the applicant's right to enter'. It is unclear what this means, and what assessment could be in mind, other than the determination of the claim which is referred to in '(b) determining the elements of the claim'. Specifying absconding risk not as a ground, but rather an element of detention to determine the asylum claim, seems problematic also, given that detention is liable to impede access to the sorts of information, support, and advice that facilitates the open communication and trust that is a necessary feature of reliable refugee status determination. Including such an expansive list leaves it to the judges to interpret the necessity of detention on these wide grounds.

The Dublin System, as mentioned, sets up further incentives and opportunities for detention. As asylum seekers become deportable under the Dublin System, they may be detained in order to facilitate that removal. In practice, asylum seekers may resist Dublin removals, for good reasons in light of the human rights shortcomings detailed in Chapter 5. The categorization of Dublin detention illustrates tensions between the ECHR and the EU framework, and indeed the perspective of UNHCR. Strasbourg's ruling in *RU v Greece* deemed asylum seekers as falling outside pre-deportation detention, but left the relationship between 'Dubliners' and the ECHR in other respects unclear. For UNHCR, asylum seekers transferred back under the Dublin Regulation should not be detained, as they cannot be regarded as unauthorized entrants in the receiving State, contrary to the practices of some States such as Bulgaria. [133] The position of those awaiting transfer to other Dublin States ought to be treated similarly, and as long as their substantive asylum claims are yet to be determined, they cannot be held in pre-deportation detention, a view endorsed by the ECtHR and national courts increasingly.[134]

As far as grounds for Dublin detention are concerned, Article 28 of the Dublin III Regulation does not clarify whether 'significant risk of absconding' is the only

[131] Art 8(3) RRCD. [132] Art 28(2) Dublin III Regulation.

[133] UNHCR, *Submission of UNHCR in the Case of Said v Hungary (Application No. 13457/11)* (UNHCR, 2012) 8–9.

[134] See, e.g. *BGH, Beschluss vom 26. 6. 2014—V ZB 31/14*; *LG Saarbrücken*, where the Administrative Court of Saarbrucken held that the criteria for pre-deportation detention cannot be used for the purpose of Dublin detention. (With many thanks to Minos Mouzourakis for providing this reference.)

ground for detention. Given that Article 28(1) prohibits detention on the sole ground that an applicant is subject to a Dublin procedure, however, one would assume that the Regulation has exhaustively defined the grounds of detention.[135] Yet, even detention on that limited ground could sit uneasily with the ECHR provisions, if 'Dubliners' are neither unauthorized entrants nor deportees.

## 2. Pre-deportation detention and the CJEU detention rulings

The RD sets out rules governing the conditions and procedures for the return (i.e., deportation) of illegal TCNs.[136] Once a Member State deems someone 'illegal' in their residence, the RD sets out 'a horizontal set of rules, applicable to *all* [TCNs] who do not or who no longer fulfil the conditions for entry, stay or residence in a Member State'.[137] Like the asylum directives, it took prolonged negotiations to reach agreement on the RD, though involving the European Parliament as a co-legislator.[138] Some of the standards in the RD are lamentably low, prompting a broad-based international campaign against its adoption, during which it was condemned as a 'shameful' and 'outrageous' measure.[139] The eighteen-month outer time limit for detention has been the focus of the most criticism.[140] While Member States are not obliged to permit such long detention, in practice several

[135] ibid.

[136] For detailed analysis, see A Baldaccini, 'The Return and Removal of Irregular Migrants under EU Law: An Analysis of the Returns Directive' (2009) 11 EJML 1. See also A Baldaccini, 'The EU Directive on Return: Principles and Protest' (2010) 28 RSQ 114; M Schieffer, 'Chapter V. Termination of Residence' in K Hailbronner (ed), *EU Immigration and Asylum Law: Commentary on EU Regulations and Directives* (Beck and Hart Publishing 2010).

[137] Recital 5 RD.

[138] See generally D Acosta, 'The Good, the Bad and the Ugly in EU Migration Law: Is the European Parliament Becoming Bad and Ugly?' (2009) 11 EJML 19 (discussing the different steps in the adoption of the Directive); see also F Lutz, *The Negotiations on the Return Directive: Comments and Materials* (Wolf Legal Publishers 2010); A Ripoll Servent, 'The European Parliament and the Returns Directive: The End of Radical Contestation; The Start of Consensual Constraints' in B Anderson, MJ Gibney, and E Paoletti (eds), *The Social, Political and Historical Contours of Deportation* (Springer 2013).

[139] See, e.g., 'No to the Outrageous Directive', Document prepared by 14 European pro-migrant NGOs, subsequently supported by 400 European organizations and more than 8000 citizens. <http://www.statewatch.org/news/2007/dec/eu-returns-ngo-compilation.pdf> accessed 12 April 2015. See also European Council on Refugees and Exiles (ECRE), *Returns Directive: EU Fails to Uphold Human Rights*, Press Release (2008); UNHCR, *UNHCR Position on the Proposal for a Directive on Common Standards and Procedures in Member States for Returning Illegally Staying Third-Country Nationals* (UNHCR, June 2008); UN, 'UN experts express concern about proposed EU Return Directive' *UN Press Release* (18 July 2008).

[140] See, e.g., PACE, Resolution 1707 (2010), para 5. 'The European Union Return Directive, which provides for a maximum length of detention for irregular migrants of up to eighteen months, can be criticised for adopting the lowest common standard with regard to length of detention...and increasing the possibility for states to increase their minimum duration of detention.' WGAD (n 14), para 56: 'The Working Group has also publicly expressed, together with other mandate holders of special procedures, its concern regarding a law-making initiative of a regional organization comprising mainly receiving countries which would allow concerned States to detain immigrants who are in an irregular situation for a period of time of up to 18 months, pending removal. It would also be permitted to detain unaccompanied children, victims of human trafficking, and other vulnerable groups.'

have increased detention times in implementing the Directive.[141] Further, re-entry bans reinforce the impression of a repressive measure.[142]

Yet, the RD integrates human rights principles,[143] in particular the principle of proportionality.[144] It aims to encourage voluntary return, so the coercive moves to detain and deport may only be engaged after a waiting period.[145] The preamble cites the Council of Europe's Twenty Guidelines on Forced Return.[146] Concerning detention, Recital 16 RD provides:

> The use of detention for the purpose of removal should be limited and subject to the principle of proportionality with regard to the means used and objectives pursued. Detention is justified only to prepare the return or carry out the removal process and if the application of less coercive measures would not be sufficient.

Article 15 RD requires that detention only be used as a last resort, for as short a period as possible, with the specific purpose of preparing and carrying out the return process and crucially for as long as it is 'necessary to ensure successful removal'. Two specific purposes are given as examples of when detention would be necessary: when there is a risk of absconding, or when the individual concerned avoids or hampers the preparation of return or of the removal process. Reflective of the ECtHR case law, detention is only permissible 'as long as removal arrangements are in progress and executed with due diligence'.[147] In the absence of a 'reasonable prospect of removal', detention must cease.[148] The terms of Article 15 are clearly stricter than the ECtHR case law in incorporating a necessity requirement.

However, the impact of the implementation of the RD on the average length of detention across the Member States is highly variable. In its 2014 Communication *On EU Return Policy*, the European Commission noted wide disparities between EU countries, ranging from an average five to six days in Finland and seven days in the UK, to at least 180 days in Greece.[149] The Commission has in fact found that the implementation of the RD has led to longer outer detention time-limits in Greece, Spain, Finland, France, Italy, and Luxembourg; although Bulgaria, the Czech Republic, Denmark, Estonia, Lithuania, Latvia, Romania, Slovenia,

[141] See Flynn and Cannon (n 3), 5: 'Greece, Italy, and Spain have all increased detention times since adopting the Return Directive. A fourth country, Hungary, is set to double maximum detention terms when newly adopted legislation enters into force at the end of 2010.' For a detailed overview of detention time limits, see FRA (n 21), 31–35. On implementation more generally, see K Zwaan (ed), *The Returns Directive: Central Themes, Problem Issues, and Implementation in Selected Member States* (Wolf Legal Publishers 2011).

[142] Art 11 RD, explaining the issuing of entry bans.

[143] Recital 2 RD refers to 'full respect for…fundamental rights and dignity'; see also Recital 24 RD, asserting that 'This Directive respects the fundamental rights and observes the principles recognised in particular by the Charter of Fundamental Rights of the European Union.'

[144] Recital 13 and 16 RD.

[145] Recital 10 and Art 7 RD. The period envisaged is between seven and thirty days.

[146] Recital 3 RD. See also Council of Europe Committee of Ministers (n 17). On many contentious issues in the negotiations, the 'Twenty Guidelines on Forced Return' adopted by the Committee of Ministers of the Council of Europe provided compromise solutions. See Schieffer (n 136) 1506.

[147] Art 15(1) RD. [148] Art 15(4) RD.

[149] European Commission, *On EU Return Policy*, COM(2014) 199, 17.

Slovakia, and Norway have shortened their detention periods following the entry into force of the Directive.[150]

The CJEU has given eleven rulings on the legality of pre-deportation detention under the RD. *Kadzoev*,[151] and *Arslan*[152] dealt with the scope of the RD, in particular its interaction with detention of asylum seekers, while *Filev and Osmani*[153] considered the applicability of the RD in the context of re-entry bans. *El-Dridi*,[154] *Achughbabian*,[155] *Sagor*,[156] and *Mbaye*[157] clarify the pre-emptive relationship between pre-deportation detention and criminal incarceration for immigration reasons. *G and R*[158] and *Mahdi*[159] dealt with judicial control of the grounds of detention and extensions of detention, while *Bero and Bouzalmate*[160] and *Pham*[161] ruled on detention conditions. Several of the cases were decided under accelerated procedures,[162] the third under the ordinary accelerated procedure.[163]

### *i. The scope of the RD*

**Kadzoev, Arslan, and Filev and Osmani**

Kadzoev's prolonged detention in Bulgaria shows the sharp end of EU detention practices.[164] At the time of the reference, he had spent thirty-four months

[150] ibid, 20.

[151] Case C-357/09 PPU *Kadzoev* [2009] ECR I-11189. For analysis, E Mincheva, 'Case Report on *Kadzoev*, 30 November 2009' (2010) 12 EJML 361; G Cornelisse, 'Case Comment' (2011) 48 CMLRev 925.

[152] *Arslan* (n 98).

[153] Case C-297/12 *Filev & Osmani* [2013] OJ C 344/31.

[154] C-61/11 PPU *Hassen El-Dridi alias Karim Soufi* [2011] ECR I-3015. For analysis, see R Raffaelli, 'Criminalizing Irregular Immigration and the Returns Directive: An Analysis of the *El Dridi* Case' (2011) 13(4) *EJML* 467.

[155] Case C-329/11 *Alexandre Achughbabian v Préfet du Val-de-Marne* [2011] ECR I-12695. For analysis, see R Raffaelli, 'Case Note: The *Achughbabian* Case: Impact of the Return Directive on National Criminal Legislation' (2012) Diritto Penale Contemporaneo, available <http://ssrn.com/abstract=1998324> accessed 1 November 2015.

[156] Case C-430/11 *Sagor* [2013] OJ C 26/13.

[157] Case C-522/11 *Mbaye* [2013] OJ C 156/16.

[158] Case C-383/13 PPU *G and R* [2013] OJ C 325/8.

[159] Case C-146/14 PPU *Mahdi* [2014] OJ C 253/14. For analysis, see ML Basilien-Gainche, 'Judicial Control of Detention: A Deceptive Upheaval?' (*EU Law Analysis*, 10 June 2014) <http://eulawanalysis.blogspot.gr/2014/06/marie-laure-basilien-gainche.html> accessed 12 April 2015.

[160] Joined Cases C-473/13 and C-514/13 *Bero and Bouzalmate* [2014] OJ C 315/22.

[161] Case C-474/13 *Pham* [2014] OJ C 315/23.

[162] See Art 267 TFEU: 'If such a question is raised in a case pending before a court or tribunal of a Member State with regard to a person in custody, the Court of Justice of the European Union shall act with the minimum of delay.' See also Rules of Procedure of the Court of Justice [2012] OJ L265/1, Art 104b Rules of Procedure of the CJEU. For a general discussion, see C Barnard, 'The PPU: Is it Worth the Candle? An Early Assessment' (2009) 34 ELRev 281.

[163] Rules of Procedure of the Court of Justice [2012] OJ L265/1, Art 104a.

[164] Concerning his particular case, see Amnesty International, 'Bulgaria: Fear of forcible return/ fear of torture or ill-treatment: Said Kadzoev (m)' (2008) AI EUR/15/001/2008, <http://amnesty.org/en/library/asset/EUR15/001/2008/en/90cd1485-0d65-11dd-a114-e974a1f25b3e/eur150012008eng.pdf> accessed 12 April 2015. See also the complaint in the Report of the Special Rapporteur on torture and other cruel, inhuman or degrading treatment or punishment, Manfred Nowak, UN Doc A/HRC/10/44/Add4, 17 February 2009, 42. Concerning Detention Practices in General in Bulgaria, see V Ilareva, 'Bulgaria's Treatment of Asylum Seekers' (2007) 29 Forced Migration Review 60.

in detention, despite bringing unsuccessful asylum claims and judicial reviews in order to secure his release. The reference arose when the interior ministry requested a domestic court to rule *ex officio* on the duration of detention. The questions referred concerned the temporal and material scope of Article 15 RD in light of the particular facts of the case. The first two questions concerned the determination of which periods were covered by the prescribed maximum detention period. The first question concerned periods predating the Directive's entry into force, while the second question raised the crucial question of how the periods while asylum applications were pending should be regarded. The third question concerned periods when the execution of the removal was suspended pending appeal. The fourth question went to the meaning of removal being 'reasonably possible', raising fact-specific concerns pertaining to the non-cooperation of the Russian authorities. The fifth and final question asked what the Bulgarian authorities were to do if the maximum detention period had passed and 'there [was still] a doubt as to [the applicant's] identity, he [was] aggressive in his conduct, he [had] no means of supporting himself and there [was] no third person who has undertaken to provide for his subsistence?'[165]

The specific answers may be summarized quickly: the period spent in detention prior to the entry into force of the RD did count toward the maximum period, when proceedings were ongoing after its entry into force.[166] Periods spent as an asylum seeker did not count towards the period, as a separate regime addressed this issue, and, crucially, asylum seekers were not 'illegal', so they did not fall under the RD. If, however, no specific decision had been taken to retain Kadzoev under the asylum rules, the time under the RD would continue to run.[167] Similarly, periods in detention when deportation was suspended pending appeal did count toward the RD time limit.[168] The 'reasonable prospect of removal' meant a realistic prospect, which would not pertain if the receiving country was unlikely to admit the individual within a 'reasonable period' (according to AG Mazák)[169] or the period set out in the RD (according to the Court).[170] Once the detention period was up, there was no further basis to detain the individual under EU law, and immediate release was required,[171] notwithstanding the facts the Bulgarian government sought to rely on.[172] In a footnote, the AG acknowledged the possibility of residual Member State competence to detain 'because of aggressive behaviour on the basis of national legislation intended to maintain public order or the criminal law, for example'.[173] The Court was silent on this crucial question of the extent to which Member State action had been pre-empted by the RD.

In *Arslan,* the referring Czech court sought guidance on the applicability of RD to asylum seekers, asking whether, if the RD does not apply, pre-deportation detention must be terminated if the person concerned applies for asylum and there are no other reasons to keep him or her in detention. The CJEU clarified that a

[165] *Kadzoev* (n 151) para 30. [166] ibid, paras 34–39. [167] ibid, paras 40–48.
[168] ibid, paras 49–57. [169] ibid, paras 95–99. View of AG Mazák.
[170] ibid, paras 65–66. [171] ibid, paras 68–71. [172] ibid, para 71.
[173] ibid, para 101, footnote 28. View of AG Mazák. See G Cornelisse (n 151), 933.

TCN who has applied for asylum cannot be regarded as illegally staying in the Member State concerned until a negative decision on his or her application or a decision terminating his or her right of stay is taken.[174] Accordingly, asylum seekers may not be regarded as in pre-deportation detention until the outcome of their application.[175] An exception was contemplated, however, where the asylum seeker sought international protection after having been detained under Article 15 RD. Given that the RRCD authorizes Member States to detain an asylum seeker who lodges an application with the sole purpose of frustrating a return procedure,[176] detention may be maintained (albeit no longer on pre-deportation grounds):

> where it appears, after an assessment on a case-by-case basis of all the relevant circumstances, that the application was made solely to delay or jeopardise the enforcement of the return decision and that it is objectively necessary to maintain detention to prevent the person concerned from permanently evading his return.[177]

*Filev and Osmani* concerned an optional provision contained in Article 2(2)(b) RD, which confers discretion upon Member States not to apply the RD to TCNs who are 'subject to return as a criminal law sanction or as a consequence of a criminal law sanction, according to national law, or who are the subject of extradition procedures.' The case concerned two TCNs subject to criminal conviction following their entry into Germany in violation of re-entry bans.[178] The questions referred by the national court concerned the impact of Article 11(2) RD. The CJEU found that, under Article 11(2) RD, the five-year time-limit on re-entry bans runs 'independently of an application made for that purpose by the relevant [TCN]',[179] and that re-entry bans past five years cannot give rise to criminal sanctions, except for where those bans were made against TCNs constituting a 'serious threat to public order, public security or national security'.[180]

The Court also clarified that the exemption provided in Article 2(2)(b) RD, if not formally implemented in national law before the expiry of the Directive's transposition deadline, could not be invoked against TCNs who would already fall to benefit from the RD's provisions to restrict the RD's scope and thus worsen their legal situation.[181]

**Pre-deportation detention cf criminal incarceration:**
***El-Dridi*, Achughbabian, Sagor, Mbaye**

*El-Dridi* delves even more deeply into the criminal incarceration for irregular presence in Italy, raising precisely those pre-emption questions that were left unanswered in *Kadzoev*.

[174] *Arslan* (n 98) para 44. [175] ibid, para 49.

[176] ibid, para 55–56. The Court recalled that Directive 2003/9 confers discretion upon Member States as to the definition of grounds for the detention of asylum seekers. However, the same ground for detention would apply under the RRCD, in accordance with Art 8(1)(d) RRCD.

[177] ibid, para 63.

[178] Art 11(2) RD provides that re-entry bans cannot in principle exceed five years, except for cases where the TCN represents a serious threat to public policy, public security, or national security.

[179] *Filev and Osmani*, para 27. [180] ibid, paras 44–45. [181] ibid, paras 53–55.

Italy has been at the forefront of the criminalization of irregular migration, a trend seen increasingly across Europe.[182] Incarceration in the criminal context is conceptually and legally distinct from immigration detention, as Article 5 ECHR reflects. However, immigrant populations increasingly fall foul of criminal laws specifically designed to criminalize their presence.[183] In Italy, it is a criminal offence for a foreigner to remain in the country once a legal order to leave the territory has been issued.[184] Although the Italian Constitutional Court has tempered the strictness of the offence, the crime of illegal presence remains.[185] Notably, the Italian Constitutional Court has recently issued a number of rulings undermining some elements of the repressive anti-immigrant legislation, known as the 'security package'.[186] *El-Dridi* may be viewed as part of this process of judicial action to constrain the States' immigration decrees. Italian judges sent a raft of similar preliminary references on the topic.[187] The questions referred merit setting out in full:

In the light of the principle of sincere cooperation, the purpose of which is to ensure the attainment of the objectives of the directive, and the principle that the penalty must be proportionate, appropriate and reasonable, do Articles 15 and 16 [RD] preclude:

- the possibility that criminal penalties may be imposed in respect of a breach of an intermediate stage in the administrative return procedure, before that procedure is completed, by having recourse to the most severe administrative measure of constraint which remains available?
- the possibility of a sentence of up to four years' imprisonment being imposed in respect of a simple failure to cooperate in the deportation procedure on the part of the person

[182] See generally Council of Europe Commissioner for Human Rights, *Criminalisation of Migration in Europe: Human Rights Implications* (Council of Europe 2009).

[183] FRA Report on Criminalisation; A Aliverti, *Crimes of Mobility: Criminal Law and the Regulation of Immigration* (Routledge 2014).

[184] See *El-Dridi* (n 154) para 17 for the full text of the synopsized provisions.

[185] See Report of the WGAD (n 14), paras 57–67 for an extensive discussion of both Italy's 'extraordinary measures in the fight against crime by irregular migrants' and immigration detention *stricto sensu*. The Italian Constitutional Court has reviewed this law, and precluded its application in cases where non-compliance with the order to leave was justified. See 17 December 2010, Case No 359/2010.

[186] All, bar one (Case C-144/11 *Abdallah* [2011] OJ C152/17), have been terminated in light of *El-Dridi* (n 154). See Y Maccanico, *Statewatch Analysis: Italy—Series of defeats in court for the 'security package'* (Statewatch 2011). See generally Italian Constitutional Court, 25 July 2011, No 245 (striking down a law restricting the right to marry of irregular migrants); Italian Constitutional Court, 8 July 2010, No 249 (striking down a law imposing additional criminal penalties on irregular migrants); Italian Constitutional Court, 4 April 2011, Case No 115 (striking down a law conferring excessive powers on local government to combat irregular migration).

[187] See Case C-43/11 *Assane Samb* [2011] OJ C113/7; Case C-50/11 *Lucky Emegor* [2011] OJ C113/7, [2011] OJ C252/28 (withdrawn); Case C-61/11 *Mrad* [2011] OJ C113/8, [2011] OJ C252/28 (withdrawn); Case C-63/11 *John Austine* [2011] OJ C120/5, [2011] OJ C252/28 (withdrawn); Case C-94/11 *Survival Godwin* [2011] OJ C139/14, [2011] C252/29 (withdrawn); Case C-113/11, *Cherni* [2011] C238/4 (withdrawn); Case C-120/11 *Yeboah Kwadwo* [2011] OJ C145/17 (removed from register); Case C-140/11, *Demba Ngagne* [2011] OJ C152/16, [2011] OJ C252/29 (removed from register); Case C-156/11 *Ibrahim Music* [2011] OJ C269/20 (removed from register); Case C-169/11 *Conteh* [2011] OJ C173/8 (removed from register); Case C-187/11 *Vermisheva* [2011] C211/11 (removed from register).

concerned, in particular where the first removal order issued by the administrative authorities has not been complied with?[188]

The Italian Government argued that its use of criminal law put the detention outside the scope of the RD, relying on Article 2(2)(b).[189] In one sentence, the Court rejected that plea.[190] AG Mazák clarified that the exception only applied where the return obligation was applied as a result of a criminal conviction. In the instant case, the return obligation was the predicate act to the criminal offence, and so the exception was not applicable.[191]

The CJEU characterized the national provisions as providing for criminal incarceration 'on the sole ground' that the migrant was in breach of the order to leave.[192] In contrast, the Court described the RD as establishing a 'fixed order' of 'various, successive stages' of the removal process,[193] which must employ the 'least coercive measures possible'.[194] Detention, the 'most serious constraining measure' was 'strictly regulated' in order to ensure observance of fundamental rights.[195] Having confirmed the direct effect of Articles 15 and 16 of the RD,[196] the CJEU identified various ways in which 'the removal procedure provided for by the Italian legislation at issue in the main proceedings [was] significantly different from that established by that directive'.[197] These differences included the absence of a period for voluntary departure[198] and the recourse to criminal detention.[199]

The CJEU reassured the Member States that they may still take '[coercive] measures, including criminal law measures, aimed *inter alia* at dissuading those nationals from remaining illegally on those States' territory'.[200] However, those measures, even in the criminal law field, must be adjusted to ensure compliance with EU law,[201] and ensure its effectiveness.[202] The principles of proportionality and effectiveness precluded any national rule that provided for a custodial sentence 'on the sole ground' that the TCN continued to stay illegally after the order has been issued. Instead, Member States must 'pursue their efforts to enforce the return decision, which continues to produce its effects'.[203] The CJEU noted that detention in this circumstance risked making removal more difficult.[204]

The result is startling: the RD precludes the Italian law. As EU law is supreme over national law, national courts are obliged not to apply those provisions of the Italian law which are incompatible with the RD, taking into account the general principle 'of the retroactive application of the more lenient penalty'.[205] This duty, incumbent on all national judges irrespective of their position in the national judicial hierarchy, has been a hallmark of EU law since its early years.[206]

188 *El-Dridi* (n 154) para 25.
189 ibid, para 49.
190 ibid, paras 48–49. At issue was the exclusion of those facing deportation for criminal reasons under Art 2(2)(b) RD.
191 ibid, paras 22–28.
192 ibid, para 29.
193 ibid, para 34.
194 ibid, para 39.
195 ibid, para 42.
196 ibid, paras 44–47.
197 ibid, para 50.
198 ibid, para 51.
199 ibid, paras 52–60.
200 ibid, para 52.
201 ibid, para 54.
202 ibid, paras 55–56.
203 ibid, para 58.
204 ibid, para 59.
205 ibid, para 61.
206 See Case C-106/77 *Simmenthal* [1978] ECR 629.

EU law's capacity not only to penetrate the domestic legal order, but also to shift aside other domestic norms and make way for its own 'full effectiveness' is truly distinctive. The question left unasked and unanswered in *Kadzoev* is of great constitutional significance for the relationship between the EU and its Member States. If Kadzoev can no longer be detained under the RD, what residual power does the Member State have detention-wise?[207] *El-Dridi* takes up this issue in regard to criminal detention. The AG and the CJEU are not *ad idem* on the extent of pre-emption. The AG notably took issue with the inherent nature of criminal law, described as a 'repressive reaction'.[208] For the AG, both criminalization per se and imprisonment as the specific penalty were liable to impede the achievement of the RD's aim.[209] In contrast, the Court expressly leaves more leeway for national criminal measures in this field.[210] Indeed, in emphasizing that the offending aspect of the Italian legislation was that detention was 'on the sole ground' of staying in the face of the order to leave, the CJEU seems to implicitly allow for other criminal offences based on illegal residence coupled with some other elements of wrongdoing, provided that this did not make deportation more difficult.

While the approach in *El-Dridi* seems capable of taming some of the punitive excesses of the moves toward the criminalization of migration, much depends on its scope, and in particular the extent to which the Court treats criminalization of migration at other stages as also subject to EU law. In addition, if criminalization was demonstrated to be effective in achieving deportation, then one would fall back on the principle of proportionality alone to restrain it under EU law, in which case the notion that the RD would pre-empt the national rules would be much more difficult to sustain.

The Court returned to these issues in the case of *Achughbabian*. Alexandre Achughbabian was arrested in June 2011 and placed in police custody on suspicion of having committed the criminal offence under French law of entering without proper authorization or remaining when a visa has expired.[211] On investigation, it was discovered that he had been refused a residence permit, and requested to leave the territory in February 2009. Following his arrest, a deportation order and administrative detention order were issued in July 2011. Achughbabian argued that the French criminal provision was incompatible with the RD, in light of *El-Dridi*. The Paris Appeal Court referred the matter to the CJEU, asking whether the RD precluded 'national legislation [such as that at issue], which provides for

[207] A Arena, 'The Doctrine of Union Preemption in the EU Single Market: Between *Sein* and *Sollen*' (2010) Jean Monnet Working Paper 03/10, 31. This form of pre-emption, where the EU rules pre-empt national ones because the latter impede the effectiveness of the former, is 'the most hazy and ill-defined' form of pre-emption in EU law. The other forms are field pre-emption (where EU rules in the field preclude national action in that field) and rule pre-emption (where an EU norm precludes a contradictory national one.) Arena's account focuses on pre-emption in the context of the EU's single market. He notes in his conclusion that investigating the 'preemptive effects on EU legislation in the area of freedom, security and justice' is of 'paramount importance'. ibid, 90.

[208] *El-Dridi* (n 154), para 40. [209] ibid, para 43. [210] ibid, para 52.

[211] Art L. 621-1 CESEDA (Code de l'Entrée et de Séjour des Etrangers et du Droit d'Asile Français), set out in *Achughbabian* (n 155) paras 10–14.

the imposition of a sentence of imprisonment on a third-country national on the sole ground of his illegal entry or residence in national territory'.[212]

The Court began with a general statement that the RD did not preclude Member States from making illegal stay a criminal offence and from 'laying down penal sanctions to deter and prevent such an infringement of national rules on residence'.[213] The Court too accepted the French Government's argument that the investigative detention leading up to the determination of illegal stay was a matter for national law, but was in keeping with the aim of the RD.[214] The Court too required States to act 'with diligence and take a position without delay on the legality or otherwise of the stay of the person concerned', followed by a return decision (subject to the exceptions under Article 6 RD).[215] The Court then clarified that Member States may still criminalize illegal stay and impose penalties of imprisonment, but not such as to undermine the objectives of the RD, which would arise if the imprisonment was in the course of the return procedure.[216] As the applicant was subject to a return procedure, the imprisonment for a criminal offence was, like in *El-Dridi*, liable to thwart the effectiveness of the RD by delaying removal.[217] Criminal imprisonment, falling outside the RD under Article 2(2)(b), had to be for offences other than illegal staying.[218]

In addition, in rejecting arguments of the German and Estonian Governments, the Court also ruled out the imposition of terms of imprisonment *before* a removal is carried out.[219] However, after the process envisaged under the RD was over, and if removal had still not been possible, the Court cast back to the Member States their punitive power, with a caveat: the RD did not preclude penal sanctions under national criminal law against those 'illegally staying in the territory of a Member State without there being any justified ground for non-return'.[220] The Court reminded finally that any such sanctions must comply with the ECHR.[221] The bald reference to the ECHR (rather than the EUCFR and general principles of EU law) indicates that the CJEU is keen to avoid further references on this topic, and regards it principally as falling within national competences.

So, whilst ruling out criminal imprisonment (but not necessarily initial investigative detention) before and during the process envisaged under the RD, the CJEU in *Achughbabian* reassured Member States that they may impose penal sanctions against 'illegals' if return is impossible and, crucially, there are no 'justified grounds for non-return.' Clearly, if there are legal reasons precluding removal, be it under the CSR, IHRL, or any other source of protection against *non-refoulement*, that would suggest that detention is ruled out as deportation itself is. As well as impediments due to human rights risks, removal is often impossible for reasons relating to the conduct of the envisaged State of return. In these situations too, the migrant would seem to have 'justified grounds for non-return'. The CJEU merely alludes to the ECHR standards, rather than elucidate the notion of 'justified grounds for

[212] *Achughbabian* (n 155) para 25. [213] ibid, para 28. [214] ibid, para 30.
[215] ibid, para 31. [216] ibid, paras 32–33. [217] ibid, paras 36–39.
[218] ibid, para 41. [219] ibid, paras 44–45. [220] ibid, para 48.
[221] ibid, para 49.

non-return'. Concerning the criminalization of illegal presence in Italy, the Italian Constitutional Court countenanced an exemption for migrants who lacked the means to return.[222]

**Residual public order detention**

As for the notion of residual 'public order' detention powers, as mentioned by AG Mazák in *Kadzoev,* there is certainly no general 'public order' power to detain under Article 5 ECHR. The grounds for detention set out there are finite.[223] The Court has interpreted the potentially broadest ground, which permits detention 'to secure the fulfilment of an obligation prescribed by law' narrowly, requiring a specific identifiable legal obligation in view.[224] Even in times of emergency, detention powers must be exercised in a non-discriminatory fashion. Singling out foreigners for special forms of detention, other than under Article 5(1)(f) ECHR, is not permissible. This is best illustrated by the rulings in the *Belmarsh* litigation saga,[225] culminating in the ECtHR Grand Chamber ruling in *A v UK.* Nonetheless, many Member States do have anomalous detention grounds that cannot be subsumed under the ECHR purposes,[226] and so are of questionable legality under the ECHR. If such grounds impede the effectiveness of the removal, the RD may also preclude them.

*Sagor* follows directly from *El-Dridi* and *Achugbabian*, also concerning the Italian criminalization of illegal stay. The referring court asked whether, under the duty of sincere cooperation and the principle of effectiveness, the RD precluded national legislation that penalized TCNs' illegal stay by means of a fine, which might be replaced by an order for expulsion or home detention. Concerning the penal fine for which an expulsion order may be substituted under Italian legislation, the CJEU reiterated that the RD concerns 'only the return' and not all the rules on the stay of foreigners in the EU. Thus, reiterating *Achughbabian,* it stated that the RD does not preclude Member States from criminalizing illegal stay and penalizing it in a deterrent manner,[227] as long as the criminal sanction in question does not undermine the effectiveness of the RD.[228] While *El-Dridi* and *Achugbabian* established that criminal incarceration would impede the effectiveness of the RD, the CJEU held that a fine for which an expulsion order may be substituted had 'markedly different effects';[229] in particular it did not delay return

[222] See *Kadzoev* (n 151). [223] For a discussion, see FRA (n 21) 19.

[224] *Engel and others v the Netherlands* (1976) 1 EHRR 647.

[225] *A v Secretary of State for the Home Department* [2004] UKHL 56; *A v Secretary of State for the Home Department (No 2)* [2005] UKHL 71; *Secretary of State for the Home Department AF* [2009] UKHL 28.

[226] FRA (n 21) 19–20. As the FRA has recently highlighted, in the Czech Republic, Finland, Greece, Germany, and Hungary, additional reasons (such as the threat posed to public order) are used to determine whether to place individuals in pre-deportation detention. The practices are difficult to square with the requirement that detention be strictly necessary for the purpose of effectuating removal. In other Member States (Latvia, Lithuania, and Malta), public order and other non-Article 5 grounds, seem *per se* to justify detention of foreigners.

[227] *Sagor* (n 156) para 31, citing *Achughbabian* (n 155) para 28.

[228] ibid, para 32, citing *El-Dridi* (n 154) para 55 and *Achughbabian* (n 155) para 39.

[229] ibid, para 33.

measures.[230] The Court also ruled that criminal legislation providing for home detention during a return procedure would be akin to penal incarceration in terms of its impact on deportation, and would therefore hamper the effectiveness of the RD.[231]

Return in substitution for the fine did not include the waiting period for voluntary departure set out in the RD, as pointed out by the Commission.[232] However, the Court in *Sagor* seemed to suggest that such a criminal provision could be brought within the requirement of Article 7(4) RD, which enables Member States to waive the waiting period if there is a risk of absconding.[233]

The CJEU revisited this issue in *Mbaye*, where it reiterated *Sagor*.[234] *Mbaye* also constitutes a straightforward confirmation of the ruling in *Achughbabian*.[235]

### *ii. Judicial protection*

In *G and R*, the applicants challenged a decision extending their detention by a maximum of twelve months pending removal from the Netherlands,[236] on the ground that the authorities had infringed the rights of the defence by depriving them of the right to be heard. The reference came from the Dutch highest court, the *Raad van State*, which accepted that the extension procedure violated the right to be heard. At issue were the consequences of that violation, in particular whether violating this procedural right meant that 'automatically and in all cases…the detention must be lifted', or whether 'the general principle of respect for the rights of the defence [left] scope for a balancing of interests in which, in addition to the seriousness of the infringement of that principle and the interests of the foreign national adversely affected thereby, the interests of the Member State served by the extension of the detention measure are also taken into account'.[237] The Court reiterated the usual position in EU law to the effect that a violation of the rights of defence only results in annulment if the outcome of the process might have been different had the rights been respected.[238] Accordingly, the Court concluded that 'the national court responsible for assessing the lawfulness of that extension decision may order the lifting of the detention measure only if it considers, in the light of all of the factual and legal circumstances of each case, that the infringement at issue actually deprived the party relying thereon of the possibility of arguing his defence better, to the extent that the outcome of that administrative procedure could have been different.'[239] The ruling is orthodox, if disappointing, and follows closely the line proposed by the Raad van State.

[230] ibid, para 35. [231] ibid, paras 43–47. [232] ibid, para 40.
[233] ibid, para 41. [234] *Mbaye* (n 157) paras 30–33. [235] ibid, paras 18–22.
[236] Detention was extended on the ground of 'lack of cooperation' under Art 15(6) RD.
[237] *G and R* (n 158) para 21.
[238] ibid, para 38, citing, to that effect, inter alia, Case C-301/87 *France* v *Commission* [1990] ECR I-307, para 31; Case C-288/96 *Germany* v *Commission* [2000] ECR I-8237, para 101; Case C-141/08 *Foshan Shunde Yongjian Housewares & Hardware* v *Council* [2009] ECR I-9147, para 94; Case C-96/11 P *Storck* v *OHIM* [2012] OJ C 331/7, para 80.
[239] ibid, para 45.

The second case on judicial remedies, *Mahdi,* has more profound implications. The reference arose out of proceedings before the Sofia City Administrative Court, which was requested to rule of its own motion on the continuation of the detention of Mr Mahdi, a Sudanese national being held in an immigration detention centre in Sofia. Mr Mahdi was arrested on 9 August 2013 at a border post in Bregovo, near the Serbian border. He did not have any identity documents but presented himself as Bashir Mohamed Ali Mahdi, a Sudanese national. On the same day a deportation and re-entry ban was made. Three days later, whilst in detention, he signed a statement consenting to voluntary return. However, the Sudanese embassy official refused to issue him a travel document, 'apparently based on the fact that Mr Mahdi was not willing to return to Sudan.' A Bulgarian national, Ms Ruseva, swore an affidavit that Mr Mahdi would be provided with accommodation and his own means of support during his stay in Bulgaria, and requested his release against provision of security. This statement was checked and validated by the police on 26 August 2013. The Director of the relevant migration section at the Interior Ministry suggested he be released and subject to an ATD, namely a reporting obligation. More senior officials refused this option, due to Mahdi's immigration law infractions, and previous rejected asylum claim.[240]

The RD expressly requires detention decisions to be in writing and reasoned. The Court extended this requirement to extensions of detention, as it was a requirement of the rights of defence.[241] Concerning judicial supervision, the Court reiterated that Article 15 RD was directly effective,[242] and that detention under the RD was 'strictly circumscribed' to ensure compliance with the principle of proportionality and fundamental rights.[243] Judicial supervision then had to take place irrespective of the detaining authority's request[244] to ensure that one of the two grounds of permissible extension were made out,[245] and that the basic overarching requirement of a 'reasonable prospect of removal' still existed.[246] The judicial supervision also had to assess the viability of ATDs.[247] Crucially, the judge had to be able to order release and substitute ATDs. Thus *Mahdi* clarifies the meaning of judicial 'supervision' of decisions prolonging detention in a passage worth citing in full:

> It follows that a judicial authority deciding upon an application for the extension of detention must be able to rule on all relevant matters of fact and of law in order to determine...whether an extension of detention is justified, which requires an in-depth examination of the matters of fact specific to each individual case...To that end, the judicial authority ruling on an application for extension of detention must be able to take into account both the facts stated and the evidence adduced by the administrative authority and any observations that may be submitted by the third-country national. Furthermore, that authority must be able to consider any other element that is relevant for its decision should it so deem necessary. Accordingly, the powers of the judicial authority in the context of an examination can under no circumstances be confined just to the matters adduced by the administrative authority concerned.[248]

240 *Mahdi* (n 159) paras 16–24.
241 ibid, paras 44 and 46.
242 ibid, para 54, citing *El-Dridi* (n 154) para 47.
243 ibid, para 55.
244 ibid, para 56.
245 ibid, para 58.
246 ibid, para 59.
247 ibid, para 61.
248 ibid, para 62.

*Mahdi* also contains some guidance on the grounds of detention. After all, judicial control and necessity tests may be superficial unless courts are required to carefully assess whether detention is necessary to meet its particular aim. Concerning the risk of absconding and its relationship with lack of identity documents, the Court reiterated that lack of documents could not be equated with flight risk, and was not in itself a ground for extension of detention.[249] However, it could be taken into account in the assessment of flight risk. This is crucially important, as it appears that lack of documentation is the most frequently used criterion for assessing absconding risk in the EU.[250] All renewals of detention were also subject to the ATD assessment.[251] The assessment had to be on a case-by-case basis.[252] Another case is pending before the CJEU on how flight risk is to be assessed.[253]

*Mahdi* also dealt with the other ground for extension, 'lack of cooperation'. The CJEU found that the lack of identity documents cannot be equated with 'lack of cooperation'. However, it emphasized that Article 15(6)(a) is only triggered where the following conditions are satisfied: (1) 'the removal operation is lasting longer than anticipated, despite all reasonable efforts' on the part of the Member State,[254] (2) an examination of the TCN's conduct during the period of detention shows a lack of cooperation in the implementation of the removal operation, and a causal link is established between the TCN's conduct and the delay in the implementation of the removal operation.[255] However, the CJEU characterized this principally as a question of fact for the national court to assess, leaving considerable uncertainty on how the lack of cooperation from the Sudanese authorities was to be taken into account.

On the final question, concerning the issue of a residence permit on release, the RD does not establish such an obligation. For someone in Mr Mahdi's situation (a TCN without identity documents, released from detention if there is no reasonable prospect of removal), the only concession is that the State should provide him 'written confirmation of his situation'.[256] According to AG Szpunar's view, such a written confirmation would be necessary to 'prevent that person from being arrested again... if he were asked to prove his specific situation in the event of an administrative control or check'.[257] In its latest Communication *On EU Return Policy*, on this topic of 'non-removable' returnees, the Commission undertakes to 'collect best practice, based on existing best practices at national level, to avoid protracted situations and to ensure that people who cannot be removed are not left indefinitely without basic rights and do not risk being unlawfully re-detained'.[258]

249 ibid, para 73. 250 Commission 2014 (n 149) p 15.
251 *Mahdi* (n 159) para 67. 252 ibid, para 70, citing *Sagor* (n 156) para 41.
253 Case C-554/13 *Zh & O* [2014] OJ C9/20, in which the CJEU will answer some questions sent by the Dutch *Raad van State* lodged on 28 October 2013 about the way the 'risk of absconding' can be or must be defined.
254 *Mahdi* (n 159) para 83. The Court explains further: 'that means that... the Member State in question should have sought, and should still actively be seeking, to secure the issue of identity documents for the third-country national'.
255 ibid, para 82. 256 ibid, para 89. 257 ibid, para 96. View of AG Szpunar.
258 European Commission (n 149) 8.

### *iii. Places of detention*

In *Bero and Bouzalmate*, the applicants had been detained in prison. Ms Bero, a rejected asylum seeker, described as 'probably a Syrian national', had been detained with ordinary prisoners for almost a month, while Mr Bouzalmate was in an area of prison dedicated for immigration detention.[259] The key aspect of German law was that although pre-deportation detention was generally to be in specialized detention facilities, if the particular *Land* had no such facilities, 'other custodial institutions' could be used. The law also required that such detainees 'be accommodated separately from prisoners serving criminal sentences.' The CJEU treated the questions as going to the issue of how this requirement was to be implemented in a federal context, where the Land in question did not have such dedicated detention facilities.[260] The Court held there was a general duty on the Member State to set up detention facilities.[261] The national authorities responsible for applying the national legislation transposing Article 16 RD must therefore be able to detain TCNs in specialized detention facilities. This did not require each *Land* to have such facilities, but rather through agreements, the Member State could ensure that detainees were placed in such centres.[262]

*Pham* concerned a Vietnamese national who had also been detained in ordinary prison for over three months but had, by a written declaration, 'consented to being accommodated in a prison together with ordinary prisoners, because she wanted contact with compatriots who were in that prison'.[263] The CJEU reiterated that the requirement to use specific migration detention facilities created an 'unconditional obligation.'[264] The German and Dutch Governments argued that waiver was suitable to vindicate the interests and welfare of the detainee.[265] However, the Court noted the requirement as 'not coupled with any exception',[266] and so was 'a substantive condition for that detention, without observance of which the latter would, in principle, not be consistent with the directive'.[267] Accordingly, the Member State was precluded from taking into account the 'wishes of the [TCN] concerned.'[268]

## 3. CJEU–ECtHR interactions

Overall, the early CJEU rulings were characterized by a fundamental rights reticence, with the Court tending to focus on the text of the RD. However, over time, the Court asserts the importance of limiting detention and ensuring that ATDs are examined, also by the national courts, as seen in *Mahdi*. Nevertheless, the grounds of detention have not been fully scrutinized, so while EU law requires that detention be necessary, until the grounds are properly elucidated, the necessity test will

[259] *Bero and Bouzalmate* (n 160) paras 9–23.
[260] ibid, para 24.
[261] ibid, para 29.
[262] ibid, para 31.
[263] *Pham* (n 161) para 8.
[264] ibid, para 17.
[265] ibid, para 18.
[266] ibid, para 19.
[267] ibid, para 21.
[268] ibid, para 22.

not bite. Also, the creative role of the CJEU has its limits—the RD's purpose is not to constrain detention per se, but rather to ensure that deportation is effective. In this context, some criminal detention has been precluded, in a rather stunning manner in *El-Dridi* and *Achughbabian,* but where detention is necessary for deportation, the RD requires it if ATDs will not work. Also, the question of what to do with non-removable persons in terms of legal status remains unresolved, even after *Mahdi*, as the EU anti-regularization ethos remains.[269]

Luxembourg engages with the Strasbourg standards.[270] In *Kadzoev,* the reasoning of AG Mazák and of the Court are similar, but, as is typically the case, the AG's View is more elaborate, particularly in its engagement with the ECtHR authorities. In regard to the 'reasonable prospect of removal' under Article 15(4) RD, the AG cited the Council of Europe material, in particular the Council of Europe's Twenty Guidelines on Forced Return.[271] AG Mazák noted that EU law also incorporated the Article 5(1)(f) ECHR standards,[272] citing *Chahal* and *Mikolenko*. The AG emphasized the ECtHR requirement of due diligence, in order to ensure that periods in detention are as short as possible.[273] The AG's view was decided on 10 November 2009, less than a month after the ECtHR ruled in *Mikolenko* that detention was unlawful as there was no reasonable prospect of removal. Given the proximity in time, it is unsurprising that the AG would cite this case, particularly since both cases concern impediments to removal due to insufficient cooperation from the receiving country. Unlike the Court, AG Mazák gave a strong indication that the detention should be regarded as unlawful in the absence of a reasonable prospect of removal.

However, *Kadzoev* signals that the RD standards are *higher* than the ECHR in other crucial respects, namely in requiring that detention is necessary to effectuate removal,[274] and in imposing a strict time limit. In *El-Dridi*, the Court noted that the RD was intended to take account of both the Strasbourg case law,

> according to which the principle of proportionality requires that the detention of a person against whom a deportation or extradition procedure is under way should not continue for an unreasonable length of time, that is, its length should not exceed that required for the purpose pursued,[275]

and the guideline providing that detention is to be 'for as short a period as possible'.[276] In this way, the CJEU reads in the Strasbourg requirements as to the duration of detention, making clear that the eighteen-month time limit is the outer limit, which will not be justified in all cases. However, as we have seen, the ECtHR rejects the requirements of necessity and proportionality in its case law, but reads

[269] See further Chapter 2.

[270] Based on the interpretation of the RD as transposing ECtHR jurisprudence. See Opinion of AG Bot in *Bero and Bouzalmate* (n 160) para 84; Opinion of AG Szupnar in *Mahdi* (n 159) para 45.

[271] *Kadzoev* (n 151) View of AG Mazák, para 52, footnote 17, citing Council of Europe Committee of Ministers (n 17) Guideline No 7.

[272] *Kadzoev* (n 151) para 53.

[273] ibid, para 52.

[274] *Kadzoev* (n 151) para 64.

[275] *El-Dridi* (n 154) para 43; *Saadi v UK* (n 71) paras 72 and 74.

[276] *El-Dridi* (n 154), citing Council of Europe Committee of Ministers (n 17), Guideline No 8.

the requirement of 'reasonable time' into its conception of non-arbitrariness. It would be regrettable if the distinctive EU version of proportionality were to be sapped of vigour by converging on the weak ECHR non-arbitrariness standard.

The AG in *Kadzoev* also cited the Strasbourg case law to clarify that, although asylum seekers could not be detained under the RD, 'detention of an asylum applicant [was] not, as such, prohibited under the international and [EU] law of asylum'.[277] While the judgment is crucially important in delimiting the detention of asylum seekers from the detention of those facing deportation, it should not be taken to endorse the view that the ECHR standards in *Saadi* should be incorporated into EU law *in toto*. Rather, as demonstrated above, the EU legislative framework contains the building blocks for more rigorous scrutiny of detention of asylum seekers. Constructive human rights pluralism stands for critical engagement, not automatic integration. The EU legislative framework and its immanent commitment to rigorous proportionality review warrant a different approach.

On the other hand, pluralism has revealed positive interactions where Luxembourg relies on the ECtHR's experience in fact-sensitive assessments, such as in the assessment of the legality of detention conditions. In *Bero and Bouzalmate*, AG Bot refers to Strasbourg case law to identify 'the criteria by the yardstick of which it assesses the adequacy of the place, conditions and regime of detention'.[278] Moreover, AG Szupnar in *Mahdi* emphasized ECHR standards on the requirement of due diligence, by citing ECtHR rulings in particular cases where Bulgaria had been found to be dilatory in trying to get travel documents for deportees. [279]

## VI. Conclusion

The proliferation of rights sources and adjudicative bodies with overlapping jurisdiction may give the appearance of a rights surfeit. Yet, the cases reveal a burgeoning practice of immigration detention. The HRC has used a vague, capacious notion of 'arbitrariness' to condemn automatic detention of migrants, instead demanding individual justification. But, the permissible aims of detention remain open under its jurisprudence. Regrettably, neither the ECtHR nor the CJEU gives due weight to the HRC authorities. The ECtHR takes an eccentric course, particularly in refusing to apply its standard proportionality approach, and in allowing the State unlimited leeway to deem migrants unauthorized. The two leading rulings, *Chahal*

[277] *Kadzoev* (n 151). View of AG Mazák, para 85, citing e.g. *Saadi v UK* (n 71), *Riad and Idiab v Belgium* (n 58), *A v Australia* (n 25).

[278] Opinion of AG Bot in *Bero and Bouzalmate* (n 160) para 87. The AG cites *Popov v France* App No 39472/12 (ECHR, 19 January 2012). ibid, para 88.

[279] AG Szupnar in *Mahdi* (n 159) para 90, footnote 33, citing *Auad v Bulgaria* [2011] ECHR 1162, para 132 and *Raza v Bulgaria* (n 104) para 73. He noted that in *Auad*, the ECtHR deemed three letters insufficient for the purpose of demonstrating that the Bulgarian authorities had followed up the case actively or that they had made every effort to negotiate the applicant's rapid transfer or admission to a third country.

and *Saadi*, sit poorly with the authority of the HRC and the CSR, as well as with the standards now binding on the bulk of its members via EU law. A necessity test and authorized presence at least for asylum seekers once admitted to the procedure are acknowledged features of the EU regime.

Constructive human rights pluralism would have Strasbourg engage in a less perfunctory manner with the IHRL standards and align with them, when appropriate. The existence of the EU standards should exert pressure for that movement from within. EU law, despite the apparently unpromising legislative framework, has integrated the better aspects of the ECtHR jurisprudence, superimposing the necessity requirement that the ECtHR erroneously rejected. Guiraudon's prediction of the 'bold' CJEU and the 'tamer' ECtHR seems to be playing out.[280] It would be wrong for the EU to converge on the ECHR minimum when it is called upon to articulate its own interpretation of the right to liberty. In its early RD cases, given the nature of the claims before it, textual fidelity to the RD produced outcomes that are evidently more rights-protective than the ECHR. In later cases, *Mahdi* in particular, it has bolstered national judicial control over detention and emphasized the importance of assessing ATDs in detention reviews. As it sets its own course, it should be wary of the overblown statism that animates the Strasbourg case law.

Much depends on national judges. They trigger preliminary references, and their questions not only dictate the scope of the CJEU's jurisdiction, but may nudge the Luxembourg judges in particular directions. While the referring court in *Kadzoev* seemed incredulous that release from detention was required as a matter of EU law, the questions referred in *El-Dridi* seem part of a concerted judicial effort to thwart the criminalization of irregular migration in Italy. The Italian Government's argument in *El-Dridi*, that its criminal law was immune form EU scrutiny, has a naïve ring to it. The outcome, wherein the RD instead 'precludes' the Italian law, shows that the state *qua* EU Member no longer controls the exception. At the other end of the enforcement spectrum, we might contrast the distortion of the scope of the RD by governments keen to treat 'asylum seekers' as presumptively 'bogus' rather than presumptive refugees. *Mahdi* seems like a classic EU case of domestic judicial self-empowerment: A case referred from a lowly administrative Tribunal concerned to ensure that its detention review powers, apparently constrained to a tick-box effort under domestic practices, actually allowed the judge to assess the full facts, and give effect to a presumption of liberty if ATDs were available. Recall too that on the facts in *Mahdi*, the Director of the detention sector was also in favour of releasing Mr Mahdi.

This book opened with the statist assumption, and the migrant's vulnerability to naked State power. EU law takes a different view of the State, unsettling statist assumptions, and opening up space for greater normative contestation. The universal subject, the rights-bearer, appears a more vivid prospect under EU law than

[280] V Guiraudon, 'European Courts and Foreigners' Rights: A Comparative Study of Norm Difference' (2000) 34 International Migration Review 1088, 1094.

under IHRL. The RD fits this model in some respects, by creating directly effective judicially protected rights.

And yet, I have not described a continent at ease. Immigration detention continues to increase, and Member States are raising detention time limits in response to the RD. EU law brings us '[d]etainees [who] have more rights, but they are detained for longer periods of time.'[281] But at least, once the maximum period of detention expires, release is required. But then what? Once Kadzoev, El-Dridi, and Mahdi are released from detention, their irregular status remains. They get a 'document' explaining their legal predicament. As Chapter 2 discussed, periodic regularizations of irregular migrants are routine in EU Member States,[282] and increasingly justified in human rights terms.[283] Mincheva suggests the implicit next step for *Kadzoev* should be regularization.[284] Yet, that step is not taken in *Mahdi.* EU law offers no solution at present, in spite of the wording of the RD,[285] and may even be seen to exert an anti-regularization ethos over its Member States.[286] As mentioned above, the Commission goes no further than to suggest, weakly, that it will 'collect best practice, based on existing best practices at national level, to avoid protracted situations and to ensure that people who cannot be removed are not left indefinitely without basic rights and don't risk being unlawfully re-detained'.[287]

The ECHR protects some migrants from removal based on their long residence, but does not provide them with a formal status in the host State.[288] There is no clear supranational legal remedy at present.[289] It appears the best we can hope for is that supranational courts and authority will prompt inclusive political and judicial moves at the domestic level.

[281] Flynn and Cannon (n 3) 9, reporting the statement of an EU workshop participant.

[282] For an overview of regularization practices, see M Baldwin-Edwards and A Kraler, *REGINE: Regularisations in Europe: Study on Practices in the Area of Regularisation in the Member States of the EU—Final Report* (ICMPD 2009).

[283] See A Kraler 'Fixing, Adjusting, Regulating, Protecting Human Rights—The Shifting Uses of Regularisations in the European Union' (2011) 13 EJML 297.

[284] See Mincheva (n 151).

[285] Art 6(4) RD: 'Member States may at any moment decide to grant an autonomous residence permit or other authorisation offering a right to stay for compassionate, humanitarian or other reasons to a third-country national staying illegally on their territory.'

[286] The problems posed by non-removable irregular migrants have long been noted, but even a suggestion to study the various Member State practices concerning non-removable migrants with a view to developing some common principles at the EU level was dropped. See Kraler (n 283) 301.

[287] European Commission (n 149) 8.

[288] See, e.g. *Bonger v the Netherlands* App No 10154/04 (ECHR, 15 September 2005). In rare cases, Art 8 ECHR may provide a basis for a claim to regularize a migrant's stay. See generally D Thym, 'Respect for Private and Family Life Under Article 8 ECHR in Immigration Cases: A Human Right to Regularize Illegal Stay?' (2008) 57 ICLQ 87.

[289] Indeed, but limiting the scope of the QD and instead noting that some migrants are non-returnable under the RD, the CJEU could be viewed as exacerbating the precariousness of non-deportability without formal status.

# 8

# Conclusions

## I. Beyond Statism

This book has examined how human rights law responds to challenges to migration control and migration status. A central premise of this work is that, to the extent that they reflect the statist approach to migration control, the European Court of Human Rights (ECtHR) rulings fail to scrutinize official actions appropriately. Arguably, on several key issues, the ECtHR case law can be criticized for privileging State prerogatives over human rights, producing internally inconsistent case law. Even more so, the statist assumption sits ill in the European Union (EU) context. Examining *migration status* and *migration control* illuminates the breadth and pervasive impact of official actions masked under this sovereigntist logic. *Migration control* refers to the enforcement apparatus which surrounds migration and asylum, which extends far beyond the territorial borders, from visa officers in faraway embassies and immigration officers posted at airports outside Europe, to detention centres for interdicted migrants in third states.[1] Migration control also pervasively takes place within the State, routinely reaching into family life, workplaces, and educational establishments. *Migration status* refers to the fact that immigration and asylum law create particular statuses (or none), packages of rights, and obligations of enduring significance. Migration status dictates not only the nature, extent, and duration of rights of entry and residence, but also often determines rights in other contexts, in the political realm, in family life, in the workplace, and economic life generally.[2] Establishing status-based hierarchies for the distribution of important rights and goods undermines equality, and in future work I will examine how equality guarantees may be invoked to challenge migration-status hierarchies. EU law offers greater potential than Article 14 European Convention on Human Rights (ECHR) in this context, given that equality and non-discrimination have a strong constitutional position under the EU Treaties. The pending Grand Chamber

[1] Consider UN Committee against Torture, *JHA v Spain*, Communication No 323/2007, 10 November 2008, discussed in Chapter 6.

[2] This book focuses on admissions (rights of entry and residence), but for a collection examining the impact of migration status in work, see C Costello and M Freedland (eds), *Migrants at Work: Immigration and Vulnerability in Labour Law* (OUP 2014).

ruling in *Biao v Denmark* will be important in testing whether the ECtHR will apply its more robust anti-discrimination approach to migration status matters.[3]

The functions under scrutiny in this book—authorizing entry and stay—are traditionally understood as intrinsic and central to statehood. This characterization has meant that oftentimes when human rights law is invoked, there is excessive deference to States' sovereign prerogatives. The statist assumption works from the premise that a particular power exists as part of the established understanding of statehood, to regarding its manifestations and consequences as a necessary feature of that power. A central premise of this book is that the statist migration control assumption obscures the impact of both migration status and migration control on the human rights of migrants and refugees, and ought to be abandoned. Even if we treat the control of immigration and some aspects of asylum as subject to a degree of discretionary power, this does not mean we should not scrutinize the impact of the exercise of those powers on human rights, just as other exercises of public power are scrutinized.

If competence over migration is shared and disaggregated, as it now is in the EU, it is hoped that these actions are more visible, and subject to greater political and legal accountability. To illustrate, if detention is no longer treated as the 'necessary adjunct' of the State's power to control admissions or deport, but rather must be demonstrably compliant with a range of norms which test its effectiveness to meet certain specified aims and objectives, it is *potentially* limited, just as the other powers of the State are limited and constrained by human rights and the rule of law.

The caveat *potentially* is important: sharing competences is not a panacea, it could lead to congealed, enhanced coercive enforcement capacity bearing down on migrants,[4] to the detriment of their rights. However, if properly designed, there is potential for greater accountability and human rights protections in systems of divided power. Accordingly, when EU law is added to the mix, it opens up not only an additional layer of legal regulation and complexity, but also an important justificatory space and site of contestation. Migration control and status are no longer the exclusive domain of States—they are increasingly regulated by EU law in a shared manner, subject to greater legislative articulation and judicial scrutiny. These are changes in nature, not merely of venue: allocating legally defined, judicially enforceable residence rights is to confer a form of membership as of right. The statist migration control assumption, which veils the human rights impacts of migration status and migration control measures, is unsettled in this pluralist context.

[3] *Biao v Denmark*, Application No 38590/10, 25 March 2014; ECtHR, 'Grand Chamber Panel's Decisions', Press Release ECHR 250 (2014), 9 September 2014.

[4] For example, contemporary contestation under US federalism is exclusionary: local and State power to enforce federal immigration laws is limited, and local and State moves to join in the enforcement of federal migration control and status matters have a predominantly exclusionary dimension. See J Chacon 'The Transformation in US Immigration Federalism: A Critical Reading of Arizona v US' (2013) 21 Wm & Mary Bill Rts J 577. Reprinted in S Bagley and D Nakacha (eds), *Immigration Regulation in Federal States: Challenges and Responses in Comparative Perspective* (Springer 2013).

## II. Constructive Human Rights Pluralism

This book has sought to articulate and defend a version of human rights pluralism. In Chapter 2, a constructive human rights pluralism, in which mutual engagement and interaction across different human rights regimes is encouraged. Crucially, divergence is also embraced, in particular where there are good reasons for higher standards of protection within the EU system. In the interactions between the ECtHR and the Court of Justice of the European Union (CJEU) on the human rights of migrants, we have seen a whole gamut of interactions, but often the dialogue is too muted to be constructive. As the CJEU has ruled that accession to the ECHR is not permissible (effectively rejecting a draft agreement which took many years to negotiate),[5] the two systems will continue to interact informally, but intensively, as they have for decades.

While it might be tempting to see uniformity in human rights protections as desirable, my central contention is that there are good constitutional, institutional, and legal reasons why the CJEU's approach should be distinctive and more rights-protective. In the migration context, these differences mean that the statist migration control assumption is inapt in the EU. It is ill-fitting in the EU's distinctive constitutional and institutional constellation. Once admissions are a matter of shared competence, the Member States ought no longer to be able to invoke *ipso facto* justifications for their acts *qua* states. The Area of Freedom, Security and Justice offers space for reconceptualization; indeed, it demands it. It demands reasoned argument as to why particular restrictions are justified, not pre-emptive assertions that the State may act in pursuit of its sovereignty. We should expect that the troublesome 'weightiness' attached to migration control and the pervasive impact of migration status should be open to scrutiny in the normal way, just as other official actions are for their impact on individuals' human rights.

## III. Migration Status in a Multi-level System

Chapter 3 examines how migration status is formed in the multi-level polity that is the EU. EU law now creates many statuses, such as for student migrants, long-term residents, refugees and subsidiary protection beneficiaries, seasonal workers, and intra-company transferees. EU law is not merely juris-generative (that is rights-generative), but also status-generative. This capacity means that national authorization is no longer constitutive of residence rights, at least for those privileged migrants with EU residence rights. However, the granting of these statuses remains the role of national authorities, as is commonplace in the EU's decentralized administrative system.

5 Opinion 2/13 (Accession to the ECHR) [2015] OJ C 65/2.

When it comes to nationality matters, EU law also now plays a role. By creating secure migration statuses, it enables more migrants to claim the lawful residence that is a normal prerequisite for naturalization under domestic law. While decisions on naturalization remain predominantly with individual States, they no longer exclusively control who may live in their territory. Furthermore, when and if they choose to exercise powers to denaturalize, if this decision affects EU rights, then they must respect the EU principle of proportionality, and arguably other EU principles.[6]

If naturalization is the most visible act of legal inclusion, regularization is its less formal, but no less significant, companion measure. While Member States remain competent to regularize irregular migrants, the protections against removal in ECHR and EU law[7] in particular create an inclusive dynamic. Regularization remains a key corrective, which ought to be seen as a requirement of justice, rather than an act of pure executive beneficence. The jurisprudence of the ever-tentative ECtHR lends some support to this contention, although Strasbourg's endorsement of the statist assumption prompts high deference to State's authorization of residence, even in those cases where individuals may not be deported. As Chapter 3 reveals, the EU adopts two strikingly different approaches to regularization. On the one hand, EU law creates secure rights of entry and residence for certain people, and in effect regularizes them. However, the EU also bolsters Member States' admission control prerogatives, producing greater restrictiveness. As regards regularization *stricto sensu*, that is large regularization programmes, the EU discourages, and at least formally, demands deportation over regularization in its 'fight' against 'illegal immigration'.

As the scope of inclusion is always finite, acts of inclusion also inevitably exclude. The frictions between inclusion/exclusion at the EU level and national level are also evoked in this work. We see, for instance, that as family reunification at the national level has been restricted, including for Member States' own nationals, challenges before the ECtHR occasionally limit the restrictive turn, but in the main ECHR protections have deferred to the statist assumption. In contrast, although EU legislation was drafted in the climate of national restriction, in practice the case law has exerted a liberalizing pull. Of course, not all fall within the scope of EU law. EU Citizens (initially only mobile ones, but static ones too since *Zambrano*)[8] and those covered by the Family Reunification Directive have relied on EU law to challenge domestic restrictions, in some surprising ways given the drafting of that measure.

The immanent features of EU law, its strong individual rights-based approach and robust standard of proportionality analysis, tend to protect migrants' rights better than the Strasbourg approach in this context. The argument for higher EU standards is again rooted in the CJEU's constitutional and institutional context.

[6] Case C-135/08 *Rottmann* [2010] ECR I-1449.
[7] Latterly made manifest in Case C-562/13 *Abdida* [2015] OJ C 65/13.
[8] Case C-34/09 *Zambrano* [2011] ECR I-1177.

The first pertinent feature of EU law, a manifestation of its embrace of the individual, is its concern with secure rights of entry and residence, even for third-country nationals (TCNs) who derive rights from EU measures. As Chapter 4 reveals, unlike the ECtHR, the CJEU case law on the residence rights of EU Citizens and their TCN family members exemplifies migration as of right, with the significance of national authorization downplayed. This approach is equally applicable under other EU measures that create rights of residence.[9] This does not mean there are no limitations to the scope of these entitlements, or that States no longer control who may come and go if they have good reason. But where individuals fall within the scope of these measures, they are no longer objects of discretionary migration control, but legal subjects who may bear claims of right against the public authorities of the Member States.

The second crucial immanent feature of EU law is context-sensitive proportionality analysis. EU-style proportionality offers much more than Strasbourg's multi-factor balancing under Article 8 ECHR (examined in Chapter 4 on family migration) or its anti-arbitrariness standard under Article 5 ECHR (discussed in Chapter 7 on detention). On these two key issues, the CJEU ought to take a different approach to Strasbourg, simply to be faithful to its own conception of legality. To a significant extent, the CJEU is taking that approach in its interpretation of the EU rules on family reunion and on pre-deportation detention under the Returns Directive.[10] However, a real challenge would be the examination of detention of asylum seekers on arrival, where the woefully weak Strasbourg case of *Saadi v UK* reflects the worst of Strasbourg's deference to statist approaches to migration control and status.[11]

## IV. Human Rights vs Migration Control—Four Flashpoints

This discussion of migration status in the early chapters of this work is a prelude to the examination of the human rights flashpoints in the later chapters. Migration controls and migration status determine the legal predicament in which migrants

[9] This was evident with regard to migrants subject to a Europe Agreement in Case C-327/02 *Panayotova* [2004] ECR I-11055, and has been confirmed as regards students in the crucial case of Case C-491/13 *Ben Alaya* [2014] OJ C 409/18. That case established that once individuals fulfilled the criteria for grant of the residence right, Member States were normally obligated to accord it. See *Ben Alaya*, para 36. As regards long-term residents too, the LTRD has been interpreted in a manner that confers a status which can be claimed as of right. See D Acosta, 'Civic Citizenship Reintroduced? The Long-Term Residence Directive as a Postnational Form of Membership' (2015) 21(2) ELJ 200.

[10] For examples on family migration, see C-578/08 *Rhimou Chakroun v Minister van Buitenlandse Zaken* [2010] ECR I-01839, and for pre-deportation detention, see Case C-357/09 PPU *Kadzoev* [2009] ECR I-11189.

[11] (2008) 47 EHRR 17. Admittedly, the CJEU has not used EU proportionality in all contexts. In Joined Cases C-57/09 and C-101/09 *Germany v B* and *D* [2010] ECR I-1097, its decision on exclusion from refugee status, the Court did not explicitly apply proportionality. Nonetheless its approach in para 99, which required a case-by-case assessment of individual responsibility for acts amounting to a serious non-political crime, is an important refugee-protective move.

and refugees find themselves. The remainder of the book has examined four flashpoints of human rights contestation, where EU law interacts with ECHR protections. There are many more issues I could have examined, such as access to social rights or workplace protections, but these were chosen as they illustrate the closest connection with migration status and control.

At each of these flashpoints, I have explored the interaction between EU legislative norms, EU human rights law, and ECHR standards, thereby illustrating both the importance and shortcomings of Strasbourg standards for the EU's admissions rules. Much of the existing scholarship on European human rights pluralism has focused on the court-to-court, i.e. Luxembourg-to-Strasbourg, interactions. I take this interaction as a given, and also explore EU legislative norms.

As Chapter 4 illustrates, EU law has long dealt with the migration of family members of EU Citizens within the EU, irrespective of their nationality, now in the Citizenship Directive.[12] The Family Reunification Directive has set out minimum standards for the entry of family members of TCN migrants who have a 'reasonable prospect' of acquiring a right of permanent residence. The CJEU in the *Family Reunification Directive Ruling* engages with the Strasbourg jurisprudence under Article 8 ECHR. I contend in Chapter 4 that it ought to have developed a distinctive higher EU human right to family reunion. That distinctive EU right emerges in later cases, in particular *Chakroun*, where Dutch financial restrictions on family reunion were deemed incompatible with the Directive. Subsequent cases have vacillated between rights and discretion, but the former is more appropriate to the EU legal framework. There is now clear divergence between and within EU and ECHR standards on family migration, despite glimpses of convergence in *Jeunesse v the Netherlands*.[13]

Chapter 5 examined the scope of protection under international refugee law, the ECHR, and the EU Qualification Directive (and its Recast), which establishes statuses for refugees and those fleeing other forms of serious harm. Chapter 5 reveals that the greatest transformation of refugee law is that, given the manner in which at least the definitional aspects of the Refugee Convention form part of EU law, the CJEU can truly be characterized as a refugee law court. In this context, *Qurbani* is a real disappointment:[14] The manner in which the Court treated Article 31 of the Refugee Convention as outside the scope of EU law is dubious. Nonetheless, concerning the definitional aspects of refugeehood as codified in EU law, the CJEU's rulings on persecution, exclusion, and cessation have made significant contributions to the development of refugee law. On Article 1D, in its *Bolbol* and *El Kott* rulings on Palestinian refugees formerly in UNRWA areas,[15] it has developed a nuanced approach to a highly complex and contested provision of the

[12] Directive 2004/38/EC of the European Parliament and of the Council of 29 April 2004 on the right of citizens of the Union and their family members to move and reside freely within the territory of the Member States (CD) [2004] OJ L229/45.

[13] *Jeunesse v the Netherlands* App No 12738/10 (ECHR, 4 December 2012).

[14] Case C-481/13 *Qurbani* [2014] OJ C 31/24.

[15] Gaza Strip and Lebanon respectively.

Refugee Convention. While its approach departed in some respects from the line advocated by UNHCR, and has not gone without critique,[16] the CJEU's approach will nonetheless protect these refugees much more readily than the previous practices in some European countries.

On subsidiary protection, the Court has worked within the limited confines of the Directive. In *Elgafaji,* it made an admirable attempt to render Article 15(c) intelligible and workable. Rather than a provision designed to protect those fleeing armed conflict in general, the wording requires applicants to demonstrate that they are at individual risk of indiscriminate violence. *Elgafaji* provides workable guidance on that provision, while *Diakité* also helpfully rules out the relevance of International Humanitarian Law conceptions of armed conflict, which some national authorities were using to limit the scope of Article 15(c). Overall, though, the impact of Article 15(c) has been patchy and muted, not least as many fleeing conflict are Convention refugees,[17] or may be at risk of inhuman and degrading treatment and warrant protection under Article 15(b), as the analogue of Article 3 ECHR.[18]

More ominously, this chapter also reveals attempts by the EU legislature to limit the Strasbourg jurisprudence, or at least to freeze it. Concerning subsidiary protection, the EU legislature has attempted to tidy up the Strasbourg case law, and avoided having to give an EU status to all those who benefit from ECHR protection from removal, as has now been exemplified in *M'Bodj.*[19] The tensions include, first, the rights violations that create obligations of *non-refoulement*: The Qualification Directive does not contain a general human rights clause to track the Strasbourg case law on 'flagrant breaches'. Secondly, the Directive only covers certain types of targeted killing rather than the full potential of the Article 2 ECHR jurisprudence. Thirdly, its re-formulation of the Article 3 ECHR protection seems to exclude the so-called 'health cases' and other possible cases concerning socio-economic conditions under Article 3 ECHR, as has been confirmed by *M'Bodj*. Fourthly, although the ECtHR has unequivocally reiterated the absolute nature of the Article 3 ECHR protections, the Qualification Directive allows for exclusion from subsidiary protection on wide grounds. While this move cannot in and of itself undermine the absolute nature of the protections against removal under Article 3 ECHR, it brings back insecurity of status for many non-removables.

Chapter 6 dealt with access to protection for refugees, examining both the barriers to lawful entry in the EU, and the Dublin System which ostensibly allocates responsibility for processing asylum claims across the EU. Access to asylum depends practically on access to a place of refuge. Securing access to territory means overcoming both physical and legal barriers. In practice, safe, legal access to

[16] JC Hathaway and M Foster, *The Law of Refugee Status* (2nd edn, Cambridge University Press 2014) 509–523.

[17] UNHCR, *International Protection Considerations with regard to people fleeing the Syrian Arab Republic, Update II* (UNHCR 22 October 2013).

[18] See *Sufi and Elmi v UK* (2012) 54 EHRR 9.

[19] Case C-542/13 *M'Bodj* [2015] OJ C 65/12.

the EU for those fleeing war and persecution is virtually impossible, due to EU visa policies, carrier sanctions, and other aspects of the EU entry control system. The Refugee Convention's *non-refoulement* guarantee applies at the border and beyond. The ECtHR provides a forum to scrutinize extra-territorial border controls, and vindicate the right to seek protection. In light of the evolving jurisprudence on the meaning of 'jurisdiction' under Article 1 ECHR, the potential to subject many extraterritorial border control activities to Strasbourg standards is evident. *Hirsi v Italy*[20] also breaks new legal ground in finding the prohibition of collective expulsions applicable extraterritorially.

Once in Europe, the Dublin System is a significant barrier, which elongates procedures and often requires asylum seekers to remain in States where their claims are likely to be rejected for want of proper examination. The mechanisms of allocating responsibility under Dublin are legitimized as mutual recognition. In Chapter 1, I suggested that mutual recognition requires more than bare adherence to the ECHR minimum in order to be acceptable. Under the guise of mutual recognition, individuals are exposed to another State's coercive measures with enduring consequences. In this context, human rights protections above the ECHR minimum are imperative. Regrettably, in Opinion 2/2013,[21] the CJEU has seemingly elevated mutual recognition from an adaptable tool in certain areas of EU policy designed to meet particular aims, to a constitutional necessity, requiring strict duties.

As Chapter 6 illustrates, the ECtHR has played an important role in limiting the human rights violations that emerge from the Dublin System. The Grand Chamber ruling in *MSS v Belgium and Greece*[22] was a vindication of human rights, albeit one which publicized what all knew: that behind the façade of EU standards and masking device of 'mutual recognition' lay serious violations of human rights. It broke new legal ground in recognizing the legal vulnerability of asylum seekers and the concomitant obligations on States to avoid leaving them languishing in inhuman living conditions. And crucially, it set a standard to ensure that one European country could not return asylum seekers to another where such conditions were known to prevail, under the guise of mutual recognition. However, it was followed not with a re-think of Dublin, but with persistence in returns to other States where asylum systems were of concern, leading to much further litigation to test the scope of *MSS*, including before the CJEU in *NS/ME*,[23] and back to the Grand Chamber of the ECtHR in *Tarakhel v Switzerland*.[24] The battleground for asylum seekers' rights took place in the interstices of the two supranational courts' rulings. Governments pushed the limits of the rulings, exploiting subtle linguistic differences between the otherwise apparently consistent judgments. The

[20] (2012) 55 EHRR 21.
[21] Opinion 2/13, para 191 et seq.
[22] (2011) 53 EHRR 2.
[23] Joined Cases C-411/10 and C-493/10 *NS v Secretary of State for the Home Department and ME v Refugee Applications Commissioner & Minister for Justice, Equality and Law Reform* [2011] ECR I-13905.
[24] App No 29217/12 (ECHR, 4 November 2014).

Strasbourg Grand Chamber ruling in *Tarakhel* reasserts the importance of assessment of the conditions in the State to which return is contemplated in each individual case.[25] While this outcome can be seen as a vindication of the protection of the individual, De Schutter presciently warned that an individual human rights exception to mutual recognition tends to be 'purely reactive and *ad hoc*, rather than proactive and systematic'.[26] In this context, the Dublin litigation saga is telling. For all the successful and ground-breaking litigation, major institutional reforms have been lacking. The Dublin III Regulation was amended to reflect the *NS/ME* case law, and sets a standard to resist Dublin deportation that may not appropriately reflect human rights standards.

Finally, Chapter 7 linked back to the issues raised in Chapter 2 when considering detention on the basis of migration status. This issue reveals the intimate linkage between migration status and the enjoyment of the most basic of human rights, the right to liberty. Whether asylum seekers and other migrants to the EU may be detained depends largely on their legal status. In *Saadi v UK*,[27] the ECtHR treats authorization principally as a matter of State discretion. Although it insists that detention not be 'arbitrary', it permits detention on a range of instrumental grounds. EU law seems apt to secure the rights of residence of asylum seekers, so the CJEU ought to come to a different view on the legality of detention. Indeed the ECtHR signalled in *Musa v Malta* that there was 'some merit' to this argument.[28] The EU Returns Directive has prompted some striking rulings from the CJEU, significantly curtailing Member States' authority to criminalize and to detain irregular migrants. However, for non-removable irregular migrants who may no longer be detained, EU law, as currently construed, lacks the capacity to create a secure status, although that move would seem to be warranted.[29] We return to the question of regularization, and the capacity to authorize presence in the European condominium.

## V. Final Thoughts

This book seeks to illuminate the dynamic between the two European supranational courts, acknowledging that each is located within a distinctive institutional setting. Overall, this book reveals a complex multilevel system, in which migrants' and refugees' rights find multiple adjudicatory spaces. Like many achievements of the project of European integration, one must stand back to appreciate them.

[25] C Costello and M Mouzourakis, 'Reflections on Reading *Tarakhel*: Is "How Bad is Bad Enough" Good Enough?' (2014) 10 Asiel en Migrantenrecht 404.

[26] O De Schutter, 'The Division of Tasks between the Council of Europe and the European Union in the Promotion of Human Rights in Europe: Conflict, Competition and Complementarity' (2007) REFGOV-FR-11 Working Paper.

[27] *Saadi* (n 11).

[28] *Musa v Malta* [2013] ECHR 232, para 97.

[29] The Court seems to make such a suggestion in *Abdida*, para 60. See N Klausser, 'Etrangers malades et droit de l'Union européenne: Entre accroissement et restriction des garanties juridiques' (2015) *Revue des Droits de l'Homme* <http://revdh.revues.org/1044> accessed 12 April 2015, paras 32–38.

Binding EU standards on much of migration and asylum have the capacity to check migration controls, and afford secure migration status. EU measures are intrinsically amenable to creative, rights-protective interpretation, as the CJEU's case law to date on the Long-Term Residents Directive, the Family Reunification Directive, the Qualification Directive, and even the unpromising-looking Returns Directives testifies.

Much is left to the ECtHR and CJEU. Together, they are a powerful force, and can open up new approaches to migrants' rights, and create an inclusive dynamic. However, their capacity has its limits. Both courts are overburdened. There was a backlog of 69,900 cases waiting to be heard before the ECtHR at the end of 2014. Most cases submitted are deemed inadmissible.[30] The reform process may not meet its aim of alleviating the backlog. Noting the 'unnecessary pressure' on the Court's workload, a new system of cases deemed inadmissible was adopted.[31] Protocol 15 ECHR also contains an express reference to the principle of subsidiarity and States' margin of appreciation in the ECHR Preamble,[32] a move whose likely impact is contested.[33] In addition, Protocol 16 ECHR introduces the possibility for the ECtHR to give 'advisory opinions on questions of principle' on the interpretation of ECHR provisions.[34]

The CJEU too is overburdened, although reforms have meant that it now deals with preliminary references fairly expeditiously. Yet, acceleration risks undermining the quality of reasoning, of particular concern given that Court's already elliptical style.[35] Moreover, it should be borne in mind that national judges are European judges too, and much depends on their creativity and engagement with both the ECHR and EU law. The CJEU's preliminary reference procedure provides a remarkable forum for both national judges and the CJEU.[36] Its efficacy depends

[30] ECtHR, 'Press Conference by President Dean Spielmann, Strasbourg, 29 January 2015' (2015) <http://www.echr.coe.int/Documents/Speech_20150129_Press_Conference_2015_ENG.pdf> accessed 12 April 2015.

[31] ECtHR, 'High Level Conference on the Future of the European Court of Human Rights: Brighton Declaration' (19-20 April 2012) para 14 <http://www.echr.coe.int/Documents/2012_Brighton_FinalDeclaration_ENG.pdf> accessed 12 April 2015.

[32] 'Affirming that the High Contracting Parties, in accordance with the principle of subsidiarity, have the primary responsibility to secure the rights and freedoms defined in this Convention and the Protocols thereto, and that in doing so they enjoy a margin of appreciation, subject to the supervisory jurisdiction of the European Court of Human Rights established by this Convention.'

[33] F Fabbrini, 'The Margin of Appreciation and the Principle of Subsidiarity: A Comparison' (2015) *iCourts Working Paper No 15*. For a defence of the Protocol, see D Spielmann, 'Whither the Margin of Appreciation?' (2014) 67(1) Current Legal Problems 49.

[34] For a discussion, see P Gragl, '(Judicial) Love is Not a One-Way Street: The EU Preliminary Reference Procedure as a Model for ECtHR Advisory Opinions under Draft Protocol No 16' (2013) 38(2) European Law Review 229; K Dzehtsiarou and N O'Meara, 'Advisory Jurisdiction and the European Court of Human Rights: A Magic Bullet for Dialogue and Docket-Control?' (2014) 34(3) Legal Studies 444.

[35] Key cases in this field such as C-172/08 *Metock* [2008] ECR I-6241 have already been dealt with under truncated procedures. The first case on the Dublin Regulation, Case C-19/08 *Petrosian* [2009] ECR I-495, was decided without an AG's Opinion. The reasoning is terse, and fails to really get to grips with the underlying issues of effective judicial protection.

[36] By way of example, once the first instance judge in Budapest sought guidance on Article 1D (in both Case C-31/09 *Bolbol* [2010] ECR I-5539 and Case C-364/11 *El Kott* [2013] OJ C46/8), there

too on the receptiveness of national judges. The strength of the preliminary reference procedure, the fact that the case begins and ends in the national court, is also a source of fragility.[37] Notably, within the EU system, migrants and refugees themselves cannot bring cases directly challenging national restrictions, nor can they ordinarily directly challenge EU legislative acts.[38] National judges are guardians and gatekeepers of migrants' EU rights.

Governments have many legitimate means to influence the outcome of cases, by intervening for instance.[39] The preliminary reference procedure is increasingly crowded with national governmental interventions, raising doubts about whether it still retains its capacity as a low-visibility venue for legal transformation. The lack of clear route for public interest or other interveners is particularly worrisome in light of the governmental dominance. Even UNHCR finds itself using cyberspace to make its points to the CJEU. Although its statements may be regarded as informal *amicus curiae* briefs,[40] even it has no formal right to be heard before the CJEU. Reforms are needed to open the CJEU to range of voices, if it is to meet the institutional challenge of becoming a human rights and refugee law court.[41]

Courts' capacity to act as agents of inclusion needs political support. Without it, backlash leading to an undermining of institutional structures is not unthinkable. As well as concerns about over-burdening the supranational courts, cases on migrants' rights are often of high political salience. Governments may be tempted to try to check the decisional autonomy of courts. Currently, some of the reforms of the Strasbourg Court under discussion suggest that dealing with overburdening may become a pretext for limiting authority.[42] While this book criticizes the ECtHR, my critique is that the Strasbourg Court is too timid, not that it is too bold, and so has little affinity with the types of political swipes at the ECtHR that are common in some Member States.[43] Some of the reforms currently under discussion illustrate that limiting the Court's jurisdiction is no longer a political

was no avoiding its complexities. When the CJEU failed to address all the questions posed in *Bolbol*, the judge made the second reference in *El Kott*.

[37] Again as Case C-465/07 *Elgafaji v Saatssecreteris van Justitie* [2009] ECR I-921 reveals, the *Raad van State* seems to have undermined some of the CJEU ruling, holding that Art 3 ECHR and the domestic orthodoxy on individuation still hold.

[38] Given the *locus standi* limitations posed on individual applicants by Art 263(4) TFEU.

[39] See, for instance, interventions in *Saadi* (n 11) urged that the Court restrict its interpretation of Art 3 ECHR.

[40] e.g. by AG Sharpston in her Opinion in *Bolbol* (n 36).

[41] G de Búrca, 'After the EU Charter of Fundamental Rights: The Court of Justice as a Human Rights Adjudicator?' (2013) Maastricht Journal of European and Comparative Law 168.

[42] ibid.

[43] This book is thus out of kilter with political debates in some States, notably the UK, which seek to rein in the Court for checking States too readily. Arguably, this is because those political debates are ill-informed. For a critique of the UK Conservative Party's proposals for legal inaccuracy, see A Young, 'HRA Howlers: The Conservative Party and Reform of the Human Rights Act 1998' (*UK Constitutional Law Blog*, 7 October 2014) http://ukconstitutionallaw.org/2014/10/07/alison-young-hra-howlers-the-conservative-party-and-reform-of-the-human-rights-act-1998/ accessed 12 April 2015.

taboo,[44] so scholarly consideration of the institutional implications of this new climate is warranted.

Human rights universalism does not require open borders, but it does require that there are clear limits to what may be done in the name of migration control, and that the statuses accorded to migrants allow them to live full, dignified lives where they live. Migration controls in Europe manifestly violate human rights, in particular those of refugees. Safe access to asylum remains elusive, as migration controls prevent most of those seeking refuge from travelling legally. Many risk their lives to reach the legal protections European law affords them. If they are lucky and survive their dangerous journeys, their protection claims may or may not be recognized. If they are not, they find themselves at the sharp end of migration control, with detention used all too frequently as a means to reassert control. Courts in Europe frequently find migration-related detention conditions to be inhuman and degrading, or the detention itself to be unlawful. The urgency of the task of realizing the human rights of migrants and refugees in European law is all too apparent.

While the process of judicial dialogue has the potential to ensure enhanced human rights protection,[45] it also has risks. It may wrongly give the impression of a human rights surfeit, or become iterative and mannered, rather than transformative. Where rights restrictions are embodied in migration status and migration controls, those legal structures need political reform. Human rights and EU law provide an important supranational forum to challenge the restrictions arising out of migration status and migration controls, but vindicating human rights also require institutional and legislative changes. While this book has focused on supranational courts and litigation, it has aimed to capture the contestation and transformative potential of those processes. Litigation may serve to catalyze political activism. However, to quote Sen, 'human rights cannot be sensibly confined within the juridical model in which it is frequently incarcerated'.[46] Disruptive and innovative methods of social action are needed if the full inclusivity of human rights is to be realized.

[44] UK Conservative Party, 'Protecting Human Rights in the UK: The Conservatives' Proposals for Changing Britain's Human Rights Laws' (2014).

[45] A Torres Pérez, *Conflicts of Rights in the European Union. A Theory of Supranational Adjudication* (OUP 2009) 110–12, on the diachronic nature of judicial dialogue, with arguments developing over time.

[46] A Sen, 'Elements of a Theory of Human Rights' (2004) 32(4) Philosophy and Public Affairs 315, 319–20.

ANNEX 1

# States' Selective Participation in EU Asylum and Immigration Measures

The UK and Ireland have special arrangements, whereby they may choose to opt-in to particular legislative proposals or measures adopted by the European Union (EU) in the fields of immigration and asylum.[1] Their positions on the various legislative measures considered in this book are set out in Table 1. These special arrangements are set out in various protocols to the Treaty on the Functioning of the European Union (TFEU), which differentiate between Schengen and Schengen-building measures and general measures that form part of the Area of Freedom, Security and Justice.[2] These are principally Protocol (No 19) on the Schengen Acquis Integrated into the Framework of the European Union; Protocol (No 20) on the application of certain aspects of Article 26 of the TFEU to the UK and Ireland; and Protocol (No 21) on the position of the UK and Ireland in respect of the Area of Freedom, Security and Justice.

Protocol No 22 is on the position of Denmark. Denmark has an opt-out from EU Justice and Home Affairs law. Denmark has however become part of the Dublin System by means of an international agreement.[3] Denmark is set to hold a referendum in 2015 on replacing its complete opt-out from justice and home affairs measures with a selective one, similar to the UK and Irish opt-outs.[4]

The Dublin System comprises all the EU Member States, together with Iceland, Norway,[5] Liechtenstein, and Switzerland.[6]

[1] For an overview of the UK's selective participation, see C Costello and E Hancox, *Policy Primer: The UK, the Common European Asylum System and EU Immigration Law* (Migration Observatory at Oxford May 2014).

[2] See further S Peers, 'In a World of their Own? Justice and Home Affairs Opt-outs and the Treaty of Lisbon' (2007–08) 10 Cambridge Yearbook of European Legal Studies 383.

[3] Agreement between the European Community and the Kingdom of Denmark extending to Denmark the provisions of Council Regulation (EC) No 343/2003 establishing the criteria and mechanisms for determining the Member State responsible for examining an asylum application lodged in one of the Member States by a third-country national and Council Regulation (EC) No 2725/2000 concerning the establishment of 'Eurodac' for the comparison of fingerprints for the effective application of the Dublin Convention [2006] OJ L96/6.

[4] See further R Adler-Nissen, 'Justice and Home Affairs: Denmark as an Active Differential European' in L Miles and A Wivel (eds), *Denmark and the European Union* (Routledge 2014) 65; R Adler-Nissen, 'Through the EU's Back and Front Doors: Norway's and Denmark's Selective Approaches in the Area of Freedom, Justice and Security' in C Grøn, P Nedergaard, and A Wivel (eds), *Still the 'Other' European Community? The Nordic Countries and the European Union* (Routledge 2015) 188.

[5] Agreement between the European Community and the Republic of Iceland and the Kingdom of Norway concerning the criteria and mechanisms for establishing the State responsible for examining a request for asylum lodged in a Member State or in Iceland or Norway—Declarations [2001] OJ L93/38.

[6] Protocol between the European Community, the Swiss Confederation, and the Principality of Liechtenstein on the accession of the Principality of Liechtenstein to the Agreement between the European Community and the Swiss Confederation concerning the criteria and mechanisms for establishing the State responsible for examining a request for asylum lodged in a Member State or in Switzerland [2011] OJ L160/37; Agreement between the European Community and the Swiss Confederation concerning the criteria and mechanisms for establishing the State responsible for examining a request for asylum lodged in a Member State or in Switzerland [2008] OJ L53/3.

**Table 1** UK and Ireland's Selective Participation in EU Immigration and Asylum Measures

| EU Measure | UK | Ireland |
|---|---|---|
| **Legal Migration** | | |
| Family Reunification Directive: Council Directive 2003/86/EC on the right to family reunification [2003] OJ L251/12 111 | No | No |
| Students Directive: Council Directive 2004/114/EC of 13 December 2004 on the conditions of admission of third-country nationals for the purposes of studies, pupil exchange, unremunerated training, or voluntary service [2004] OJ L375/12 | No | No |
| Researchers Directive: Council Directive 2005/71/EC on a specific procedure for admitting third-country nationals for the purposes of scientific research [2005] OJ L289/15 110 | No | Yes |
| Long-Term Residents Directive: Council Directive (EC) 2003/109 concerning the status of third-country nationals who are long-term residents (2004) OJ L16/44 | No | No |
| Blue Card Directive: Council Directive 2009/50/EC of 25 May 2009 on the conditions of entry and residence of third-country nationals for the purposes of highly qualified employment (Blue Card Directive) [2009] OJ L155/17 | No | No |
| Single Permit Directive: Directive 2011/98/EU on a single application procedure for a single permit for third-country nationals to reside and work in the territory of a Member State and on a common set of rights for third-country workers legally residing in a Member State [2011] OJ L343/1. | No | No |
| Intra-Corporate Transferees Directive: Directive 2014/66/EU of 15 May 2014 on the conditions of entry and residence of third-country nationals in the framework of an intra-corporate transfer [2014] OJ L157/1 | No | No |
| Seasonal Workers Directive: Council Directive 2014/36/EU of 26 February 2014 on the conditions of entry and stay of third-country nationals for the purpose of employment as seasonal workers [2014] OJ L94/375 | No | No |
| Proposal for Students and Researchers Directive (recast): Proposal for a Directive of the Parliament and European Council and on the conditions of entry and residence of third-country nationals for the purposes of research, studies, pupil exchange, remunerated and unremunerated training, voluntary service, and au pairing (recast) COM (2013) 0151 final | No | No |
| **Irregular Migration** | | |
| Carrier Sanctions Directive: Directive 2001/51/EC supplementing the provisions of Article 26 of the Convention implementing the Schengen Agreement of 14 June 1985 [2001] OJ L187/45 | Yes | Yes |
| Returns Directive: Council Directive (EC) 2008/115 on common standards and procedures in Member States for returning illegally staying third-country nationals [2008] OJ L348/98 | No | No |
| Employer Sanctions Directive: Directive 2009/52/EC providing for minimum standards on sanctions and measures against employers of illegally staying third-country nationals [2009] OJ L168/24 | No | No |
| Trafficking Directive: Council Directive (EC) 2004/81 on the residence permit issued to third-country nationals who are victims of trafficking in human beings or who have been the subject of an action to facilitate illegal immigration, who cooperate with the competent authorities [2004] OJ L261/19 | Yes | Yes |

| EU Measure | UK | Ireland |
|---|---|---|
| **Asylum** | | |
| EURODAC Regulation: Council Regulation (EC) No 2725/2000 of 11 December 2000 concerning the establishment of 'Eurodac' for the comparison of fingerprints for the effective application of the Dublin Convention [2000] OJ L316/1 | Yes | Yes |
| Dublin II Regulation; Council Regulation (EC) No 343/2003 of 18 February 2003 establishing the criteria and mechanisms for determining the Member State responsible for examining an asylum application lodged in one of the Member States by a third-country national [2003] OJ L50/1 | Yes | Yes |
| Temporary Protection Directive: Council Directive 2001/55/EC of 20 July 2001 on minimum standards for giving temporary protection in the event of a mass influx of displaced persons and on measures promoting a balance of efforts between Member States in receiving such persons and bearing the consequences thereof [2001] OJ L212/12 | Yes | Yes |
| Reception Conditions Directive: Council Directive 2003/9 laying down minimum standards for the reception of asylum seekers of 27 January 2003 [2003] OJ L31/18 | Yes | No |
| Qualification Directive: Council Directive 2004/83 of 29 April 2004 on minimum standards for the qualification and status of third-country nationals or stateless persons as refugees or as persons who otherwise need international protection and the content of the protection granted [2004] OJ L/304/12 | Yes | Yes |
| Asylum Procedures Directive: Council Directive 2005/85/EC of 1 December 2005 on minimum standards on procedures in Member States for granting and withdrawing refugee status [2005] OJ L326/13 | Yes | Yes |
| Recast EURODAC Regulation: Regulation (EU) No 603/2013 on the establishment of 'Eurodac' for the comparison of fingerprints for the effective application of Regulation (EU) No 604/2013 establishing the criteria and mechanisms for determining the Member State responsible for examining an application for international protection lodged in one of the Member States by a third-country national or a stateless person and on requests for the comparison with Eurodac data by Member States' law enforcement authorities and Europol for law enforcement purposes, and amending Regulation (EU) No 1077/2011 establishing a European Agency for the operational management of large-scale IT systems in the Area of Freedom, Security and Justice [2013] OJ L180/1 | Yes | Yes |
| Dublin III Regulation: Regulation (EU) No 604/2013 of 26 June 2013 establishing the criteria and mechanisms for determining the Member State responsible for examining an application for international protection lodged in one of the Member States by a third-country national or a stateless person (recast) [2013] OJ L/180/31 | Yes | Yes |
| Recast Qualification Directive: Directive 2011/95/EU of 13 December 2011 on standards for the qualification of third-country nationals or stateless persons as beneficiaries of international protection, for a uniform status for refugees or for persons eligible for subsidiary protection, and for the content of the protection granted [2011] OJ L/337/9 | No | No |
| Recast Asylum Procedures Directive: Directive 2013/32/EU of the European Parliament and of the Council of 26 June 2013 on common procedures for granting and withdrawing international protection [2013] OJ L/180/60 | No | No |

*(Continued)*

**Table 1** *Continued*

| EU Measure | UK | Ireland |
|---|---|---|
| Recast Reception Conditions Directive: Directive 2013/33/EU of 26 June 2013 laying down standards for the reception of applicants for international protection (recast) [2013] OJ L180/96 | No | No |
| Asylum, Migration and Integration Fund Regulation: Regulation (EU) No 516/2014 establishing the Asylum, Migration and Integration Fund [2014] OJ L150/168 | Yes | Yes |

# *Select Bibliography of Scholarly Works*


A

Abizadeh A, 'Democratic Theory and Border Coercion: No Rights to Unilaterally Control your Own Borders' (2008) 36 Political Theory 37

Ackers D, 'The Negotiations on the Asylum Procedures Directive' (2005) 7 EJML 1

Acosta D, 'The Good, the Bad and the Ugly in EU Migration Law: Is the European Parliament Becoming Bad and Ugly? (The Adoption of Directive 2008/15: The Returns Directive)' (2009) 11 EJML 19

Acosta D, *The Long-Term Residence Status as a Subsidiary Form of EU Citizenship—An Analysis of Directive 2003/109* (Martinus Nijhoff Publishers 2011)

Acosta D, 'Civic Citizenship Reintroduced? The Long-Term Residence Directive as a Postnational Form of Membership' (2015) 21(2) ELJ 200

Akram S, 'UNRWA and Palestinian Refugees' in E Fiddian-Qasmiyeh, G Loescher, K Long, and N Sigona (eds), *Oxford Handbook of Refugee and Forced Migration Studies* (OUP 2014)

Akram S and Goodwin-Gill G, 'Brief *Amicus Curiae* on the Status of Palestinian Refugees under International Law' (2000–2001) 11 Pal YIL 185

Alexy R, *A Theory of Constitutional Rights* (OUP 2002)

Aliverti A, *Crimes of Mobility: Criminal Law and the Regulation of Immigration* (Routledge 2014)

Alston P and Weiler JHH, 'An "Ever Closer Union" in Need of a Human Rights Policy: The European Union and Human Rights' (1998) 9 European Journal of International Law 658

Alter K, 'The European Court of Justice's Political Power across Space and Time' (2009) 9 *Northwestern University School and Law and Economics Working Paper* 3

Alter K, *The European Court's Political Power: Selected Essays* (OUP 2009)

Anker D, 'Refugee Law, Gender and the Human Rights Paradigm' (2002) 15 Harvard Human Rights Law Journal 133

Apap J, de Bruycker P, and Schmitter C, 'Regularisation of Illegal Aliens in the European Union. Summary Reports of a Comparative Study' (2000) 2 EJML 263

Arendt H, 'The Decline of the Nation-State and the End of the Rights of Man' in *The Origins of Totalitarianism* (A Harvest Book/Harcourt, Inc 1948)

Arnull A, 'Family Reunification and Fundamental Rights' (2006) 31 ELRev 611

Avbelj M and Komárek J (eds), 'Four Visions of Constitutional Pluralism–Symposium Transcript' (2008) 2(1) EJLS 325

Azoulai L, 'The (Mis)construction of the European Individual: Two Essays on Union Citizenship Law' (2014) EUI Working Papers in Law 2014/14

B

Bader V (ed), *Citizenship and Exclusion* (Macmillan 1997)

Bader V, 'Fairly Open Borders' in V Bader (ed), *Citizenship and Exclusion* (Macmillan 1997)

Bader V, 'The Ethics of Immigration' (2005) 12 Constellations 331

Baldaccini A, 'The Return and Removal of Irregular Migrants under EU law: An Analysis of the Returns Directive' (2009) 11 EJML 1
Baldaccini A, 'The EU Directive on Return: Principles and Protest' (2010) 28 RSQ 114
Baldaccini A, Guild E, and Toner H (eds), *Whose Freedom, Security and Justice? EU Immigration and Asylum Law after 1999* (Hart Publishing 2007)
Baldwin-Edwards M and Kraler A, *REGINE: Regularisations in Europe. Study on Practices in the Area of Regularisation in the Member States of the EU—Final Report* (ICMPD 2009)
Battjes H, *European Asylum Law and International Law* (Martinus Nijhoff Publishers 2006)
Battjes H, 'Landmarks: Soering's Legacy' (2008) 1 Amsterdam Law Forum 139
Battjes H, 'In Search of a Fair Balance: The Absolute Character of the Prohibition of *Refoulement* under Article 3 ECHR Reassessed' (2009) 22 Leiden Journal of International Law 583
Bauböck R, *Transnational Citizenship: Membership and Rights in International Migration* (Edward Elgar 1994)
Bauböck R, 'Why European Citizenship? Normative Approaches to Supranational Union' (2007) 8 Theoretical Inquiries in Law 453
Bauböck R, 'There is a Mismatch between Citizens' Moral Intuitions and Their Political Views' (May/June 2009) (34)3 Boston Review 17
Bauböck R, Ersboll E, Groenendijk K, and Waldrauch H (eds), *Acquisition and Loss of Nationality: Volumes I & II* (Amsterdam University Press 2006)
Benhabib S, *The Rights of Others: Aliens, Residents and Citizens* (Cambridge University Press 2004)
Benhabib S, *Another Cosmopolitanism: Hospitality, Sovereignty and Democratic Iterations* (OUP 2006)
Benhabib S, *Dignity in Adversity: Human Rights in Troubled Times* (Polity Press 2011)
Benhabib S and Resnik J (eds), *Migrations and Mobilities: Citizenship, Borders, and Gender* (New York University Press 2009)
Besselink L, 'Entrapped by the Maximum Standard: On Fundamental Rights, Pluralism and Subsidiarity in the European Union' (1998) 35 CMLRev 629
Besson S, 'The European Union and Human Rights: Towards a New Kind of Post-National Human Rights Institution' (2006) 6 HRLRev 323
Besson S, 'European Legal Pluralism after *Kadi*' (2009) 5 European Constitutional Law Review 237
Bignami F, 'Creating European Rights: National Values and Supranational Interests' (2005) 11 CJEL 241
Bigo D, 'Border Regimes, Police Cooperation and Security in an Enlarged European Union' in J Zielonka (ed), *Europe Unbound: Enlarging and Reshaping the Boundaries of the European Union* (Routledge 2003)
Boeles P, 'Directive on Family Reunification: Are the Dilemmas Resolved?' (2001) 3 EJML 61
Bonjour S, 'Between Integration Provision and Selection Mechanism. Party Politics, Judicial Constraints, and the Making of French and Dutch Policies of Civic Integration Abroad' (2010) 12(3) EJML 299
Bonjour S, 'The Transfer of Pre-Departure Integration Requirements for Family Migrants among Member States of the European Union' (2014) 2(2) Comparative Migration Studies 203
Bosniak L, 'Universal Citizenship and the Problem of Alienage' (2000) 94 Northwestern University Law Review 963

Bosniak L, 'Amnesty in Immigration: Forgetting, Forgiving, Freedom' (2013) 16 Critical Review of International Social and Political Philosophy 344
Bryan I and Langford P, 'The Lawful Detention of Unauthorised Aliens under the European System for the Protection of Human Rights' (2011) 80 Nordic Journal of International Law 193
Byrne R, Noll G, and Vedsted-Hansen J (eds), *New Asylum Countries? Migration Control and Refugee Protection in an Enlarged European Union* (Kluwer Law International 2002)
Byrne R and Shacknove A, 'The Safe Country Notion in European Asylum Law' (1996) 9 Harvard Human Rights Journal 185
Byrne R, Noll G, and Vedsted-Hansen J, 'Understanding Refugee Law in an Enlarged European Union' (2004) 15(2) EJIL 355

C

Callewaert J, 'The European Convention on Human Rights and European Union law: A Long Way to Harmony' (2009) 6 HRLRev 768
Cantor D and Durieux JF (eds), *Refuge from Humanity? War Refugees and International Humanitarian Law* (Brill–Nijhoff 2014)
Carens J, 'Aliens and Citizens: The Case for Open Borders' (1987) 49(2) Review of Politics 251
Carens J, 'Who Should Get In? The Ethics of Immigration Admissions' (2003) 17 Ethics and International Affairs 95
Carens J, 'The Case for Amnesty' (May/June 2009) Boston Review
Carens J, *The Ethics of Immigration* (OUP 2013)
Carlier J and Sarolea S, 'Le Droit d'Asile dans l'Union européenne contrôlé par la Cour européenne des droits de l'homme' (2011) 6436 Journal des Tribunaux 353
Cassese A, 'Can the Notion of Inhuman and Degrading Treatment be applied to Socio-Economic Conditions?' (1991) 2 EJIL 141
Castles S, 'Guestworkers in Europe: A Resurrection?' (2006) 40 International Migration Review 741
Chelvan S, 'Case Comment: *X, Y and Z v Minister voor Immigratie en Asiel*: A Missed Opportunity or a New Dawn?' (2013) No5 Chambers Newsletter
Cholewinksi R, *Borders and Discrimination in the European Union* (ILPA/MPG 2002)
Cholewinksi R, 'Family Reunification and Conditions Placed on Family Members: Dismantling a Fundamental Human Right' (2002) 4 EJML 271
Cholewinksi R, 'Preventing Irregular Migration' in F Julien-Laferriere, H Labaye, and O Erdström (eds), *The European Immigration and Asylum Policy: Critical Assessment Five Years After the Amsterdam Treaty* (Bruylant 2005)
Clayton G, 'Asylum Seekers in Europe: *MSS v Belgium and Greece*' (2011) 11 HRLRev 758
Cornelisse G, *Immigration Detention and Human Rights: Rethinking Territorial Sovereignty* (Martinus Nijhoff Publishers 2010)
Costello C, 'Accidents of Place and Parentage: Birthright Citizenship and Border Crossings' in *The Citizenship Referendum: Implications for the Constitution and Human Rights* (Law School Trinity College Dublin 2004)
Costello C, 'The Asylum Procedures Directive and the Proliferation of Safe Country Practices: Deterrence, Deflection and the Dismantling of International Protection' (2005) 7 EJML 35
Costello C, 'The Bosphorus Ruling of the European Court of Human Rights: Fundamental Rights and Blurred Boundaries in Europe' (2006) 6 HRLRev 87

Costello C, 'Administrative Governance and the Europeanisation of Asylum and Immigration Policy' in H Hofmann and A Türk (eds), *EU Administrative Governance* (Elgar Publishing 2006)

Costello C, 'The Asylum Procedures Directive in Legal Context: Equivocal Standards Meet General Principles' in A Baldaccini, E Guild, and H Toner (eds), *Whose Freedom, Security and Justice? EU Immigration and Asylum Law after 1999* (Hart Publishing 2007)

Costello C, '*Metock*: Free Movement and "Normal Family Life" in the Union' (2009) 46 CMLRev 587

Costello C, 'Citizenship of the Union: Above Abuse?' in R de la Feria and S Vogenauer (eds), *Prohibition of Abuse of Law: A New General Principle of EU Law* (Hart Publishing 2011)

Costello C, 'The Ruling of the Court of Justice in *NS/ME* on the Fundamental Rights of Asylum Seekers under the Dublin Regulation: Finally, an End to Blind Trust across the EU?' (2012) 2 Asiel & Migrantenrecht 83

Costello C, 'Courting Access to Asylum in Europe: Recent Supranational Jurisprudence Explored' (2012) 12(2) HRLRev 287

Costello C, 'Article 33—Family and Professional Life' in S Peers, T Hervey, J Kenner, and A Ward (eds), *The EU Charter of Fundamental Rights—A Commentary* (Hart Publishing 2014)

Costello C, 'Child Citizens & *De Facto* Deportation: Tender Years, Fragile Ties & Security of Residence' in K Bradley, A Whelan, and N Travers (eds), *Of Courts and Constitutions: Liber Amicorum in Honour of Nial Fennelly* (Hart Publishing 2014)

Costello C, 'Migrants and Forced Labour: A Labour Law Response' in A Bogg, C Costello, A Davies, and J Prassl (eds), *The Autonomy of Labour Law* (Hart Publishing 2015)

Costello C, 'Immigration Detention: The Grounds Beneath our Feet' (2015) 68(1) Current Legal Problems 143

Costello C and Brown E, 'Comity, Convergence and Contrasts –The ECHR and European Union Law' in U Kilkelly (ed), *ECHR and Irish Law* (Jordans 2004)

Costello C and Brown E, 'The EU and the ECHR before European and Irish Courts' in U Kilkelly (ed), *ECHR and Irish Law* (2nd edn, Jordans 2008)

Costello C and Moreno-Lax V, 'The Extraterritorial Application of the EU Charter of Fundamental Rights: From Territoriality to Facticity, the Effectiveness Model' in S Peers, T Hervey, J Kenner, and A Ward (eds), *The EU Charter of Fundamental Rights: A Commentary* (Hart Publishing 2014)

Costello C and Mouzourakis M, 'Reflections on Reading *Tarakhel*: Is "How Bad is Bad Enough" Good Enough?' (2014) 10 Asiel & Migrantenrecht 404

Costello C and Freedland M (eds), *Migrants at Work: Immigration and Vulnerability in Labour Law* (OUP 2014)

Craig P, 'The Nature of the Community: Integration, Democracy and Legitimacy' in P Craig and G de Búrca (eds), *The Evolution of EU Law* (OUP 1999)

Craig P, *EU Administrative Law* (OUP 2006)

Craig P, and de Búrca G (eds), *The Evolution of EU Law* (OUP 1999)

Craig P and de Búrca G (eds), *EU Law: Text, Cases and Materials* (4th edn, OUP 2008)


## D


Dauvergne C, 'Sovereignty, Migration and the Rule of Law in Global Times' (2004) 67 MLR 588

Dauvergne C, *Making People Illegal: What Globalization Means for Migration and Law* (Cambridge University Press 2008)

P Davies G, 'The Right to Stay at Home: A Basis for Expanding European Family Rights' in D Kochenov (ed), *EU Citizenship and Federalism: The Role of Rights* (Cambridge University Press 2016, *forthcoming*)

De Bruycker P (ed), *Regularisations of Illegal Immigrants in the European Union* (Odysseus/Bruylant 2000)

De Búrca G, 'After the EU Charter of Fundamental Rights: The Court of Justice as a Human Rights Adjudicator?' (2013) 20 Maastricht Journal of European and Comparative Law 168

De Búrca G and Gerstenberg O, 'The Denationalization of Constitutional Law' (2006) 47 Harvard International Law Journal 243

De Hart B, 'Love Thy Neighbour: Family Reunification and the Rights of Insiders' (2009) 11 EJML 235

Den Heijer M, 'Whose Rights and Which Rights? The Continuing Story of *Non-refoulement* under the European Convention on Human Rights' (2008) 10 EJML 277

Den Heijer M, 'Issues of Shared Responsibility before the European Court of Human Rights' (2012) ACIL Research Paper No 2012-04 SHARES Series

Den Heijer M, *Europe and Extratteritorial Asylum* (Hart Publishing 2012)

De Jesús I and De Schutter O, 'Binding the EU to International Human Rights Law' (2008) 27 Yearbook of European Law 277

Dembour MB, 'Human Rights Law and National Sovereignty in Collusion: The Plight of Quasi-Nationals at Strasbourg' (2003) 21 Netherlands Quarterly of Human Rights 63

Dembour MB, *Who Believes in Human Rights? Reflections on the European Convention* (Cambridge University Press 2006)

De Schutter O, 'Globalization and Jurisdiction: Lessons From the European Convention on Human Rights' NYU Center for Human Rights and Global Justice Working Paper No 9, 2005

De Schutter O, 'The Promotion of Fundamental Rights by the Union as a Contribution to the European Legal Space (I): Mutual Recognition and Mutual Trust in the Establishment of the Area of Freedom, Security and Justice' (2006) REFGOV-FR-2 Working Paper

De Schutter O, 'The Division of Tasks between the Council of Europe and the European Union in the Promotion of Human Rights in Europe: Conflict, Competition and Complementarity' (2007) REFGOV-FR-11 Working Paper

De Schutter O, '*Bosphorus* post-Accession: Redefining the Relationships between the European Court of Human Rights and the Parties to the Convention' in V Kosta, N Skoutaris, and V Tzevelekos (eds), *The EU Accession to the ECHR* (Hart Publishing 2014)

Dewhurst E, 'The Right of Irregular Immigrants to Outstanding Remuneration under the EU Sanctions Directive: Rethinking Domestic Labour Policy in a Globalised World' (2011) 13 EJML 389

Dewhurst E, 'The Right of Irregular Immigrants to Back Pay: The Spectrum of Protection in International, Regional and National Legal Systems' in C Costello and M Freedland (eds), *Migrants at Work* (OUP 2014)

Douglas-Scott S, 'A Tale of Two Courts: Luxembourg, Strasbourg and the Growing European Human Rights Acquis' (2006) 43 CMLRev 619

Douglas-Scott S, 'Justice, Injustice and the Rule of Law in the EU' in G de Búrca, D Kochenov, and A Williams (eds), *Debating Europe's Justice Deficit* (Hart Publishing 2015)

Douglas-Scott S, 'The Relationship between the EU and the ECHR Five Years on from the Treaty of Lisbon' in S de Vries, U Bernitz, and S Weatherill (eds), The EU Charter of Fundamental Rights as a Binding Instrument: Five Years Old and Growing Hart Publishing 2015, *forthcoming*)

Durieux JF, 'Salah Sheekh is a Refugee: New Insights into Primary and Subsidiary Forms of Protection' (2008) Refugee Studies Centre Working Paper No 49

Durieux JF, 'The Vanishing Refugee: How EU Asylum Law Blurs the Specificity of Refugee Protection' in H Lambert, J McAdam, and M Fullerton (eds), *The Global Reach of European Refugee Law* (Cambridge University Press 2013)

Düvell F, 'Paths into Irregularity: The Legal and Political Construction of Irregular Migration' (2011) 13 EJML 275

E

Eckes C, 'EU Accession to the ECHR: Between Autonomy and Adaptation' (2013) 76(2) MLR 254

Edwards A, *Back to Basics: The Right to Liberty and Security of Person and 'Alternatives to Detention' of Refugees, Asylum seekers, Stateless Persons and Other Migrants* (UNHCR 2011)

Edwards A and Van Waas L, *Nationality and Statelessness in International Law* (Cambridge University Press 2014)

Ellerman A, 'The Rule of Law and the Right to Stay: The Moral Claims of Undocumented Migrants' (2014) 42 Politics & Society 293

Endicott T, '"International Meaning": Comity in Fundamental Rights Adjudication' (2002) 14 IJRL 280

Errera R, 'The ECJ and Subsidiary Protection: Reflections on *Elgafaji*—And After' Paper presented at the IARLJ conference, Berlin, 19–20 October 2009

Errera R, 'Cessation and Assessment of New Circumstances: a Comment on *Abdulla*, CJEU, 2 March 2010' (2011) 23 IJRL 521

Ersbøll E, '*Biao v Denmark*: discrimination among citizens' (2014) 79 EUI Working Paper RSCAS 14

F

Farahat A, 'The Exclusiveness of Inclusion: On the Boundaries of Human Rights in Protecting Transnational and Second Generation Migrants' (2009) 11 EJML 253

Fauchald O and Nollkaemper A (eds), *The Practice of International and National Courts and the (De-)Fragmentation of International Law* (Hart Publishing 2014)

Feldman G, *The Migration Apparatus: Security, Labor, and Policymaking in the European Union* (Stanford University Press 2012)

Feller E, Türk V, and Nicholson F (eds), *Refugee Protection in International Law: UNHCR's Global Consultations on International Protection* (Cambridge University Press 2003)

Ferrara A, 'Europe as a "Special Area for Human Hope"' (2007) 14(3) Constellations 315

Fischer-Loscano A, Löhr T, and Tohidipur T, 'Border Controls at Sea: Requirements under International Human Rights and Refugee Law' (2009) 21 IJRL 256

Foster M, *International Refugee Law and Socioeconomic Rights: Refuge from Deprivation* (Cambridge University Press 2007)

Fredman S, 'Human Rights Transformed: Positive Duties and Positive Rights' (2006) Autumn, PL 498

G

Gammeltoft-Hansen T, *Access to Asylum: International Refugee Law and the Globalisation of Migration Control* (Cambridge University Press 2011)

Gammeltoft-Hansen T and Gammeltoft-Hansen H, 'The Right to Seek—Revisited. On the UN Human Rights Declaration Article 14 and Access to Asylum Procedures in the EU' (2008) 10 EJML 439

Gewith A, 'Are There any Absolute Rights?' in J Waldron (ed), *Theories of Rights* (OUP 1984)

Gibney M, *The Ethics and Politics of Asylum: Liberal Democracy and the Politics of Asylum* (Cambridge University Press 2004)

Gil-Bazo MT, 'Refugee Status and Subsidiary Protection under EC Law: The EC Qualifications Directive and the Right to be Granted Asylum' in A Baldaccini, E Guild, and H Toner (eds), *Whose Freedom, Security and Justice? EU Immigration and Asylum Law after 1999* (Hart Publishing 2007)

Gil-Bazo MT, 'The Charter of Fundamental Rights of the European Union and the Right to be Granted Asylum in the Union's Law' (2008) 27 RSQ 33

Gilbert G, 'Is Europe Living Up to Its Obligations to Refugees?' (2004) 15 EJIL 963

Gilbert G, 'Exclusion and Evidentiary Assessment' in G Noll (ed), *Proof, Evidentiary Assessment and Credibility in Asylum Procedures* (Martinus Nijhoff Publishers 2005)

Goodman S, 'Controlling Immigration through Language and Country Knowledge Requirements' (2011) 34(2) West European Politics 235

Goodwin-Gill G, 'Article 31 of the 1951 Convention Relating to the Status of Refugees: Non-Penalization, Detention and Protection' in E Feller, V Türk, and F Nicholson, *Refugee Protection in International Law—UNHCR's Global Consultations on International Protection* (Cambridge University Press 2003)

Goodwin-Gill G, 'Document, *R (ex parte European Roma Rights Centre* et al*) v Immigration Officer at Prague Airport and another (UNHCR intervening)*' (2005) 17 IJRL 427

Goodwin-Gill G, 'The Search for the One, True Meaning…' in G Goodwin-Gill and H Lambert (eds), *The Limits of Transnational Law: Refugee Law, Policy Harmonization and Judicial Dialogue in the European Union* (Cambridge University Press 2010)

Goodwin-Gill G, 'Opinion: The Right to Seek Asylum: Interception at Sea and the Principle of *Non-refoulement*' (2011) 23 IJRL 443

Goodwin-Gill G and Lambert H (eds), *The Limits of Transnational Law: Refugee Law, Policy Harmonization and Judicial Dialogue in the European Union* (Cambridge University Press 2010)

Goodwin-Gill G and McAdam J, *The Refugee in International Law* (3rd edn, OUP 2007)

Gragl P, '(Judicial) Love is Not a One-Way Street: The EU Preliminary Reference Procedure as a Model for ECtHR Advisory Opinions under Draft Protocol No 16' (2013) 38(2) ELR 229

Greer S and Williams A, 'Human Rights in the Council of Europe and the EU: Towards "Individual", "Constitutional" or "Institutional" Justice?' (2009) 15 ELJ 467

Groenendijk K, 'The Directive on Mutual Recognition of Expulsion Decisions: Symbolic or Unbalanced Politics?' in P De Bruycker (ed), *The Emergence of a European Immigration Policy* (Bruylant 2003)

Groenendijk K, 'Legal Concepts of Integration in EU Migration Law' (2004) 6 EJML 111

Groenendijk K, 'Family Reunification as a Right under Community Law' (2006) 8 EJML 215

Groenendijk K, 'The Long-Term Residents Directive, Denizenship and Integration' in A Baldaccini, E Guild, and H Toner (eds), *Whose Freedom, Security and Justice? EU Immigration and Asylum Law and Policy* (Hart Publishing 2007)

Groenendijk K, 'Pre-departure Integration Strategies in the European Union: Integration or Immigration Policy?' (2011) 13(1) EJML 1

Groenendijk K and Fernhout R, van Dam D, van Oers R, and Strik T, *The Family Reunification Directive in EU Member States: The First Year of Implementation* (Centre for Migration Law 2007)
Guild E, 'Discretion, Competence and Migration in the European Union' (1999) 1 EJML 61
Guild E, 'Primary Immigration: The Great Myths' in E Guild and C Harlow (eds), *Implementing Amsterdam: Immigration and Asylum Rights in EC Law* (Hart Publishing 2001)
Guild E, 'Who is an Irregular Migrant?' in B Bogusz, R Cholewiski, A Cygan, and E Szyszczak (eds), *Irregular Migration and Human Rights* (Martinus Nijhoff Publishers 2004)
Guild E and Harlow C (eds), *Implementing Amsterdam* (Hart Publishing 2001)
Guild E, Groenendijk K, and Carrera S (eds), *Illiberal Liberal States* (Ashgate 2009)
Guild E and Garlick M, 'Refugee Protection, Counter-Terrorism, and Exclusion in the European Union' (2011) 29 RSQ 63
Guild E, Costello C, Garlick M, Moreno-Lax V, and Mouzourakis M, 'New Approaches, Alternative Avenues and Means of Access to Asylum Procedures for Persons Seeking International Protection' (European Parliament 2014)
Guild E, Peers S, and Tomkin J, *The EU Citizenship Directive: A Commentary* (OUP 2014)
Guiraudon V, 'European Integration and Migration Policy: Vertical Policy-making as Venue Shopping' (2000) 38 JCMS 251
Guiraudon V, 'European Courts and Foreigners' Rights: A Comparative Study of Norm Diffusion' (2000) 34 International Migration Review 1088
Guiraudon V, 'Before the EU Border: Remote Control of the "Huddled Masses"' in K Groenendijk, E Guild, and P Minderhoud (eds), *In Search of Europe's Borders* (Kluwer 2003)

H

Hailbronner K, 'Detention of Asylum Seekers' (2007) 9 EJML 159
Hailbronner K and Thym D, 'Annotation of Case C-34/09 *Ruiz Zambrano*' (2010) 48 CMLRev 1253
Halberstam D, 'The Bride of Messina: Constitutionalism and Democracy in Europe' (2005) 30 ELRev 775
Halberstam D, 'Constitutionalism and Pluralism in Marbury and Van Gend' (2008) Michigan Law School Public Law & Legal Theory Working Paper No 104
Halberstam D, 'Constitutional Heterarchy: The Centrality of Conflict in the European Union and the United States' (2008) Michigan Law School Public Law & Legal Theory Working Paper No 111
Halberstam D and C Möllers, 'The German Constitutional Court says "Ja zu Deutschland!"' (2009) 10 German Law Journal 1241
Hancox E, 'The Meaning of "Implementing" EU Law under Article 51(1) of the Charter: *Åkerberg Fransson*' (2013) 50(5) CMLRev 1411
Hathaway J, *The Law of Refugee Status* (Butterworths 1991)
Hathaway J, 'The Emerging Politics of Non-entrée' (1992) 91 Refugees 40
Hathaway J, 'Harmonizing for Whom? The Devaluation of Refugee Protection in the Era of European Economic Integration' (1993) 26 Cornell International Law Journal 719
Hathaway J, 'What's in a Label?' (2003) 5 EJML 1

Hathaway J, *The Rights of Refugees under International Law* (Cambridge University Press 2005)
Hathaway J, 'The Human Rights Quagmire of Human Trafficking' (2008) 49(1) Virginia Journal of International Law 1
Hathaway J, 'EU Accountability to International Law: The Case of Asylum' (2011) 33 Mich JIL 1
Hathaway J and Neve R, 'Making International Refugee Law Relevant Again: A Proposal for Collectivized and Solution-Oriented Protection' (1997) 10 Harvard Human Rights Law Journal 115
Hathaway J and Foster M, 'Internal Protection/Relocation/Flight Alternative as an Aspect of Status Determination' in E Feller, V Türk, and F Nicholson (eds), *Refugee Protection in International Law* (Cambridge University Press 2003)
Hathaway J and Foster M, *The Law of Refugee Status* (2nd edn, Cambridge University Press 2014)
Hathaway J and Pobjoy J, 'Queer Cases Make Bad Law' (2012) 44(2) NYU Journal of International Law & Policy 315
Hathaway J and Gammeltoft-Hansen T, '*Non-refoulement* in a World of Cooperative Deterrence' (2014) U of Michigan Law & Econ Research Paper No. 14-016
Hein C and Damato M, *Exploring Avenues for Protected Entry in Europe* (Italian Council for Refugees 2012)
Héritier A, 'Institutional Change in Europe: Co-decision and Comitology Transformed' (2012) 50(S1) JCMS 38
Hongju Koh H, 'YLS Sale Symposium: Sale's Legacies' (*Opinio Juris*, 17 May 2014)
Honohan I, 'Reconsidering the Claim to Family Reunification in Migration' (2008) 57 Political Studies 1
Howse R and Nicolaidis K, 'Democracy without Sovereignty: The Global Vocation of Political Ethics' in T Broude and Y Shany (ed), *The Shifting Allocation of Authority in International Law: Considering Sovereignty, Supremacy and Subsidiarity* (Hart 2008)

I

Iben Jensen U, 'Humanitarian Visas: Option or Obligation?' (European Parliament 2014)
Ippolito F and Velluti D, 'The Recast Process of the EC Asylum System: A Balancing Act between Efficiency and Fairness' (2011) 30 RSQ 24

J

Joppke C, 'Comparative Citizenship: A Restrictive Turn in Europe?' (2008) 2(1) Journal of Law and Ethics of Human Rights 128
Joppke C and E Marzal, 'Courts, the New Constitutionalism and Immigrant Rights: The Case of the French Conseil Constitutionnel' (2004) 43 European Journal of Political Research 823
Juss S, 'Free Movement and the World Order' (2004) 16 IJRL 289

K

Kesby AG, 'The Shifting and Multiple Border and International Law' (2007) 27 OJLS 101
Kesby AG, *The Right to Have Rights: Citizenship, Humanity and International Law* (OUP 2012)

Kochenov D, 'A Real European Citizenship, A New Jurisdiction Test, A Novel Chapter of the Development of the Union in Europe' (2011) 18 CJEL 56
Kochenov D, 'The Ought of Justice' in G de Búrca, D Kochenov, and A Williams (eds), *Debating Europe's Justice Deficit* (Hart Publishing 2015)
Kochenov D and Pirker B, 'Deporting the Citizens within the European Union: A Counter-Intuitive Trend in Case C-348/09, P.I. v. Overbürgemeisterin der Stadt Remscheid' (2013) 19 CJEL 369
Kofman E, 'Female "Birds of Passage" a Decade Later: Gender and Immigration in the European Union' (1999) 33 International Migration Review 269
Kofman E, 'Family-Related Migration: A Critical Review of European Studies' (2004) 30 Journal of Ethnic and Migration Studies 243
Kosař D, 'Inclusion before Exclusion or Vice Versa: What the Qualification Directive and the Court of Justice Do (Not) Say' (2013) 25(1) IJRL 87
Koskenniemi M and Castrén E, *Fragmentation of International Law: Difficulties Arising from the Diversification and Expansion of International Law* (Erik Castrén Institute of International Law and Human Rights 2007)
Kosta V, Skoutaris N, and Tzevelekos V (eds), *The EU Accession to the ECHR* (Hart Publishing 2014)
Kostakopoulou D, 'The 'Protective Union': Change and Continuity in Migration Law and Policy in Post-Amsterdam Europe' (2000) 38 JCMS 497
Kostakopoulou D, *Citizenship, Identity and Immigration in the European Union: Between Past and Future* (Manchester University Press 2001)
Kostakopoulou D, 'Floating Sovereignty: A Pathology or Necessary Means of State Evolution?' (2002) 22 OJLS 135
Kostakopoulou D, '"Integrating" Non-EU Migrants in the European Union: Ambivalent Legacies and Mutating Paradigms' (2002) 8 CJEL 187
Kostakopoulou D, 'Ideas, Norms and European Citizenship: Explaining Institutional Change' (2005) 68 MLR 233
Kostakopoulou D, 'The Area of Freedom, Security and Justice and the Political Morality of Migration and Integration' in H Lindahl (ed), *A Right to Inclusion and Exclusion? Normative Fault Lines of the EU's Area of Freedom, Security and Justice* (Hart Publishing 2009)
Kostakopoulou D, Acosta Arcarazo D, and Munk T, 'EU Migration Law: The Opportunities and Challenges Ahead' in D Acosta Arcarazo and C Murphy (eds), *EU Security and Justice Law after Lisbon and Stockholm* (Hart Publishing 2014)
Kraler A, 'Regularisation: A Misguided Option or Part and Parcel of a Comprehensive Policy Response to Irregular Migration?' (2009) IMISCOE Working Paper No 24
Kraler A, 'Fixing, Adjusting, Regulating, Protecting Human Rights—The Shifting Uses of Regularisations in the European Union' (2011) 13 EJML 297
Kraler A, Kofman E, Kohli M, and Schmol C (eds), *Gender, Generation and the Family in International Migration* (Amsterdam University Press 2011)
Kraler A, Reichel D, König A, Baldwin-Edwards M, and Şimşek M (2014): Final Report—Feasibility Study on the Labour Market Trajectories of Regularised Immigrants within the European Union (REGANE I) (ICMPD 2014)
Krisch N, 'The Open Architecture of European Human Rights Law' (2008) 71 MLR 183
Krisch N, *Beyond Constitutionalism: The Pluralist Structure of Postnational Law* (OUP 2010)
Kumm M, 'The Jurisprudence of Constitutional Conflict: Constitutional Supremacy in Europe before and after the Constitutional Treaty' (2005) 11(3) ELJ 262
Kumm M, 'The Idea of Socratic Contestation and the Right to Justification: The Point of Rights-Based Proportionality Review' (2010) 4 Law & Ethics of Human Rights 140

L

Lahav G, 'Immigration and the State: the Devolution and Privatisation of Immigration Control in the EU' (1998) 24 Journal of Ethnic and Migration Studies 675

Lambert H, 'Protection against *Refoulement* from Europe: Human Rights Law Comes to the Rescue' (1999) 48 ICLQ 543

Lambert H, 'The EU Asylum Qualification Directive, its Impact on the Jurisprudence of the United Kingdom and International Law' (2006) 55 ICLQ 161

Lambert H and Goodwin-Gill G, *The Limits of Transnational Law: Refugee Law, Policy Harmonization and Judicial Dialogue in the European Union* (Cambridge University Press 2010)

Lambert H, Messineo F, and Tiedemann P, 'Comparative Perspectives of Constitutional Asylum in France, Italy and Germany: *Resquiescat in Pace?*' (2008) 27 Refugee Survey Quarterly 16

Lansbergen A and Miller N, 'European Citizenship Rights in Internal Situations: An Ambiguous Revolution?' (2011) 7 EUConst 287

Lavenex S, *Safe Third Countries: Extending the EU Asylum and Immigration Policies to Central and Eastern Europe* (Central European University Press 1999)

Lavenex S, 'Mutual Recognition and the Monopoly of Force: Limits of the Single Market Analogy' (2007) 14 Journal of European Public Policy 762

LaViolette N, 'UNHCR Guidance Note on Refugee Claims Relating to Sexual Orientation and Gender Identity': A Critical Commentary (2010) 22(2) IJRL 173

Lawson R, 'Positieve verplichtingen onder het EVRM: opkomst en ondergang van de "Fair Balance"–Test' (1995) 20(5) NJCM-Bulletin

Lawson R, 'Family Reunification and the Union's Charter of Fundamental Rights, Judgment of 27 June 2006, Case C-540/03 *Parliament v Council*' (2007) 3 European Constitutional Law Review 342

Lawson R, 'The Monitoring of Fundamental Rights in the Union as a Contribution to the European Legal Space (III): The Role of the European Court of Human Rights' (2006) Working Paper Series REFGOV-FR-7

Legomsky S, 'Secondary Refugee Movements and the Return of Asylum Seekers to Third Countries: The Meaning of Effective Protection' (2003) 15 IJRL 567

Lenaerts K and de Smijter E, 'The European Union as an Actor under International Law' (1999-2000) 9 Yearbook of European Law 117

Letsas G, 'International Human Rights and the Binding Force of Interim Measures' (2003) 5 EHRLRev 527

Letsas G, *A Theory of Interpretation of the European Convention on Human Rights* (OUP 2007)

Levinson A, *The Regularisation of Unauthorized Migrants: Literature Survey and Country Case Studies* (COMPAS 2005)

Lindahl H, 'Finding a Place for Freedom, Security and Justice: The European Union's Claim to Territorial Unity' (2004) 29 ELR 461

Lindahl H, 'Jus Includendi et Excludendi: Europe and the Borders of Freedom, Security and Justice' (2005) King's College Law Journal 234

Lindahl H, 'Border Crossings by Immigrants: Legality, Illegality and Alegality' (2008) 14 Res Publica 117

Lindahl H (ed), *A Right to Inclusion and Exclusion? Normative Fault Lines of the EU's Area of Freedom, Security and Justice* (Hart Publishing 2009)

Lock T, 'EU Accession to the ECHR: Implications for the Judicial Review of Strasbourg' (2010) 35(6) European Law Review 777

Lock T, 'Beyond Bosphorus: the European Court of Human Rights' Case Law on the Responsibility of Member States of International Organisations under the European Convention on Human Rights' (2010) 10 HRLRev 529

Lock T, 'End of an Epic? The Draft Accession Agreement on the EU's Accession to the ECHR' (2012) 31(1) Yearbook of European Law 162

Lopatin E, 'The Changing Position of the European Parliament on Irregular Migration and Asylum under Co-decision' (2013) 51(4) JCMS 740

Lutz F, *The Negotiations on the Return Directive: Comments and Materials* (Wolf Legal Publishers 2010)

M

MacCormick N, 'Liberalism, Nationalism and the Post-Sovereign State' (1996) 33 Political Studies 553

MacCormick N, *Questioning Sovereignty: Law, State and Nation in the European Commonwealth* (OUP 1999)

Macklin A, '"Disappearing Refugees": Reflections on the Canada–US Safe Third Country Agreement' (2005) 36(2) Columbia Human Rights Law Review 101

Macklin A, 'Transjudicial Conversations about Security and Human Rights' *CEPS Special Report* (CEPS March 2009)

Maduro M, 'The Scope of European Remedies: The Case of Purely Internal Situations and Reverse Discrimination' in B Fitzpatrick, T Novitz, and P Skidmore *The Future of Remedies in Europe* (Hart Publishing 2000)

Maduro M, 'Contrapunctual Law: Europe's Constitutional Pluralism in Action' in N Walker (ed), *Sovereignty in Transition* (Hart 2003)

Maduro M, 'Europe and the Constitution: What If This Is as Good as It Gets?' in JHH Weiler and M Wind (eds), *European Constitutionalism beyond the State* (Cambridge University Press 2003)

Maduro M, 'Interpreting European Law: Judicial Adjudication in a Context of Constitutional Pluralism' (2007) 1 EJLS 1

Maduro M, 'Courts and Pluralism: Essay on a Theory of Judicial Adjudication in the Context of Legal and Constitutional Pluralism' in JL Dunoff and JP Trachtman (eds), *Ruling the World: Constitutionalism, International Law and Global Governance* (Cambridge University Press 2009)

Maduro M, 'Three Claims for Constitutional Pluralism' in M Avbelj and J Komarak, *Constitutional Pluralism in the European Union and Beyond* (Hart Publishing 2012)

Maduro M, 'In Search of a Meaning and Not in Search of the Meaning: Judicial Review and the Constitution in Times of Pluralism' (2013) 2 Wisconsin LR 541

Maiani F and Vevstad V, 'Reflection Note on the Evaluation of the Dublin System and the Dublin III Proposal' (2009) European Parliament, PE 410.690

Mantouvalou V, '*N v UK*: No Duty to Rescue the Nearby Needy?' (2009) 72 MLR 815

Marx R, 'Article 26 (Freedom of Movement/Liberté de Circulation)' in A Zimmermann (ed), *Commentary on the 1951 Convention Relating to the Status of Refugees* (OUP 2011)

McAdam J, 'The European Union Qualification Directive: The Creation of a Subsidiary Protection Regime' (2005) 17 IJRL 461

McAdam J, *Complementary Protection in International Refugee Law* (OUP 2007)

McAdam J, 'The Refugee Convention as a Rights Blueprint for Persons in Need of International Protection' in J McAdam (ed), *Forced Migration, Human Rights and Security* (Hart Publishing 2008)

McAdam J, 'Interpretation of the Refugee Convention' in A Zimmermann (ed), *Commentary on the Refugee Convention* (OUP 2011)
Meckled-García S and Çali B, 'Lost in Translation: The Human Rights Ideal and International Human Rights Law' in S Meckled-García and B Çali (ed), *The Legalization of Human Rights: Multidisciplinary Perspectives on Human Rights and Human Rights Law* (Routledge 2006)
Milanovich M, *Extraterritorial Application of Human Rights Treaties: Law, Principles, and Policy* (OUP 2011)
Milanovich M, '*Al-Skeini* and *Al-Jedda* in Strasbourg' (2012) 23 EJIL 121
Miller D, *Citizenship and National Identity* (Polity 2000)
Miller D, 'Border Regimes and Human Rights' (2013) 7(1) Law and Ethics of Human Rights 1
Milner D, 'Exemption from Cessation of Refugee Status in the Second Sentence of Art. 1C(5)/(6) of the 1951 Refugee Convention' (2004) 16 IJRL 91
Mincheva E, 'Case Report on *Kadzoev*, 30 November 2009' (2010) 12 EJML 361
Moeckli D, 'The Rules of the Game Have *Not* Changed' (2008) 8 HRLRev 534
Mole N and Meredith C, *Asylum and the European Convention on Human Rights* (Council of Europe 2010)
Monar J, 'The Dynamics of Justice and Home Affairs: Laboratories, Driving Factors and Costs' (2001) 39 JCMS 747
Monar J, 'The Area of Freedom, Security and Justice' in A Von Bogdandy and J Bast (eds), *Principles of European Constitutional Law* (2nd edn, Hart Publishing 2009)
Monar J, 'Justice and Home Affairs' (2011) 49 JCMS 145
Moreno-Lax V, 'Must EU Borders have Doors for Refugees?' (2008) 10 EJML 315
Moreno-Lax V, 'Beyond *Saadi v UK*: The "Necessity" Requirement for Administrative Detention of Asylum Seekers in the EU' (2010) Reflexive Governance in the Pub. Interest, Working Paper No. REFGOV-FR-31
Moreno-Lax V, 'Dismantling the Dublin System: *MSS v Belgium and Greece*'(2011) 13(4) EJML 1
Moreno-Lax V, 'Seeking Asylum in the Mediterranean: Against a Fragmentary Reading of EU Member States' Obligations Accruing at Sea' (2011) 23 IJRL 174
Moreno-Lax V, '(Extraterritorial) Entry Controls and (Extraterritorial) Non-*Refoulement* in EU Law' in M Maes, MC Foblets, and P De Bruycker (eds), *External Dimensions of EU Migration and Asylum Law and Policy* (Bruylant 2011)
Moreno-Lax V, 'The Legality of the "Safe Third Country" Notion Reconsidered: An Appraisal in Light of General International Rules on the Law of Treaties' in G Goodwin-Gill (ed), *International Migrations* (Martinus Nijhoff Publishers 2014)
Morris L, 'Stratified Rights and the Management of Migration' (2001) 3 European Societies 387
Morris L, *Asylum, Welfare and the Cosmopolitan Ideal: A Sociology of Rights* (Routledge 2010)
Mouzourakis M, '"We Need to Talk about Dublin": Responsibility under the Dublin System as a Blockage to Asylum Burden-Sharing in the European Union' (2014) RSC Working Paper Series No 105

N

Nafziger J, 'The General Admission of Aliens under International Law' (1983) 77 AJIL 804

Neumayer E, 'Asylum Recognition Rates in Western Europe—Their Determinants, Variation and Lack of Convergence' (2005) 49 Journal of Conflict Resolution 43

Nic Shuibhne N, 'Free Movement of Persons and the Wholly Internal Rule: Time to Move On?' (2002) 39 CMLRev 731

Nic Shuibhne N, 'Seven Questions for Seven Paragraphs' (2011) 36 ELRev 162

Nicolaïdis K, 'Trusting the Poles? Constructing Europe through Mutual Recognition' (2007) 14 Journal of European Public Policy 682

Nicolaïdis K, 'Kir Forever? The Journal of a Political Scientist in the Landscape of Recognition' in L Azoulai and M Maduro (eds), *The Past and Future of EU Law: The Classics of EU Law Revisited on the 50th Anniversary of the Rome Treaty* (Hart Publishing 2007)

Nicolaïdis K and Lacroix J, 'Order and Justice Beyond the Nation State: Europe's Competing Paradigms' in R Foot, J Gaddis, and A Hurrell (eds), *Order and Justice in International Relations* (OUP 2003)

Noll G, *Negotiating Asylum* (Martinus Nijhoff Publishers 2000)

Noll G, 'Formalism v Empiricism. Some Reflections on the Dublin Convention on the Occasion of Recent European Case Law' (2001) 70 Nordic Journal of International Law 161

Noll G, 'Fixed Definitions or Framework legislation? The Delimitation of Subsidiary Protection *Ratione Personae*' (2002) UNHCR New Issues in Refugee Research Working Paper No 55

Noll G (ed), *Proof, Evidentiary Assessment and Credibility in Asylum Procedures* (Martinus Nijhoff Publishers 2005)

Noll G, 'Seeking Asylum at Embassies: A Right to Entry under International Law?' (2005) 17 IJRL 542

Noll G, 'Diplomatic Assurances and the Silence of Human Rights Law' (2006) 7 Melbourne Journal of International Law 104

Noll G, 'Evidentiary Assessment in Refugee Status Determination and the EU Qualification Directive' (2006) 12 European Public Law 295

Noll G, 'Why Human Rights Fail to Protect Undocumented Migrants' (2010) 12(2) EJML 241

Noll G, 'Article 31 (Refugees Unlawfully in the Country of Refuge/Réfugés en Situation Irrégulière dans le Pays d' Accueil)' in A Zimmermann (ed), *Commentary on the 1951 Convention relating to the Status of Refugees* (OUP 2011)

Noll G, Fagerlund J, and Liebaut F, *Study on the Feasibility of Processing Asylum Claims outside the EU against the Background of the Common European Asylum System and the Goal of a Common Asylum Procedure* (Danish Centre for Human Rights/European Commission 2002)


## O


O'Cinnéide C, 'A Modest Proposal: Destitution, State Responsibility and the European Convention on Human Rights' (2008) EHRLRev 583

Olivas M and Kochenov D, 'Case C- 34/09 Ruiz Zambrano: A Respectful Rejoinder' (2012) University of Houston Public Law and Legal Theory Series 2012-W-1

O'Neill O, *Bounds of Justice* (Cambridge University Press 2000)

O'Nions H, 'No Right to Liberty: The Detention of Asylum Seekers for Administrative Convenience' (2008) 10 EJML 149

P

Palmer S, 'A Wrong Turning: Article 3 ECHR and Proportionality' (2006) 65 CLJ 438
Papastavridis E, '"Fortress Europe and FRONTEX": Within or without International Law?' (2010) 79 Nord JIL 75
Pastore F, 'Visas, Borders, Immigration: Formation, Structure, and Current Evolution of the EU Entry Control System' in N Walker (ed), *Europe's Area of Freedom, Security and Justice* (OUP 2004)
Peers S, 'EU Immigration and Asylum Law: Internal Market Model or Human Rights Model?' in T Tridimas and P Nebbia (eds), *EU Law for the Twenty-First Century: Rethinking the New Legal Order*, vol 1 (Hart Publishing 2004)
Peers S, 'Family Reunion and Community Law' in N Walker (ed), *Towards an Area of Freedom, Security and Justice* (OUP 2004)
Peers S, 'EC Law on Family Members of Persons Seeking or Receiving International Protection' in P Shah (ed), *The Challenge of Asylum to Legal Systems* (Cavendish 2005)
Peers S, 'Free Movement, Immigration Control and Constitutional Conflict' (2009) 5 European Constitutional Law Review 173
Peers S, *EU Justice and Home Affairs Law* (3rd edn, OUP 2011)
Peers S, 'The CJEU and the EU's Accession to the ECHR: A Clear and Present Danger to Human Rights Protection' (*EU Law Analysis*, 18 December 2014)
Peers S and S Prechal, 'Article 52—Scope of Guaranteed Rights' in S Peers, T Hervey, J Kenner, and A Ward (eds), *The EU Charter of Fundamental Rights: A Commentary* (Hart Publishing 2014)
Peers S, M Garlick, V Moreno-Lax, and E Guild, *EU Immigration and Asylum Law: A Commentary* (Rev 2nd edn, Brill Nijhoff 2015)
Pogge T, 'Migration and Poverty' in V Bader (ed), *Citizenship and Exclusion* (Macmillan 1997)
Pogge T, *World Poverty and Human Rights: Cosmopolitan Responsibilities and Reforms* (Polity Press 2002)
Price M, *Rethinking Asylum: History, Purpose and Limits* (Cambridge University Press 2009)
Provera M, *The Detention of Asylum Seekers in the European Union and Australia* (Wolf Legal Publishers 2013)
Provera M, 'The Criminalisation of Irregular Migration in the European Union' (2015) CEPS Paper in Liberty and Security in Europe No 80

R

Raffaelli R, 'Criminalizing Irregular Immigration and the Returns Directive: An Analysis of the *El Dridi* Case' (2011) 13(4) EJML 467
Rawls, *A Theory of Justice* (Harvard University Press 1971)
Reneman M, *EU Asylum Procedures and the Right to an Effective Remedy* (Hart Publishing 2014)
Rijpma J, 'Frontex: Successful Blame Shifting of the Member States?' Análisis del Real Instituto Elcano (ARI, 13 April 2010)
Rijpma J and Cremona M, 'The Extra-Territorialisation of EU Migration Policies and the Rule of Law' EUI Working Papers Law 2007/1
Ripoll Servent A, 'Point of No Return? The European Parliament after Lisbon and Stockholm' (2010) 19(2) European Security 191
Ripoll Servent A, 'Co-decision in the European Parliament: Comparing Rationalist and Constructivist Explanations of the Returns Directive' (2011) 7 Journal of Contemporary European Research 3

Ripoll Servent A, 'The European Parliament and the Returns Directive: The End of Radical Contestation; The Start of Consensual Constraints' in B Anderson, M Gibney, and E Paoletti (eds), *The Social, Political and Historical Contours of Deportation* (Springer 2013)
Risse M, 'On the Morality of Immigration' (2008) 22 Ethics and International Affairs 25
Risse M and Blake M, 'Migration, Territoriality and Culture' in J Ryberg, TS Petersen, and C Worf (eds), *New Waves in Applied Ethics* (Palgrave Macmillan 2008)
Rubio-Marín R, *Immigration as a Democratic Challenge: Citizenship and Inclusion in Germany and the United States* (Cambridge University Press 2000)
Rubio-Marín R (ed), *Migration and Human Rights* (OUP 2014)
Rubio-Marín R and O'Connell R, 'The European Convention and the Relative Rights of Resident Aliens' (1999) 5 ELJ 22
Ruhs M and Anderson B, 'Semi-compliance and Illegality in Migrant Labour Markets: An Analysis of Migrants, Employers and the State in the UK' (2010) 16 Population, Space and Place 195
Ryan B, 'The Celtic Cubs: The Controversy over Birthright Citizenship in Ireland' (2004) 6 EJML 173
Ryan B and Mitsilegas V (eds), *Extraterritorial Immigration Control: Legal Challenges* (Martinus Nijhoff Publishers 2010)

S

Sadurski W, 'Partnering with Strasbourg: Constitutionalization of the European Court of Human Rights, the Accession of Central and East European States to the Council of Europe, and the Idea of Pilot Judgments' (2009) 9 HRLRev 397
Samers M, 'An Emerging Geopolitics of "Illegal" Immigration in the European Union' (2004) 6 EJML 23
Sarmiento D, 'Half a Case at a Time: Dealing with Judicial Minimalism at the European Court of Justice' in M Claes, M de Visser, P Popelier, and C Van de Heyning (eds), *Constitutional Conversations in Europe* (Intersentia 2012)
Schütze R, 'Cooperative Federalism Constitutionalised: The Emergence of Complementary competences in the EC Legal Order' (2006) 31 ELRev 167
Schütze R, 'On "Federal" Ground: The European Union as an (Inter)national Phenomenon' (2009) 46 CMLRev 1069
Sen A, 'Elements of a Theory of Human Rights' (2004) 32(4) Philosophy and Public Affairs 315
Shachar A, *Multicultural Jurisdictions: Cultural Differences and Women's Rights* (Cambridge University Press 2001)
Shachar A, *The Birthright Lottery: Citizenship and Global Inequality* (Harvard University Press 2009)
Shacknove, 'Who is a Refugee?' (1985) 95 Ethics 274
Solanke I, 'Using the Citizen to Bring the Refugee In: *Gerardo Ruiz Zambrano* v *Office national de l'emploi (ONEM)*' (2012) 75 MLR 101
Somek A, 'Monism: A Tale of the Undead' in M Avbelj and J Komarak, *Constitutional Pluralism in the European Union and Beyond* (Hart Publishing 2012)
Soysal Y, *Limits of Citizenship: Migrants and Postnational Membership in Europe* (University of Chicago Press 1994)
Spaventa E, 'Seeing the Wood despite the Trees? On the Scope of Union Citizenship and its Constitutional Effects' (2008) 45 CMLRev 13
Spielmann D, 'Whither the Margin of Appreciation?' (2014) 67(1) CLP 49

Spijkerboer R, 'Subsidiarity in Asylum Law. The Personal Scope of International Protection' in D Bouteillet-Paquet (ed), *Subsidiary Protection of Refugees in the European Union: Complementing the Geneva Convention?* (Bruylant 2002)
Spijkerboer R, 'The Human Costs of Border Control' (2007) 9 EJML 137
Spijkerboer R, 'Subsidiarity and "Arguability": The European Court of Human Rights' Case Law on Judicial Review in Asylum Cases' (2009) 21 IJRL 1
Spijkerboer R, 'Structural Instability: Strasbourg Case Law on Children's Family Reunion' (2009) 11 EJML 271
Spijkerboer R, 'Moving Migrants, States, and Rights: Human Rights and Border Deaths' (2013) 7(2) The Law & Ethics of Human Rights 213S
Spijkerboer R (ed), *Fleeing Homophobia: Sexual Orientation, Gender Identity and Asylum* (Routledge 2013)
Stalford H, 'Concepts of Family under EU Law: Lessons from the ECHR' (2002) 16 International Journal of Law, Policy and the Family 410
Steinorth C, '*Üner v the Netherlands:* Expulsion of Long-Term Immigrants and the Right to Respect for Private and Family Life' (2008) 8 HRLRev 185
Stone Sweet A, 'A Cosmopolitan Legal Order: Constitutional Pluralism and Rights Adjudication in Europe' (2012) 1(1) Journal of Global Constitutionalism 53
Storey H, 'EU Refugee Qualification Directive: a Brave New World?' (2008) 20 IJRL 1
Stick T, Böcker A, Luiten M, and van Oers R, *The INTEC Project: Synthesis Report. Integration and Naturalisation Tests: The New Way to European Citizenship* (December 2010)
Strik R, de Hart B, and Nissen E, *Family Reunification: A Barrier or Facilitator of Integration: A Comparative Study* (Wolf Legal Publishers 2013)
Symes M and Jorro P, *Asylum Law and Practice* (2nd edn, Bloomsbury Professional 2010)

T

Tasioulas J, 'Towards a Philosophy of Human Rights' (2012) 65 CLP 1
Thym D 'Menchenrecht auf Legalisierung des Aufenthalts?' (2006) Europäische Grundrechte-Zeitschrift 541
Thym D 'Respect for Private and Family Life under Article 8 ECHR in Immigration Cases: A Human Right to Regularize Illegal Stay?' (2008) 57(1) ICLQ 87
Tiedemann P, 'Subsidiary Protection and the Function of Article 15(c) of the Qualification Directive' (2012) 31 RSQ 123
Timmermans C, 'The Relationship between the European Court of Justice and the European Court of Human Rights' in A Arnull et al. (eds), *A Constitutional Order of States? Essays in Honour of Alan Dashwood* (Hart Publishing 2011)
Torpey J, *The Invention of the Passport: Surveillance, Citizenship and the State* (Cambridge University Press 1999)
Torres Pérez A, *Conflicts of Rights in the European Union. A Theory of Supranational Adjudication* (OUP 2009)
Tsourdi E and Leboeuf L, 'Towards a Redefinition of Persecution? Assessing the Potential Impact of Y and Z' (2013) 13(2) HRLRev 402

V

Van Elsuwege P and Kochenov D, 'On The Limits of Judicial Intervention: EU Citizenship and Family Reunification Rights' (2011) 4 EJML 443

Vanheule D, 'A Comparison of the Judicial Interpretation of the Notion of Refugee' in JY Carlier and D Vanheule (eds), *Europe and Refugees: A Challenge?* (Kluwer Law International 1997)

Van Oers R, Ersbøll E, and Kostakopoulou D (eds), *A Re-definition of Belonging? Language and Integration Tests in Europe* (Martinus Nijhoff Publishers 2010)

Van Walsum S, 'Comment on the *Sen* Case. How Wide is the Margin of Appreciation Regarding the Admission of Children for Purposes of Family Reunification?' (2002) 4 EJML 1

Van Walsum S, 'Against All Odds: How Single and Divorced Migrant Mothers were Eventually Able to Claim Their Right to Respect for Family Life' (2009) 11 EJML 295

Van Walsum S, 'Transnational Mothering, National Immigration Policy, and European Law: The Experience of the Netherlands' in S Benhabib and J Resnik (eds), *Migrations and Mobilities: Citizenship, Borders, and Gender* (NYU University Press 2009)

Von Bogdandy A, 'The European Union as a Human Rights Organization? Human Rights and the Core of the European Union' (2000) 37 CMLRev 1307

W

Waldrauch H, 'Acquisition of Nationality' in R Bauböck, E Ersboll, K Groenendijk, H Waldrauch (eds), *Acquisition and Loss of Nationality*, vol 1(Amsterdam University Press 2006)

Waldron J (ed), *Theories of Rights* (OUP 1984)

Waldron J, 'Torture and Positive Law: Jurisprudence for the White House' (2005) 105 Columbia Law Review 1681

Waldron J, 'Cruel, Inhuman and Degrading Treatment: The Words Themselves' (2008) NYU School of Law Public Law and Legal Theory Research Paper Series No 08-36

Waldron J, *Torture, Terror and Trade-offs: Philosophy for the White House* (OUP 2010)

Walker N, 'The Idea of Constitutional Pluralism' (2002) 65 MLR 317

Walker N, 'In Search of the Area of Freedom, Security and Justice: A Constitutional Odyssey' in N Walker (ed), *Europe's Area of Freedom, Security and Justice* (OUP 2004)

Walker N (ed), *Europe's Area of Freedom, Security and Justice* (OUP 2004)

Walter A, *Reverse Discrimination and Family Reunification* (Wolf Legal Publishers 2008)

Walzer M, *Spheres of Justice: A Defense of Pluralism and Equality* (Basic Books 1983)

Webb P, *International Judicial Integration and Fragmentation* (OUP 2013)

Weiler JHH, 'Thou Shalt Not Oppress a Stranger: On the Judicial Protection of the Human Rights of Non-EC Nationals—A Critique' (1992) 3 EJIL 65

Weiler JHH, 'Fundamental Rights and Fundamental Boundaries: On the Conflict of Standards and Values in the Protection of Human Rights in the European Legal Space' in *The Constitution of Europe* (Cambridge University Press 1999)

Weiler JHH, *The Constitution of Europe: Do the New Clothes Have an Emperor? And Other Essays on European Integration* (Cambridge University Press 1999)

Weiler JHH, 'Does the European Union Truly Need a Charter of Rights?' (2000) 6 ELJ 95

Weiler JHH, 'Epilogue: The Judicial Après Nice' in JHH Weiler and G de Búrca (eds), *The European Court of Justice* (OUP 2001)

Weiler JHH and de Búrca G (eds), *The European Court of Justice* (OUP 2001)

Weiler JHH and Wind M (eds), *European Constitutionalism beyond the State* (Cambridge University Press 2003)

Wellman C and Cole P (eds), *Debating the Ethics of Immigration: Is There a Right to Exclude?* (OUP 2011)

Welsh M and Schuster L, 'Detention of Asylum Seekers in the US, UK, France, Germany and Italy: A Critical View of the Globalizing Culture of Control' (2005) 5 Criminology & Criminal Justice 331

Wiesbrock A, 'Court of Justice of the European Union: The Right to Family Reunification of Third-Country Nationals under EU Law' (2010) 6 European Constitutional Law Review 462

Wiesbrock A, 'Union Citizenship and the Redefinition of the "Internal Situations" Rule: The Implications of *Zambrano*' (2011) 12 German Law Journal 2077

Wilde R, 'The "Legal space" or "espace juridique" of the European Convention on Human Rights: Is It Relevant to Extraterritorial State Action?' (2005) 2 EHRLRev 115

Wilsher D, 'Immigration Detention and the Common European Asylum Policy' in A Baldaccini, E Guild, H Toner (eds), *Whose Freedom, Security and Justice? EU Immigration and Asylum Law after 1999* (Hart Publishing 2007)

Wouters K, *International Legal Standards for the Protection from Refoulement* (Intersentia 2009)

Wouters K and Den Heijer M, 'The *Marine I* Case: A Comment' (2010) 22 IJRL 1

Y

Yorke J, 'The Right to Life and Abolition of the Death Penalty in the Council of Europe' (2009) 34 ELRev 205

Z

Zetter R, 'More Labels, Fewer Refugees: Remaking the Refugee Label in an Era of Globalization' (2007) 20(2) Journal of Refugee Studies 172

Zwaan K (ed), *The Qualification Directive: Central Themes, Problem Issues, and Implementation in Selected Member States* (Wolf Legal Publishers 2007)

# *Index*